20 25 30 35

Tanais

Olbia
LAKE MAEOTIS
(Sea of Azov)
Phanagoria
TAURIC
CHERSO-
NESE
Panticapaeum
CAUCASUS MTS.
COLCHIS
Heraclea

PONTUS EUXINUS
(BLACK SEA)

Sinope
PAPHLAGONIA
Trapezus

S Y R I A
Epidaurus
CYRA
Danube R.
PHR
Byzantium
Calchedon
(Chalcedon)
Propontis
BITHYNIA
Halys R.
CAPPADOCIA
45
40

MACEDONIA
Amphipolis
Perinthus
CHALCIDICE
THASOS
Sestus
Abydus
Cyzicus
Lampsacus
Ilios
MYSIA
PHRYGIA
A S I A   M I N O R

Apollonia
Olynthus
Potidaea
Hellespont
CHIOS
LESBOS
LYDIA
Sardis
Smyrna
Ephesus
CILICIA
Tarsus

EPIRUS
THESSALY
Phocaea
Erythrai
CARIA
Halicarnassus
PAMPHYLIA
Phaselis
Soli
Salamis
Hamath
Citium
Aradus

Taras
(Tarentum)
Metapontium
Sybaris
Thurii
Croton
CORCYRA
Ithaca
CEPHALLENIA
Megara
Chalcis
EUBOEA
Athens
DELOS
Miletus
SAMOS
LYCIA
Selinus
Byblus
PHOENICIA
Sidon
Tyre
S Y R I A

Loeri
Rhegium
IONIAN   SEA
Elis
Corinth
Argos
Sparta
NAXOS
CYCLADES
Cnidus
RHODES
GRAECIA
(na)
use

CYTHERA
MELOS
Thera
Cydonia
Knossus
Itanus
CRETE

ME   A N E A N   S E A

Cyrene
Hesperis
CYRENAICA
Naucratis
E G Y P T
Nile R.
30

LIBYAN
DESERT
EGYPT
RED SEA
35

WORLD *about* 500 B.C.

VOLUME ONE

****

THE ORIENT AND GREECE TO

THE PARTITION OF THE EMPIRE

OF ALEXANDER THE GREAT

****

Under the Editorship of
WILLIAM SCOTT FERGUSON
AND THOMAS A. BRADY

A Political and Cultural

ANCIENT

VOLUME ONE

History of the

WORLD

*From Prehistoric Times to the Dissolution
of the Roman Empire in the West* ❖ ❖

C. E. VAN SICKLE
ASSOCIATE PROFESSOR OF HISTORY
OHIO WESLEYAN UNIVERSITY

HOUGHTON MIFFLIN COMPANY
The Riverside Press

D
54
.V3
v.1

HOUGHTON MIFFLIN COMPANY
Boston · New York · Chicago · Dallas · Atlanta · San Francisco
The Riverside Press Cambridge
PRINTED IN THE U.S.A.

TO MY WIFE

WHOSE AID AND ENCOURAGEMENT

MADE POSSIBLE THIS BOOK

EDITOR'S INTRODUCTION

HAVING TAUGHT a general survey course in Ancient History for twenty years, I welcome the opportunity to assist in the preparation of this textbook. It is above all clear, compact, and well organized in its presentation, and it incorporates the results of the latest excavation and research as well. The basic problem in the preparation of any textbook is the selection and organization of material. Great attention has been given here to these processes, and we have, consequently, a usable piece of work. Moreover, the book does not follow any new or radical plan of organization, nor is it the author's purpose to espouse any startling and doctrinaire hypotheses in the interpretation of the material.

There is no field of history in which the student manuals require more frequent revision than in the field of Ancient History. In times of peace, the progress of excavation is continually adding bits of very significant material to our knowledge, and this material, though not always large in amount, frequently necessitates revision in our interpretations. Although there was little if any excavation carried on during the war, significant material was discovered just before the war opened, and much of it was never fully utilized in our textbooks.

The present work is above all a sound and careful piece of historical writing, thoughtfully presented and illustrated. The aim has been to organize and present the material so that the book can be used handily for the standard college course: either the two-semester, three-hour course covering the entire Ancient World, or the one-semester, five-hour course covering the same period. It is common practice in the three-hour course to give two new assignments each week and reserve the third period for discussion of material presented earlier in the week. A similar procedure may be used in the five-hour course. The length of this volume is well adapted to such purposes.

The opening chapter attempts to introduce the student to professional techniques — especially those needed for a critical study of history. I believe we have all found that some consideration of these matters is essential in such a book as this. The chapter on Primitive Man gives a bare recital of what we know on this subject but, more important, indicates as well some of the things we do not know. Here the author abjures bizarre anthropological and psychological theories. Too many otherwise good textbooks have been marred by the inclusion of chapters on pre-history replete with fanciful and speculative material.

The second volume of this history will be devoted to the history of the Roman world down to the end of the Roman Empire in the West. Together, the two volumes will furnish a complete survey of Ancient History.

THOMAS A. BRADY

UNIVERSITY OF MISSOURI

PREFACE

A SATISFACTORY history textbook should, in the opinion of the present writer, embody three characteristics:

1. It should furnish a reliable factual treatment of the field which the author has chosen, on a scholastic level fitted to the attainments of the student group for which it is intended.

2. It should interpret thought and institutions sympathetically.

3. It should be written in an interesting, readable style. The field covered by this book is the political history and civilization of the ancient Mediterranean world, including art, religion, education, society, and economic organization, in addition to the old-style narrative of events. It is intended for use in advanced undergraduate survey courses. Text, maps, illustrations, and bibliography have all been planned with that end in view. The bibliography is not intended to be exhaustive, but has been selected on the basis of its availability to the student. For this reason, no works in languages other than English have been included.

A textbook cannot be to any great extent a work of original research. In the present work, each topic represents a careful survey of the source material, a survey of modern critical and expository works, and the author's own conclusions formed upon the basis of this evidence. Dogmatic opinions on controversial points have been avoided as much as possible, but when they occur, the instructor can easily state divergent views or assign supplementary reading in which they are stated. Similarly, it is to be expected that he will not find every point treated as fully as he thinks desirable, for no two persons can be expected to agree entirely upon the question of emphasis. In such cases the instructor will of course shift the emphasis to points where, in his opinion, it belongs. A textbook should always be a useful servant, but never a master. Direct quotations have been held to a minimum, and have been confined entirely to source material.

It has long been customary to divide the past into three parts — ancient, medieval, and modern. In this plan, ancient history begins with man's first appearance upon earth, and ends with the disappearance of the Western Roman Empire in the fifth century A.D. This division is for many reasons a faulty one, but expediency demands that for the present purpose the established convention be followed.

Ancient history, thus defined, covers a period of at least a half-million years. Of this, ninety-nine per cent is "prehistoric," in the sense that no written records preserve the memories of its events. In the present survey, a single chapter presents the bare outlines of this long and important period. This is inevitable, for little is known about it, and the historian cannot outrun his facts. The Egyptians and the inhabitants of the Tigris-Euphrates Valley were probably the first peoples to invent systems of writing, and in these countries written records began to be made shortly before 3000 B.C. In the twenty-five hundred years that followed the emergence of these peoples into the light of history, the Hittites, Assyrians, Phoenicians, Hebrews, Medes, and Persians began to produce written documents which permit us to trace the story of their development. But the records are all relatively scanty. The cultural contributions of these peoples to our Occidental civilization, while very great, have been to a large extent transmitted indirectly through the agency of the Greeks and Romans. Seven chapters have been allotted to surveys of their history and institutions. Since our knowledge of the interesting Aegean civilization of Crete and continental Greece rests almost entirely upon archeological evidence, it has received but a single chapter. In the eighth century, the Greeks, and a few centuries later, the Romans, entered the historic age. Because of the importance of their direct contributions to modern civilization and the ease with which these contributions are traced, the bulk of the present survey is devoted to them.

Large sections of the "ancient" world are purposely excluded from treatment. India and China had interesting civilizations contemporary with those mentioned above, but as they had scarcely any contacts with the ancient Occidental world, and their influence upon Western civilization has been late and relatively small, they will be left for a separate treatment. Northern Europe and Asia, central and southern Africa, Australia, and the Western Hemisphere did not enter the historic age until after the close of the period which we treat.

The author gratefully acknowledges the helpful suggestions given him by his former colleague, Professor Emeritus Trumbull G. Duvall of Ohio Wesleyan University, in the preparation of the sections dealing with Greek philosophy. He is also deeply obligated to Professor Prescott W. Townsend of Indiana University for help in the reading of proof, and to a large number of students and alumni of Ohio Wesleyan for searching and constructive criticism of the text and for help in the making of the index.

C. E. Van Sickle

CONTENTS

ILLUSTRATIONS

MAPS

****

I

Sources and Methods

for the Study of Ancient History

TAKEN IN THE BROADEST SENSE, the word "history" includes all the known facts about the human past. All phases of man's struggles and achievements, from his first appearance upon earth to the present, are proper subjects of investigation by the historian, for they all throw light upon the steps by which he lifted himself from primeval savagery to civilization. Agricultural and manufacturing methods in ancient Babylon are as truly a part of his field of investigation as the wars of King Hammurabi; and the technical processes used by the Athenian sculptor interest him no less than the achievements of the Athenian statesman Pericles. No fact is so unimportant that it may not form a useful part of the human record.

The foregoing broad definition of history does not, of course, mean that every historian must or can treat the whole field. To write a full or adequate summary of all that is known about the past of our race is clearly beyond the powers of any individual. Instead, the task is divided both chronologically and topically. The historian tends more and more to specialize upon the study of a single age, or people, or phase of human life. The field in which he can hope to do productive research and discover new facts is necessarily a narrow one, and even in it he must carefully check the work done by other investigators. In other fields, even when they are closely related to that of his special interest, he must depend to a still greater extent upon the works of others, which he should supplement by a careful evaluation of their methods and by close observation of the sources from which they drew their materials. If he writes a history covering an extended field, it must consist largely of borrowed material, and only to a slight extent of his own original findings. It is only when he is exploring previously uncharted portions of the human record that he relies entirely upon historical sources.

VARIETY OF SOURCES OF ANCIENT HISTORY

Kinds of Written Sources

A historical source is the agency from which information regarding a given fact is ultimately derived. It may be either a written document, an artistic representation of a material object, or the object itself. For the present, we may well confine our attention to written documents. The acid test which establishes the character of a document as a source is this question: Did the agency from which this information came derive it from another agency which is now extant? If so, it is not, strictly speaking, a source, but a secondary work, and we must go back yet another link along the chain of transmission. Only when the last link now in existence has been reached have we arrived at the source. Hence, the character of a given record as a source is a purely relative matter, due in many cases to nothing but the loss of one or more links in the chain of transmission which once existed.

It follows that written sources vary widely in their relative proximity to the subject with which they deal. One may be an eye-witness account of an event, the authenticity of which is vouched for by every possible test, while another may be a fourth-hand transcription, made centuries later and badly garbled. Yet the latter is as truly a source as the former if we cannot follow beyond it the chain of transmission of the account which it gives. Of course the relative values of two such sources may be different. Only by weighing each on its merits can its worth be determined.

On the basis of content, written sources are divided into two principal classes. The first, which will henceforth be referred to as *narrative sources*, includes all accounts composed for the purpose of conveying historical information to their readers. Such are contemporary histories, chronicles, biographies and autobiographies, memoirs, diaries, commemorative inscriptions, and similar materials. The second class, which may be termed *documents*, includes all written records which are not primarily designed to convey historical information, but which contain material of which historians may make use. Examples of documentary source materials would be speeches, laws, proclamations, letters, business accounts, judicial decisions, contemporary fiction, religious literature, and didactic essays. Each class serves to supplement the other, and both are of value to the historian.

Narrative Sources

The advantages of a carefully composed narrative source are obvious. Events are placed in their proper order and are described with some effort at continuity. The succession of kings or other public officials is given, and a serviceable framework is provided upon which to arrange all the other facts which one may learn regarding the subject. If the author was a capable, reliable, and discerning contemporary, he no doubt saved for posterity a mass of information gathered from eye-witnesses and from documents afterward destroyed. Even if he had to rely upon earlier sources, his work will rest upon a mass of material which we could not use under any other circumstances.

But each source of this class must be subjected to careful study before its true value can be ascertained. Was the author a contemporary of the events which he describes or did he live in another age and use the works of others? If he were the former, was he an eye-witness of the events and conditions which he treats; or if not, how did he get his information, and what was his personal viewpoint? In some cases he may have been a careful and methodical investigator, and in others slovenly and credulous. His judgments may have been made with judicial impartiality, or he may have been misled by prejudices of various types. If he lived long after the age about which he writes, the number of factors to be considered become much larger. One must determine the character of the sources which he used as nearly as possible, and ancient historians often neglected to tell their readers anything whatever on this point. If the age of which he wrote differed greatly from that in which he lived, there is danger that he failed to understand the spirit of the earlier time, and unconsciously altered the thought of his sources to fit his own preconceived ideas. Lastly, ancient and medieval historical works were long circulated in manuscript, and the texts which we have are usually the result of numerous transcriptions. Each copy added a few errors to those of its prototype. Ignorant copyists, finding on the margins of a manuscript notes made by previous readers, not infrequently copied them into the texts which they produced. A rather complex science of text criticism has grown up to place before the modern reader as nearly as possible the sense — and if possible, the exact words — of writers whose works have been subjected to such contamination.

Autobiographies and memoirs are usually compiled by public men who wish to interpret their acts and policies either to their contemporaries or to posterity. The potential value of such work is high, for the author should be better informed on the subject matter than anyone else could be. A few of them (such as Caesar's *Gallic War*) are really first-rate sources, but as a rule they have serious weaknesses. Only vanity or the anticipation of unfavorable criticism is likely to spur one to compose such a work. If the former, he will certainly magnify his own achievements, while in the latter case he will be tempted to defend and exculpate himself at the expense of sober truth.

In the ancient world — particularly in the Orient — memoir-writing of a sort was to be found in the so-called "Display Inscriptions," carved at the order of kings or other public men to record their important deeds. A large part of the political history of Egypt, Babylonia, Assyria, Persia, the Hittite Kingdom, and other states of the ancient East is recovered from such works. There can be little doubt that in the main they furnish reliable information, but the statement must be carefully qualified. They are subject to all the faults of other personal memoirs, and to some which are peculiarly their own. One becomes suspicious when one notes that in all their many wars these Eastern kings seldom, if ever, confess to having suffered defeat in battle. The truth is that in these countries unsuccessful kings faced almost certain rebellion or assassination, and the fact, together with personal vanity, caused them to gloss over defeats or turn them into victories. Usually a careful study of the circumstances of a campaign will expose the hollowness of their claims in this, as in certain other matters wherein they were prone to exaggerate or falsify.

Emphasis of Chronology in Narratives

Modern historians are often baffled by the meagerness of the data which the literary sources furnish upon certain points in which present-day readers are deeply interested, and by their emphasis upon matters which interest the modern student very little. Ancient writers, for example, more often than not stress war and government and neglect all other considerations. The historian in any age of the world is tempted to pass over the facts of his environment, which are too familiar to his readers to warrant description, but which readers in some subsequent century are able to recover only by the most laborious research and by indirect means. Cultural data given by the ancient historians are frequently embodied in incidental remarks, and are tantalizingly incomplete.

Another serious problem which arises from the use of literary sources is that of constructing a reliable chronology from the data which they furnish. Nowhere in the ancient world did writers adopt a uniform system of dating events by a fixed era, as we do from the reputed year of the birth of Christ. In early Egypt and Babylon it was customary to name each year after its most important event, which was designated early in the year by the state. To ascertain the date of an event, we need a table of such year-names, and even when we have it, we cannot always transfer it into terms of the pre-Christian era. Later it became customary to date by the regnal years of kings. This was better than the older custom, but co-regencies and other accidents might still render a date uncertain. In Assyria and in many of the Greek cities it was customary to name the year after the holders of certain annual magistracies in the states involved, and the reader is lost without a table of such magistracies. Fortunately, we possess such tables for both Assyria and Athens, and it is possible to transfer their dates into terms of the pre-Christian era. Toward the end of their history, the Greeks sometimes dated events from the reputed year of the institution of the Olympic Games (776 b.c.), but the practice never became universal during the period covered by the present volume. Often no dates of any kind are given, and the reader is left without a chronological guide.

Documents, Accounts, and Fiction

The value of documents not historical in intent lies chiefly in the vivid light which they frequently shed upon everyday life and thought, but they are also useful at times in the study of political history. Laws record the customs of a people and embalm their faults; for they are designed to regulate ordinary human relations, and their prohibitory clauses are leveled against acts which are not only considered prejudicial to the welfare of society, but which are also common enough to call for repression. Much can be learned about the habits of a people by simply observing the relative space allotted in their laws to social and economic matters as compared to crimes of violence. A highly civilized people will require a complex commercial code, elaborate laws on inheritance and family relations, and relatively small emphasis upon crimes of violence, while among barbarians the reverse will be true. In some cases legislators fixed prices, wages, and rent. If we could be sure that such enactments were practicable and successful, they would furnish us with the raw material for social and economic histories.

Business accounts, contracts, mortgages, and title deeds largely supplement our knowledge in the social and economic fields. A Babylonian marriage contract is an excellent source for the study of both of these phases of life in the Tigris-Euphrates Valley, while the cost accounts of the building of the Athenian *Erechtheum* give us a clear picture of labor conditions in Athens shortly before 400 B.C. Such materials tell us much that the professed historian would never take the trouble to record, and they have an unconscious naturalness which his work can never attain.

Fiction also has its value for the study of social life, for when it deals with contemporary situations it must furnish the reader or theater audience with convincing pictures of actual conditions. Examples of this type of literature that have proved useful to the social historian are the comedies of Aristophanes, which in more than one respect illustrate Athenian customs in the fifth century.

Archeological Sources

Our second important class of sources is material remains. Their study has been reduced to a science with elaborate methods of procedure, to which is applied the name *archeology*. Not only does it check, supplement, and illustrate the information furnished by the written sources, but for the whole prehistoric period and for the Aegean cultures it furnishes our only guides.

Only the briefest sketch of the work of the archeologist can be given here. He explores the sites formerly inhabited by men, as well as the graves or tombs in which their bodies were laid to rest, in order to learn everything possible about their material cultures and habits of life. The public knows his work chiefly through his occasional sensational discoveries, but such finds are rare, and are by no means the chief objective of his work. Most of his investigations produce little that is of interest to newspaper readers. He undertakes to survey every shred of material remains found on the sites which he is investigating, with a view to piecing together a picture of the life led by their ancient inhabitants. The actual digging is done by expert workmen, who take elaborate precautions to prevent the destruction of so much as a single broken piece of pottery. The superintendent of the enterprise carefully locates the site of the discovery of each object, indicates the other objects found near it, and takes copious notes on the circumstances of the discovery. These notes are later collated and published, and the objects which have been discovered are, if important, deposited in museums.

On most ancient sites the inhabitants seldom bothered to remove the débris from a ruined building. Instead, they merely leveled it off and built over it. Thus, such a site is covered with layer after layer of refuse, in which are found all manner of objects lost or thrown away by the former inhabitants. Each layer tells its own story, and it is the archeologist's task to wring that story from the objects which the spades of his workmen turn up. Burial places are often full of interesting material, for the ancient peoples usually tried to equip the departed with objects which he would need in the world beyond. Because of the temptation which such wealth presented to tomb-robbers, these burial places were often carefully secreted in inaccessible places and are not easily discovered.

The remains which are found vary widely in character with the nature and location of the site. Only in Egypt and in similar arid lands can one hope to discover well-preserved human bodies, wood, leather, paper, cloth, or other perishable materials. Even in such surroundings they may have suffered damage unless artificially preserved and protected. But human skeletons will, under favorable conditions, last thousands of years, even in humid climates, and anthropologists can reconstruct the vanished profiles of specimens on the basis of the known relation of skeleton to surface structure. Even when perishable material has completely vanished, it often leaves traces to prove that it once existed. Thus, in the caves once occupied by Paleolithic man, the finding of bone needles and of scrapers like those used by modern savages to prepare skins points to the conclusion that the former inhabitants wore skins, which they sewed together to form robes. Likewise in late Neolithic and Bronze-Age sites, the finding of loom weights and spindles proves that some kind of cloth was woven. In certain kinds of soil, decaying objects formed casts which preserved their shape and texture.

Archeological Remains: Pottery, Metals, Sculptures

Of the durable materials, pottery is the most common, and for the purposes of the archeologist, the most valuable. An entire pot or jar is very fragile. It shatters easily, and it is so easy to replace that no one tries to repair it. In ancient cities the fragments were often thrown into the streets and trampled underfoot. But these very fragments are among the most durable of the works of man. Especially when buried, they will last for many thousand years, and they can be easily cemented together. Of all the signs by which the distinctive character of a culture and its relations to other cultures can be told, pottery is perhaps the most certain. The styles and methods of manufacture are quite distinctive and instructive. There is little danger of mistaking an Athenian piece of the fifth century for one of the same period made in Corinth or Samos. Its presence far from the place of manufacture is a sure index to the scope of commercial relations. Thus, if one finds Athenian pottery of the mid-fifth century in

Etruscan tombs in Italy, in burial mounds in eastern Germany and southern Russia, in Egypt and Cyrene, one can gain from this fact alone a picture of the tremendous spread of Athenian trade. It likewise helps to solve chronological problems. The discovery in Egyptian tombs of pottery manufactured in Minoan Crete is the safest means of dating the various periods of a culture of which the written records are still illegible. Greek pottery paintings are almost the only examples of ancient painting pre-served outside of Egypt and Pompeii, and they provide us with scenes from common life which are as realistic as photographs.

Metals are, of course, durable, but their chances of survival in any given form are poor. Their intrinsic value, and the ease with which they can be worked over into other forms, caused ancient raiders and tomb-robbers to collect them carefully for resmelting. Nevertheless, some pieces have escaped the hand of the spoiler, and even much-rusted iron implements offer to the investigator valuable information about the cultural condi_tion of their makers. Because of their small size, and the tendency of men in all ages to bury them for safe-keeping, coins have a better chance of survival than other forms of metal. In them, too, we have valuable indices to the artistic skill and taste of their makers.

Statues, reliefs, and other carved stones also form part of the possible findings of the archeologist. They are almost always in a mutilated con-dition with the noses, ears, heads, arms, or legs most often suffering dis_figurement. Modern artists can often replace the missing parts, but in doing so they must be careful to preserve the form and spirit of the orig-inals. Sculptures are enormously valuable bases for judgments regarding the manual skill and sense of beauty of their makers, while reliefs, in par-ticular, often serve to illustrate daily life in much the same way as Greek pottery paintings. Thus our knowledge of many phases of Egyptian, Assyrian, and Hittite life rests largely upon the information furnished by their extensive reliefs.

But the archeologist's range of interest is all-inclusive. He investigates sewers as well as temples, and Roman roads or ruined farmhouses as readily as the Colosseum. His task is a laborious one, but it provides a more cer-tain approach to the past than any other method.

THE SOURCES FOR THE STUDY OF ANCIENT HISTORY

Chronological Order of Availability

To understand the use of sources in the study of the ancient world, one must first realize the chronological order in which the various types of source material became available. Since, in the beginning, man did not possess the art of writing, we can study his story only through the material remains which he has left. Prehistory is almost exclusively the field of the archeologist. When written records began to appear, they first took the form of short royal inscriptions, manuals of religious ritual, or documents dealing with everyday transactions. At a very early date, governments began to keep records for their own convenience, and from these court diaries, treasury records, and other such writings, chronicles were compiled. The earliest extant chronicle (the *Palermo Stone Inscription*) was composed in Egypt, apparently about 2750 B.C. It is a list of kings, with the regnal years of each, and the events by which the individual years were named. Only gradually do these written documents and records supplement to any large degree the data furnished by archeology, and in no part of the ancient world did they ever become full enough to render its aid unnecessary.

The Earliest Records: Babylonia

The oldest written records come from Egypt and Babylonia, which seem to have been first to develop the art of writing. They may be dated roughly at about 3200 B.C. In each country they first take the form of royal inscriptions. One of the first from the Tigris-Euphrates region, which will serve as an example of its kind, was carved on a vase dedicated in a temple at Nippur by Utug, king of Kish. Such an inscription does little more than identify the person named in it. But the inscriptions of Ur-nina, king of Lagash, carved about three centuries later, tell us much about the king's activities as a priest and as a builder of temples and canals. The use of clay tablets as writing material has preserved many business documents from this early age of Babylonian history, and from them we can trace with fair accuracy the evolution of economic and social institutions in Babylonia. The dates of such documents are usually fairly definite, and when one is found in a given layer of ruins, it serves to date the other objects found there. Thus, written documents early came to the aid of archeology. The earliest extant attempt at chronicle writing was made much later. Scribes from the Sumerian cities of southern Babylonia composed, between 2200 and 2000, a series of "king-lists," purporting to give the names of all the kings who had held the suzerainty over the whole country from the beginning, but with little or no information about them except the number of years that each had reigned. Even a work of this kind must have been based upon earlier ones now lost, and the sources in this case seem particularly weak in chronology. The first eight kings were said to have ruled 241,200 years, and reigns of from a hundred to fifteen hundred years continue to occur throughout the early dynasties. But at a date which would correspond roughly to 3200, we begin to hear of kings with reigns short enough to be in harmony with the normal span of human life, and for them an occasional inscription is found to verify a royal name and to show that from this point onward the lists are not all fiction.

Law codes form an important source of information for the study of Babylonian society and government. Various city codes are preserved in fragmentary form, while about 2225, King Dungi of Ur issued a code for all of his subjects, and about 1900, King Hammurabi of Babylon revised and expanded the laws of Dungi to form the famous *Hammurabi Code*. From these collections of laws, the modern investigator can learn how the ancient inhabitants of the Tigris-Euphrates Valley conducted their business affairs, the details of family life, social organization, class relationships, and many other significant facts.

Religious literature and fiction play a very large part in the reconstruction of Babylonian history. Tables of omens with their alleged meanings not only tell us much about the current superstitions, but often fortify their predictions by citing previous events otherwise unknown which had been preceded by the same phenomena. The frequent mention of eclipses is important in the solution of chronological problems, for a modern astronomer can reckon the dates of eclipses for thousands of years with great precision. Charms and penitential psalms played a large part in the religion of the people, and from them we are not only enabled to reconstruct the beliefs of those who used them, but also to learn the relationship which existed between Babylonian and Hebrew beliefs. Fiction plays its age-old rôle of portraying the ideas, life, and manners of the people for whom it was composed.

Egyptian Inscriptions and Chronicles

Egyptian records followed a process similar to that observed in Babylon, but with variations. Not only do we find an unbroken series of display inscriptions set up by the kings, but the nature of Egyptian funeral rites led to the creation of a series of very elaborate frescoes and relief sculptures on tomb walls, with ample explanatory texts. Not infrequently, Egyptian nobles caused autobiographical sketches to be engraved on the walls of their tomb chapels, and from them one can learn much Egyptian history.

For example, in about 2550 a noble of southern Egypt recorded his trading journeys into central Africa, and included in it a copy of a complimentary letter sent him by the king. About one thousand years later, two officers in the army which freed Egypt from the Hyksos invaders caused similar sketches of their lives to be written, and from these works we catch our only close view of one of Egypt's most acute crises. Similar sketches are found at intervals all through Egyptian history. Religious inscriptions also play a large part in Egyptian epigraphical collections. From the walls of the tomb chamber of King Unis (about 2650) come a series of charms intended to protect the dead monarch in the world beyond, and similar "pyramid texts" occur in other royal tombs of the age. The walls and columns of temples were covered with reliefs and explanatory inscriptions, some of which glorified the reigning king (who was himself a god of sorts), while others contained prayers and incantations. Such material places before us some phases of Egyptian religion which otherwise could not be discovered.

In the field of formal chronicle writing the Palermo Stone was undoubtedly followed by a series of similar works, but it is probable that these were written upon perishable materials and most of them have vanished. Their existence may be inferred from the fact that in the third century before the Christian era the Graeco-Egyptian historian Manetho found sufficient materials available to enable him to write a complete history of the country from its unification to his own time. Occasionally the Egyptian chroniclers have left traces of their work, as in the excerpts from the history of the wars of King Thutmose III (1501–1447) engraved on the wall of a temple in the capital city of Thebes. The original must have been a spirited and graphic narrative, for even the random fragments which have been preserved contain scenes of great interest. Never again (if we may trust the surviving remains) did an Egyptian author come so near to Western standards of historiography. Manetho, although Egyptian in blood and cultural background, was inspired by Greek precedents and wrote in the Greek language.

A source of great importance for the history of Egyptian foreign relations is the diplomatic correspondence of the Egyptian kings Amenhotep III and Amenhotep IV. Some three hundred letters of this correspondence have been discovered, which are known as the "Amarna Letters" from the modern name of the place of their discovery. Being written in the Babylonian cuneiform script on clay tablets, they have largely escaped damage by the accidents of time, and their contents open to us a phase of Oriental history which could have scarcely been explored either from the chronicles or from other purely Egyptian sources. Similar discoveries of diplomatic dispatches at the Hittite capital of Kheta (modern Boghaz Keui) in Asia Minor and at the Assyrian capital of Nineveh have likewise proved enormously useful to historians.

Later Assyrian and Babylonian Chronicles

With the rise of the Assyrian Empire came fuller and more informative histories of the Tigris-Euphrates region. They had not discarded the disjointed annalistic style of narration, but the statements were somewhat more definite, and the range of the material was broader than in the surviving specimens of the earlier works. Shortly after 800 an Assyrian scribe compiled the *Synchronous History*, a record of the relations of Assyria with Babylon during the preceding eight centuries. The author's pro-Assyrian bias is evident and his statements may have been distorted, but the chronicle preserves much valuable information. Somewhat later came the dry but informative *Assyrian Chronicle*, and various lists of eponymous magistrates after whom the years were named. On the Babylonian side we have the *Babylonian Chronicle* which treats the years 745 to 668 inclusive with considerable objectivity, and the *Gadd Chronicle* which tells in a fair and straightforward manner the story of the last years of the Assyrian Empire and that of the rise of the New Babylonian Empire. These are but examples of a much larger body of chronicle literature which seems to have been extant in the third century before the Christian era. At that time King Antiochus I of the Seleucid state commissioned a Babylonian priest named Berosus to write a history of his country, just as Manetho was doing for Egypt at about the same time. This work, of which only fragments have been preserved, apparently went back to the beginning, telling the confused story with the aid of a long series of chronicles and "king-lists" now lost. Like Manetho's work, it was composed in Greek.

Jewish Historiography

The Jews, like their neighbors, had their chroniclers. But they also had at least one historian who could weld the scattered data together into a connected narrative. It is doubtful whether they had any written records of importance until the tenth century. There are indeed records for the earlier period of the Old Testament, but they were probably not reduced to writing until after the time of King David (1000–960). The traditions embodied in the books of Joshua and Judges undoubtedly contain varying amounts of historic truth, but we cannot check them by any other written narratives and can only supplement them with archeological data. With the rise of the monarchy came government archives, which made possible the compilation of chronicles.

Yet not later than the reign of Solomon, David's son, there arose a historian who produced an account of the rise of the Hebrew Kingdom, comparable to the masterpieces of Greek historiography. At present it comprises the cores of the Old Testament books of First and Second Samuel, but the text is badly garbled with later material inserted by an unskillful editor. The author began with the Philistine conquest of Israel, traced the rise and fall of Saul, the creation of a powerful kingdom by David, and David's later years. His narrative is coherent and closely knit, and the style is simple and powerful. His portrayal of the character of David is masterly, and is achieved by simple narration rather than by labored characterization. There is an almost complete lack of prejudice for any person or class, and the writer handles his subject with the sure hand of one who knew the story from the inside. To judge by the surviving remains of his work, neither the Jews nor any other Oriental people ever afterward produced his equal.

Later Hebrew history is to be gleaned from the books of Kings and Chronicles, supplemented by historical notices in the prophetic books. Because of their continued use for religious purposes, these books have suffered extensive interpolations, but originally they rested upon much the same foundations as the Babylonian and Assyrian chronicles. The same process of interpolation has rendered the so-called "Mosaic Law" practically useless as a source for the study of any single period of Hebrew history.

Less Known Cultures: the Persian and Aegean

Although the Persian government kept written records from the beginning, there is no evidence that they inspired any chroniclers to compile narratives tracing its growth. Persian history is learned from the works of Greek historians, supplemented by notices in the Babylonian chronicles and by display inscriptions of the Persian kings. The most important of the inscriptions is that carved on a cliff at Behistun by order of King Darius I (522–485), in which he tells the story of his accession to the throne. The others contain little of historical interest.

Although the Aegean region was the home of a civilization almost as old as that of Egypt, it was one of the last parts of the eastern Mediterranean world to emerge, for modern investigators, from the prehistoric age.

This is because of our inability to read the records which the people of Minoan Crete left behind them, although they do not seem to have been very full or informative. In fact, all over the Aegean area the period prior to about 750 can be studied only through two media: archeology and oral legends recorded centuries later by the Greek poets and historians. The Minoan Cretans had commercial contact with Egypt, Cyprus, and other near-by lands, but the records of these neighbors have little or nothing to say about them. Archeology has uncovered for us the remains of a civilization here which for sixteen hundred years (3000–1400) flourished in wealth, luxury, and splendor, and which produced many fine art treasures, yet its political history is still a blank to us. The civilization of the mainland Greeks during the latter part of the same period (1600–1100) is somewhat better known because of the wealth of oral legend — much of it substantiated by archeological evidence — which illustrates political, social, and economic conditions and preserves the names of important individuals. It cannot be said that the Greeks of the thirteenth century B.C. are as well known to us as the Egyptians of the same period, but their history is by no means an entire blank.

The Middle Age and the Dawn of Historic Greece

With the fading of the older civilization of Greece, which occurred about 1100, there ensues a period for which legend has preserved few facts. Not until about 750 does the veil begin to lift, and even then the various parts of the Greek world do not come into view at once. The alphabet used by the historic Greeks appears to have been first developed on the coast of Asia Minor and it was the eastern Greeks who first made extensive use of it. We cannot be certain what kind of written records they used, but it is reasonable to suppose that records of sorts existed. As the knowledge of alphabetic writing spread, the practice of recording simple facts would spread with it. Epitaphs, lists of magistrates, business accounts, and similar matters would naturally be set down before other facts. Shortly before 650, a movement to codify the laws of the various cities became evident, and by the end of the seventh century a number of written codes were to be found. In the early sixth century we find public men like the Athenian lawgiver Solon composing autobiographical sketches to justify their careers to posterity, and even writing books on philosophy. For the same age we have a great deal of lyric poetry which contains allusions to contemporary events. Before 500, prose genealogies of noble families and other avowed records of the past were being compiled. Not until 450 did

Herodotus compose the oldest Greek historic work now in existence, but his fund of accurate information for some of the Greek world goes back to three centuries before that date. From these incomplete records, supplemented by archeology, the history of Greece during the three centuries after 750 can be written.

Except for the solitary Hebrew historian of the tenth century B.C., the Greeks were the originators of the art and science of historiography, for it was they who, first of all Occidental peoples, adopted the practice of writing the story of the past as a connected narrative instead of in a series of choppy and disconnected notices. From the fifth century onward the Greeks were never without their historians, but this is not the place to evaluate their work. Herodotus, Thucydides, Xenophon, and their fellow historians demand extensive treatment, and the proper place for it is in connection with Greek literature.

METHODS OF CHRONOLOGICAL RESEARCH

Chronological Aids: Name-Lists and the Greek Olympiads

In view of the chronological shortcomings of ancient historians, the art of determining and verifying the dates of the events which they record has to be highly developed. But for all that, its foundation principle is a simple one: the historian must in each case proceed from the known to the unknown. The early centuries of our Christian era overlap with two other eras — that which began with the foundation of Rome, and that which began with the first regular holding of the Olympic Games in Greece. A comparison will soon show that the Roman era began in the year 753 B.C. and the Olympic era in 776 B.C. For present purposes it will be sufficient to confine our attention to the latter. As the Olympic Games were held every four years, a given year would be designated as the first, second, third, or fourth of a given Olympiad. Let us now take a given event — the battle of Leuctra — and see how its date can be determined. Two methods of dating are given by ancient historians. It is said to have taken place in the second year of the one hundred and second Olympiad, when Phrasiclides was archon at Athens. Now the first date gives us the year 371 B.C., and as the Athenian year began in July, we must assume that Phrasiclides became archon in July, 371, and served until about the same month of 370. As the battle occurred in the fifth day of the first month of the Attic year, it must be placed in July, 371. But in most cases the name of the Athenian archon alone is given. There are in existence tables showing the order in which the archons succeeded to office, and double-dating like that given above enables us to work forward or back on the archon tables to place any given archon in his proper year of the pre-Christian era. Where no dates at all are given, events may be dated indirectly by their relation to those whose dates are known.

For the Oriental countries, more roundabout methods are necessary, and the results are often only approximate. As previously indicated, the Assyrians had the practice of naming each year after an official called a *limmu*, and kept tables of such officials like the Athenian archon lists. They also kept records of eclipses of the sun and moon with their dates, and astronomers are able to give the exact dates of these phenomena. By these and other means, all of which give substantially identical results, the *limmu* tables can be correlated with the years of the pre-Christian era, and dates in Assyrian history can be determined as far back as the tenth pre-Christian century. But the Assyrians themselves frequently give us dates for events which happened before the beginning of this system of chronological reckoning. Thus, King Sennacherib (705–681) tells us that his predecessor Tukulti-enurta reigned six hundred years before him — a fact which would place the latter shortly after 1300. Such Assyrian dates for early events are not always correct, but by checking them with all available data, mistakes can usually be detected.

Egyptian chronology is determined by several kinds of data. One can begin by adding up the regnal years of the kings as given by Manetho, but this method is not at all exact. Manetho's sources did not always give correct figures, and even if they had done so, it is likely that they would have been garbled in the process of transcription. But here again the astronomer comes to the aid of the historian. Until a very late date the Egyptians used a calendar of exactly 365 days, which therefore lost approximately one day every four years, or a year every 1461 years. Now the star Sirius rises with the sun on the same day of the true solar calendar each year, and the Egyptians celebrated the event with an annual feast. We know that a cycle of 1461 years ended in either A.D. 139 or 143. Accordingly, when we learn from Egyptian sources that in the ninth year of King Amenhotep I the rising of Sirius occurred on the ninth day of the eleventh month, astronomical calculations set the year at either 1550 or 1546, and the king's accession at 1557 or 1553. Such astronomically fixed dates carry us back as far as 2000, beyond which our chronology becomes liable to an increasing margin of error. For the early period of Egyptian history we have only Manetho's reckonings, rechecked by inscriptions and the laws of probability, and most dates are subject to an uncertainty which may amount to a century either way.

The Aegean Civilization: Evidence from Commerce

In view of the entire lack of narrative and documentary sources for the study of the Aegean civilization, its chronology must be tentative and approximate. As a rule the round dates which are given for the beginning and ending of its periods are gained by observation of its contacts with Egypt and other lands whose chronology is fixed. Commerce between the Egyptians and the peoples of Minoan Crete was fairly constant before 2000. Egyptian objects, the approximate dates of whose manufacture are known, have been found at Knossos and other Cretan sites, and Cretan objects have been found in Egypt associated with Egyptian articles the dates of whose manufacture can be easily determined. Similarly Cretan objects were exported to mainland Greece and the Aegean islands. By such evidence the archeologist is able to prove that the period of Cretan history known as "Early Minoan" was roughly contemporary with the Egyptian Old Kingdom period and the age of disorder which followed it (3000–2200), that the "Middle Minoan" period was contemporary with the Egyptian Middle Kingdom (2160–1788), and that the "Late Minoan" age began about the time of the rise of the Eighteenth Dynasty in Egypt. After 1400, there was a complete stoppage of imports of artistic Minoan pottery from Crete into Egypt, a fact explained by the destruction of the Cretan cities by invaders about that time. When once a certain type of Minoan pottery has been dated by the finding of specimens in Egypt, or of Egyptian articles of known date associated with it in Crete, the discovery of specimens of the same style in mainland Greece or elsewhere would point to the fact that the strata of remains in which it is found were deposited at about the same time as that in which the pottery was made. Such results can only be regarded as rough approximations, but if this fact is kept in mind, they are of great value.

Combined Methods: Babylonian and Hebrew Chronology

Babylonian chronology has to be determined by means like those used in the cases of Assyria and Egypt and by comparison with the latter. As far back as 1600, the *Synchronous History* correlates it with the chronology of Assyria. Likewise several of the Babylonian kings of the fifteenth, fourteenth, and thirteenth centuries of the pre-Christian era carried on diplomatic relations with Egyptian and Hittite rulers whose dates are known. By using such data, and by dead reckonings from the known lengths of the reigns of various kings, we can secure a fairly exact chronological reckoning which takes us as far back as the sixteenth century. If, in addition, we accept the figures given by a late Babylonian chronicle for the duration and terminal date of the Kassite Dynasty of Babylonian kings, we may reach the year 1746 B.C. as the tentative date of the accession of the first Kassite ruler. Before that time the dates are all problematical, the possible margin of error increasing the farther back one goes. At first glance it might appear that the "king-lists" and the work of Berosus would help greatly in eliminating this uncertainty, but the former are prone to record as consecutive many dynasties which were undoubtedly contemporary, and the latter in its present state is too fragmentary and confused to serve the purpose. Thus, we find in modern histories of Babylonia dates as far apart as 2123 and 1940 given for the accession of King Hammurabi, while that of his great predecessor Sargon of Agade is variously placed at 2872, 2650, 2630, and 2500.

Hebrew chronology would, if the Old Testament figures were accepted without question, be a very simple matter. The lengths of the reigns of the kings of Israel and Judah are given quite definitely in the books of Kings and Chronicles, and even in Joshua and Judges the duration of each period prior to the rise of Saul is stated in exact terms. But the appearance of clarity is somewhat deceptive. The figures are not always consistent with themselves and vary in the different versions of the Old Testament. Hence it is advisable to check them carefully by other available data. A number of Phoenician, Egyptian, and Assyrian sources either mention the Hebrews directly or refer to persons mentioned in the Old Testament narrative, and in some cases such notices lead to changes in the accepted dates. An example would be found in the terminal dates of King Ahab of Israel. By the literal Old Testament chronology he reigned from 899 to 877, but a statement in an inscription of Shalmaneser II of Assyria shows that Ahab was reigning in 854. Again, the Assyrian records state that Samaria fell in 722, and the notice in Second Kings declares that this was the sixth year of Hezekiah, king of Judah. But elsewhere we hear that Sennacherib's invasion of Judea took place in the fourteenth year of King Hezekiah, and Assyrian sources date this invasion at 701. Hence the correct date of Hezekiah's accession seems to have been 715 instead of 728.

Such is the brief outline of the critical method by which chronological problems connected with ancient history are solved. It cannot in all cases result in conclusions which are above criticism, but it has already solved many problems and brought others closer to solution, and with new data it will no doubt solve many more.

2

Primitive Man and

the Birth of Civilization

IN THE BEGINNING, if we may trust our scanty evidence, man was completely uncivilized, living very much as did his cousins, the anthropoid apes. It requires a considerable exercise of the imagination to grasp the meaning of this statement. We must conceive of a state of human life without tools, fire, clothing, artificial shelter, agriculture, tame animals, government, religion, or any other features of that enormous cultural heritage which even the lowest of the present-day savages possess. Our first human ancestors began on a cultural plane no higher than that of the other animals, and only after ages of slow progress did their descendants accumulate knowledge sufficient to assure relatively secure mastery of their environment. The story of man's first halting steps along the road to civilization will be told, so far as meager data and limited space permit, in the present chapter.

Qualifications for Survival

Since mankind has developed along lines so different from those followed by the other animals, it may be well to determine what characteristics the species possesses which will account for its matchless achievements. At first glance the human body appears poorly equipped for the struggle for existence compared with that of the bulky elephant, the swift horse, or the well-armed tiger. In fact, this is not the case. It is true that man does not possess any of the qualities which fit these animals so efficiently for their respective environments, but the latter have achieved a certain limited superiority by extreme specialization and have thereby largely sacrificed the ability to adjust to changed conditions. Man's physical makeup is not, biologically speaking, highly specialized. Therefore, although he is not perfectly adapted to any one set of circumstances, he can, with artificial help, survive under climatic conditions varying from extreme humidity to the barren desert and from tropical heat to sub-arctic cold. His digestive tract has accommodated itself to a range of diets from entirely carnivorous to strictly herbivorous. His powers of sight are among the best in the animal kingdom and, under pressure of necessity, his senses of smell and hearing can be tremendously developed. Opposable thumbs allow him to apply his hands to uses impossible in the forelimbs of other animals. But above all, his mental powers make him supreme. All other animals depend almost entirely upon instinct to guide their actions, but man makes extensive use of both reason and imagination, faculties which allow him to foresee future needs and to provide for them. His power of speech enables him to secure the effective co-operation of his fellows and to transmit the accumulated experiences of the past to each new generation with a degree of accuracy impossible for other species of animals. Thus he builds up a cultural heritage which grows appreciably with each generation.

As a result of these unique qualities, the development of the human race has no close parallel anywhere among living things. Man overcomes his natural deficiencies by artificial means, and where the other animals can meet the challenge of changed conditions only by migration or modification in physical structure, he creates for himself an artificial environment. Clothing and a heated dwelling allow him the indispensable advantages of the tropics in a cold climate; tools and weapons make him dominant over the animal and vegetable kingdoms; and agriculture and stock-breeding supply him with food in abundance greater than unaided Nature could ever provide.

Shadowy Origin of the Earliest Human Types

The present state of archeological knowledge makes it impossible to state in what part of the world man first became differentiated from the other primates, but the remains of types with decided ape-like characteristics have been found in Java (Pithecanthropus Erectus), England (Piltdown Man), China (Peking Man), and elsewhere. The dates of their existences are largely matters of conjecture, but there are indications that they lived hundreds of thousands of years before recorded history. It is uncertain whether the crudest stone implements that survive are their handiwork, but at best their cultural attainments appear to have been few and rudimentary. Not until ages after his first appearance upon earth did man first attain anything approaching his present mental development and with it the faculty to create efficient artificial aids for the mastery of his environment.

Wherever the place of its origin, the human race soon spread over all the land masses of the globe except those nearest the North and South poles. The time and circumstances of the migrations which carried mankind so far can, in most cases, never be known, for they occurred long before the dawn of history. Indeed, it may well be said that over most of the world its human inhabitants produced few if any ideas or inventions which helped to raise the cultural level of the race. The primitive inhabitants of Australia, central and southern Africa, North and South America, the Pacific islands, and northern Asia, had, it is true, cultures of a sort, but these races, when first observed by Europeans and civilized Asiatics, were poorly developed in the practical and fine arts and in intellectual matters. Even the civilization of China and India, although advanced, has had very small influence upon the growth of the high and complex culture which is now becoming the common property of all nations. The leaders in the creation and development of this early civilization were the peoples of southwestern Asia, Europe, and northern Africa, and it is to them exclusively that the present study will be devoted.

THE OLD STONE AGE

The continuous development of civilization in Europe and the Near East can be traced with somewhat greater certainty from the beginning of what is commonly called the *Paleolithic* or Old Stone Age (roughly 30,000 B.C.). The earlier part of this period coincides in northeastern North America and northern Europe with a series of extreme climatic changes collectively known as the *Glacial Age*. Four times these lands were invaded by masses of ice from the polar regions, which covered them as thickly as interior Greenland is today. Between glaciations, temperate or even subtropical conditions would prevail at times, and plant and animal life varied accordingly. In the warm interglacial periods, tropical animals, such as the elephant, rhinoceros, and hippopotamus, found their way into France and England, but later the returning cold drove out or exterminated these tropical visitors and replaced them by the reindeer and other arctic forms of life.

The land masses of the Northern Hemisphere underwent similar catastrophic changes. At times the sea receded so far that the British Isles

DRAWING OF A MAMMOTH
From a cave in France

formed a part of the adjoining continent and the bed of the North Sea was a broad river valley. But on the other hand, the ocean covered portions of what is today dry land. Land bridges connected Spain as well as southern Italy and Sicily with Africa, permitting the distribution of plants and the migration of animals and men from south to north under conditions now impossible.

Glacial Age Men: Neanderthal and Cromagnon Races

Near the beginning of the Glacial Period, a new race of men (known from the place where their remains were first discovered as the *Neanderthal Race*) entered Europe. Although more primitive, physically and mentally, than present-day Europeans, they made notable progress in the arts of life. They had acquired considerable skill in manufacturing flint axes, scrapers, and other tools, which they made by the "percussion" method. A piece of flint was broken into long, narrow flakes. Each suitable flake would be further reduced by striking off small fragments until the desired shape and sharpness were secured. The Neanderthals must have had efficient spears and other weapons and a profound knowledge of trapping. The sites of their camps are strewn with the bones of the elephant, rhinoceros, hippopotamus, horse, and other animals, which they evidently slew for food. They understood the use of fire and cooked their meat. It is probable that they knew how to make clothing out of skins, and during the colder part of the year lived in natural caves. They buried their dead, placing with

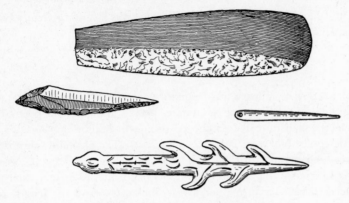

PALEOLITHIC TOOLS AND WEAPONS

them implements and ornaments for use in the world to come. This fact indicates that they had a religion of sorts, and it is to be regretted that time has left no glimpse of their other social, political, and religious institutions. These would, we may be sure, have been at least as highly developed as those of many modern savages.

Toward the close of the Glacial Age a new race appeared in Europe which superseded or absorbed the Neanderthals. The *Cromagnon* (or *Aurignacian*) *Race* (so called from two caves in France where their remains have been found) introduced decided improvements into European culture. Physically and mentally they were not inferior to modern Europeans and applied their skill to both practical and aesthetic purposes. Their flints were better chipped than those of their predecessors, and they made fine weapons and domestic implements of bone. On the walls of the caves which formed their winter homes they painted striking and realistic sketches of the animals with which they were familiar, occasionally interspersing them with human figures. These paintings probably had a magical significance, for among them is a figure which evidently represents a magician costumed in an animal mask and skin. They carved corpulent female figurines in soapstone which may represent a deity whom they worshiped. They wore clothing that had been sewed with bone needles, and for personal adornment necklaces, bracelets, and other articles which were also buried with the dead.

As the climate grew warmer after the last glaciation, the distinctive features of Cromagnon culture disappeared. The last, or *Azilian*, phase of the Old Stone Age contains little of interest. It was a time of transition. New races were entering Europe from both east and south, bringing with them novel and stimulating ideas. The time was ripe for a great advance in arts, living standards, and thought.

THE NEW STONE AGE

About 6000 B.C., Europe was beginning to assume something of its present appearance with regard to climate, plants, animals, and population. The glaciers had retreated to the position which they now occupy and climatic conditions were much as at present. The elephant, rhinoceros, reindeer, and other exotic animals were gone, succeeded by the present fauna. Likewise, the human inhabitants had begun to assume their present racial character. In the northwest, the ancestors of the long-headed, blond Nordics had taken possession of the lands vacated by the glaciers. In the south and along the western coast in a belt reaching as far north as the British Isles, the short, dark, long-headed Mediterranean stock was predominant. A third group, the stocky, broad-headed, brunette Alpine race, was pushing in from the east and occupying the center of the continent. Apparently, in their original Asiatic home, the Alpine peoples had been in contact with a higher culture than any in the Europe of that day, and they brought with them the knowledge of improved forms of flint-working, several varieties of tame animals, and possibly a primitive form of agriculture. These groups all belonged to the Caucasian Race. Their descendants, very much mixed, form the population of most of the continent today.

First Craftsmanship: Implements, Pottery, Weaving, Building

The New Stone Age, which grew out of these conditions, was marked by comparatively rapid and thoroughly revolutionary progress. Instead of using any chance piece of flint which came to hand, men began to mine the chalk seams in which the best quality flints were to be found, and in districts where such seams occurred, a mining industry developed. With picks of deer horn the miners sank shafts to tap the chalk seams, and followed them for long distances in transverse tunnels.

Once brought to the surface, the flint was worked into various implements which were exported to distant communities. The tools were highly specialized and were made by a new and improved process of flaking. After the instrument had been roughly shaped by the percussion method, a piece of wood or bone was pressed against it at various points, causing a series of very fine flakes to fly off shaping the blade to a keen and

Oriental Institute, Chicago

NEOLITHIC TOOLS, AND NEOLITHIC POTTERY WITH GEOMETRIC DECORATIONS

uniform edge. In some instances the blade was polished smooth on a whetstone. Axes were attached to handles in various ways. Sometimes a hole was bored in the handle, one end of the flint head inserted, and the handle tied above and below to prevent splitting. Or a hole might be drilled through the axe-head and the handle inserted, as in modern axes. Other kinds of stone were used in certain localities and for specific purposes. Thus, in Italy, Sicily, the Aegean region, and elsewhere, much use was made of obsidian — a brittle volcanic rock which takes a very sharp edge. On the shores of the Baltic Sea amber was collected and exported as far as the Mediterranean lands.

An equally important improvement in living conditions resulted from the discovery of the art of pottery-making of which Paleolithic man knew nothing. When carrying liquids he had to use gourds, skin-bottles with greased seams, hollow horns or bones, or his stomach. The boiling of food was almost impossible. The first jars were entirely hand-made. On a flat surface a layer of stiff mud was spread to serve as a bottom, and the sides were built up gradually with strips of the same material and baked in an open fire. Such jars were porous and no doubt the pores were sealed with animal fat, which is the process used by some of our Western Indians. But the Neolithic housewives soon found a wide variety of uses for these crude vessels. They provided rat-proof storage for food, and with proper care could be used for cooking-vessels. Gradually, rude ornamentation — usually of geometric design — was added for beautification.

In central Europe the Neolithic Age witnessed the birth of still another art which was to add greatly to human comfort — that of weaving. Linen thread and cloth of various kinds have been found on the sites of the Swiss lake-dwellings of this period, and it is safe to assume that woolen cloth was also woven. The fabric was dyed black, yellow, red, or blue; or sometimes the threads were dyed in various colors and woven into patterns.

A revolution likewise occurred in housing. We do not know what dwellings other than natural caves had been used in the Old Stone Age, but the more progressive Neolithic people almost entirely abandoned these shelters, and built houses. They were usually flimsy structures of poles covered with plaited twigs, with an outside coat of mud, and thatched roofs. The dwellings were grouped in villages frequently surrounded by stockades to repel animal or human intruders. In the lake region of Switzerland the need for defense led to still more drastic steps. Far out in the lake the inhabitants drove piles into the bottom, built their timber platforms on them, and on these erected their houses. Removable bridges or boats provided the residents with means of reaching the shore.

Agriculture and the Domestication of Animals

Permanent settlements imply the possession of a dependable food-supply. Hunters and fishermen have to follow the game and the fish, remaining more or less nomadic. In the Neolithic Age two new sources of livelihood developed: agriculture and stock-raising. Both had started probably in central Asia, where excavations indicate that crops were grown as early as 8000 B.C. The domestication of the cow, pig, sheep, and camel came much later in this region. And the horse was not added to the list of tame animals until later still. In its earliest stages, agriculture was one of the main occupations of the Neolithic woman, who cultivated the ground with picks, digging-sticks, and hoes. Necessarily, only a small patch of ground (an acre or less) could be cultivated by each woman, and the vegetable food which she produced merely supplemented the game and fish which the men provided.

The domestication of animals changed all this. A team of oxen, dragging a primitive plow made from the fork of a tree, could accomplish as much in a day as a woman with a hand-tool could in two weeks. But as woman's strength was not equal to the task of guiding the plow, the men took over this phase of the cultivation. In doing so they lost the old happy-go-lucky freedom of the primitive hunter and developed new qualities: patience, industry, shrewdness, and devotion to home. Wheat, barley, oats, rye, peas, beans, and many edible herbs largely replaced meat in the diet of the people. Methods of cultivation were usually crude, and the land in many localities was soon exhausted. In Egypt, the Tigris-Euphrates Valley, and parts of the Aegean region, however, this was not the case. There irrigation was used to mature the crops, and the natural fertility of the soil, aided by careful and intelligent labor, kept productivity high over long periods of time. Somewhere in this region the olive and grape were domesticated, and have since been important features of the agriculture of the Mediterranean lands.

The domestication of animals gave to the Neolithic populations new sources of food, motive power, and raw materials for textiles. In addition to the species reduced to man's service in central Asia, the peoples of western Asia and northern Africa tamed two others which have since been commonly used there — the donkey and the goat. In various localities different breeds of wolves and jackals were admitted to human society and became the ancestors of our present-day dogs. They served to guard the flocks and herds and aided their masters in tracking game.

Later there appeared on the steppes of eastern Europe and western Asia, and in the semi-desert lands of Arabia and North Africa, a new group of nomadic herdsmen, who depended entirely upon their "moving farms" for sustenance. When at last the possession of horses made it possible for these people to move about rapidly, they varied their activities by raiding the lands of their settled neighbors and robbing them of their possessions. Thus, the age-long struggle between nomad and farmer began — a struggle which was to deluge with blood and ruin the civilized lands of Europe, Asia, and Africa.

Beginnings of the Family, Society, and Government

But it was not enough that the human race should acquire dominion over the other animals and dependable means of supplying its material necessities. Its members had to learn how to live harmoniously together, to co-operate for the common good, and to satisfy spiritual cravings which, though vague, were real and urgent. The first two of these needs led to the evolution of social and political institutions, and the third gave birth to religion. It is probable that mankind felt all of these needs and attempted to meet them at a very early stage of his existence.

How social organization and government originated can, in the present state of our knowledge, only be described hypothetically. It is reasonable to suppose that some form of family group existed among the human species from the beginning, but the steps in its evolution are unknown. In the present-day world an infinite variety of such institutions exist, but it seems probable that the races to which we owe the origins of Occidental civilization had from a very early period leaned toward the polygamous or monogamous patriarchal family in which the father was not only the head of the group, but the channel through which descent and relationship were traced. But such a kinship group could be expanded readily to much larger proportions.

When the sons of the same father became in time the heads of new families, their children continued to acknowledge the relationship of all these descendants of a common ancestor, and a clan was formed. Similarly a group of clans claiming descent from a common ancestor would form a tribe. Often the blood-kinship of the members of such a group was fictitious rather than real, for adoption of outsiders was always possible, and common interests would lead in time to the wholesale amalgamation of unrelated neighboring groups.

Out of these expanded kinship groups came man's first form of government. Within the society customs developed regulating the mutual relations of its members, and certain individuals, distinguished by age, wealth, wisdom, or warlike valor, became chiefs or elders. To them, individually or collectively, were delegated the tasks of interpreting and applying customs, arbitrating disputes, formulating policies, and taking the lead in offensive or defensive war. Morality was rather strictly a group affair and every stranger was an enemy. Property rights begin to gain recognition, first in personal possessions and later in landed property, but respect for property rights was confined within the home group. Plundering others was not only permissible but honorable. For this reason wars were common in the Neolithic Age.

War profoundly modified the composition of human society. To wage it successfully, one had to submit to leadership and discipline, and the victorious tribe of one day would occasionally find itself in a state of near servitude to its own chief the next. The fate of conquered peoples varied. Sometimes the whole tribe migrated so far that it was beyond pursuit. Again, it might accept an inferior position under the suzerainty of the conquerors, paying them tribute and perhaps swelling the forces with which they fought subsequent wars. At worst, the men of the conquered group would be killed and the women and children distributed as slaves among the conquerors. Thus, there grew up in some regions a class of slaves who, in return for the barest subsistence, toiled for the benefit of their masters, and slavery became a recognized feature of human society.

By such means successful war chiefs came to dominate large numbers of people with nearly absolute power, and other influences contributed to the same result. In lands where irrigation or flood-control was practiced, men had to co-operate in masses to perform the work upon which the life of the community depended, and this could only be achieved by submission to leaders capable of directing such activities. Religion, as we shall presently see, strengthened the authority of rulers by giving to their acts divine sanction. Thus, by the end of the prehistoric period a few communities were under the rule of absolute divine-right monarchies. Especially in Egypt and Asia this tended to become the prevailing form of government.

Origins of Religion and Custom

The second great need, no less urgent than the first, was to find a means of living in harmony with the powers that ruled the universe. This problem was not entirely new. Very early in his earthly career man had begun to feel that he was in contact with powerful, intelligent, and invisible beings whose good-will brought him prosperity, and whose anger meant misfortune, suffering, and death. His utter ignorance of the laws of nature, and the seemingly inexplicable blows of famine, pestilence, and other misfortunes, led him to study the ways of these beings to propitiate them. His quest was greatly intensified when he began to cultivate the soil and to breed livestock. There had been sorcerers and medicine-men even in Paleolithic times, but now the power and influence of these people grew enormously. They claimed to know by what rituals, charms, and sacrifices the "powers" could be made friendly to man so that they could bestow prosperity and safety. They also professed to foretell the future, and by the possession of these occult powers they exercised a tyrannical authority which we can hardly conceive. When in Egypt or western Asia we later find the priests manipulating governments to their own advantage and becoming enormously wealthy landlords, or when we consider the stupendous labors which the people of Europe and the Near East performed in erecting the huge stone circles which formed their places of worship, we realize the awe which these priestly tyrants inspired. While there were no doubt many tricksters and conscious cheats among them, they probably helped to enforce the laws which contributed to the general welfare and thus formed a necessary agency of social control.

It must be assumed that the spirits in which the Neolithic Europeans believed were seldom clear-cut and widely recognized gods, but rather a host of hazy and mysterious beings, without human form or qualities.

Yet this primitive religion was all-pervading and all-powerful. "Taboos" were numerous and were mercilessly enforced. Human sacrifices were common, as well as self-torture, sacramental sexual license, ritual cannibalism, and other primitively obscene rites. Every act of life called for the propitiation of the unseen powers and when the matter was of general and lasting importance, the result was the establishment of a holiday or festival. Sacred stones, springs, trees, caves, and mountains abounded. We may smile at the more puerile features of such a religion and feel disgust at its darker phases, but we must remember that it satisfied needs far more intimate and pressing than later and more refined worships have done. Proof of its vitality is to be found in the fact that it was the real religion of the masses until the advent of Christianity, that it offered to the latter far more resistance than the official pagan gods could inspire, and that many of its less objectionable features were later incorporated into the practice of the Church. Many of our Christmas, May-Day, Easter, and other customs go back to the Neolithic Age.

The belief in a future life must have become increasingly vivid in Neolithic Europe, for burial customs and tomb furniture became more elaborate. Wealthy persons were laid to rest in tombs consisting of chambers made of rough stones, covered with mounds of earth. Into these burial places were put weapons, jewelry, clothing, and other possessions of the deceased, to be used by him in the other world. Monuments of this character are found throughout western Europe, northern Africa, and Asia as far east as India, indicating the existence of ancestor- and hero-worship throughout this region.

If the foregoing description of Neolithic life is compared with that of the Paleolithic hunting tribes on the one hand and with the life of today on the other, we can see that during this period men had acquired most of the arts essential to civilization. Agriculture and the possession of tame animals freed them from the necessity of wandering in search of food and improved weapons made them superior to the most dangerous beasts. They had learned to co-operate in performing tasks for which their individual strength was inadequate, and they regulated their lives by law and religion. Crude as was their existence, they needed only to make a few more discoveries, in addition to developing the arts they already possessed, to make life comfortable and refined.

The End of an Age

But we may well suppose that at the end of the Neolithic Age the human race had reached a temporary *impasse* which could only be overcome by new discoveries. Skillful as was the manipulation of stone, bone, wood, and horn, these materials could not be fashioned into delicate or complicated instruments and their efficiency was limited. A stone axe could, with great labor, be used to cut down a tree, and with the aid of fire it might be the instrument for hollowing a dugout canoe, but a better material had to be found for cutting trees before wood could be shaped into planks to build ships and houses. Again, as long as men had to depend entirely upon the spoken word and memory for the transmission of knowledge, they labored under an insuperable disadvantage. Some other and more dependable means of recording and transmitting their thoughts was essential. The first need was to be met by the discovery of the art of smelting and casting metals, and the second by the invention of the art of writing.

THE AGE OF METALS

Nature has never provided mankind with a sufficient supply of any of the metals in a pure state. Occasional deposits of pure native copper have been found in North America, Australia, and a few other places, but the natives of these localities have never learned to melt the metal or to make tools from it. With a few exceptions it may be said that copper, tin, iron, silver, and gold occur in nature only as ores, from which they have to be released by mechanical and chemical treatment.

The Chalcolithic and Bronze Ages

It is not known where the first steps in metal-working were taken, and we can only guess at the date. Gold, which sometimes occurs in a free state in nuggets, and which can be easily hammered into desired shapes, was used for jewelry by those fortunate enough to possess it in the later Neolithic Age, but it is too soft for use in cutting-tools. Copper is very easily separated from some of the ores, and it is not surprising that it was the first of the metals to be worked in important quantities. Stones containing hematite or other copper compounds would, when exposed to fire, break down and so yield lumps of more or less pure copper. Experiments would soon show that, by remelting, these lumps could be cast into any desired shape. On the Iranian Plateau, in what was later to be Persia, the rudiments of this art were known thousands of years before they were practiced in the Mediterranean world, but it is not certain that it was discovered there, and it may have been worked out independently in several places.

The new material had several decided advantages over stone in the manufacture of weapons and domestic implements, but it also had certain disadvantages which slowed its spread. Pure copper is almost useless for cutting-tools, since it is too soft to hold an edge. Fortunately, Nature helped the primitive metal-workers to overcome this handicap. The ores from which they obtained their supplies of copper also contained antimony, tin, zinc, arsenic, and other minerals which melted out with the copper, forming natural alloys. These were harder than pure copper, and for many centuries such alloys formed the best material for axes, saws, knives, and many other objects. These tools could, with care and patience, be made to perform tasks far more complicated and difficult than those which could be done with stone implements. The stone which faced the Egyptian pyramids was probably cut with saws of this low-grade copper alloy. In fact, both the Egyptians and the peoples of the Tigris-Euphrates Valley used similar implements until about 2500 B.C., long after the historic age had begun and found them fairly adequate to the needs of a high civilization. But they never entirely replaced stone and other materials used in the Neolithic Age. The latter were cheaper than the new tools and satisfied the requirements of the poorer classes and backward communities. Hence, this period may be termed the Chalcolithic or Copper-Stone Age.

Meanwhile, continued experiments had shown that a mixture of approximately nine parts of copper and one part of tin produced an alloy (bronze), far superior to any other then known in toughness and durability. About 2500 B.C., it began to displace the other copper alloys in the markets of western Asia and the Mediterranean world, and for over a thousand years thereafter dominated the scene. This period is generally known as the Bronze Age.

The spread of bronze-working was gradual but steady. From its earliest centers in Egypt and Asia, traders carried bronze utensils and weapons to the Aegean region and Cyprus. There the natives soon began to work their local deposits of copper ore, and obtained the tin from Spain, Italy, and the Aegean countries. From these new centers as well as from the old, the art spread along the trade routes by sea and by land in all directions. Bronze was sent to the Baltic countries in payment for amber. All the other sections of northern Europe had entered the Bronze Age by 1500 B.C. No violent break in the evolution of civilization resulted, although the possession of better and more effective weapons may have had some effect upon the greater prevalence of wars in these regions, henceforth.

The Dawn of Recorded History

In Egypt and the Tigris-Euphrates Valley, the latter part of the Chal-colithic Age and all of the Bronze Age lie outside the prehistoric period, for the peoples of these lands had by this time evolved efficient and dependable systems of writing. Written records of a rudimentary type go back to about 3300 B.C., and through them the surrounding countries emerged dimly into the light of history a few centuries later. In the western Mediterranean lands and in central and northern Europe, thousands of years were to elapse before the veil was lifted. But at this point let us take up the thread of history in those lands where the materials for it were already committed to writing.

3

****

Early Babylonia (ca. 3500–1750 B.C.)

The Land of the Two Rivers

It is a striking fact that the two earliest historic civilizations of the world, those of Egypt and the Tigris-Euphrates Valley, arose in rather close proximity to each other and in very similar environments. We may well begin our study of these two cultures with a glance at the countries which gave them birth.

Terrain and Climate

At the southwestern corner of Asia lies the Arabian peninsula with an area of over a million square miles, most of which is a desert. Although the peninsula joins the continent at about thirty degrees north latitude, the desert extends some five degrees farther north, forming a semicircular expanse of waste land to which has been applied the very apt name of the "Desert Bay." This whole region is in the same rainless belt as North Africa and is almost entirely unfit for cultivation. From the earliest known times it has been the home of nomadic tribes of Semitic speech and culture, who have wandered from one oasis to another, living on the produce of their flocks and herds, supplemented by the spoils of war or the income from trading ventures. So narrow is their margin of subsistence that every unusually dry year is certain to send them forth as desperate and starving robbers to attack and plunder the lands of their settled neighbors. This process, continued over a period of thousands of years, has resulted in the Semitization of all the neighboring lands and has given rise to such settled agricultural Semitic peoples as the Babylonians, Assyrians, Syrians, Phoenicians, and Jews.

Along the eastern, northern, and western sides of the Desert Bay lies the "Fertile Crescent." It is a strip of land which varies from a few miles to one hundred and fifty in width, and can be rendered productive either by the utilization of the natural rainfall or by irrigation. Its eastern extremity is at the head of the Persian Gulf, from which it stretches to the northwest until it touches the mountains of Asia Minor and continues southwestward between the desert and the Mediterranean Sea to the Isthmus of Suez. Indeed, it may be said to continue up the Nile Valley to the southern border of Egypt or beyond. Thus, the two regions in which man first emerged from barbarism lay at opposite ends of this fertile strip. As the civilization of the Tigris-Euphrates Valley is presumably the older of the two, let us examine it first.

Both the Euphrates and the Tigris rivers rise in the mountains of Armenia and flow southeastward into the Persian Gulf. They preserve roughly parallel courses between the Desert Bay and the Iranian Plateau. At one time the Persian Gulf extended over three hundred miles farther inland than at present, but before the dawn of history the silt deposited by the rivers had driven it back, forming a plain some two hundred miles long and from fifty to one hundred and fifty miles wide of light, loose, and very fertile soil. Each year in March, the melting snows of the northern highlands swell these streams to flood stage and the Euphrates remains high throughout the summer. In a state of nature they inundate the plain indiscriminately, cutting numerous side-channels and depositing new layers of silt. In this condition the rivers are useless or even dangerous to man, but as he develops the intelligence to plan dikes and canals, and the industry to build them, their waters cause the soil to produce enormous crops. Such was the land which later became known as Babylonia.

The plain of the Tigris and the Euphrates at that time had the thirty-first parallel of north latitude as its southern boundary and the thirty-fourth as its northern. It was about as far from the Equator as our states of Georgia, Alabama, and Mississippi. Babylon lies in about the same latitude as Savannah, Georgia. This fact, together with the low elevation of the plain, its proximity to the Arabian Desert, and the protection from cold north winds which the mountains afford, determines the climate. In summer the noonday temperatures often rise above 120° Fahrenheit, though the nights are cool. The winters are mild, with no snows and only an occasional light freeze. From November to March showers are frequent, but little or no rain falls at other times. The wealth of this region is almost exclusively agricultural. All kinds of grain, garden produce, and orchard fruits thrive and yield enormous returns. In the valley itself and on the adjoining steppes great herds of livestock find pasturage. Here the Babylonians reared cattle, sheep, goats, donkeys, and

MAP OF BABYLONIA

pigs. The horse was unknown until about 2000 B.C., and apparently the camel was either unknown or but little used.

In keeping with its alluvial character, the plain had little or no mineral wealth. Both stone and metalliferous ores had to be imported, sometimes from considerable distances. Asphalt was so plentiful that the ancient inhabitants used it as mortar to lay up walls, but they knew next to nothing about the petroleum which is now found in the same geological formations. Timber always had to be imported from Asia Minor or northern Syria. Nor were the advantages which the land possessed available for exploitation without considerable labor on the part of the recipients. Irrigation canals and flood-control works required constant attention. To secure safe sites for cities, the inhabitants had to heap up huge mounds of earth, which were often hundreds of acres in extent and fifty or more feet high.

In addition to the task of making the land habitable and productive, there was the equally strenuous one of defending it. From the western desert the Semitic nomads looked greedily upon the fertile soil of the plain, while the eastern mountains harbored hardy and predatory tribes (related to the Alpine peoples of central Europe) who seized every opportunity to invade the land of plenty. The struggle with nomads and mountaineers never ended. Century after century and millennium after millennium, any sign of weakness in the peoples of the plain was followed by an invasion, which frequently resulted in the conquest of all or part of the land and the establishment of a foreign dynasty and aristocracy. Thus, the soil of the valley was the object of bitter strife at all times and only the strong could preserve their lands and liberties from the hand of the spoiler. Even in the intervals between invasions, peaceful immigrants continued to flock in and contribute new blood to the population.

Sources for the Study of Babylonian History

The "Lost Period" of Babylonian History, and Cuneiform Writing

While the peoples of the Tigris-Euphrates Valley at a very early date evolved a system of writing and began to keep written records, their history was for a long time almost entirely lost. Only within the last century has much progress been made toward its recovery. The chief reason for this peculiar situation was that about the beginning of the Christian era the *cuneiform* system of writing, in which these records had been kept, was replaced by a more convenient alphabetic system, and thereafter men completely forgot how to read the older script. For nearly two thousand years the Western world derived its scanty knowledge of the history of this region from the Old Testament, the works of the Greek writers Herodotus and Ctesias, and from a history written in Greek by the Babylonian priest Berosus. The last of these survived only in the form of excerpts made by other authors, and all of them together gave but a shadowy and quite unreliable outline of the past of this crucially important region. Only by finding some way to read the original records could modern men hope to dispel the mystery.

The discovery of the key to the Babylonian and Assyrian languages and system of writing was accomplished indirectly. When the Persians wished to reduce their language to writing (in the sixth century B.C.), they selected forty-two cuneiform signs, assigned alphabetic values to them, and for a long time wrote their records in this manner. Later they too abandoned this alphabet and forgot how to read it, but in the meantime a number of inscriptions had been made, including a long one cut by the order of King Darius I on the cliff of Behistun, on the border between Babylonia and Persia. Part of the importance of the Behistun Inscription arises from the fact that the Persian text is accompanied by translations into the Babylonian and Elamitic tongues. If the first could be deciphered, it could be used to solve the mystery of the other two.

About 1802, George Grotefend, a German scholar, began work on the Persian cuneiform and succeeded in identifying a number of proper names. By so doing he was able to assign correct values to eleven signs and within the next thirty years the labors of other scholars had led to the identification of the rest. It was now found that the Persian language of the inscriptions was quite similar to that of the *Avesta*, or sacred book of the Parsee sect. Aided by this knowledge, the Englishman, Sir Henry Rawlinson, made a complete copy of the Behistun Inscription which he published with a translation in 1844. The first necessary step had been taken.

The way was now open for the decipherment of the Babylonian and Assyrian scripts and languages. Both tongues proved to be members of the Semitic family to which Aramaic, Hebrew, and Arabic belonged. So marked are the similarities of grammar and vocabulary between the member tongues of this family that it is possible to discover the meanings of many unknown words in the extinct ancient representatives of the group by reference to the corresponding modern Semitic terms. Rawlinson, Edward Hincks, and a number of other scholars attacked the task. Little by little they identified the six hundred or more syllabic and ideographic signs used by these peoples and mastered the languages. The year 1857 saw the work so far advanced that four scholars, working independently, were able to make translations of the same text which were in substantial agreement with each other. Since then much additional light has been thrown on the subject, but the test of 1857 showed that the essential work had been done.

Each advance in the conquest of the cuneiform script has opened the way for still further progress. While the decipherment of the Assyrian and Babylonian texts was in progress, other documents were found, written in an archaic cuneiform or ideographic script and in a non-Semitic tongue. The Semitic Babylonian priests themselves used it as a sacred language (much as Roman Catholic priests use Latin), and studied it with the aid of bilingual lexicons. Once the Babylonian language had been deciphered, these textbooks made possible the understanding of the older tongue. It proved to be the idiom of the early non-Semitic inhabitants of southern Babylonia, the *Sumerians*. Continued excavations have brought to light enormous numbers of documents in all these languages and it is now possible to translate them with substantial accuracy.

Babylonian Excavations

Equally important with the linguistic studies have been the excavations of cities, temples, and palaces in the Tigris-Euphrates region. Beginning in 1842, when the Frenchman, P. E. Botta, undertook to dig among the ruins of Nineveh, an almost continuous series of excavations by English, French, German, and American investigators have laid bare the ruins of most of the important centers in the region. The earlier workers in this field sought principally for museum pieces and worked rather unsystematically. But increasing experience has resulted in more careful and methodic procedure. The present-day archeologist makes it his business to survey every scrap of material recovered. All the earth removed from excavated sites is carefully sifted to make sure nothing is lost. As it was customary to erect new buildings on the ruins of old ones without removing the débris, the remains on the average site rise in successive layers which correspond to the various eras in the history of its occupation. The thickness of each layer is measured and the objects found in it are catalogued. Reports of operations are published and are available to interested persons throughout the world. Many years will probably elapse before the archeological survey of the Tigris-Euphrates Valley is reasonably complete, but enough already has been done to open a new chapter in human history. Utensils, sculptures, weapons, building-plans, and written records have been unearthed in quantities which make it possible to reconstruct with substantial accuracy the lives of the peoples who produced them and to clarify many chapters in the political history of the region which would otherwise be unknown.

THE ACCADIANS AND SUMERIANS (ca. 3500–1940 B.C.)

There is no positive evidence that the alluvial plain of the Tigris and Euphrates was inhabited until near the end of the Neolithic Age, but that was solely because until then it had not fully emerged from the sea. In near-by lands there were people who were waiting for an opportunity to avail themselves of its amazing fertility. As land slowly emerged from the waters, one band after another moved into the plain and took possession. From the upper Euphrates Valley and the near-by Syrian Desert came a Semitic people who in later times were to be known as Accadians.

They occupied the northern part of the alluvium and there founded permanent settlements. In their previous homes they had passed through the early Neolithic stage of culture and at the time of their entry were as far advanced along the road to civilization as was possible without the use of metals. Before the dawn of history they had used copper alloys and had acquired several other features of Chalcolithic culture.

Farther down the valley another and more primitive Semitic group moved in from the Arabian Desert, but they were not left long in undisputed possession. During prehistoric times they had been conquered and absorbed by the Sumerians. The original home of these invaders is unknown and for the present purpose need not concern us. When we first make their acquaintance, they seem to have been in the country a long time, but there are indications that originally they had come from a mountainous country, where they worshiped the gods on hilltops. They spoke an *agglutinative* language like modern Turkish or some of the American Indian tongues. A sentence consisted of a number of monosyllables, each of which expressed a complete idea and all were strung together to express a thought. An example would be:

> *Sumerian:*   E-gal-Ur-gur-ur-gal-Un-gal-e-Anna-in-ru-a-ka-ta.
> *Literal English:*   Palace-Urgur-King-Ur-man-Eanna-he built-(genitive particle)-in.
> *Standard English:* In the palace of Urgur, the King of Ur, the builder of Eanna.

Physically, both the Accadians and Sumerians belonged to the dark-complexioned, long-headed Mediterranean race, with minorities of various broad-headed groups from the mountains of Asia Minor and the Iranian Plateau. In historic times the Semites were the more robust and energetic of the two. The Sumerians shaved their hair and beards and wore flounced woolen skirts of ankle length, to which in later times they added long mantles of the same material.

Sumerian Culture: Government and Military Science

Whatever the place of their origin, the Sumerians were the bearers of an advanced civilization. When the light of history falls upon them, we find them using various copper alloys, silver, and gold, from which they fashioned both implements and weapons. In the manufacture of pottery they used both the potter's wheel and the closed oven and painted or glazed their wares. The scarcity of stone compelled them to use baked or sun-dried bricks for building material, but from them they constructed elabo-

rate dwellings, temples, and palaces. They made wheeled carts and chariots, which were drawn by donkeys. They were proficient farmers, who
originated the system of irrigation and flood-control in use in the valley.
In addition, the Sumerians bred cattle, sheep, pigs, goats, and poultry, and
used oxen to draw plows. To them is apparently due the practice of constructing artificial mounds of earth to use as building sites.

In government, religion, and thought they were no less advanced than
in material culture. Long before the dawn of history, Sumer was divided
among a host of city-states, each of which consisted of a district with a
city as its political and religious center. Each had a complete set of political institutions, and not only aspired to complete independence of outside
authority, but whenever possible tried to conquer and rule its neighbors.
As all could not be first at the same time, this bellicose ambition made war
almost the normal condition of the Sumerian community. Usually one
state exercised a shadowy suzerainty over the others, but its authority was
seldom strong enough to prevent wars among its vassals.

The internal government of a Sumerian city-state had as its chief functions war, religion, the control of irrigation, and the regulation of commerce. Its institutions were all centered about the administration of its
leading temple, for while the Sumerians were polytheists like their neighbors, each city had a patron god who was treated with especial honor and
whose temple was more imposing than the others. The chief priest of this
temple, the *patesi*, was also the head of the secular government, combining
the functions of a general, chief engineer, and judge with those of his
priesthood. His office was hereditary, although, if the city were overcome by an enemy, he might be deposed or killed and a successor appointed
by the conqueror. A patesi who ruled several cities often assumed the
title of *lu-gal* (king).

Constant wars led to great development of armament and military tactics. Our earliest information on the subject comes from a mosaic panel,
the so-called *Standard of Ur*, found in a royal grave in that city and dating
from about 3500 B.C. In its crude, but expressive, figures we are shown the
army of Ur in battle and later celebrating its victory over the foe. First
came a charge of chariots, four-wheeled vehicles with high fronts and
sides, each drawn by four donkeys. In each chariot stood a warrior armed
with an axe and four javelins, while a charioteer handled the vehicle.
Next came the lightarmed skirmishers, armed with axes, short spears,
swords, and daggers; and behind them marched the heavy-armed infantry,
protected by conical copper helmets and heavy cloaks, and carrying short
spears.

Seven centuries later, another sculptor from the city of Lagash fashioned
the famous Vulture Stela, on which he portrayed the victory of his patesi
Eannatum over the people of the neighboring city of Umma. In Eannatum's army apparently only the king rode in a chariot, while all others
marched on foot. Few lightarmed troops are shown and the scene is dominated by the phalanx of heavy-armed infantry, drawn up in six ranks, the

Bettmann

FRAGMENT OF THE VULTURE STELA

front protected by heavy wooden shields. The soldiers wear copper helmets, seem to be protected by armor, and fight with long spears. With the
victorius Eannatum at their head, they push relentlessly forward over the
bodies of their slain foes. The battle must have been a bloody one, for in
the accompanying inscription the victor informs us that he buried twenty
heaps of his own slain soldiers, while the enemy's loss was 3600 men.
Little or nothing is known of the details of military administration in the
Sumerian cities.

Writing; the Ideograph

Among the Sumerians writing was in everyday use. Small tablets of clay took the place of paper and a stylus made from a piece of bone or a water reed was used to print signs upon it. At first a number of such strokes were used to make a rude picture of the object represented; but the need for rapid writing and the wedge-shaped marks made by the stylus soon resulted in wholly conventionalized signs, each of which stood for a word, but usually bore no recognizable resemblance to the object for which it stood. Such a sign is an *ideograph*. When a tablet was completed, it was dried in the sun for several days and then baked like any brick. Business accounts, legal documents, religious texts, and royal inscriptions were in fairly common use before 3000 B.C., and furnish the data for a rather sketchy history of the Sumerian people.

Political Geography and the Unification of Sumer and Accad

There are indications that at some time before the dawn of history, the Sumerians had for a time controlled the whole of both Sumer and Accad, but before 3000 B.C. they had lost their hold upon their Semitic neighbors and at times had even been compelled to submit to the latter's suzerainty. Certain Sumerian cities prospered, while others never emerged from obscurity. *Eridu*, near the seashore and west of the Euphrates, was a revered religious center but not otherwise important. Its nearest neighbor, *Ur*, had at times held the suzerainty of the whole plain and continued to be outstanding as long as the Sumerian people existed. East of the Euphrates lay *Erech*, famous for its temple of Ishtar (the goddess of love), and several times suzerain of the land. Farther east, on a canal which brought water from the Tigris, was *Lagash*, which between 2900 and 2650 B.C. was the seat of a race of strong and able patesis, who conquered most of the other cities of Sumer. It was one of them, Eannatum, who commemorated his victory over the neighboring city of Umma by setting up the Vulture Stela, which has already been mentioned. *Nippur* was famous for its temple of the earth-god, *Enlil*. Isin and Larsa acquired importance at a later time only as the seats of dynasties of foreign conquerors. The chief cities of Accad were *Kish, Cutha, Sippar,* and *Babylon*; but of these only the first acquired importance in the early historic period. It seems to have been at one time a Sumerian city but was later Semitized. Several families of its kings had at various times held the suzerainty of the valley. We must, of course, remember that neither for Sumer nor Accad is the above list com-

University Museum, Philadelphia

SUMERIAN TEMPLE OF THE FIRST DYNASTY, 2900 B.C.

plete. Each had many smaller centers which, in a brief sketch like the present, merit no particular mention.

The first well-attested movement toward the effective unification of Sumer and Accad began about 2650, and in its first phase was dominated by the Sumerians. *Lugal-zaggisi*, the patesi of Umma, conquered all of Sumer and most of Accad, and led a raid up the Euphrates which may have taken him as far as the Mediterranean coast, but his success was short-lived.

At Kish there lived an Accadian who later took the name *Sharrukin-lubani* ("A lawful-king-is-truly-created"), or *Sargon*. He was an orphan who had been reared by a gardener, but his talents were too great to allow him to remain in obscurity. He usurped the rule of his native city, founded another at *Agade* in northern Accad, and embarked upon a career of conquest. About 2630, he overthrew Lugal-zaggisi and in the next few years conquered the whole valley up to the Taurus Mountains, as well as northern Syria and the tribes along the edge of the eastern highlands. While Sargon adopted a conciliatory attitude toward the Sumerians, the Empire of Agade was a Semitic state in which the Accadians were foremost. For nearly two centuries Sargon and his descendants held sway over their extensive dominions, but at no time did they succeed in putting an end to the ingrained separatist tendencies of their subjects. Every king had to put down rebellions in Sumer and occasionally even in Accad, while in the later years of the dynasty the outlying districts fell away and formed independent and hostile states. About 2470, the Accadian supremacy disappeared in a whirlwind of confusion and civil war. "Who was king? Who was not king?" is the graphic summary which a later Sumerian chronicler gives of the ensuing chaos.

Accadian Civilization and the Guti Invasion

Although the Accadians had not so long a tradition of civilization behind them as had the Sumerians, the Empire of Agade was by no means a barbaric state. In their long association with their southern neighbors, the Semites had learned much, at the same time retaining a virility and progressiveness which the Sumerians were gradually losing. That the Northerners had mastered the art of relief sculpture is proved by the well-known Stela of Naram-Sin, a limestone slab erected by Sargon's grandson and found in the Elamitic capital of Susa. On it is portrayed the capture of a stronghold in the mountainous district of Lulubu. The royal army, with the giant figure of Naram-Sin at its head, advances up a rocky and tree-clad slope. It marches in open skirmish order, the soldiers carrying, in addition to their spears, the characteristic weapon of the Semites, the bow. On the hill are two puny enemy figures, one of whom strives vainly to pull the king's spear from his throat while the other begs for mercy. The grouping of the figures is somewhat childish, but the towering figure of Naram-Sin, with its swelling muscles, horned helmet, and majestic pose, is an artistic triumph of which a Sumerian artist would hardly have been capable. Similar attainments may be credited to the Semites in literature, religion, and economic organization, while the Empire of Agade was governed far more effectively than any previous state of its size in history. The period is one of the high points in the civilization of the Tigris-Euphrates Valley.

The confusion which followed the fall of the Sargonid Dynasty afforded an opportunity to the eastern mountaineers of which they were not slow to avail themselves. The *Guti*, a barbarian tribe from the Zagros Range, invaded both Sumer and Accad and plundered them from end to end. Later chroniclers gave graphic pictures of the slaughter and devastation which these destroyers inflicted upon the peoples of the valley, but the invaders soon fell under the spell of a superior civilization and a sem-

University Prints   *Oriental Institute, Chicago*

STELA OF NARAM-SIN, AND THE STELA CONTAINING THE
HAMMURABI LAW CODE

blance of order returned. The Gutian kings held the suzerainty over
Sumer and Accad for well over a century. For the first part of this period
there is little of interest, as the invasion had impoverished the land and
retarded its culture, but its later stages were marked by rapid recovery.
At Lagash the patesi *Gudea* ruled a prosperous community, fostered temple-
building, sculpture, and irrigation works, and in general so benefited his
subjects that in later times he was worshiped as a god. But the Sumerians
were never reconciled to Gutian rule. About 2280, they rose in revolt
under the leadership of *Utu-Khegal* of Erech and drove the last of the foreigners from the land.

High Point of the Civilization of Ur

For over a century after the expulsion of the Guti (2280–2170), Sumerian
kings again ruled the lower Tigris-Euphrates Valley. The supremacy soon
passed to Ur, from which a dynasty of able kings held sway over nearly
the same lands that the Semitic Sargon had once ruled. The capital and

University Museum, Philadelphia

GOLD VASES
From the Royal Graves at Ur

the other Sumerian and Accadian cities were adorned with splendid temples, the irrigation system was restored, and both commerce and manufacturing prospered. But while the rulers of Ur were Sumerians, and no doubt favored their own people as much as possible, it is obvious that they were steadily losing ground before the more virile Semites. Large colonies of the latter were to be found in the old Sumerian centers and the kings of Ur were compelled to advance them to high positions in both the army and the civil service. With these concessions they seem to have been contented and harmony prevailed between the two peoples. These fortunate conditions were reflected in the well-being of all classes of the people. Excavations show that at this time not only the rich, but also the middle class and the poor, enjoyed the highest standard of living ever known in the region.

The Rise of Babylon

Splendid as was the Empire of Ur, it was doomed, however, to a relatively short life. Both the Sumerians and the Accadian Semites seem to have been unequal to the task of maintaining their imperial state among hostile and often barbarous neighbors. Despite their activities as builders, neither people seem to have had any creative artistic genius left, and this fact probably reflected decadence in other lines. After 2200, the rulers of Ur lost their grip upon the outlying provinces and about thirty years later the end came. From the upper Euphrates a new Semitic group, the Amorites, invaded the kingdom and simultaneously a revolt broke out in Elam. Ur was sacked and burned, her last king was led a captive to Elam, and the victors divided the spoils. An Amorite king, with his capital at Isin, and a ruler of unknown origin at Larsa, succeeded to the inheritance of the Empire of Ur.

The states of Isin and Larsa lasted, with various changes of fortune, for two centuries and a half. Their histories are at best obscure, the kings bearing at various times Sumerian, Semitic, and Elamite names. The period marked the death struggle of the Sumerian people, who progressively lost ground before the northern Semites until the cities of Sumer at last became entirely Semitized in speech and culture. During this last phase of their history, Sumerian scribes compiled the traditional accounts of their country's past in chronicles and king-lists, and wrote religious manuals which preserved for later times the knowledge of their beliefs and rituals. In these activities they were supported by their rulers, who may have hoped to keep the older element of their subjects contented by this means. Meanwhile, foreign powers, Elam and Babylon, were overshadowing the monarchies of Isin and Larsa. Not long after 2000, the Elamites conquered Larsa and installed a branch of their royal house on its throne. The second of these, Rim-Sin, also captured Isin. The kings of Babylon were Amorites who had seized this Accadian city about 2040 and greatly extended their sway over the surrounding region. The stage was set for a decisive struggle between the Amorites and the Elamites for the mastery of the valley.

Hammurabi and the First Dynasty of Babylon (1940–1750 B.C.)

It was *Hammurabi* (1940–1897), the sixth Amorite king of Babylon, who decided the issue. In a series of successful wars which occupied the greater part of his reign, he defeated and captured Rim-Sin and conquered all of Sumer, Accad, Elam, Assyria, and the upper Euphrates Valley to the Taurus Mountains. Thus, in his later years, he ruled an empire which entitled him to a place beside Sargon and the kings of Ur as a conqueror. His descendants, although by no means as strong rulers, continued to rule the core of his empire for a century and a half after his death and are known in history as the First Dynasty of Babylon.

Hammurabi was a statesman as well as a legalist and a conqueror. He says in the epilogue to his law code:

> I was neither careless nor neglectful of the black-headed people whom Bel presented to me and whose care Marduk gave to me. I expelled the enemy north and south; I made an end of their raids; I made the people to rest in habitations of security; I permitted no one to molest them.[1]

This was no vain boast. He was a great builder of temples, fortifications, and irrigation canals, and he kept a vigilant eye upon his subordinates in all these activities. His letters to Sin-iddinam, his governor of Larsa, show that few details of administration escaped his notice, and he brooked no neglect, corruption, or laxity on the part of his officials. Private letters and business documents show that the country was thriving and prosperous under his efficient rule.

The Hammurabi Code

Toward the end of his reign, Hammurabi published a code of laws which was to be the basis of the Babylonian legal system for the next fifteen hundred years. In the main it consisted of old Sumerian laws, with a few changes to bring it up to date. But whereas law had hitherto been essentially a local matter, varying from city to city, this Code was intended to apply to the whole of his extensive dominion. In general the penalties for criminal offenses were more severe than in the Sumerian laws, and like them it continued to recognize concubinage and slavery. In some cases ordeals were used to settle disputes. But its 282 paragraphs are characterized by a very large measure of justice and common sense and by great care for the rights of widows, orphans, and other helpless persons. The position of woman described in it is high in most respects. It devotes relatively large space to such matters as wages, inheritances, and business transactions, as well as to agricultural questions. This is sure evidence that it was planned for a society which had long since emerged from barbarism. The provisions of the Code and the light which they throw upon Babylonian society will be treated more fully farther on. The history of the text of the Hammurabi Code from which our knowledge is gained is peculiar. In the temple of Marduk at Babylon there stood a black diorite slab about eight feet high, on which a copy of the Code was engraved.

---

[1] Luckenbill and Chiera, in J. M. P. Smith's *Origin and History of Hebrew Law*, Appendix II, pp. 218–19. By permission of the University of Chicago Press.

In the twelfth century B.C., an Elamite king carried it away to Susa, where
he erased five of the paragraphs but did the stela no other damage.   In
1901, it was found by excavators and is now in the Louvre in Paris.

Hammurabi's Political Achievement

Hammurabi was not the first ruler to unite all peoples of the Tigris-
Euphrates Valley under a single government, but his achievement trans-
cends mere conquest.   More than any other one man he was the creator of
that moral unity which was to characterize the people of Sumer and Accad
from that time forth.   It is true that in this he was helped by circumstances.   By his time the Sumerians had been almost completely absorbed
by their Semitic neighbors and a single language was spoken everywhere.
But he gave to all his subjects unity of laws and a sense of equality of privileges and benefits which reconciled them to the subordination of local
interests to those of the whole group.   Thereafter political unity might
often be broken, but spiritual unity remained to render a political restoration relatively easy and one might speak with propriety of Babylonia and
of a Babylonian people.

Soon after the death of Hammurabi, the First Dynasty fell upon evil
times.   None of his descendants equaled him in ability, and the task which
they were called upon to face was very difficult.   Rebellions in the outlying
provinces and raids by barbarian neighbors repeatedly weakened their
position, until about 1750 they were overthrown by a raid of Hittites
from Asia Minor.   Babylon and her neighbor cities were taken and sacked,
and when the invaders withdrew the land was ready for a new master.
The Kassites, a hill tribe from the Iranian highland, placed their chief
upon the vacant throne, where his race was to remain for nearly six centuries (1750–1169).   Many centuries were to elapse before Hammurabi's
one-time capital would emerge again to the leadership of the Near East.

Such was the political history of the lower Tigris-Euphrates Valley during a period of nearly sixteen centuries, an endless struggle of city-state
against city-state, of Sumerian against Accadian, and of both peoples
against external invaders.   But it was not all chaos and destruction.   Here
was evolved one of the first effective systems of government in the world,
with organized might to protect the people from external enemies and laws
to regulate their dealings with each other.   By these means, and by active
encouragement, the small and bellicose city-states made possible the emergence of a civilization that has influenced the whole subsequent history of
mankind and to which brief consideration will now be given.

BABYLONIAN CIVILIZATION

The culture which prevailed among the united Babylonian people of Hammurabi's time was, like the people themselves, of mixed ancestry and, necessarily, it contained elements taken from both its parent stocks. The spoken tongue was Semitic, but Sumerian, as we have seen, continued to be used for religious purposes. The fine arts, the mechanical arts, agriculture, literature, law, and religion were predominantly Sumerian products, although modified by Semitic influences. Government was a rather equal mixture of elements drawn from both peoples and springing naturally from the conditions prevailing in the region.

Government and the Structure of Society

As we have seen, after Hammurabi's time, political unity was the normal condition of Babylonia. Within this united land the prevailing form of government was absolute, divine-right monarchy. The king did not as a rule claim personal divinity, but rather took such titles as "Favorite of Shamash," or "Beloved of Marduk." Hammurabi and his successors were not irresponsible despots — his laws and correspondence indicate quite the contrary. Hammurabi was a conscientious, hard-working ruler and the same may be said of most of his successors.

The king's will was carried out by an elaborately organized staff of governors, patesis (now reduced to unimportance), town mayors, and judges of several different grades. All were appointed by the king and might be removed or punished by him. To protect the people from oppression by this bureaucracy, Hammurabi allowed them to appeal directly from the local courts to his own tribunal in Babylon, and severe penalties were ordained against officials who were guilty of wrong-doing.

Hammurabi's Law Code contains a clear picture of the organization of Babylonian society and of the rights and privileges of its component parts. It consisted of three classes: gentlemen, commoners, and slaves. Though all received some protection from the law and had certain privileges, these differed decidedly from class to class.

Gentlemen included officials, priests, and soldiers. Apparently they held landed estates on a kind of feudal tenure and owed in return certain specified services. Soldiers and administrative officers were forbidden to sell such holdings, but could buy and hold other land on the same terms as others. They were under strict discipline, death being the penalty for attempting to hire a substitute to perform one's services or for disobedience to orders. They were protected from injury by heavier penalties than were commoners, but on the other hand they suffered heavier punishments for wrong-doing than did the lower classes. Thus, the accidental killing of a gentleman cost the slayer one-half a mina; but if the victim were a commoner, the fine was only one-third of a mina. But a gentleman who struck one of his own rank was fined sixty shekels, while a common man who struck his equal paid but ten shekels. For major surgical operations a gentleman paid a fee of ten shekels, though a commoner paid but five. The property of gentlemen and of commoners enjoyed equal protection at law. Thus, the relations of these classes legally, at least, were characterized in the main by a spirit of justice and fairness.

Slaves, of course, suffered the greatest disabilities and had the least legal protection. They were reduced to servitude by capture in war, as punishment for certain crimes, or in satisfaction for debts. In the last case, a whole family might be enslaved, or the head of a family might hand over his wife and children to his creditors for a period of three years, at the end of which they became free. Little or no social stigma was attached to a slave, who could, and sometimes did, marry a free woman. In such cases, or if a slave woman bore children to her master, the children were free. Slave concubines who had borne children could not be sold and became free at the master's death. Slaves were protected from violence except on the part of their masters and could not be sold into a foreign country. They could accumulate property and with it could buy their freedom.

Marriage and the Family

The Babylonian family was monogamous with certain reservations. Under ordinary circumstances a man might have but one wife, but if she were a hopeless invalid, he might marry again during her lifetime, though remaining liable for her support. A childless wife might be divorced with no difficulty, and for a man, divorce was easy under any circumstances. On the other hand, a woman had to have a strong cause before she could divorce her husband. But in practice divorce laws were no doubt greatly modified by the custom of giving dowries. Before marriage a prospective bridegroom gave his fiancée's father a sum of money in return for the privilege of marrying her, and the father in turn gave the girl a dowry which after marriage remained her property. As a rule she turned it over to her husband, but if he divorced her, he had to return it, and if she died childless, it reverted to her family; otherwise, her children inherited it. In no case did it become the absolute property of the husband. A childless wife might, like Sarah, the wife of Abraham, hand over one of her slaves to her husband as concubine, but her rights in such instances were carefully protected against usurpation. In fact, the family relations of Abraham seem to have been regulated throughout by the provisions of the Babylonian law under which he had lived in his native Ur. Married women were in economic matters nearly on an equality with men; they could use their own property, conduct business in their own names, and sue or be sued in the courts. Children, on the other hand, had few rights and were under severe legal restraints. Thus, a son who struck his father had his hand cut off, and an adopted son who attempted to disown his foster parents was in some cases liable to lose his eye or have his tongue cut out. But a father could not disinherit his son without the consent of a judge, and then only after a second serious offense.

Agriculture and Manufacturing

Babylonian economic life rested about equally upon agriculture, commerce, and manufacturing. In districts which could be irrigated, the land was cultivated intensively, producing wheat, barley, garden vegetables, and orchard crops. Of the latter, dates, figs, and grapes were the most important. Some slave labor was used in agriculture, but most of the work seems to have been done by small landholders and free tenants. The rent on land planted to grain was from a third to a half of the crop, but if the tenant after leasing land failed to plant it, he was liable for a rent based on the yield of adjacent fields. Careless farmers who flooded the lands of their neighbors while irrigating their own fields were liable for damages. Grain was cut by hand and threshed by driving over it sledges set with sharp stones. Straw was cut up and fed to animals. The yields were large, but one can hardly believe the statement of the Greek Herodotus when, fifteen hundred years after Hammurabi's time, he wrote that the soil of Babylonia yielded wheat crops of two hundred to three hundred times the seed.

Stock-raising was highly developed, the animals being fed in part from the produce of artificial meadows and in part pastured on the steppes which lay between the alluvium and the edge of the desert. The need for wool from which to make clothing caused sheep-raising to be popular, while pigs, cattle, and goats were raised in great numbers. The donkey, as always, was bred for riding and driving purposes, his popularity being all the greater because of the ease with which he could be supported on weeds and plant refuse from the fields. The horse was unknown until Hammurabi's time and only became common during the Kassite period.

From the wool of their sheep the Babylonians wove great quantities of cloth of various grades, the finer varieties bringing high prices in the export market. Leather goods were also produced in quantities, as were pottery, jewelry, objects of copper and bronze, household furniture, and many other articles. The metal, stone, and wood used in the manufacture of these commodities had to be imported from Arabia, the Iranian Plateau, Syria, and Asia Minor, but to pay for them the shops of the Babylonian cities exported manufactured products. In Hammurabi's time political mastery gave to Babylonian merchants the control of the markets of many of the districts whence these raw materials came.

Commerce and Banking

But the Babylonians were more interested in buying, selling, and money-lending than in either agriculture or manufacturing. These activities were carefully regulated by the government, which required that all agreements had to be in writing before they were enforceable in the courts. As a consequence, untold thousands of business documents of all kinds survive, and from them we can obtain a very clear picture of the business life of nearly every period of the region's history.

As coined money did not exist, various other media of exchange were in use. Small trade was carried on by barter, but for larger transactions commercial rings of gold, silver, and copper were in use and were weighed anew at each transaction. The table of weights, which was the same for precious metals as for other commodities, was as follows:

> 180 grains = 1 shekel
> 60 shekels = 1 mina
> 60 minas   = 1 talent (about 68 pounds)

In many cases both wages and prices were set by the government, but where such was not the case, an agreement was reached by the age-old Oriental method of haggling. In buying an article, the purchaser was expected to give the seller a gift in addition to the price agreed upon. Elaborate legislation governed the contracting and repayment of loans. If one borrowed grain, he had to pay thirty per cent interest in case his fields yielded a crop, but if, through no fault of his own, they failed to do so, the year's interest was canceled. Then, as always, bankers financed merchants and peddlers, who used the credit thus obtained to buy goods for export to far-off lands. On loans of this character, the maximum interest was twenty per cent, but if the debtor could prove that he had suffered ill-fortune through no fault of his own, the interest might be remitted for a time.   Often a merchant with excess means would lend funds to a peddler to make a venture in which his whole stock might be carried on his own back or on that of a donkey; but again the merchant himself might send shiploads of goods to points along the shores of the Persian Gulf, or cara-van-loads to Syria, Asia Minor, or the Iranian Plateau.   As the result of these contacts, the Babylonian language and the script in which it was written came into international use in western Asia and even Egypt.

Housing, Food, and Clothing

Living standards were surprisingly high for all classes of Hammurabi's subjects.   The houses of the upper and middle classes were commodious structures of baked or sun-dried brick, the outer walls covered with stucco and the roofs made of poles with a covering of matting and a top dressing of mud.   Many of the more commodious were two stories in height and

Society of Antiquaries, London

CROSS SECTION AND RECONSTRUCTION OF A PRIVATE HOUSE IN UR

contained from twelve to twenty rooms, arranged around an open central court as in modern Spain or Italy. Heating facilities were poor, the only fire being that which blazed on a brick hearth in the kitchen, but furniture (if one may judge by reproductions in painting and sculpture) was plentiful and comfortable. Such a house had a private chapel in which the family worshiped the gods, and under it would be the family burial vault, which was entered through an opening in the chapel floor.

The food of the common people was largely of a vegetable character: bread, porridge, garden produce, and fruit, with cheese and a little honey. Meat was rarely tasted by any but the rich and powerful, and to have it as a regular article of diet was an evidence of high rank. The water-supply must have been unspeakably bad, coming as it did from shallow wells sunk into soil polluted by human remains, sewage, and garbage, or from the rivers and irrigation ditches. Probably for this reason a great deal of wine was drunk. It was made from dates or grapes and sold in public shops kept by women of bad character and frequented by ruffians and criminals as well as by respectable workingmen. Wool rather than linen was used for the manufacture of clothing, and by Hammurabi's time the voluminous robes of the Semite had driven the lighter costume of the Sumerian from use.

Streets and Ziggurats

The streets of a Babylonian city would doubtless have appeared repulsive to a modern Englishman or American. They were narrow, crooked, and usually unpaved. Underground drains in some places carried off the water from the surface, but there was no means of removing garbage or even sewage from them. No windows broke the bare expanses of wall, although there were occasional doors, kept closed when not in use. Even the palaces of kings and nobles probably differed from the others only in size.

One of the few breaks in the monotony of a Babylonian city was the temple of the city's patron god which, if not beautiful, had a grandeur resulting from its tremendous size and unusual construction. In most respects such a structure was but a dwelling-house on a colossal scale, for it was the god's house, and served much the same purposes as the houses of men. Dominating the rest of the temple was the *ziggurat*, or elevated sanctuary, of which a good example is to be found in the temple of Nannar at Ur. It consisted of a platform of sun-dried bricks faced with baked bricks, and was about 200 feet long, 150 wide, and 70 high. Toward the

University Museum, Philadelphia

ZIGGURAT
Temple of Nannar at Ur (Restored)

top it tapered to a series of terraces, on the highest of which stood a small building — the "holy of holies." At the front of the platform three converging stairways afforded access to its summit. Not all temples had their ziggurats, but they continued to be characteristic of the most pretentious temple architecture throughout Babylonian and Assyrian history. The Babylonians used several architectural principles, such as the arch, vault, and dome, which both the Romans and modern peoples have used to good effect.

Art

In Hammurabi's reign Babylonian sculpture had begun to decline, but its level was still creditable. The best surviving piece for this period is the relief at the top of the stela containing the Code, which represents the king standing in an attitude of adoration before the god Shamash, who is handing him an object symbolic of the Law Code. But it lacks the fiery spirit of the Stela of Naram-Sin or the power and pathos which redeem the crudity of the Vulture Stela. Closely allied to sculpture was the art of seal-cutting. The nature of cuneiform writing made it impossible for an individual to have a distinctive signature, but this disadvantage was remedied by two devices. The signer of a document might impress his thumb-

Oriental Institute, Chicago

BABYLONIAN CYLINDER SEAL

nail in the wet clay, or he might use a cylinder seal. Into the surface of such a cylinder was cut a series of figures which usually composed a scene together with the name of the owner. When the seal was rolled over the moist surface of a tablet, the figures were printed in low relief on the clay. A specimen would be designed somewhat as follows: The scene would portray the owner being led by one of the minor gods into the presence of Anu, Marduk, or some other important figure of the Babylonian pantheon. With it would be the name, for example, "Shamash-uballit, servant of the daughter of the king." Such a signature could not be forged, and the carvings with which they were adorned are among the finest products of Babylonian art.

Religion and Moral Standards

Both Sumerians and Semites had always been religious to the point of groveling superstition and this trait continued to dominate their descendants. To them, religion was a thing of magic, gloom, and terror. In a general way the universe was governed by a group of great deities, such as *Ea*, the god of waters, wisdom, and the arts; *Shamash*, the sun-god; *Nergal*, the god of death; *Ishtar*, the goddess of love and of reproduction of human and animal life; and *Marduk*, the warrior. Ea was looked upon as the friend of mankind and Ishtar had her more tender moods, but as a rule the gods were not calculated to inspire affection in mankind. They had, according to Babylonian belief, once trembled with fear of a monster named Tiamat, until Marduk, fortified by potent charms, had killed her and used her carcass to create the world. In the story of the Universal Deluge, we find them becoming terrified at the violence of the storm which they had raised:

> The gods are terrified at the hurricane; they flee to the heaven of Anu; the gods crouch like dogs. . . . The gods sit down, sad and weeping.

Beneath them were hordes of demons, ghosts, and monsters, ever ready to injure mankind, who had to be placated or driven off with charms. Sickness was a visitation of the spirits and was generally treated with spells and incantations to banish these unwelcome visitors. Portents of good or evil were sent by the gods in the forms of dreams, eclipses, the birth of misshapen animals, etc., and these had to be interpreted by persons skilled in the art of augury. Hence, the Babylonians may be described as "priest-ridden" in a sense that few other peoples have ever been, for only the priests could conduct the delicate relations between man and the gods so as to ward off evil and bring good. A favorite method of foretelling the future was by means of the liver of a sacrificed animal. The organ was marked off into squares, and if discolorations or other abnormalities were found in a given square, the sign had a definite significance. Clay models of livers, all properly marked off and with the significance of each portent noted, were used for the instruction of beginners. Thus arose the enormous power of the priests, who formed an important part of the government of the country and were by far its largest property-holders.

Babylonian religion was, after all, strictly a thing of this world, for in the world beyond the grave the gods had nothing to offer. It was not a place of rewards and punishments for deeds done in this life, but a gloomy subterranean prison, where good and bad alike led a miserable and cheerless existence. A Babylonian poem, *The Descent of Ishtar into the Lower World*, thus describes it:

> Ishtar the daughter of Sin [went] to the house of shadows, the dwelling Irkalla, whence no one who enters ever goes out, to the road whence there is no turning back, to the house without light for him who enters, where dust is their nourishment, and clay their food. They have no light, but dwell in darkness. They are clothed in feathers like the birds. Over door and bolt the dust has gathered.[1]

---

[1] Adapted and condensed from C. D. Gray's translation in *Assyrian and Babylonian Literature* (Aldine ed., New York, 1901), p. 408. By permission of the D. Appleton-Century Company.

But it must not be forgotten that beside this gloomy fatalism there are traces of another belief — that the souls of the departed can be made comfortable by burial rites and sacrifices. According to this second view, those who were neglected by the living wandered about the world feeding on garbage and vented their wrath upon the living by causing pestilences and other misfortunes. In the *Gilgamesh Epic* we find both views stated side by side, without a hint of their incompatibility. But in either case men prayed only for earthly blessings and never for eternal life. It was enough to ask the gods for prosperity, for the aversion of misfortune, or for vengeance upon one's enemies. Eternal happiness was a gift which they could not or would not give.

As gods were only human beings drawn on a colossal scale and endowed with immortality, provision had to be made for their wants, and they required extensive staffs of servants. The average temple had a large staff of both priests and priestesses, including the children of kings among their upper ranks. The staff was headed by a group of ministers patterned after those of a king, and below them were more than thirty different classes of high priests, votaries, musicians, diviners, anointers, and so forth. The priestesses were looked upon as wives and concubines of the god, and in some degree all were sacred prostitutes. This practice was observed in the form of religion in the precincts of all temples, and its votaries — at least those in the higher ranks — enjoyed the respect of the public. Aside from their religious duties, they were expected to observe the same rules of conduct as other women, and the Hammurabi Code decreed that one of them who entered a wineshop should be burned alive.

Babylonian religion had not the stern sanctions for moral living which Christianity, Judaism, and Mohammedanism possess, but that is not to say that the Babylonians had no moral standards. Their standards of conduct were by no means low, yet they sprang from secular rather than religious considerations. Law and custom commanded men to practice justice and honesty, and the commoner vices were interdicted. While a priestess who was a temple prostitute was honored and revered, other women lived by a standard of virtue not below that of peoples whose religions were free of such ceremonials.

The importance of religion in Babylonia is evidenced in the character of personal names. Such names were phrases or sentences which placed the bearers under the protection of certain gods or proclaimed their enjoyment of divine favor. Thus, the name of Eannatum, the famous patesi of Lagash, meant "Worthy of [the temple] E-anna." That of Naram-Sinf the grandson of Sargon of Agade, meant "Beloved of the Moon-god."

Sin-muballit, the name of Hammurabi's father, meant "The Moon-god is the giver of life." The same principle governed the formation of names among the Phoenicians, Assyrians, and Jews.

Literature, Science, and Education

We have already had occasion to see that the Babylonians possessed an extensive body of poetic literature, although only scanty fragments remain. First in importance among the surviving portions comes the great *Gilgamesh Epic*, the work of an unknown poet of no small power. The hero was a legendary king of Erech, whom the gods sought to punish for his tyrannical rule by creating as his rival a giant wild man named Eabani. But Gilgamesh foiled them by making friends with the monster, who became his companion in various adventures. The goddess Ishtar fell in love with Gilgamesh, who repulsed her advances with a coarsely realistic story of her cruelty and treachery to a long series of former lovers. The wrath of the jilted deity seems to have resulted in the death of Eabani, while Gilgamesh himself was smitten with a loathsome disease. In his efforts to regain his health and to win immortal life, he journeyed to the home of his divine ancestor, Ut-napishtim, the Babylonian prototype of the Hebrew Noah. The latter favored him with the long story of the Universal Deluge, which is identical in its general plan and in many details with the story found in Genesis 6:5–9:1. Of the two, the Babylonian account far excels the Hebrew narrative in poetic power, but the latter contains an ethical significance which the former altogether lacks. The *Creation Epic* has been mentioned, but in addition we must not overlook such poems as *The Descent of Ishtar into the Lower World*, the story of Adapa who broke the wings of the south wind because it had upset his boat, or that of Etana, who, somewhat after the manner of the Greek Icarus, flew to heaven on the back of an eagle, only to fall to his death. A large number of hymns, prayers, and penitential psalms assure us that this type of literature was old when the Hebrews first adopted it, and the Babylonian prototypes are as full of poetic power and religious fervor as the Old Testament psalms. It is significant that there are also prose chronicles which furnished the outlines of the country's history, intermingled with much fable and poorly arranged. Even so, the remaining fragments of these works furnish useful hints toward the reconstruction of Babylonian history as far back as the last centuries of the fourth millennium B.C.

Science in the true sense hardly existed, though there was considerable real or alleged factual lore from which science might have been developed.

Thus, surgeons were already attempting operations, and as Hammurabi felt called upon to regulate fees for successful surgery, we may presume that the patients sometimes recovered.   But the usual custom was to recite spells and charms over the sick, and as an unsuccessful surgeon was punished with the loss of his hand or with a heavy fine, we can hardly blame those who used the safer method.   The priests were already observing the heavenly bodies and had discovered that some of them followed regular courses, but their interest was chiefly in portents and omens.   Time was measured by a lunar year of 354 days, which was divided into twelve months, of twenty-nine or thirty days each.   As this was eleven days short of the true figure, the calendar year was soon out of touch with the course of the seasons.   To remedy the defect, an additional (intercalary) month would be added at intervals.   A letter of Hammurabi illustrates the custom: "Since the year has a deficiency, let the month now beginning be registered as a second Elul."   Thus that year would have thirteen months.

A written literature presupposes a reading public, and such a group, although far smaller than in these days of state-supported schools, certainly existed in Babylonia.   Then, as in medieval Europe, schools were controlled by the priests, and usually they were adjuncts of the temples. The task of learning to read and write was not easy.   Out of the Sumerian ideographs the Semites had evolved a cumbrous set of more than six hundred characters, some of which were ideographic, while others were syllabic.   Sometimes several signs would stand for the same syllable, and

Keystone

MESOPOTAMIAN CLAY TABLET

again the same sign could be read several ways. A sign was placed before the name of a god, which warned the reader that he was dealing with divine things, while another would indicate that the word which followed was the name of a country. Such characters are now known as *determinatives*. Children learned to read and write by the familiar method of first learning the simpler signs, then framing words, and from that point reproducing whole sentences. Girls as well as boys attended school. Probably few ever finished the process, and the masses, as always in the Orient, depended upon public letter-writers to indite the epistles which they wished to send or to read what they received.

Brilliant and prosperous as seemed the Babylonia of Hammurabi's time, its greatest period already lay in the past. In art, literature, and other fields of human endeavor, convention was beginning to throttle originality to a dangerous degree. Babylonia was still to be the teacher of many peoples in southwestern Asia, but her day as the creator of a new culture was nearly done.

4

Early Egypt (to about 1580 B.C.)

THE NILE VALLEY

THE SECOND early historical civilization developed in the lower valley of the Nile River, to which the Greeks, Romans, and modern Europeans have given the name *Egypt*. Its physical environment in some respects resembles that of the plain of the Tigris and Euphrates rivers, but with striking and important differences. To understand Egypt, we must first consider the Nile, which is the source of its soil and the nourisher of its life.

The River and Its Importance

Far up in the jungles of central Africa there lies a chain of freshwater lakes fed by tropical rains. From them the Nile pursues a northward course for some four thousand miles to the Mediterranean Sea. A tributary, the Blue Nile, joins it about 1350 miles from the sea, bringing with it the flood waters and silt of the Ethiopian highlands, but for the last twelve hundred miles of its course it flows across the North African Desert in a deep, canyon-like valley carved out of the sandstone plateau of the region. The upper part of its course across the desert is interrupted by a series of rapids (the "cataracts"), but about seven hundred and fifty miles from the sea it leaves the last of these behind. Thereafter, its valley measures from ten to thirty miles in width, with high cliffs on either side. At one time it emptied into a bay of the Mediterranean Sea about a hundred miles south of its present mouths, but continual deposits of silt have replaced the bay with a low, broad plain, bounded along the coast with a rim of swamps. From its resemblance to the shape of the fourth letter of their alphabet, the Greeks named this plain the *Delta*. At its southern end the ancient Nile divided into seven branches, by which it entered the sea. Egypt, in the strict sense of the word, is the Nile Valley from the sea to the First Cataract. It has an area of less than ten thousand square miles — about as large as the state of Maryland.

Egypt lies between 24° and 31° 30' north latitude — about the same distance from the Equator as peninsular Florida. Eastward from the head of the Delta, nearly nine hundred miles of desert stretch away to the banks of the Euphrates, and to the west, a similar barren waste, broken only by a few oases, extends to the Atlantic Ocean. The climate of Egypt is similar to that of the deserts on either side of it. Except in the Delta, rain scarcely ever falls. In the valley, summer temperatures at midday often reach 120° Fahrenheit, but the nights are cool. A striking peculiarity of the region is the extreme dryness of the air which prevents even the highest temperatures from becoming oppressive and preserves perishable substances from decay for thousands of years. For this reason archeologists have been able to unearth a far greater wealth of material in Egypt than in any other country.

The Annual Flood: Its Importance to Egyptian Life

That Egypt is not a desert like the lands around her is due entirely to the annual flood of the Nile. Each year the tropical rains and the melting snows of the Ethiopian mountains swell it to flood stage. In the lower valley the river begins to rise about June, and in November it is from twenty-five to fifty feet higher than at low water. When the inundation recedes, it leaves a thin coat of alluvial mud to enrich the land. It is hardly too much to say that this annual flood dominates Egyptian life. If it does not rise high enough, famine follows. If it rises too high, the villages are flooded and men and animals are drowned. Thousands of years of continued silt deposits have built up the soil of the valley floor to a depth of many feet, with boundless agricultural possibilities.

Labor and Other Resources

But in Egypt as in Babylonia, Nature's bounty depends entirely upon man's co-operation. The waters of the inundation furnish the moisture necessary to start a crop, but the flood has dried long before the crops can mature. A network of irrigation canals covers the country, but they are far above the level of low water in the river. The water must be lifted. In ancient Egypt this work was done entirely by hand and for this purpose the peasants used the *shadoof*, a device like an old-fashioned well-sweep,

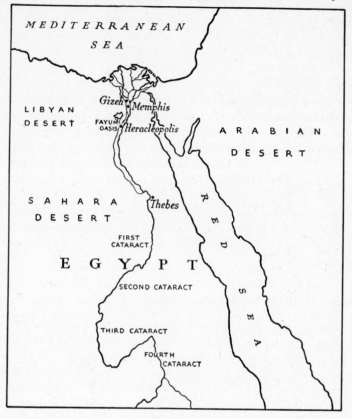

MAP OF EGYPT

the end of the pole opposite the bucket weighted with a ball of dried mud. By this primitive device toiling peasants raised from sixteen hundred to two thousand tons of water each year to the level of the fields for each acre of arable land. The canals had to be cleaned and repaired periodically. Hence, the nature of the country compelled the Egyptians to work, taught them to co-operate toward common ends, and made them anticipate future needs. Once they had developed these qualities, the returns were fabulously rich. Wheat, barley, garden vegetables, poultry, and other kinds of livestock were so plentiful that they provided a large exportable surplus.

Although her wealth was mainly agricultural, Egypt was not lacking in other resources. Stone for architectural and sculptural purposes could be found in the eastern desert within a short distance of the valley's edge or in quarries near the First Cataract. Copper was mined in the near-by Sinai peninsula, and gold was dug in both the eastern desert and the southern district of Nubia. The valley had little or no timber, but cedar was imported from Syria, and ebony was brought down the Nile from central Africa.

The Historical Influence of Egyptian Geography

Both the position and shape of Egypt profoundly influenced her political history. With deserts on either side and a harborless seacoast on the north, she was vulnerable to invasion at few points. At the northwest corner of the Delta, the Libyans were sometimes dangerous, and at the opposite corner, the Asiatic Semites several times invaded the land. From the south the Egyptians had to fear the Negro tribes of Nubia. But under a strong government they could easily repel all these invaders. As a rule, the foreigners who entered the valley came in small groups and as peaceful immigrants. The extreme length and narrowness of the valley might have proved an obstacle to political unity, but the Nile itself promoted unification by providing an easy means of communication between its various parts. Another force which promoted unity was the need for centralized control of the irrigation system, which functioned best under a single head. Egypt very early attained union under a strong central government and kept it during most of her long history. For this reason her civilization was not subjected to strong or continuous foreign influences as the result of conquest.

THE SOURCES FOR THE STUDY OF EGYPTIAN HISTORY

Like the peoples of the Tigris-Euphrates Valley, the Egyptians had written records of sorts at a very early date, the nature of which has been explained.[1] The Egyptian system of writing (which will be treated later) was used until about the fourth century A.D., when it was abandoned and forgotten. In the meantime the Greek historians Herodotus and Diodorus had gathered the materials for sketches of Egyptian history from priests who had access to the records, and upon these records Manetho based his history of Egypt. Manetho's work was lost, but extensive excerpts survive in the form of quotations by Greek and Roman authors, and by the Jew, Josephus. Egyptian remains — especially the Pyramids of Gizeh — contin-

[1] Chapter 1.

ued to attract the attention of travelers throughout the ages, and Egyptian inscriptions piqued their curiosity. But aside from the scanty and confused data furnished by these foreign historians, there were no clues to Egyptian history.

The Rosetta Stone and the Philae Inscription

The recovery of the key to the ancient Egyptian writing was an indirect result of Napoleon Bonaparte's Egyptian campaign of 1798–99. A number of scholars accompanied the army and made extensive researches and topographical surveys. Most important of all, a soldier digging trenches at Rosetta, near the western mouth of the Nile, found a stone bearing an inscription in two varieties of Egyptian script with a Greek translation of the Egyptian text. The *Rosetta Stone* found its way into the British Museum. In 1822, a second bilingual inscription was found on the island of Philae. As the Greek versions could be read, they served as a key to the Egyptian language and writing.

Work on the decipherment of the Rosetta Stone inscription began in 1802 and continued for over twenty years. The chief workers were the Frenchmen, De Sacy and Champollion, the Englishman, Thomas Young, and the Swede, Akerblad. As in the Persian cuneiform, proper names were used as a starting point. The Rosetta Stone contained the name *Ptolemaios* in the Greek version, and the Philae inscription had both *Ptolemaios* and *Kleopatra*. In the Egyptian version there was a group of characters surrounded by an oval ring (the *cartouche*) corresponding to each name. A comparison showed that the Egyptian writing was alphabetic. As the letters were identified, the Egyptian texts could be written with essential accuracy in Latin letters. Champollion then pointed out that the ancient Egyptian language was the ancestor of the modern Coptic tongue. From the latter he could identify the meanings of many common words used in the inscriptions and could master Egyptian grammar. When Champollion died (1832), the pioneer work had been done; later discoveries have been more of details than of fundamental additions to the knowledge of the language.

Excavations

Excavations in Egypt since 1850 have been supervised by the government far more carefully than have those in the Tigris-Euphrates Valley. In that year Auguste Mariette was made director of the Cairo Museum and continued in office for thirty years. He was succeeded by Sir Gaston Maspero, another distinguished scholar. These men had the direction of all excavations carried on in the country and both made important discoveries. Later the Egyptian Excavation Society, together with various German, French, Swiss, and American groups, secured permission from the Egyptian government to work special fields. Such enterprises have always been carefully co-ordinated and directed by the authorities of the Cairo Museum. Temples, royal tombs, and cities yielded enormous numbers of inscriptions, papyri, statues, reliefs, paintings, mummies, jewelry, and implements, illustrating the development of Egyptian civilization in all its phases.

Using the skeleton history supplied by Manetho, scholars began to fit the kings into their proper places and to construct a systematic chronology. The difficulties, especially in the chronology of the early period, are very great. The methods employed, and the limitations to which they are subject, have been treated elsewhere. It might be well to repeat that up to 2000 B.C. all dates are subject to a margin of error, which may amount to as much as a century either way. Practically all the written material is either official or priestly in origin, and so gives us the viewpoint of the government or the hierarchy, but seldom or never that of the people. But what written sources fail to do is often supplied by art. Never did a people supply to future ages a more complete and lively panorama of their lives than did the Egyptians in the paintings, reliefs, and statuettes of their tombs. Hence, while the political history of the country is sketchy and incomplete, our knowledge of everyday life in ancient Egypt has a satisfying completeness.

Early Egypt (to about 3200 b.c.)

When the Egyptians first emerged into the light of history, they were already in possession of a culture which must have been many centuries old, and its character indicates that, for the most part, it had been evolved in the land itself. Far back in the Neolithic Age, the Nile Valley had been occupied by a group which belonged to the short-statured, long-headed Mediterranean race, with possibly a touch of Negroid blood. They had attacked the problems presented by their new environment with intelligence and energy, and, before the discovery of metals, had reached perhaps the highest cultural level ever attained by a Neolithic people. Their flints were carefully shaped, and they used obsidian, ivory, bone, and wooden implements. Although their pottery was hand-made, the clay was thoroughly cleansed and mixed and the vessels were well shaped and tastefully decorated. They wove linen cloth, built houses of sun-dried bricks or of wattles plastered with mud, and practiced agriculture and stock-raising. Their religion was a crude nature-worship, of which magic and totemism were parts. They had temples and shrines and buried their dead with rites which showed that they believed in a future life.

At first these primitive Egyptians were probably divided into numer- ous tribes and clans, but at an early date political unification had been achieved. (Two kingdoms absorbed the smaller states and dominated the land: Upper Egypt, which controlled the entire valley to the head of the Delta, and Lower Egypt, which included the Delta itself. Asiatic immi- grants brought with them their language (which profoundly influenced later Egyptian grammar and vocabulary), and the knowledge of copper- and gold-working. Egypt entered the Chalcolithic Age centuries before the age of writing and with tools fashioned from the copper alloys, Egyp- tian craftsmen were able to do fine and handsome work.)

The Solar Calendar; Alphabetic Writing

The other outstanding discoveries of the prehistoric period were the solar calendar and the art of writing. Primitive peoples almost always reckon time by the moon, but this practice is open to a very grave objec- tion. The original purpose in devising a calendar would be, of course, to secure a reliable method of predicting the changes of the seasons, but since these changes are governed by the relative position of the earth and the sun, the moon has nothing to do with them. If the moon made an exact number of revolutions around the earth while the earth was making one revolution around the sun, the lunar calendar would be a useful guide, but such is not the case. Twelve lunar months make roughly 354 days and 8 hours, while thirteen lunar months amount to 384 days. The first is nearly eleven days short of the true solar year and the second is almost nineteen days too long. An example of the confusion which results from the use of this lunar year is to be found in the history of the Romans, who continued to use it to the end of 45 B.C. Shortly before that date, Cicero informs us that the spring equinox (by our calendar March 21) came on May 16! The priests of Lower Egypt had discovered the true length of the solar year within less than a quarter of a day as early as 4241 B.C., and about that time worked out a calendar on the basis of a year of 365 days. This was the closest approximation of the actual length of the solar year that was made until the fifth century — nearly four thousand years later.

To appreciate the magnitude of this achievement, we must remember that it was made with few or no instruments.

At the dawn of history the Egyptians had long had a system of writing. It had already passed through the pictographic, ideographic, and syllabic stages of development, and before 3000 B.C. was on the verge of developing a true alphabet of consonants. From the stalks of the papyrus reed the Egyptians had learned to make a tough and serviceable paper, on which they wrote with reed pens and ink. All this was far in advance of the clumsy Babylonian syllabary and clay tablets. A people who could make such discoveries was both alert and progressive and gave promise of great things in the future. In this respect, the subsequent history of Egypt is disappointing. Never in the historic period did its people again display such keenness of mind and progressiveness of thought as they did in the morning twilight of their existence.

THE OLD KINGDOM (3200–2450 B.C.)

As previously indicated, we owe the co-ordination of our data on Egyptian history largely to Manetho. He grouped the kings of Egypt into thirty *dynasties*, or families, which he said had ruled the land consecutively. We now know that this concept is faulty. For example, Dynasties VIII and IX seem to have ruled different parts of Egypt simultaneously, and a change of family (which Manetho fails to record) probably took place in the middle of Dynasty XVIII. But since his concept is not only convenient, but also widely used by ancient and modern historians, we shall follow it in this discussion.

The Union of the Two Lands; the Old Kingdom

Later Egyptian tradition ascribed the union of Egypt entirely to *Menes*, a king of Upper Egypt who conquered Lower Egypt and founded the First Dynasty. But this is oversimplification of what was, in fact, a very long and difficult process. We cannot even be sure which of several kings had Menes for one of his names. It would seem that the kings of Upper Egypt first conquered the North about 3200, but the union which they established was loose and unstable, interrupted by frequent rebellions. It required two centuries of conquest and conciliation to effect a lasting union, but after the reign of King *Khasekemui*, the founder of the Third Dynasty (about 2980), we hear of no more wars between the two sections. The line of demarcation between them, it is true, was never obliterated. The king was always "*King of Upper and Lower Egypt*," and other traces of the former division were preserved. Yet the significance of this hard-won unity in Egyptian history can hardly be overestimated. Thereafter, while Egypt had her periods of disorder, order and union were considered the normal condition of the country, and only occasionally do we hear of the strife and chaos which were the ordinary state of the Tigris-Euphrates Valley.

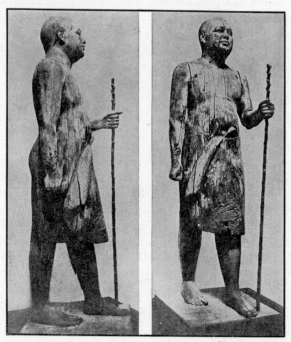

University Prints

THE SHEIKH-EL-BELED

The union of all Egypt under a single head which endured without interruption for over five centuries (2980–2450) is commonly termed the period of the *Old Kingdom*. During the first two hundred years of this time, the Third and Fourth Dynasties held the throne and the kings were absolute monarchs. Their dominions were divided into about forty administrative districts, called *nomes* and named after animals or birds, such as Nome of the Jackal, Nome of the Swan, Nome of the Mouse. Over each nome was a deputy or *nomarch* appointed by the king, who collected taxes, dispensed justice, commanded the local militia, and administered royal property. The royal palace, which was always situated near the city of Memphis, was the center of the system. Into the treasury came grain, cattle, copper, gold, silver, linen, and other products of the land, for coined money was unknown there as it was in contemporary Babylonia. Appeals from the local courts were often made to the king, with the evidence and arguments written on papyrus rolls. Every peasant in the land was called yearly to work for the king for a specified length of time without pay other than his food. This forced labor was intended for nationally useful activities such as cleaning the irrigation canals or mining copper in Sinai, but not infrequently it was to mold bricks for the royal palace, quarry stone for the king's tomb, or otherwise minister to the king's vanity and love of display. (In short, the whole material wealth of the country was at the disposal of the monarch.)

Pyramid-Building

It is in this setting that we must view the building of the Pyramids of Gizeh. The Egyptians always believed that the life after death was in some manner dependent upon both the preservation of the body and provision for the material welfare of the soul in the world beyond, through offerings made by the living. To achieve happiness in the world to come, those who could afford to do so built tombs which constantly became more elaborate as civilization progressed. Beginning with graves lined with sun-dried bricks, kings and nobles gradually evolved rectangular tombs of stone (*mastabas*), in each of which was a shaft for the reception of his body and a chapel for the worship of the dead man's spirit. For the nobles, such structures had to suffice, but the kings could and did do much better. Under *Zoser*, the second king of the Third Dynasty, the royal minister *Imhotep* (later deeply revered because of his wisdom) planned a structure consisting of a series of mastabas of progressively smaller size, one above the other. This "terraced pyramid" was nearly two hundred feet in height. The pyramid form was also used in the tombs of the later kings of the Third Dynasty, with gradual improvements in form and structure. (But it was under the Fourth Dynasty that the desire for magnificent pyramids reached its culmination. *Khufu* (the Cheops of Herodotus) devoted the resources of his kingdom to the building of his tomb throughout most of his reign. At Gizeh, near Memphis, he constructed on the edge of the desert a structure 755 feet square on the base and 481 feet high, containing 2,300,000 blocks of limestone weighing approximately two and a half tons each.   Legend says that the task required the services of a hundred thousand men for twenty years, which is probably true.   The surface was covered with blocks of dazzling white limestone, the joints so closely fitted that in the surviving fragments a penknife blade cannot be inserted into them.   Within, a complicated series of passages led to the tomb chamber.   In front of the pyramid was a temple for the worship of the king's spirit, and near-by were ranged the smaller stone tombs of the king's wives, children, and courtiers.   A gigantic covered ramp led to this "city of the dead" from the valley below.   *Khafre*, the son of Khufu, erected a similar pyramid, and *Menkaure*, a later member of the same family, executed a third and smaller one.   Both are exquisitely planned and executed, though neither equals that of Khufu.   The nation must by this time have been nearly exhausted by this long-continued waste of its energies, for the later kings of the dynasty could not complete any monuments of comparable size and splendor.

The Pyramids of Gizeh stood intact for at least thirty-five hundred years.   To the Greeks and Romans they were at least as great a curiosity as to us, and then, as now, many a tourist went to see them.   Later still, the Arabic conquerors of Egypt stripped them of their beautiful coverings, leaving them as we see them today.   The royal remains were plundered and destroyed, in all probability not long after they were deposited there.

Fifth and Sixth Dynasties; Decline of Royal Power

About 2750, a revolution, dimly hinted at in tradition, placed the Fifth Dynasty on the throne.   It was evidently brought about by an alliance of the nobles and priests of the kingdom, headed by the priests of the sun-god *Re*, and it had far-reaching effects.   Re became the head of the official pantheon and each king claimed to be his son.   A reaction also took place against the extreme centralization observable under the two preceding dynasties.   At least, under the later kings of the Fifth Dynasty, the office of prime minister was hereditary in another family, and the governors of the nomes also passed their offices and lands on to their sons.   This tendency became even more pronounced under the Sixth Dynasty (2625–2450).   The nomarchs now called themselves "hereditary princes" of their respective nomes, and although ostensibly loyal to the kings, they ruled their own domains like feudal lords.

Inevitably, the royal power declined.   The tombs of the kings of the Fifth and Sixth Dynasties (in those days a sure index to their power) were small and poorly constructed pyramids, while the tombs of the nobles

were built on their estates. In art and other fields of culture the improvement was great and continuous. Sculpture grew finer and more realistic,
and in architecture, new devices, such as the clerestory and the colonnade,
made their appearance. The kings sent exploring parties far up the Nile,
and their merchant fleets brought rare foreign products from Punt (East
Africa) and Phoenicia.

Three Centuries of Chaos

But this feudal monarchy had a fatal weakness. It depended upon an unbroken succession of strong kings, and this could not always continue.
Probably in the later years of King Pepi II, who ruled, according to tradition, ninety-four years, there was a rebellion of the nobles. The Sixth
Dynasty lost control of the country and each nome became in effect an independent state. Civil wars broke out and chaos descended upon the land.

Nearly three centuries of internal disorder and foreign invasion followed
the overthrow of the Sixth Dynasty. In general, the period was marked
by a struggle between the rival families of Memphis (Dynasties VII and
VIII), Heracleopolis (Dynasties IX and X), and Thebes (Dynasty XI). As
none of them were able to control the country effectively, every powerful
nomarch took advantage of the confusion to become a law unto himself.
The Asiatic Semites and the Nubian Negroes invaded the land. All classes
suffered misfortunes, and the literature of the time betrays the blackest
pessimism. At last the nomarchs of Thebes pushed down the Nile, captured Heracleopolis, and compelled the nobles everywhere to acknowledge
their suzerainty. A measure of order returned and a new age dawned.

THE MIDDLE KINGDOM (2160–1788 B.C.)

When Egypt emerged from chaos, it was with a constitution considerably like that which she had had under the Sixth Dynasty but with a
new center of political gravity. Feudalism was so well established that
the kings of the Eleventh and early Twelfth Dynasties made little effort
to overthrow it. Each nomarch was the immediate ruler of his nome.
He collected its taxes, commanded its army, and was the fountain of law
and justice to his subjects. Some of his land was held by a revocable grant
from the king and some was his private possession. Naturally the kings
tried to see that only persons friendly to them inherited these principali-
ties, but in general, hereditary succession was the rule. The king had estates in all of the nomes, but the nomarchs collected the income from them

and turned it over to him. Revenues from gold mines, returns from commercial ventures, and the spoils of war further swelled the royal treasury. The king kept a small military force which formed the nucleus of an army. The rest of the soldiers were supplied by the nomarchs. In short, the king was again strong enough to maintain order and obedience, but he was not an absolute monarch.

The Theban Feudal Monarchy

With the triumph of the Theban nomarchs, their capital became that of the kingdom. It was located in Upper Egypt, about one hundred and forty miles north of the First Cataract. In the Old Kingdom it had been a place of little importance. Its patron god, *Amen*, was identified with Re and became the head of the official pantheon. By one means or another, it was to retain its religious and political prestige for over a thousand years.

The feudal social order was, if we may trust our evidence, an equitable one. The peasants had as little voice in government as before, but the nomarchs were ready to hear complaints and were cognizant of conditions. No doubt some ruled despotically, but they insisted that they ruled justly and benevolently. One of them says in an inscription found in his tomb:

> There was no citizen's daughter whom I misused, no widow whom I oppressed, no peasant whom I turned away. . . . There was no one wretched or hungry in my time.[1]

Another says:

> I was rich in grain. When the land was in need I maintained the city with kha and heket [grain measures]. I allowed the citizen to fetch for himself grain, and his wife, the widow, and her son. I remitted all arrears of imposts which I found counted by my fathers.[2]

Under their personal supervision agriculture and industry throve. A middle class of free citizens arose, many of them comfortably well-to-do, but without noble titles. Art had declined during the long period of anarchy, but it now revived and reached a level comparable to that of the Old Kingdom.

The Twelfth Dynasty

After a century and a half of rule, the Eleventh Dynasty was supplanted by another Theban family, the Twelfth Dynasty (2000–1788). While local government long continued to be in the hands of the nobility, royal con-

[1] Breasted, *Ancient Records of Egypt*, I, 523, condensed. By permission of the University of Chicago Press.   [2] *Ibid.*, I, 408.

trol over it progressively tightened. A series of able kings (Amenemhet I and III, Sesostris I and III) restored the royal power. A new capital (*Ithtowe*) was built near the head of the Delta. Nubia was conquered and made a province. Relations with Syria, Palestine, Cyprus, and Crete were fairly close. Before the death of Amenemhet III, Egyptian feudalism had been abolished as a political institution and the king was once more an absolute monarch.

A notable accomplishment of the Twelfth Dynasty kings was the reclamation of the Fayum and the construction of irrigation works there. Near the new royal capital was an extensive depression in the western plateau (called today the *Fayum*), connected with the Nile Valley by a narrow gorge. When the Nile was in flood, the depression was filled with water, but up to this time the water had retreated as the river fell, leaving the Fayum empty. Amenemhet III constructed a dam and locks in the gorge which enabled him to let out the water gradually, thus doubling the volume of the Nile below the Fayum during the hundred days of lowest water. In the Fayum itself, dikes reclaimed twenty-seven thousand acres of fertile land. To the later Greeks the body of water in the Fayum was known as Lake Moeris.

When the Twelfth Dynasty ended, Egypt was a rich, prosperous community, with art, literature, and religion flourishing more vigorously than ever before.

Renewed Disorder. The Hyksos Invasion (1788–1580 B.C.)

In Oriental lands, good government is dependent upon the strength, wisdom, and benevolence of the sovereign, and for two centuries after the death of Amenemhet III, Egypt did not have strong sovereigns. For a century, one pretender after another assumed royal titles and strove to make good his position. The nobles regained the powers of which the kings of the Twelfth Dynasty had deprived them, and the helpless people were once more visited with all the miseries of civil war.

The times were singularly inauspicious for a country in such a condition. Far up in the steppe country north of the Black and Caspian seas, tribes of Indo-European nomads had begun to migrate southward in search of new and more attractive homes. The Iranian Plateau, the Balkan Peninsula, Asia Minor, and western Europe all felt the effects of these disturbances, as tribe after tribe was thrust out of its territory and moved forward to escape annihilation. This movement was probably the chief cause of the invasion which, shortly after 1700, descended upon Egypt. A horde of

Syrian and Palestinian Semites, driven from their homes by invaders from the north and east and probably accompanied by a few Indo-European chiefs, fell upon the cities of the Delta region, devastating, killing, and plundering. When the *Hyksos*, as the Egyptians named the invaders, finally settled down, they controlled Lower Egypt from their capital at Avaris and exacted tribute and obedience from Upper Egypt. This domination continued for about a century, after which the Hyksos were expelled.

Destructive as was the Hyksos invasion, it probably served as a stimulant to Egypt. The newcomers brought with them the horse and the chariot, both of which had previously been unknown in the Nile Valley. As the horse had been known in Babylonia several centuries earlier and the chariot drawn by donkeys had apparently been in use among the Sumerians before recorded history, we may assume that Egypt's geographical isolation had been the cause of this cultural lag. This crust of isolation was now broken. Above all, the invasion produced a reaction in the Egyptian mind which was later to cause the expulsion of the foreigners, the restoration of national unity, and the building of a powerful and brilliant empire. This phase of Egyptian history will be treated in a later chapter.

EGYPTIAN CIVILIZATION

The Use of Metals; Craftsmanship

When the Egyptians first emerged into the light of history, they were acquainted, like the Sumerians and Accadians, with various alloys of copper, from which their finer and more effective tools were made. The

Museum of Fine Arts, Boston

EGYPTIAN STONE VASES

University Prints

DIADEM OF A PRINCESS

variety of uses to which they put this metal is astonishing. From it they made drills with which, aided by sand, water, and endless patience, they produced stone vessels so thin as to be translucent. With saws of the same material they mastered not only wood but stone, and their chisels shaped columns, statues, and reliefs from the hardest volcanic rock. Not until near the end of the Old Kingdom did they come to use bronze. Even then the poor seldom owned bronze tools but continued to use other copper alloys or flint.

Of the other metals, the Egyptians early learned the use of gold, silver, and, to a small extent, iron. The gold was obtained from deposits near at hand and was at first less valuable than silver, which was imported from Asia Minor. Iron was probably secured from fallen meteorites and seems to have been considered a precious metal, for it was seldom worked into tools. From the gold and silver the royal goldsmiths fashioned exquisitely beautiful crowns, bracelets, and other jewelry, which they set with precious stones. As in Babylonia, the precious metals were used as a medium of exchange, but there was no coinage, and the metals had to be weighed and tested anew at each transaction.

In all the useful arts the Egyptian craftsmen developed a skill and good taste that have seldom been surpassed. From imported wood they fashioned furniture which would do credit to a modern cabinetmaker. At an early date they discovered the art of glassmaking, and they glazed their pottery. At the beginning of the historic period, stone vessels had driven the finer kinds of pottery from the market, but before the end of the Old

Kingdom, the introduction of the potter's wheel had restored the balance between them. Flax was grown in large quantities and linen was used by all classes. The poorer grades were coarsely woven, but the finer varieties could hardly be distinguished from silk and were almost transparent. The manufacture of paper from the papyrus reed has been mentioned, and papyrus was also used for the making of ropes and cables.

Agriculture and "Planned Economy"

Agriculture was the staple industry of Egypt, and it was pursued intelligently and methodically. Wheat and barley were the common grain crops, but sorghum was also grown. Although the olive was probably known, the chief sources of cooking-fat were castor beans, sesame, linseed, and similar field-grown plants. Among the garden vegetables were beans, onions, garlic, vetches, and lentils. Grapes were grown in favorable localities, and wine was a common drink among the aristocracy. As sugar was unknown, bee-culture was important, nor was animal husbandry neglected. Cattle, sheep, goats, and donkeys were bred extensively, and poultry-farming was followed with a care and intelligence not found anywhere else in that day. The irrigation system was, of course, the farmer's chief concern, for if it functioned well, the fertility of the soil made good crops almost a certainty. But for all that, he did not neglect artificial fertilizers. Manures were carefully saved and applied to the soil, and a pungent dust, rich in phosphates (called *sebakh* by the modern Egyptians), was gathered from the ruins of abandoned villages to supplement animal wastes. Grain was sometimes sown on the mud left by the retreating flood and trampled into the ground by the hoofs of farm animals, but where this was not practicable, an ox-drawn plow was in use. Other agricultural implements were simple and clumsy, as they have tended to be the world over until very recent times. The Egyptians cut their grain with sickles, threshed it by spreading it out on the ground and driving cattle over it, and separated it from the chaff by throwing it into the air on windy days. The chaff was gathered and used for stock-feed.

At all times the economic activities of the people were directed from above. Except in the later years of the Middle Kingdom, there were few if any untitled landowners. Kings, priests, and nobles monopolized the ownership of the soil, and the peasant bore the burden of the whole social structure. Although there were some slaves, the peasants were regarded by law as free men, but their freedom meant little or nothing to them. They worked under supervision of overseers and were used to being beaten.

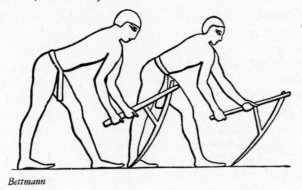

Bettmann

PEASANTS WITH HOES
The Earliest Form of Plowing

They paid rent for the land they lived on, and the government collected both taxes and forced labor from them. Their lords were obliged by self-interest to provide them with subsistence in hard times, and no doubt often treated their charges kindly, for the prevailing mood of the peasant seems to have been a happy one. The sculptors show him singing as he worked and even record some of his rude verses. Only contentment and good humor could have produced these.

The Egyptians were not so much given to commerce as were the Babylonians, and their business was differently organized. While there must have been private merchants, the only export and import trade of which we hear was conducted by the government. The king monopolized mining of all kinds, and it was he who equipped the expeditions to Sinai, Punt, Phoenicia, and the Sudan which brought back rare and valuable goods. There were private markets which enjoyed wide patronage. Small purchases were made by barter, and large ones, as previously stated, were paid for in uncoined gold or silver.

Family Life and Living Standards

The Egyptian family was organized along lines common in the Orient but with a few differences. For the average man, monogamy was the rule. Often his wife was also his sister, and such marriages were not only permissible but very common. The upper classes practiced both polygamy and concubinage, yet unlike many other polygamous peoples, they preserved strong traces of an earlier matriarchal social organization. Sometimes, the eldest daughter was the heiress-at-law to the family title and estates. Women of all classes occupied a fairly high legal position, and much of the private business of the country was in their hands.

Living standards varied widely from class to class. The king, nobles, and priests lived in huge palaces of sun-dried brick which were luxuriously furnished. They had beautiful gardens, swimming pools, and pleasure boats, and plentiful and varied food. As early as the Old Kingdom we hear of a menu consisting of "ten kinds of meat, five kinds of poultry, sixteen kinds of bread and cakes, six kinds of wine, four kinds of beer, eleven kinds of fruit, and miscellaneous articles." [1] Clothing, on the other hand, was very simple. The men shaved their heads and faces clean, and wore knee-length kilts. The women wore a garment resembling the "slip" of their modern sisters, except that it had only one shoulder-strap instead of two.

The leisure moments of both sexes were enlivened by games, music, dancing, boating, or, for the men, hunting and fishing. But the Egyptian gentleman was neither an idler nor an ignoramus. He could read and write, and probably had at least some manuals of religious ritual in his library. Either in the service of the king, or as priest or landlord, his days were filled with activity. He might lead a military expedition or an exploring party, supervise building or quarrying operations, or share civic and community activities. Manuals of etiquette and rules of good conduct show that he had a reasonable amount of sophistication and a fairly exacting moral code.

The peasants naturally lacked the refinements which graced the lives of their superiors. Small huts of sun-dried brick — usually of only one room — scanty furniture, and simple food fell to their lot. Their diet was chiefly unleavened barley bread, vegetables, and, rarely, a little meat. Nile water and beer were their drinks. When not engaged in hard work, the peasant wore a loincloth and his spouse a humbler version of the aristocratic woman's garb, but when strenuously employed, both sexes reverted to primeval nudity.

Religion

Rich or poor, the Egyptians were extremely religious. Like most of the human race in all ages, they were polytheists, with an infinite number of gods of varying degrees of importance. A few, such as *Re* the sun-god, *Ptah* the divine craftsman, or *Nut* the sky-goddess, enjoyed fairly general

---

[1] Erman, *Aegypten*, p. 265, as quoted in Breasted, *History of Egypt*, p. 88. By permission of Chas. Scribner's Sons.

OLD KINGDOM WALL PAINTING
Milking Scene from the Tomb of Ti

recognition, but in addition, each city and nome had its patron deity, often unknown elsewhere. When a new royal family came to the throne, it was likely to introduce the worship of its patron god into the state cults, as the Fifth Dynasty had done with Re, and the Twelfth Dynasty with Amen. Many of the gods were represented as grotesque compounds of man and animal, and their religious literature and mythology explain the reasons for this. Re had a human body and a ram's head; Horus, a human body and a hawk's head; and Anubis (a god of the dead) had the head of a jackal.

The gods were thought to have human needs and desires and were treated accordingly. Their temples were their homes and the priests were their servants. At sacrifices, a god was fed, and at other times he was clothed, anointed, or amused. Except for the chief priest of each temple, the priests and priestesses were often laymen who gave part of their time to religious activities. Nomarchs and other nobles sometimes held priesthoods among their other titles. Temples were supported by endowments of land and by the offerings of the worshipers.

The Egyptian, like the Babylonian, expected the gods to grant him earthly blessings in return for his prayers and offerings, but he also hoped to win happiness in the world to come. His religion combined primitive savagery with some of the most advanced moral teachings known to the pre-Christian world. He never gave up the idea that his future life and happiness depended upon the preservation of his body and upon offerings made to his spirit by the living. The tombs of the wealthy were furnished with vessels of food and wine, furniture, clothing, jewelry, boats, weapons, and means of amusement. The walls of the tomb chapel were decorated with paintings and reliefs showing the activities of a great estate — plowing, sowing, reaping, stock-breeding, hunting, fishing, arts and crafts, and amusements — a moving panorama of contemporary life created with a view to furnishing the deceased with his accustomed style of

Brown Brothers

THE MUMMY CASE OF KING TUTANKHAMEN

living in the hereafter. Until near the end of the Middle Kingdom, a noble could order his slaves or concubines to be butchered at his tomb so that their spirits might accompany him to the hereafter. The journey into the Great Beyond was beset with perils, which could only be averted by potent charms. These were engraved upon the wall of the tomb chapel, or written upon the inside of the great cedar coffin in which the corpse rested. At first no effort was made to preserve the body from decay, but in the Middle Kingdom embalmment was producing the first of the mummies which we associate with the name of Egypt. To take the place of the body, should it be destroyed, there were images of the dead in which his soul might reside.

The Osirian Hereafter

Such beliefs were crude and materialistic, but in the Middle Kingdom another concept of the hereafter developed, diametrically opposed to the first. To understand it, we must begin with the Osiris myth. *Osiris*, according to the story, was a divine king of Egypt in former days. *Isis* was his sister and wife, while their brother *Set* was the "black sheep" of the family. Osiris, a just and beneficent ruler, was murdered by Set, and his mangled remains were scattered over all Egypt. Isis by potent charms restored the dead god to life, but instead of resuming his earthly career he went to the Underworld to be the judge and king of the dead. *Horus*, the son of Osiris and Isis, overthrew Set and became king in his father's place. Originally, no doubt, this dying and resurrected god represented the annual death and rebirth of vegetation, but he gradually acquired a deeper significance. As Osiris rose from the dead, so might any mortal do with his aid. But as Osiris was good and just, so only the good and the just might hope to be resurrected. In his judgment hall the heart of the dead man was put upon one side of a balance, with a feather, the symbol of truth, upon the other, and at the same time he had to declare himself innocent of a long series of evil deeds. If the scale showed that he lied, he was devoured by a hideous monster; if not, he entered the Land of the Blessed.

Writing and Education

Religious and secular documents alike were written in a mixture of ideographs, syllabic signs, and alphabetic signs. At an early date the Egyptians had evolved an alphabet of twenty-four letters, each of which represented a consonant. As the vowels were not written, the reader might often be left in doubt as to which of a series of possible words a given set of consonants represented. To understand the dilemma in which a reader might find himself, let us suppose that English were written similarly. *P-r-* might mean *par, per, pear, pore, pour, poor,* or *pure,* and perhaps other words in addition. To avoid confusion, a series of suggestive pictures was devised to guide the reader's choice. A small human figure with the finger pointed toward the mouth meant *hunger,* or *famine.* Such a picture, if placed with *-p-r-,* would show that *poor* was intended. Each letter had originally been itself a picture, and in inscriptions or highly formal documents of all kinds it continued to be so. This was the *hieroglyphic* style. But in ordinary writing the pictures were conventionalized

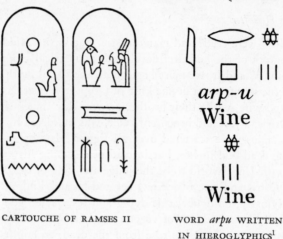

CARTOUCHE OF RAMSES II

arp-u
Wine

Wine

WORD *arpu* WRITTEN
IN HIEROGLYPHICS[1]

into signs without any pictorial realism. This was the *hieratic* style. Not until late in Egyptian history was the third or *demotic* style developed.

Writing was a rare accomplishment among the lower classes, but to learn it was a sure road to advancement. Women rarely emerged from illiteracy. School discipline was rigorous. "A boy's ears are on his back," ran an Egyptian proverb, "and he listens when he is beaten." But once he had learned to write, a young man need no longer follow the dull round of peasant toil. Scribes were always in great demand, and they boasted of the ease of their lot. Theoretical education could scarcely be said to exist. All the knowledge taught in the schools was of a practical character, designed for the most part to fit one either for an official career or to guide him in religious affairs.

Science and Literature

This preference for the practical rather than the theoretical aspects of knowledge entirely dominated Egyptian science. Astronomy was used to determine the dates of the feast-days and other dates of religious importance. Geometry was precisely what its Greek name suggests — the art of land-measurement. Egyptian scholars knew several of the geometric theorems which Greek mathematicians were later to include in their theoretical treatises on the subject, but the idea of compiling a textbook of

[1] The lower set of characters, which also appears with the hieroglyphic spelling, is the determinative for wine.

Oriental Institute, Chicago

WALL PAINTING
From the Tomb of Khnumhotep at Beni Hasan, Egypt 1920–1900 B.C.

theoretical geometry probably never occurred to an Egyptian. In arithmetic the four elementary processes of addition, subtraction, multiplication, and division were used, but with few exceptions the only fractions which were employed were those having 1 as a numerator. More complicated fractions were broken down into series, each member of which had a numerator of 1. Thus, seven-eighths would be represented by a half, a fourth, and an eighth. Simple algebraic problems were also solved. As in Babylonia, medicine was a mixture of empirical wisdom and magic. Disease was thought to be the work of evil spirits, and a priest or magician was as likely to be summoned as a physician. Indeed, the two callings were often combined. But a large number of rational and useful remedies were in use, and simple surgical operations were performed. This real and pseudo-medical knowledge was collected in textbooks and manuals for the use of practitioners, and was taught in the temples.

Outside of a few official biographies and collections of proverbs, the Old Kingdom produced nothing that approximated the character of pure literature. An interesting example of "wisdom literature" is the *Admonitions of Ptahhotep*. The author, a prime minister to a Fifth Dynasty king, laid down the rules for a happy and prosperous life, including table manners, court etiquette, social tact, and how to get along with one's wife.

The Middle Kingdom Egyptians did much better. The existing *Prophecies of Ipuwer* describe in moving terms the miseries of the people in the anarchy which preceded the rise of the Twelfth Dynasty, and predict the peace and prosperity to be experienced under a future king — probably Amenemhet I, in whose reign it may have been written. The *Tale of the Eloquent Peasant* tells the story of a poor man who suffered oppression at the hands of a petty official, but who, by persistence and persuasive eloquence, finally carried his case to the king's court, where he secured redress. The *Shipwrecked Sailor* is a yarn worthy of a place in the *Arabian Nights*, and the story of *Sinuhe* recounts the wanderings of an Egyptian exile among the Semites of Syria. There is some poetry, of which easily the best is the *Song of the Harper* — in some respects a worthy precursor of the *Rubaiyat* of Omar Khayyam. It is an exhortation to men to enjoy the present, for death is certain, and no one knows what comes after it.

> The gods [deified kings] who were aforetime rest in their pyramids, likewise the noble and the wise, entombed in their pyramids. As for those who built houses, their place is no more; behold what has become of them. I have heard the words of Imhotep and of Harzozef, whose utterances are of much reputation, yet how are the places thereof? Their walls are in ruin, their places are no more, as if they had never been. None cometh from thence, that he might tell us of their state, that he might restore our hearts, until we too depart to the place, whither they have gone.[1]

But this uncertainty regarding the hereafter should only spur us to greater enjoyment of the present:

> Encourage thy heart to forget it, and let the heart dwell upon that which is profitable to thee. . . . Increase yet more thy delights, let not thy heart be weary, follow thy desire and thy pleasure, and mould thy affairs on earth after the mandates of thy heart, till that day of lamentation cometh, when the stilled heart hears not their mourning. For lamentation recalls no man from the tomb. Celebrate the glad day. Rest not therein! For lo, none taketh his goods with him; yea, no man returneth again, that is gone thither.[2]

Art in Architecture

We have already had occasion to discuss certain aspects of Egyptian art, including tomb paintings and sculptures and the Pyramids of Gizeh. Pyramid-building died out soon after the end of the Twelfth Dynasty. Already in the Middle Kingdom it had been largely superseded by tombs

[1] Breasted, *History of Egypt*, p. 206. By permission of Chas. Scribner's Sons.
[2] *Ibid.*

Brown Brothers

EGYPTIAN PAINTING
From Tomb of Men-na

cut into the cliffs along the edge of the Nile Valley, the sepulchral chamber being located at the foot of a shaft sunk at the rear end of a long tunnel. The paintings and sculptures of the chapel walls, for all that their purpose was purely magical, breathe the spirit of true art. Their makers were careful observers of everyday life, and they represented it with a zest and vigor seldom equaled. There were rigid conventions to be adhered to. A standing statue had to be posed with the arms at the sides, the left foot forward, and not otherwise. Human figures shown in profile must have the eye and shoulders done in full view. The body was done sketchily, but the face was usually a careful likeness, and some of the royal portraits, such as the Old Kingdom statues of Khafre, or the Middle Kingdom statues of Sesostris III and Amenemhet III, are masterpieces. With servants and other lesser characters, the artists had more freedom than with gods and kings, and they used it to good effect. The so-called Louvre Scribe, an Old Kingdom statue in limestone, is a triumph of realism. The eyes are inlaid with rock crystal to produce the illusion of reality, and the face is shrewd, hard-featured, and full of character.

The architecture of the Old Kingdom has been treated in part, but its most significant contributions to the art of building have yet to be discussed. Wonderful as were the Pyramids of Gizeh, the world at large has made very little use of pyramidal forms in its buildings. But it has derived from Egypt some of its most important architectural devices, among them the arch, the colonnade, and the clerestory. The arch was known and used as early as the Third Dynasty. The clerestory made its appearance in the mortuary temple of King Khafre, the successor of Khufu and builder of the second Gizeh Pyramid. Its floor plan consists of three parts, a central hall or nave, flanked on either side by side-aisles. The nave is divided from the side-aisles by two rows of square stone piers, with heavy stone lintels above them. Above the lintels rises a low clerestory, its walls pierced with small windows designed to light the interior of the building. In the temples of the Fifth Dynasty period the piers have been replaced by columns shaped like palm trunks, the capitals representing the foliage of the trees. The clerestory was destined, four thousand years later, to be used by the Romanesque and Gothic architects of medieval Europe, while the colonnade was employed by Greeks, Romans, medieval cathedral-builders, and many other schools of architects.

In general it may be said, although with significant exceptions, that by 1600 B.C. Egyptian civilization was displaying distinct traces of old age in the form of hardening conventions and reluctance to accept new ideas. But its life-cycle was not yet complete, and it was to enjoy a marvelous, though temporary, rejuvenation in the three centuries which followed.

5

The Egyptian Empire and Its Neighbors

(1580-1100 B.C.)

THE FOUNDATION OF THE EMPIRE

IT WILL BE REMEMBERED that about 1700 B.C. the Delta region was invaded by a horde of Semites known as the Hyksos. After about a century of Hyksos domination, the Egyptian people arose and expelled their conquerors. Little is known about most phases of the war, but several facts stand out clearly. The movement began in the upper valley, and as it proceeded, the princes of Thebes (the Seventeenth Dynasty) gradually assumed the leadership. As they slowly pushed back the Asiatics, the Theban rulers tightened their hold upon their brother dynasts, eliminating some and reducing others to impotence. At some time during the war they assumed the royal title. About 1580 B.C., Ahmose I of Thebes and Upper Egypt captured Avaris and shortly afterward drove the Hyksos far back into Asia. Rebellious nobles were put down with a strong hand. Egypt was not only free from the presence of the invader, but was united under a single master. Moreover, in achieving independence and unity she had developed new forces of energy and military zeal, which were later to urge her to foreign conquests. Although Ahmose I was of the Seventeenth Dynasty, Manetho makes him the founder of the Eighteenth.

Egypt emerged from the Hyksos period with a new form of government and a new social order. Her ruler was not only the head of the state but the owner of all the land, from which he drew rent rather than taxes. His power was absolute. The nobles were military and civil officials of his own choosing, who enjoyed the royal favor but had no independent power. From their ranks and from the middle class, the king created the first well-organized army in history. A vast bureaucracy, enlisted from all classes, enforced the royal will.

If there was a check of any kind upon the power of the king, it was the priesthood. No longer was the service of the gods a part-time employment of laymen. Each temple now had a staff of professional priests who controlled its endowment and performed the acts of worship. As Amen was again the chief god of the state, his priests enjoyed primacy over those of the other deities, and, next to the sovereign, his high priest was the religious head of the kingdom. In this situation lay future danger to the state, but centuries were to elapse before the peril became acute.

War Against Syria and Palestine

The first two kings of the Eighteenth Dynasty did no more than establish their authority in Egypt, reconquer Nubia, and raid the adjacent parts of Asia, but this limited policy did not satisfy the nation. Public opinion demanded that the former suffering and humiliation of the people be avenged upon the Asiatics whose ancestors had caused them, and the military class knew that rich spoil was to be acquired in the process. A war of conquest against these northeastern neighbors was imminent.

That this enterprise did not develop sooner was due to strife within the royal family. Thutmose I raided Syria and claimed dominion over it as far as the Euphrates River, but his authority in Egypt rested entirely upon marriage with a princess of the old royal line. From 1540 to 1480 B.C., he and his children, Thutmose II, Thutmose III, and Hatshepsut, were contending for the throne. During the last twenty years of this period, Queen Hatshepsut ruled Egypt and relegated her brother and husband, Thutmose III, to inactivity. As she could not lead the army abroad and would not allow her husband to do so, the Asiatics overthrew the authority which Egypt had been exercising over them. At last, by some method unrevealed, Thutmose III disposed of the imperious queen and thenceforth ruled alone. Vigorous prosecution of the war against the Asiatics was now certain.

With the Asiatic campaigns of Thutmose III, military history may be said to begin. He was a genius in war and administration, and his campaigns were carefully planned efforts with well-defined objectives toward systematic conquest. Official journals, excerpts from which still survive, recorded in detail the events of each year. Thutmose found Syria and Palestine divided into numerous city-kingdoms, inhabited by a people of Semitic speech and customs, but considerably mixed in blood and with little political cohesion. In the years just preceding the Egyptian invasion, only southern Palestine had been under the king's control. Farther north, the king of the city of Kadesh had formed a coalition of Syrian and Phoenician cities to defend the independence of the country. Syria, at its northern extremity along the Taurus Mountains, bordered upon the dominions of the Hittite king, and across the Euphrates to the east were the lands of the king of Mitanni. These two states were enemies, and only Mitanni offered resistance to the progress of Egyptian arms. Even so, the task was difficult and taxed the full power of Thutmose.

Beginning in 1479 B.C. with a smashing victory over the forces of the Kadesh confederacy at the Palestinian city of Megiddo, the Egyptian king pursued his career of conquest for nineteen years, during which period he invaded Syria seventeen times. Kadesh, Aleppo, and the other Syrian and Phoenician cities were captured, rebellions were crushed, and the country organized as an Egyptian dependency. The king of Mitanni was overpowered. The last embers of resistance were extinguished when Kadesh was captured for the second time, about 1460 B.C. Egypt now controlled an empire reaching to the northern limits of Syria and bounded on the east by the Syrian Desert and the Euphrates River. On the south, Thutmose extended his frontier nearly to the Fourth Cataract of the Nile.

The financial gains from these conquests had been considerable. Thousands of pounds of gold, silver, and copper, an immense number of slaves, horses, cattle, sheep, and chariots, and enormous quantities of timber and ivory had been landed at Thebes. After the spoils came tribute from the new provinces and, in addition, gifts from the Assyrian, Cretan, and Hittite rulers. The Egyptian king was now one of the richest sovereigns in the world.

The Government of the Egyptian Dependencies

The government of Egypt's Asiatic and Nubian dependencies, as organized by Thutmose, was a combination of centralized control and local self-government. The king was represented in Asia by a "Governor of the North Countries," and in Nubia by a "Viceroy of Kush and Governor of the South Countries." Egyptian posts and garrisons were established throughout both regions, and temples of Amen were built at central points and endowed. Local government was left to the local princely families, aided in each city by a council of "elders," which acted as an advisory body and a court of justice. Each vassal prince had to send one or more of his sons to Egypt as hostages for the loyalty of their parents. While in Egypt, the youths were educated as Egyptian nobles. When a prince died, one of his sons was sent home to take his place. A stated annual tribute was imposed on each community. A similar plan was applied to Nubia, with some differences which our data do not make clear. The chief fault of this system was that it left tempting opportunities for revolts in the hands of the subject peoples, but so long as a strong ruler occupied the Egyptian throne, it worked smoothly. By preventing wars among the Syrian and Palestinian princes, the arrangement probably more than repaid them for the tribute which was exacted. Egyptian civilization took a stronger hold in previously barbarous Nubia than it did in the Asiatic provinces, which had for two thousand years been under the cultural influence of Babylonia.

The Empire Under the Successors of Thutmose

The interval between the death of a king and the proclamation of his successor has always been a precarious period in Oriental countries, and the Asiatic Empire of Egypt was no exception to the rule. When news of the death of Thutmose III arrived in Asia (1447 B.C.) it was the signal for the revolt of many of the local chiefs, but his successor, Amenhotep II, sternly suppressed the movement. The next king, Thutmose IV, probably had to begin his reign under similar conditions, but thereafter a long period of peace ensued, and Amenhotep III, the last of the great imperial rulers of the Eighteenth Dynasty, did not have to repeat the preliminary campaigns of his father and grandfather. When Egypt lost her empire in Asia, it was attributable not so much to disaffection among the natives as to her own weakness and to Hittite interference.

THE WORLD OF THE AMARNA LETTERS

Beginning in the reign of Thutmose IV and extending through the succeeding seventy-five years, Egypt was in close diplomatic relations with the other powers of the eastern Mediterranean region and of western Asia. Our knowledge of Egyptian foreign relations during this period arises from the discovery in 1888 of some three hundred letters, written in Babylonian cuneiform on clay tablets. They originally formed part of the archives of the "foreign office" of Amenhotep III and his son, the heretic king, Ikhnaton. As the modern name for the place where the letters were discovered is Tell-el-amarna, they are usually known as the "Amarna Letters." Let us glance at the world which they reveal to us — the "state system" of the Near East about 1400 to 1350 B.C.

In material power and civilization, Egypt was by far the most important of the Near-Eastern states. Her empire extended from the Fourth Cataract of the Nile to northern Syria — a distance of about two thousand miles. Nubia, the southern province, was docile, and in Syria and Palestine there had been no outward sign of trouble for many years. But the strength of kings and people in the Nile Valley was beginning to diminish. We shall see presently that neither Amenhotep III nor his subjects were actuated by the military ardor which had enabled Thutmose III to acquire his Asiatic empire. Only the prestige of her great name still protected Egypt's interests in Syria and Palestine.

Relations With Babylon, Assyria, Mitanni

Babylon, under the Kassite Dynasty, was a weak power. Her territory included only the alluvial plain of the lower Tigris-Euphrates Valley, and although she claimed Assyria as a dependency, her kings were unable to enforce their pretensions. Amenhotep III of Egypt was in constant communication with the Kassite sovereigns Kurigalzu, Kadashman-enlil, and Burnaburiash. He married two Babylonian princesses, and his Kassite "in-laws" constantly wrote to beg for gold or to complain about the small amounts which they received. Egyptian vassals in Syria-Palestine did not always protect Babylonian merchants and envoys, and protests were sometimes lodged against Amenhotep's recognition of the rebel Assyrians. But as a rule the Kassites recognized their inferiority to Egypt and adopted a humble tone when dealing with her ruler.

Just above the Babylonian territory, on the middle Tigris, lay Assyria, a small city-kingdom inhabited by a Semitic people similar to the Babylonians, but more warlike and less civilized. Although the Assyrians were able to maintain their independence against Babylon, they were less fortunate in their relations with their northern neighbor, Mitanni. At one time during Amenhotep's reign, Tushratta of Mitanni was so manifestly in control of Assyria that he sent the image of the goddess Ishtar of Nineveh on a state visit to Egypt. Later in the same reign, however, the Assyrians regained their independence, and their king, like his neighbor sovereigns, begged gold from the Egyptian monarch.

Mitanni was located just east of the Euphrates River and south of the Taurus Mountains. It had been founded, during the disturbances which produced the Hyksos invasion of Egypt, by a band of Indo-European warriors who ruled a non-Semitic subject population. Mitanni's kings had fought against the Egyptians when the latter conquered Syria, but Thutmose IV had established friendly relations between the two royal families, and had married a Mitannian princess who probably became the mother of Amenhotep III. The latter married one or two ladies of the same family. The letters of Tushratta, king of Mitanni, to Amenhotep have a tone of warm and almost obsequious friendship.

Relations With the Hittites, Crete, and Cyprus

The one power which might prove dangerous to Egyptian interests in Asia was the Hittite Kingdom. Although its early history is obscure, evidently the people, like the Mitannians, consisted of an Indo-European aristocracy and a commonalty of native Armenoid stock. Its lands lay in central and southeastern Asia Minor, and during periods of expansion included districts on the southern slopes of the Taurus Range. It had long been quiescent and offered no opposition to the northern conquests of Thutmose III, until about 1411 B.C., when an able and energetic king named Shubbiluliuma ascended the throne and began a policy of aggression against both Egypt and Mitanni.

Active relations were also maintained by the Egyptian monarch with both Cyprus (*Alashiya*) and the Minoan Kingdom in Crete. Letters from the Cyprian king to Amenhotep reveal that he exported copper to Egypt in return for gold and Egyptian products, and that he was practically a vassal of his great southern neighbor. The kings of the Eighteenth Dynasty had long been receiving gifts from the Minoan sovereigns of Knossos, but at some time during Amenhotep's reign, invaders from the north destroyed the Cretan capital and these relations abruptly ceased.

In the reign of Amenhotep III, Egypt was the one state in southwestern Asia strong enough to offer serious resistance to the rising power of the Hittites, and to her support of the balance of power, as well as to subsidies and royal marriages, we may attribute the warm friendship shown her by Babylon, Mitanni, and Assyria. Rebellious Asiatic vassals could not hope for support from these powers. It was only when Amenhotep III and Ikhnaton ceased to show interest in their northern empire that the Hittite Shubbiluliuma could pursue his ambitious projects south of the Taurus Mountains with any hope of success.

THE GOLDEN AGE OF AMENHOTEP III

At home the reign of Amenhotep III saw his subjects enjoying a prosperity caused by two centuries of internal peace and by nearly a century of empire in Nubia and southwestern Asia. Each year the Nubian viceroy and the Asiatic vassals poured their tribute into the coffers of the king, and war captives furnished abundant labor for public works. With few or no military expenditures, Amenhotep could enjoy unparalleled luxury and construct some of the largest buildings ever known.

Court Life; the Growth of Art

The royal court acquired at the same time a dazzling splendor and an unconventional manner unknown to earlier ages. Styles of dress and personal adornment became increasingly elaborate, and the palaces of the king and his courtiers became constantly larger and more ornate. Amenhotep, while still officially a god like his ancestors, had little divine aloofness. He issued a proclamation enumerating his "bag" of lions and other wild animals — an act of extreme condescension in a god-king. His queen was a woman of low degree, and he must have shocked his more conventional contemporaries by publishing the fact in a series of proclamations. Queen Tiy obviously was a woman of great intelligence and

WALL PAINTING OF MUSICIANS AT A BANQUET
From the Tomb of Amenemhet

political ability, for she played a large part in affairs of state — something almost unknown in Oriental countries, ancient or modern.

The reign of Amenhotep III was one of the high points in the history of Egyptian art. At no other period did architecture combine the qualities of colossal size, pleasing proportions, and fineness of finish to so great a degree. Sculpture and painting kept pace with the art of the builder. Statues, both large and small, exhibit a faithfulness of portraiture and a delicacy of modeling that equal or surpass the best Old Kingdom work. Relief sculptures and paintings set before us the pageant of contemporary life with vivid realism or merciless caricature. Under the guidance of the royal architects and engineers, Thebes became a "monumental city" of carefully planned and integrated buildings and sculptures. Only the royal palace was of sun-dried brick and wood. The gods were housed in splendid structures of imperishable stone.

Temple-Building: Karnak and Luxor

In this era the floor plan of the Egyptian temple became stereotyped and can be traced in most of the shrines which date from this and succeeding ages. However, the ambition of later kings frequently led them to deface the works of their predecessors or to mar them with unsymmetrical additions. As one approached such a building toward the front, one first passed between a pair of tall obelisks, covered with reliefs and hieroglyphic inscriptions commemorating the king who had built the temple. The temple front consisted of a pair of high, oblong towers, forming the *pylon*, with walls sloping inward along the front and outer sides. Between them was a massive portal, closed at night with doors of cedar covered with bronze. Within, the visitor found a forecourt surrounded by a cloister, the columns of which imitated bundles of papyrus stalks with the buds for capitals. Beyond lay a great colonnaded hall, or *hypostyle*. The two rows of columns on either side of the axis were somewhat higher than those in the wings, making possible a clerestory with a row of windows in each wall. At the rear of the building lay the sanctuary of the god, flanked by a series of rooms used for purposes of the ritual and for the storage of supplies. Pylon, columns, walls, and ceiling were covered with painting and sculptures — the king smiting his enemies, leading victorious charges, worshiping the gods and receiving gifts or blessings from them. The ceilings were painted a brilliant blue, studded with stars to represent the sky, while the other paintings were in black, red, blue, or yellow. The whole structure was surrounded by a high wall. Thus, the

Egyptian artist lavished his attention upon the front of the temple and upon its interior, leaving the sides and the back usually without decoration. That this was not the only type of temple known to this age is proved by the exquisite little building which Amenhotep constructed on the island of Elephantine, near the First Cataract. It consisted of an oblong room surrounded by a portico, which was supported by piers resting on a stone balustrade.

Near the royal palace in western Thebes were the tombs of previous kings, and the plain was lined with mortuary temples built for the worship of their spirits. That of Amenhotep towered above the others and far surpassed them in splendor. It was approached from the river along an avenue lined on both sides with statues of jackals. In front of the pylon were two colossal, seated statues of the king, weighing seven hundred tons each. Time and the vandalism of Rameses II (who used it as a quarry for building materials) have left nothing but the statues, but when intact it was probably one of the finest products of the age.

East of the river, about a mile and a half apart, stood two temples of

University Prints

RESTORATION OF THE GREAT HYPOSTYLE HALL OF KARNAK

Amen, known today by their Arabic names of Karnak and Luxor. Karnak had been the recipient of many favors from previous kings, and Amenhotep did no more for it than to erect a pylon. Luxor had hitherto been unimportant, but he determined to make it the equal of its neighbor shrine. The old temple was demolished and a splendid new one was begun on the site. One approached the Luxor temple through a huge, covered colonnade, the side-walls of which were decorated with excellent reliefs depicting the New Year festival in honor of Amen. A forecourt 168 feet long and 147 wide ushered the visitor into a hypostyle hall lighted by clerestory windows and supported by 32 papyrus-cluster columns. The sanctuary behind this hall was defaced when later it was converted into a Christian church. A striking feature of the building is the "birth-room," which is still preserved, with its reliefs showing the divine birth of Amenhotep and his nurture in infancy by various deities. This giant structure was unfinished when the great king died, and it suffered later from the religious fanaticism of his son and from the tasteless additions made by Ramses II. Karnak and Luxor were connected by an avenue flanked by recumbent statues of rams, interspersed with occasional small temples.

High Point of Painting and Sculpture

The custom of hewing the tombs of kings and nobles in the cliffs along the edge of the valley continued, and excellent paintings and reliefs are found in their chapels. The artist, in most of his endeavors, was still hampered by conventions, but when unrestricted he showed a vivid realism tempered by satiric humor. Asiatic and Nubian slaves and vassal princes were so faithfully depicted that modern scholars can use their portraits as guides to the complex racial situation in these Egyptian dependencies, and their peculiarities were at times exaggerated with a touch as skillful as that of any modern cartoonist. In the tomb of a high priest of Ptah, near Memphis, is a series of reliefs depicting the funeral procession of the deceased. It is a fine character study, from the weeping sons of the dead man to the bored and elegant dignitaries who followed the bier as a matter of custom and official duty. Paintings from the ruins of Amenhotep's palace display a sympathetic love of nature equal to the best of the Old Kingdom productions.

If considerable space has been allotted to the art of this period, it is not because the output was larger than that of any other portion of Egyptian history or because more has been preserved than from other ages. The succeeding dynasty produced far more that has survived and its works were larger and better preserved than those of Amenhotep's day.   But never again was Egyptian art to combine such stupendous size with such remarkable beauty.   In small art objects, only the reign of his son produced anything comparable to the sculptures and paintings which his subjects gave to the world.   After his death the fine arts slowly but steadily declined.

THE DECLINE OF THE EMPIRE

While Amenhotep III was playing the part of the "sun-king" in Thebes, his Asiatic empire was beginning to crumble.   It is doubtful if he ever visited these dominions, and he soon ceased to accord them the attention which they required.   The more ambitious vassal princes seem to have lost their fear of him, and in his later years there were ominous rumblings of revolt and foreign invasion.   In the north, the Hittite king raided Mitanni and northern Syria, but his first attempt was repulsed by Amenhotep's ally Tushratta.   Out of the eastern desert came Bedouin nomads (the *Habiru* — possibly Hebrews), to ravage his lands and form settlements in them.   In the northern vassal state of Amurru, a family of crafty and able princes was embarking on a career of conquest against their fellow vassals.   Vigorous action was needed to repel these dangers, but the luxury-loving old king was incapable of the effort, and in 1375 B.C. he died.

Amenhotep IV (Ikhnaton) and the Religious Reform

It was the misfortune of Egypt that at this crisis, when above all things she needed a strong sovereign with the ability to fight and govern, she was ruled for nearly two decades by a religious visionary who entirely lacked these qualities.   Amenhotep IV (1375–1358) was a man of bold and original ideas and inflexible courage, which he demonstrated by making a complete break with the religious past of his country.   In place of the many gods, headed by Amen, whom the Egyptians worshiped, he saw evidence in the world about him of only one god — a beneficent and kindly father to mankind, devoid of all the primitive characteristics associated with the deities of popular belief.   To this deity he gave the name of *Aton* and made the sun-disk his visible symbol.   All other gods were but figments of the human imagination, and he declared ruthless war on them.   Their shrines were closed, their images destroyed, their priests dispossessed, and their endowments confiscated.   Ikhnaton caused the name of Amen to be chiseled out of inscriptions, although it involved the defacement of some of his father's monuments.   He caused hymns and liturgies

KING IKHNATON WORSHIPING THE SUN

to be composed in honor of Aton, temples to be built and endowed, and priesthoods to be established.

It requires but little imagination to picture the confusion which this movement, supported by an omnipotent king, must have caused in the religious life of the people. A small clique of courtiers followed the heretic, either from conviction or from self-interest, but the priests and the people viewed the revolution with confusion and horror. Thebes, the center of the Amen cult, must have become intolerable to Amen's arch-enemy. The king changed his name to *Ikhnaton* ("Aton-is-pleased"), and deserted his hostile capital. Nearly two hundred miles north of Thebes, on the eastern bank of the Nile, he founded a new city, *Akhetaton*, dedicated to his new god. There he spent the remainder of his days among a congenial circle, propagating the faith. A new school of art, noted for its ruthless realism, enjoyed his unqualified encouragement. One of its products is a series of busts, statues, and reliefs depicting the scrawny features of Ikhnaton and his queen *Nefertiti* in what may be caricature, but can never have been flattery. Splendid hymns in honor of Aton emanated from this circle, anticipating by many centuries some of the sayings of the Hebrew prophets. It must have been a charming and intellectual court which frequented the halls of Akhetaton, but while it was engaged in religious and artistic reforms, the Asiatic empire had all but ceased to exist and Egypt itself was falling into chaos.

The Loss of the Asiatic Empire

Whoever else may have profited from Ikhnaton's innovations, they provided a golden opportunity for two men — the Hittite *Shubbiluliuma* and the Amorite *Aziru*. The latter, a vassal of Egypt, began by attacking his fellow vassals, killing them and annexing their lands. The loyal princes sent frantic appeals to their Egyptian suzerain, but without results. It is impossible to avoid the suspicion that some of Ikhnaton's subordinates in Egypt and Asia deliberately deceived him regarding Aziru, for the latter was able to pursue his plans while posing as a loyal subject until he had conquered most of Syria and Phoenicia.

Shubbiluliuma seems to have encouraged this intrigue, meanwhile conspiring against the Mitannian king Tushratta. The latter was assassinated and Mitanni fell into anarchy. Shubbiluliuma promptly made the land of his former enemy a vassal state. Then, waiting until Aziru had conquered the northern lands of Egypt, he attacked the Amorite and made him a vassal as well. The Hittites now controlled a considerable empire south of the Taurus Mountains. In Palestine, the inroads of the Habiru had so desolated the land that thousands of homeless wretches sought refuge in Egypt. Then Ikhnaton died. Several ephemeral successors (including Tutankhamen, the discovery of whose tomb created a sensation in 1923) followed him, but in less than a decade, the Eighteenth Dynasty was extinct.

The Nineteenth Dynasty (1350–1215 b.c.)

Throughout the period of the Atonist upheaval, a general named *Harmhab* had been rising to power. He was capable, blunt, realistic, and possessed a high sense of duty. With the aid of the priests of Amen, he seized the throne and founded a new dynasty (the Nineteenth). Atonism had been rejected by the Egyptian people, and Harmhab recognized the fact. The temples were reopened, their endowments were restored, and Egyptian religion resumed its usual character. During the confusion of the preceding twenty years, soldiers and officials had practiced the most shocking oppression of the poor. Harmhab undertook to end such practices by cutting off the noses of offenders and banishing them to a remote fortress on the edge of the desert. Law and order returned and the people breathed freely again. As it was useless to attempt to reconquer Syria, Harmhab made peace with the Hittites.

Ramses II and the Hittite War

The next two kings, Ramses I and Seti I (1315–1292 b.c.), continued the work of rehabilitation, and were contented with reconquering those portions of Palestine and Phoenicia not claimed by the Hittites. But Ramses II (1292–1225 b.c.) made a determined effort to restore the empire of Thutmose III. It was hopeless from the beginning, for the Hittites had thoroughly colonized their Syrian provinces. The Egyptians, on the other hand, had never been able to send settlers to Asia, and could not have done so now even if they had reoccupied their former provinces. The highlight of the war was a battle fought at Kadesh (1288), in which Ramses was drawn into an ambush and saved his army by good luck and prodigies of personal valor. The vain monarch made much of his personal exploits in this encounter, and commemorated them in reliefs and inscriptions which are familiar to every tourist who visits Egypt, but Kadesh was either a drawn battle or an Egyptian defeat. Sixteen years of war left Ramses with only Palestine and southern Syria, which his father had possessed.

In 1272, a treaty ended the destructive struggle. Thereafter, Ramses was on friendly terms with the Hittite king Hattushil, whose daughter he married later.

Ramses II reigned forty-seven years after the end of the Hittite war. He was a man of boundless self-conceit, who surpassed Amenhotep III in the size and number (although not the quality) of his buildings. At times, as we have seen, he even resorted to the destruction of the works of his predecessors to secure building material. His principal memorials were the gigantic colonnaded hall at Karnak and his mortuary temple in western Thebes. These are only the outstanding examples of a policy which furnished every important town in Egypt with one or more temples, obelisks, statues, or other tokens of royal esteem. The great hall at Karnak was the largest structure of its kind ever undertaken. Its floor measures 338 by 170 feet — an area large enough to permit the Parisian Cathedral of Notre Dame to be placed within its walls. On top of each of the columns of the nave a hundred men could find standing room, and each of the blocks of the architrave above it weighs one hundred tons. Clerestory windows nearly thirty feet high lighted the interior. It lacked the refined proportions of earlier work, but its enormous size helped to disguise the fact. The *Ramesseum*, or mortuary temple of Ramses, is a far superior creation. It may be presumed that he seriously depleted the resources of the nation by his extravagance, as his successors were unable to continue his program.

Decline and End of the Nineteenth Dynasty

Under Ramses the center of political gravity shifted to the north, and Thebes, while still the first city of Egypt, ceased to be the royal residence. A new residence city, Per-Ramses, was built in the eastern Delta region. Commerce with Syria and Phoenicia was very active and Semitic influence was apparent in every phase of national life. Thus, the great king grew old amid pomp, ostentation, and servile flattery. For the pressing ills of his country he knew no remedy and sought none. His people were losing their warlike spirit, but he contented himself with the hiring of barbarian mercenaries. The wealth and power of the priesthood were growing to dangerous proportions and he aggravated the evil by making enormous grants to Amen and the other gods. During the last twenty years of his life, northern pirates and Libyan tribesmen threatened the Delta, but the senile king did nothing to defend his lands. For all the splendor of his reign, its end came none too soon.

After Ramses' death the decline of Egypt became even more apparent.

His son *Merneptah* (1225–1215 B.C.) struggled valiantly with some success against the Libyans, the Northerners, and rebellious Asiatic subjects. With him the Nineteenth Dynasty ended and at least a decade of anarchy and civil war followed. The Twentieth Dynasty (probably a branch of the Nineteenth) restored order and its second king, Ramses III, resumed the hard task of repelling the invaders from Egyptian shores.

FOREIGN PERILS AND INTERNAL DECLINE

A New Northern Migration and Its Defeat

The danger to Egypt from without in the late thirteenth and twelfth centuries B.C. arose largely from waves of migration starting far in the barbarian North, as in the time of the Hyksos. New cultural forces, among which was the discovery of iron-smelting, had caused vast dislocation of population. One wave rolled down through Asia Minor, bringing the Indo-European Phrygians into the peninsula and smashing the Hittite Kingdom. Gathering new volume as it progressed, the migration swept into Syria and headed for Egypt. It seemed as though the Hyksos conquest was about to be repeated.

But in Ramses III, Egypt had found a man capable of meeting the danger. Gathering a fleet and army, he advanced into Phoenicia and gave battle to the invaders, destroying their fleet and capturing their land forces. Egypt was saved and her authority in Palestine and Phoenicia was re-established. One group of the defeated horde, the Philistines, settled down in the coast cities of Palestine, where they developed a culture with strong similarities to those of Crete and western Asia Minor. We shall hear more of these people in connection with the rise of the Hebrews. The repulse of the northern invasion was to be the last great military feat of the Egyptians for over five centuries, and it was accomplished almost entirely by mercenary forces, with little or no help from the native population.

National Decay and Rise of the Priests of Amen

After the death of Ramses III (1167 B.C.), nine more kings of his name and family reigned in Egypt. Their history is a painful one. The real rulers of the land were the priests of Amen, who had greater wealth and power than the kings. As one weakling succeeded another on the throne, Egyptian prestige abroad vanished and disorder reigned at home. The Delta became an independent kingdom. At Thebes the law was so little respected that all the more important royal tombs were plundered. At last, the high priest of Amen, *Hrihor*, seized the throne, founding the Twenty-First Dynasty, but the change brought little improvement. Centuries of disorder, disunion, and foreign invasion ensued, but their story must be told in a later chapter.

The empire period was the last age of creativity in Egyptian history. Its artistic achievements have been briefly considered. In literature it produced a number of popular stories, such as the *Doomed Prince* and *The Two Brothers* — the latter embodying the same theme as the story of Joseph and Potiphar's wife. The splendid hymns of the Aton-worshipers also entitle the ill-fated cult to a place of eminence in the literary history of the world.

Aside from Atonism, most of the developments in Egyptian religion were pernicious. The growing wealth of the priests made it possible for them to neglect the poor, who were excluded from all share in the official cults. Priestly rascals undermined the moral influence of the Osiris cult by undertaking to show men how to cheat the divine judge and win eternal happiness in spite of vicious living. Charms and incantations, intended to ward off the perils of the hereafter, had long formed part of the equipment of a corpse. There was now one added to the list, beginning, "Oh, my heart, rise not up against me as a witness!" By repeating it at the moment when one's heart was being weighed, one could secure a favorable verdict without regard to one's conduct while on earth. Small statuettes called "answerers" were placed in the tombs of the wealthy, so that when the deceased was called upon to do manual labor in the world beyond the grave, an "answerer" was always ready to say, "Here I am," and to do the work for him.

In short, Egyptian civilization was not merely old but senile. Egypt was later to teach the Greeks the rudiments of many of the manual arts and to enjoy a partial revival of political power, but in the civilization of the world her leadership had ended.

6

···

Syria, Phoenicia, and Palestine

ON THE WESTERN HALF of the Fertile Crescent lay Syria-Palestine, a political and cultural battleground of the Hittites, Egyptians, and Babylonians. The history of this region has been determined largely by four major geographic factors:

1. Its location on the great commercial and military route between Egypt and the Tigris-Euphrates Valley, which has subjected it to invasion and occupation from both sides.
2. Its broken surface, which is crossed by high mountains and deep valleys. This feature has always made political unity difficult, and has forced the people to live in small and mutually hostile groups.
3. The Mediterranean Sea, over which have come numerous invaders and which has afforded commercial opportunities to the peoples on its coasts.
4. The Desert Bay, whence came most of its peoples and many phases of its culture.

The Country of Palestine

Palestine was the southernmost of the three divisions of the country. It was bounded on the south and east by the desert, on the west by the Mediterranean Sea, and on the north by a line running from Mount Carmel to the headwaters of the Jordan, and thence eastward to the desert. Its greatest length was not over one hundred and fifty miles, its maximum width not above eighty miles, and its area about 10,500 square miles. Physically, it is divided from east to west into four well-defined zones. First comes the narrow but fertile Mediterranean coastal plain. East of the plain, the land rises to a great central mountain ridge which occasionally attains a height of three thousand feet. The third zone is the volcanic rift-valley of the Jordan which, at its deepest, is thirteen hundred feet below sea-level. Beyond the Jordan the land rises again, and there is a narrow belt of fertile land which merges with the desert. Most of the soil is wretchedly poor, and there are considerable areas of "wilderness," or waste land, suitable only for pasturage.

Palestine lies between 31° and 33° 15' north latitude — about the same as southern Georgia, Alabama, and Mississippi. Jerusalem is in nearly the same latitude as Natchez, Mississippi. In general, the climate is that of the warm Temperate Zone, with rainy winters and hot, dry summers. At Jerusalem the temperature has been known to vary from 112° to 25° Fahrenheit, and snow falls occasionally. The rainfall — twenty-three inches annually — is about that of central Kansas. Drought is a dreaded calamity, and water-supply a serious problem. Wells and springs are highly prized, and villages are usually located near them.

Nature does not compensate the Palestinian people with other resources for the poverty of their soil. Timber, though formerly more plentiful than now, has always been scarce. Some iron ore is found, but little or no other metal. Potter's clay and building stone are about the only valuable raw materials. It is a difficult land in which to make a living, and to better one's condition one would have to become a trader, a manufacturer, or a conqueror of one's neighbors.

Syria and Phoenicia

North of Palestine, the topography is as strongly diversified as in the south. The coastal plain in ancient times was the country of Phoenicia. The coastline, which in the south is devoid of good harbors, becomes more irregular, and there are adequate ports at Acre, Tyre, Sidon, Byblos, Arvad, Amuru, and Beirut. Eastward the land rises rapidly to the Lebanon Mountains, and some of the peaks attain an altitude of over ten thousand feet. Here were found in ancient times the famous "cedars of Lebanon," which were in demand all over the Near East. The great volcanic rift through which the Jordan flows is continued in the fertile valley of the Orontes River. The latter flows northward for a long distance parallel to the Mediterranean coast and then turns abruptly westward to enter the sea. On the eastern side of the valley rises the ridge of the Anti-Libanus, beyond which the land slopes to the Syrian Desert. At the desert's edge is the rich Damascus Oasis, watered by streams which flow from the mountains. In the north a plain, which in some places is swampy, affords the traveler from the south a passage between the Orontes and the Euphrates. Syria is a much richer land than Palestine, and its climate is usually

cooler and more invigorating. It has some mineral wealth, but its chief
source of both wealth and woe in ancient times was the fact that it lay at
the crossroads of the ancient world. Here converged the great commercial
routes along which moved goods from Asia Minor, Egypt, the Mediterranean islands, Babylonia, and Arabia, and the armies of conquerors followed the merchants. Syrian history and civilization reflect the varied
influence of all these lands.

Early Phoenician and Canaanite Culture

We have learned something regarding the peoples of Palestine and southern Syria in connection with our study of Egyptian history. At some time
previous to 2500 B.C., Semitic nomads from the Desert Bay had swept into
Palestine and Syria in force sufficient to absorb the native Mediterranean
population and to Semitize the language of the land. Those who settled
on the Syrian seacoast were known to the Egyptians as *Fenkhu* (whence the
Greek word *Phoenices* and our Phoenicians). The inhabitants of Palestine
were called Canaanites.

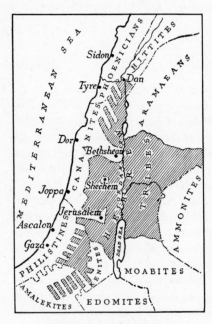

MAP OF PALESTINE BEFORE   MAP OF PALESTINE AFTER
THE RISE OF THE MONARCHY   DIVISION OF THE HEBREW KINGDOM

Religion and Government

Both groups soon acquired cosmopolitan cultures. They brought with them the pastoral economy, enforced simplicity of life, and unaffected, austere religion of the desert. Their new homes were already occupied by an agricultural people, possessed of the rudiments of civilization, and having a religion largely designed to stimulate by sympathetic magic the reproductive powers of nature. Every community worshiped a *Baal* and *Baalat* (Lord and Lady) of its own. There were also the fertility goddess *Ashtart* and her husband, the vegetation god *Adonis*. Every year Adonis died and, after being frantically mourned by his worshipers, was resurrected amid delirious rejoicing. The firstborn offspring of man and beast were sacrificed to the gods. Self-torture and mutilation, together with sacramental sex indulgence, were part of the ritual. The Hebrew prophets vigorously denounced such practices, but other rites — the Passover, fasts, sacrifices, and the Sabbath — passed permanently into Hebrew religion.

We have already seen something of the government of this region. In the more backward districts the clan system of the desert prevailed, with its feuds and internal strife. But in each city there was a king, with nearly the same powers as an early Babylonian patesi, and a council of elders that aided and advised him. At a very early date, some of these communities had regular codes of law, which often showed marked Babylonian influence.

Culture

The clothing, manners, and personal appearance of these Semitic Canaanites were a never-failing source of mirth to the Egyptians. They wore voluminous and gaudily colored robes of wool or linen and let their hair and beards grow long. When speaking, they gesticulated more than an Egyptian thought proper, and used an inflated, ornate style of diction. But they were shrewd merchants, with whom an Egyptian could only deal to advantage when backed by a victorious army.

Foreign influences in their region were strong. Babylonian merchants spread the cuneiform writing and a knowledge of the laws of their native land, along with Babylonian manufactured goods. A similar culture current flowed from Egypt, reinforced by conquering armies and the enforced residence of Semitic hostages in Egypt. A knowledge of Egyptian writing and writing materials was one of the most valuable contributions from this quarter. From Minoan Crete came the knowledge of many useful arts. The peoples of Asia Minor added a new strain of blood, from which probably came the traditional "Jewish" type of face, really an Armenoid profile, with close analogies in eastern Anatolia to this day.

In one respect the Syrian Semites soon improved upon their teachers. Before 1200 B.C. they had abandoned both the cuneiform and hieroglyphic styles of writing in favor of a true alphabetic method of their own invention. For centuries the western Semites had been experimenting with alphabets of mixed Egyptian and Babylonian derivation, and the result bears traces of influence from both sides. A conventionalized sign was adopted to represent each of the twenty-two consonantal sounds in their language, and each received a name which embodied the sound for which it stood. Thus, the first letter was *aleph*, meaning ox; the second was *beth* (house); the third, *gimel* (camel), and so forth. There were no signs for vowel sounds, but this was not as serious a disadvantage as it would have been in an Indo-European language. Determinatives, such as the Egyptians and Babylonians used, were discarded. In place of the low-cost, clumsy clay tablet, they used Egyptian papyrus, on which they wrote with pen and ink, and from right to left, as in modern Hebrew. Such was the famous "Phoenician" alphabet — the ancestor of all modern alphabets.

The Decline of the Great Powers

So long as Egypt, Babylon, and the Hittite Kingdom were the great powers of the Near East, Syria-Palestine had no chance for independent development. In our previous studies, we have seen it merely as a dependency of Egypt or the Hittite state, but by 1150 B.C. this was no longer true. Babylonian influence was no longer strong, the Hittite state had ceased to exist, and Egypt was decadent. Except for an Assyrian raid about 1100 B.C., Syria-Palestine was not threatened by the great powers for nearly three centuries, and in that period it had an opportunity to develop a culture of its own.

THE HEBREWS AND THE ORIGIN OF JUDAISM

The Hebrew Invasion: the Northern and the Southern Tribes

We have seen that in the reign of the Egyptian king Ikhnaton, Palestine was entered by nomads from the eastern desert, whom the natives called *Habiru* (nomads), or *Shasu* (robbers). Both names are descriptive of the invaders' habits. Beginning with settlements in the lands east of the Jordan, they spread west of the river, occupying the country districts of the central highland north of Jerusalem. Some of the cities, like Jericho, were taken and destroyed, but Jerusalem, Schechem, Beth Shan, and other Canaanite strongholds held out successfully. On the coastal plain the newcomers had very little success. Their early tribal organization was not that with which Old Testament readers are familiar, but this group later included the Biblical tribes of Asher, Dan, Naphtali, Zebulon, Issachar, Ephraim, Manasseh, Benjamin, Reuben, and Gad. Although at first devoid of unity, they gradually acquired a loose sense of solidarity based upon community of language and religion, and later were to form the Kingdom of Israel.

South of Jerusalem another group of tribes of similar lineage and habits conquered a domain from the Canaanites. Bible readers are familiar with the component parts of this group as the tribes of Judah, Simeon, and Levi. Simeon was later absorbed by Judah, and the Levites soon became a priestly caste, without any land of its own. The traditional lawgiver *Moses* was a Levite, and the incident of the captivity in Egypt may have involved this tribe. It certainly did not apply to all the Hebrews.

Thus, from the beginning there were two Hebrew peoples, separated from each other by the unconquered Canaanite city of Jerusalem. This fact was to be of great importance in later Hebrew history. When at length the two groups attempted to form a united state, the tradition of division was too strong to be overcome, except for a few years.

The Yahweh Cult

Early in the history of the Hebrew settlement in Palestine we find some of the newcomers worshiping *Yahweh*, a god of the desert and the storm. His cult originated somewhere in the south and spread northward. For many centuries he did not have undisputed sway anywhere. The Hebrews, like earlier Semitic immigrants, adopted the cults of the Baals and the fertility gods, with all their emphasis upon sexuality and cruel but impressive rites, and when they recognized Yahweh, it was merely as one of a host of deities. His importance lay as yet in the future, but he had one quality which distinguished him from his divine colleagues. He was a "jealous god," who resented the honor paid to others, and herein lay the germs of monotheism. North of Jerusalem his principal shrines were at Gilgal, Bethel, Shiloh, and Dan.

"The Period of the Judges"

From the first the Hebrews were in a state of chronic war. On the one hand, they had to fight the settled Canaanites, and on the other, the nomadic Moabites, Ammonites, Midianites, and Amalekites who crowded in behind them. When other enemies were lacking, they sometimes fought each other. For a time they must have recognized Egyptian suzerainty, and Merneptah lists them among the Palestinian peoples whom he had conquered. Shortly after 1200 b.c., the Philistines appeared on the seacoast and conquered the plains up to the edge of the plateau.

The centuries which elapsed between the settlement and the rise of the monarchy of Saul is generally known as "the period of the Judges." Later Hebrew tradition preserved considerable scraps of history from this age, but they are entirely disconnected, and their appearance of cohesion is deceptive. The Judges were popular leaders who arose in times of peril to lead the people to victory and moral reform. Of the many whose names have been preserved, one of the most important was *Barak*, who, with the prophetess *Deborah*, led some of the northern tribes to victory against the Canaanite Sisera. A splendid war song, preserved in the book of Judges, commemorates the event. Likewise, we hear of *Gideon, Jephthah, Samson*, and *Samuel*, each of whom played a part in the troubled and anarchic affairs of the people of Israel.

The Israelites could fight on equal terms with Canaanites and nomads, but the Philistines were more formidable enemies. After their defeat by Ramses III, they had settled in the coast cities of Gaza, Ascalon, Ashdod, Ekron, and Gath, while a similar group, the *Zakkalu*, occupied Joppa and Dor. In their old homes they had been under the influence of the Mycenaean Greeks, and their arms, pottery, clothing, and buildings show the Aegean stamp. The Philistines were tall and strong — "giants," the Hebrews said. Their warriors wore helmets, corselets, and greaves, and carried spears whose size astonished their enemies. The five cities of Philistia formed a confederation, for which their chiefs acted as a council. Thus, in war as in other matters, they were centuries ahead of the barbarous highland Hebrews. In the Biblical narratives we naturally learn only the Hebrew side of the story, so to be fair, we must remember that both peoples were intruders, and that to the Philistine the Hebrew was an uncivilized robber against whom he had to defend himself. Before 1050 b.c., the Hebrews who lived west of the Jordan had been conquered by the Philistines and were ruled by governors appointed by them.

The Reign of King Saul

After some years of subjection, the tribes north of Jerusalem began a movement toward union and independence. The first step was to choose a king, and at the instigation of Samuel they elected *Saul*, a brave and handsome Benjaminite. After repulsing an Ammonite raid upon the east Jordan lands, he fell upon the Philistines and won a series of great victories. War with them continued throughout his reign, but for many years his leadership afforded the land a respite from nomad plunderers and Philistine tyranny. Even Judah recognized his authority. Saul established his capital at Gibeah, a little north of Jerusalem, where his palace has been excavated.

Saul's later years were stormy. Samuel had promoted him in the hope that he would prove a pliant tool in the hands of priests and prophets, but the king, while deferential to Samuel, had a mind of his own. Repeated clashes between them ended in a complete break. Toward the end he became involved in another quarrel, this time with his son-in-law, David of Bethlehem. The latter was handsome, able, and crafty, and had the support of the priests. At last David fled to the Philistines, and Saul and his son Jonathan were killed in battle at Mount Gilboa. Israel and Judah relapsed into servitude, with David as a Philistine vassal prince in Judah, and a younger son of Saul in the same capacity in Israel.

The Reign of King David

Such a condition, with David in a position of influence, could not continue. A Judean army under David's nephew, Joab, attacked the armies of Israel and won a succession of victories. Treachery disposed of David's rival, and the northern tribes called upon the Bethlehemite prince to rule over them as well. So keen was the sense of separatism that his title was "King of Israel and Judah."

His reign (about 1000–955 B.C.) inaugurated the brief but glorious Hebrew Empire. In this age of small states, David had no overwhelming opposition to fear, either from neighbors or foreigners. A series of successful campaigns disposed of the Philistines, who were glad to make peace. Then David attacked and took the Canaanite fortresses of Jerusalem, Beth Shan, and Megiddo, which divided the land into disjointed fragments. Jerusalem became the royal capital and the religious center of the nation. For the first time the Hebrew territory was free from enclaves of foreigners. Following the liberation and unification of Israel and Judah, David and the faithful Joab subjugated the Edomites, Mo-

COLOSSAL STRIDING LION
Hittite Sculpture

abites, Ammonites, and the Aramean states of eastern Syria, including Damascus. His frontier may, for a short time, have reached the Euphrates, and on the south touched the Red Sea and the boundary of Egypt. Internal organization was also effected. A governor was appointed for each of the tribes, and a census was taken. Aside from subject peoples, David probably had about six hundred thousand subjects. Taxes and the *corvée* were exacted regularly. The army was carefully organized and disciplined by the loyal but bloodthirsty Joab. David began the embellishment of Jerusalem and strove to make it a worthy metropolis for a great kingdom.

The latter days of the great king were not happy. Like many another Oriental ruler, he found his harem a major problem. He became involved in a clandestine affair with the beautiful Bathsheba, who later became his queen. His sons Absalom and Adonijah made unsuccessful bids for the throne, the former leading a formidable rebellion in which he lost his life. Bathsheba secured the succession for her young son Solomon, and amid such scenes the old king sank into dotage and closed his eventful career. Solomon and Bathsheba murdered Joab and Adonijah, banished David's friend, the priest Abiathar, and installed their own partisans in power.

Solomon's Reign and Death

Once securely seated on the throne, Solomon proved to be a peaceful ruler, who delighted in courtly luxury, foreign merchandise, fine buildings, and his harem of a thousand wives. He constructed a new royal palace and near it a temple for the worship of Yahweh. The temple was of modest size — ninety feet long, thirty feet wide, and forty-five feet high, and was entered by way of a porch fifteen feet wide. The walls were of stone, and the roof and inside paneling were of cedar. Around this central shrine, but separated from it on all sides by a court, were rooms used for the purposes of the cult. Splendid bronze and gold furnishings were made by Tyrian workmen. The altar and walls of the innermost sanctuary (Holy of Holies) were plated with gold, but there was no mention of any image of Yahweh himself. Evidently, even at this early date, there was a feeling that the god of Israel could not be represented in human or animal form.

Solomon in later times was considered Israel's wisest king. Yet, with all his splendor and wisdom, he was not his father's equal in war and statesmanship. Edom and Damascus became independent in his reign. Forced labor and heavy tribute bore severely on his subjects, and there were rumblings of discontent in the north. A certain Jeroboam attempted a revolution, failed and fled to Egypt. When the "Wise King" died, only a great statesman could have held the Hebrew state together, but none appeared.

With the accession of Solomon's son Rehoboam, the storm broke. When the reckless youth refused Israel's demand for a redress of grievances, the eight northern tribes declared their independence and chose Jeroboam for their king. It was a natural result of the deep-seated differences between the north and the south, which had been so recently and so imperfectly overcome by David. Judah and Benjamin, including the capital city of Jerusalem, continued to acknowledge Rehoboam.

The Kingdoms of Israel and Judah

The northern kingdom was much the larger, richer, and more populous of the two. Jeroboam built temples in honor of Yahweh at Bethel and Dan, with bull idols to represent his deity. Israel retained her independence about two centuries (until 722 B.C.). During much of this time her kings held the suzerainty over their weaker Judean rivals. There were repeated revolutions and changes of dynasty. The ablest king of Israel was Ahab (874–852), who warred successfully with the Arameans of Damascus and held an important place in the coalition which defeated an invasion of the Assyrian king Shalmaneser. Ahab disagreed with the prophets of Yahweh on religious matters, and so has failed to receive due recognition for his merits. After his death, his family was soon overthrown, and a century later the disintegration of the kingdom began. In 732 B.C., Israel became tributary to the Assyrians, and ten years later its capital at Samaria was taken and destroyed by the Assyrian Sargon II. The cities were destroyed, the upper classes were deported (the Ten Lost Tribes), and their places were filled with Syrian and Babylonian exiles. Mingling with the remaining Israelites, the newcomers adopted a variant form of the Yahweh cult and became the ancestors of the Samaritans of later times.

Judah continued to acknowledge the House of David. Her kings were usually men of mediocre ability, and she was surrounded by enemies who took advantage of her weakness. Under King Uzziah and his son Jotham (782–736 B.C.) the land enjoyed prosperity, but soon afterward it became involved in the struggle between Assyria and Egypt. In this battle of the "great powers," Judah was no more than a pawn and suffered accordingly. When Assyria fell, the change brought little relief. After a period of vassalage to the Egyptian Necho II, Judah fell under the influence of the Babylonian Nebuchadnezzar and later was drawn by Egyptian intrigues into new rebellions. In 586, Nebuchadnezzar's patience was exhausted. Jerusalem was destroyed, her king blinded and deported, and her nobles and landowners carried to Babylonia. The Jewish people were yet to make their unique contribution to the culture of the world, but for the time it seemed as if their national existence was at an end.

The Evolution of the Yahweh Cult

Throughout this brief sketch of Hebrew history, repeated mention has been made of the cult of Yahweh. As we have seen, in its earlier stages it differed but little from those of other gods. Yahweh's austere desert character was soon overlaid with features borrowed from the gods of the Canaanites. Scattered through the land were shrines and "high places" where he was honored with rites like those of his fellow deities. Passover, burnt offering, sin offering, fasting, and even human sacrifices were celebrated there. He had little moral influence and his worshipers had no assurance of a blessed hereafter. They expected to pass at death into the same cheerless subterranean *sheol* as their Babylonian cousins.

The evolution of Yahwehism began with the rise of the monarchy. David and Solomon gave the cult a center at Jerusalem, and Jeroboam did the same for his kingdom at Bethel and Dan. A priesthood, which claimed descent from the Levite lawgiver Moses or his brother Aaron, served these shrines. For ages the "high places" where Levites performed the rites were the centers of popular religion. Monotheism, together with many other features of modern Judaism, was still unheard of, but the ritual of these temples was probably not so crude as that of the older shrines.

Far more potent was the influence of the prophets. We are accustomed to think of a prophet as one who foretells the future, but this was not the major function of a Hebrew prophet. His duty was to proclaim the will of God as he saw it, on all matters, present or future. There were among them some charlatans, like the official prophets of Ahab mentioned in First Kings. Others, like Elijah the Tishbite in Israel, or Hosea in Judah, devoted their lives to fighting against the worship of gods other than Yahweh, or to uprooting from his cult objectionable practices borrowed from heathen worship. Again, Isaiah and Amos denounced the moral wrongs and social injustice current in the Hebrew states, and the former acted as a censor of the foreign policy of Hezekiah. While the priests were, as a rule, conservative and thought more of the privileges of their order than of ennobling the attributes and worship of their god, the prophets thought little of ritual, but much of the matters which the priests neglected. Theirs was no easygoing tolerance of many gods. Their viewpoint was expressed by Elijah in his challenge to the men of Israel: "If the Lord be God, follow him; but if Baal, then follow him." [1] They waged merciless war upon the injustice and immorality of men in high places. It was the prophet Nathan who denounced David for his adultery with Bathsheba, and Elijah foretold woe to the House of Ahab for the judicial murder of Naboth. Good conduct, and not sacrifices, was what Yahweh demanded of his people. Especially did the prophet fulminate against cruel and immoral rites practiced by the peasantry in honor of both Yahweh and his rival gods. It is in this light that we must interpret the charge made with such terrible effectiveness by Hosea, that Israel had become a prostitute.

[1] I Kings, 18:21.

Progress Toward Monotheism

These prophetic thunders at last bore fruit. The followers of Elijah fomented the revolution which placed the cruel but thoroughly devoted Yahwist, Jehu, on the Israelite throne, and Isaiah's prophecies infused courage into the Judean Hezekiah in dealing with the "high places" of his kingdom. Hezekiah and his great-grandson Josiah at last destroyed all local shrines, forbade the worship of other gods, and centralized all religious rites of importance in the Temple of Jerusalem. The step was not an unmixed blessing, for it worked great hardship on the people in remote districts, yet it outlawed all other cults except that of Yahweh and was a long step toward monotheism.

In general, it may be said that before the Babylonian captivity the people of Judah had made great progress toward monotheism, and that their more progressive thinkers had given their religion a moral content, but neither feature had achieved an established place in Hebrew religion. Yahweh was still only a Palestinian god. It required many years of residence abroad to convince men that his power extended throughout the universe and that there were no other gods.

The Origins of the Old Testament

Religious writings reflected this evolution. As early as David's time the first attempts had been made to record the legendary history of the Hebrews. Some of David's poems were recorded in writing, later to be included in the book of Psalms. Historical works resting on reasonably good authority and recording the story of the monarchy were probaby composed in Solomon's time, and official chronicles were kept by the kings of Israel and Judah. Manuals of civil and religious law were compiled, and their authorship was attributed to Moses in order to give them authority. The practice of assigning one's works to some great figure of the past in order to secure their acceptance was not, we must remember, considered morally wrong until modern times. Stories of the creation of man and of the universal deluge were compiled — the latter a surprisingly close copy of the analogous story in the Babylonian *Gilgamesh Epic*. Collections of prophecies were compiled at or soon after the time they were delivered. Thus, when Nebuchadnezzar broke up the kingdom of Judah, its people had a body of writings which centuries later were recast or edited to form Genesis, Exodus, Deuteronomy, First and Second Samuel, First and Second Kings, and the earlier prophetic books, with fragments which were incorporated into other parts of the Old Testament. Hebrew religion was still much more backward than one might suppose from an uncritical reading of the Old Testament, but the rudiments of later developments were already apparent.

THE PHOENICIANS

The Great Sea Power of the Early Near East

While the invading Hebrews were settling down to civilized life, the narrow plain of Phoenicia had become the seat of one of the greatest sea powers of the ancient world. We have seen how its Canaanite inhabitants had evolved a culture of their own, and how it had been subjected to foreign influences. The twelfth century B.C. brought to the Phoenicians freedom and prosperity. Before 1150 B.C. Egyptian suzerainty was a thing of the past. Tyre, Sidon, Byblos, Arvad, Amuru, and some of the lesser centers once more became independent city-states, ruled by their own kings and free to advance their own fortunes.

Conditions abroad favored them. The Mycenaean Greeks had been vigorous competitors, both in legitimate commerce and on account of their piratical activities, but a new series of invasions from the north reduced the Greek world to barbarism for several centuries. Such commerce as survived in the Aegean region, along with that of the western Mediterranean, was thereafter monopolized by Phoenician traders. Spain, Gaul, North Africa, and (later) the British Isles proved to be virgin fields for commercial exploitation, while Egypt, Palestine, Syria, and the Tigris-Euphrates Valley were open to caravans and the ships which unloaded at their ports. In addition, the Phoenicians held a monopoly of the valuable cedar forests of Mount Lebanon.

Tyre, Sidon, and Carthage

In this new world of opportunity the lion's share fell to two cities — Tyre and Sidon. At first Sidon was predominant, but by 1000 B.C., Tyre had gained supremacy. Hiram, her king in the days of David and Solomon, was an ally of the Hebrew kings, and drew great advantages from this relationship. He furnished many of the materials for the Temple of Jerusalem in return for wheat and olive oil, but Solomon was heavily in debt to him and had to cede territory to make up the balance. A later Tyrian king, Itto-baal, ruled both Tyre and Sidon and his daughter Jezebel married the Israelite king Ahab.

Tyre and Sidon had been active in colonization from the first. Their colonists shared Cyprus with the Mycenaean Greeks. About 825 B.C., a revolution at Tyre sent Elisa, the sister of King Pumyaton, into exile with her supporters to the Phoenician colonies which already existed in North Africa. On the Bay of Tunis they founded Carthage, which later became the chief city of the region. Carthage in turn sent colonists to Sicily, Spain, Sardinia, and the Balearic Islands.

Phoenician Vassal Policy; Greek Rivalry

Toward the great imperialistic powers of the Near East, which in the ninth century began again to reach out toward Syria, the Phoenicians adopted a shrewd and practical policy. Having no imperialistic ambitions themselves, they never hesitated to become vassals or pay tribute if the economic opportunities afforded thereby overbalanced the cost. In this way they gained access to the vast territories governed by Assyria, and later by Babylonia. But if the tribute was too high or the opportunities too meager, they could and did fight with indomitable courage and persistence. Tyre stood a thirteen-year siege by Nebuchadnezzar, and in such cases one city often aided the invader against another.

In the eighth century the Greeks once more became serious rivals of the Phoenicians. The markets of the Aegean Islands, eastern Sicily, southern Italy, Gaul, and Egypt were lost to these northern rivals. A furious struggle ensued, but by 500 B.C. a balance had been reached between the contestants. The Carthaginians and their Etruscan allies had the advantage in the western Mediterranean and Tyrrhenian seas, while the Greeks controlled most of the commerce of the eastern Mediterranean.

Phoenician culture contained little that can be called original. Its elements were derived from many sources, and it added scarcely anything new to them. Tyrian and Sidonian workshops imitated Egyptian, Assyrian, Babylonian, or Hittite models, and Phoenician merchants often handled goods which were not made in their native cities. In art and literature they created little or nothing. We are greatly indebted to them, however, for the dissemination, if not the invention, of true alphabetic writing.

THE ARAMEANS

When the Egyptian and Hittite empires dissolved, northern and eastern Syria were occupied by a mixture of Hittites, Semitic Amorites, and Indo-Europeans. These groups were organized into small states of the traditional Syro-Palestinian type, with little or no unity. By the twelfth and early eleventh centuries all this was changed. A new wave of Semitic nomads — the *Arameans* — rolled in from the Desert Bay, destroying the Amorite Kingdom, submerging most of the other elements in Syria, and founding settlements along the Euphrates as far south as Babylonia.

Only one Aramean state can be treated here, and that one but briefly. In eastern Syria arose the Aramean kingdom of Damascus, which David conquered and Solomon lost. It long continued to have its own kings, who sometimes fought against Israel and Judah, and occasionally became their ally. In the end (732 B.C.), Tiglath-Pileser III of Assyria took Damascus, and its territory was made an Assyrian province. The Aramean states of northern Syria shared the same fate.

The cultural significance of the Arameans rests upon two facts. With the borders of the Desert Bay in their possession and with contacts in the desert itself, they became the middlemen and carriers of goods in the inland country, as the Phoenicians were by sea. Their Semitic dialect became the international tongue of southwestern Asia and gradually supplanted several of the older Semitic languages, including Hebrew. It became a secondary official language for both the Assyrian and Persian governments. In the time of Christ it was the spoken language of all Palestine and Syria and so continued until the Mohammedan invasion (seventh century A.D.).

With the language went an alphabet, derived from that used by the Phoenicians and Canaanites, and written on papyrus with pen and ink. The convenience of such a medium, compared with the clumsy cuneiform syllabary and clay tablet, soon assured it wide acceptance. Before the beginning of the Christian era the Aramean system of writing had completely displaced its rival. Thus, without having founded an extensive empire, the Arameans imposed the distinctive features of their culture upon southwestern Asia.

7

The Assyrian Empire

THE DECLINE of the Egyptian, Babylonian, and Hittite empires, which allowed Syria-Palestine several centuries of independence, also gave to the Assyrians an opportunity for a career of empire. Assyria was a triangular district, less than a hundred miles long on each side, situated on both banks of the upper Tigris River. On the north it was bounded by the Armenian Mountains, on the east by the Zagros Mountains, and on the south by Babylonia. On the west, where it faced the Mesopotamian steppes, it had no well-defined natural boundary. Physically, this region is divided into two distinct parts. West of the Tigris is an undulating plain with plentiful pasturage but too dry for extensive cultivation. Along the Tigris and its eastern tributaries are narrow but fertile valleys, in which are found metal-liferous ores and building stone. The climate is more bracing than that of Babylonia, as the summer heat is tempered by the neighboring mountains, and the winters are cold enough to afford occasional snowfall. With wild mountain tribes on the north and east, and equally wild desert nomads on the west, the Assyrians were compelled to develop warlike qualities, and the climate helped to develop in them the physical vigor needed for self-defense. Under the conditions which prevailed in the ancient world, Assyria was a suitable home for a race of conquerors.

ORIGINS AND EARLY HISTORY

The origins of the Assyrian Kingdom are hidden in the mists of pre-history. As early as 2400 B.C., the region was occupied by a people of Semitic speech and culture, who showed traces of Sumerian and Accadian cultural influence, but were of sturdier physique and more warlike habits than their southern neighbors. Its cities of Ashur, Kalhu, Nineveh, and Arbela were smaller and cruder replicas of provincial Babylonian centers. Of its history during these early ages, only disconnected incidents are

known. At times the country was subject to the great empires which arose
in the lower Tigris-Euphrates Valley, but occasionally it would assert its
independence and assume temporarily an important part in the affairs of
its neighbors.

After a century of moderate good fortune as an imperialist power (about
1350 to 1250 B.C.), Assyria, like her near-eastern neighbors, had to cope
with the invasions from the north and from the Desert Bay which destroyed the Hittite Kingdom and reduced Babylonia and Syria-Palestine
to disorder. In her exposed position the struggle for existence was certain
to be longer, more continuous, and more severe than for the other states
of southwestern Asia, for she had to contend with both groups of invaders,
and enjoyed little or no natural protection. For three centuries after 1200
B.C. she was engaged in a fight for the right to exist, and she emerged
from it with her territory intact and her people unconquered. Survival
under such circumstances was no mean accomplishment, and the qualities
which made it possible were certain, under more favorable circumstances,
to give her a commanding position among the welter of small and disorgan-
ized states which had arisen as a result of the invasions.

Contemporary Babylon

Her nearest civilized neighbor, Babylon, did not fare so well. In the
early twelfth century the Kassite Dynasty came to an end, and not one. of
the native dynasties which followed it was able to preserve order or promote culture. Aramean tribes from the desert settled in the land, and the
Elamites from the eastern mountains invaded it at frequent intervals.
These unhappy circumstances, following the long rule of the semi-barbaric
Kassites, reduced the Babylonians to a miserable condition and all but destroyed the civilization in which they had previously played so brilliant
a part. Yet the tradition of her glorious past still survived and made her
people unwilling to submit to foreign domination, even when it was exercised by their near relatives the Assyrians. The latter, on their part, rev-
erenced Babylon as their teacher in the arts of civilization, and displayed
in their dealings with her a far more tolerant and humane attitude than
that which they showed to their other neighbors. In the days of Assyrian
greatness Babylon was to present a problem as baffling and as dangerous
as that of Ireland in the modern British Empire.

PREDATORY IMPERIALISM (885–746 B.C.)

About 900 B.C. conditions both at home and abroad tempted Assyria to
a program of expansion. The crisis of her struggle for existence had

passed, but she was still beset with enemies. Aramean tribes were raiding her southwestern frontier, and in the northern mountains a civilized state was being formed, known to the Assyrians as *Urartu* or *Haldia*, and normally at enmity with them. The Assyrian kings had met these perils by creating an efficient army. They had an abundant supply of iron from which to make arms and armor. The hardy race of small farmers and shepherds which inhabited their territories furnished the manpower for a body of infantry, well disciplined and armed with bow, spear, and sword. In place of the clumsy chariots of an earlier age, they had developed mobile and effective cavalry. Their siege engines, which included the formidable battering-ram, enabled them to breach with ease the mud-brick walls of the Mesopotamian cities. With such an army it was possible not only to repel invaders, but to raid the lands of wealthy neighbors, carry off their goods, and impose tribute upon them. The temptation to make this war machine pay its way and yield dividends was irresistible.

Assyrian history in the century and a half following 900 B.C. is, therefore, the record of defensive wars against age-long enemies from mountain and desert, alternating spoil and tribute-collecting raids into Syria-Palestine with unsystematic interference in the troubled affairs of Babylonia. Little or no continuous effort was expended upon the organization of dependencies in conquered territory. Instead, the native rulers were usually reduced to vassalage and left in immediate control of their former dominions. It was the crudest and most frankly predatory form of imperialism known to civilized man.

Calculated Cruelty

To encourage submission without resistance and to discourage future revolts, the Assyrian kings had resort to a policy which has been aptly termed "calculated frightfulness." War has always involved brutality, but civilized contestants have rarely made deliberate attempts to increase its horrors. Beginning with Ashur-nasir-apal (885–860), however, the Assyrian kings made the torture, mutilation, and massacre of conquered enemies a regular feature of their policy, and boasted of the fact in inscriptions and reliefs. Thus, Ashur-nasir-apal himself records his treatment of a captured city:

> With battle and slaughter I stormed the city and captured it. Three thousand of their warriors I put to the sword; their spoil and their possessions, their cattle and their sheep I carried off. Many captives from among them I burned with fire, and many took as living captives. From some I cut off their fingers, and from others I cut off

their noses, their ears, and their fingers; of many I put out the eyes.   I
made one pillar of the living and another of heads and I bound their
heads to posts around about the city.   Their young men and maidens
I burned in the fire.[1]

Hostile chiefs and rebels were in many cases flayed alive.   Whether and
to what extent these horrors were deliberately exaggerated by their perpetrators for effect, it is, of course, impossible to determine.

Assyrian history in this period is a record of extreme vicissitudes.   At
one time kingdoms as distant as Israel and the Philistine states were on the
tribute lists, while at another the homeland was ravaged by a pestilence,
torn by the strife of nobles and free cities, and invaded by Haldians who
came within twenty miles of Nineveh.   Toward the middle of the eighth
century the old royal line had lost its vigor, and chaos at home was added
to misfortunes abroad.   A revolution at last disposed of the elderly and
incapable Adad-nirari V, and replaced him with a vigorous upstart who
assumed the title of Tiglath-Pileser III.   With his accession a new age
began.

THE MAKING OF THE ASSYRIAN EMPIRE

Beginning with the accession of Tiglath-Pileser III (746–727), the
Assyrian kings evolved a new and more coherent imperial structure than
that of the preceding age.   Ferocious cruelty was still practiced to discourage resistance and rebellion, but it was supplemented by new and more
effective measures for the control of dependencies.   The Assyrian homeland had always been divided into provinces, which were administered by
governors appointed by the king.   This system was now applied to many
of the regions previously governed by vassal kings.   The tribute was collected and justice administered in these provinces by Assyrian officials,
upon whose loyalty the king could usually depend and who could prevent
or quickly suppress rebellions.   Thus, the subject peoples were deprived of
the leadership of their native rulers, who in the past had always been
ready to revolt when the occasion offered.   The upper classes in conquered
countries were frequently deported to distant lands where they would be
powerless to stir up trouble, and their places would be taken by other exiles in whom the common people could feel no confidence.   In Assyria a
strong effort was made to curb the privileges of the nobles and the cities,
which had proved so destructive of national unity.

Under Tiglath-Pileser these policies worked well.   Unity was restored

[1] Luckenbill, *Ancient Records of Assyria and Babylonia*, vol. I, p. 147, no. 445.   By
permission of University of Chicago Press.

at home, Syria-Palestine was set in order under a combined system of provincial governors and vassal kings, and the Haldians were driven back to the mountains. In Babylon the new king tried to end the prevailing anarchy by assuming the crown himself, a policy which his successors followed whenever possible. Yet his centralizing policy so offended the Assyrian people that within five years after his death they overthrew his son and placed on the throne another usurper, who assumed the name of Sargon II.

The Sargonid Dynasty: Policy and Problems

Sargon and his descendants occupied the Assyrian throne until the fall of the empire (722–612). Except in so far as Sargon relaxed a few of Tiglath-Pileser's restrictions upon the nobles and free cities, there was no change of policy. From her location and the character of her people, the career of Assyria was certain to be one of continual war, and, given the policy of imperialism, the character of the wars was largely predetermined. To preserve the possessions which she had previously won, she must be

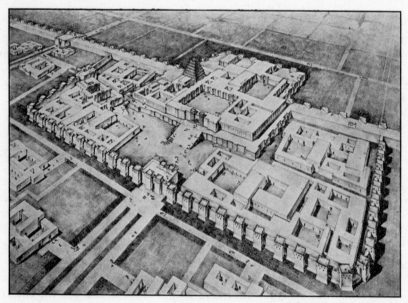

Oriental Institute, Chicago

RESTORATION OF DURSHARRUKIN, CITY OF SARGON II
Modern Khorsabad

forever on guard to suppress rebellious subjects and to beat back the foreign princes who instigated revolts within the Assyrian Empire and attempted to conquer its lands. The Haldians, who had given former kings so much trouble, soon ceased to be a source of danger, for they were attacked by hordes of barbarians from north of the Black Sea and their strength was effectively sapped. Nevertheless, the inhabitants of the Haldian border provinces long continued to wage a petty war of raids and sieges against their neighbors in the Assyrian Empire, and the situation became even more dangerous when the Medes took the place of the Haldians in the northeast. The Babylonian problem was incapable of any lasting solution, for the southerners could neither govern themselves nor submit to the government of others. In the rare intervals when they might have co-operated with their Assyrian suzerains, their Elamite neighbors were always at hand to provoke new strife.

In Syria-Palestine, Egypt played a rôle analogous to that of the Elamites in Babylonia. Her Ethiopian kings were weak and much of the government was in the hands of feudal lords, but Egyptian emissaries were constantly busy stirring up the Assyrian vassal princes of the region to revolt. The dupes of this policy never received effective aid from Egypt, but so long as she was independent, Assyria could never hope to rule her western provinces in peace.

Sargon (722–705) continued the Babylonian policy of his immediate

Brown Brothers

RESTORATION OF PALACE OF SARGON II
Khorsabad

predecessors and assumed the title of "King of Babylon." After years of trouble with Merodach Baladan, an energetic Aramean chief who claimed the crown, Sargon temporarily quieted the southern kingdom. In the west he put down disorder with a strong hand, and on the northern frontier chastised the Haldians and their Phrygian allies. In the eastern highlands the Median tribesmen were reduced to vassalage. Yet in the intervals between these strenuous activities, Sargon found time and energy to erect a splendid new capital (*Dursharrukin* or "Sargonsburg") a few miles north of Nineveh, with a palace covering twenty-five acres of ground and an excellent library. On one of his expeditions to the eastern mountains he was ambushed and slain.

Sennacherib

His son Sennacherib (705–681), like his predecessors, had to begin his reign by settling difficulties in Babylon. Various experiments intended to soothe the tender susceptibilities of the southern kingdom failed. His son, whom he had made king of Babylonia, was betrayed to the Elamites and slain. Losing patience, Sennacherib sacked Babylon, massacred its inhabitants, and destroyed it utterly. In the west he had to cope with rebel vassals and their Egyptian ally. Tyre was reduced, the Philistine cities were taken, and Hezekiah of Judah had to seek a humiliating peace. But in attempting to invade Egypt, the Assyrian king lost most of his army from bubonic plague, and his efforts in that region produced no lasting results. Along the northern frontier there were only punitive expeditions against individual tribes, for the common danger from northern invaders had brought peace between the Assyrians and Haldians. Moving the capital back to Nineveh, Sennacherib adorned the city with a palace and a library and supplied it with water by means of an aqueduct. Like his father, he died a violent death. Two of his sons, whom he had passed over when choosing a successor, murdered him as he prayed in a temple.

Esarhaddon (681–669) reversed his father's policy in both Babylon and the west. He restored the city which Sennacherib had destroyed and showed it marked favor. With Egypt he could have no peace except by conquest, and he prepared to face the issue squarely. His invasion of the Nile Valley was a temporary success, but no sooner had he returned to Asia than a new revolt recalled him to the west. On the way he fell sick and died, but his army continued the expedition and reduced Egypt to obedience.

Assyria's Peak and the Collapse of the Empire

Soon after Esarhaddon's death the Assyrian Empire reached the greatest extent which it was ever to attain. The whole Fertile Crescent, including Egypt, was under effective control, and an ill-defined "sphere of influence" had been established in the adjacent mountainous areas of the north and east. Although most of this wide domain was administered by Assyrian governors, some states, such as Judah, were ruled by vassal princes. The population was a motley array of tongues, kindreds, and peoples, with no bond of unity except common subjection to the Assyrian king. In spite of the fact that his rule was strong and reasonably just except in cases of revolt, few of his subjects had any affection for him. Every misfortune was certain to be followed by a wave of revolts, and foreign agents found receptive hearers when they attempted to incite the subjects to rebellion.

The reign of Ashur-bani-apal (669–625) vividly illustrates the working of both the centrifugal and centripetal forces within the empire. After crushing several rebellions in Egypt, the Assyrians found that they had only paved the way for a strong and capable native ruler, who was to wrench it from their grasp. Among the vassals whom they set up was a

University Prints

WINGED MYTHOLOGICAL FIGURE OF THE TIME OF SARGON II

certain Psamtik, who proceeded to employ Greek mercenaries, unite Egypt, and drive the Assyrian garrisons from the land. Before 650, Egypt was once more independent. To pacify the Babylonians and a disgruntled elder brother at the same time, Ashur-bani-apal made the latter king of Babylon. The two malcontents joined forces, with the Elamites as a third party, and Babylon became the scene of a terrible rebellion, which terminated only when the rebel king set fire to his palace and perished in the flames. Elam was mercilessly devastated and Babylon was partially depopulated. The real beneficiary of this act was Belibni, a descendant of Merodach Baladan. Appointed to a post in the exhausted land, he soon made himself so powerful that a few years later his son, Nabopolassar, was able to assume the crown and to found the Chaldean (Neo-Babylonian) Empire. Ashur-bani-apal's later years were clouded by the approach of Scythian tribes through Asia Minor and by ominous signs of dissolution in Babylonia and the west. Assyria was nearing exhaustion. Her manpower was so depleted that the ranks of the army were filled with conscripts drawn from the conquered peoples. Most of her free commoners had either sunk into tenancy or left their bones on foreign battlefields. Her kings were physically weak, and Ashur-bani-apal, while well educated, was mentally mediocre. Only a vigorous foreign power was needed in her neighborhood to give her the death-blow.

Twenty years after the death of Ashur-bani-apal, Assyria had ceased to exist. A competent chief, Cyaxares, united the Median tribes under his rule and organized an army on the Assyrian model. With his Scythian allies he descended from the mountains, while Nabopolassar advanced to his aid from Babylon. Nineveh was taken and destroyed (612), and after a flicker of national vitality at Harran, the whole Assyrian power collapsed, never to revive. The victors divided the spoils. A new age had dawned, and a new drama occupied the historical stage which the Ninevites had so long dominated.

Assyria's Reputation for Cruelty

Assyria has a bad reputation in the modern world. To many her name is a synonym for cruelty, rapacity, and tyranny. On the score of cruelty it is impossible to acquit her, for her kings have condemned her by their boasting. But we must remember that cruelty and rapine have attended wars in all ages, and certainly the people of this age have no vantage-point of self-righteousness from which to reproach the warriors of the ancient world. Although the Assyrians may have surpassed many of their neigh-

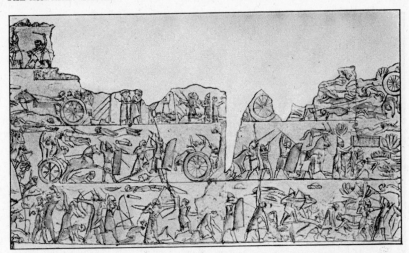

BATTLE SCENE SHOWING ASSYRIANS AND ELAMITES

bors in calculated ferocity, one has only to read the Biblical account of David's wars to realize how common such acts were. Assyria's existence depended upon success in war. That success was attained by better arms, organization, and fighting spirit than her enemies possessed, and her fall exemplified the tragedy which is the inevitable end of all empires.

Assyrian Civilization

Assyrian civilization was a close but not slavish copy of that of Babylon. From the latter she acquired cuneiform writing, and with it the whole of Babylonian literature. Her architecture was Babylonian in origin, but into it were incorporated elements borrowed from the Hittites, the Egyptians, and possibly even the Greeks. Likewise her sculpture owed its original impetus to Babylon, but in this field she far surpassed her teacher. Especially did her sculptors excel in their treatment of animal forms, both in relief and in the round. The relief figures of wounded and dying lions breathe a pathos hardly to be expected from a people whose name is synonymous with disregard for suffering. Her sculptors never equaled the Greeks in ability to portray the human form, but their reliefs tell stories with an accuracy and a wealth of detail which make them rival written history as sources of information. The Babylonians never achieved this quality except for a short time in the third millennium B.C. — two thousand years before Sennacherib and Ashur-bani-apal. Neither people had

University Prints

DYING LIONESS

any interest in abstract science, and neither produced any philosophy more profound than wise maxims regarding the prudent conduct of one's affairs. But Assyrian astronomy and medicine made considerable progress along empirical and practical lines over their Babylonian originals. In law the Assyrians had a code of their own which displays Babylonian influence, but was clearly an outgrowth of the local scene. In many respects it was more primitive than the Code of Hammurabi, with more emphasis upon crimes and family relationships and less upon economic activities and organization. The position of women was definitely lower in Assyria than in Babylonia. Babylonian religion was taken over completely, but the chief god of the Assyrians was always the local deity Ashur, and so important was he in Assyrian life that the deities borrowed from the south were always in a subordinate rank. In short, while we must recognize the close resemblance between the Babylonian and Assyrian civilizations, it is proper to speak of the latter as a distinct entity.

Commerce and manufacturing, which the Babylonians had cultivated assiduously, the Assyrians completely neglected. Their whole economic structure remained backward throughout their history. When they indulged in peaceful pursuits, they devoted their whole attention to agriculture and herding. Trade and manufacturing were entirely surrendered to

the Phoenicians, Arameans, Babylonians, and Greeks. In fact, one of the
most lasting results of Assyrian imperialism was to create an economic
and cultural empire for the Arameans.

At a time when the Babylonians were decadent and half-barbarized,
their virile relatives took over the more significant features of their ancient
culture. The Assyrians adapted, improved, and blended them with features borrowed from other sources, transmitting them to the later Babylonians and to the other peoples of Asia and the outside world. In addition, we must not forget that the Assyrian kings and armies, heavy-handed
and cruel though they were, for centuries acted as guardians of the civilized world against the barbarians from the northern steppes, the eastern
mountains, and the Arabian Desert. By doing so they performed a service
which, in part at least, compensated for the suffering and destruction
which they caused. In both respects they made appreciable contributions
to the development of civilization.

8

The Near-Eastern State System of the
Early Sixth Century B.C.

FOR OVER FIFTY YEARS after the fall of Assyria, no power appeared in western Asia capable of occupying the place which she had vacated. Instead there were a number of kingdoms of moderate size, existing side by side in a condition which approached peace and amity, with only occasional wars and with international relations reminiscent of the days of Amenhotep III. The chief powers of the region at this time were the Medes, the Neo-Babylonian Empire, Egypt, and Lydia.

The two immediate participants in the overthrow of Assyria — the Medes and Babylonians — divided her territories between them. Cyaxares took as his share the lands east of the Tigris, while Nabopolassar received the remainder of the Fertile Crescent. Nebuchadnezzar, the Babylonian crown prince, soon occupied Syria-Palestine and drove out the Egyptians who had come to claim it.

Asia Minor had been little molested by the Assyrians, but had suffered cruelly from the raids of the Cimmerians and their enemies, the Scythians, shortly before the middle of the seventh century. In these convulsions, the Haldian Kingdom and Phrygia, which had previously dominated that region, had disappeared. The chief power was now, in the west, Lydia, and in the east, the Medes. A third but much smaller kingdom in the same area was Cilicia, which occupied the plain along the southern coast and the mountain belt immediately behind it.

Egypt had not, on account of her geographic position and internal conditions, shared in the partition of Assyria. In fact, she had aided the Assyrians against the allies to the very end, and was fortunate to avoid invasion or other calamity. By 600 B.C. the successors to Assyria were in possession of their respective shares of the partition of that country, and the war-torn lands of western Asia had settled down to a half-century of relative stability and nearly constant peace. Such a condition was very unusual, especially when there were so many independent powers. Let us survey briefly the kingdoms which formed this state system.

EGYPT UNDER THE TWENTY-SIXTH DYNASTY (650–525 B.C.)

When Psamtik I united Egypt and expelled the Assyrians, he terminated a period of disorder and decadence which had existed nearly five centuries. As in the days of the Eighteenth Dynasty, the feudal lords who had divided the land were destroyed or made politically impotent, and the king's word was again law in the land. Agriculture, manufacturing, and commerce, along with art and religion, could now revive under his strong rule.

Egypt's Cultural Senility

The Egypt of Psamtik and his successors was not, however, that of Ahmose I or Thutmose III. She was now old and afflicted with the ills of cultural senility. Her people, except for a short time after the expulsion of the Hyksos, had never been fighters, and their disinclination toward military life had grown with the years. For ages such armies as her kings had led had been composed principally of foreign mercenaries. The descendants of these hirelings now formed a military class which enjoyed great privileges but were almost useless on the battlefield. The effective part of the army was composed of Greek and Carian mercenaries, who had been hired directly from their native lands. Moreover, the priesthoods were an incubus upon the country. The Libyan and Ethiopian kings had indeed broken the political power of the priests of Amen, but they and the other priestly colleges were still richly endowed. They consumed the resources of the people, but in return contributed to them only a set of degraded superstitions. All that was noble or inspiring in the old religion was now dead, and in its place had come the worship of sacred animals. Psamtik and his successors were powerless to cure these evils, but they dealt with them as intelligently as possible.

Egyptian culture was completely dominated by a blind love of ancient times. Neglecting the great period of the empire, the people sought to revive the "good old days" of the Old Kingdom. Art became studiously archaistic and imitated the styles prevalent in the days of the pyramid-builders. Similarly, they revived old religious texts, official titles, and other phases of early Egyptian culture, and did everything within their power to revert their country's life to ancient customs. When recent elements were included, as sometimes they had to be, they were carefully disguised with an appearance of antiquity. Hence, considerable self-deception was necessary and it was willingly practiced. With this unreasoning love of the past went a hatred of foreigners and their customs which at times rose to fanaticism.

Even a cursory glance at sixth-century Egyptian life will show how inadequately this archaistic mania suited the conditions of the time. Try as they would to revive the artistic conventions of two thousand years earlier, the Egyptians never quite succeeded. Architecture, sculpture, and painting had made adequate advances which left their traces upon even the most careful imitations of older work. Portrait sculpture attained a degree of excellence never before known. The sculptor-artist could now cast hollow metal statues, which the Old Kingdom sculptor could not, and his work displayed a freedom from convention and a perfection in modeling which had earlier been lacking. It was from the Egypt of the Twenty-Sixth Dynasty that Greek artists learned many principles of technique which they afterward so effectively executed.

Unwelcome Foreign Influence

Since the army was constituted of Greek mercenaries, and Greek merchants were crowding into the Nile mouths, their countrymen exerted a powerful influence in Egyptian affairs. During the disorders of the years preceding the rise of Psamtik I, Ionian Greek pirates had established a settlement on the Canopic branch of the Nile, known as the Fort of the Milesians. Psamtik himself quartered a large mercenary garrison at Daphnae, in the eastern Delta. Sais, the capital, and Memphis had their Greek residents. Needless to say the ingenuity and tact of the kings were taxed to the uttermost to repress quarrels between their native subjects and these aggressive foreigners.

Psamtik I and his son Necho II (609–593 B.C.) participated, as we have seen, in the closing struggles of the Assyrian Empire. In an effort either to save his failing ally or to gather some of the spoils for himself, Necho invaded Palestine and Syria. In 608 B.C., Josiah of Judah was defeated and killed, and Necho advanced to Carchemish. There he met the Babylonian crown prince Nebuchadnezzar in battle and suffered an overwhelming defeat. Nebuchadnezzar advanced to southern Palestine and took possession, but the death of his father recalled him and he made a treaty of peace which left Egypt independent. Two other brief struggles left conditions unaltered.

In the reign of Apries (588–569 B.C.), the anti-foreign sentiment of the Egyptian people reached its climax. The king was impetuous and imprudent, unfortunate in his wars, and openly favorable to the Greeks. A revolt of the military class led to the dethronement and death of Apries and the crowning of Ahmose, or, as the Greeks called him, Amasis. With his accession the last period of the Twenty-Sixth Dynasty begins.

Amasis: Egypt Conquered by Persia

Amasis (569–526 B.C.) was tactful enough to satisfy his native supporters and at the same time remain friendly to the Greeks. He abolished the camp at Daphnae, but founded a new and splendid Greek city at Naucratis on the site of the old Fort of the Milesians. It was the sole port of entry for Greeks trading with Egypt. Nevertheless, his personal friends were Greeks and he manifested deep interest in the affairs of the Hellenic world. Polycrates, tyrant of Samos, was his ally, and he contributed liberally to public projects in Greece. When Cyrus of Persia overthrew the Medes, Amasis formed an alliance with Babylon and Lydia to check the progress of the upstart, but both allies were overthrown before he could aid them. Amasis, however, succeeded in preventing a Persian invasion as long as he lived. He had been dead only a few months when the Persian king, Cambyses, annexed Egypt to the empire which had already engulfed the other independent states of the Near East.

THE NEO-BABYLONIAN (CHALDEAN) EMPIRE

In Babylonia during the sixth century the people were obsessed with a reverence for ancient times similar to that which prevailed in Egypt, but

Museum of Fine Arts, Boston

BABYLONIAN LION IN GLAZED BRICK

altered somewhat by local conditions. Unlike the Egyptians, the Babylonians had been in close and constant contact with other nations and the old stock had been modified by extensive and continued immigration from neighboring districts. The royal house belonged to a tribe of Arameans called Chaldeans, whence the state is sometimes called the Chaldean Empire. Furthermore, the real preservers of Babylonian culture in the dark centuries which preceded Nabopolassar's rise had been the Assyrians, who had not allowed this culture to stagnate. Medicine, astronomy, and art — to mention but a few phases — made some progress, and when, about 600 B.C., Babylon arose from her ruins, she received the improved product back from her former pupil. Despite these alleviating circumstances, the forces of conservatism were formidable. The priesthoods of the great gods were, like their Egyptian counterparts, highly privileged and richly endowed corporations, but unlike the Egyptian priests they could wield dangerous political influence against a recalcitrant king. As in Egypt, the older stock among the population had lost its military habits and was absorbed in manufacturing, commerce, and agriculture. In such a country only an unbroken succession of able rulers could arrest the forces of dissolution, and such a phenomenon was not to be expected.

Consolidation; Babylon Rebuilt

Nabopolassar (625–604 B.C.) and his son Nebuchadnezzar II (604–562 B.C.) were strong and able rulers. The latter garnered the inheritance of Assyria in Syria-Palestine, drove back the Egyptians, and destroyed the kingdom of Judah. Tyre stood a thirteen-year siege, and finally submitted to him without being captured. But the latter part of his reign was a period of peace, so we may infer that he realized his subjects were lacking in military ardor and acted accordingly.

Babylon, his capital city, was rebuilt on a sumptuous scale. Its walls may be traced today as a square over two miles long on a side and the Greek historian Herodotus asserts that the fortified area had a perimeter of fifty-six miles. This defense was both high and thick, constructed of sun-dried bricks with a coating of burnt bricks. A splendid processional street for religious pageants ran the entire length of the city. It was elevated above the ordinary ground-level and paved with stone. Near the royal palace stood the famous Hanging Gardens, a terraced structure planted with trees, grass, and shrubs, and intended to allay the homesickness of Nebuchadnezzar's Median queen. Ziggurats in honor of Marduk and the other gods broke the skyline. The walls of temples and palaces were

From Unger's "Babylon"

RESTORATION OF ANCIENT BABYLON
Time of Nebuchadnezzar II

veneered with glazed brick colored red, white, blue, or yellow, and the surfaces were ornamented with figures of men, animals, or weird, composite monsters, executed in warm, rich colors. The smaller cities of Babylonia were honored with temples and fortifications.

Measured by the standards of his time, Nebuchadnezzar II was a good ruler. He was sincerely and humbly religious and worked for the welfare of his people. Occasional outbursts of cruelty against enemies and rebels were in keeping with the character of his age and people. The making of the Chaldean Empire was principally his work and it did not long survive him.

The End of the Empire

When Nebuchadnezzar died, the splendid imperial structure of which he was the head immediately began to totter. His son, Amil-Marduk, offended the priests. In less than two years after his accession he was murdered and replaced by a more compliant brother-in-law, Nergal-shar-usur. After a reign of five years, the usurper was succeeded by his minor son, who was soon deposed. The priests then secured the coronation of an elderly Babylonian named Nabonidus, who was very religious and even more superstitious. Although occasionally awakened to his responsibil-ities, Nabonidus devoted his time to the revival of old religious rites and building temples in the provincial towns. He was keenly interested in archeology and constantly sought mementoes of former kings in the tem-ples which he restored. After 550, when the Persian king Cyrus overthrew the Medes, the fall of Babylon was only a question of time, but this absent-minded antiquarian took few if any steps to avert the calamity. The priests of Marduk, who felt that their ruler's preoccupation with other gods and cults endangered their position, secretly encouraged Cyrus in his designs upon Babylon. In 539, the city surrendered without a contest. Nabonidus was exiled and the Neo-Babylonian Empire was at an end.

Lydia

The earliest historical reference to Lydia describes a pastoral, agricul-tural, and mining community, located in the valleys of the Hermus and Caicus rivers, a short distance from the western coast of Asia Minor. Its people were apparently a mixture of native Asiatics and Indo-European immigrants from the Balkan peninsula. At one time they had been polit-ically subject to the Phrygians of the central plateau.

Our first authentic knowledge of Lydia begins about 683 B.C., with the revolution which placed King Gyges on its throne. During a reign of over thirty years he was engaged in active relations with the Asiatic Greek cit-ies on the one hand and with Ashur-bani-apal of Assyria on the other. While warring with the Greek cities on his border, Gyges dedicated rich offerings in the Greek temples of the old homeland. His reign witnessed the coming of the Cimmerians, against whose raids he sought aid from Ashur-bani-apal. Their alliance broke down, however, and Gyges was killed by the barbarians. His successor, Ardys, drove them from the kingdom.

The Medes and Asiatic Greece

When Assyria disappeared, the Lydian kings advanced their frontier eastward some two hundred and fifty miles to the river Halys (Kizil Irmak), which brought them into contact with the Median kingdom of Cyaxares. A five years' war between the two powers (590–585 B.C.) ended in a drawn battle. Taking advantage of a portent furnished by an eclipse of the sun, the contestants ended hostilities, and the daughter of King Alyattes married Astyages, the son of Cyaxares. Thereafter, peace prevailed between the two powers.

While wars between the Greeks of Asia and the Lydians had been chronic ever since Gyges' time, it was Croesus, the fourth king of the dynasty, who first undertook a systematic conquest of Asiatic Greece. In a reign of fourteen years he subdued all but one of the cities. Miletus was the exception, and with it he formed an alliance. Thus, the seaward ends of the trade routes leading into the interior came into his possession, and the tribute which he exacted tended to neutralize the gains which the Greek merchants and their governments had been exacting from his own subjects.

But there was another side to this relationship. Croesus' court was frequented by Greek visitors and he gave lavishly to Greek temples. His Hellenic subjects found that their access to the markets of Lydia gave them practically a monopoly of many lines of goods. His friendship for the Greeks was an outstanding trait of his character and they accepted him almost as a compatriot.

"As Rich as Croesus"

The rich soil of his kingdom, the gold-washings along its streams, the timber on the mountain slopes, and the tribute from his Greek subjects established the name of Croesus as a synonym for wealth. If the Greek tradition is to be trusted, Lydia was the original home of the art of coinage, although its invention antedated Croesus' reign. He was at peace with his neighbors and apparently had nothing to fear from any source. To his Greek friends he seemed to have all the blessings which a mortal could enjoy. So much the more startling was his sudden downfall before the forces of Cyrus the Persian (546), the story of which must be reserved for a later chapter.

MEDIA

The strongest of the successors of Assyria was the Median Kingdom. Even before the fall of Nineveh, it had included all territory along the western edge of the Iranian Plateau. Among its vassal states was the principality of Persia to the east and south of Elam. Soon after the collapse of Assyria, Cyaxares extended his rule into the Armenian Mountains and westward through Asia Minor to the Halys River. Eastward, his dominions stretched for an undefined distance over mountain and desert.

Media, to judge from our available evidence, was a loosely organized feudal state. The actual administration of each community was vested in a local prince, who in turn owed allegiance, tribute, and service to the king. Cities were few, and culture was at a low ebb. Whatever civilization the Medes enjoyed was largely an importation from Assyria.

After the death of the conqueror Cyaxares, his son Astyages (585–550) ascended the throne. The events of his reign, except for its disastrous close, are lost to the modern historian, which alone would indicate that he was tyrannical and unpopular. Apparently he kept peace with both Babylon and Lydia.

Cyrus and the Persian Revolt

Among the southern vassals of Astyages was a prince named Cambyses, whose state was called Persia. It was a poor, hilly land, which bred a hardy race of farmers and shepherds, speaking a language closely akin to that of the Medes. In 559 or 558, Cambyses was succeeded by his son Cyrus who eight years later revolted against his suzerain. Only a few unreliable legends of the cause of the revolt survive and they may be disregarded. One fact is clear: Astyages could not rely upon his own soldiers, for they surrendered him to Cyrus and submitted to the latter as their lord. Henceforth the Persians were to be the leaders and the Medes their vassals.

This was no mere change of dynasty, although the Medes and Persians probably so regarded it. Cyrus had the genius of a great conqueror, and in all the neighboring states there was no king of pre-eminent ability at the head of a strong people who might check him. Within a little over a decade after his victory, the "state system" of the Near East was no more, and a quarter of a century enabled him and his successors to absorb its last members in an all-embracing empire.

9

The Persian Empire (550-323 B.C.)

FOUNDATION AND CONSOLIDATION

WHEN CYRUS THE PERSIAN overthrew Astyages the Mede, he embarked upon a career of conquest which was to result in the formation of the largest empire the world had yet known. The victory gave him control of a wide domain and paved the way for more extensive conquests. Even before the overthrow of Astyages, Cyrus had had an army of devoted followers, to which was now added the armed force of the Medes. Media submitted quietly to her new lord and had little reason to regret the change. Cyrus assumed the title of "King of the Persians and of the Medes," and both races shared in the high dignities of the empire which he was founding.

Cyrus, a Great Leader

In war and statesmanship alike, Cyrus was a genius of the first rank. That he was a great general may be taken for granted, but he knew how to conciliate as well as to conquer. His merciful treatment of conquered rivals marks him as a unique figure in the history of the ancient Orient. Astyages the Mede, Croesus the Lydian, and Nabonidus the Babylonian were spared and treated with humanity. Cyrus was careful not to inflict needless humiliation upon the peoples whom he conquered. At Babylon he disguised the fact of conquest by paying homage to Marduk, the patron god of the city, and by assuming the crown and titles of a legitimate Babylonian king. He likewise permitted the Jewish exiles in Babylonia to return to Jerusalem and rebuild the temple of their national god Yahweh. Once active resistance had ceased, he was a model of tolerance and kindliness to vanquished foes.

The revolution in Media had not passed unnoticed among her neighbors. Under the leadership of Croesus of Lydia, they formed an alliance to preserve the balance of power against the potential threat to their independence. It included Lydia, Babylonia, and Egypt. In 547 or 546, Croesus and Cyrus were at war, but the league was no match for Cyrus. Its members were widely scattered and Nabonidus in particular was no soldier. The Lydian campaign was quickly terminated. After an indecisive battle on the frontier, Croesus supposed that the campaign was over for the winter and disbanded his forces. But cold and inclement weather was no impediment to Cyrus. Pushing quickly forward, he defeated Croesus, drove him into Sardis, and after a siege captured both the city and its king. The only active member of the league was now eliminated. Within the next few years all of Asia Minor except a few inaccessible strongholds was added to the Persian Empire.

The Conquest of Babylon and Egypt

It was now the turn of Babylon. The inept Nabonidus had offended priests and people alike and Cyrus was assisted by treason within the ranks of the enemy. In 539, he entered Babylon almost unopposed. Because of his magnanimous and conciliatory conduct, the Babylonians accepted him as a legitimate national king, and thereafter he made Babylon the winter capital of his dominions. With this conquest went the control of Syria-Palestine.

Cyrus was now lord of all southwestern Asia, but his ambition was still unsatisfied. To the east of Persia lay Bactria, Parthia, and other districts inhabited by Iranian peoples akin to the Medes and Persians. In the last ten years of his life Cyrus brought them under his rule, thus extending his frontier to the border of India and to the edge of the central Asiatic steppes. There, in 529, he was killed while fighting the wild tribesmen of the grasslands.

Cyrus left two sons, Cambyses and Smerdis (Bardiya), and two daughters, Atossa and Roxana. Cambyses (529–522) succeeded to the throne, and according to a questionable later account, murdered his brother. He also married his two sisters, and then set out to conquer Egypt, the only important power in the eastern Mediterranean which remained independent.

Egypt proved to be nearly as easy a conquest as Babylon. Amasis had died shortly before the invasion, and there was treason among the Greek mercenaries. One battle and two short sieges made Cambyses master of the country. At first he displayed the same politic humaneness and consideration for the feelings of the vanquished which had marked his father's conquests. He took an Egyptian royal title and paid homage to Egyptian gods. For him Egypt was to serve as a base from which to conquer the lands to the west and south. One expedition was sent against Nubia, another against the western oases, and a third was planned against Carthage. But in all these enterprises misfortune dogged his steps. The Nubian expedition failed disastrously, and the force sent against the oases was utterly destroyed — probably by a desert storm. The Phoenicians who formed the most effective part of the royal navy completed Cambyses' discomfiture by refusing to serve against their daughter city of Carthage. The conquest of Egypt was the net result of the western expedition. But when this last important independent state in the Near East had been subjected to Persian rule, Cambyses could claim universal dominion as the term was then understood.

His last days were tragic. The disastrous failures of his projected conquests in Africa unsettled his reason, and he committed senseless outrages against his Egyptian subjects. While returning to Persia, he learned that a man who claimed to be his brother Smerdis had usurped the throne and had won the support of the whole eastern part of the empire. Shortly afterward Cambyses died, possibly by suicide. The pretender ruled for at least a year, and gained general recognition as king.

DARIUS AND THE ORGANIZATION OF THE EMPIRE

Among the courtiers of Cambyses was his distant cousin, a young man named Darius, whose father, Hystaspes, was the governor of Parthia. With six other Persian nobles, Darius formed a conspiracy, and Smerdis, whether the real heir to the throne or not, was killed. Darius assumed the crown, and each of the other conspirators was given a highly privileged position, which descended to his heirs.[1]

The coveted place was not lightly won. The western part of the empire remained passive or supported Darius, but in the eastern and central provinces a perfect epidemic of revolts broke out. It was only after several years of fierce fighting that Darius I (521–484) established his authority. To commemorate his rise to power, he carved the Behistun Inscription of which we have heard.[2] The leaders of the various revolutionary movements were punished with savage cruelty.

[1] Professor A. T. Olmstead, in an article, "Darius and his Behistun Inscription" (*American Journal of Semitic Languages and Literature*, October, 1938), maintains that Darius deliberately falsified the story of his accession, and that the man whom the conspirators slew was really the brother of Cambyses.

[2] Chapter 3.

DARIUS I AND THE REBELS
From Behistun

Darius as Statesman and King

Once in power, Darius proved to be a constructive statesman of the first rank. The rapid growth of the empire under his two predecessors had not been followed by the evolution of a practicable system of imperial organization. The civil wars which accompanied the rise and fall of the pretender Smerdis had displayed in the plainest fashion the weakness of the bond between the provincial governors and the king, and Darius found it necessary to put to death at least two subordinates who had assumed in their respective provinces a position of semi-independence. As soon as conditions permitted, he undertook to establish an efficient system of control over his officials and to define their duties and obligations. The system of imperial administration which he set up lasted until the overthrow of the Persian power two centuries later.

At the head of the state was the king, who like other Oriental sovereigns claimed and exercised absolute power. His official title was "The Great King, King of Kings." At his court an elaborate system of etiquette prevailed, including the practice of falling prostrate before the king when one approached his person. Aside from the families of his fellow conspirators, there were no persons in his dominions whose rights he was bound to respect. He made laws, levied taxes, exacted services, and was a judge from whose sentence there was no appeal. Actually, of course, his authority was limited by many forces — the lack of information, the influence of persons and cliques at court, the fear of rebellion or assassination, and the passive resistance of officials to orders of which they disapproved. As a rule, he could work his will upon any individual, whatever his rank, but it was unsafe to pursue policies which would offend large and powerful classes. As the king had the supreme direction of all the affairs of his extensive dominions to attend to, the amount of work necessary to perform his duties efficiently was very great and required enormous physical strength and tenacity of purpose. Darius, who had risen from a subordinate position through his own talents, possessed these qualities, and understood the feelings of his subjects well enough to avoid oppressive conduct. His weaker successors, however, were usually tyrannical *débauchés* who found it easier to leave the conduct of public business in the

Keystone

PALACE OF DARIUS I AT PERSEPOLIS

hands of concubines and eunuchs, for whom the nominal sovereigns were too often only supine instruments.

Government; Military and Naval Service

As organized by Darius, the empire contained twenty provinces or satrapies. Over each was a satrap, or governor, appointed for an indefinite term. As the king's representatives, the satraps had previously exercised complete military, judicial, and financial powers within their provinces; and in the main they continued to do so under the new system. But Darius, profiting by his experiences with them during the civil wars, imposed various checks upon their authority. An imperial postal service kept the king informed of their actions. The secretary of the satrap was appointed independently and had separate access to the royal ear. Garrisons of Persian troops, under commanders not responsible to the satraps, were stationed at strategic points throughout the empire. At intervals, an inspector, known significantly by the title "The King's Eye," visited each satrapy and reported his findings. Under the satraps were district governors; while in some districts vassal kings were left in power with limited authority. In local government the Persians were, at least in the earlier period of the empire, tolerant of local prejudices and customs and just in their dealings with their subjects.

The royal army and fleet were levied on the basis of universal and compulsory service at the wish of the king. The fleet was furnished by the Egyptians, Phoenicians, and Asiatic Greeks. Each satrap had to provide a fixed quota of men or ships for either arm when called upon. Each nationality represented in this motley array was armed after its own fashion. The native Persians, Medes, and a few other warlike peoples were the only effective fighters in the whole force. The army was never welded together into a well-integrated fighting force comparable in effectiveness to the disciplined Greek armies. In matters of discipline a sharp distinction was made between the Medes and Persians on the one hand and provincial levies on the other. The former were well treated if not pampered, while the latter were driven into battle by officers armed with whips and fared no better in other respects. Whatever its failings, the Persian army was, in Darius' hands, a formidable weapon, and he seldom lost a campaign.

Tribute and the Monetary System

In financial matters the imperial government was a strange mixture of the old and the new. Each province had to pay annually, over and above the cost of local government, a fixed sum as tribute to the king. In the western provinces, where either coined money or precious metal in bulk was used in business, the tribute was paid in cash. The eastern provinces had no monetary system and their tribute was paid in kind. Thus, one province owed the king three hundred and sixty white horses a year with other similar obligations. The tribute was collected by the satrap and was forwarded to the king. As government services cost little and provisions for the royal court, army, and navy were requisitioned without pay, the kings amassed huge reserves of gold and silver at the royal cities of Susa, Persepolis, and Ecbatana. Likewise, the provincials had to support the satrap and his subordinates — often a heavy burden. When an army passed through a region there was an additional levy in kind for its support.

Darius, responsive to the importance of the new economic currents of his day, instituted the first Persian system of coinage. The right to strike gold pieces was a royal monopoly, but silver and bronze might be coined by the satraps or by local units. The standard gold coin, the *daric*, weighed .2744 troy ounces, and was worth at the present price of gold about $9.60. Between gold and silver the ratio of value was 13 1/3 to 1. The importance of Persian coinage was limited to the western part of the empire. The Semitic and Iranian peoples long continued to use barter or to weigh precious metals at each transaction, as they do in some places to this day.

Darius annexed an additional strip of territory along the border of India and began the conquest of Thrace on the European side of the Dardanelles and the Bosporus. His later years were marked by a revolt of the Asiatic Greeks, which his generals suppressed, and by a similar movement in Egypt, which was put down by his successors. His efforts to punish the European Greeks for their part in the Ionic revolt failed at Marathon, and he died during the preparation of another effort which he was to have led in person. No man of equal ability ever again wore the Persian crown.

XERXES AND THE DECADENCE

With Xerxes (484–465 B.C.) the first signs of decay became apparent. He had been born after his father's accession and he had the weakness, tyrannical character, and love of luxury to be expected in a prince reared at court. He put down the Egyptian rebellion and gathered immense forces for an expedition against European Greece. This effort (480–479) was a complete failure. His army and fleet were nearly destroyed and the Greek allies wrested Asiatic Greece from his control. Babylon revolted and was partly destroyed. In later life, Xerxes became a besotted *débauché* and his career was closed by assassination.

Thereafter, the decline proceeded more rapidly. The Greek war continued another thirty years and cost the Persians dearly in men and money. Then came a series of rebellions, conspiracies, and court intrigues which showed a decided weakening of the central government. In 408, Egypt revolted, and not until 341 was it again reduced to subjection. In several mountainous districts of the empire, some of them near its center, the people reasserted their independence and made good their claim.

Succession Disputes and the Satrap War

A constant source of danger to the throne was the presence of many ambitious brothers and half-brothers of the ruling kings. Darius II gained the crown by overthrowing Xerxes II, and after the death of Darius, his younger son Cyrus tried to take it away from the older son Artaxerxes II. The lucky chance that Cyrus was killed in battle alone saved Artaxerxes.

A further threat was the insubordinate character of the satraps. Many of them ruled almost as independent sovereigns, supporting private armies and making treaties with foreign powers. They even fought private wars with each other, unhampered by their common lord.

In only one field did Persian affairs prosper. The Greeks were so weakened by their suicidal wars that, in 404, Darius II was able to regain control of Asiatic Greece. In 387, the Peace of Antalcidas made Persia the arbiter of Greek affairs. But the advantages gained by this treaty were partially offset by the use of Greek mercenaries in the imperial and provincial armies. The commanders of these ready-made armies often acquired great influence, especially in the western part of the empire.

The Empire Under Succeeding Kings

Thus affairs stood under Artaxerxes II (403–358 B.C.), when the forces of decadence almost destroyed the Persian power. At court, the influence of the queen-mother Parysatis and of the king's women and eunuchs produced a lurid round of intrigue, treachery, and murder. Later his son and successor Ochus gained the upper hand. He hanged his brother who stood in his way and finally massacred eighty of his father's one hundred and twenty children to secure the throne. A formidable rebellion among the satraps of Asia Minor and Syria and aided by the Egyptians was crushed, more by the treachery of the rebels toward each other than by the feeble exertions of the king.

Artaxerxes III, Ochus (358–337), was a stronger ruler than his father, and in other respects a tiger in human form. Once securely seated on the throne, he undertook to crush the remaining rebels of Syria and to bring Egypt back into subjection. The last embers of the Satraps' War were quenched in blood, the citizens of Sidon even committing mass suicide rather than trust themselves in the king's hands. Egypt was reconquered, her temples desecrated, her second Apis bull slain and an ass installed in his place. Everywhere the satraps were reduced to a closer obedience than they had shown to any king since Xerxes I. But though he gained decisive victories over the forces of dissolution, he could not control his own courtiers. A eunuch named Bagoas, who aspired to dominate the government, poisoned Artaxerxes III and all but one of his sons at a single banquet.

The regicide did not long enjoy the fruits of his crime. The one son whom he had spared to act as a puppet king proved refractory, and was likewise poisoned. A distant cousin of Artaxerxes III was crowned with the title of Darius III (336–330). His first act was to provide for his own safety by poisoning Bagoas. The new king came to the throne just in time to meet the irresistible attack of the Macedonians under Alexander the Great. For such a crisis, Darius had neither sufficient strength nor courage, yet perhaps no one else could have done much better. He saw his dominions overrun by his young antagonist and was at last stabbed by his own officers. But the story of his fall will be told elsewhere.

The collapse of the Persian Empire marked a revolution in human affairs. Alexander transferred the scepter of universal power from Asia to Europe. It was destined to remain in the hands of Europeans — first of Macedonians and Greeks and later of Romans — until the seventh century A.D., when the Mohammedans restored the domination of western Asia to the Asiatics.

Persian Culture

"The Persians," says the Greek historian Herodotus, "teach their boys only three things — horsemanship, archery, and truth-telling." It was a narrow curriculum, but well fitted for an imperial people. In war and government the Persians achieved much, although they founded few political institutions which the world at large has adopted. Their art was borrowed from the Assyrians and Babylonians, and their alphabet, which they derived from the same source, was never used to record a great national literature. But in religion they made a lasting contribution to civilization.

Iranian Paganism; Zoroaster

Originally, both the Medes and the Persians were pagans like their neighbors, with a professional priesthood known as *magi* (whence our word "magic"). Fire was worshiped as an emblem of deity, and sacrifices were made to the gods as in other pagan cults. There was nothing in the primitive worship of either people to indicate that they would be the propagators of a great religion or of an advanced standard of ethics.

In the sixth century B.C. there appeared in Media a great religious leader, known to us as *Zoroaster*. He rejected the polytheistic faith of his fathers entirely. There is, he said, only one god, *Ahura Mazda*, the personification of wisdom, goodness, truth, and light, and the creator of all good things. But opposed to him is *Ahriman*, the personification of evil, darkness, and falsehood. Between the two spirits there is continual warfare, with the domination of the universe as the prize. In this struggle every man must take a part, and it is his duty to help Ahura Mazda. He can do this by moral living, steadfast truth-telling, improving the world as a place of human habitation, and destroying the works of Ahriman. In the end Ahura Mazda will triumph, and his helpers will enjoy an eternity of happiness. The partisans of Ahriman, on the other hand, will suffer eternal punishment.

It was a virile, stimulating faith, and Zoroaster lived to see it widely accepted. The satrap of Bactria, *Hystaspes*, became a convert, and Hystaspes' son Darius became king of Persia. Soon it became the official religion of the Persian people, but it paid dearly for the honor. The magi, willing to be priests of any religion which would assure them paying positions, reluctantly accepted it and became its clergy, and with them there crept back into it many of the superstitions which Zoroaster had abhorred. Among these was fire-worship, which continued to be popular. Before the fall of the Persian Empire, even the old gods had partially regained their sway, probably by the devious route of the royal harem, where impressionable kings adopted the superstitions of their mothers and concubines. Later, in the third century A.D., the worship of Ahura Mazda was stripped of some of the cruder polytheistic beliefs which clung to it and became the basis of the present-day *Parsee* religion. Some parts of its sacred book — the *Avesta* — probably go back to Zoroaster, but much more was added after his time.

The Contribution of Persia

Thus, the phases of world civilization which have been most strongly affected by the Persians are government and religion. Their system of provincial administration was widely copied by the Macedonian successors of Alexander the Great, and through them it found wide acceptance among the Romans of the empire. The Persian system of court etiquette set a fashion which has been followed, with modifications, at European courts ever since. Zoroastrianism profoundly influenced its sister religions. Heaven and hell, a personal devil, and many other features of Judaism, Christianity, and Mohammedanism have been derived from it. In addition, it remains one of the great religions of the world in its own right.

THE JEWISH RESTORATION; JUDAISM

When Cyrus the Great permitted the Jewish exiles in Babylonia to return home, he encouraged a movement of great importance in the religious history of mankind. During the exile of the Jews in Babylon, their religion had not been static. Two great prophets, Ezekiel and Deutero-Isaiah, had taught them a spiritualized monotheism such as they had never known in their old homes. They had learned to regard Yahweh not as a local or national god, but as the supreme ruler of the universe, beside whom there is no other. The glorious prophecies of Deutero-Isaiah had foretold the return of the Chosen People to their rightful homes, and had promised the establishment of a divine kingdom upon earth in a future age. Much probably dates from this period which today passes as the work of Moses.

The Jews who returned to Palestine were but a fraction of those who at that time lived in Babylonia. Their adopted country was a rich land, where many of them had prospered, and they had no desire to leave it for the stony hills and lean fields of their native Palestine. Those who went were zealots, to whom their religious faith and national existence were more important than economic prosperity. They rebuilt the altar of Yahweh and re-established his cult. Jerusalem rose from her ashes. Then the curtain dropped upon the scene for nearly eighty years, during which the movement languished. The Jews who had been left in the country did not take kindly to the novel customs and beliefs of their fellow countrymen, and the surrounding Gentiles were hostile.

About 458, another and more successful attempt was made to reorganize the Jewish community in Palestine. Ezra and Nehemiah (the latter a cup-bearer of King Artaxerxes I) came to Jerusalem within a few years of each other, armed with royal decrees authorizing the necessary work, and with a new code of laws known to modern Biblicists as the *Priests' Code*. The temple and the walls of Jerusalem were rebuilt and the ceremonial law was rigorously enforced. Not without severity, and against considerable opposition from within and without, the Jewish community was reorganized. The priesthood was re-established, subjected to rigorous regulations as to religion and morals, and granted extensive authority over the people in religious and secular matters.

Thus was born the religion which we call Judaism. It was an outgrowth of the older Hebrew faith, but richer, nobler, and more fully charged with ethical content than ever before. To this period we owe the Old Testament books as they exist today. Judaism was made possible by the kindly tolerance of the Persian kings.

10

The Aegean Civilization

THE AEGEAN WORLD

JUST as the Nile and Tigris-Euphrates regions left their respective indelible stamps upon the Egyptian and Babylonian civilizations, so the culture of the Greeks bore no less plainly the features impressed upon it by the basin of the Aegean Sea, where it arose. This region exerted a powerful influence upon every phase of their lives, material, intellectual, and spiritual. Therefore to understand the unique quality of this gifted people, we must first become acquainted with the land in which their national character developed.

Ancient Greece: Extent and Character

The classical Greeks thought of Hellas (Greece) as including all lands where intelligible forms of their language were spoken and where men followed the Greek way of life. But that was after a period of colonization had spread their speech and customs over an area much greater than that in which the salient and lasting features of their national temperament had been formed. The cradle of Hellenic civilization and of the Hellenic people was the Aegean Basin, and especially the peninsula which forms its western side.

The Greek peninsula, a southern projection of the Balkan peninsula, is about two hundred and fifty miles in length, and one hundred and eighty wide at its broadest part. The fortieth parallel of north latitude (near which are located the American cities of Philadelphia, Pittsburgh, Salt Lake City, and San Francisco) passes through its extreme northern part. Athens, in central Greece, is almost the same distance from the Equator as Louisville, Kentucky. The peninsula is ribbed with parallel mountain ranges, which bend to the southeast from its eastern shore toward the coast of Asia Minor. In prehistoric times, when the basin of the Aegean Sea sank below water-level, the tops of the mountains formed the two great chains of islands and the numerous smaller groups with which the sea is dotted. The first chain includes the large island of Euboea (1438 square miles) and the Sporades and Cyclades groups. South of it is the other chain, which consists of Cythera, Crete (3328 square miles), Carpathos, and Rhodes. The northern Aegean has remnants of other sunken ranges which form the islands of Lemnos, Imbros, Scyros, Samothrace, Thasos, Lesbos, Chios, and others.

Nature made the Greeks seafarers, but she also directed them in their early wanderings abroad. In a lean and mountainous country, fish was a welcome addition to the larder. The rugged eastern coast, with numerous harbors suitable for small boats and with islands visible from almost every point, induced the people to be sailors, and the island chains led them toward the more civilized south and east — to Asia Minor, Syria, and Egypt. The western coast, on the other hand, has few good harbors, although the long, narrow Gulf of Corinth, which opens from it, runs straight up into the heart of the country. Only the narrow Isthmus of Corinth prevents the region south of the Gulf (the Peloponnesus or Island of Pelops) from being an island in fact as well as in name. Thus, it was not until relatively late in their history that the Greeks and other Aegean peoples ventured westward to trade with the rude inhabitants of Italy and surrounding countries.

Terrain and Climate

The Greek peninsula is a land of striking scenery and grueling poverty. There are only a few small areas of fertile soil, such as the valleys of the Peneus River in Thessaly, the Alpheus, Pamisus, and Eurotas in the Peloponnesus. Most of the streams flow through narrow ravines carved in the rocks. They are dry much of the year, but become raging, destructive torrents after heavy rains. Several inland districts, like Arcadia and Boeotia, have no adequate drainage systems aboveground. Shut off by mountain ranges from the sea, they discharge their waters through natural underground channels worn in the soft limestone which underlies so much of the country. Such channels clog easily, and as a result the areas which they drain may be subjected to disastrous floods. The mountains are seldom more than five thousand feet in height, the loftiest chains being in the north. Thus, their summits are below the level of perpetual snow. The forests which once clothed their slopes have been destroyed extensively by fires, overcutting, and the pasturage of sheep and goats. This has allowed the winter rains to wash away the soil, leaving the bare rock protruding. Not many years ago it was estimated that only eighteen and a half per cent of the land of the peninsula was arable. The ancient Greeks did much better, for by means of terraces they farmed steep slopes where today nothing can be grown. At best, cultivable land is to be found in areas of from a few square miles to a few hundred, separated by wide expanses of mountain, forest, or scrub.

Nature partly compensates the Greeks for the barrenness of their country by the attractiveness of their climate. The latitude of the peninsula is in general that of central United States, but its central and southern parts are protected by the mountains from the cold north winds, while the Mediterranean Sea and the Libyan Desert still further modify the winter temperature. Except in the north, the climate of the lowlands is that of the warm Temperate Zone, with rainy winters and hot, dry summers. At Athens, snow falls only about five days in an average year, and about three hundred days are prevailingly sunny. The summer heat is tempered by the Etesian (annual) winds, which blow from the northeast during July and August. Lack of moisture renders the air crystal-clear, so that even distant objects stand out distinctly. On the mountain slopes and in Thessaly and Epirus, lower temperatures prevail and conditions more nearly approximate those of central Europe.

Plant, Animal, and Mineral Resources

The Aegean region as a whole is a land of few agricultural and animal resources, wherein it is difficult to earn a livelihood. Wheat yields but little return and barley only a moderate amount. Grapes and olives, while probably not native to the country, do better because they thrive on rocky slopes. The grape furnishes the wine which is so important in the Mediterranean lands, while the olive is either eaten raw or pressed for its oil. To the ancient Greek, olive oil served as food, soap, and a means of illumination. The vast areas of uncultivable land have always furnished pasture for herds of cattle, sheep, goats, and swine. As elsewhere in the Mediterranean world, these animals are driven to the high mountain pastures in summer to escape the drought and returned to the lowlands in autumn. Thus, the herdsmen have always formed a semi-nomadic class in the midst of a settled agricultural population. Timber was more plentiful in ancient than it is in modern Greece, although the supply was never equal to the demand. The principal trees are the oak, elm, pine, fir, ash, and cedar. The plane tree served as shade in ancient as in modern Greece. The fig was probably an early importation from the east, and the date palm has been found from early times in the southern Peloponnesus. The orange, lemon, walnut, and several other trees found in modern Greece were unknown in classical days.

Mineral resources are as scanty as those of plants and animals, though the mountains contain many kinds of building stone in large quantities. Marble of several varieties is found, the most valuable being the yellow-white Pentelic of Attica and the white of the islands of Paros and Naxos. Deposits of limestone and tufa (calcareous volcanic rock) are to be had almost everywhere. An abundance of potter's clay makes possible the use of jars for many purposes for which we employ wood and metal containers. From the clay the ancient Greeks wrought those exquisite jars and vases which constitute one of the finest accomplishments of their artistic genius. Metallic ores, however, have always been scarce. Copper was available in small quantities in Euboea and Crete, but tin for the making of bronze had to be imported. Iron was found in Euboea, Boeotia, in several of the islands, and particularly in the Taygetus Range in the Peloponnesus. Most of the iron ores were of poor quality, but at one time enough of the metal was produced to allow some for export. The only known gold deposits in the Aegean world were on the northern islands and the neighboring coasts of Thrace and Asia Minor. Silver ores were found in Attica and on the islands of Thasos and Siphnos.

Environment and the Greek Character

With these modest resources the Greeks had to be content. Although the mild climate made existence easier than in colder regions, there was little for subsistence, and it required energy and ingenuity to secure even that. The inhospitable soil drove them to seafaring, piracy, and trade. Compelled to make the most of their natural abilities, they developed initiative, industry, perseverance, and self-control. Yet Nature never oppressed the Greeks, as she did most of the Near-Eastern peoples, with phenomena so overwhelming as to instill in them a sense of their own insignificance. Their world was small enough and its conditions were sufficiently stable for them to gain self-confidence through continued successful mastery of their environment. Their very poverty precluded the establishment of a vast, impersonal governmental machine like those prevalent in many Asiatic states and in Egypt. Hence, it was an easy transition from monarchy to democracy. The concentration of population on the isolated patches of productive soil, with stretches of barren land and often barriers of mountain or sea between them, hindered communication and engendered a narrow, local patriotism in each group. Under such circumstances, hatred and suspicion of outsiders, especially near neighbors, was inevitable. Thus, the Greeks while free were never able to gain political unity. Their internal struggles wrote many a tragic chapter into their history, culminating in their conquest by Macedonia and later by Rome. Not all the traits displayed by the historic Greeks were developed in this environment, for the country frequently received immigrants who contributed to the national character elements that had originated in their native lands. But most of the salient features of the Greek temperament were indigenous and owed their existence to the nature of the country.

THE STONE AGE IN THE AEGEAN REGION (*ca.* 6000–3000 B.C.)

So far as can be determined, it was not until the Neolithic Age that man first found a home in the Aegean Basin. The first settlers were members of the short-statured, long-headed, brunette Mediterranean race, and probably crossed from Africa to Crete. The date of their arrival can hardly be placed later than 6000 B.C. The other Aegean islands and the Peloponnesus remained uninhabited for ages thereafter. Somewhat later, a group of broad-headed wanderers from central Europe settled in the valley of the Peneus River in northern Greece. They too were in the Neolithic stage of development and for many centuries did not progress beyond it. Few, if any, of these northerners penetrated the peninsula south of Mount Othrys, and not until much later did extensive contacts take place between these two races.

Stone Age Culture of the Earliest Greeks

For thousands of years after their first appearance in Crete and the neighboring islands, the inhabitants of the southern Aegean region lived the rude life characteristic of the late Stone Age. Their earliest dwellings were caves in the mountains, but these were superseded by round huts of mud, with stone floors and thatched roofs. Their original implements, made of sandstone or limestone, were subsequently abandoned for the harder serpentine, jadeite, hematite, and obsidian, the last of which is a hard volcanic glass, easily shaped into serviceable knife-blades and axe-heads. The only available supply in the neighborhood of Crete was on the island of Melos, about eighty miles to the north, whose obsidian quarries had been worked by the Neolithic Cretan colonists. They also had cattle, sheep, goats, and swine, and they supplemented their supply of meat and skins by hunting. The surrounding waters provided a plentiful store of fish. Agriculture was unknown or little practiced, but the early Cretans probably gathered such wild grains and other vegetable foods as Nature provided. What clothing they wore consisted principally of skins, but the presence of spindle-weights and bobbins among the débris of their settlements indicates that some cloth was woven. Pottery was still handmade, but underwent a striking evolution. In the lower strata of the rubbish that forms our only record of Neolithic man are found only crude shapes made of impure clay, but in the upper layers the forms become more artistic and the clay is carefully cleansed. Although unglazed, the finest specimens of this early Cretan pottery were carefully stroked to smoothness with pebbles and were decorated with incised lines filled with white clay. Religious practices were represented by crude and gross female figurines of baked clay, which apparently portrayed the mother-goddess so prominent in the cults of this region in later ages.

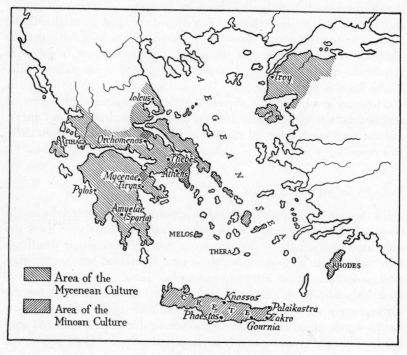

MAP OF THE AEGEAN WORLD

Shortly before 3000 B.C. this primitive culture was subjected to a series of foreign influences and spread to new areas. Waves of immigration from the north occupied central and southern Greece, at the same time that the Mediterranean Cretans also sought the coasts of the Peloponnesus. Both groups, as well as immigrants from Asia Minor, populated the Sporades and Cyclades. Commerce sprang up between the Aegean peoples and Egypt. From this source they secured tools of impure copper and somewhat later learned to extract the metal from their native ores. They began to improve the quality of their pottery and to use a primitive pictographic system of writing. A brilliant civilization was in the process of evolution.

The Minoan Civilization (3000–1400 b.c.)

The civilization which flourished in Crete and the near-by islands from about 3000 to about 1400 is commonly called Minoan, from Minos, a legendary Cretan king. It formed one division of a much more extensive Aegean culture, the others being the Helladic (on the mainland of Greece) and the Cycladic (on the Aegean islands). As the Helladic culture did not achieve prominence until about 1400, its early stages can be treated briefly, and the Cycladic does not warrant extensive description in the present work.

Sources of Knowledge

Our knowledge of Aegean civilization is derived for the most part from its material remains like that of the Neolithic culture which preceded it. The writing of the Minoans has never been deciphered and is practically useless as a guide to their history. Egyptian records barely mention them, and the classical Greeks knew only a few artless stories about the splendor of their royal palaces, the power of their kings, and their man-devouring monster, the Minotaur. Accordingly, modern historians know little more about them than can be learned from the remains. Hence, unless a key to their language and writing is found, we cannot know their literature or more than vague outlines of their political, social, and economic history. It seems reasonably certain that they did not speak any form of the Greek language, although some of their words were later adopted by the Greeks.

Not until about 1870 did the modern world know anything definite regarding the prehistoric Aegean civilization. For a long time it had been the fashion to dismiss the stories of such a civilization found in classical Greek literature as myths and the episodes described by Homer as purely

fanciful. The proof that such a culture had existed is due primarily to a
brilliant amateur archeologist, Doctor Heinrich Schliemann. As a young
man he was an avid student of the Homeric poems, and in spite of the in-
credulity of the scholastic world, he believed that they told a true story.
After making a fortune from Russian oil wells, he determined to excavate
the hilltop of Hissarlik (in northwestern Asia Minor), where legend said
that ancient Troy had stood. He had little training in archeology and
he made gross blunders, but he opened an entirely new chapter in the history of the Aegean world. His beloved Homer was triumphantly vindicated. Above the virgin rock were the remains of nine successive settlements, each built above the ruins of its predecessor. The oldest dated
from the Neolithic period, and the most recent was a Graeco-Roman city.
Later investigations showed that the sixth of these was the city destroyed
by the Achaean chiefs.

From Troy, Doctor Schliemann went to Mycenae and Tiryns in southern
Greece, where he made equally startling discoveries. His work was carried on by Doctor Dörpfeld and other able investigators. Before the end
of the century the late Helladic culture known as Mycenaean had been
rescued from oblivion. In 1900, Sir Arthur Evans began excavations at
Knossos in Crete. Within the next ten years he and other European and
American scholars had proved that the age of which Homer wrote was
merely the "Indian summer" of a brilliant civilization which had flourished for nearly two thousand years before the Trojan War, and of which
Homer knew next to nothing. Research in this field has continued ever
since; and almost every year reveals new data.

Minoan Chronology; the Early Period

On the basis of excavations at Knossos and other Cretan cities, with approximate dates determined by Egyptian and other foreign objects found
at various levels, Evans worked out the following chronological scheme
for the Minoan culture:

I. Early Minoan (3000–2200 B.C.)
II. Middle Minoan (2200–1600 B.C.)
III. Late Minoan (1600–1200 B.C.)

He divided each of these periods into three sub-periods. In our present
survey, these sub-periods may be ignored, except III, Late Minoan, which
marks the introduction of Helladic, or mainland, civilization into Crete
and merits special consideration.

The culture of the Early Minoan period flourished most extensively in eastern Crete, Melos, and the Cyclades, no one of these areas displaying any marked superiority over the others. It was characterized by the use of impure copper for cutting-tools, the manufacture of stone vessels (with a partial decline in pottery-making), and the introduction of a system of pictographic writing modeled after Egyptian hieroglyphics. In fact, the nascent Minoan culture displayed a number of striking similarities to that of the Nile Valley, with which it was in constant communication. Architecture developed slowly, but even at this early date certain features became apparent which, in a more highly developed form, were to characterize the edifices of Knossos and other Minoan centers a thousand years later. Particularly is this true of the floor plan, in which rooms were arranged around a central court — the so-called *patio* plan. In eastern Crete, huge communal houses were the rule, each probably sheltering a whole clan rather than a single family.

Far off on the outskirts of the Aegean world the Early Minoan Age witnessed the rise of the "Second City" of Troy, with a civilization strikingly different from that of the Cyclades and Crete. There the palace of the ruler was built on a plan which had originated in central Europe, with a great hall and fireplace taking the place of the Minoan courtyard. The Trojan palace was plainly not a communal dwelling, but the residence only of the king with his family and servants. The early Trojans already knew the use of bronze (perhaps even earlier than the people of the southern Aegean), but like several other important features of their culture, the knowledge probably resulted from a local discovery or was derived indirectly from the Tigris-Euphrates Valley. The "Second City" was destroyed about 1850 B.C.

Museum of Fine Arts, Boston

EARLY MINOAN POTTERY

The Middle Minoan Period

Toward the end of the Early Minoan period the Cretans and their neighbors also learned to use the more serviceable bronze in place of copper and obsidian. With implements made from the new alloy, it was now possible to build and adorn edifices of stone and to practice other arts hardly feasible before. Simultaneously, a new technique appeared in the field of pottery manufacture. The potter's wheel enabled the workman to fashion perfectly round products with walls of eggshell thinness. Instead of baking his vessels in an open fire, he now enclosed them in an oven, where they could be fired in a high, even heat.

By 2200 B.C., these and other developments had carried the Minoan culture into a new stage, characterized by greater achievements and growing originality. The foreign elements which had hitherto played so important a part had been assimilated and the Minoan people had attained cultural maturity. Meanwhile, eastern Crete and the Cyclades, with the exception of Melos, declined in importance.

Halfway between the eastern and western ends of Crete two cities rose to pre-eminence: Knossos on the northern coast and Phaestos on the southern. The former seems to have traded with Greece and the Aegean islands, while the latter was in communication with Egypt. Other cities of central Crete shared this prosperity in varying degrees. The rulers of Knossos, Phaestos, and Mallia erected pretentious palaces. What the political condition of Crete may have been at the time can only be inferred. Evidently it had not attained unity, for life was highly competitive and dangerous. The kings of Knossos erected strong fortifications around the palace, but these failed to save it from destruction (about 1750 B.C.), when the other palaces of central Crete met the same fate. The details of this catastrophe are unknown.

Middle Minoan Culture

In every field of art the Middle Minoan period was one of fearless experimentation, intelligent receptivity, and rapid advancement. The potters began to make full use of the advantages to be obtained from the wheel, the oven, and improved facilities for decoration. Some of their creations have walls less than four one-hundredths of an inch thick — the so-called "eggshell ware." They imitated the practices of the metalworkers and shaped their products like gold and silver bowls. New coloring matter was discovered which could be applied with a brush, making possible polychrome decorations. Spirals, scrolls, and representations of

LATE MINOAN POTTERY

natural objects completely displaced geometric designs from the repertoire of the pottery painter. Fine vases were carved from the stone called *steatite* and decorated with reliefs. Frescoes of great beauty adorned the walls of the First Palace of Knossos, and surviving examples of gold-smith's work from the same period indicate that it was not inferior to other branches of the fine arts.

The increasing complexity of government promoted the use of writing for accounts and official correspondence. Thus, there was a transition from pictographs to a simpler and more practicable form of conventional hieroglyphs. They were approximately one hundred and thirty-five in number and were probably syllabic. About 1700 B.C. an even simpler form came into use, with ninety signs, written in a linear script. While some form of paper may have been used, no trace of it has survived. The only existing specimens of Minoan writing are engraved on hard objects, prin-cipally clay tablets. There is no record that the Minoans ever had an ex-tensive literature, as the only surviving documents are apparently book-keeping entries and other government accounts.

Greece and the Achaean Migration

While this refined, yet virile, culture was growing up in Crete, the peo-ples of the Greek peninsula were developing to a lesser extent along similar lines. Before the end of the Early Minoan period (Early Helladic on the mainland), they were using bronze implements and had made progress in other directions. As yet they probably did not speak any form of the Greek language or possess other Indo-European institutions. About 1800 B.C. Indo-Europeans from the steppes of southern Russia and western Asia swept out westward, eastward, and southward. We have seen how they hurled the Hittite and Kassite tribes into Babylonia and the Hyksos into Egypt. This migration also brought the Greek-speaking Achaeans into the Greek peninsula. While still partially nomadic, they were not entirely uncivilized, and they had great capacity for advancement. They knew the use of bronze, which they probably taught to the Neolithic tribes of Thessaly. For two centuries their bands continued to advance through the peninsula, conquering as they went, and leaving a trail of chaos and destruction. About 1600 B.C., however, settled conditions returned. The invaders founded a group of states in which they formed the ruling classes. Intercourse with Crete taught the mainlanders once more the arts of civilization. Agriculture revived, and Orchomenos, Thebes, Athens, Mycenae, Tiryns, and Pylos were either newly founded or rose from their ashes. At some places, especially Thebes and Orchomenos, there may have been actual conquests of mainland territory by Cretan invaders. Cretan arts and fashions gained such strong ascendancy that the reviving civilization of the peninsula in early Achaean times is regarded as a variety of the Minoan culture. There was a difference, how-

Brown Brothers

THE VAPHIO CUPS

ever, as the Achaean kings and nobles strongly influenced the structures which grew up under their dominion. Their dwellings, like the palace of the "Second City" of Troy, were of the hall or *megaron* type. Arms, clothing, and many other features of Achaean life differed from those of Knossos or Phaestos. As a whole, the mainlanders were cruder, but more vigorous, than their southern neighbors.

The Late Minoan Age

About 1600 B.C. Crete entered upon its last and most brilliant period of prosperity, the Late Minoan Age. The damage done by the catastrophe which destroyed the Cretan palaces in the late eighteenth century B.C. had been fully repaired. Knossos, Phaestos, Gournia, Tylissos, Palaikastro, and other cities flourished once more. By a process, the details of which must remain unknown until Minoan writing can be read, the whole island was unified under a line of kings who ruled from Knossos, although they had a smaller palace at Phaestos and a villa at the near-by town of Hagia Triada. The later Greeks, usually ignorant of the affairs of the non-Hellenic Minoans, had a number of legends regarding the power and splendor of Minos, king of Knossos. Probably the name was not that of a single king, but a title applied to the whole dynasty that ruled Crete in the days of her greatness, just as the early Jews tended to call all Egyptian kings Pharaoh. Not only did Minos rule the great southern island, but with his fleet he mastered the Aegean islands and the coasts of Greece. He exterminated pirates and collected tribute from the islanders and the chiefs on the mainland. So orderly was his government that, in spite of occasional legends of cruelty, his name became a symbol of justice to the Greeks. They believed that after death he became the judge of the souls in Hades. With political domination went commercial monopoly. The whole carrying trade of the eastern Mediterranean was in the hands of his sailors. Even Thutmose III, the Egyptian conqueror, hired them to carry cedar logs from Phoenicia to Egypt.

The Palace of Knossos

Under the stimulus of the wealth secured by these means, the Cretan capital attained the apogee of its greatness. The city of Knossos must have had a population not far short of one hundred thousand persons. Like other Cretan cities, it was unwalled, for the fleet kept enemies at a distance. The royal palace, known in Greek legend as the *Labyrinth*, covered an area

STAIRWAY TO QUEEN'S APARTMENT
In Palace at Knossos, Crete

of five acres, and was several stories high. It was built on a hill and skill-fully accommodated to the irregularity of the ground. The walls were of sawed limestone. In spite of its size, the building was not grand or im-posing and little attention was paid to symmetry. Originally it must have centered about a great courtyard, 195 by 94 feet, but as need arose, new courts and rooms were laid out, until it formed a veritable maze of rooms, courts, light-wells, and corridors. The king who lived in this palace was not an aloof or haughty master like the Egyptian Pharaoh. The throne-room contained a simple chair of gypsum for his use, and a divan to seat his courtiers extended around the room. Beautiful frescoes, large and small, adorned the walls of the palace. But perhaps the most striking feature of this unusual structure was its highly developed system of water-supply and sewage-disposal. Terra-cotta pipes brought pure water from hillside springs, while stone-covered drains, latrines, and bathrooms en-abled the inhabitants to enjoy bath and toilet facilities unknown anywhere else until the middle of the nineteenth century A.D.

The palace of Knossos was not merely a royal residence; it also served as storehouse, factory, arsenal, and artistic center. Not far from the royal apartments were rooms containing huge jars for the storage of grain, oil, and wine. Thousands of bronze arrowheads, with other war supplies,

THE THRONE ROOM
Palace of Knossos, 15th Century B.C.

enabled the king to equip an army on short notice. Order and system prevailed in the palace storerooms, and careful accounts were kept of all supplies. There were royal potteries, sculptors' studios, and bronze foundries.

A whole school of art owes its name to these palace factories and studios. The potters of the Palace Style abandoned polychrome decoration in favor of black figures on a light or buff background. In place of the earlier scrolls and spirals, they painted flowers, papyrus plants, marine animals, and other natural objects. A favorite theme was the cuttlefish, which in the best work was treated with glaring realism. The palace sculptors rarely attempted large pieces, but instead produced exquisite figurines and statuettes such as the Bull-Leaper or the Snake Goddess now in the Museum of Fine Arts in Boston.

Minoan Religion

Religion also claimed its place at the center of government. Three deities appear to have enjoyed especial honors — the mother-goddess, a young vegetation god, and a young goddess, "The Sweet Maiden." The god's symbol was the double-axe (Labrys, whence Labyrinth), and it was frequently used as a decorative motive. There is no definite evidence that the Minoans had a professional priesthood, but the king himself was probably a high priest. Chapels in the palaces took the place of temples, although caves in the mountains were also used as sanctuaries. The belief in an afterlife was such as to require elaborate funeral rites, for the corpse was buried with a profusion of grave furniture, and at intervals the relatives offered sacrifices to the departed spirit. By analogy, we are led to infer that the ghosts of the unburied and uncared-for dead were believed to be dangerous to the living.

The Life of the People

But no superstitious terrors restrained the Minoans from full enjoyment of their life on earth. Then, as always, fine clothing was a source of pleasure and a means of display. The feminine costume was elaborate and in some respects astonishingly modern in appearance. Long and ample skirts, with flounces and ruffles, gave the lady of Knossos a superficial resemblance to the belles of the "Gay Nineties," although her frontless bodice would hardly have passed without censure in that modest decade. Masculine garb was simple, consisting of a short skirt, secured by a belt

Museum of Fine Arts, Boston

THE SNAKE GODDESS
Knossos, Crete

at the waist and covering the hips. High boots protected the lower part of the leg, but in compensation for his scanty raiment, the Minoan dandy adorned himself with rings and bracelets. Both sexes belted their waists to a wasplike slenderness.

Amusements were many and varied. In his idle hours the king played a game resembling chess. For group sports, the palaces of Knossos and Phaestos were provided with open-air theaters, which had stone seats and pavements and a capacity of about five hundred spectators. There the women gathered with the men to enjoy music, dancing, and games. Boxers, their heads protected by leather helmets and their hands encased in padded leather gloves, amused the "fans" of 1500 B.C. There are indications that some form of gladiatorial combat existed. But the most popular sport was bull-leaping. As the maddened animal charged down a runway, an acrobat seized him by the horns, turned a somersault over his back, and was caught in the arms of a waiting comrade. Many a performer must have been gored to death in this dangerous pastime. It is probable that the human participants were slaves, and the story of the tribute of youths and maidens collected by Minos from his Greek vassals to serve as food for a monster bull can only refer to this practice. In the country at large, if we may trust the evidence of the reliefs on the Harvester Vase, there were gay

Bettmann

Metropolitan Museum

METAL VASE MADE IN CRETE
ABOUT 1500 B.C.

THE CUP BEARER FRESCO
SHOWING MINOAN MALE
COSTUME
Palace of Knossos

and noisy processions of peasants at the great seasonal and religious festivals.

In the Late Minoan Age, war within the island of Crete had gradually subsided, and after 1450 practically ceased. The small, wiry Minoans never took kindly to the heavy armor of more stalwart races and cooler climates. The spearmen wore no body armor and probably no helmet, but protected themselves with huge, "man-covering" shields of leather stretched over wooden frames, contracted in the middle to form a figure-of-eight. Chariots were used to transport them and their bulky equipment to the field of battle. Archers and slingers formed an important part of the armed forces

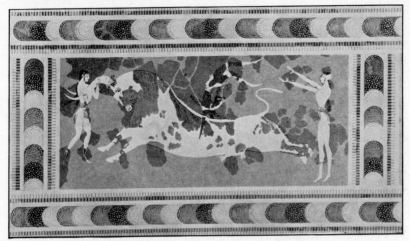

Metropolitan Museum

BULL-LEAPING SCENE FROM A MINOAN CIRCUS
A Fresco from Knossos

and probably had no defensive equipment of any kind. No definite evidence on the nature of Minoan naval tactics exists.

A striking symbol of the power and intelligence of Minos' government was the construction of a number of excellent roads in Crete, particularly between Knossos and Phaestos. Here a forty-mile section of highway with culverts and bridges led travelers over the mountains with an ease and speed never equaled on the roads of historic Greece. The Mycenaean states on the mainland took a similar interest in road-building, and several highways can be traced in the neighborhood of Mycenae and Tiryns.

Decadence

It was a gay and active civilization which flourished in the royal courts of Crete in the fifteenth century B.C., yet signs of decay were not lacking. Apparently all creative effort had become centered in the palace, and this led to decadence and stagnation elsewhere. This tendency is shown clearly in contemporary art which, in spite of technical perfection, is full of triviality and conventionalism. The evidence points to a people whose energies were being drained to maintain a splendid court and a bureaucratic administration. Such a condition is always dangerous. Where everything depends upon a central government, one mistake or moment of weakness on its part may easily precipitate universal ruin. The government of the Cretan monarch must have been unpopular, not only with his vassals, but with the Egyptians and others who paid him extortionate profits for merchandise.

No one knows just how Knossos and her sister cities were destroyed, but about 1400 B.C. foreign invaders — probably mainland Greeks — descended upon the island and in a short time spread destruction everywhere. The ruins of the palaces tell the melancholy story of a people caught off their guard: of potters, bakers, jewelers, and masons surprised while at work and killed or enslaved, leaving their unfinished work to be found by excavators over three thousand years later. After carefully looting the captured palaces, the invaders burned them to the ground.

The calamity did not utterly destroy Cretan civilization, but it inflicted a blow from which the island never recovered. Knossos was reoccupied by a poor and discouraged remnant of her inhabitants, who lived as squatters in the ruins of the palace. Later on a measure of revival took place, but never again did the grandeur and prosperity of the great age return. Eventually, Greek chiefs from the mainland came to settle in Crete, introducing their own language and customs. Thus arose the Crete that Homer knew — a poor reflection of her former eminence.

Metropolitan Museum

MYCENEAN VASE

The Mycenaean Civilization (1600–1100 b.c.)

Whatever part the mainland Greeks may have had in the destruction of the Minoan civilization, they were the chief beneficiaries of the deed. Mycenae, Tiryns, Thebes, Orchomenos, Pylos, and many other cities of the peninsula rose to new heights of prosperity and splendor. Their manufactured wares of all kinds — arms, armor, pottery, and trinkets — were spread by commerce and piracy to Italy, Sicily, Egypt, Palestine, and other lands of the eastern and central Mediterranean. Never before had the Aegean region produced such quantities of goods for the export trade. A fairly uniform culture prevailed within the peninsula, except in the mountainous center of the Peloponnesus and some of the more backward northern districts.

The Mycenaean Civilization

In origin and character, the Mycenaean civilization was a vulgarized form of the Minoan culture, with a large mixture of elements brought by the Greek invaders from the north. All its artistic and intellectual background was Cretan and it adhered to this phase of its Minoan heritage to

University Prints

GALLERY IN THE WALL
Tiryns, Greece

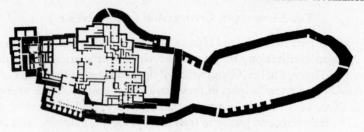

University Prints

PLAN OF PALACE AT TIRYNS

the end. But in certain important respects it differed widely from its prototype. As previously indicated, the palaces were of the megaron type. Even in elaborate structures like the palace of Tiryns, the best that the architect could do was to construct several halls instead of one.

Unlike the Cretans of the Late Minoan age, the Mycenaean Greeks lived in perpetual danger of attack from civilized neighbors or from mountaineers and northern barbarians. Hence, their princes were men of war and their cities were encircled by massive and elaborate fortifications. Large storerooms permitted the accumulation of provisions and secret passages afforded access to water during sieges. The walls of Mycenae were sixteen feet thick and thirty-five high, and the famous Lion Gate, which gave access to the citadel, was topped by a block of limestone sixteen and a half feet long, eight feet wide, and over three feet thick. It was high enough to allow a man to stand upright in a chariot and pass under it. Similar massiveness characterized the royal tombs, which were huge, beehive-shaped, underground chambers, approached by passages cut into the hillsides and roofed with false arches of stone. The Mycenaean tomb which Doctor Schliemann called the *Treasury of Atreus* was fifty feet in diameter at the floor line, fifty feet high, and had a lintel block over the door weighing over a hundred and thirty tons.

In dress and armor, as in architecture, the Mycenaean Greeks showed the influence of central Europe as well as that of the Minoan south. Until a late date the women followed the styles prevalent in Knossos. The men, however, never took kindly to the scanty raiment of the Cretan men, wearing instead the *chiton*, a loose shirt which at full length reached to the calf of the leg, but which was belted so as to fall only to the knee. Unlike their southern neighbors, they let their beards and mustaches grow long. In warfare some of them used the Minoan style of armament; more frequently, however, they preferred a suit of bronze armor consisting of a

TREASURY OF ATREUS
Mycenean Royal Tomb

THE LION GATE
Mycenae

Metropolitan Museum

THE WARRIOR VASE

helmet adorned with a tall horsehair plume, a corselet for the body, greaves to cover the lower part of the leg, and a small, round shield, made of leather over a wooden frame and bound in bronze. The shield could be carried on the left arm, leaving the right arm free. The bow was less popular than in Crete. Instead, the Mycenaean warrior depended upon a spear and a sword, both of bronze, for he preferred close combat. Some of their inlaid bronze sword blades are masterpieces of artistic beauty.

The Mycenaean Age in Greek Legend

Greek legend has preserved a surprisingly extensive and connected body of stories of the Mycenaean rulers, and when proper allowance has been made for the confusion of incidents and chronology inevitable in all legends, and for the nature-myths and tales of superhuman strength and courage which they contain, they probably have a large residue of fact. From them come many of the nursery favorites: Perseus the Gorgonslayer; Bellerophon who rode the winged horse; Jason and the Argonauts; and Hercules the strong man. When we strip these legends of the glamour imparted to them by poetic genius and fanciful adventure, they portray a hard, brutal, and violent society, torn by wars and addicted to piracy and murder. Frequently, the royal and noble houses were stained by deeds of blood and horror so shocking that the classical Greeks believed that these

Metropolitan Museum

GROOM WITH HOUNDS SHOWING MYCENEAN
MALE COSTUME
From Tiryns

families had been under hereditary curses imposed by the gods in punishment for their crimes. This theme was to be used repeatedly by the Athenian dramatists of the fifth century B.C. It is only fair to say that the legends, for the most part, relate events of the thirteenth and twelfth centuries B.C. and hence may not represent the age at its best.

The Theban and Trojan Wars

Two episodes of the later Mycenaean Age which strongly impressed the imagination of the classical Greeks were the wars of the Achaean chiefs from the Peloponnesus against Thebes, ending in its destruction, and the siege of Troy. The former apparently occurred about 1200 B.C., and is important as an example of the disorder that prevailed until the rising power of Mycenae, under the family of Pelops, established a measure of peace. The Trojan War is a good example of the piratical and predatory methods by which the Achaean chiefs increased their wealth. As we have seen, there is strong reason for believing that Troy was actually destroyed at about the time and in the manner indicated in the legend (1184 B.C.), and the same may be true of the Theban War. Both stories furnished themes for the later Greek poets.

Massive and splendid as were some phases of the Mycenaean civilization, its history from the fall of Knossos to its disappearance was one of steady decline. Examples of this fact are numerous. In the beginning, the Minoan system of writing was extensively used by the Mycenaean Greeks. Later, for no apparent reason, it disappeared, and surviving traditions of the Trojan War show, with one doubtful exception, universal illiteracy. Ceramic decoration retrogressed from beauty and naturalism to the crude, geometric figures abandoned by the Minoan potters fifteen hundred years before. Homer's descriptions of Achaean palaces, which presumably apply to the twelfth century B.C., describe much ruder living conditions than those which archeology indicates existed a century or two earlier, and while he knew of finely wrought inlay metal-work such as the earlier Mycenaean workmen had produced, he could only attribute it to the god Hephaestus. Obviously, twelfth-century workmen no longer achieved the earlier high standard.

The End of the Mycenaean Civilization

It was formerly customary to attribute the fall of Mycenaean civilization to a single calamity — the Dorian invasion. But archeological discov-

University Prints

DEATH MASK
From Mycenae

eries have proved that it was not overthrown by one particular catastrophe. Instead, Mycenaean culture simply underwent a continuous decline until it disappeared. Of course, this process was accelerated by the series of invasions from the north which began in the thirteenth century and continued for about two hundred years, but they were not primarily responsible for the decline. Even before the Trojan War these migrations had begun. The Thessalians, a rude people from the Balkan peninsula, moved into the valley of the Peneus River, driving out or enslaving the older inhabitants. The destruction of Thebes had so thinned the population of central Greece that fugitives from Thessaly moved into the vacant region and founded the Boeotian group of later times. These and other movements of a similar character had introduced half-civilized conquerors into northern and central Greece before the Trojan War, in which some of them participated. About two generations after that event, western Greece and the Peloponnesus began to suffer. The Aetolians of the northwest, driven from their homes by enemies, crossed the Gulf of Corinth and fell upon the Mycenaean kingdom of Pylos, which they ultimately destroyed, replacing it with the historic state of Elis. Lastly — and most important of all — a group of tribes, known collectively as Dorians, crossed the Gulf and fell upon the eastern and southern Peloponnesus. Mycenae, Tiryns, and Sparta were sacked and burned and the decadent Mycenaean civilization gave way to complete chaos. How long the process took to complete its course can only be conjectured. The island of Aegina, for example, seems to have escaped destruction for nearly two centuries after Mycenae fell. The backward Arcadians of the central Peloponnesus, who had never yielded to the blandishments of Mycenaean culture, escaped conquest, as did Attica beyond the Isthmus of Corinth. But throughout the peninsula, the Mycenaean civilization came to an end.

II

The Greek Middle Age

The Death of an Old Order and the Birth of a New One

THE DECLINE of the Mycenaean culture, which was sketched at the close of the preceding chapter, continued until about 900. Population must have declined sharply, and economic and social life sank to a primitive level. The only commerce which survived this age of disorder and violence was controlled by Phoenician traders, who supplied all the finer manufactured goods and many common articles. Native craftsmanship became progressively cruder and less artistic. Buildings were made of wood or sundried brick and were small and mean. Sculpture almost disappeared. It is indicative of the breakdown of communication between the various parts of the peninsula that, in place of the uniform styles of workmanship which had formerly prevailed throughout the Mycenaean world, numerous local styles made their appearance. For more than three centuries the Greeks could scarcely be called a civilized people.

It would, however, be misleading to conclude that this was a period only of deterioration and decay. The collapse of the old order coincided with the first steps in the creation of a new one. As the northern invaders merged with the older population, the historical division of the Greek people into Ionians, Dorians, Aeolians, and Arcadians crystallized. Each group spoke a dialect intelligible to other Greeks, but clearly distinguished by peculiarities of vocabulary, grammar, and pronunciation. Likewise, each of these divisions had its characteristic social and religious institutions. The Dorians held the southern and eastern parts of the Peloponnesus, the Isthmus of Corinth, and most of Crete. The Ionians and Arcadians were remnants of the pre-Dorian population. On the mainland, the Ionians held only Attica, but, as we shall see, they greatly expanded their possessions through colonization. Although the Arcadians were restricted to the mountains of the central Peloponnesus, a nearly related group had introduced its dialect and customs into faraway Cyprus, which it partly Hellenized. Later Greek geographers assigned to the Aeolian stock the northern and western parts of the Peloponnesus and the lands north of the Gulf of Corinth, an extensive district in which the population was by no means uniform in culture. Important subdivisions of this people would be the Aetolians of the western Peloponnesus and the adjacent region north of the Gulf of Corinth, the Achaeans of the northern Peloponnesus, the Boeotians whose territory adjoined Attica on the north, and the Thessalians in the valley of the Peneus River in the extreme northern part of the peninsula.

. A new political order likewise came into existence. While the Mycenaean kingdoms had been relatively large, the states of the new, barbaric Greece were usually small. As indicated in the previous chapter, the nature of the country tended to strengthen the new order by encouraging the concentration of population in isolated groups, separated from each other by areas of waste land. Since these states protected the political freedom of their members, and also promoted their economic, social, and religious interests, they had tremendous internal solidarity. The local patriotism which they inspired in their citizens was so strong that throughout the classical period of Greece, it rendered the political unification of the peninsula impossible. In this respect it was one of the most potent forces in the development of Hellenic civilization. As the Greeks colonized neighboring lands, they introduced their political institutions along with other phases of their culture.

Perhaps the strongest influence exerted by this hard age upon the subsequent history of the Greeks was that which it had upon the national temperament. For several centuries poverty and strife ruthlessly eliminated unfit individuals, leaving only the strongest members of each generation to propagate the succeeding one. Ultimately, it produced a hardy race, endowed with strong bodies, clear heads, abundant energy, and indomitable resolution. Adaptability and creativeness, already stimulated by the poverty of the country, were greatly intensified. From this harsh school emerged the race which was to occupy so prominent a place in the subsequent history of the Mediterranean world.

Progress in the Arts and Crafts

From the northern invaders the Greeks learned the art of smelting iron and shaping it into efficient cutting-tools. Before the end of the period the new metal was produced from local ores. This innovation marked a

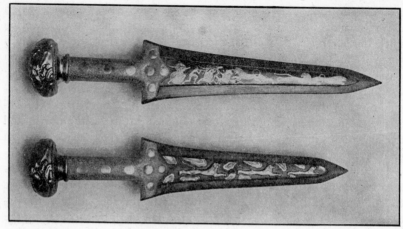

University Prints

INLAID BRONZE DAGGERS
From Mycenae

positive advance in civilization, for although iron had long been in use in Asia Minor, the Mycenaean Greeks had been very slow to adopt it. At first, the metal was used only for weapons, and even armor continued to be made of bronze. Not only was the potential supply of iron more abundant, but the tools made from it were more durable and efficient than those of bronze. Many of the artistic achievements of the later Greeks were facilitated by the possession of iron implements.

An equally revolutionary change was made in woman's clothing. The introduction of the safety-pin, or brooch, coincided with the abandonment of the form-fitting, low-necked Mycenaean costume and the adoption of the Dorian *peplos*. This was a woolen garment consisting of two strips of cloth, sewed or pinned along the sides and fastened together over the shoulders with large, decorative brooches. This simple, graceful dress occasionally was covered by a plain mantle of cloth wound around the body and held in place by one hand.

Literature and Religion

The disappearance of the art of writing in the late Mycenaean Age confined literary production entirely to poetry, which could easily be memorized. Yet in this restricted field much was accomplished. Ballads, sung by minstrels at the courts of kings and later by *rhapsodists* in the market-places, preserved the legends of the later Mycenaean Age with surprising fullness. Before the period ended, Homer and other bards had combined these older songs into a number of epics, of which two — the *Iliad* and *Odyssey* — rank among the world's greatest masterpieces.

During this period religion underwent significant developments. Without considering in detail the emerging religion of the Hellenic peoples, we may mention certain aspects of it as illustrating the fusion of Aegean and northern elements in Greece. This process had begun early, and while it is unknown precisely how far it had progressed at the beginning of the Middle Age, certain facts seem fairly clear. The later Greek gods had qualities borrowed from the northern Indo-European gods, and at the same time other characteristics adapted from the analogous deities of the primitive Aegean peoples. Thus, the Zeus worshiped in classical Greece was a blend of the northern sky-god and of the Minoan god of the double axe. Such goddesses as Athena, Artemis, Aphrodite, and Demeter seem to have been predominantly Aegean in origin and character. In addition, the Aegean peoples had apparently worshiped a number of semi-divine heroines of whom Atalanta and Ariadne are typical, and these cults, together with those of innumerable lesser nature-spirits (nymphs, fauns, satyrs, etc.), remained popular among the later Greeks. As some gods and goddesses became more popular and widely recognized, they tended to acquire definite personalities and characteristics and to be pictured as magnified human beings. Probably the great majority of the spirits to whom homage was offered were not personified, but the small minority of *anthropomorphic* divinities who thus emerged into prominence were later to serve as sources of inspiration to poets and artists, and as patron deities of the Greek states.

Evidently, a new belief regarding the future life was brought into Greece by the invading northerners, and with it came funeral rites previously unknown in the Aegean region. The newcomers cremated their dead and believed that the spirits of the departed went to the far-off land of Hades, whence there was no return. This system did not entirely displace the Aegean practice of inhumation, with its accompanying beliefs in ghosts and the worship of the dead. Indeed, these Aegean ideas later regained much of the ground which they had lost, and from them grew the cult of the heroes: great men of former ages who, because of their services to their fellowmen, were honored after death with temples, prayers, and sacrifices. Naturally, the citizens of the states which they had served during life paid them special regard and looked to them for protection. Typical demigods were Theseus at Athens, Adrastus at Argos, and Menelaus at Sparta.

Not only did local feeling produce lesser divinities in each region, but also profoundly altered the nature of the greater gods themselves. For one reason or another, each of them developed widely different attributes in different localities. Thus, in Arcadia — and nowhere else — Zeus had the additional name of Lycaeus (the wolf-god), and was worshiped with human sacrifices and cannibal feasts. Artemis of Ephesus was a fertility goddess who had nothing but the name in common with the virgin huntress of the continental Greeks. To the modern student this bewildering variety of names and rituals presents one of the most baffling, and at the same time fascinating, problems connected with the classical Greek religion.

In short, the Greek Middle Age was by no means a period of utter stagnation. It witnessed the beginnings of those arts, institutions, and habits of thought which were to characterize Greek culture in its later and more mature stages.

THE GREAT MIGRATION

The disorder produced by the invasions in the Greek peninsula caused a colonization movement which was not only a potent influence in the history of the classical Greeks, but also a factor in modern Greek history until the Lausanne Treaty of 1923. Great numbers of dispossessed Achaeans, Aeolians, Ionians, and, later, Dorians took possession of the Aegean islands and the coast of Asia Minor, establishing there a new Greece which in time was to be fully as important as the old. The date of this movement can only be given as sometime between 1125 and 900.

Conditions existing in the Aegean region at this time strongly favored Hellenic expansion. The chaos which had descended upon the Greek peninsula had also overwhelmed Asia Minor. About 1200, the Hittite Empire had gone down before the wave of invaders whose progress Ramses III had finally checked on the coast of Phoenicia. A few years later the destruction of Troy had removed the last strong power from northwestern Asia Minor. Minoan and Mycenaean influences had long been potent on the islands and eastern coast of the Aegean Sea. Hence, their populations culturally had much in common with the Greek immigrants and invaders.

Methods of Colonization

These earliest Greek colonies displayed several characteristics which were to mark all subsequent Hellenic colonial enterprises. Each group of settlers established a politically independent state, so that there was no more unity in the new Greece than in the old. Since the area which the invaders occupied never extended more than a few miles inland, the native Phrygians, Lycians, Carians, and Lydians still held the interior. The Asiatic Greeks later owed many misfortunes to this condition, for as soon as the inland people began to re-establish strong states, their kings were compelled to seek access to the sea by conquering the intruders who held the good harbors. In other respects, the colonization of the islands and the Asiatic coast did not follow any fixed pattern. Sometimes the Greeks came as peaceable settlers, who crowded into existing cities in numbers sufficient to Hellenize the language and customs of their Asiatic fellow citizens. In other instances they intervened in the dynastic quarrels of native princes and thereby secured land for settlements. Occasionally they stormed the cities, killing the men and marrying the women. They were a hybrid group when they arrived and they became still more mixed by intermarriage with the natives. Herodotus, writing in the fifth century, ridicules the race pride of the Asiatic Ionians of his day. He says:

> It is very foolish to say that these are more truly Ionian or better born than other Ionians. For a considerable part of them are Abantians from Euboea, who are not Ionians even in name, and mixed with these are Minyans from Orchomenos, Cadmeans, Dryopians, Phocian emigrants, Molossians, Pelasgians from Arcadia, Dorians from Epidaurus, and many other tribes. Indeed those who set out from the town hall at Athens, and deem themselves the best born of the Ionians, brought no wives with them to the settlement, but married Carian women whose parents they slew. And for kings some of them chose Lycian descendants of Glaucus the son of Hippolochos, and others Caucones of Pylos, descendants of Codrus the son of Melanthos, and some both.[1]

The civilization of Asiatic Greece was as thoroughly mixed as the blood of its inhabitants. Native religious ideas were adopted and the gods were worshiped in huge temples served by wealthy professional priesthoods of a kind not to be found in old Greece. Asiatic styles of clothing, arts and crafts, and household furniture were likewise adopted by Greek colonists. In later times the Ionians in particular were known for their luxurious standard of living, their trailing robes, and fine jewelry.

The Asiatic Greek Colonies

The Asiatic Greek settlements were divided into three groups: Aeolian, Ionian, and Dorian. The Aeolians occupied the northern section of the

[1] *History*, I, 146–47.

Metropolitan Museum

VASE SHOWING ARCHAIC GREEK COSTUME

Asiatic coast, together with the islands of Lesbos and Tenedos. In all, they founded twenty-three cities, of which the most important were Mytilene, Cumae, Notium, and Smyrna. The Asiatic Aeolians carefully preserved the legends of the Trojan War, and it is probable that Homer learned from them the songs from which his epics were compiled. Mytilene, the chief city of the island of Lesbos, was later noted for her wealth, the freedom accorded to her women, the brilliant literary circle which she produced, and the bitterness of the party strife which raged within her walls.

The central part of the Asiatic coast, with most of the Aegean islands, was settled by the mixed group who later called themselves Ionians. On the mainland, their chief cities were Ephesus, Miletus, Colophon, Phocaea, and later Halicarnassus and Smyrna, with Samos, Paros, Naxos, and Delos on the islands. Consciousness of a common origin and culture was strengthened by the establishment of religious festivals at which representatives from all Ionian cities were present. The most important of these were held at the Panionion (a temple of Poseidon near Miletus), at the temples of Apollo at Branchidae, Mycale, and Delos, and at the temple of Artemis at Ephesus.

The Dorians occupied the chain of southern islands which extended from the Peloponnesus to the Asiatic coast, including Melos, Thera, Crete, Carpathus, and Rhodes, and founded several cities on the Asiatic mainland. Like their Ionian kinsmen, they had a common center of worship at the temple of the Triopian Apollo.

For four centuries after its foundation, Asiatic Greece was to be the cultural leader of the Greek world. The location protected it from the worst of the disorders which for several centuries beset the continental Greeks. Its mixed population was virile and enterprising, and the material resources at their disposal were vastly greater than those of the old homeland. The Aegean islands greatly facilitated the movement of marine commerce, while the Asiatic cities were advantageously located at the seaward ends of trade routes leading into the interior. Hence, they could act as middlemen between the peoples of Asia Minor and the outside world. Ionian merchants and pirates sailed to all parts of the Mediterranean Sea, and these adventurers were soon followed by colonists. Wealth gained from trade and piracy, from the sale of manufactured goods, and from farming the rich soil of the Asiatic river valleys enabled them to produce comforts and luxuries which their kinsmen of the Greek peninsula could not afford. Contacts with the Orient made them familiar with both the material and the intellectual phases of the older cultures. The fine arts were to blossom sooner in Asiatic than in European Greece. The Greek alphabet was evolved in Ionia, and Ionian poets and philosophers were long pre-eminent in the Greek world in their respective callings.

The Homeric Epics

Any adequate discussion of the formative period of Greek civilization must devote considerable attention to the *Iliad* and the *Odyssey*. Their enduring popularity has but few parallels in the literary history of the world. Throughout the classical period of Greek history these poems held a position somewhat analogous to that of the Bible among Christian peoples. The Roman poet Virgil borrowed heavily from both when composing his immortal *Aeneid*, and through the *Aeneid*, they exercised an indirect influence upon Dante's *Divine Comedy*. Today, more than twenty-seven centuries after their composition, they are still included in the short list of the world's greatest poems. Aside from their unique literary interest, they are valuable sources of information for the study of early Greek culture. The charm of these epics is many-sided. A child may enjoy the story of Odysseus and the Cyclops, while the most exacting critics must admire their melodious cadences, finely drawn characters, vigorous narration, sustained grandeur, simple pathos, and occasional subtle humor. Thus their appeal is almost universal.

The Authorship

The Greeks with little hesitation assigned the authorship of the *Iliad* and *Odyssey* to Homer, a blind bard whose life was spent entirely in the new settlements on the eastern side of the Aegean Sea. His birthplace is unknown, and while many legendary accounts of his life survive, few of them can be trusted. It is, however, reasonably certain that his career fell within the ninth century, and for this reason his works may be treated as the crowning literary triumphs of the Middle Age. For a long time hypercritical modern scholars subjected the Homeric epics to a ruthless analysis which led some of them to deny the poet's existence, and to consign the Trojan War of which he sang to the realms of myth. As we have seen, archeological research has proved the story of the war surprisingly accurate, and has vindicated the essential accuracy of the Homeric description of society at the beginning of the Middle Age. In fact, modern scholarship feels little doubt that Homer existed, although both the *Iliad* and the *Odyssey* have been extensively revised by later minstrels, editors, and copyists.

Form and Language

The Homeric epics are written in dactyllic hexameter verse — a meter so admirably adapted to the telling of a long story that it has since become a favorite medium of expression for narrative poets. They were composed in the Ionic dialect, with numerous Aeolic forms. In all probability they were not committed to writing until centuries after their composition, but were handed down orally by a succession of bards, who made incidental changes or additions, leaving the main body of each poem unaltered. At present, each epic is divided into twenty-four books, a practice which appears to have been devised by later editors.

Neither singly nor collectively do these poems tell the whole story of the Trojan War. The *Iliad* narrates incidents from the latter part of the ninth year of the siege: the quarrel between Agamemnon and Achilles, the latter's refusal to take further part in the fighting, the death in battle of his friend Patroclus, Achilles' magic suit of armor, and the slaying of the Trojan hero Hector. It rings throughout with the clash of arms and the din of battle. This is to be expected, for the older songs upon which the poet depended were full of war and slaughter, and his audience enjoyed gory scenes. Yet there is much in them besides bloodshed. We see the Achaean chiefs in council, at the festive board, dominating an assembly, or mourning the dead. They are not a group of lay figures, but finely drawn individual characters. Each is given a personal touch which marks him as a living personality. The quick-tempered but warm-hearted Achilles, the haughty Agamemnon, the wise though garrulous old Nestor, the weak and kindly Menelaus, and the wily Odysseus: each is seen as a man of flesh and blood, with human virtues and failings. On the Trojan side we meet the noble Hector, his devoted wife Andromache, his worthless brother Paris, and his aged parents. Homer is not narrow in either sympathies or understanding. He can appreciate the heroism of Hector as well as that of Achilles, both of whom are doomed to die in a quarrel not their own. Achilles thus states the case to Agamemnon:

> I did not come here because of the brave Trojans; for they never wronged me. They did not steal my cattle or my horses; nor did they plunder fruitful Phthia. We came with you, Shameless One! To win glory against the Trojans for you and for Menelaus.[1]

Fatalism

A gloomy fatalism overshadows everything. The gods have determined the lots of Greeks and Trojans alike, and these are more often evil than good. So says Achilles when he tries to comfort Priam, whose son he has slain:

> Such is the thread which the gods spin for mortals — to live in woe while they are free from pain. Two chests stand before Zeus's door. In one is good, in the other, evil. When the Lord of the Thunderbolt gives a man something from each, then he has some good fortune and some evil; but if from the bad alone, then disgrace and misery pursue him over the earth.[2]

Death is the common lot of all. Again it is Achilles who speaks:

> You, too, my friend, must die. Why wail thus? Patroclus is dead, who was far better than you. And look at me, who am so tall and

[1] *Iliad*, I, 151–160; condensed.   [2] *Ibid.*, XXIV, 525–533.

fair and strong. My father was noble, and my mother is a goddess. Yet I too must yield to death and stubborn fate.[1]

Observation of Life and Nature

With all its brutal quarrels, its copious bloodshed, and its dark pessimism, the *Iliad*, nevertheless, has its brighter side. The author was a keen and understanding observer of life in all its phases. The best examples of this trait are found in the similes, which are inserted to give emphasis to his descriptions. They range from battles of boars and lions in the forests, or storms which send great trees crashing to the earth, to reapers at work in the fields, smiths at their forges, or children playing by the seashore. Again, there are occasional incidents and scenes which illustrate, not merely the customs of an age, but universal and unchanging human nature. The visit of Thetis to the workshop of the blacksmith god Hephaestus, and the god's bluff welcome to his benefactress, is a masterpiece of kindly realism which needs but slight modification to apply to any age or country. Again, nothing can surpass in vivid and sympathetic verisimilitude the description of Hector's meeting with Andromache on the walls of Troy, their baby's fright when approached by his armored and helmeted father, and the interview between the heroic pair.

The *Odyssey* relates the adventures of Odysseus on his homeward journey from Troy, his slaying of the suitors who were devouring his substance while they sought the hand of his wife, and his restoration to wife and kingdom. It belongs to a more peaceful environment than the *Iliad*, and from it the student of social and cultural history can obtain a convincing picture of the domestic life of the age with which the epics were concerned. The adventures of Odysseus were drawn from a store of folk-tales and legends which had no doubt been attached to the names of many other heroes before him. Examples of this tendency are his encounters with nymphs, goddesses, and the one-eyed, cannibal giant whose eye he bores out, or his meeting with the departed spirits at the gates of Hades. Through these and many other vicissitudes of shipwreck and peril he wins his goal by indomitable resolution, crafty guile, and divine favor. But no mere description can do justice to Homer. To be appreciated he must be read.

The Lesser Epics

The *Iliad* and *Odyssey* are the only survivors of a larger group of epics which were once extant, and which dealt with the legendary history of the

[1] *Ibid.*, XXI, 106–110.

Mycenaean Greeks. The others are known to us only by report and were of two cycles: the Theban and the Trojan. The former consisted of the *Oedipodeia*, *Thebaid*, and *Epigonoi*, and related the causes and incidents of the Theban wars. The latter included the *Cypria*, *Aethiopis*, *Little Iliad*, *Sack of Ilios*, *Nostoi*, and *Telegonia*. Collectively, they told the story of the Trojan War and the adventures of the participating heroes. Some of these poems were attributed to Homer, though he was not their author. Probably they were all composed in imitation of his works, and certainly most of them were of inferior merit. Not for over two centuries after Homer did the creative impulse in this field entirely fail. The chief value of these minor epics is that the Attic tragedians of the fifth century used them as a source for dramatic themes.

HOMERIC CIVILIZATION

As a background for his stories, and quite incidentally, Homer sketched the outlines of a society and civilization with convincing realism. Although he lived nearly three centuries after the age in which his heroes had played their parts, it is conceded that he used the older poems and ballads so intelligently and sympathetically that he scarcely ever attributed to the age of which he sang the customs of his own time. Accordingly, the Homeric epics may be relied upon to furnish a dependable picture of the civilization of the Heroic Age — a stage in the decadence of Mycenaean culture which existed just before the coming of the Dorians, and differing only in minor details from the civilization of the Greek Middle Age.

Homer's heroes lived in a profoundly aristocratic society. In each community there was a group of noble families who claimed descent from gods through their unions with mortal women. Many centuries later such stories were to scandalize the philosophers and Christian moralists, but at that time no discredit was attached to them. In reality, the superiority of the nobles over the other elements of society rested chiefly upon wealth and skill in war. They supplemented their incomes from agriculture by raiding their neighbors' possessions and by the entirely honorable calling of piracy. Theirs was a crude and brutal existence, and even in their more peaceful moments they were likely to prefer drinking, feasting, and hunting to more refined occupations.

Family Life and Economy

At home, the life of an Achaean lord was a mixture of barbaric splendor and rude simplicity. His house was of the megaron type, large and commodious, but plain. Earthen floors were the rule. Building and furniture were made by the noble and his servants. Each establishment included the head of the house, his wife and children, and a large staff of servants, both free and slave. Married sons often remained at home with their parents. The wife was bought from her father, and to be called "worth-many-cattle" was a compliment to a young girl. On the other hand, the bride brought her husband a dowry and she could refuse the advances of an unwelcome suitor. In addition to his legal wife, a noble often had one or more slave concubines, but the rights of the wife were carefully protected, and she was the mistress of the house. The entire household, including the master and mistress, worked. Odysseus, though a king, could plow, sow, reap, and was skilled in carpentry and several other trades. Penelope, Helen, and Arete, though queens, were constantly busy supervising the servants, spinning, weaving, and doing fancy-work. Slave women ground grain in the hand-mills and did the cooking, baking, and sewing.

Some crops were produced, but stock-raising was the chief source of wealth. Agricultural methods were crude. Half the land was allowed to lie fallow each year to regain its fertility, and it required three plowings with the primitive instruments in use to produce a crop of grain. Oxen served as draft animals and donkeys as burden-bearers. Horses were used only to draw chariots and as breeding-stock for mules. Huge herds of cattle, sheep, goats, and hogs were kept, for meat was a favorite article of diet. Odysseus had only twelve slaves at work in his fields while fifty herdsmen were required to tend his livestock. Money was unknown, and prices were set in kind, with cattle as the preferred unit of value.

Social Stratification

The lot of the slave was not especially hard. Old and trusted servants, like the swineherd Eumaeus or the nurse Euryclea, had much freedom and not a little authority. Eumaeus had a house and slave of his own and looked forward to the time when his master would provide him with a wife and a plot of ground. Usually the slaves were acquired as captives in war or bought from traders who had kidnaped them.

The lot of the freeman was sometimes less desirable than that of the slave. Skilled workers fared reasonably well, traveling from place to place in search of employment. Minstrels, who entertained the nobles at their feasts, were treated with marked consideration, and the same was true of soothsayers. But behind the brilliant pageantry of Homer's poems we occasionally catch glimpses of a large group of unfortunates for whom life was an endless and losing struggle with want. A class of small land-holders existed who were often in need, and to be a servant of one of them was considered the most wretched lot on earth. Even lower were the homeless wanderers who alternately begged their bread and found odd jobs as laborers. Their only reward was sufficient food when employed, and they were in constant danger of being seized and sold into slavery. Rags, hunger, and contemptuous treatment from the more fortunate classes were, under ordinary circumstances, all that they could expect.

In the homes of the great an openhanded hospitality reigned. A stranger of respectable appearance might be entertained for a long period without the host's taking the trouble to inquire his name. Plentiful feasts of roast meat, bread, and wine were served, and as the wine cup passed from hand to hand a minstrel would chant ballads commemorating the great deeds of the heroes of old or the adventures of the gods.

Government

So aristocratic a society would naturally be regulated by a government of the same character. The word *basileus*, which we commonly translate as "king," was applied impartially to every great landholder. Each state had many kings, one of whom exercised a loose primacy over the rest. He might claim divine ancestry and absolute power, but these were meaning-less echoes from an earlier age. In fact, he owed whatever power he pos-sessed to his wealth, physical strength, courage, and wisdom. When he was too old to perform his duties efficiently, he might, like Laertes, the father of Odysseus, abdicate and retire to the country. In war, the king (to use the word in its modern sense) commanded the army, over which in actual combat he had absolute power. In peace, he presided over certain religious rites and assumed a leading part in the formulation of state poli-cies. There was little or no legislation, as the law was handed down from father to son as a sacred tradition. But when questions such as peace or war were to be settled, the king was bound by tradition to consult the no-bles who formed his council. After he and they had arrived at a decision, the free warriors of the state were summoned to an assembly to hear it; but they did not debate the issue, and had little influence over the ruling class. Here, then, we have the three elements in the government of a Homeric state: king, council, and assembly, a type of government common to many other Indo-European peoples. Its importance in the history of Greek polit-ical thought would be difficult to overestimate, for, although the system underwent many changes as republics succeeded monarchies, the division of governmental agencies into three parts analogous to those of the Homeric state was, for a long time, carefully preserved.

State Functions and Welfare

Protection from external enemies and propitiation of the gods were the chief functions of the state. Vengeance for personal wrongs devolved upon the injured man or his kinsfolk, but the resulting feuds could be averted by the payment of compensation. The state was just beginning to concern itself with the administration of justice, as indicated by the following scene from the "Shield of Achilles" in the *Iliad*:

> A fierce dispute had arisen between two men about the price of a man slain. One appealed to the people, saying that he had paid all; while the other denied that he had received anything. Both wished the matter to be judged. Partisans encouraged both sides with noisy shouts. The heralds silenced the crowd. The reverend elders sat around in a solemn circle on polished stones, holding the wands of the loud-voiced heralds in their hands. They waved these as they heard the pleadings of each side. Two talents of gold lay in their midst, to be taken by the one who should prove his cause righteous.[1]

The amount involved, at least 115 pounds of gold, worth at present prices about $84,000, seems absurdly large, though not when compared with other sums mentioned in the epics. The procedure is clear — it was a damage suit, and not a criminal action. Each party posted a sum equal to the amount claimed by the plaintiff and the winner took all. Usually, however, a man's best protection was his own strength and numerous kinsmen.

In spite of the frequency of wars — many of them mere cattle-lifting expeditions — armies were poorly organized and military tactics were practically unknown. The nucleus of each army was a few heavily armed chiefs, who in peace formed the council of the ruler, and their immediate dependants. Armament varied, with the small shield, helmet, corselet, and greaves forming the usual defensive equipment of a well-armed soldier. His offensive weapons consisted of two spears — either for throwing or thrusting — a sword, and a dagger. The metal parts of these weapons were of bronze. Most of the soldiers were poorly armed and the bulk of the fighting was done by the heavily armed chiefs. War chariots, each occupied by a driver and a warrior, were in frequent use. Sieges were rarely more than blockades or ambuscades in which starvation or surprise attacks were relied upon to reduce strongholds.

[1] *Iliad*, XVIII, 497–508.

Religion: the Greek Gods

The loose, inefficient governments on earth were reflected in the easy-going government of heaven. We have seen some aspects of the religion of the Homeric Age, but the subject deserves further consideration. As the religion of the epics represented a stage in the evolution from the beliefs of the Mycenaean to those of the classical Greeks, it was not exactly like either. To Homer, the number of gods seemed infinite. The lesser ones — spirits of trees, streams, rocks, sea, or mountains — were in some cases mere impersonal forces, but in others had become personalized and acquired definite human or animal forms. It is possible that these lesser divinities seemed much more important to the masses than to the aristocrats whose viewpoint dominates the epics. At any rate, the religion of the *Iliad* and *Odyssey* is largely the worship of the anthropomorphic Olympian gods, so called from the fact that they were supposed to dwell upon lofty Mount Olympus, in northern Thessaly. Homer thought of the Olympian divinities as a family with definite mutual relationships and clear-cut personalities.

At the head of the family was *Zeus*, "the father of gods and men." He punished those who offended him by hurling them to the lower world with his thunderbolts, and exercised a loose authority over the other members of the group. His wife, *Hera*, was a virtuous but jealous matron, who chafed under the many infidelities of her husband and tried to take vengeance upon his mistresses and their children. *Hermes* was the messenger of the gods; *Apollo* was the divine archer and the god of music, prophecy, and medicine; and *Artemis*, Apollo's twin sister, was also an archer and a huntress. *Hephaestus* was the lame smith of the gods, who constructed wonderful works, but excited the laughter of the other deities as he hobbled about. *Hestia* was the goddess of the fire that sparkled on the hearth. *Ares* was a brutal god of predatory warfare who occupies a poor place in Homer's poems. *Aphrodite* was the goddess of love and the heroine of many an amorous adventure with gods and men. Second only to Zeus in power and importance was *Athena*, the virgin goddess born from the forehead of Zeus, and patroness of those arts which promote civilization. She was also a warrior, but always fought in good causes and hence enjoyed a respect which was denied Ares. *Demeter*, goddess of the earth, was the spirit through whose help grew the grain which furnished man's food. *Hades* was the god of the underworld, and *Poseidon* of the sea.

None of these divinities were awe-inspiring or aloof like the Hebrew Yahweh. Neither individually nor collectively were they omnipotent,

and except for Athena and Apollo, they could not even foretell the
future. Although immortal, they could feel pain, and in the Trojan War
Aphrodite was wounded by the Greek hero Diomedes. Their government
of the universe was very lax. In the Trojan War, some of each side in the
earthly struggle had partisans among the gods, while Zeus vainly endeavored to enforce strict neutrality upon his scheming and unruly family.
Their moral standards were, of course, those of their worshipers. Hermes,
in particular, was an accomplished thief, and falsehood and deceit were
prevalent on Olympus. They were capricious and revengeful, and punished insults or neglect on the part of their human worshipers with plague,
famine, or other misfortunes.

Such as they were, they were powerful to help or hurt mankind, and
one had to worship them. Fortunately, all of them could easily be approached by personal prayer, without the aid of professional priests. The
father acted as priest for the household, and the king for the state. Prayer
and sacrifice usually went together, for the whole act constituted a contract between the god and his worshiper, by which a favor was exchanged
for a sacrifice. Thus, when Agamemnon insulted the priest Chryses, the
latter prayed to Apollo:

> Lord of the Silver Bow, hear me! If ever you were pleased with the
> offerings which I made you; if ever I burned the fat of bulls and goats
> for you, grant me this favor: let your unerring arrows avenge my
> tears upon the Greeks! [1]

As a sacrifice was a gift made to a god by a worshiper, it might be almost
any piece of valuable property. The commonest form of the rite was that
of killing an animal and burning part of it on an altar in the god's honor
with an appropriate prayer. As a rule, the god's share of the sacrificed
animal was not large, and consisted of bones and fat, with only a little
meat. The remainder of the carcass served the worshiper, his family and
friends, as a feast. In fact, the Greeks so often offered to the gods parts of
animals slain for food that the same word came to be used for a sacrifice
and for the act of butchering an animal for ordinary consumption.

Religion, to the Homeric Greek, was a means of solving the problems
of this world whereby one avoided calamity and gained prosperity. Its
ethical value was confined to a narrow field, for while the gods punished
heinous crimes like the murder of parents or wrongs done to guests, they
were blind to ordinary human failings. Divine help was confined entirely
to mundane affairs, since the ordinary man had no hope of happiness after
death. The common lot of souls in the hereafter was to lead a cheerless,

[1] *Iliad*, I, 37–42; condensed.

shadowy existence in the subterranean realms of Hades in a semi-conscious state. By drinking fresh blood, the shades could be restored temporarily to conscious life, but they soon sank back again. The ghost of Achilles thus expressed the common opinion of the world beyond to Odysseus:

> Do not try to comfort me about death, noble Odysseus. I would rather live on earth as the hired servant of a man without inheritance or resources than to reign over all who have ever died.[1]

But a few of the departed spirits received either better or worse treatment than the majority. Perpetrators of terrible crimes, such as Tantalus who had killed his son Pelops and tried to feed his cooked flesh to the gods, suffered eternal torture in the subterranean prison of Tartarus. At the other extreme was Menelaus, to whom the gods promised an eternity of happiness in the far-off Islands of the Blessed because he had married Helen, the daughter of Zeus.

Moral Standards

In spite of the fact that their gods gave only the most shadowy sanctions to moral living, Homer's heroes had a definite moral code. It was suited to the habits of the warrior aristocracy, for it stressed positive rather than negative virtues. The qualities which made a man respected were bravery, energy, wisdom, and generosity. As in most backward civilizations, a sharp distinction was made between those within the clan or family of an individual and those outside it. Toward kinsfolk one had to show kindliness, loyalty, and co-operation, for he would need the same treatment from them in the future. Hospitality to the passing stranger was an act of kindness and also of wisdom, as who knew how soon the host himself would need similar aid? As a rule, there was no obligation to members of other groups except in the case of guest-friendship. Toward guest-friends a host owed many of the privileges of relatives, but toward others he could gratify his predatory instincts without scruple. He needed no excuse other than his own will to plunder their homes, to steal their women, their livestock and other possessions, and to leave whole districts in ruins. Such rapine was, indeed, the most honorable means of acquiring wealth. Personal faults were regarded with great tolerance, provided they did not impair social usefulness or prove irritating to neighbors. Lying was under most circumstances hardly considered a vice and, under many conditions, might even be a virtue. Odysseus was a fluent and convincing prevaricator, to whose fabrications even the goddess Athena listened with open

[1] *Odyssey*, XI, 488 ff.

admiration. Yet the frank Achilles not only told the truth himself, but expected to hear it from others. In spite of the quantities of wine the Achaean heroes consumed, drunkenness was rare, and other forms of self-indulgence were not common. Affection toward parents, wives, and families was as prevalent as in most modern homes. Such maxims of conduct, though based upon secular motives, adequately served their purpose.

12

The Greek Renaissance:[1] Economic

Revival and Colonization

AN ECONOMIC CRISIS

THE CESSATION of the northern invasions in the tenth century made possible a return to relatively orderly conditions in the Greek peninsula. Wars became less frequent, property was safer, and productive enterprise was freer from interruption than at any time since the Mycenaean Age. The population, which had been toughened by centuries of hardship and danger and had learned to live under the most rigorous conditions, now began to increase and to fill the half-depopulated land.

Overpopulation and Poverty: Hesiod

In an agricultural country a rapid growth of population is certain to cause drastic economic changes, for the land must be more efficiently exploited to feed the increasing number. All the more fertile land was quickly occupied, and men began to lay out farms on rocky slopes formerly devoted to forest and pasture. Many family estates were divided and subdivided, until only in good years would they produce enough food to supply their owners. Pastureland became scarcer and more inaccessible. By the end of the ninth century, large parts of the Greek world on both sides of the Aegean were in the grip of an economic crisis which was to last for

[1] The term "renaissance" is used, in the present and succeeding chapters, merely to emphasize the parallel between the age under discussion and the fourteenth and fifteenth centuries A.D. in western Europe. It is not meant to imply that the new Greek civilization was a "rebirth" of its Aegean predecessor. Its literal accuracy might be difficult to defend in either instance.

the better part of three centuries and to exert a decisive influence upon later Greek history.

It is fortunate that we have what appears to be an authentic record of a case from the early part of the period — the family history of the poet Hesiod. Dios, Hesiod's father, had been a citizen of the Asiatic Greek city of Cyme, which he had to leave because of poverty. After trying seafaring, Dios settled on a farm in the Boeotian village of Ascra, near Thespiae. When he died, his elder son, Perses, bribed the magistrates to give him far more than his share of the paternal estate, leaving the smaller and poorer part to Hesiod. Later, Perses squandered much of his ill-gotten gains in strife and dissipation, and Hesiod wrote the *Works and Days* to teach profitable husbandry to the spendthrift. The tone of the poem is one of dour pessimism. Hesiod's farm is large enough to employ a few slaves besides the owner, but too small to afford more than a bare subsistence in return for incessant labor and hard-fisted thrift. The farmer who would avoid want and debt must be up early and down late, planning his work with care, foreseeing his future needs, and resting only for short periods in the hottest month of summer and the coldest of winter. Mindful of his own family troubles, our poet advises landowners to rear only one son.[1] A farmer must live to be very old in order to accumulate property enough for two.

Hesiod felt that the lot of man had grown steadily worse throughout the ages. Zeus first brought evil into the world through the creation of woman. Since then the race has passed through the ages of gold, silver, bronze, and the Heroic Age. His own age was that of iron, when "men rest not ever from toil and grief by day and destruction by night."[2] Throughout the poem he alludes bitterly to the greed of the aristocrats who give unfair judgments in return for bribes and on whom the vengeance of the gods will fall in punishment for their evil deeds. Hesiod expects no improvement in conditions. Wrong and injustice will increase until shame and justice desert the world, and Zeus destroys mankind. The idea that one's own age is one of degeneracy is common to much of the world's literature, but Hesiod's specific allegations show that his own times were badly out of joint. Population was too large for the country under a system which allowed the noble families to monopolize the best land. On the poorer soils, the repeated division of the estates among heirs reduced many to poverty. We shall consider Hesiod again in other connections.

The end of the eighth century found Sparta also suffering from an excess of population. A century later, Athens was in a similar plight, and there

---

[1] *Works and Days*, I, 376.   [2] *Ibid.*, II, 176-177.

is evidence of the same condition in many other places. Much of Greece was overpopulated, but the term, we must remember, is purely relative. A thousand savages may starve on an area which would support a million civilized men in comfort, and Greece later supported a much larger population than the one which distressed her in the eighth and seventh centuries. The trouble lay in faulty social organization and inefficient exploitation of resources; but the immediate consequences were none the less real — poverty, oppression, and unrest.

Varied Reactions to New Conditions

When the people of a country are confronted with an entirely new and unaccustomed set of conditions, individuals and communities may be expected to react in a variety of ways. The Greek landed aristocracies did not, as a rule find the new conditions unfavorable to them, and they often profited considerably from the distress of their fellow citizens. They limited the size of their families, made profitable marriages, participated in the spoils of war and piracy, and gained what they could from their influence in government by taking bribes and administering the laws in their own favor. Having a surplus of food, they lent it to less fortunate neighbors, and when the debtors could not pay, annexed their lands or sold the owners into slavery. Thus, their wealth and power grew incessantly, enabling them to overthrow the monarchies under which they lived and to domineer over the other classes of society. The lower classes had to meet the crisis in various ways. Insolvent debtors, illegitimate sons, and other unfortunates wandered about as traders, pirates, and mercenary soldiers. In the latter half of the eighth century the city-state governments began to organize expeditions of their poorer citizens to found colonies in other lands, and each colony was swollen by exiles whom poverty, crime, revolution, or foreign conquest had driven from their homes. Thus, the phenomenal expansion of the Greek people in the eighth, seventh, and sixth centuries was a direct result of the need for more land. Sometimes, as in the case of Sparta, the whole community solved the problem by conquering a neighboring state and reducing its inhabitants to serfdom. If a small landholder had sufficient capital, he might plant his land in grapes and olives, which yielded much more per unit of area than grain. Lastly, the poor might devote their spare time to manufacturing useful articles for sale, and thus after a time become full-time tradesmen or merchants.

There was, however, a large class who, through stupidity, conservatism, or ill-fortune, did none of these things. They continued to follow the customs of their ancestors, fell into debt, and died tenants or slaves. In every city there was a seething mass of human misery, frantic with suffering, and ready for any desperate blow against their oppressors. The class hatred resulting from this condition may be counted as one of the most important facts in Greek history, for in many places it persisted until the Greeks fell under the domination of Macedonia or Rome. Nothing better explains the bitterness of political strife in such cities than the misery of the masses, and the realization by the upper classes that they dwelt above a social volcano which might erupt at any time. But this phase of the subject must be reserved for a later chapter. In the meantime let us examine in somewhat more detail the means by which large classes of the Greek people overcame their misfortune.

Greek Colonization

As might be expected under the circumstances, the most energetic or adventurous members of the depressed classes of Greek society sought homes in foreign lands. While the more productive districts of their homeland were either too crowded or in the control of aristocratic landlords, there were broad areas of rich but thinly populated land on the shores of the Mediterranean and Black seas which offered them the livelihood which they lacked at home. Later, it was commercial opportunities that encouraged the planting of colonies.

Exploration

Intelligent colonization must be preceded by exploration and the accumulation of geographic knowledge. For the Greeks, this service was performed during the ninth and eighth centuries by a host of adventurers, traders, and pirates — much as Portuguese, Spanish, and English colonization in Africa and America was preceded by the explorations of Vasco da Gama, Columbus, Drake, and Sir Walter Raleigh. Nearly all the names of these Greek adventurers have been lost, but the presence of Greek pottery of the ninth century in Etruscan tombs proves that about the year 800 the old Aegean trade route to the west had been reopened. Homer knew of Sicily and the Strait of Messina, although he was ignorant of Spain and Gaul. Before the year 600, Ionian navigators had reached the Spanish coast. Nearer home, the shores of Thrace and Macedonia had been known from prehistoric times. Even the Black Sea had been visited by Mycenaean sailors, as we may infer from the legend of the Argonauts, but in the ninth century Homer knew so little about it that he believed the home of the Cimmerians (the modern Crimea) to be in the western Mediterranean. Wild stories were current regarding the perils of the Inhospitable Sea (*Pontos Axeinos*), yet in the eighth century, hardy adventurers were again sailing their ships along the track of the *Argo*, and the wealth which they found drew others to what soon was called the Hospitable Sea (*Pontos Euxinos*). The southern shore of the Mediterranean had been visited by pirates from Crete and Greece ever since Mycenaean times, and about 650 B.C. intercourse with Egypt was greatly facilitated by the fact that King Psamtik, founder of the Twenty-Sixth Dynasty, enlisted an army of Ionian and Carian mercenaries to aid him in expelling the Assyrians. The northwest coast of Africa was closed to the Greeks by the Phoenician colonies of Carthage and Utica, and the shores of Syria and Palestine by the Phoenicians themselves, backed by their Assyrian or Chaldean suzerains. Nevertheless, broad stretches of land awaited civilized settlers.

The Aegean Colonies

The colonies which spread the Greek tongue, customs, and commercial products over so large a part of the Mediterranean world were the work of comparatively few city-states of old Greece. The most important were Miletus, Chalcis of Euboea, Corinth, and Megara. The Achaeans of the Peloponnesus, the Spartans, the Locrians, and a number of others participated to a lesser extent.

Nearest and most attractive of the fields open to Greek colonists was the northern shore of the Aegean Sea. Just east of the coast of Thessaly lies a three-pronged peninsula, the surface of which is interspersed with fertile plains, and whose coast is indented with small harbors. Before 700 B. C., Chalcis of Euboea had established colonies so thickly over this region that it became known as the Chalcidice. Here also Corinth founded Potidea. Farther east lay the island of Thasos, with its gold and silver mines. This rich prize became a colony of the island of Paros and the home of the poet Archilochos. Other colonies, founded by various cities, were planted along the coast of Thrace. Of these, Amphipolis, a late Athenian project, was destined to attain the greatest prosperity. The northern Aegean coast produced grain, fish, wine, timber, slaves, and gold.

As soon as commerce with the Black Sea region became important, settlement began along the Hellespont, the Sea of Marmora, and the Bosporus. At the mouth of the Hellespont, Mytilene founded Sestos on the European side, and Miletus planted Abydos on the opposite shore.

Farther east, on the Asiatic coast, Miletus established Cyzicus in the early seventh century. On the Asiatic coast at the mouth of the Bosporus, Megara founded Chalcedon, a purely agricultural colony which never attained great prosperity. Some years later, however, when commerce had assumed greater importance, the Megarians recognized the supreme importance of the site on the opposite side of the strait. There they founded

FEATURES OF RURAL LIFE IN THE SIXTH CENTURY B.C.
Scene from a black-figured cup

Byzantium, which was to become one of the world's great cities. Not only did the new city have a splendid harbor, but the swift current which flowed through the strait from the Black Sea beat against the European shore, forcing ancient shipping, coming toward the Aegean, to run into the Byzantine port, and affording the citizens an inexhaustible supply of tunny-fish for domestic consumption and export. Nearly a thousand years after its foundation, the Roman emperor Constantine changed the name of Byzantium to Constantinople.

Black Sea Colonies

From the Bosporus, a natural step led the Greeks into the Black Sea. With few exceptions, all the colonies on its coast were founded by Miletus whose economic empire included the whole region. On the southern shore, the chief settlement was at Sinope, which soon became important enough to send out colonies of her own. Amisus, Trapezus (Trebizond), Phasis, and Dioscurias were also Milesian foundations. Like Miletus herself, these colonies were located where trade routes from the interior reached the coast. All grew into important cities, exporting timber, fruit, iron, slaves, and manufactured products from inland Asia.

The northern shore of the Black Sea offered other attractions to settlers. The climate, it is true, was harsh and cold — utterly unlike that of the Aegean region. But the black soil of the southern Russian plain has always produced fabulously rich harvests of grain, and the rivers were natural trade routes over which raw products could be brought hundreds of miles from the interior. The sea afforded a large supply of fish. Near the mouth of the Bug River the Milesians founded Olbia, and on the eastern side of the Crimea, at the outlet of the Sea of Azov, Panticapaeum. At the mouth of the Don they established Tanais, the most distant of their colonies. The western shore was dotted with smaller cities of Milesian foundation — Tyras, Istros, etc. These settlements on the edge of the southern Russian steppes were of little or no cultural value, for their rugged environment precluded the development of the characteristic Greek artistic and intellectual activities. Yet they were of enormous importance in the Greek economic system, for they instituted the Black Sea grain trade. They either raised or bought immense quantities of wheat and barley which they exported to the Aegean cities in return for olive oil, wine, and manufactured products. From these bases traders carried manufactured goods far northward, and brought back gold, amber, and other valuable merchandise. Ionian (later, Athenian) pottery and other products have been found as far north as the headwaters of the Oder River. The discovery of a bountiful food-supply was important to the cultural development of sixth-century Ionia and fifth-century Athens. Miletus alone founded ninety colonies on the coast of the Black Sea.

Naucratis and Cyrenaica

Throughout the Middle Age the Greeks had never lost touch with Egypt. The eighth century saw Ionian pirates harrying the Nile Delta and seeking employment as mercenaries under Egyptian princes. Before 700, Miletus had established a post on one of the distributaries of the Nile — the "Fort of the Milesians." After the rise of the Twenty-Sixth Dynasty, the favor of King Psamtik and his successors allowed the "Fort" to become a city — Naucratis, although Miletus did not monopolize this colony. Samos, Aegina, and other naval powers had quarters there, and individuals came from all over the Greek world. King Amasis (569–525) enhanced the importance of Naucratis by compelling all Greeks who landed in his country to use it as a port of entry and by concentrating all the trade between Egypt and the Greek world in its harbor. The king was a consistent phil-Hellene, whose favors to Greeks were the theme of many stories. Naucratis throve. The influence which Egypt exerted upon the Greeks through this strange city was profound. Hellenic workmen learned there the technical processes which made possible their great progress in industry and the fine arts. Merchants and travelers from the Aegean toured the Nile Valley, where they marveled at the huge monuments and at the people's pretensions to wisdom. From guides and priests they gathered some facts and much fiction concerning Egypt's past, together with a smattering of mathematics, medicine, and astronomy. Greek philosophers from Thales to Plato were to find in Egypt a potent intellectual stimulus. Miletus long enjoyed a privileged position there, as she did on the shores of the Black Sea.

About five hundred miles northwest of the Nile Delta, the African coast rounds off into a huge promontory. It has fertile soil and enough rain in regions near the coast to nourish field crops and trees. For some distance inland the back country supports grass for pasturage. The Greeks had long known the spot, but not until about 630 was the city of Cyrene founded

Brown Brothers

TRADE AT CYRENE
King Arcesilaus superintending the weighing and the sale of goods.

near there by the Dorians from the island of Thera. Successive waves of immigrants from other parts of Greece and the islands brought in so many people that by 500 the whole coast of the promontory had been settled. Although grain and livestock enriched the settlers, the distinctive Cyrenean product was *silphium*, a plant which modern botanists have failed to identify, but which was used as a medicine and as a flavoring for food. For many centuries its exportation was a government monopoly, and a spirited local vase painting shows King Arcesilaus seated under a canopy overseeing the weighing of the precious plant while servants stow it aboard ship.

Italy, Sicily, and the Ionian Seacoast Colonized

Exploration of the Italian and Sicilian coasts was followed by the foundation of colonies. Indeed, several of the Italian Greek cities claimed to have been founded shortly after the Trojan War — an assertion which in a few cases may preserve the memory of actual Mycenaean settlements. Archeological evidence usually disproves it.

The stepping-stones between the Greek peninsula and Italy were the western islands of Zacynthos, Leucas, Cephallenia, and Corcyra. At Corcyra, Dorian Corinth (about 735) displaced an earlier Chalcidian colony and founded one of her own. Because of its strategic position, this city was to play an important part in early Greek history. Her relations with Corinth were usually unfriendly, and she incurred an unenviable reputation for the bitterness of the political strife within her walls. Corcyra and Corinth co-operated in founding on the near-by coast of Epirus (whose population was not really Greek) the colonies of Apollonia, Epidamnus, Anactorium, and others.

Although the Adriatic shore of Italy was not suited to Greek colonization because of the scarcity of good harbors, the western shores of the Ionian Sea abounded with favorable sites. The seventh century witnessed the foundation of an almost continuous line of Greek cities from Tarentum (Taras) at the top of the "heel" of the peninsula to Rhegium at the end of the "toe." Tarentum, which claimed to be a Spartan colony, contained fertile land for the raising of sheep and her fine harbors encouraged shipping and commerce. She became the most prosperous city on Italian soil and her manufactures of metal-work, cloth, pottery, and other articles did much to introduce civilization among the Oscan peoples of southern Italy. Farther west was a group of cities which claimed to have been founded by the Achaeans of the Peloponnesus: Metapontum, Sybaris, and Croton. Their primary importance was agricultural, for they were located in fertile though malarial lowlands, but their geographical position soon made them commercial centers as well. The perils of the Strait of Messina made it convenient for shippers to unload goods at these points and carry them across to the coast of the Tyrrhenian Sea. There Sybaris founded Laos, Skidros, and, farther north, Posidonia, and connected them with a practicable road. Croton did likewise, with Terina and Temesa as her northern termini. To these points came Etruscan traders to buy imported wares. Sybaris, in particular, ruled over a large group of native Italian tribes and Greek cities and her name has ever since been a synonym for wealth and luxury. About 510 B.C. rivalry over these two routes destroyed Sybaris. The city was taken and razed by the Crotonians. South of Croton was Locri, a colony founded by the Greek Locrians about 680. She long remained a conservative community, and Pindar [1] cites her as an example of good morals for the rest of the Hellenic world. Archeological evidence, however, indicates that before 500 she too had conquered a strip of land reaching across the peninsula of Bruttium, and was participating in the lucrative overland trade. Posidonia deserves separate mention. Located on a fertile, though malarial site like that of her mother-city, she was never important in the ancient world, but her huge and well-preserved Doric temple of Poseidon is one of the best-preserved monuments of Greek architecture.

Even earlier than the Dorians and Achaeans, the Chalcidians had begun to colonize the Italian coast. About 740, in conjunction with some other Ionians and a Boeotian group called *Graioi*, they founded Cyme (Cumae), just north of the Bay of Naples. The new settlement prospered from the beginning. It was too far from the Greeks of the Ionian seacoast to fear their rivalry, and not for a century and a half after its foundation did the Etruscans become a source of danger. Cyme's manufactured wares, together with those imported from old Greece, found a ready market among the Italian natives, and with the merchandise went the intellectual products of the Greek world. Early Roman legend frequently refers to contacts with Cyme, through which the Romans probably received their knowledge of the alphabet and of many Greek gods and goddesses with rituals for their worship. Apparently the Graian element in the population furnished the Romans with the names which they were later to apply to the whole Hellenic people — *Graii* or *Graeci*. Cyme soon sent out colonies of her own. On the near-by bay, with some Athenians, she settled Neapolis (new town), now Naples. Before long she seized the sites which commanded the Strait, founding Rhegium on the Italian shore and Zancle on the Sicilian side. Cyme was the northernmost Greek colony on the western coast of Italy. Above it the Etruscan sphere of influence prohibited further expansion.

Colonies in Sicily, Gaul, and Spain

In Sicily the Chalcidians began colonization by founding Naxos (near Mount Etna), Catana, and Leontini. Zancle founded Himera, the only

[1] *Olympian Ode*, X, XI.

Greek colony on the northern coast. The Ionian colonies were concentrated about the northeastern corner of the island. Not long after 650, so many Messenian exiles crowded into Zancle that the city's name was changed to Messene.

The Dorians undertook the colonization of the southern and southeastern coasts. Corinth led the way about 735, when the same expedition which founded Corcyra occupied the small island of Ortygia and established the city of Syracuse. With an excellent harbor and a copious water-supply from the fountain of Arethusa, the city soon outgrew its island and spread to the neighboring Sicilian mainland. The Sicel natives were reduced to serfdom, and the Syracusan aristocrats (*Geomoroi* or "Sharers of the Land") became the lords of large estates. Later settlers built up manufacturing and commerce. Throughout its stormy history, Syracuse was to be the chief city of Greek Sicily. On the southern shore of Sicily a mixed colony in which Rhodians predominated was founded at Gela. From Gela, in turn, emigrants went forth and established Acragas, farther west on the same coast. It became the second city in importance in Greek Sicily.

Three sources of trouble were to harass the Sicilian Greeks throughout their history: party strife at home, the Sicel and Sican natives, and the Carthaginians. Since the Greek settlements formed only a narrow fringe along the southern and eastern coasts of the island, the hills behind them were full of barbarian natives, whose hostility at times caused serious trouble. Furthermore, the Carthaginians saw themselves deprived of good markets and fertile fields which they longed to recover. Among the Greeks themselves, city fought against city and class against class, with even greater bitterness than in the homeland. Yet in the face of all these obstacles, the Sicilian Greeks prospered.

Only the Ionians undertook to colonize the coast of Gaul and Spain. About 600, Massalia (Marseilles) was founded near the mouth of the Rhone River by Phocaean colonists whose leader married the daughter of a native Ligurian chief. Within a century, Massalia was sending out colonies of her own: Hemeroscopion, Rhode (Rosas), and Emporiae (Amporias) in Spain, and Agathe (Agde), Antipolis (Antibes), Monoikos (Monaco), and Nicaea (Nice) in Gaul and Italy. Massalia herself, situated at the end of a trade route which went by way of the Rhone and Saône to the Seine Valley and the English Channel, became an *entrepôt* for tin, amber, furs, slaves, and other northern products. Her people introduced the culture of the grape and olive into southern Gaul, and from them the natives learned many of the arts of civilization.

Relations Between Colony and Metropolis

So much colonization over so long a period resulted in the evolution of a traditional method to be followed in the foundation of a new settlement. The founding city sent to Delphi to secure the advice of Apollo about the enterprise. When his approval had been gained, a noble of the mother-city was chosen to lead the emigrants; or, if it was itself a colony, its own mother-city might provide a founder for them. Fire from the altars of the mother-city (*metropolis*) and some earth from her soil were carried along. On arriving at the destined site the leader (*oikistes*, founder) assigned land to the colonists, established the laws and religious rites of the mother-city among them, and set the machinery of government in motion. After death he would be worshiped by the colony which he had founded.

The relations between the metropolis and the colony varied widely with circumstances. At all times the cultural bonds were close and intimate. Their people spoke the same dialect, worshiped the same gods, and had similar institutions. Usually the two cities were on terms of intimate friendship, though politically the great majority of Greek colonies were entirely independent. The chief exceptions to this rule were the Athenian *cleruchies* — military settlements founded to hold conquered territory, in which the colonists retained their Athenian citizenship. The colonies of Sinope were also dependencies of their metropolis and had to pay her tribute. This tendency of colonies to strike out for themselves made it impossible for important colonizing centers like Chalcis, Miletus, or Corinth ever to build colonial empires in the sense that Portugal, Spain, the Netherlands, or Great Britain were to do. Hugging the coasts, ill-at-ease when out of sight of the sea, the Greeks could never Hellenize whole countries in the way that Rome was later to Latinize Gaul and Spain. Their mission seemed rather to be that of acting as a stimulus to the development of other civilizations.

COMMERCE AND INDUSTRY

If thus far only incidental attention has been paid to the expansion of commerce and industry in the Greek world, it is because colonization preceded and largely stimulated any important development in either field. The time was now favorable to the growth of commerce. Shipping facilities were improving rapidly. Naval architects had begun to differentiate between the cargo boat, built for capacity rather than speed and moved principally by sails, and the warship, which was long and slim, armed with a bronze ram, and moved in crucial moments by oars alone. The sailing season, which in Hesiod's time had included only the months of August and September, now began in March and ended in October. Devices like the anchor added to the mariner's safety, and when necessary he could steer a course by the sun and stars. Increasing geographical knowledge disclosed accessible lands with large surpluses of grain and other raw materials which the Greeks needed, and in exchange for which the inhabitants were willing to take wine, oil, pottery, arms, trinkets, and textiles.

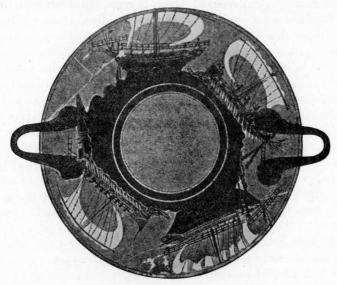

GREEK WARSHIPS AND MERCHANTMEN

Even in 500 B.C., we must remember, pirates, enemy states, storms, and unknown coasts made sailing hazardous, but land transport was even more arduous and more expensive. Greek roads were always wretchedly poor, and the chaotic political condition of much of the country added other dangers to land travel. Hence, whenever possible, travel and transportation were by water.

Early Hellenic commerce, like that of Elizabethan England, was often difficult to distinguish from piracy. Phoenician sea power was declining as a result of attacks of the Assyrians and Chaldeans upon the cities of the Phoenician homeland. By force as much as by superior bargaining power, the Greeks drove their rivals from the Aegean and Ionian seas. Sailors of different cities tried to eliminate each other in similar fashion.

Commerce and Manufactures

Alike in the eastern and western Mediterranean, the mariners of the Ionian cities of Chalcis, Samos, and Miletus were the first to resume maritime commerce on anything larger than a purely local and occasional basis. The far-flung colonies of Miletus early became collection depots and centers for her shipping. From Naucratis, her sailors carried pottery, papyrus, scarabs, and other Egyptian products to points as distant as the Black Sea colonies. In return, they received cargoes of grain, salted fish, iron, timber, slaves, furs, and other products of the region. Inland Lydia supplied the Ionian cities with wool, gold, slaves, and Oriental goods brought overland from the Tigris-Euphrates Valley. From the wool, cloth was woven and dyed with the blood of the *murex* to the color known to the Greeks and Phoenicians as "purple" (actually bright red). Other brilliant colors were used as well. The textiles thus produced were luxury goods and commanded high prices. From Naucratis the Ionians learned the art of welding and hollow-casting metals, while Egyptian stonecutters taught them to carve statues of stone with a sure hand and a high degree of perfection. Pottery was manufactured for export, both in Miletus and in other Ionian cities, and geometric decoration was succeeded by figures of men and animals arranged in friezes, imitated from Oriental models. In the seventh century, Ionia far surpassed any other part of the Greek world in wealth and luxury, and her goods were found as far west as Italy.

On the western side of the Aegean Sea, about the year 700, Chalcis of Euboea was not far behind Miletus in economic activity. Copper deposits (from which the city took her name) made possible a flourishing bronze industry, especially in the production of armor. Pottery and purple-dyed textiles added to her wealth as it did to that of Miletus. Chalcidian ships traded with the colonies in the northern Aegean, and for a time bid strongly for the commercial monopoly of the western seas. By 650, however, Chalcis was giving way in Italy and Sicily to the rising power of Corinth.

The Dorian island of Aegina also developed a flourishing bronze industry, and her ships shared with Miletus the carrying trade of Naucratis. In Sparta the iron from Mount Taygetus was worked into arms, keys, and domestic utensils. Spartan bronze-work was justly famous, and she produced popular household furniture. Woolen cloth and leather goods were also made in this inland town, which has been chiefly known in later times for its narrow militarism. But the militarism was the work of the aristocracy, while commerce and industry were confined to other classes.

The commercial and industrial center of continental Greece in the last half of the seventh and the first half of the sixth centuries was Corinth. Her position astride the Isthmus gave her harbors on both the Aegean and Ionian seas. The dangers encountered by ships sailing around Cape Malea, at the southern tip of the Peloponnesus, made many a captain willing to take advantage of two stretches of calm water by transporting his ship and goods across the Isthmus. Corinth made this easy by building a tramway over which vessels could be hauled without unloading. Her government — an oligarchy under the merchant family of the Bacchiadae — did everything possible to further commercial and manufacturing interests. Corinthian shipyards led the Greek world in naval architecture, being the first to produce vessels with three banks of oars (*triremes*). Her potters had never entirely succumbed to the geometric style of decoration, and their wares, painted with figures that show strong Oriental influence, for a century monopolized the export market. Bronze-work, arms, and splendid robes dyed in many colors, added to the wealth of this busy city.

The rival which overthrew the commercial supremacy of Corinth in the later sixth century was Athens. Up to that time the Athenian navy had been overshadowed by that of Aegina, and her pottery, although it far surpassed that of Corinth in quality and beauty, had only a limited demand outside her own territories. The tyrant Peisistratus changed all this. By encouraging manufactures at home and by intelligent diplomatic and military activities abroad, he secured for his city control of the Black Sea pottery market and a growing share of the western trade formerly monopolized by Corinth.

Economic Changes; the Invention of Coinage

The growth of manufacturing and commerce produced profound effects upon the economic and social life of the Greek world. We must, of course, guard against the tendency to visualize the economic processes of the sixth century B.C. in terms of the twentieth century A.D. The craftsmen of Miletus, Corinth, Chalcis, and Athens worked on a very small scale. The working force of one of them seldom exceeded a dozen free workmen or slaves, and the shop contained little or no machinery. Mass-production methods were unknown. Throughout its history Greek industry remained subordinate to agriculture, both in economic importance and social standing, and even in democratic Athens the stigma placed upon industrial labor was never entirely removed. Even when proper allowance has been made for these facts, there is no mistaking the vital importance of these

MINING OF POTTER'S CLAY, SIXTH CENTURY B.C.
From a Vase Painting

new developments. They enabled states that were burdened with excess population to import food and pay for it. They opened the door of opportunity to many a poor man who, like Hesiod, was fighting a losing battle with want on a barren farm. The successful tradesmen and craftsmen soon came to equal in wealth the greatest nobles, but it was a new kind of wealth, for which a new measure of value was invented — coined money.

The use of precious metals as a medium of exchange was not new. The Oriental peoples had long employed them for this purpose, as we have seen, but there was no guarantee of the weight or purity of the metal. Each piece had to be weighed and tested anew at each transaction, until about 700, the kings of Lydia, just east of Asiatic Aeolis and Ionia, conceived an epoch-making device to facilitate trade. Their dominions produced large quantities of *electrum* — a natural alloy consisting of about seventy per cent gold and thirty per cent silver. Lumps of this metal were cast, uniform in size and value, and then stamped with the royal seal to guarantee their worth. These could be accepted without weighing. From Lydia the new practice spread to Ionia, where the city-states began to strike both electrum and silver coins. In continental Greece and the Aegean islands, however, gold was too scarce to be used in coinage, but in the sixth century rich silver mines on the islands of Thasos and Siphnos, and at Laurium in Attica, produced enough of the pale metal to allow its use as a standard of monetary value. Hence, throughout the greatest age of its history, the Greek world operated upon a silver standard, just as modern Mexico and China have done. Where gold was used, its value was long reckoned as thirteen and one-third times that of silver. The units of value were derived from the old Oriental system of weights, with smaller subdivisions. The smallest unit was the *obol*, originally an iron spit, and later coined in copper or bronze. Its multiples were as follows:

$$6 \text{ obols} = 1 \text{ drachma (silver)}$$
$$100 \text{ drachmas} = 1 \text{ mina (not coined)}$$
$$60 \text{ minas} = 1 \text{ talent (not coined)}$$

Two systems of coinage, both of which employed these denominations, dominated continental Greece. The first was the *Aeginetan*, in which the standard coin was a two-drachma piece weighing 194 grains or 97 grains per drachma. At current world prices for silver, therefore, an Aeginetan drachma would be worth about ten cents. The Aeginetan standard was current in most of the Dorian states, although rejected by Corinth. Chalcis of Euboea, on the other hand, adopted a standard two-drachma piece weighing only 135 grains, or 67½ grains per drachma. The intrinsic worth of a Chalcidian drachma would therefore be about seven cents.[1] This standard was popular in the Chalcidian colonies, but it derived its chief importance from its adoption by Athens. Athenian four-drachma pieces, stamped on the reverse with a crudely shaped owl, were so well known for the unfailing honesty of their weight and purity that in the fifth century B.C. they became practically an international currency. Other states were rarely so honest, and their coins were often acceptable only within their own domains.

The Influence of a Money Economy

The rise of a money economy produced its full effects only in the more progressive states. Backward communities were long without coinage, and Sparta used an iron currency for internal trade until late in her history. Where coinage was adopted, it aided patently in destroying the old order and building a new one. A rising aristocracy of trade began to undermine the position of the old aristocracy of birth and land. The ruling classes of many states had to open their ranks to successful commoners whose wealth reposed in strong-boxes, or was represented by ships, slaves, or industrial equipment. Thus, beside the old patriarchal slavery of Homeric

[1] The values stated here are based upon the world price of silver in a free market on October 1, 1946.

times, there grew up a capitalistic slavery, the aim of which was the earning of profits, and beside the free agricultural peasantry there appeared a class of free workmen who were paid money wages. A new Greek civilization was coming into existence, and the developments reviewed in this chapter are among its most significant features.

13

The Greek Renaissance: Political Evolution

EARLY IN THE EIGHTH CENTURY the expanding culture of the Greek people created a situation for which their traditional political institutions were no longer adequate. In the more advanced communities the economic progress outlined in the preceding chapter destroyed the social basis upon which the patriarchal monarchies of Homeric times had rested by redistributing population and by creating new and aggressive classes who had no place in the old order of things. In the next century the economic crisis and the need for more extensive government service still further intensified the problem. This social and political maladjustment increased the unrest which marked the three centuries between 800 and 500 B.C.

As the Greeks met the crisis of economic maladjustment by founding colonies and by developing commerce and industry, so in the field of government they responded to the stimulus by creating a lavish variety of new political institutions designed to introduce order and justice into the new world which was coming into being. They evolved the free city-state, made it a republic, and enabled large classes of its population to participate in its government. Such accomplishments entitle them to a high place among the world's political thinkers. On the other side of the account, though, we must charge the frequent warfare between states and the rancorous party strife, punctuated by bloody revolutions, which shock the modern reader. This significant phase of Greek civilization can be best understood if one begins by a general survey and proceeds from that to a detailed study of the governments of the two chief states, Sparta and Athens.

THE TRIBAL STATE (ETHNOS)

Our study of Homeric society in Chapter 11 has already acquainted us with the broad outlines of Greek government in the Middle Age; but the society of the Homeric period deserves further consideration. While some of the cities of Mycenaean Greece, such as Thebes, Athens, Argos, and Corinth, existed continuously throughout the Middle Age, they must have been small and their influence upon forms of government negligible. Society was predominantly rural and was organized upon a basis of real or fancied relationship.

Related Groups and Social Classes

Each state of the period consisted of an ascending hierarchy of related groups: family, clan, phratry, and tribe. The clan (*genos*) was theoretically composed of a number of families descending from a common ancestor in the male line. Actually, its numbers were increased by emancipated slaves and by the adoption of strangers. Its real bonds of unity were common secular and religious interests. Together its members worshiped their human and divine ancestors. Family and clan usually held land in common ownership, individuals having lots assigned to them in usufruct. The clan undertook to protect its members from injury and assumed collective responsibility for their acts. Their chiefs were the "elders" who formed the council of the king.

A group of related clans formed the *phratry*. Again the members participated in common religious rites, from which non-members were barred. Several phratries constituted a tribe (*phyle*). At its head was a tribal king, who enjoyed especially high standing in the counsels of the greater king who ruled the state.

The number and arrangement of tribes and social classes in a state varied with circumstances. In those states founded by the Dorians, three tribes of the conquering people were always to be found (*Hylleis, Pamphyloi,* and *Dymaneis*), along with one or more tribes of the older population. Athens, on the other hand, had four (*Hopletes, Geleontes, Aegicoreis,* and *Argadeis*); and some or all were carried over into the Ionian states. In some cases additional tribes were established to take care of groups not of Athenian origin. But to dismiss the subject at this point would be to oversimplify a very complex situation. In some of the Dorian states the pre-Dorian inhabitants were left personally free, as at Sicyon, while Argos and Sparta each had, in addition to the three Dorian tribes, a class of free but depressed *perioeci* ("dwellers-around") and another of serfs. In short, though all the tribal states had many features in common, it is doubtful if any two were exactly alike.

The territorial organization of such a state reflected its group organization. The lands of a clan formed a village community, of which the clan chief was the head, and the lands of the phratry formed a canton (*systema*), whose common affairs were administered by an assembly of village chiefs. The tribe itself naturally had a certain jurisdiction over the combined lands of its member groups. Where a conquered people retained their personal freedom, they frequently lived apart from their conquerors on lands devoted to their use, under clan and tribal governments of their own which performed collectively their obligations to the conquerors. Although some features of the tribal state existed in all later Greek city-states, it soon began to lose ground, and in the fifth century was found only in half-Greek Epirus and Macedonia. Elsewhere its place was usually taken by the city-state.

The City-State (Polis)

Throughout the Middle Age powerful forces were developing a more satisfactory state than that described above. In continental Greece, as we have seen, fertile soil is found only in small, isolated patches, and drinking water can be obtained only at cèrtain points. In a rude and warlike age people needed defensible places of refuge from enemies and pirates. If a site, like the Cademia of Thebes, Acro-Corinthus, or the Acropolis of Athens, possessed these advantages, it became a center of worship, business, and government for the people of the neighborhood. Through combined efforts it was fortified against attack. In this secure retreat several clans or phratries built altars and worshiped their gods in common. From defense x and religion it was but a step to make this central point a meeting place for political purposes. Wealthy chiefs built houses in or near the stronghold, and soon merchants and craftsmen settled there. A town was formed, to which the people of the surrounding tribes and phratries became economically, religiously, and politically subject. A new and more effective bond united them, making possible a higher civilization than that which had existed in the old days of isolation. A city-state (*polis*) had come into existence. Once formed, it annexed a much larger area by conquest or negotiation. The people of this territory, who lived many miles from the civic center, were still counted as citizens of the city-state. All important business was transacted in the city, and they looked to it for government and defense.

Area and Population of the Greek City-State

Natural conditions strictly limited the amount of land which could be administered by a city-state and the population which it could support.

It had to be small enough so that the more distant of its inhabitants could reach its administrative center in about a day's journey on foot or by donkey. Sparta, at her greatest, was the largest state in continental Greece, but her territorial area was less than 3000 square miles. Athens, with Salamis and Oropos, controlled about 1060 square miles; Thebes, about 400; Corinth, 352. Of the smaller city-states, Phlius had 72 square miles, and the Boeotian cities, except Thebes, averaged 52 square miles each. Yet these were not the smallest states. Boeotia, Thessaly, Achaea, Argolis, and Arcadia, which appear as unities on modern maps, were at best only loose leagues of independent states, and often, as in the case of Arcadia, were no more than " geographical expressions." The populations of most city-states were small in proportion to their territories, though figures are lacking in most cases. It is probable that Athens at her greatest (and she was, no doubt, the most populous state in Greece) had no more than four hundred thousand inhabitants, free and slave. Many of the cities which figured prominently in history had less than ten thousand free male citizens, and the Boeotian city of Plataea, in 490 B.C., had only one thousand.

The total number of city states in the Greek world is unknown, but it was very great. About 335 B.C. Aristotle and his students made studies of one hundred and fifty-eight city-state constitutions, and there were probably several times that number of states in all. From one end of the Mediterranean world to the other, wherever men followed the "Greek way of life," the city-state was the prevailing form of government.

The formation of the city-state appears to have been an evolutionary process. At first the union of clans, phratries, and tribes was very loose, and each continued to perform many of its old functions. The government was a monarchy of the Homeric type, with the usual council and assembly, and its activities were but little more extensive than those performed by Odysseus or Menelaus. Such a state of affairs could not survive the impact of new conditions. The three centuries following the year 800 B.C. saw far-reaching changes in three directions:

1. The state established new religious cults and took control of the old ones, thus weakening the authority of the clans and phratries and offering the benefits of the state religion to persons not included in these organizations.

2. It usurped the right to administer justice, put an end to collective responsibility, and strove to abolish blood feuds and other forms of disorder.

3. The monarchies everywhere gave way to republics, which involved

greater or less popular participation in government (aristocracy, oligarchy, timocracy, and democracy), with occasional lapses into one-man rule in the form of tyranny.

These transformations — especially the last — were to make the Greek city-states the most productive political laboratories in the history of the human race.

The Evolution of the City-State Government

The Abolition of the Kingship

The first of the institutions of tribal society to disappear from the strange atmosphere of the city-state was the patriarchal monarchy. It had endured only while it served as a rallying point for isolated groups who had no other bond of unity, and the common interest which had led to the creation of the city-state took its place. About 800 B.C. the aristocracies of clan chiefs and tribal kings began to strip their nominal overlords, the city kings, of their powers. The details of the process varied widely from city to city, but almost everywhere it was slow and gradual rather than swift and revolutionary. Sometimes a royal family died out and was not replaced. At Sparta, some unrecorded accident resulted in the establishment of two kings chosen from different families. Of course, each acted as a check upon the other, and in addition, there was an elective board of *ephors* to supervise both. Usually the king was divested of his military and judicial powers, which were given to new officials chosen from the aristocratic class. After a time the kingship ceased to be hereditary in most cities, and in any case became a mere political office, filled by election and held for a term of one year only. Yet it is significant that, in spite of its degradation, the royal office was seldom abolished. Many, if not most, Greek city-states had obscure officials called kings until relatively late in their history. The reason for this astonishing bit of conservatism was religious. The gods were accustomed to receive sacrifices and prayers on behalf of a state from a king, and who could be sure that they would be satisfied if these acts of worship were offered by anyone else?

The Aristocracies

Notwithstanding this shadowy survival of the kingship, the average city-state had, before 700 B.C., become an aristocratic republic, with power vested in the noble families whose heads had formerly acted as advisers to the king. As in Homeric times, they continued to form the effective part of the state's armed forces, although improvement in the military art had substituted cavalry for chariots. Often the aristocrats among men specialized, as in Thessaly and Euboea, in the breeding of the horse, the aristocrat of the animal kingdom. Participation in government was restricted to certain families, who traced their descents from gods and heroes, and proudly preserved their genealogies for as many as fifteen or twenty generations. Beneath them was a group composed of the poorer members of the recognized clans, together with those whose kinship groups had been reduced by conquest to an inferior position, and the large class whom illegitimate birth or some other accident had deprived of clan connections. These commoners were either tenant farmers, holders of small farms in unproductive areas, or petty merchants and tradesmen in the cities.

Aristocratic government was adapted to a land economy, and only in predominantly agricultural districts could it long survive. Yet occasionally the nobles encouraged colonization, commerce, and manufacturing. A good example is the case of the Bacchiadae who, for nearly a century, monopolized the government of Corinth. No doubt at one time their chief had been king of the city. In the eighth century the whole clan seized the sovereignty, deprived the other clans of all share in the government, and refused to intermarry with them. The Bacchiadae founded colonies, built the two harbors of Corinth, and constructed the tramroad by which ships were carried across the Isthmus. They also fostered potterymaking, shipbuilding, and other lines of manufacturing. The nobles of Chalcis in Euboea, significantly known as "horse-feeders," acted similarly. Many aristocratic governments encouraged colonization as a means of freeing their cities from the presence of the discontented poor.

The Development of Oligarchy

As the economic revolution progressed, it transformed the aristocracies of the more advanced communities into oligarchies. This word — which basically means the rule of the few — denotes a system of government in which political rights are determined by a property qualification, regardless of pedigree. Commerce and manufacturing produced groups of men whose wealth, while not in land, was very great. They were able to live better than many of the old agrarian nobility, to own horses, and to equip themselves for war. To exclude such men from a share in the government was dangerous, and when attempted, as in Corinth, produced revolutions. An innovation in military tactics hastened the fall of the aristocracies. By the middle of the seventh century, the progress of the bronze and iron industries had put arms and armor on the market at so low a price that men of moderate means could own them. This development vastly increased the number of possible recruits for the heavy-armed infantry (*hoplites*), and a new formation, the *phalanx*, was invented for them. Disciplined masses of armored spearmen, fighting in close formation, proved more than a match for the cavalry of the aristocratic states, and once their superiority had become established, all the more important states had to adopt the new system. The cavalry was used only to guard the wings of the army and to pursue a beaten enemy. With army service went political privilege. Within a few years many of the Greek city-states had divided their populations into classes, depending upon the amount of property which they held, and apportioned both military obligations and political rights accordingly, without regard to family connections. Everywhere the poor were exempt from regular service and usually had no part in the government. In other respects the operation of the system varied widely. In the mildest form of the oligarchy (a *timocracy*), all who could serve at their own expense in the heavy-armed infantry might vote in the assembly, while the important offices were reserved for the wealthier classes, who formed the cavalry. In some of the more extreme oligarchies the assembly might consist of a fixed number of the wealthiest citizens — often a thousand; or council and assembly might be merged in a single body, chosen for life, whose members elected the magistrates and governed the state. Such a body were the six hundred *Timouchoi* at Massalia, who had to be fathers of families and the descendants of two generations of citizen ancestry. From their number was chosen an executive committee of fifteen, whose members administered the state.

Oligarchy, while not a liberal form of government, marked a definite advance in many respects. It substituted personal qualifications for family connections as a basis for the distribution of political rights. This development, however, was itself a part of a larger tendency to liberate the individual from the political authority of kinship groups, and to place him under the direct power of the state. In keeping with this trend, in the late seventh century a number of states abolished the collective responsibility of these groups for the acts of their members, and made appeals to the courts a compulsory substitute for private vengeance. The importance of this development may be appreciated when we remember that in every state a considerable portion of the population had never shared even the imperfect protection which clan or phratry had extended to their members. In that age the law was unwritten tradition, which could be arbitrarily altered by the judges with every new case and was generally manipulated in the interests of the privileged classes. Yet its protection, such as it was, was now extended to all. The change was not made without a struggle. The proud noble, whose most cherished privilege was that of wearing a sword, submitted with bad grace to the ban upon private feuds. Only after many vicissitudes did even the most progressive cities establish the reign of law, and in backward regions like Crete or Aetolia it was never established at all.

The Formation of Political Parties

The weakening of the clan and family ties coincided with the formation of political parties, usually organized along class lines. The poverty and misery of the depressed classes everywhere generated a seething mass of discontent, which needed only leadership to become dangerous. The shortsighted contempt of the upper classes for the common man may be judged from the poems of the Megarian noble Theognis, who describes the peasantry of his native state as "grazing like deer outside the walls, clad in goatskins," and laments the admission of this vile herd into the city. But the contempt of Theognis and his class was not confined to the peasants. It included the successful middle class, whose growing wealth was making it a power in society. This aristocratic exclusiveness often drove all of the non-noble elements into an alliance against their oppressors. Thus, the seventh century saw the beginning of a relentless party struggle between the privileged and the unprivileged classes of Greek society, which was to continue with varying intensity until the end of national independence. The violent passions to which it gave expression may be judged by incidents like the massacre of the adherents of Cylon at Athens, or the revolt of the serfs at Miletus. These latter, having captured a number of their masters' children, laid them on a threshing-floor and drove a herd of oxen over them; the masters, when they regained the upper hand, smeared their prisoners with pitch and burned them alive. The reason for this cruelty is not far to seek. The poverty-stricken masses at times attempted the utter extermination of their oppressors and the redivision of the land, and the upper classes responded with repressive measures of corresponding severity. That these destructive forces did not entirely overturn the budding civilization of the Greeks was largely due to the appearance of a number of statesmen of transcendent genius, some of whom are known to us as lawgivers and others as tyrants.

Codification of the Laws

The demand of the middle and lower classes for the codification of the laws arose from the fact that because the laws were unwritten they were certain to be changed with every case to the advantage of the privileged classes. The first code to be reduced to writing, that of the Italian-Greek city of Locri, was compiled by Zaleucus (663–662). It was crude and severe, with death as the penalty for an unsuccessful attempt to change it or for an unsuccessful appeal from the sentence of a magistrate. Luxury of dress and ornament were forbidden, and every injury was punished by a similar injury to the culprit. Another popular law code in western Greece was that of Charondas framed at Catana in Sicily. Thebes, Corinth, Athens, and many other states of continental Greece and the Aegean area reduced their laws to writing before the end of the seventh century. Most of the early law codes were, like that of Zaleucus, rigorous and uncouth, with little recognition of the new money economy and with extravagant safeguards for property rights. In these respects they reflected the aristocratic background from which they sprang. But they could now be consulted freely, and the magistrates were no longer at liberty to distort them to favor personal and class interests. Furthermore, since the law had ceased to be a mystery, it could be altered whenever the popular demand became sufficiently strong.

The Tyrannies

The unrest occasioned by the misery of the masses and the unsatisfied ambitions of the middle class was seldom quieted by the codification of the laws. The later seventh and sixth centuries witnessed continued outbreaks of violent class warfare in various parts of the Greek world, with massacres, exiles, confiscations of land, and frequent changes of government. Out of these disorders grew the tyranny and the elective dictatorship. The word tyrant (*tyrannos*) was probably of Asiatic origin, and denoted a ruler who held supreme power by violent means in defiance of tradition. In itself, the term had no unfavorable meaning. Tyrants might be either good or bad, and in fact they ranged in character all the way from bloodthirsty monsters like Phalaris of Acragas to beneficent statesmen like Cleisthenes of Sicyon or Peisistratus of Athens. Two characteristics they all had in common: they had won their power in defiance of the laws, and they ruled without legal restraints.

Tyranny was usually the product of revolution. Most often the tyrant was a member of the nobility who espoused the cause of the depressed classes and gained ascendancy by their aid. Sometimes he was a magistrate who illegally prolonged his term of office, while in other instances he was a successful plotter or revolutionary leader. He was usually the enemy of the nobility, who resented his domination over them, and the friend of the lower and middle classes. The tyrant ordinarily maintained a splendid court, erected fine buildings and other public works, patronized the arts and literature, and encouraged the growth of commerce and industry. As a rule, they were men of peace, who strove to strengthen their positions by alliances abroad, particularly with other tyrants. Yet, capable and popular as many of them were, they were rarely able to establish families that would last more than a generation after their founders. Their office had no roots in tradition, and was often repugnant even to the classes who supported them. Only their ability to redress the grievances of their adherents and increase the prosperity of the people kept them in power, and in practically every case they found it necessary to rely on mercenary soldiers. Usually the son of the founder had been spoiled by luxury, vice, or suspicion before he came into power, and often the jealousy of his father had kept him from securing any preliminary training for the task of government. He would rule harshly and cruelly, his popular partisans would desert him, and the tyranny would be overthrown. In continental Greece, the Spartans, who favored the upper classes in neighboring states, helped to overthrow several tyrannies.

Cleisthenes of Sicyon

But the institution can best be studied by a survey of a few outstanding cases. The little city of Sicyon, located on the Corinthian Gulf just west of Corinth, was inhabited by a mixed population of Ionians and Dorians, of whom the latter were the dominant element, and was politically dependent upon Argos. About 660, Orthagoras, a member of the Ionian element, transformed his office of general into that of a tyrant. The family which he founded lasted a full century — longer than any other known tyrannical dynasty. His descendant, Cleisthenes (about 590–560), was the organizing genius of the family and won the independence of his city from Argos. As religious sentiment was a powerful force in politics, he undertook to make Sicyon religiously as well as politically free from her former mistress. To do this, he put an end to the richly endowed cult of the Argive hero Adrastus and transferred his favor to the Theban hero Melanippus, who in life had been Adrastus' enemy, and to Dionysus, the god most popular among the peasantry. In other respects as well, his rule had a strong anti-Dorian tendency. The three Dorian tribes had their names changed to Hogs, Porkers, and Asses, while his own tribe, formerly the Shore men, were called Rulers (*Archelaoi*).

A charming story is told by Herodotus about the marriage of Cleisthenes' daughter Agariste. When she was of marriageable age, her father proclaimed at the Olympic Games that a year and two months later he would choose a husband for her, and bade all who thought themselves worthy of marrying into his family to come to his court prepared to stay until the appointed time. Many noble youths from all over the Greek world came, and Cleisthenes carefully tested their accomplishments and observed their characters until the allotted time had expired. When the time for the choice came, he had tentatively decided upon an Athenian named Hippocleides, but at the feast at which the announcement was to be made, the favored suitor became intoxicated and gave so revolting an exhibition of dancing that Cleisthenes in anger exclaimed, "Son of Tisander, you have danced yourself out of your marriage!" "Hippocleides cares not!" answered the young man, and the saying became a proverb at Athens. Thereupon the tyrant arose and spoke with gracious courtesy to the suitors, thanking them for the honor done to his house by them in seeking a wife from it, and deploring that he had not a daughter to give to each of them. Agariste's hand went to the Athenian Megacles, and each of the disappointed candidates received a talent of silver as a consolation prize. To Megacles and Agariste was born a son, Cleisthenes, who became the Athenian legislator. The tyranny at Sicyon ended with the death of Cleisthenes and was succeeded by a moderate oligarchy.

The Tyranny at Corinth: Periander

At Corinth the power of the Bacchiadae was overthrown, about 655 B.C., by Cypselus, a descendant of the clan through his mother. There the tyranny lasted something over two generations. Its most brilliant figure was Periander, the son of Cypselus. Of him the story is told that he sent to Thrasybulus, tyrant of Miletus, to learn the secret of the latter's success. Thrasybulus led the envoy through a wheat field, and with his staff broke off all the tallest heads. Periander took the hint and slew or exiled the Corinthian nobility. Again we see all the symptoms of an anti-Dorian reaction. Dorian social and religious customs were forbidden, and the worship of Dionysus was encouraged. Splendid public works commemorated the rule of Periander. Commerce and industry flourished, and in the interest of the free workingmen the importation of slaves was restricted. Periander conquered Epidaurius, Aegina, and Corcyra, and founded numerous colonies, which he ruled through members of his family. Dissensions between Periander and his designated successor ruined the family, and a few years after the great tyrant's death, the Spartans aided in the establishment of an oligarchy at Corinth.

Not all tyrannies were as stable as those described. Theagenes, who became tyrant of Megara shortly after Cypselus mastered Corinth, was overthrown by the populace. Phalaris, tyrant of Acragas, was guilty of such cruelty that he was murdered by his enraged subjects. Polycrates, tyrant of Samos, fell a victim to the treachery of a neighboring Persian satrap. A long list of others could be compiled, who either failed to establish themselves or perished after a few years of rule.

An Evaluation of the Tyranny

In its very nature the tyranny was an extraordinary government whose fatal weakness was that it ran counter to the whole spirit of Greek civilization. As soon as it solved the problems which led to its establishment, its former supporters were willing, as a rule, to see it overthrown. But we must remember that, in spite of bad features, the Greek tyrannies conferred great and lasting benefits upon the cities in which they existed. Their lavish building and patronage of art and literature did much to advance Greek civilization. They constantly strove to improve the economic condition of their subjects. By confiscating the lands of the nobles and giving them to the poor, they righted the wrongs done by conquest or economic privileges in former ages, and these unfair conditions were scarcely ever re-established in full when a tyranny came to an end. By bending the upper classes to their iron rule, they helped to establish the reign of law and to make future constitutional government possible. Usually their encouragement of popular religious cults helped to break the monopolies of clans and phratries in this field, and thus to strengthen the patriotism of the citizen body. Truly, the Greeks owed much to these unmoral and revolutionary statesmen. Although the period between 650 and 500 B.C. was the Age of Tyrants *par excellence*, we must not suppose that later ages were entirely free from this form of government. Any Greek state might revert to it in times of stress, and the fifth and fourth centuries saw many examples, especially in western Greece.

Closely resembling the tyrant was the elective dictator (*aesymnetes*), chosen for a term of years to rectify the affairs of disordered states. From this office an unscrupulous man could easily pass into the tyranny. An outstanding example of the honorable elective dictator was Pittacus of Mytilene. After a prolonged civil war and a short-lived tyranny had reduced the state to chaos, he was chosen to restore order (589). At the end of ten years of rule he had accomplished his task, and after recalling the banished nobles, he laid down his power. Similar in character, if not in name, was the place held at Athens by the lawgiver Solon, of whom more will be said subsequently. Sometimes a strife-torn city would choose an individual or a committee from another city to improve conditions, and might accept a law code or even an entire constitution from such a source.

Timocracies, Democracies, and the Party System

As time passed, many of the oligarchies were broadened into timocracies by lowering the property qualifications, and these in turn sometimes passed into democracies. One must, however, guard against giving modern meanings to ancient terms. A Greek democracy was a state in which the whole citizen body had a decisive voice in the government. Every adult male citizen had a seat in the popular assembly and was usually eligible for the magistracies of the state. To avoid invidious distinctions, certain states went so far as to choose some of their officials by lot. But these facts do not make what we call a democracy. The slaves and resident aliens, who together might comprise more than half of the population, were disfranchised. Woman suffrage was of course unknown. Salaries for officials were almost unheard of, and rarely did the state furnish them even bare subsistence while on duty. Thus, a poor man was barred from an official career by the necessity of earning a living. To exercise his voting rights in the assembly, the citizen might be compelled to walk or ride many weary miles to the city and lose two or three days a month. While the representative principle was not unknown, it was seldom practiced. Greek democracies were as far from our definition of the term as was our average southern state of pre-Civil War days.

The party system of the Greek states was a permanent feature of their political structure. The peculiar bitterness of party warfare, so hard for a present-day American or Englishman to understand, arose from the sweeping character of party aims. In a modern democracy, the party in power accepts the established form of government and the fundamental institutions of society, and merely tries to carry out policies for the operation of that government under the established system. Among the Greeks, a change of party frequently involved a radical change in the form of government and might even result in a complete redistribution of all property, with the massacre or exile of the leaders of the defeated group. Hence, each group tended to look upon the other as an outlaw organization, and to treat it accordingly. As the oligarchic party was always the less numerous of the two, it was inclined to depend upon outside aid to keep itself in power. Much of the importance of Sparta in Greek history arose from the part which she played as upholder of the rule of the few over the many. The popular party in continental Greece and the islands came, in the fifth century B.C., to look to Athens as their champion. Other states at times played a similar part in producing or preventing revolutions among their neighbors. So vitriolic was this strife that frequently a besieged city would be betrayed to the enemy by some of its citizens who were members of the party which was dominant in the besieging force. Wars between cities were frequent, and a victorious state often compelled a vanquished rival to alter its form of government in order to put the partisans of the victor into power. Thus, Hellenic civilization grew up in the midst of bitter struggles within and without.

By the end of the sixth century, the Greek world was a welter of city-states and tribal states, of leagues and alliances, of aristocracies, tyrannies, oligarchies, timocracies, democracies, and states whose governments would fit none of these classifications. No portion of the human race had ever before, or has since, produced such a profusion of political institutions.

The Citizen and His City

All of the foregoing discussion fails to convey, however, the love and reverence which the Greek had for his city. To him it was church and state in one. Within its limited territory, usually smaller than an American county, lay all that was nearest and dearest to him. On its Acropolis stood the shrines of the city's patron gods, who might be his own ancestors, and within its bounds were spots where they had once held communion with mankind. All the citizens were, in a sense, his kinsmen, while the men from the city which lay a short day's journey away were often his hereditary enemies, against whom his forebears had waged war and whom he, too, would probably meet on the battlefield. As exile severed all these ties, it was considered as little less severe than death. One might hate one's fellow citizens for political reasons, but toward the city herself one felt an affection far transcending the patriotism of which modern man is capable. It is no wonder that the Greek city-states attained an inner unity and cohesion which for centuries not only defied all attempts at national unification, but when unification had at last been achieved by foreign spears, preserved city-state boundaries and consciousness intact, until Christianity and the northern barbarians consigned the whole ancient civilization to oblivion.

14

Sparta, the Champion of Militarism

and Oligarchy

EARLY HISTORY

FROM THE VIEWPOINT of war and politics, the strongest state in continental Greece from the seventh to the fourth century B.C. was Sparta. With the largest territory and the most powerful army of any state in the peninsula, she usually enjoyed unquestioned supremacy over her neighbors. Her government remained practically unchanged for many years, and the uniqueness of her political and social structure made it the model for the Utopian dreams of aristocratic philosophers. She championed the cause of the upper classes of other states in their strife with the commons, and in the Persian Wars served as a rallying point of Greek nationality against the invader. In short, she occupied a more influential place in the Greek world than any other state except Athens.

Origins

The cradle of Spartan power was the valley of the Eurotas River, in the southeastern Peloponnesus, known as Laconia or Lacedaemon. In Mycenaean times this region had been part of the kingdom of Menelaus and Helen. Somewhat before 1000 B.C., bands of Dorian invaders entered it from the north and spread throughout the length of the valley, subduing or combining with the Achaean population. The nucleus of the later Lacedaemonian state was a group of Dorian villages located on the western bank of the Eurotas, three miles above Amyclae, the former capital of Menelaus, and twenty-five miles from the sea, which came to be known collectively as Sparta. For nearly three centuries, Amyclae barred these Dorians of the upper Eurotas Valley from southward expansion, but about

750 B.C. the balance of power shifted in the Spartans' favor. Probably as the result of a closer union, the Dorians were enabled to capture Amyclae, and within a few years the whole valley and the adjoining slopes of the Parnon and Taygetus ranges were in their hands. Scarcely any details of the process of unification are known, but there are indications that some of the other Lacedaemonians were peacefully amalgamated with the Spartans and received their citizenship. Of those conquered by force, some were allowed to retain personal freedom and local autonomy in return for submission, while others were reduced to serfdom. These groups were called respectively *perioeci* and *helots*.

The tide of Spartan conquest was not stayed by the subjugation of Laconia. The same overpopulation and land-hunger prevailed there as in other parts of Greece, and the situation called for still further expansion. Across the Taygetus Range lay Messenia, which was smaller in area but more fertile than Lacedaemon. The population was a mixture of Dorians and pre-Dorians, with the latter in the majority. Later legends assigned plausible causes for the war which broke out between Lacedaemonians and Messenians about 700 B.C., but the Spartan poet Tyrtaeus bluntly admits that the fertility of the Messenian soil was the real cause. After twenty years of conflict, the whole country fell into Spartan hands, its best lands were divided among the conquerors, and the inhabitants were reduced to the status of perioeci or helots.

Sparta the Home of Wealth and Culture

Sparta was now the mistress of the whole southern part of the Peloponnesus, and surpassed all her immediate neighbors in wealth and culture.

IVORY RELIEF REPRESENTING A SPARTAN WARSHIP ABOUT 600 B.C.

Contemporary poetry and modern excavation have proved that there was, in the first half of the seventh century B.C., scarcely a trace of the rustic crudity and harsh self-denial for which the Spartans were later to be so famous.   Manufactures flourished and overseas commerce brought in articles of luxury from abroad.   In intellectual accomplishments the Spartans stood as high as in material well-being.   The poet and statesman Tyrtaeus was probably a native of the country.   In addition, two foreigners, the Lydian Alcman and the Lesbian Terpander, settled in the city and composed their poetry there — a proof that they found in it a sympathetic environment.   Splendid religious festivals, graced with elaborate choral singing by both men and women, were instituted.   It was a promising beginning, but fated to be blighted prematurely.

The Second Messenian War

Later in the seventh century this wealthy and cultured state was subjected to a peril which threatened its very existence, and which probably marked the turning point in its history.   Aristocrates, king of the Arcadian Orchomenos, had united most of the Arcadian states under his leadership.   In the western Peloponnesus a feud was raging between Pisa and Elis for the control of the temple of Zeus at Olympia and for the presidency of the games held there every fourth year.   Sparta was the ally of Elis. On the other side of the peninsula, Argos had become a formidable power under her able king, Pheidon.   Orchomenos, Pisa, and Argos alike resented the growing power of Sparta, and when, about 650, the Messenians broke out in revolt, all these states gave them aid.   Pisa with Argive aid gained control of the Olympic Games.   The Spartans suffered defeat from the Messenians and their allies and there was danger that Lacedaemon herself would be invaded.

In this deadly peril the Spartans owed their salvation largely to the efforts of Tyrtaeus.   Music and poetry always affected the Greeks more powerfully than they do modern men, and Tyrtaeus made them the vehicles of his appeals to his fellow countrymen.   But he was not merely a versifier. He led armies and planned campaigns.   In fiery elegies he castigated the youth of his city for their apathy.

> Youths, stand side by side and fight.   Give not away to fear or disgraceful flight, but rouse the great, staunch hearts within your breasts, and when fighting against men do not play the coward.   Do not flee, and desert not the older men whose knees are no longer supple.   For it is shameful that an older man should be struck down

among the fighters in the front ranks, and should lie before the young men, his hair white and his beard gray, breathing forth his stout spirit in the dust.[1]

Heartened by his exhortations and shamed by his reproaches, the countrymen of Tyrtaeus finally got the upper hand. It is probably to this period that we should attribute the evolution of the phalanx formation, which was soon to spread throughout the Greek world, and it almost certainly originated in Sparta. The Messenian stronghold of Eira, the center of the rebellion, fell. Aristomenes, the hero of the Messenian struggle for independence, died in exile at Rhodes. Some of the conquered people fled over the sea and the remainder resigned themselves to servitude.

Spartan Supremacy

During the remainder of the seventh century and the first half of the sixth, the Lacedaemonians asserted their supremacy over the Peloponnesus. Their allies, the men of Elis, recovered Olympia and all but destroyed Pisa. The lands on the upper Eurotas were conquered, and a determined attempt was made to subjugate Arcadia, where the kingdom of Aristocrates had fallen. After half a century of warfare with the Arcadian border city of Tegea, the Spartans had to content themselves with an advantageous alliance with the Tegeans and the other states of the region. After the death of Pheidon, Argos declined rapidly. We have already seen how she lost Sicyon. From her the Spartans won the region east of the Parnon Range (Cynuria) and the island of Cythera, and inflicted upon her defeats so decisive that she sank to a second-rate power.

After the defeat of Argos, the Lacedaemonians were recognized as the leading power in the Greek world. Two-fifths of the Peloponnesus was in their possession, while Elis, the Arcadian states, Sicyon, Phlius, Corinth, Megara, Aegina, and others were close allies. They assumed the rôle of mediators in the war between Athens and Megara over the island of Salamis (*ca.* 570 B.C.). Even Croesus, king of far-off Lydia, recognized their leadership in continental Greece and sought their alliance. In the meantime they had adopted a unique set of political and social institutions, which we shall now consider.

---

[1] Translated from the text in Wright, *Golden Treasury of Ancient Greek Poetry* (Oxford, 1867), p. 95, ll. 1-10.

LACEDAEMONIAN SOCIETY

Origin of the Class System

The Spartans were known to the classical Greeks as the possessors of a harsh, rigid, and carefully planned society, which was designed for military efficiency and sacrificed all other interests to this aim. Later, legend attributed this peculiar organization of Spartan society to a single law-giver, Lycurgus, who was supposed to have lived in the ninth century B.C. The legend is, however, without foundation. While some features of the Lacedaemonian class system may have been a heritage from Mycenaean times, the system as a whole was undoubtedly the product of a long evolution, and did not achieve its final form until after the Messenian wars. It was forced upon the Spartans by the fact that they were a ruling minority in the midst of a vastly more numerous subject majority.

As we have seen, the inhabitants of Lacedaemon were divided into three classes:

1. Spartiate citizens, who were collectively the governing body of the state.
2. *Perioeci*, who, while personally free, were collectively subject to the Spartan state, of which they were not citizens.
3. *Helots*, who were state-owned serfs, allotted to the lands of the Spartiates as laborers and tenant farmers.

In itself this class system was not peculiar to Lacedaemon. Communities of free vassals and classes of serfs existed in Thessaly, in early Argos, and elsewhere. Some of its features were remarkably like the institutions of the Dorian cities of Crete. What distinguished the Spartan system from these others was the strict subordination of the interests of all classes — particularly the Spartiates and helots — to the military needs of the state.

Spartan Citizenship

Ordinarily, to be a full citizen of Sparta one had to be of citizen ancestry on both sides. Foreigners were very rarely naturalized, and the perioeci never. Helots who showed outstanding bravery in war were sometimes freed and became *neodamodes*, or "new citizens," but they had no political rights. The *mothakes* — children of Spartan fathers and helot mothers — received the same training as the young Spartiates, and, while not citizens by birth, were often granted full citizen rights. The full citizens, who enjoyed both civil and political rights, were known as "equals" (*homoioi*), and were divided into nobles and commons. As late as the seventh century, class strife within the citizen body was in evidence, and one of Tyrtaeus' poems (*Eunomia*, or "Law and Order") was written to quiet the discord. Then came a reallotment of lands, under circumstances unknown to the later Greeks. Each of the nine thousand to ten thousand adult male citizens received a share of the citizen land, with a staff of helots to work it for him. If Tyrtaeus' statement about the Messenians is to be applied generally, the produce was to be divided equally between helots and landlord, but in effect the allotment was expected to pay its holder seventy *medimni* of grain (105 bushels?) for his own support, twelve for that of his wife, and a proportionate amount of wine and oil, regardless of the total yield. No citizen might perform manual labor or enter business, for his whole time had to be at the disposal of the state. The only money in circulation was an iron coinage which was worthless outside Sparta.

The state took charge of the male citizen at birth, and never relaxed its grip until he died. In other Greek communities the father of a newborn child had the right to expose it by the wayside, either to die or to be picked up and reared by others. At Sparta the elders of the tribe examined the child, and if it were weak or deformed, laid it in a glen on Mount Taygetus to die. If allowed to live, it was sent home to be reared until seven years of age. Then its training for the business of life began. A boy was sent to live in the barracks, where he was enrolled in a training company under the supervision of a young man chosen by the state. His condition was purposely made as hard as possible, in order to toughen him for the hardships of warfare. He was barefoot and poorly clad, summer and winter, and slept on a bed of rushes which he gathered along the Eurotas. His food was scanty and he was encouraged to supplement his allowance by stealing, though flogged unmercifully if caught. Once a year he had to undergo a ceremonial beating before the altar of Artemis Orthia to teach him uncomplaining endurance of pain. Occasionally a boy would die under the lash rather than make an outcry. Athletic exercises toughened his frame, but of intellectual training he had little except Homer and a few war songs and moral poems. The aim of this system was to make the youth hardy, brave, and modest, and the young men of Sparta became famous for these qualities. At eighteen, military drill began, and at twenty he was a full-fledged soldier. He was now expected to marry, but for the next ten years might see his wife only by stealth. He also must join one of the public messes of the city.

The Spartan Adults

The public messes of Sparta (*syssitia* or *pheiditia*) were famous everywhere, although a similar institution existed in the cities of Dorian Crete. Each mess had not more than fifteen members, and vacancies were filled by vote of the surviving members. Bread crumbs rolled in the hand served as ballots and a single adverse vote barred a candidate from membership. Once admitted, he had to make monthly contributions of food to the mess and furnish cash for meat and other "extras." These were fairly heavy, and probably included subventions to the state which we would class as taxes. Any person who failed to keep up his quota lost his right to vote in the assembly, and became known as an "inferior," but had still to perform the duties of a citizen. The members of a mess always ate together, shared the same tent, and fought side by side in battle. They prided themselves upon avoiding unnecessary words, so that "laconic" has become a synonym for brevity and pithiness. The fare at a public mess was plain and simple, an important item being the famous "black broth." Game taken by the members at times relieved the monotony of the diet, and the rules were relaxed somewhat when the men were on campaign, but an Athenian wit once remarked, after eating at a Spartan *syssition*, that it was no wonder the Spartans faced death so bravely in battle — life had so little to offer them!

At thirty years of age the Spartiate became a man, with a vote in the assembly and a home of his own. But he continued to eat and sleep in the barracks up to the age of sixty and was under the same rigorous discipline as in youth. Bravery in battle was enjoined by law and cowardice was punished as a crime. Many instances are on record of small bands, outnumbered by enemies, who would suffer annihilation rather than retreat; and cowards, even when not actually punished by the authorities, were so humiliated by their fellow citizens that they were often driven to suicide. As an army left for a campaign, wives and mothers exhorted their dear ones to return "with their shields or on them."

"Lycurgus," said Aristotle ironically in his *Politics*, "tried to reduce the [Spartan] women to obedience to his laws, but when they refused, he yielded to them." [1] Certainly this was an exaggeration with an element of truth in it. To give the girls strong bodies they were compelled to practice running, jumping, and boxing, but once married they were left largely to their own devices. By purchase and inheritance they came into possession of a large share of the citizen land, and the concentration of property in their hands later became an acute economic and political problem.

[1] Aristotle, *Politics*, II, 9, 1270.

The Perioeci and the Helots

The perioeci must have been more than three times as numerous as the Spartiates. They furnished cash contributions to the state and each of their communities provided a contingent of soldiers for the army. Although free from rigorous Spartan training, they achieved high military efficiency, and also served as sailors and marines in the fleet. Their city governments were about one hundred in number. They took charge of all

YOUNG MEN CARRYING A SLAIN WARRIOR
From a Laconian black-figured cup, sixth century B.C.

local affairs and were organized like other city-states, with nobles and commons. The Spartan government could put members of this class to death without trial, but the right was seldom abused, and as a rule the perioeci were loyal to their masters. The poorer lands of Laconia and Messenia were left in their possession, although they did not farm extensively. Instead, they were devoted to herding, manufacturing, and commerce. In these lines they had a monopoly, for neither Spartiates nor helots could compete with them. They could never become Spartan citizens, and were allowed to reside at Sparta only for business purposes. Their artists produced fine work in stone and bronze, and occasionally members of this class rose to pre-eminence in literature and philosophy.

The helots, as previously mentioned, were state serfs, stationed on the lands of Spartiates, but not owned by them. Their number was very great, a contemporary estimate counting them a hundred times as numerous as their masters. In some respects their position was tolerable, for their contributions to the landlords were fixed and any increase in the yield went to them. They served as lightarmed soldiers in the army and thus not only gained plunder, but might be freed for bravery. Even with these privileges, their lot was wretched. Every year the ephors declared war on them so that they might be killed without incurring the guilt of murder. A helot who showed the slightest discontent or incurred suspicion of disloyalty was ruthlessly struck down by the secret police. On one occasion, some two thousand, who had distinguished themselves in war and had received a promise of freedom, were mysteriously done away with. They wore a distinctive garb, and each year their masters compelled them to give disgusting exhibitions of intoxication and lewd dancing as a warning to young Spartiates. They were not even allowed to repeat the great national poems and war songs.

The resentment of the helots against their oppressors no doubt varied in intensity, being stronger in Messenia, where memories of independence survived, than in Laconia. That it was everywhere formidable, is proved by the large number of recorded revolts and the statements of contemporary writers. No doubt it was the recognition of this fact which made the Spartiates willing to submit to their harsh round of drill and privation, and certainly it invested the methods of the government with an air of arbitrary tyranny.

THE SPARTAN STATE

When one considers the timid conservatism of the Spartiates in general, it is not surprising that their constitution preserved more of the features of the Homeric polity than did any other in continental Greece. The Spartan government consisted of four parts:

1. The kings.
2. The board of ephors.
3. The council of elders (*gerousia*).
4. The assembly (*apella*).

Spartan Constitution and Rule

While the origin of the double kingship is unknown, it probably resulted from the amalgamation of two groups of the Dorian conquerors of Laconia on equal terms. There were two royal families, the *Agiads* and the *Eurypontids*, each of which furnished one king. The rule of primogeniture was not, however, always followed. The kings were commanders-in-chief of the army, but after 510 B.C. both could not participate in the same expedition. Without the power to declare war or make treaties, they merely executed the orders of the ephors, the council, or the assembly. At home they presided over religious rites and were *ex-officio* members of the council of elders. The encroachments of the council and the ephors left them very few judicial powers. They had to take a monthly oath to obey the laws and were subject to punishment for transgressing them. Several kings were deposed from office at various times on one pretext or another. Such were the poor remnants of the once extensive royal power.

One group that gained by the degradation of the kingship was the council of elders. It consisted of thirty members in all. The two kings, as indicated, were members *ex officio*, while the other twenty-eight were nobles over sixty years of age, elected for life by the assembly. The method of election was peculiar. The candidates for a vacant place were made to pass before the assembly and as each one passed he was received with applause. A returning board, concealed in a near-by building and supposedly ignorant of the order in which the candidates passed, gave the vacant place to the one for whom the loudest applause had been given. No doubt this permitted the returning board to decide the election as they chose. The gerousia decided what business was to be brought before the assembly and might reverse a decision of that body. It also advised the kings and ephors and acted as a court of criminal justice. As Spartan law was unwritten and no appeal could be made from its decisions, this power was enormous.

The assembly consisted of all male citizens over thirty years of age who kept up their contributions to the public messes. It could only meet when summoned by the ephors, considered only such business as was proposed by the gerousia, and voted by acclamation without debate. Under such circumstances it is not surprising that its power was small.

The real organ of popular control in the Spartan state was the board of five ephors, elected annually by the assembly. They began their term of office with a stereotyped proclamation:

> Shave off your mustaches and obey the laws,
> that they may not prove grievous to you.

Individually, they acted as judges in civil suits; collectively, they had the right to summon the gerousia and the assembly, to supervise the other executive agencies, and to represent the state in foreign affairs. As guardians of the Spartan tradition they set themselves resolutely against social and political changes, and to them and the gerousia we may probably attribute the fact that society and government remained nearly static for centuries, in spite of frequent attempts at revolution, while other Greek states were undergoing such numerous and far-reaching changes.

The Army and the Secret Police

Every phase of Spartan life centered about the army after the era of its organization as a disciplined body — probably during the Second Messenian War. The poems of Tyrtaeus enable us to see something of its character in his day. The heavy-armed infantry fought in phalanx formation, but since each warrior took whatever place he chose, the poet exhorts the brave to choose the front ranks. The lightarmed infantry fought in open formation with stones and javelins. Cavalry is not mentioned, although it undoubtedly existed. In later times the lightarmed troops were helots, and the cavalry, while composed of citizens, occupied a very low rank in the service. The heavy-armed citizen infantry was organized into a well-disciplined phalanx, divided into six battalions (*morae*) — one for each tribe and an additional one to serve as a bodyguard to the kings. The infantry furnished by the perioeci for each expedition was at first equal in numbers to that of the Spartiates, but later, because of the decrease in the number of male citizens, greatly exceeded them. Expeditions abroad usually included considerable numbers of allies from other states. Military affairs, like other branches of the administration, were shrouded in secrecy, and rarely did accurate information about them leak out.

Characteristic of a state whose ruling class lived in constant fear of revolts by the subject population was the ill-famed *crypteia*, or secret police. Only the most active young men were chosen for this service. They ranged the country, sleeping by day and traveling by night. Any helot suspected of rebellious sentiments was struck down by their daggers without trial.

Such were the main outlines of the Spartan constitution. It was, at least in the fifth and fourth centuries, in constant danger of being overthrown by rebellious helots, outside powers, or discontented citizens, and it was administered with a secrecy and rigor which bears comparison with collectivist states of contemporary Europe. Little is known of the internal history of Sparta. The ephors periodically expelled all foreigners who could

MAP OF THE PELOPONNESUS UNDER SPARTAN LEADERSHIP

not justify their presence in the country, and in general discouraged contacts with the outside world.   Yet it is significant that almost every time
the veil is lifted from Lacedaemonian history, we see the state undergoing
a severe crisis of some kind, and no doubt there were many more of which
Greek historians knew nothing.   The wonder is not that Spartan government was so harsh and arbitrary, but that in the face of so many perils it
lasted so long.

SPARTAN FOREIGN POLICY

The Peloponnesian League

The importance of Sparta in Hellenic history rests principally upon two
facts:

1. Her efforts to weld the other states of continental Greece into a
   harmonious state system under her own leadership.
2. Her policy of upholding oligarchies and aristocracies in neighboring states in opposition to tyrannies and democracies.

Both policies were, in the last analysis, the fruits of her domestic situation, and both were closely interrelated.   As a small aristocracy governing

a large subject population, the Spartiates were bound for the sake of self-preservation to oppose in principle the leveling influences of both tyrannies and democracies, for these might easily spread to her own perioeci and helots. The best defense against all these subversive tendencies was to put the upper classes in control of as many neighboring states as possible and to form a combination of such states to resist the march of revolution.

In the sixth century, the Lacedaemonians actively or indirectly aided in the overthrow of tyrannies at Sicyon, Corinth, and Athens, and in each instance they endeavored to replace the fallen government by a government of the upper classes. In the Peloponnesus, by the end of the century, the only really democratic government was found at Argos, which steadily resisted Spartan influence.

After the defeat of Argos and Tegea, the Lacedaemonians began to draw the Peloponnesian states into alliance with them. Elis was a friend of long standing. The defeat of Tegea led to treaties of alliance with all the Arcadian states, and with Sicyon and Corinth after the overthrow of their tyrannies. Megara, Phlius, Aegina, and (for a time) Athens were drawn into the same circle. The Achaean cities and Argos obstinately remained outside. Thus arose the Peloponnesian League.

The League's Constitution

Many articles in the constitution of this powerful organization are unknown, although the intent of some may be inferred from recorded instances of their operation. Sparta was the president and dominant member. The separate treaties of the member states with her were supplemented by regulations adopted by their delegates in general congresses. Each state had complete local autonomy, and might even go to war with another member of the league, provided no war was in progress against an outsider. The assembly of the league, in conjunction with Sparta, made war or peace, but in doing so it could not violate the religious scruples of members. Each state furnished for the common army a contingent which was commanded by its own officers, but the army as a whole was led by a Spartan. The size of the contingent was fixed by the assembly of the league. No tributes or contributions were levied and hence a fruitful source of discontent was avoided.

The Peloponnesian League was the most successful and enduring political combination in Greek history, lasting, with vicissitudes, nearly two centuries. It made Sparta the foremost power in Greece, stayed the onward march of the democracies, and provided a nucleus around which the otherwise disunited Hellenes could rally when, in 480–479, they were in danger of being conquered by Persia.

15

Athens Becomes a Democracy

HER EARLY HISTORY

As IMPORTANT AS SPARTA in Greek history, and vastly more so in the history of civilization, was Athens. Between the middle of the eighth and the end of the sixth centuries, she evolved a government which protected the rights of all classes and achieved a satisfactory solution for the social problem which tormented so many of her neighbors. At the same time she laid the foundation for a surpassingly brilliant culture and a career of successful empire-building. To understand her later greatness it is essential to consider her early historical development.

Attica, the Land of the Athenians

The territory of Athens was practically coterminous with the triangular peninsula of Attica, which forms the eastern side of the Saronic Gulf. From north to south, Attica's greatest length was a little less than forty miles and its greatest width was about the same. No part of it was much more than twenty-five miles in a straight line from the city of Athens. With the exceptions of the small plains of the Mesogeia, Eleusis, and Marathon, the surface is rough and the soil poor. The Parnes and Cithaeron ranges, which form its northern boundary, attain heights of over forty-six hundred feet above sea-level, and in the center of the country Mount Pentelicus is more than thirty-six hundred feet high. The best harbors are on the western side, being clustered about the little peninsula of the Piraeus.

The Athenians always boasted that they were the descendants of the original inhabitants of the land. Their ancestors, they believed, had never been conquered by outsiders, and had withstood triumphantly even the shock of the Dorian invasions. On the other hand, they had received some of the noblest families of the pre-Dorian Peloponnesus as peaceful immi-

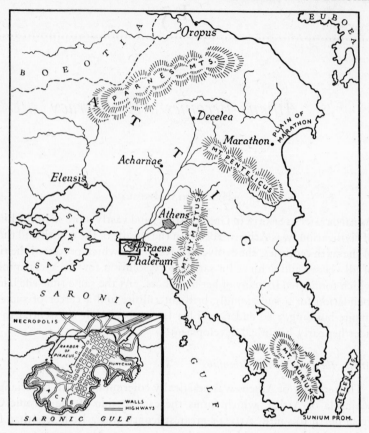

MAP OF ATTICA WITH INSET MAP OF HARBORS OF ATHENS

grants, and had bestowed kingship upon one of them. Thus, the Athenians of later times might well be proud of their state, with an unbroken record of independence since the beginning of its history. A tangible effect of this fact was that Athens, unlike the Dorian states of the Peloponnesus, had no invidious system of social and political classes based upon conquest. Hence, she could work out solutions to her problems without having to deal with the terrible hatreds to which these gave rise.

The Unification of Attica

Originally, according to the Athenian legend, Attica had been a confederacy of twelve cities or tribes, which the hero-king Theseus (thirteenth century B.C. or earlier) had closely unified. The legend abridges what was no doubt a long and gradual process. The most important of the Attic cities was Athens, located some four miles from the western coast, and centering about a defensible limestone plateau which was to become famous as the Acropolis of the united Athenian state. By conquest, negotiation, and the clever use of religious bonds, successive kings of Athens incorporated all the outlying territories of Attica into their domains until the whole district formed a compact political unit. It is probable that the need for common action against the Dorians assisted materially in the achievement of this end. The last portion of Attica to be annexed was Eleusis, which was conquered about the eighth century, while the island of Salamis was not acquired until the sixth century. The unified Attica was not a loose and discordant confederation, like Boeotia, nor a tyranny of one community over others, like Lacedaemon. From the Parnes Range to Sunium and from Eleusis to Marathon, all the people alike were Athenians, for whom the political and religious center was Athens. As the Athenians were Ionians in culture, they were divided into the four traditional Ionian tribes, and these in turn into phratries and clans.

From Monarchy to Timocracy

The destruction of the Athenian monarchy was accomplished by slow stages over a period of nearly a century. During the Dorian invasions of the Peloponnesus, the Medontidae, an immigrant clan from Pylos, had gained the royal power. Its second king, Codrus, had endeared his race to the people by heroically repelling a Peloponnesian invasion, in the course of which he was killed. For several centuries thereafter his descendants occupied the throne. Indications point to the existence at this time of a typical Homeric monarchy, with a council of tribal kings and clan chiefs and an assembly of freemen. Collective responsibility of clans and phratries and the principle of private vengeance encouraged disorder and closely limited the powers of the government. As in other states similarly organized, the army was a mere levy of fighting men of the type familiar to readers of the *Iliad*.

The Overthrow of the Athenian Monarchy

The encroachments of the Athenian aristocracy upon the monarchy first became apparent, according to tradition, early in the period of the Medontidae, when the kings were deprived of their military powers. These were given to elected officials, the *polemarchs*, or war chiefs. About 752 B.C., the life tenure of the royal office was abolished. Henceforth, the kings, while still chosen from the Medontidae, were elected by the council for a period of ten years only. Forty years later, the Medontidae were deposed, and the royal office was made accessible to all members of the aristocracy. About 700, a third office — that of *archon* — was instituted, to which the king's judicial and administrative functions were transferred. About 683, the terms of office of the king, polemarch, and archon were all reduced to a single year. At the same time, probably to end the discontent of the masses with the arbitrary decisions of the magistrates, a board of six *thesmothetae*, or recorders of decisions, was instituted, "to reduce the customs to writing and keep them for the trial of offenders." All these officials were chosen by the council and had to be wealthy aristocrats. The monarchy had come to an end: Athens was an aristocratic republic.

The overthrow of the royal power was followed by the rise of the council, which originally was only an advisory body to the king. However, after the royal power was abolished, the council elected the magistrates, supervised their conduct, and determined the policies of state. Gradually, it became customary for the councilors to co-opt all outgoing magistrates (king, polemarch, archon, and thesmothetae) to its ranks for life, provided no fault was found with their conduct while in office. The assembly for a time lost most of its functions and may have passed almost out of existence. The century between 750 and 650 was the golden age of the Athenian aristocracy.

The Aristocratic Republic

The stratification of Athenian society under the aristocracy has to be deduced largely from indirect evidence. Every citizen was associated with a clan, but some were full members, while others were only permitted to participate in certain of its religious rites. A few clans had, by means of wealth or other considerations, come to be recognized as noble. Their members were *eupatridai*, or "sons of good fathers," and to them went the important political offices and priesthoods. The nobility furnished the cavalry, which formed the effective part of the military forces. Beneath it were the commons, whom a tradition dating back to the Middle Age divided into farmers (*georgoi*) and craftsmen (*demiourgoi*). Some of the farmers were small landholders, who usually worked the poorer lands and were generally indigent. Others were tenants on the lands of the wealthy. They were called *hectomeroi* ("sixth-share men"), but whether this means that they paid one-sixth of their produce as rent, or that they were only allowed to keep that amount for themselves, is uncertain. The first possibility, in a country as poor as Attica and with the inefficient means of cultivation that prevailed, would have been a severe hardship to them, while the second seems impossible. At any rate, their persons and those of their families were security for the payment of the rent, and upon failure to pay they were reduced to slavery. The craftsmen were few in numbers, for this period — the golden age of Corinthian, Milesian, and Chalcidian industry, commerce, and colonization — found Attica still an agricultural country, which planted no colonies.

The Timocracy

The prevailing tendencies about 650 B.C. were hostile to aristocracy. The introduction of the phalanx formation into contemporary armies was a particularly important factor in political evolution, and ended the unrestricted rule of the nobles about the middle of the seventh century. To maintain themselves against foreign aggression they were compelled to call to arms all who could furnish themselves with the equipment of heavy-armed infantrymen, and with military service went political rights. The aristocracy was replaced by a timocracy. Fourth-century Athenian political pamphleteers have left us descriptions of seventh-century government which appear to contain much more propaganda than history, for they were usually eager to abolish universal suffrage and described the earlier time in terms of what they wanted for their own. It seems, however, reasonably certain that the assembly took a new lease on life, and that membership in it was open to all who could equip themselves with arms and armor. The poor, who could not do this, were excused from regular military service and excluded from all part in the government. Special property qualifications confined the important magistracies to the wealthier class. To make the reconstruction of the assembly something more than a form, a new council of four hundred and one members was established, to prepare business for the assembly's consideration. All voters were eligible for membership. The old council, known as the *Council of the Areopagus* from the hill on which it met, lost the right to choose the magistrates, who were thereafter elected by the assembly. A navy was being developed, and this, with the increasing complexity of other government functions, necessitated the creation of a territorial administrative system. The territories of the four tribes were divided into twelve *trittyes* (thirds), and each *trittys* was in turn subdivided into four *naucraries* (ship

districts), with elected *naucrars* at their heads to collect taxes and enforce
the orders of the central government in other matters.   This "timocracy
of the heavy infantry" met the military needs of the state, and broke the
governmental monopoly of the aristocrats by birth, but it did little or
nothing toward solving the economic and social problems which afflicted
the rest of the population.   The privileges of the upper classes and the
abuses to which they gave rise were as great as ever.

Lawgivers and Tyrants

Contending Rulers and Class Strife

With revolutions occurring on all sides of her, Athens could not long
escape the ferment of discontent which was abroad in the Greek peninsula.
In neighboring Megara ruled the tyrant Theagenes, the leader of a popular
revolution against the Dorian aristocracy of his city.   His daughter was
married to the Athenian aristocrat Cylon, who had won prestige by a victory at the Olympic Games.   About 630, Cylon and his supporters, probably with aid from Theagenes, attempted to seize the Acropolis and establish a tyranny.   The time was not propitious for such a move.   The farmer-
soldiers rallied at the call of the magistrates and the attempt failed.   Cylon
escaped, but his partisans had to surrender.   In spite of a promise that their
lives would be spared, they were massacred at the instigation of the archon
Megacles, chief of the great clan of the Alcmeonidae.   A few years later,
Cylon's supporters were powerful enough to bring the clan of Megacles,
who had died meanwhile, to trial for sacrilege in connection with the
affair.   The living Alcmeonidae were banished from the land, and even the
bones of their dead were cast from their tombs to a point beyond the frontier.   With these violent outbursts of hatred, Athens entered upon more
than a century of intermittent class warfare.

The suppression of Cylon's attempted *coup* did nothing to quiet the discontent of the masses.   As elsewhere, the first demand of the commons was
for a codification of the law.   Sixty years after the establishment of the
thesmothetae, this had not been done, but in 621, under circumstances
unknown to us, a special effort was made toward this end.   Draco was
elected thesmothete, with full powers to reduce the legal customs of
Athens to writing, and in a few months he finished the work.   No changes
were made in the form of government, but the rules by which civil and
criminal actions were decided were at last open to the public.

In later ages the name of Draco became a synonym for rigorous severity,
and the adjective "draconic" has that meaning in our own tongue.   This

unenviable reputation results from two characteristics of his work. In the first place, the laws which he reduced to writing were those already in force in the state, and were undeniably severe. Death was the penalty for even the pettiest thefts, and the person of a debtor was entirely at the disposal of his creditor. Secondly, Draco put a ban on blood feuds, and compelled injured persons or their kinsmen to resort to the courts rather than to private vengeance. This point is best brought out in his law of homicide, which was to be the most permanent part of his work. Cases involving wilful murder came before the Areopagus, and the condemned were punished by death and confiscation of goods. Various other courts tried cases in which extenuating circumstances were alleged. There is a touch of primitive superstition in the provisions which compel a murderer, already in exile, but charged with a second offense, to plead his case from a boat moored near the shore, or in that which directs the trial of animals or inanimate objects which have caused the death of a man. But the law, by abolishing collective responsibility and the blood feud, established a milestone on the road from chaotic barbarism to the ordered régime of civilized life.

For nearly a generation after Draco's code was completed, the slow-moving Athenian society endured its growing ills. To social disorders at home was added a war with Megara over the island of Salamis. For a time the Athenians had little success, and suffered from invasions, piratical descents, and the loss of markets. The discontent of the masses, who bore the brunt of these calamities, reached its climax about 600, and civil war began. The commons, guided by examples in other states, were ready to set up a tyrant to redress their wrongs, and desired nothing less than the confiscation and equal division of the lands.

Solon: Affairs at Athens

The eruption of a catastrophic revolution at this point was prevented mainly by the statesmanship and character of Solon. The son of an impoverished noble, he had become a merchant and had traveled to Egypt and other countries to recover his patrimony. Noble birth, mercantile experience, and sterling honesty recommended him to all classes. He was a man of broad culture, the author of numerous poems and popular sayings, and later ages included him among the "Seven Wise Men" — an arbitrary list of the best intellects which the Greek people had produced. The longest and best-known of his works, actually a book of memoirs, was written in verse because the Greeks had not in his day developed a prose literature. To

Solon, the distracted Athenians were willing to accord the office of archon with full power to reform the laws and constitution of the state (594 B.C.).

The picture of Athenian conditions which Solon gives us in his poems is a dismal one:

> The nobles, persuaded by their love of money, recklessly wish to destroy this great city. And as for the people, the minds of their magistrates are corrupt. These magistrates are destined to suffer great evils because of their terrible violence. . . . They grow rich through unjust deeds. They spare neither sacred nor public property, but rob and steal — one here and one there. . . . This wound comes inevitably upon the city, namely evil slavery into which the state has fallen, which stirs up civil war, destroying thus large numbers of our noble young men. . . . These evils are common to all, but large numbers of the poor are going into a foreign land, sold and bound in unseemly chains, and suffer hateful woes in slavery.[1]

But the poor were not blameless. They wanted Solon to become a tyrant and divide among them the confiscated property of the rich:

> They came for plunder, cherishing a hope of riches, each imagining that he would get great prosperity, and that I, who now smoothly flattered, would disclose a harsh purpose. . . . It is not right! With the help of the gods I performed what I promised.[2]

So demoralized was the whole social structure by the greed, corruption, and cruelty of the upper classes and the revolutionary aims of the lower elements that drastic action was necessary to prevent a general collapse of society. Solon chose a moderate course of remedial legislation to meet the most pressing needs of the commons. As nearly all were in danger either of losing their land or falling into slavery from debt, he canceled all debts secured upon land or person, and forbade the mortgaging of one's freedom in the future. This was the famous *seisachtheia* ("shaking-off-of-burdens"). There were in Attica many people already in slavery because of debt, and many more either had been sold abroad or had gone into exile to avoid this fate. To such slaves he gave freedom, and restored the exiles to their homes:

> In the just fullness of time the mighty mother of the Olympian gods will bear me witness, even the most excellent black Earth, that I removed from her numerous mortgage pillars. She who was formerly in slavery is now set free. To our divinely founded country, Athens, I restored many men who had been sold, some legally and

---

[1] Solon, Frag. 4: ll. 5–26. Adapted from G. W. Botsford's translation in Botsford and Sihler, *Hellenic Civilization*, pp. 141–42. By permission of the Columbia University Press.   [2] *Ibid.*, p. 148.

some illegally, and others who had been forced into exile by dire need, who in their far wanderings had forgotten the Athenian tongue. I set free others held here in unbecoming slavery and trembling beneath their masters' caprices. I did these things by force of law, uniting force with justice, and I fulfilled my promise.[1]

Constructive Economics and New Legislation

But it was not enough to right past wrongs. Measures were necessary to prevent their recurrence. Recognizing the economic trends that were reshaping other Greek cities, Solon undertook to develop commerce and industry. To strengthen the connection between Athens and the great commercial centers of Euboea and Ionia, he abolished the use of the Aeginetan system of weights, measures, and coinage which had previously been used, and substituted the Chalcidian standard in its place. Special favor, including rights of citizenship, was shown to craftsmen from other cities who would settle in Athens, and a law was enacted which provided that every father must teach his son a trade or else forfeit all claim to support from him in old age. To loosen the bonds which hindered the free movement of property, Solon enacted a law permitting childless persons to bequeath their property to whomever they chose instead of the previous law which gave it to their collateral relatives. To assure an adequate food-supply in a land where it was a pressing problem, he forbade the exportation of grain, but encouraged the new agriculture by permitting olive oil to be sold abroad.

The poverty of the Greeks made sumptuary laws popular with the masses, for it was felt that the luxury of one person was purchased by the misery of many. Solon responded to this demand by enacting measures forbidding rich gifts of clothing and jewelry to brides and extravagant show at funerals. The rich were thus compelled to refrain from displaying their wealth in an offensive manner and deprived of the opportunity to overawe their less fortunate neighbors.

In the field of criminal law, the harsh provisions of Draco were all repealed except that for homicide, and a more enlightened set of laws took their place. A further blow was struck at the power of the kinship groups by a provision which allowed anyone to institute proceedings in behalf of an injured person, instead of confining this power to kinsmen as Draco had done. For religious reasons, however, Solon restricted to relatives of the victims the right to prosecute murderers.

[1] Edmonds, *Solon*, 36, ll. 13–17, Loeb Classical Library. By permission of the Harvard University Press.

Reorganization of Government

Having remodeled the entire legal system of Athens, Solon proceeded to make drastic changes in the form of government. If the commons were to benefit by the measures which he had enacted in their behalf, they needed a check upon the activities of the magistrates and a voice in the determination of government policies. The aim of the legislator was not to turn the state over to the poor, but merely to give them sufficient power to protect their legitimate interests. "The commons," he said, "ought best to follow their leaders, having neither too much rein nor yet being oppressed." With this end in view, he liberalized and systematized the timocracy which he found in force. It was not certain whether his predecessors had attempted to classify the population on the basis of income as an index to political rights, but Solon did so. His classification was made upon the basis of combined income from grain, wine, and olive oil. The unit of dry measure was the *medimnus* (1½ bushels), and that of liquids the *metretes* (8½ gallons). On this basis four classes were established: the *thetes*, with less than two hundred measures; the *zeugitai*, with two hundred to three hundred measures; the knights (*hippeis*) with three hundred to five hundred measures; and the *pentacosiomedimnoi*, with five hundred measures or over. All classes were admitted to the assembly and the popular law courts. The thetes served the state only in time of emergency as lightarmed infantry or rowers in the fleet, and could hold no offices. The zeugitai served on demand as heavy-armed infantry and might hold minor offices. The two upper classes served in the cavalry, were liable to special taxes and services, and monopolized the higher offices.

None of the old agencies of government were abolished, but all were systematized. Measures were taken to prevent the recurrence of the abuses which had formed one of Solon's grounds of complaint against the aristocrats. The king, polemarch, archon, and thesmothetae were combined into a board of nine archons, who jointly or individually constituted the chief executive of the state. They were to be chosen annually by lot from a list of forty names submitted by the four tribes; and, as before, exarchons formed the Council of the Areopagus. It retained wide judicial powers and in general acted as guardian of the constitution. The Council of the Four Hundred and One was reorganized and lost its extra member, originally intended to guard against a tie vote. The most important of the changes in the government made by Solon, however, was the institution of the popular courts (*heliaea*). Official corruption and oppression were two of the counts upon which he had most bitterly assailed the aristocratic magistrates, and the new court was intended to guard against these evils. It consisted of a body of citizens of good character, over thirty years of age, and sworn to uphold the laws. Little or nothing is known about their number or procedure in Solon's time, but from the first, the court must have been large, and was later fixed at six thousand. To this popular body appeals might be taken from the sentences imposed by the magistrates. At the close of their terms of office, these same magistrates had also to go before the court for audit of their accounts and investigation of their official conduct. With this powerful weapon in their hands, the commons not only checked the corruption of which Solon had complained, but were later able to subject the whole state to their control. Having published an amnesty which permitted the return of all exiles, except those guilty of murder or attempts to overthrow the government, Solon withdrew into private life and soon afterward left the country to travel abroad.

An Evaluation of Solon's Work

Two of Solon's sayings record his own estimate of the character of his work. In his memoirs he says:

> I gave the commons enough power, and did not either detract from nor add to their honor. I planned that those who were mighty and of great wealth should not endure anything unbecoming. I also stood with my strong shield over both parties, allowing neither to gain an unjust victory.[1]

It was this spirit of fairness and impartiality which paved the way for the later reconciliation of the classes that was to save Athens from the barren round of revolutions and counter-revolutions that convulsed so many of the Greek states. Solon's constitution, with its evenly balanced powers for high and low, eliminated the worst evils of Athenian government without becoming a mere partisan instrument for the lower classes. No wonder that it retained its form even after successive liberalizations had changed the government into a radical democracy. Again Solon escaped the pitfalls which usually engulfed Greek lawgivers, in that he envisioned possibilities of growth and change in Athenian society and government. Asked whether his laws were the best possible, he is said to have replied that they were not, but only the best that the Athenians would receive. Unlike Zaleucus or the authors of the Spartan system, he did not attempt to found a tyrannical and unchanging "way of life" for the Athenians.

[1] Edmonds, *Solon*, 5, ll. 1–6. Loeb Classical Library. By permission of the Harvard University Press.

Instead, he left them with a constitution and a set of laws which were flexible enough to invite growth and change. The institutions which he established had many future possibilities, although some were not realized until long after his death. Not without reason did the later Athenians look upon him as one of the founders of their democracy, even though the constitution which he established was not itself a democratic one.

The thirty years following Solon's archonship, however, were not peaceful. Neither party was satisfied with a settlement which awarded only a part of its demands. The poorer landholders of the mountains, disgusted with Solon for his failure to become tyrant and give them a share of the more fertile plain land held by the nobles, formed the "Hill" party, under the leadership of the noble Peisistratus. Their adversaries, the rich landlords, were the backbone of the "Plain" party, led by Lycurgus. Between the two was a moderate group, the "Shore" party, with the Alcmeonid Megacles as its chief. Of the three, only the last upheld Solon's arrangements. Family feuds aggravated the disorder. In 582, Damasias was elected archon and tried to transform his office into a tyranny, but in the third year of his tenure he was ousted by a coalition of all classes. This, however, soon dissolved and war with Megara was resumed. In spite of Damasias' failure, conditions were gradually becoming ripe for a tyranny.

Peisistratus Rises to Tyranny

The decade between 570 and 560 witnessed the steady rise of Peisistratus. He was an able warrior, who had won fame in the struggle with Megara; and his affable manners and championship of the interests of the poor assured him wide popularity. Yet he was not really an extreme radical, as events were to show. Patient and resourceful, he could on occasion cheat and lie with a facility which offends our modern sense of propriety, but which the Greeks regarded with tolerance. He saw the needs of Athens more clearly than any other man of his time, and his understanding of conditions in the Greek world at large was profound. Only toward implacable opponents did he show cruelty. Toward others he was willing to be merciful as soon as active resistance had been overcome.

Having wounded himself and the mules that drew his chariot, Peisistratus drove headlong into the meeting place of the assembly and announced that his opponents had tried to kill him. The people voted him a guard of club-bearers, with which he seized the Acropolis and became tyrant (560). He was twice expelled; but the first time a secret "deal" with Megacles restored him, and the second time he overcame opposition with the aid of mercenary soldiers. He died of old age in 527, having held the tyranny in all about nineteen years and having been in exile about fourteen.

Athens Under Peisistratus

The administration of Peisistratus, Aristotle informs us, was more like a constitutional government than a tyranny. All previous institutions remained in operation, but the supporters and relatives of the tyrant filled the offices and carried out his wishes. The laws of Solon were strictly enforced, and Peisistratus, with a large force of mercenaries at his disposal, was able to end feuds and disorders. He was probably responsible for raising the corps of three hundred Scythian slaves, who, armed with bow and dagger, acted as night patrolmen in the Athens of the next century. For the convenience of the rural populace and to keep them away from the city, he sent out traveling justices to settle minor lawsuits on the spot. He was popular with the masses and even with most of the nobility, although a few families, like the Alcmeonidae, proved refractory and were banished.

During the last years of Peisistratus, Athens was the center of a network of colonies and alliances which affected most of the Greek peninsula and the Aegean coasts. The tyrant cultivated friendly relations with Thessaly, Argos, the Boeotian cities, and Sparta. He had extensive personal possessions, including rich gold mines, on the coasts of Macedonia and Thrace. He sent a colony to occupy the Thracian Chersonesus (Gallipoli peninsula), and another to Sigeum, on the other side of the Hellespont. Both districts were governed by his representatives. Lygdamis, tyrant of Naxos, was his dependent. Thus, Athens acquired markets for her products, especially in the Black Sea region, and her pottery began to replace that of Corinth and Miletus in the export trade.

At home, Peisistratus wrought what amounted to an economic revolution. His private fortune was very large, and he supplemented it by confiscating the lands of banished opponents and by levying an income tax of ten per cent, which was afterward reduced to five per cent. The lands were sold on easy terms and in small tracts to the poor. Landless men were likewise encouraged to lay out vineyards and olive orchards on the hill slopes, receiving loans from the treasury to give them a start. By these measures, he created a large class of small landholders, and not for centuries after his time did the land question arise in Attica. The pottery industry flourished as never before. Skilled workmen, both natives and immigrants, brought the black-figured red style to the greatest perfection that it ever attained; and shortly after his death occurred the change to the red-figured black style in which the ceramic art at Athens was to achieve its most splendid triumphs. Metal-working, shipbuilding, and many other industries were established in the city and the near-by harbor settlement of Phaleron. Probably the silver mines of Laurium were now worked systematically for the first time.

Culture kept pace with industry and commerce. The temple of Athena on the Acropolis (the *Hecatompedon*, "Hundred-Foot House") was surrounded with a colonnade of marble and adorned with sculptures. A huge temple was begun in honor of the Olympian Zeus southeast of the city, but it remained unfinished for nearly seven centuries, until completed by the Roman emperor Hadrian. Like other tyrants, Peisistratus honored Dionysus, for whose worship he constructed a temple south of the Acropolis. A splendid festival, the Greater Dionysia, was instituted, with choral performances from which the Athenian tragic drama was gradually evolved. In honor of Athena, Peisistratus either originated or greatly elaborated the *Panathenaea*, marked by a magnificent procession from the city up to the Acropolis. Poets from other parts of Greece lent luster to the Athenian court, and under the auspices of the great tyrant a complete text of the Homeric poems was written out — probably the first ever made. In a more practical field, Peisistratus constructed an aqueduct which gave the city its first adequate water-supply, with a fountain (the "nine spouts") for its distribution. Roads were laid out to many parts of Attica. For the first time in her history, Athens was in a prominent position among Greek states.

The Decline of the Tyranny

After Peisistratus' death the government remained in the hands of his family for seventeen years. At first his two elder sons, Hippias and Hipparchus, shared the tyranny between them, but as Hippias was an able man of affairs and Hipparchus a frivolous dilettante, the former had by far the greater authority, and administered the state for thirteen years (527–514). A trivial personal quarrel brought the prosperity of the Peisistratid family to an end. A snub administered by Hipparchus to a young aristocrat named Harmodius roused the latter and his friend Aristogeiton to seek vengeance. A plot was formed to assassinate the whole family of the tyrants, but at the last moment it miscarried. Hipparchus was killed, but

the guards slew Harmodius, and Aristogeiton was executed with a number
of other participants in the conspiracy. This incident changed the whole
character of the tyranny. Hippias became suspicious of everybody, and
his cruelty alienated his supporters. The Peisistratid family was ripe for
overthrow, and its enemies were prepared to act.

Among the Athenian exiles were the Alcmeonidae, now led by Cleisthenes, the grandson and namesake of the great tyrant of Sicyon. His
first attempt to dislodge Hippias failed, but by a clever ruse he succeeded
in enlisting the aid of the priests of Apollo at Delphi. Each time the
Lacedaemonians came to consult the oracle, they were told to free Athens
from the tyrant. This advice exactly suited their proverbial policy of be-
friending aristocrats and overthrowing tyrants, and, furthermore, the
Peisistratidae had of late been rather too friendly to Argos. Under their
king Cleomenes, the Spartans succeeded, after a preliminary defeat, in
blockading Hippias in the Acropolis. Distrusting his ability to hold out,
he tried to smuggle his children to a place of safety, but they fell into the
hands of the besiegers. To gain their freedom, he agreed to leave the country and retired to Sigeum. Athens was once more free (510).

THE DEMOCRACY

The departure of the tyrant was the signal for the reappearance of the
party strife which Peisistratus had repressed. The exiled nobles returned,
fully expecting to recover lands and privileges and to consign the upstart
masses again to subjection. The work of the preceding half-century was to
be undone, but events soon proved that this was impossible. The returned
exiles under Cleisthenes were opposed by Isagoras, the partisan and relative of Hippias. For a time both parties confined their efforts to the political clubs of the city, over which Isagoras had control. He was elected
archon for the year 508. While Cleisthenes had returned to Athens as the
leader of the exiled nobles, his background did not fit him for the part of
a reactionary. From his grandfather, the great tyrant of Sicyon, and his
father who had led the moderate party in the days before the rise of Peisistratus, he had inherited more liberal opinions than those of his allies, and
the victory of Isagoras gave him an excuse for putting them into effect.
He appealed to the masses, promising citizenship to the foreigners and
freedmen who either never had had it or had lost it at the hands of his partisans. With their support he overcame Isagoras. The vanquished faction
appealed to Sparta. Cleomenes returned, and in co-operation with Isagoras
expelled Cleisthenes and seven hundred families of his party from the coun-

try, while to insure the ascendancy of Isagoras, he established a Lacedae-monian garrison on the Acropolis. At this the populace rose in arms, blockaded the Spartan garrison, and compelled them to withdraw. Cleis-thenes was again at liberty to carry out his plans.

The Constitution of Cleisthenes: Local Government

The constitution which Cleisthenes established, probably while holding the office of thesmothete, was the keystone of the Athenian democracy. It was the logical outgrowth of the work of Solon and Peisistratus. The former had given to the Athenians a practicable body of civil law, while the latter had broken the power of the aristocracy, strengthened the ad-ministrative machinery of the state, and fostered a class of independent small landholders and tradesmen. It now remained to work out a system of local government free from the destructive influences of sectionalism and the old kinship groups. In accomplishing this purpose, Cleisthenes dis-played a wise mixture of ruthless radicalism and tolerant conservatism. The religious and social functions of clan and phratry were not dangerous, and with them he did not interfere. Each year, as from time immemorial, the phratries continued to celebrate the feast of the Apaturia, at which marriages were solemnized and fathers announced the coming-of-age of their sons and had their names entered upon the citizen rolls. But these groups were no longer exclusive, and in one way or another every Athenian citizen could belong to them. At the same time Cleisthenes completely abolished the political structure based upon them. As we have seen, a half-hearted attempt had already been made to accomplish this purpose in the establishment of the naucraries. These had been part and parcel of the old Ionic tribes, and the redistribution of population in the sixth cen-tury rendered them no longer adequate. In place of the previous system, Cleisthenes established one which was purely territorial.

The land of Attica was divided into more than a hundred *demes*, or wards. All free inhabitants of a deme at the time of its establishment were its citizens, and even slaves living apart from their masters were in some cases enrolled. Citizenship in a deme carried with it citizenship in the state. Thereafter, the state, in registering a citizen, ignored his clan con-nection and placed the emphasis upon his deme. Each deme had a com-plete local organization with an elected *demarch* at its head, treasurers, priests and priestesses, and assembly of citizens. It might own corporate property, had charge of local shrines, and conducted petty local adminis-tration. Several contiguous demes constituted a *trittys*, which did not, however, have any political functions. There were in all thirty trittyes, of which ten occupied territory inhabited by Hill men; ten more, that of the Shore men; and the remaining ten, that of the Plain men. Three trittyes — one from each division — constituted a tribe, and thus there were ten tribes. As the tribes were electoral divisions for the choice of various officials, it followed that the local interests of any given trittys would, at the time of an election, be kept in the minority by those of the other two. As the parts of a tribal territory were not contiguous, had divergent interests, and had no traditional background, it could never in itself become a rallying point for local feeling, any more than a modern French *département*, which is laid out on a somewhat similar principle. The only claimant for the devotion of a citizen was henceforth to be the state.

A Reorganized Government

A new local organization necessitated considerable readjustment in the central government. The archons were, under the tyranny, again elected by the assembly, and Cleisthenes continued the practice. In the Areopagus, no change was made except to diminish its functions. But the Council of Four Hundred had proved to be one of the foundation stones of popular control, and it was thoroughly reorganized, with greatly enlarged powers. Its number was increased to five hundred — fifty from each tribe. The members were chosen by lot, as before. In addition to its previous powers, it was now invested with a wide range of administrative functions. The year was divided into ten arbitrary periods of approximately equal length (*prytaneiai*), and the fifty councilors of each tribe had a period assigned to them by lot during which they were continuously on duty, acting as the chief executives of the state. In cases of emergency, the whole council was called into session. Decrees passed by it, when not contrary to existing laws, were valid for the current year, and when ratified by the assembly became actual laws. As the army was organized into ten tribal regiments and ten squadrons of cavalry, officers were elected by the tribes to command. There were ten generals (*strategoi*), with subordinate officers for each tribe. The supreme command remained in the hands of the polemarch, although the reform greatly diminished his importance. Each tribe likewise elected a treasurer, the ten *apodektai*, to supervise the collection and care of funds.

The assembly continued to be the supreme legislative and policy-determining body of the state, and the popular courts established by Solon retained their organization and prerogatives with little or no change. A host of minor officials were chosen by lot.

Ostracism

Cleisthenes had been the leader of a movement to overthrow the Athenian tyranny and he tried to prevent the rise of any future tyrant. For this purpose he devised the law of *ostracism*.[1] Each year the assembly was summoned and asked whether it wished to declare any person dangerous to the state. If six thousand members or more were present and the vote was affirmative, a second vote was taken. No name was proposed publicly, but each member picked up a piece of broken pottery (the assembly met for this purpose in the market-place, where the ground was strewn with them), and wrote on it the name of the person whom he considered a public menace. If anyone received a majority of votes, he was sent into honorable exile for ten years without other punishment. This was a humane and effective substitute for the barbarous proscriptions which prevailed in other cities. So moderate were the Athenians in its application that nearly twenty years elapsed after its establishment before it was used.

To sum up the government after the establishment of the constitution of Cleisthenes: the Athenians were living under the civil laws of Solon and under a system of local government consisting of territorial units (demes, trittyes, and tribes), which had certain powers of local administration and acted as electoral units for the central government. The latter had as its mainspring the popular assembly, consisting of all adult male citizens who could attend, with the Council of Five Hundred (*Boulé*) as its executive committee. The archons acted both as executive officers and judges, and the Council of the Areopagus was not only a court for the trial of cases of homicide and sacrilege, but an executive body some of whose functions overlapped those of the Council of Five Hundred. The generals, while nominally subordinates of the polemarch, were really his rivals, and the powers of both archons and Areopagus were severely curtailed by those of the popular courts. This curious duplication of offices and powers, the effect of religious feeling and other forms of conservatism, was to exist throughout Athenian history, but in each case the newer office or council was to sap the vitality of its older rival, leaving it little more than a phantom. This system was called a democracy, yet it was so only to the extent that power ultimately reposed in the whole citizen body. The fact that no salaries were paid to officials, assemblymen, or jurymen was in itself enough to exclude the poor from extensive participation in the gov-

[1] It is urged by some that ostracism was not originated by Cleisthenes, but by the enemies of the tyrannist party, in 487, when we first hear of its use. Our Greek sources, however, attribute it to him. Aristotle, *Constitution of Athens*, 22, 3, 6; Glotz, *The Greek City*, pp. 169–171.

ernment, while the census classification of Solon still barred them from the higher offices. On the other hand, the lower classes no longer feared the oppression of the higher, and what amounted to a reconciliation of the two took place. The old nobility for the most part cheerfully and loyally served the new government, and the lower classes regularly elected them to the highest offices. For a century after Cleisthenes, Athens was almost entirely free from the strife, the plots, and the bloodshed which so often convulsed her neighbors. At the end of the sixth century she was, in her foreign relations, still a docile follower of Sparta. Her rôle as defender of democracies in neighboring states was to be played in the next century.

****

16

The Dawn of Greek Civilization;

Learning, Religion, and Ethics

THE VIGOR AND CREATIVE ABILITY, which in the three centuries following 800 B.C. led the Greeks to such great achievements in colonization, commerce, industry, and government, also found expression in the fields of art and intellect. The practical and fine arts rose from the low levels of the Middle Age and developed new forms. Poetry adapted itself to the expression of new thoughts and emotions, and the introduction of alphabetic writing stimulated the evolution of a prose style. Intellectual curiosity led men to question the validity of their religious ideas, to modify them to fit the needs of more mature minds, and, in a few cases, to discard mythical explanations of the origin and character of the universe for philosophical hypotheses. The philosophers did not stop with speculations on material nature, but attempted also to solve the problems of human life and conduct, and even to pierce the mysteries of the hereafter. Interest in geography and history began to awaken, and the Greeks learned, through contact with foreigners, to recognize themselves as a distinct people. In short, this period witnessed the first promising steps toward the creation of the Greek civilization which was later to astonish the world.

But in one respect the Greeks of this new age lagged far behind their Aegean predecessors. Of the household conveniences and decencies which the Minoans had possessed, the historic Greeks knew little or nothing. Drinking water, even in the larger cities, came from easily contaminated wells and springs, and the streets were crooked, unpaved, and filthy. The fine roads of Minoan Crete and the Mycenean Greek kingdoms were not imitated by the new city-states. Land travel and transport were served in most places by crooked lanes and footpaths which made wheel traffic almost impossible and drove men to sea voyages wherever practicable.

Few features of Greek life are more astonishing than the barbarous disregard of this richly endowed people for their material comfort and well-being.

Alphabetic Writing and Its Influence

The coming of the Middle Age to the Greek Peninsula and its neighborhood had been marked by the complete disappearance of the art of writing. For several centuries the only literate branch of the Greek people was the Arcadian colonists in Cyprus, who used a syllabic script derived from that of the Minoans. When the Aegean world, about 800 B.C., again began to record its thoughts in writing, it was in an entirely different medium derived from the Orient.

Greek Writing

We have seen how the Semitic peoples of Syria, Palestine, and near-by countries had evolved a true alphabet instead of the clumsy Babylonian cuneiform and the equally unserviceable Egyptian characters. Commercial contacts between the Phoenicians and the Asiatic Ionians acquainted the latter with the system, and from them it spread, before 700 B.C., to the remainder of the Greek world.

But in this, as in other cultural elements borrowed from their neighbors, the Greeks were not content with slavish imitation. The alphabet underwent in their hands changes so radical that it became in a true sense their own. The Semites had symbols for the consonants only and the reader had to fill in the vowels as best he might. One can realize the inconvenience of such a system if he imagines a similar plan in vogue for writing English. The characters -p-n- might stand for *pan, pen, pin, upon, open, pain, pane,* and several other words, with only the context to guide the reader's choice. The Greeks did not long tolerate this condition. Five of the twenty-two Semitic characters represented consonants which did not exist in the Greek language. These were given vowel pronunciations, and although the innovation did not entirely meet the need for vowel sounds, it did so reasonably well. A series of additional consonant signs was invented to represent sounds not found in the Semitic languages (*phi, xi, chi,* and *psi*). The Phoenician names of the letters were deformed to fit the Greek tongue. Thus, the Phoenician name for the first letter (*aleph* — "ox") became *alpha,* and for the second (*beth* — "house") *beta.* None of these letter-names had any independent meaning in Greek. The Semites wrote from right to left across the page, and for a short time the Greeks did likewise.

Soon it became customary to run alternate lines in opposite directions: right to left and left to right. This was called the *boustrophedon* or "ox-turning" system, from the practice of driving a plow team back and forth across the field and turning it at the end of each furrow. Ultimately, all writing was from left to right.

The diversity of dialects and customs in the new Greece was soon reflected in the local variations which appeared in the alphabet. Two chief groups developed — the eastern and the western. The former included the Ionian and Athenian alphabets, and was the parent of the Greek alphabet which we know. The latter included two letters, *digamma* and *koph*, which were soon dropped out of the eastern group. When the Romans took up the art of writing from the western Greeks, the former became *f* and the latter *q*.

Uses and Influence of Writing

Only gradually did the Greeks discover the possibilities of their new possession. For a long time its use was probably confined to merchants' account books. The oldest inscription — from the island of Thera — cannot have been made long before 700, and few were carved before the seventh century. In the latter part of the seventh century, public opinion had forced the governments of many cities to reduce the laws to writing; and before 600, poetry was being preserved in the same manner. Since it was now no longer necessary to use metrical forms as an aid to memorization, it was possible to employ prose instead of verse in the treatment of non-poetic subjects. Conservatism, however, long prevented the spread of the new medium of expression, and the Greeks never confined the use of verse rigidly to what modern peoples consider its proper field.

The possession by the Greeks of an effective means of recording and preserving their thoughts accelerated their progress along all lines. Although they could transmit oral tradition with marvelous exactness for many generations, written records were far superior. They established direct contact between minds separated by centuries of time and many miles of space, without the inevitable adulteration which accompanies oral transmission, and on a scale impossible where the only means of communication was personal contact.

Numerals

The weakest element in the Greek system of writing was the numerals. Until the end of the fourth century the numbers under five were designated by an appropriate number of vertical strokes, while five (*pente*), ten (*deca*), one hundred (*hecaton*), one thousand (*chilioi*), ten thousand (*myrioi*), were designated by their respective initial letters. A Δ with a ⊓ inside it stood for five tens, or fifty, and an M inside a ⊓ denoted 50,000. The number 30,500 would be written MMM⊓⊢⊓. There was no symbol for zero. Usually, the numbers were simply spelled out. It was practically impossible to employ this clumsy system of notation for mathematical operations, and in practice it was used only to record results. The arithmetical processes were performed mentally, with the aid of mechanical devices like counting-stones, the fingers, or the *abacus*. This weakness retarded the progress of Greek mathematics throughout its history.

Religious Evolution

While the anthropomorphic religion of Homer and Hesiod continued to hold a privileged position among the Greeks throughout their history, it did not completely monopolize the field nor remain unaffected by the current of progress which transformed other phases of Hellenic life. The influence of these poets, it is true, preserved old myths and concepts and brought them to the attention of the educated classes in each generation. This, however, does not mean that they had to be accepted uncritically or that they excluded the existence of rival beliefs. Although the Homeric poems have been called the "Greek Bible," they never attained the adamantine authority of the Hebrew Scriptures. In spite of them, Greek religion remained chaotic, and in the chaos there was the possibility of evolution and growth.

The gods of Homer, in all probability, had always been more popular among the ruling aristocracies, who claimed descent from them, than among the middle and lower classes. The commons, it is true, did not reject his picture of Olympian society, but they modified it to suit their needs, and introduced other gods to supplement it. The Arcadians, as mentioned in Chapter 11, worshiped Zeus in the form of a wolf, and in one of the popular Athenian cults he appeared as a snake. Such practices were permissible, for there was no creed, church, or powerful priesthood to curb them. The common people also assigned great prominence to deities who in Homer were of little importance — Demeter and Persephone, Dionysus, Hephaestus, Hestia, and Hermes. The rise of the submerged classes in the centuries following 800 B.C. brought this popular religion to the front, and the growing complexity and sophistication of society demanded that the gods provide a sanction for moral living which had hitherto been lacking.

Dionysus and the Orphists

Most remarkable of all the gods whom the new age brought into prominence was Dionysus. Originally a Thracian deity, the spirit of wine or beer and the patron of intoxication, he had an inferior place in the aristocratic Homeric epics. By the end of the seventh century, however, he had become the popular object of worship among the peasantry of central Greece. The tyrants in particular encouraged his progress. The myths and ceremonies connected with him were unusual. He was the son of Zeus and a mortal mother, and so he was at once human and divine. When torn to pieces by the Titans, he had risen from the dead. His rites were violently emotional. The worshipers, inflamed with wine and excited beyond control, wandered about in bands with streaming hair, carrying torches, yelling, and singing. At his festivals elaborate choral performances by masked choirs resulted in the creation of the drama, of which Dionysus became the patron. Such a cult could take on a deeper significance, which ultimately it did. In the unbridled excitement of the revels, men felt that they were no longer themselves, but had become mystically united with the god. If so, could they not rise from the dead as he had done and enjoy eternal life and happiness?

To reduce this chaotic cult, so rich in possibilities, to order, and to give it a moral content, was the work of the Orphists. This society took its name from a legendary Thracian bard, Orpheus, whose love for Eurydice is the theme of one of the most touching stories in all literature. The Orphists found in the Dionysus myth a key to the mystery of the universe and the destiny of man.

The Greek Moralist Cults

Dionysus was, in a sense, the supreme being, mystically identified with Zeus and yet distinct from him. He had gone through several incarnations, in one of which he had created the world. Like him, the soul of man was subject to rein arnation and in each existence suffered punishment for the misdeeds committed in previous ones. But Dionysus could free men from this dreary round of birth and death, for the human soul was also in part divine — "the child of Earth and Starry Heaven," as the Orphists phrased it. By abstaining from things that defile, by ritual purification and sacraments, and by mystic union with the god, one could assure himself of eternal happiness in the hereafter. The Orphists had a book of revealed scriptures, prescribed rituals and ceremonies, and an organization for the conduct and propagation of the cult. The faithful took with them to the grave, charms and directions to aid them in the world beyond. The following is a sample:

> You will find a spring under a white cypress to the left of Hades' house. Do not go near it. But you will find another by the Lake of Memory, with cold water flowing out, but there are guards before it. Say "I am a child of Earth and Starry Heaven, but I am of heavenly lineage. You yourself know this. I am dying of thirst. Give me quickly the water that flows from the Lake of Memory." Then they will voluntarily give you a drink from the holy spring, and thereafter you will rule among the other divine spirits.[1]

The influence of Orphism is hard to estimate. Its adherents, in easygoing Greek fashion, combined their faith with belief in the other gods. We do not even know the names of the leaders of this cult, yet the movement must have served to lighten the trials of life for thousands of unfortunates and it contributed to Hellenic religion one of its most significant elements.

Similar in character were the Eleusinian Mysteries, which were a part of the cult of Demeter and Persephone. As Persephone was queen of the Underworld, but was restored to earth for a time each year, she became a symbol of resurrection from the dead, and by her aid mankind might attain eternal life and happiness after death. In the temple of Demeter at the Attic town of Eleusis there was enacted annually a solemn ritual, the participants in which were supposed to gain the protection of the deities, and hence the promise of a blessed hereafter. It was sponsored by the Athenian state. Those to be initiated underwent a solemn purification, partook of various sacraments, and witnessed a mystic drama in which probably they were acquainted with the story of Persephone and her rôle of protectress of souls. Those who had undergone initiation felt that they had gained a priceless possession.

Apollo and the Delphic Oracle

In spite of the prominence of these and other mystery cults, it would be a mistake to think that Greek religion was dominated by mysticism. Diametrically opposed to this tendency in many ways, and of even greater importance for everyday affairs, was the cult of Apollo. As god of prophecy,

[1] Translated from Kaibel, C.I.G.I.S., no. 641.

he had numerous oracles, or shrines, at which advice was given about affairs present and future. Chief of these was the oracle of Delphi, located in the state of Phocis. From a chasm in the rocks there arose a stupefying vapor, which caused those who inhaled it to babble incoherently. The temple of Apollo was built over this spot. His priestess, the Pythia, when about to declare the judgment of the god, was seated on a tripod and swung over the chasm until apparently in complete subjection to his will. Her ravings were then arranged by the priests in the form of hexameter verses, and we may suppose that when the oracle was finally delivered to the inquirer it bore little resemblance to the words of the Pythia. In predicting the future, the Delphic priests were, of course, not infallible, and they could maintain the god's reputation only by wording their responses so ambiguously that they would fit any possible outcome of a given situation. An example of this quibbling is the response given to the Lydian king Croesus when he asked the outcome of his projected attack upon the Persians. The answer was that "he would destroy a great empire." He went to war, but the empire which he destroyed was his own.

The real significance of the Delphic oracle lay in its advice upon current problems. There the priests assumed the rôle of censors of morals and arbiters of interstate relations. Almost without exception their advice was characterized by kindliness, moderation, mercy, decency, and common sense. Numerous instances of their exhortations on the side of righteousness are recorded. Thus when the Milesians burned alive the leaders of their rebellious serfs, they were long forbidden access to the oracle, and when they asked the reason, the god replied:

> My heart is touched for the hapless Gergithae [serfs], poor wretches smeared with pitch.[1]

Again, when a man asked the god's advice about wrongfully retaining money that had been entrusted to him, he was solemnly warned of the awful consequences that would follow, and when the would-be sinner apologized for asking the question, he was threatened with punishment for trying to make Apollo his accomplice in so unsavory an affair. Over the door of the temple were chiseled the mottoes, "Know thyself," and "Nothing in excess," and these may be taken as embodying the principles which the oracle strove to establish. It exerted its influence to abolish weird and cruel religious rites, to prevent wars, and to heal party strife. Greek states and foreign kings vied with one another in the richness of their gifts to it, and a special combination of neighboring states, the Del-

[1] Heracleides Ponticus, quoted by Athenaeus, XII, 26.

phic Amphictyony, protected it from the encroachments of enemies and oppressors.

An Estimate of Greek Religion

In Greek polytheism generally, some progress in the direction of greater spirituality and a higher moral tone was apparent, although it was not strong enough to transform the old beliefs and practices. Even Homer looked upon Zeus as the punisher of flagrant sins: perjury, unfilial conduct, and oppression of the helpless stranger. Hesiod threatens unjust rulers with the anger of Zeus, who was the guardian of family life and the enemy of all who injured their kinsmen. Most implacable of all, the Furies, snake-haired goddesses from the dark regions beneath the earth, hounded the perpetrators of great and shocking crimes through life and carried them to eternal torment after death. Pride and arrogance were sins toward which no mercy was shown; and once a family had thus incurred the divine anger, it was pursued from generation to generation with a weight of inherited guilt.

The patron gods of a city expected patriotic loyalty from its citizens. Like Apollo, the other Olympian gods helped to abolish many barbaric rites intended to promote the fertility of plants, animals, and the human race, rites which teemed with sex-symbols, indecent rituals, and cruelty. Especially was the influence of Athena on the side of better and more humane conduct. The myth of the wars between the gods and the giants was spiritualized and made to typify the struggle between the growing forces of world order and civilization, and those of chaos and barbarism. It is, therefore, apparent why the seventh and sixth centuries were marked by an outburst of religious fervor which can be traced in the impassioned hymns of the poets and in the growing splendor of temples and ceremonies. Yet the darker side of Homeric and pre-Homeric religion, while weakened, still remained. As always, it was impossible to rid the gods of attributes dating from ages of lower moral standards and embodied in popular legends. The homeric *Hymn of Hermes* tells with gusto the story of the young god's theft and successful perjury. The loves of Zeus and the other gods with mortals, which shocked the finer spirits and called down the wrath of some of the philosophers, could not be forgotten. Too many noble families traced their origin to such a source and the authority of the poets was too great to permit a purification of the current mythology; therefore religion remained an odd blend of the primitive and the civilized so long as paganism existed.

SCIENCE AND PHILOSOPHY

The Greeks Create Pure Scholarship

Notwithstanding the approaches which the Egyptians and Asiatics made toward science and philosophy, the Greeks may be properly called the creators of both. The Oriental "Wise Men" had gathered bits of concrete information by empirical means and for practical purposes. The true philosopher and scientist seek knowledge for its own sake, by reason and observation. They are not satisfied with individual facts, but try to understand underlying principles. It was the Greek thinkers who first observed these conditions. Likewise they were the first to endeavor to explain the origin and nature of the universe in the light of such thought and knowledge, without invoking the instrumentality of personal divinities. They entered upon this untrodden path about the end of the seventh century B.C., and began by assimilating the lore accumulated earlier in mathematics and astronomy by their more civilized neighbors.

It was only natural that the first steps toward a rational understanding of the universe should have been made in Ionia, in the great commercial and manufacturing city of Miletus. Contacts with foreign lands enriched her economically and intellectually. In their travels, the Ionians had learned from Egypt or Babylonia to forecast eclipses of the sun and moon with tolerable accuracy, and they had also accumulated geometric knowledge such as the approximate numerical ratio between the diameter and circumference of a circle. Meeting with men of other ideas and beliefs made them reflective and skeptical. In short, it was by absorbing the thoughts of others that the Greeks were trained to think for themselves.

Gnomic Poetry

Their first faltering steps along this path took them no farther than their Oriental models — to the compilation of immediately useful knowledge and rules for good living. In this connection, we have only to recall similar procedure in Egypt and Babylonia. Hesiod's *Works and Days*, with its agricultural lore and exhortations to thrift and justice, is the earliest surviving Greek example of this type of literature. In the seventh and sixth centuries a whole class of writers, the so-called *Gnomic Poets*, followed his example. Pittacus, who is best known as a lawgiver of Mytilene, also wrote gnomic verses, one of which reads:

One should only face a wicked man with a well-bent bow and a quiver of arrows. For his tongue says nothing true and he is prompted by a deceitful heart to utter tricky speeches.[1]

His saying, "It is hard to be a really good man," became a popular proverb. His contemporary, Bias of Priene, was remembered for the following:

Try to please all the citizens, in whatever city you live. For this will win you the favor of all, but haughty manners often produce ruin.[2]

Choose your course with deliberation, but when you have made a choice, then persevere firmly in it.[3]

Theognis of Megara (see Chapter 13) indulged in the following reflections:

Do not associate with the bad, but always with the good. Drink with them, sit with them, eat with them, and be agreeable to them. For you will learn noble lessons from noble men. If you associate with bad men, you will lose what sense you have.[4]

We seek rams, asses, and stallions of noble breed, Cyrnus — but a noble man does not hesitate to marry a low-class woman of low birth if she has plenty of money.[5]

From such observations, it is but a short step to true philosophy.

The First Greek Philosopher

The first Greek who is known to have taken this step was Thales of Miletus (about 636–546 B.C.). Little is really known about his life, and the later Greeks concealed their ignorance behind a mass of apocryphal anecdotes, some of which deserve mention in this discussion. He is known to have been well versed in mathematics and astronomy, both of which he probably learned in Egypt. He served as a military engineer for two Lydian kings, and in 585 B.C. predicted an eclipse of the sun for King Alyattes. Nearly forty years later he tried, unsuccessfully, to form a union of the Greek states against Persia.

In his disinterested thirst for knowledge and his dependence upon orderly reason and observation, Thales has a valid claim to the name of philosopher. The story-tellers of later Greece showed their appreciation of the epoch-making character of his works by telling about him the first "absent-minded-professor" story in history: how, while gazing at the stars, he fell into a well. The partisans of philosophy, however, told another, equally apocryphal, to the effect that one winter he determined from his

[1] Quoted in Diogenes Laertius, *Lives of the Philosophers*, I, 78.
[2] *Ibid.*, I, 85.   [3] *Ibid.*, I, 88.   [4] *Elegies*, I, ll. 31–36.
[5] *Ibid.*, I, ll. 183–186; condensed.

knowledge of the stars that there would be an abundant olive crop the next summer. He hired all the available olive presses at a low price and cleared a large sum on his monopoly.

The problem which Thales attempted to solve was a stupendous one, being nothing less than that of determining how the universe had originated. Observing how large a part water played in nature and how silt is deposited by standing water, he concluded that in water he had found the original form of all matter, some of which had evolved into other forms. Eventually, he believed, these variant forms would return to water. He believed that the earth rested upon the ocean like a floating block of wood, that the heavenly bodies consisted of burning earth, and that the moon received its light from the sun. As Thales apparently did not reduce his ideas to writing, we may assume that we have here only scraps of what must have been a far more extensive body of conclusions.

The Ionian School

The mixture of philosophy and physical science which characterized the teachings of Thales was still further elaborated by his fellow citizen and pupil Anaximander (early sixth century). He embodied his conclusions in a book to which later generations gave the name *Nature*. In seeking the first form of matter, Anaximander rejected the idea that one of the existing forms gave rise to the rest. The first principle of all things, he taught, is the "Infinite," which is different from any known form of matter. In it are embodied all the qualities which matter can possess, even opposite qualities. From it the heavens and the earth had their beginning, and into it they will some day return. Even the gods are subject to this inexorable law. The earth, he taught, is cylindrical in shape, and the heavenly bodies are circles of fire which surround it. They have opaque coverings in which are holes like the holes of a flute, and the fire which shines through them is all that we can see. Partial or complete stoppage of the holes in the "sun-circle" and "moon-circle" is the cause of eclipses and of the phases of the moon. Anaximander had a crude idea of the evolution of animals, including man, from lower forms of life. In astronomy and geography he did significant work aside from his theories, including a chart for making sundials and a map of the world.

Anaximenes, who like his two predecessors was a native of Miletus, flourished in the later sixth century. Like them he attempted to find the first form of matter and decided that it was air. From it, he said, other forms of matter are produced by condensation and rarefaction.

The last important member of the Ionian school of natural philosophers, Heracleitus, was a native of Ephesus, and was active about 500 B.C. He, too, sought the primary form of matter and thought that he had found it in fire. The most significant facts in the universe, he said, are change and struggle. Everything is in a perpetual state of flux. At intervals the whole physical universe is reconverted to fire, only to resume its former shape. As it is a world of change, so it is a world of strife — a struggle between opposite qualities, which is the essence of life. Their opposite character is only apparent. Life and death, sleeping and waking, existence and nonexistence, youth and age, are all basically the same, because each one of a pair of opposites can change into the other. But this endless change is governed by a supreme law. "The sun," he said, in the naïve language of his time, "will not overstep his bounds. If he does, the Furies, allies of justice, will find him out." This universal law is God and all nature is but varying forms of Him. Heracleitus was the first Greek to make a distinction between knowledge and wisdom, and he claimed that Homer, Hesiod, and several of his contemporaries had the first without the second.

With Heracleitus, the Ionian school of physical philosophy closed. This was in part owing to the calamities inflicted upon the Asiatic Greeks by the Persians; although there were other causes. The problem which they had attacked was too formidable to be solved by the aid of reason alone, and even our own age, with its immeasurably greater command of factual knowledge and methods of reasoning, has not yet solved it. Their conflicting hypotheses are in themselves of small value to us, but that does not greatly detract from the splendor of their achievements. They were the creators of philosophy in that they pursued knowledge for its own sake, and tried to free its gold from the dross of mythology by the use of reason. Subsequent ages have far surpassed them, but only because they built upon the foundation which the Ionians had laid.

Pythagoras

Contemporary with the later members of the Ionian school was Pythagoras of Samos (about 550–475 B.C.). While still relatively young he migrated to the Greek city of Croton in Italy, where he spent the remainder of his life and where his work was done. His life and teachings are obscured by legends. The philosophy of Pythagoras was a mixture of mathematics, natural science, and religion. He organized his disciples into a monastic brotherhood with a strict ascetic discipline. They rapidly assumed political functions, and dominated the city. Other cities, including

Tarentum, eventually submitted to a similar régime, although the men of Croton exterminated their local Pythagorean society in a bloody revolution.

Pythagoras made *numbers* one of the fundamental points in his system. He is said to have been the first to demonstrate the geometric theorem that "the square erected upon the hypotenuse of a right triangle is equal to the sum of the squares of the other two sides," and probably did other work in the same field. But he went farther. For him, *number* held the place that water, fire, air, or "the Infinite" held for the physicists — the primary substance of the universe. Mystic properties were assigned to the numbers and geometric figures. Thus he was led into fantastic vagaries. In the field of physics he or his followers determined by experiment the relation between the length of a taut string and the pitch of the notes which it could be made to emit when plucked. He recognized that the earth is a sphere, and worked out an elaborate explanation of the movements of the heavenly bodies, but here again his mysticism proved a stumbling-block.

Pythagoreanism, being more nearly a religion than a true philosophy, also concerned itself with the nature and fate of the human soul. Its founder was a firm believer in the doctrine of transmigration, and in other respects held views similar to those of the Orphists. His identification of God with "the One" points toward monotheism. The later Pythagoreans no doubt elaborated the doctrine, and some of their views were credited to their founder.

Xenophanes

In Xenophanes of Colophon (later sixth century) we may see the echoes of the Ionian tradition mingled with religious and moral teachings. Although an Ionian by birth, he spent the last sixty-seven years of his life in exile. As a wandering poet, he visited many parts of the Greek world, and his sensitive, independent temperament did not always win friends. In his opinion, matter is indestructible, and the universe has always existed. The land periodically rises from the sea and sinks back into it. He supported this conclusion in a thoroughly scientific manner by pointing to the presence of marine fossils in rocks high above the water. He seems to have attempted a scientific collection of data on the volcanoes of Sicily and the Lipari Islands. His views on scientific questions, interesting as they are, are secondary in importance to his opinions on religion and morals. With the zeal of a missionary, the keen insight of an anthropologist, and the embittered scorn of an exile, he lashed the vices and foibles of his country-men and their gods. Homer and Hesiod, he said, had disgraced the divine nature by attributing to the gods vices and crimes shameful even to men. Such stories are false. There is but one God, and He is all mind and knowl-edge, without beginning and without end. The reason for the misrepre-sentation of the deity, he said, is that men attempt to make Him in their own image. Ethiopians make the images of their deities black, pug-nosed, and woolly-haired. "And if cattle and lions had hands, so as to produce works of art as men do, they would represent their gods in forms like their own — horses like horses, cattle like cattle." He castigated the luxurious habits of his countrymen, and in particular the extravagant honors paid to victors in the athletic games. Permenides, who founded the Eleatic School, may have been his pupil.

Thus, the keenest minds of Ionia and the remainder of Greece had re-jected before 500 B.C., wholly or in part, the traditional mythology as a means of explaining the universe and of furnishing a basis for conduct. But we must not exaggerate the influence of philosophy upon the masses of the population. Only a few of the better-educated people came into con-tact with the philosophers. The vast majority clung to their old beliefs or absorbed new religious ideas; they knew little and cared less about the innovations of Thales and his kind.

Geography and Genealogy

From philosophy, the spirit of rational criticism soon extended to geography and history. In an age of exploration it was but natural that men's interests in distant lands should be stimulated, and as early as the middle of the seventh century, Aristeas of Proconnesus had composed a geographical poem on Scythia. The pride of cities and of noble families had led to poetical accounts of their origins, and a group of authors known as "genealogists" had arisen to cater to the demand. The first writers of this class composed their works in verse and were wholly uncritical. But the later sixth century saw a significant change. Hecataeus of Miletus undertook to apply rationalistic principles to both genealogy and ge-ography, and to broaden their scope. Travel, study, and practical experi-ence had fitted him for the task, and his determination to write in prose freed him from the cramping influence of poetic conventions. His *Gene-alogies* open with a significant statement: "I write here what I think is true, for the Greeks have numerous stories which in my opinion are ridicu-lous." Thus his aim was precisely that of all true historians: to tell the exact truth, without romantic coloring or personal bias. His treatment of old myths, it is true, was less radical than that of Xenophanes, and he usually did no more than rationalize the more fantastic and improbable parts of them. In his book *The Circuit of the Earth* he described all known countries and gave a sketch of the historical development of each down to about 500 B.C. Thus, although his work cannot be said to be pure history and only partly met the rigid test which he had established for it, he laid the foundation upon which the historians of the next century were to build. A whole class of *logographers* or "writers in prose" appeared in the later sixth century, and treated, for better or worse, the same subjects on which Hecataeus had written.

— MORALITY AND NATIONALISM —

Religion, philosophy, and political progress alike contributed to the improvement of morality in the Greek world during the sixth century. We have seen how the first two raised the ideals of the people. The leveling of harsh class distinctions by lawgivers and tyrants, and the political stabilization of the Peloponnesus by the Spartans made it possible to put these ideals into practice to a greater extent than ever before. The repression of lawless feuds and piracy by the strong arm of government allowed men to cultivate the virtues of peace. The consequence was a marked improvement in all lines of conduct.

It is hard to determine how far individual conduct was influenced by this improvement of conditions. The Greek had at all times an unabashed frankness in preaching what he practiced, whereas our modern world veils many of its doings behind a decent cloak of hypocrisy. To justify lying and deceit, he had the unimpeachable authority of Homer, and such worthies as Peisistratus were masters of guile, even when they used it for humane and statesmanlike ends. His sex morality was certainly as strict as that of the contemporary Jews: though neither was precisely puritanical. Practices such as the abandonment of unwanted babies were not even seriously denounced. All in all, it is safer to seek for evidence of higher ethical standards in public than in private life.

The most striking manifestations of this ethical progress were moderation, self-restraint, and humanity. In many places luxury in food, clothing, and household equipment were restrained by law. Wars between states and occasional revolutions continued to occur, but the former, at least, were robbed of much of their barbarity by the growth of a well-recognized international law, upheld by public opinion and the stronger city-states. Thus, unprovoked attacks upon neighbors were discredited. In war it became customary for captors to allow the ransom of Greek prisoners instead of enslaving or massacring them. After a battle the victorious army usually gave up the bodies of their slain enemies to the vanquished under a flag of truce.

Greek Nationalism; Festivals and Games

Indeed, the latter part of the sixth century witnessed a marked tendency toward cultural — but not political — nationalism among the Greeks. Their thin line of colonies, spread along thousands of miles of the Mediterranean coastline, showed them quite clearly the essential similarity of all Greeks as opposed to the endless variety of foreign peoples with whom they were in contact. Recognition of this fact was not long in coming. They adopted a common name, *Hellenes,* and to account for it invented a common ancestor, *Hellen.* From him, through his three sons (Dorus, Aeolus, and Xuthus), the various branches of the Hellenes were said to be descended. A common name for all Greeks called for one to designate all non-Greeks. They were *barbaroi* — people who could not talk intelligibly. As yet the name implied no stigma. That was to come in the next century.

Hellenic cultural unity was fostered by many factors, among which great importance must be assigned to the national religious festivals and athletic games. Of the latter, four were predominant: the Olympic, Pythian, Isthmian, and Nemean. The Olympic Games were held in honor of Zeus near his shrine at Olympia in Elis, and were the most important of all. The Pythian Games were held in honor of Apollo at Delphi; the Isthmian, in honor of Poseidon at Corinth; and the Nemean, in honor of Zeus at Nemea near Argos. The first two were celebrated at intervals of four years and the others at intervals of two years. All were very old. Only free Greeks could participate in the contests, which consisted of races on foot and in chariots, jumping, boxing, wrestling, and the *pancration* — a sort of rough-and-tumble fight in which no tactics were barred. The proudest aristocrats were glad to enter their names for these events. Warring states observed truces while they were in progress and visitors traveled to and from them unmolested. They were places of general resort for the cultured classes. The victors were recipients of the most extravagant honors from their native cities, and sections of the city walls were broken down to admit them on their return. Statues were erected in their honor, poets sang their praises, and they were feasted at public expense.

To win the simple crown of bay or laurel, young aristocrats spent weary years of practice. No other people ever put such emphasis upon a thing of so little practical utility, or glorified so extremely the perfection of physical strength and agility. From the figure of the naked athlete, the sculptors acquired the knowledge of anatomy which enabled them to surpass the artists of all other nations in the realistic portrayal of bodies in action.

17

****

The Dawn of Greek Civilization;

Art and Literature

THE PRACTICAL ARTS

ANY DESCRIPTION of manufacturing methods and technical skill in ancient Greece must be confined largely to such activities as metal-work and pottery, specimens of which have been able to withstand the ravages of time. Although the Greeks were skillful workers in both wood and textiles, in both fields the perishable character of the material used has compelled us to rely for our knowledge upon paintings, sculptures, and written descriptions. Even the larger pieces of bronze or gold-work have gone into the melting pot and are lost to the world. In the arts of coinage and pottery, however, sufficient evidence survives to enable us to trace their progress with considerable exactness.

Early Coinage

Coinage, in the strict and accepted sense of the word, had probably never existed until after 700 B.C. In the seventh and sixth centuries it became an important force in the economic evolution of the Greek people and furnished the die-cutter with a splendid opportunity for artistic expression. The earliest coins were merely pieces of precious metal of known weight and fineness which had been heated red-hot, laid upon a striated metal surface, and punched on the upper side with three square or oblong marks. As the invention spread from one city-state to another, it became necessary for each government to stamp its coins with a distinctive device which would identify them. At this point the die-cutter became an artist. A representation of the city's patron god or some other unmistakable symbol

Numismatic Society

Left: ACRAGANTINE AND ATHENIAN COINS   *Right:* EARLY LYDIAN
AND IONIAN COINS WITH PUNCH MARKED REVERSES

was cut into the surface of the bronze or soft iron die, and with it all or part of the city's name. This was to stamp the obverse side of the coin. A similar die, bearing some other device, was cut out for the reverse side. A blank coin was laid upon one of these dies, the other was placed above it, and the upper die was struck one or more heavy blows with a hammer. Thus, both sides of the coin would be shaped by one operation. Little care was taken to secure a round coin or to protect the edges from clipping. Indeed, the practice of milling the edges of valuable coins to protect them from the shears of the coin-clipper was unknown until modern times.

As coined money originated in Asia Minor, it was natural that the earliest and crudest specimens in existence would be from Asiatic mints. The Phocean coins, marked on the obverse with a seal and the letter *phi*, and on the reverse with three punch-marks, or those of Chios (obverse, a sphinx and a vase; reverse, punch-marks), are so rude that they can hardly be classed as art. On the other hand, the Italian and Sicilian Greeks began at an early date to strike pieces of good shape, bearing neatly executed and pleasing images. Examples of their work are the Syracusan *staters* (four-drachma pieces) of the later sixth century, bearing on the obverse the head of the patron nymph Arethusa within a border of dolphins and on the reverse a four-horse chariot whose driver is being crowned by the goddess of victory. The artistic quality of such a piece is fully equal to that of the

Museum of Fine Arts, Boston

SYRACUSAN COIN

sculptures of the same period. The silver coins of Athens, however, while noted for their honest weight and pure metal, never attained such excellence of design. The Athenian stater was stamped on the obverse with a crude head of Athena and on the reverse with an owl of equally poor design. Before the end of the sixth century nearly all important Greek states had their own mints, and as the dies wore out rapidly, hundreds of cutters must have been employed. Yet in the entire history of Greek coinage, only a few are known to us by name and none from the period before 500.

Developments in Pottery

The other practical art of which many remains exist today was pottery-making. We have seen that the Minoan and Mycenaean potters had attained perfection of technical methods and a mastery of delicate naturalism in the decoration of their work. At no time in the Middle Age did the potter forget how to cleanse his clay, how to shape it on the wheel, and how to fire it thoroughly. But for several centuries the shapes of pots, vases, and jars were rude and awkward, and the prevailing style of decoration was the primitive geometric. During this period three schools of decoration were pre-eminent: the Athenian, the Corinthian, and the Ionian.

As late as the end of the eighth century, the Athenian school was the chief exponent of the geometric style. Near the Dipylon Gate of Athens was a cemetery in which, during the ninth and eighth centuries, a number of huge vases were set up as tombstones. Their outer surfaces were divided into parallel bands, each of which was filled with meanders, zigzags, and other patterns rendered in straight lines. Occasional attempts at naturalistic drawing relieved the monotony. A band might be filled with human or animal figures instead of geometric motifs, or a scene would be represented: a wedding procession, a funeral, or a battle. The drawing was childish. A human torso was represented by two triangles with the apexes joined, the arms and legs being mere lines, and the head a shapeless knob. But the vessels were shaped with a simple dignity and a grandeur which redeem many of their faults.

The Corinthians and Ionians were strongly influenced by Phoenician and other Oriental contacts. They soon emerged from the geometric stage, and began to imitate the human, animal, and monster forms which they found on their models. At Corinth this style is known as "proto-Corinthian," and its best examples display a high degree of artistic merit. Both Corinthians and Ionians soon passed beyond this stage and evolved styles of their own. Somewhat later than the others, perhaps about 700, the Athenians abandoned their geometric style and followed the trends prevalent in other centers.

During most of the seventh and sixth centuries, the Corinthians were the chief producers of pottery for export, with the Ionians of Samos, Chios, and Miletus strong rivals. All these centers used the style known to modern students as "black-figured red." The decorations were usually in black, although relieved at times by brown, red, or even white. The field was the red of the baked clay. The artist no longer attempted, as in the geometric style, to cover the outer surface completely with ornamentation. Instead, he concentrated his attention upon one or two large scenes with occasional borders of geometric motifs. His subjects were taken from mythology, legend, or everyday life, and his drawing, while it retained certain archaic features, gained rapidly in grace and sureness of touch. Sixth-century specimens of this style throb with life, motion, and humor. Unlike the modern pottery painter, who may stencil the same device upon thousands of pieces, the Greeks never made two pieces exactly alike. The gods, the adventures of Heracles, the Trojan War, street scenes from his native city, the interior of his shop, farmers at work in the fields, ships at sea or tied up at the dock — these and thousands of other scenes furnish us with an endless panorama of the world, real and imaginary, in which the artist lived. To make sure that his meaning would not be mistaken, he labeled the characters in each scene. Beginning with the Corinthians, it became the practice in many places for the potter to "sign" his work, and thus the names of some of the greatest of them are known. After the middle of the sixth century, the superior work of the Athenians and the

FRANÇOIS VASE ABOUT 560 B.C.

(*left*) DIPYLON VASE, 800 B.C.

HERCULES AND ANTAEUS (*Red-figured black jar*)

HERCULES AND KING BUSIRIS (*Clay jar from Ionia*)
Pictures from University Prints

shrewd diplomacy of Peisistratus gained one market after another, and before 500 B.C., Athenian mastery of the export trade was an accomplished fact.

Before the end of the sixth century, the "black-figured red" style was losing ground before a rival — the "red-figured black" style. As the name indicates, it meant a reversal of colors between ground and figures. The former was now painted black and the latter was left with the red of the clay the prevailing tone. This practice permitted much finer shading than its predecessor. Fine lines could be used to bring out details. Drawing and grouping improved greatly, and the increasing variety of the scenes reflected the growing richness of contemporary life. The older style lingered on for a long time but the new one dominated the field.

THE FINE ARTS

As the Greek world emerged from the crude conditions of the Middle Age, religion and civic pride stimulated the revival of architecture, sculpture, and, to some extent, painting. Of the splendid achievements of the older civilization of Crete and Greece, little or nothing remained. Wood and sun-dried brick were the best materials which the builders of the Middle Age knew how to use, while rudely carved and gaudily painted treetrunks or blocks of wood served as images of gods and heroes. When, in the eighth century, men once more began to feel the urge toward more beautiful and more durable works of this kind, they were compelled to begin their artistic training almost from the start and to learn anew the fundamentals from the Egyptians, Phoenicians, and the people of Asia Minor.

The Greek Temple: Origins

The history of Greek architecture up to 500 is principally concerned with the evolution of the temple, and here there were few or no precedents from the older civilization of the Aegean world upon which to build. As we have seen, the gods of Knossos and Mycenae had been housed almost exclusively in chapels in private houses or palaces. During the Middle Age, however, a few communities had followed the Oriental practice by erecting buildings to protect sacred images and utensils. These were at first only modest cells constructed of the cheapest materials. Such was the temple of Artemis Orthia at Sparta, built before 900 B.C. It was a small imitation of a megaron palace, about fifteen feet in width and thirty in length. The foundation was of stone, the framework and roof of wood, and the walls of sun-dried brick. The roof was gabled and supported within by a row of wooden columns running lengthwise along the center of the building. No windows were needed, for the worship of the deity was performed at an altar outside the door. The image of the goddess was of wood, so small that the priestess carried it out in her hands at each ceremony. The walls of such buildings were protected from the weather by a coat of dazzling white stucco. They were very durable and by no means ugly when viewed from without. No doubt there were temples of similar character in other cities in the Middle Age.

These primitive structures had certain features which persisted as artistic conventions long after their usefulness had passed, and traces of them may be seen in modern buildings which embody the classical tradition. Because of the softness of the sun-dried brick, the top of the wall was covered by a broad wooden beam — the *architrave* or top beam — which spread the weight of the roof evenly and prevented the rafters from damaging the wall. In the later stone temples it persisted as a distinct band of stone at the top of the wall, or directly over the columns of the colonnade. To prevent the roof from spreading and thus collapsing, a row of beams was laid across the structure from side to side, their ends resting on the architrave and attached to the ends of the rafters. The ends of these cross-beams were visible from the outside and between them were holes, each of which was probably filled with a block of wood. When stone replaced wood and sun-dried brick as building material, these beam-ends were represented by blocks of stone, each of which was divided by vertical grooves into three parts — a *triglyph*. The blocks which had formerly stopped the holes between the beam-ends (*metopes*, "openings between") were likewise continued in the stone temples and later covered with relief sculptures. A band of these alternating triglyphs and metopes constituted a Doric frieze. In the primitive temple it had been customary to protect the lower part of the wall from injury by a veneer of wooden planks. This practice was continued in the later structures by covering the lower courses of the wall with an additional veneer of stone, the corners mitered in imitation of the earlier wooden veneer.

The Evolution of Temple Plans

Modifications soon began to be made in the simple plan just described. To provide a comfortable loitering place for the worshipers on hot and sunny days, a porch was constructed before the door. This was done by

In Asiatic Greece, the Ionic order took form. In general it was lighter, less massive, and more highly ornamented than the Doric order. The columns rested upon sculptured bases, the flutings were more deeply cut, and the capitals were shaped like scrolls. The frieze, instead of alternating triglyphs and metopes, was a plain band of sculpture.

Temple Sculpture

Temple architecture afforded the sculptor a splendid opportunity for the exercise of his talents. The friezes of both Doric and Ionic buildings were decorated with reliefs. The gabled roofs left triangular spaces, the *pediments*, to be filled with high reliefs or with figures done in the round. Last, and most important of all, were the images of the gods, upon which the best artistic talent was lavished. It is not surprising that the development of sculpture went hand-in-hand with that of architecture, or that the sixth century saw extraordinary progress in both.

Although the Greeks of the Middle Age had continued to make a few crude figures of bronze, wood, or ivory, their descendants in the seventh century had to learn anew some of the simplest rudiments of the art of sculpture from Egyptians and Asiatics. The colonists at Naucratis and visitors from the Aegean region were in touch with Egyptian artists and craftsmen who had at their disposal the accumulated skill and knowledge of thousands of years, and whose secrets were gradually learned and applied by the Greeks. There the Greek stonecutter learned to control his materials with a sure hand, and there he acquired the artistic conventions which were to influence his work until the fifth century. From Egypt, the Ionians of Samos and Miletus learned how to cast hollow statues of various metals, and from the Ionians the art passed to the other Greeks.

The oldest Greek relief sculptures now in existence date from about 600 and represent the art in its infancy. The figures are gross and awkward, the elevation is nearly uniform, and there is little or no attempt to show depth. Conventional attitudes and facial expressions predominate. Thus, in the group "Perseus Beheading Medusa" from a metope at Selinus, all the figures face the spectator, but the feet are in profile. The same group also illustrates a striking artistic convention of the period — the "archaic smile." As it was used until the end of the sixth century to denote all kinds of emotion from joy to the agonies of death, we need not be surprised to see on the face of the dying Gorgon a bright smile, while the faces of Perseus and Athena are entirely expressionless. Sculpture in the round is equally uncouth. A female figure from Delos is little more than a rounded

University Prints

PERSEUS BEHEADING MEDUSA
From Temple of Selinus

shaft, with a featureless face and with arms which cling closely to the
sides. In both male and female figures the sculptor long adhered to Egyptian conventions. This tendency may be illustrated from a series of male
statues, conventionally termed "Apollos" or "Kouroi," which date from
the first half of the sixth century and come from various parts of the Aegean
region. They stand stiffly upright, the hands at the sides, and the left foot
of each figure is thrust forward.

While these and other conventions long persisted, progress was steady
and fairly rapid throughout the sixth century. The "Apollos" show a
steadily increasing knowledge of anatomy and mastery of material. The
reliefs of the "Harpy Tomb," an Asiatic Greek production of about 550,
display delicacy as well as finish. At Athens the age of Peisistratus was a
period of remarkable progress. The great tyrant invited the most skillful
sculptors of the Greek world to Athens and gave them opportunities to

MALE FIGURE FROM TENEA ABOUT 575 B.C.

work. The result was to make that city the art center of the Aegean region. Marble replaced limestone as the popular medium. A touch of archaic stiffness long peristed in the Athenian work of the period, but it was redeemed by the improved rendering of faces, limbs, and draperies. Characteristic of this school is a series of female figures discovered by modern excavators on the Acropolis and now in the local museum. These "maidens" are elaborately dressed and the sculptor has reproduced their costumes and coiffeurs with meticulous care. The same foppish elegance is to be observed in the arrangement of the hair and beard of the so-called "Rampin Head," now in the Louvre. Details have been carefully mastered and we may readily suppose that we have before us realistic representations of the shallow but graceful "socialites" of Peisistratid Athens. Of emotion or power there is little trace, but that was no doubt the fault of the environment and not of the artist. By the end of the century, Greek sculpture was nearing maturity. The foreign influences under which it arose had been assimilated. The pupil had become the equal of his teacher, and in the next century would surpass him.

Painting

Aside from pottery, the sixth-century painters found in the coloring of statues and reliefs the most important outlet for their talents. All sixth-century sculptures, whatever the material, were painted. The colors, however, were not in any sense naturalistic. Remains from the Athenian Acropolis show such startling effects as green bulls, blue horses, and red lions. Human figures were often colored a bright pink. The purpose was probably to catch the eye rather than to impart to the figure a semblance of reality.

LITERATURE

In the works of Homer, the heroic epic attained its greatest perfection, and thereafter, although imitations long continued to appear, it was plainly decadent. The stories of heroes of old could not hold man's interest indefinitely. The stirring of new interests demanded new forms of expression. While the post-Homeric epics were net all devoid of literary merit or of influence upon later Greek writers, they were far below the level of the *Iliad* and *Odyssey*, and the decline was progressive. When Eugammon of Cyrene finished his insipid *Telegonia* about 570, the stream of epic inspiration had run dry. Long before his time the poets had turned to more fruitful fields.

Didactic Poetry: Hesiod

Even before the end of the ninth century, while kings and nobles were still listening greedily to tales of old wars, Hesiod was composing his *Works and Days*. We have already examined this poem for the light which it sheds upon economic and social conditions at the time of its composition.[1] It is the oldest surviving example of a type of poetry whose appeal was to the middle and lower classes, and whose aim was to put into literary form rules of conduct and directions for the performance of necessary tasks — in short, didactic poetry. The meter, like that of the Homeric epic, is dactylic hexameter. Aside from the knowledge of agricultural methods which it imparts to the modern reader, it provides him with a priceless picture of the laborious existence of the Boeotian small farmer, and of the qualities which characterized the class: shrewdness, persistence, keen observation, superstition, and dour pessimism. It abounds in wise and pithy sayings:

> Do not put off your work until tomorrow or the day following, for a lazy worker does not fill the barn . . . Industry makes work go well, but a delayer always faces ruin.[2]

[1] Chapter 12.

[2] *Works and Days*, I, 405–412, condensed.

FEMALE FIGURE FROM THE ATHENIAN ACROPOLIS

Invite your friends to a meal, and especially your neighbor, but not your enemy. If a misfortune happens, neighbors come without waiting to put on their clothes, but relatives stop to dress. A bad neighbor is as great a pest as a good one is a blessing.[1]

Take fair measure from your neighbor when you borrow, and pay him back fairly with as good measure, or better, if you can. Thus, if you are afterward in need, you will find him ready.[2]

To Hesiod, as to the author of Genesis, woman is the source of all man's ills. This belief is embodied in the story of Pandora's jar. Zeus was angry with the human race, and to punish mankind he caused Hephaestus to fashion the first woman. Each of the gods gave her some attractive characteristic, except Hermes, who endowed her with "lies, crafty words, and a deceitful nature." She was named Pandora ("All-endowed" or "Gift of all"), and Zeus deceitfully gave her to the man Epimetheus as a gift. Until then mankind had suffered no evils, for every misfortune was imprisoned in a huge, covered jar, and Hope was their fellow prisoner. But Pandora took the lid from the jar, and released all the prisoners except

[1] *Ibid.*, I, 467–473.   [2] *Ibid.*, I, 479–482.

Hope, so that now men live in misery, with only Hope to solace them.

The wretchedly inadequate lunar calendar of the Greeks compelled the farmer to become versed in a crude astronomical lore as a means of apportioning his work throughout the year. Thus:

> When the Pleiades, daughters of Atlas, are rising, begin your harvest, and your plowing when they are ready to set.[1]

> When Zeus has completed sixty winter days after the solstice, the star Arcturus leaves the ocean and first rises brilliantly at dusk. After him . . . the swallow appears to men when spring is just beginning. Before she comes trim your vines.[2]

Rural life was ruled by a host of superstitions, to which the last one hundred and fifty lines of the *Works and Days* are devoted. Lucky and unlucky days played an important part in life:

> The sixth day of the mid-month is very unfavorable for plants, but it is good for the birth of males, though unfavorable for a girl either to be born or married.[3]

> Do not trim your nails at a festival of the gods.[4]

Several other works were attributed to Hesiod by later Greek literary critics, but of these only the *Theogony* ("Birth of the Gods") need concern us. It is a hexameter poem of 1022 lines, which traces the generations of the gods and demigods from Chaos and Earth down to the Olympian gods and their children. Its chief importance is that it was perhaps the nearest approach to systematic theology that the classical Greeks ever achieved and served as a source of religious lore for the poet's successors.

Lyric and Elegy

For nearly a century after Hesiod, no poet of importance appeared. Monarchies passed away, the age of colonization began, and life became complicated by interstate wars and class strife. For better or worse, contemporary interests were absorbing men's thoughts, and personal feelings demanded expression. Current issues provided subjects for the poets, but they could not be treated in the old manner. New forms of composition became popular — the elegy, the iambic, and several forms of *melic* poetry. All will be treated under the general heading *monodic* lyrics, those intended to be sung or recited by a single performer, to distinguish them from the *choral* lyric, which was adapted to group rendition.

[1] *Ibid.*, II, 525.   [2] *Ibid.*, II, 783–786.

[3] *Ibid.*, II, 1089–91.   [4] *Ibid.*, II, 1029–30.

Metropolitan Museum

STATUE OF MAIDEN IN IONIC COSTUME
Acropolis, Athens

The nearest of these to the epic in form was the elegy. It consisted of a series of couplets, each made up of a hexameter line followed by a pentameter line. It seems to have been invented in Ionia some time before 700 B.C. and in the following century spread to the remainder of the Greek world. It was particularly adapted to songs of war, love, and grief, but could be employed for didactic purposes. The first known elegist, Callinus of Ephesus, is a shadowy figure, whose career seems to have fallen within the seventh century. Only one fragment survives — a war song — which may be the work of Tyrtaeus, the Spartan poet, to whom it has been ascribed by authorities. Of the latter, and of Solon the Athenian elegist, mention has already been made. With Mimnermus of Colophon (about 630 to 600) the elegy became devoted entirely to the expression of personal feelings. His poetry breathes a spirit of languorous melancholy:

The murky fates stand by our sides, one holding the goal of troublesome old age, the other of death.   Small is the harvest of youth, as
far as the sun lights up the earth.   But when its bloom is past, it is
better to die than to live.[1]

The elegy was used by certain other seventh- and sixth-century poets.
It was revived by the Hellenistic writers of the third and second centuries
B.C. and was continued by the Roman poets.   Both associated it more
closely with the sad reflections of Mimnermus than with the manly exhortations of Callinus, Solon, or Tyrtaeus.

The Iambic Lyric

The iambic measure, each foot consisting of a short, followed by a long
syllable, originated among the common people, who found it well adapted
to impromptu satirical verse.   Its elevation to literary respectability was
the work of Archilochus, known to have been living in 648.   This colorful
personality was the first literary man in Greek history, except Hesiod, to
tell us anything about himself, and he laid bare his life to the world with
a shameless frankness which far surpassed the great Boeotian.   Archilochus was the son of a Parian aristocrat and a slave woman, and he accordingly grew up without a recognized place in society.   He was proud, headstrong, witty, hot-tempered, and reckless.   In his youth he joined a colony sent by his countrymen to the island of Thasos, where they mined
gold and silver.   But Archilochus was ill-adapted to a settled career of any
kind.   He despised Thasos:

This island stands like a donkey's back covered with forests.   There
is no lovely spot, nor a charming one like those along the stream of
the Siris.[2]

He quarreled with his neighbors, and in battle with a Thracian tribe on
the mainland threw away his shield and ran for his life.   This was the
height of disgrace, but Archilochus characteristically boasted of it:

Some Saian [Thracian] now boasts of the shield which I left behind
a bush, without a scratch on it and against my will.   But I saved my
skin, so good riddance to the shield!   I'll soon have a better one.[3]

Thasos soon grew too hot for the reckless youth and he probably had excellent reasons for not returning to Paros.   He adopted the life of a mercenary soldier which he followed through many vicissitudes until his death
in battle.

[1] *Elegies*, II, ll. 5-10.   [2] Archilochus, 21.   [3] *Ibid.*, 6.

At some stage of his career, Archilochus had a love affair with Neobule, the daughter of the Parian, Lycambes. After giving his consent to their marriage, Lycambes withdrew it, but this proved to be a mistake. Archilochus attacked father and daughter in a series of verses so scathing that they were said to have been driven to suicide.

Archilochus wrote on many different subjects. His iambic *Hymn to Heracles* was greatly admired. Of the extant fragments of his verses, several refer to the life of a mercenary, or perhaps of a pirate:

> Bread is kneaded in my spear; in my spear is Ismarian wine; and I lean on my spear as I drink.[1]

> But come, go through the rowers' benches of the swift ship with an earthen cup, pull the lids from the jars, and draw out the red wine; for not even we can remain sober in this watch.[2]

Again he comforts friends in distress, or preaches moderation:

> For incurable ills, my friend, the gods have set endurance as a remedy. Sometimes one is afflicted, and again another. Now it is our turn, and we lament a bleeding wound. But another time it will be someone else's turn; so bear up, and thrust away your womanish sorrow.[3]

> I don't care if King Gyges is rich in gold, nor am I jealous of the doings of the gods. I shall not speak of the power of tyrants, for it is far from my eyes.[4]

The Greeks thought Archilochus second only to Homer, and in his chosen field of the personal lyric he was no doubt as unapproachable as Homer in the epic. But the churchmen of medieval Constantinople, offended by his unblushing coarseness, destroyed so much of his work that only fragments remain.

The Lesbian Poets: Alcaeus and Sappho

About 600, Mytilene, on the island of Lesbos, was one of the most brilliant cities in the Greek world. Its nobles were cultured and luxury-loving, and the women of the upper classes enjoyed free and unconstrained lives in no respect inferior to those of the men. The city had a reputation for free-and-easy morals which it may have deserved to a certain extent. Party strife raged with unusual ferocity. Such was the environment which produced Alcaeus and Sappho. Both lived during the later decades of the seventh century and the first decades of the sixth.

[1] *Ibid.*, 2.   [2] *Ibid.*, 4.   [3] *Ibid.*, 9-13, ll. 5-10.
[4] *Ibid.*, 25. The translations are the author's own.

The life of Alcaeus was full of storm and stress, which explains much of his work. He was a fierce and arrogant partisan of the nobility and felt that his country's welfare was bound up in that of his own class. At the same time he was, in his own way, a sincere patriot. He fought against the Athenians in an early struggle for Sigeum and, like Archilochus, threw away his shield, but the greater part of his active career was spent in class struggles. Several leaders of the commons at various times attempted to set up tyrannies, only to be overthrown or murdered. Of one of these, Myrsilus, Alcaeus says:

> This man, with his longing for great power, will quickly overturn his country. She is tottering now.[1]

The warning went unheeded, and Myrsilus forced Alcaeus and his partisans into exile. From the near-by town of Pyrrha, Alcaeus issued a spirited address to his troubled fatherland:

> What purpose or intent is in thee, my Country, that thou hast been so long time distraught? Be of good cheer, for the son of Cronus himself did tell thee that thou hadst no need to fear warfare howsoever it should seize thee, nor should neighbor foeman, nay nor oarsmen from over the far-bounded sea, maintain for long the woeful conflict with the far-flung spear, unless thou shouldst of thyself send afar all the best of thy people. . . . And now I make this prayer concerning thee, that I may no longer see the daylight, if the son of Cleanax, or yonder Splitfoot, or the son of Archeanax, be suffered yet to live.[2]

The fierce hatred for political opponents which blazes in the last lines of the preceding quotation is again in evidence in a song composed upon receipt of news of the death of Myrsilus:

> 'Tis time for wine and time for women, for Myrsilus is dead.[3]

Alcaeus returned to Mytilene, though not for long. His rank partisanship soon caused him to be exiled again, and he became one of the leaders of a group who were trying to effect a return by force of arms. The populace made the wise Pittacus dictator (*aesymnetes*), with power to set the distracted state in order. After ten years of arbitrary rule, he completed his task and relinquished his powers. Alcaeus and his fellow exiles were recalled, and the poet spent his last years in peace.

[1] Fragment 50. Edmonds, J. R., *Lyra Graeca*, Loeb Classical Library, New York and London, 1922. By permission of the Harvard University Press.

[2] Fragment 41, *op. cit.* By permission of the Harvard University Press.

[3] Fragment 42, *op. cit.* By permission of the publisher.

In addition to his songs of party strife, Alcaeus wrote some charming nature poetry, interwoven with exhortations to his audience to spare not the wine. One of the best examples is in his *Winter Song*:

> Sleet is falling, the streams are frozen, and a great storm comes down from the sky. Cast off the winter, build up the fire, mix the sweet wine plentifully, and bind wool about your brow. You should not give yourself up to melancholy. For we gain nothing by tiring of you, Bacchus; but the best medicine for those in distress is to call for wine and get drunk.[1]

Although Sappho lived through the same upheavals as Alcaeus and suffered exile at least once, her surviving poems contain few references to political strife. She was of noble birth, and after a few years of married life was left a widow with a daughter. Thereafter, she became the center of a brilliant circle of intellectual young women, and may have been the head of a kind of girls' boarding school. She had rivals, one of whom had lured away a favorite student of Sappho's. There was a story, originating in a later age, that Alcaeus fell in love with Sappho and that she rejected his advances.

Sappho took a warm personal interest in her pupils, which continued long after they had left her. She addressed charming verses to several of them, including Atthis, Gongyle, and Anactoria. She had the professed intellectual's contempt for the uneducated woman, and expressed it with brutal frankness:

> When you die you shall lie forgotten by future ages. For you have no part in the rose which blooms on Pieria, but in Hades' house you shall wander obscurely among the dim shades.[2]

She was, nevertheless, a keen and sympathetic observer of nature. In her poems we meet with references to apples hanging on orchard trees, hyacinths in mountain dells, sunrise, moonlight, and leaves rustling in summer breezes by the banks of streams. But she could indulge in scathing denunciation and biting satire when the occasion arose. One of the best known of her works is a severe attack upon her brother Charaxus, who, while in Naucratis, had become involved with a courtesan and was wasting money upon her. Again she treats us to a burlesqued description of a man with enormous feet:

> The doorkeeper's feet are forty feet long, and it requires five ox-hides to make him a pair of sandals, with ten shoemakers to sew them up.[3]

[1] Athenaeus, quoting Alcaeus, X, 430a.
[2] From Edmonds, Greek text, 71. Loeb Classical Library.
[3] *Ibid.*, 154.

Yet after all, Sappho's chief interest was love and her love songs are her masterpieces. Her one completely preserved poem is a hymn to Aphrodite, in which she addresses the goddess of love as her patroness and helper:

> Immortal Aphrodite on thy beautiful throne, daughter of Zeus, deceiver, to thee I pray. Do not distress my spirit with weariness or sadness, O Queen. Nay, come to me if ever before you heard my distant voice, and left your father's mansion to yoke the doves to your golden chariot.[1]

She is thrown into transports of passion at the sight of her beloved:

> When I gaze at you, Brocheo, my speech falters or entirely fails me. My tongue is broken, and at once a delicate fire spreads through my flesh. My eyes see nothing, and my ears roar. Sweat pours from me, my limbs tremble, and I grow pale green like grass. Death itself seems near.[2]

A later legend told how Sappho, her advances rejected by a youth named Phaon, committed suicide. The story, although untrue, is significant as a part of the "Sappho Legend." In every age subsequent to her own, this Lesbian poetess has been rated highly for her excellences of form and expression. Catullus and other Roman poets used her works as models and she was often hailed as the "tenth muse." Among modern writers who owe much to her influence may be mentioned Wordsworth, Byron, Tennyson, Mrs. Browning, and Swinburne. But some two centuries after her death there arose in Athens or Ionia, where respectable women were secluded within their homes, a legend which made her a woman of doubtful morals. Apparently it rested entirely upon the ardent passion of her love poems and the feeling that a good woman could not have produced such work. Modern scholarship has shown that the reproach should not be taken seriously. Perhaps this story was partly responsible for the destruction of Sappho's works, which in the eleventh century shared the fate of those of Archilochus and Alcaeus at the hands of the Byzantine churchmen. Only one complete poem, a large part of another, and some fragments survive from her nine books of poetry.

Other Lyric Poets

Brief mention must be made of Simonides of Amorgus (seventh century), whose ill-natured satire on women is his chief surviving work. He divided the fair sex into nine classes, which resemble respectively the hog, the fox, the dog, the earth, the sea, the donkey, the horse, the monkey, and the

[1] *Ibid.*, 1.   [2] *Ibid.*, 2.

bee. Each class has the qualities of its animal prototype. Of these, only the last is good, but Simonides partly redeems himself by the warm praise which he bestows upon the faithful, loving, and industrious wife.

The courts of the sixth-century tyrants fostered a school of charming but shallow poetry, which celebrated the joys of love and wine and exhorted men to enjoy the present moment. The chief members of this school were Simonides of Ceos (about 556–466), and Anacreon (about 550–465). Simonides graced the courts of Hippias and of the Thessalian nobles. About 490 he returned to Athens, where for a number of years he composed stirring patriotic verses to celebrate the victories of the Greeks over the Persians. He died while the guest of Hiero, tyrant of Syracuse. Even in his earlier career he was a master of restrained pathos, as one may see by perusing his famous *Lament of Danae*. Perhaps the best-known of his works is the epitaph which he composed for the Spartans who fell defending the Pass of Thermopylae:

> Stranger, report to the Lacedaemonians that we lie here in obedience to their laws.[1]

He was a master of the *epigram*, which to the Greeks was a short, expressive, occasional poem, without the satirical implications which we attach to the word. An epitaph of a young girl illustrates his ability in this field also:

> Gorgo, your arms lay about your mother as through your tears you made your last speech: "Mother, stay with my father and bear him other children, who will be happier than I in that they will live to soothe his old age."[2]

The finer qualities of Simonides were lacking in Anacreon. He wrote love poetry, which lacked the passion and fire of Sappho's lyrics and was plainly composed only for effect. Few of the genuine works with which he charmed Polycrates and Hipparchus have survived, but his success inspired imitators whose works, called *anacreontics*, long passed among modern scholars as the products of the poet's own pen.

The Choral Lyric

While the poets of eastern Greece were developing the personal lyric, those of the Greek peninsula, of Italy, and Sicily were favoring the choral lyric. The latter was sung or recited as part of a religious ceremony by

---

[1] Herodotus, *History*, VII, 228.

[2] Quoted by Perry, *History of Greek Literature* (New York, 1890), p. 190.

choirs of costumed performers who accompanied their words with appropriate gestures — usually a ritual dance. Naturally, the choral lyric was composed to express the religious sentiments of the audience rather than the personal opinions and feelings of the poet.

Choral performances were older than recorded history, and the original choral odes were probably nothing but rude folk songs. As we have seen in the preceding chapter, the cults of Demeter and Dionysus gave strong impetus to such performances, and the Dorian states, followed by Athens, placed them under government supervision. At Sparta, the poets Thaletas, Alcman, and others composed, during the seventh century, a series of splendid choral odes which retained their popularity even during the harsh militaristic régime which began in the latter part of the century. At Corinth, Sicyon, and in Greek Sicily the *dithyramb* was the popular form. Originally, it was no more than a rude hymn in honor of Dionysus; but in the hands of Arion, Stesichorus, and others it became a polished performance rendered by a trained and costumed choir. Stesichorus (about 635–565) in particular directed his attention to the refinement of its literary content. His hymns treated the old myths with considerable freedom and he preferred a series of striking word-pictures to bare narration of a story. His stanzas were arranged in groups, each composed of a *strophe*, *antistrophe*, and *epode* — a plan afterward embodied in the drama. The dithyramb gradually acquired a dramatic character in other respects as well.

The Origin of the Drama

The most significant development of this form of composition took place at Athens under the tyrants. There the festivals in honor of Dionysus, particularly the *Great Dionysia*, attained unexampled splendor, with a corresponding elaboration of the choral performances. The songs in which the adventures of the god were told were recast, so that the chorus did not appear in their own proper persons, but as characters re-enacting the scenes described in their songs. The leader of the chorus would assume the part of Dionysus or some other character in the story, and clarify the narrative by conducting a dialogue with the other members as a body. Such a person was an "answerer" — *hypocrites*, whence our word "hypocrite," in reality, an actor.

Thespis, a writer of odes who lived at the court of Peisistratus, is usually credited with having taken the decisive step from the pure choral ode to the drama. Actually, the change was evolutionary, and was still in progress in the fifth century. Not until Sophocles introduced a third actor upon the stage in 468 can it be said to have been complete.

The Greeks had, by the end of the sixth century, built up a virile and aggressive culture. They had, it is true, not attained the level of personal comfort and refinement in domestic life that seem to have characterized the Aegean peoples of an earlier date. In other matters they had already surpassed them, while in some fields they were doing things which the Minoan and Mycenaean peoples had not attempted. Their greatest triumphs were yet to be won; but only time and a strong stimulus were needed to make such triumphs possible. The preliminary work had been accomplished.

18

The Greeks Defeat Persia, Carthage,

and the Etruscans

THE PERSIAN CONQUEST OF ASIATIC GREECE

IN THE CENTURY between 550 and 450 B.C., the Greek people successfully withstood the threat of a disaster which had repeatedly overwhelmed the promising civilizations of the Near East — conquest and exploitation by a foreign people of lower culture than themselves. Hellenic civilization had, fortunately, grown up in a region so far from the Nile and Tigris-Euphrates valleys that none of the great Oriental empires had been able to crush it in its helpless formative stage. When, at length, the Persian Empire attacked the Greeks from the east and the Carthaginians and Etruscans from the west, their culture was too highly developed and firmly rooted to bow before the storm, and in overcoming the peril, it developed still further its energy and creative power.

The Lydian Conquest of Asiatic Greece

For five centuries after the fall of the Hittite Kingdom (1200–650 B.C.), no power strong enough to subjugate the Asiatic Greeks had arisen in Asia Minor. It was during this period that they colonized the islands and the eastern coast of the Aegean Sea. But about the middle of the seventh century B.C. their period of peace came to an end. A dynastic revolution in the inland state of Lydia brought to its throne an able king in the person of Gyges. For a century thereafter he and his descendants made Lydia one of the leading states of the civilized world, with territories stretching from the coast of the Aegean Sea to the Halys River. Because the Greeks controlled nearly all the harbors of the peninsula and the seaward ends of the trade routes reaching into the interior, any state which controlled inland Asia Minor was compelled either to master Asiatic Greece or to suffer economic strangulation. In the century of Lydian ascendancy, practically all Hellenic cities in that region became tributary to these back-country neighbors. Lydian suzerainty was not oppressive. The kings who ruled at Sardis were themselves partly Hellenized, worshiped Greek gods, and gave the Greeks a privileged position in their dominions. Croesus, the last of the dynasty, was so staunch an admirer of Greek ways that they looked upon him almost as one of themselves. Economically, the Asiatic Greeks were even better off than before and their civilization suffered no appreciable check.

Persian Domination in Asiatic Greece

When the Persians conquered Asia Minor (546 B.C.), all this changed for the worse. Our previous study of Persian provincial government has indicated its general character. Compared with that of other Asiatic empires, it was unusually mild and humane. Practically the only obligations which it imposed were tribute, occasional military or naval contingents to the armed forces of the king, and a few other matters of a similar character. There was very little interference with local government.

The Asiatic Greek cities, along with some of the native peoples, formed a part of the Ionic satrapy. In each city the Persian conquerors appointed a native Greek governor as their representative. Under other circumstances this would have been a wise concession to the feelings of local independence, but to the Greeks such a ruler was a "tyrant," and although he would be sure to have some friends and partisans among the citizens, his presence as a visible representative of a foreign power would certainly tend to make Persian rule unpopular. Furthermore, the Greeks were no longer a favored people as they had been under the Lydian kings. They were merely the outer fringe of a gigantic empire, ruled by a people of alien speech and ideas. The surprising fact is that they did not revolt until forty years after the conquest. Even the convulsions into which the Persian Empire fell at the accession of Darius did not stir the Asiatic Greeks into action. In 512 B.C. their tyrants provided ships and men to accompany Darius upon his expedition against the Scythians.

The Scythian Expedition of Darius

The reasons which led Darius to attempt the conquest of the region north and west of the Black Sea are not clear, and little is known about its

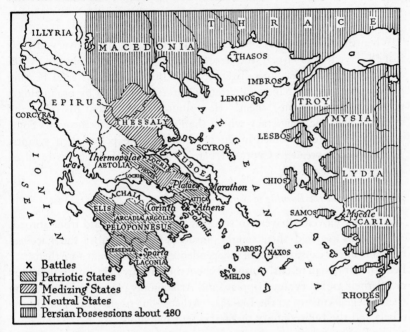

MAP OF GREECE AND THE AEGEAN WORLD DURING THE PERSIAN WARS

incidents. It failed of its immediate object, but on his return, the Great King determined to add to his dominions the portion of Europe which lay across the Hellespont and the Bosporus. He left an army under Megabyzus in Thrace, and it soon reduced the northern shore of the Aegean to a Persian province as far west as the river Strymon, while the semi-Hellenized state of Macedonia became a Persian vassal kingdom. The tide of Oriental conquest had reached the threshold of peninsular Greece, but events elsewhere were to prevent it from further advances for the next twenty years.

Meanwhile, individual Greeks had found great favor with Darius. A physician named Democedes cured him of an injury, and a Greek captain commanded a fleet which explored the entire northern coast of the Indian Ocean. Greek exiles sought the Persian court, where they urged the king to intervene in the political struggles of their native cities. Hellenic cultural influence might have improved the uncouth Persians if peaceful relations had not been interrupted by a bitter struggle which lasted for a half-century (499–449 B.C.).

THE IONIC REVOLT (499–494 B.C.)

When the Asiatic Greeks finally struck a blow for the recovery of their lost liberty, it was largely the result of an accident. Aristagoras, tyrant of Miletus, had fallen into disrepute with his Persian masters. Fearing punishment at their hands, he attempted to save himself by organizing a general uprising against them. He voluntarily abdicated his office and re-established the democracy which the Persians had overthrown. Some other cities of Ionia joined in the movement and expelled their tyrants. The rebellion spread to Cyprus, where all but one of the cities revolted against the Great King.

Aristagoras and the Burning of Sardis

If such a movement were to succeed, it must receive aid from abroad. Aristagoras realized this, sought unsuccessfully to enlist the Lacedaemonians in the cause of Ionian independence, and then went to Athens. A Persian satrap had recently insulted the Athenians by demanding that they recall their exiled tyrant Hippias, and Aristagoras played skillfully upon their alleged kinship to the Ionians. Athens sent twenty ships to aid the rebels and the Euboean city of Eretria sent five more.

The Ionic rebels began the war by taking the offensive. They attacked Sardis, the capital of the Lydian satrapy, and took all of it but the citadel. During the fighting a fire broke out among the flimsy buildings of the city and reduced it entirely to ashes. The Greeks retreated, but on the way to the coast they were overtaken by Persian reinforcements and disastrously defeated. Thereupon the Athenians and Eretrians deserted the cause and went home. They had insulted the Great King by invading his lands and had thereby incurred his vengeance, without aiding the Ionic cause to any appreciable extent. Herodotus, who fifty years later wrote the story of the rebellion, relates that when Darius heard of the burning of Sardis he asked who the Athenians were, and when told, he shot an arrow into the air and prayed that his god would grant him vengeance for the wrong done him. Thereafter, a slave was appointed to say to him each day at dinner, "Master, remember the Athenians." True or not, the story illustrates the bitterness of the hate which later made him hurl the whole strength of his dominions upon European Greece in an effort to obtain vengeance.

The Suppression of the Revolt

The revolt soon began to weaken. Cyprus was reconquered, and a Phoenician fleet under Persian commanders sailed against Miletus. By this time all Asiatic Greek cities had joined the movement and a rebel fleet had been collected to resist that of the Persians. But incompetence, levity, and treachery were at work to ruin the cause. Messages from the banished Ionian tyrants to their countrymen induced many of the crews to desert, and in the battle of Lade, the patriotic portion of the Greek armada was defeated (494 B.C.). Miletus, besieged by land and sea, was taken and destroyed. Her men were slain and the women and children enslaved. Everywhere the Great King's authority was restored. Yet the victors had learned much from the incident and they put their knowledge to good use. Instead of re-establishing the hateful tyrannies, they organized democracies in the conquered cities. A careful survey was made to serve as a basis for the levying of tribute and intercity wars were forbidden.

In spite of this generous treatment, the damage done to Asiatic Greece was irreparable. Hitherto, its people had led the Greek world in art, science, philosophy, and poetry. Thereafter, the cultural primacy of the Hellenes passed to the continental Greeks, principally to Athens. It cannot be said that the suppression of the revolt was entirely responsible for this fact, for several other causes were at work. Yet the destruction of Miletus and the re-enslavement of her sister cities signalized its accomplishment.

The Marathon Campaign and Its Results (492–490 B.C.)

The suppression of the Ionic revolt did not finish the task of Darius in the Aegean region. To secure his hold upon Asia Minor he had to recover his Thracian and Macedonian possessions and punish the cities of continental Greece which had insulted his authority. No sooner had the last remnants of the rebellion been stamped out in Asia than he undertook to complete his work in Europe. Mardonius, an able Persian commander who had lately married Darius' daughter, was placed in command of a combined military and naval force and sent across the Hellespont (492). With little difficulty he recovered his master's former possessions and added to them the island of Thasos. Then he moved his forces westward along the coast toward Attica. At this point misfortune befell him. His fleet was caught in a storm as it was rounding Mount Athos, with the loss of two hundred ships and twenty thousand men. Attacks by the wild Thracian tribes destroyed many more, and Mardonius abandoned the second part of his program. For a time he was in disgrace, but Darius did not give up his purpose to punish Athens and Eretria. Two years later he was ready to try again.

Athens Becomes a Strong Power

Athens in the meantime had grown strong since the expulsion of the tyrants, and conditions marked her as the coming leader of central Greece. Even before the constitution of Cleisthenes was completed, she had decisively defeated a coalition of Chalcidians and Boeotians. Chalcis became for a time an Athenian dependency, and four thousand Athenian colonists were settled upon land taken from her. From the Boeotians, Athens took the port of Oropus on the eastern coast and compelled them to cease their attacks upon the little Boeotian city of Plataea, which refused to join their league. With Aegina, she was fighting a bitter struggle for the naval supremacy of the Saronic Gulf. Her sea power, however, was still in its infancy, and her heavy-armed infantry as yet constituted her chief offensive and defensive weapon. Athens was a member of the Peloponnesian League and recognized the right of Sparta to judge disputes between herself and other members. Although she had withdrawn ingloriously from the Ionic revolt, her sympathies were still with her Asiatic kinsmen. When, after the capture of Miletus, the tragedian Phrynicus wrote a drama describing the catastrophe, his audience wept; and the Athenian people

Metropolitan Museum

GREEK FOOT SOLDIER

not only forbade the further production of the play, but fined the poet a thousand drachmas "for reminding them of their misfortunes."

The Rise of Miltiades

In 492, there had returned to Athens a man who had lived for many years abroad and who was to do her signal service. During the tyranny of Peisistratus a tribe living in the Thracian Chersonesus (Gallipoli peninsula) had appealed to Athens for aid against their wild kinsmen of the interior. An Athenian aristocrat named Miltiades had responded to their call and had become their ruler. His nephew, Miltiades the son of Cimon, in time succeeded him, and ruled both the Greeks and barbarians of the region. As a Persian vassal he participated in the Scythian expedition of Darius. During the Ionic revolt he had become compromised, and the approach of Mardonius caused him to flee to Athens with his family and possessions. There he was accused of oppressive government in the Chersonesus, but the court acquitted him, and in 490 B.C. he was one of the generals. He was a brilliant tactician, and his worth to Athens was enhanced by his familiarity with Persian methods of fighting. As his father had been murdered by Hippias, he was a bitter enemy of the family of Peisistratus. This fact was of great importance, for Hippias had become a Persian protégé after his expulsion from Athens, and his partisans were sure to favor the Persian cause.

The Persians Capture Eretria

In 490, Darius made his second effort to invade continental Greece. It would seem that his only objective was to punish Athens and Eretria and not to make a general conquest of the country. In view of the recent failure of Mardonius, the command of the new expedition was entrusted to the king's nephew and a Mede named Datis. To avoid the dangerous passage around Mount Athos, the fleet was to ferry the army straight across the Aegean. Later Athenian legend magnified the number of the invading army to 120,000 men and the enemy fleet to six hundred warships and a number of transports for horses. As a preliminary measure, heralds were sent by Datis and Artaphernes throughout the Aegean islands and continental Greece to demand "earth and water" (the customary tokens of submission) from the chief cities. Most of them complied with the demand, and by so doing they at least pledged themselves not to aid the Athenians and Eretrians. The overthrow of both cities seemed certain.

As the Persian armada sailed across the Aegean, subduing the islanders in its path, the Athenians and Eretrians did little to prepare for the emergency. Athens directed her colonists who had settled on Chalcidian land to aid Eretria, but instead, they fled home. The Eretrians retired within their walls and allowed themselves to be besieged. Seven days later, two citizens treacherously opened the gates and admitted the enemy. The Persians destroyed Eretria and enslaved the inhabitants.

The Persians Defeated at Marathon

From Euboea it was but a short step to the eastern coast of Attica, and thither Hippias led the Persians. They formed a camp on the plain of Marathon, while their fleet was beached on the seashore. The Athenians, fearing the worst, sent a long-distance runner to Sparta to ask for immediate help. He is said to have covered the one hundred and seventy-five miles between these two cities in the incredibly brief space of two days, but in vain. Religious scruples prevented the Lacedaemonians from beginning an expedition until after the next full moon, which was six days

PERSIAN ROYAL GUARD

off. Athens would have to defend herself for the promised aid would come too late. Her generals had only nine thousand heavy-armed infantry with which to repel the invaders, and the Persians were reputed to be invincible. Athens was without defensive walls, and to await attack near the city was to give the tyrannist party a chance to betray it. Led by the polemarch Callimachus, the Athenian army crossed Attica and encamped on the hills above the camp of the enemy. There they were joined by the whole Plataean army — one thousand heavy-armed infantry.

At this point Miltiades came into prominence. In the council of war he and four other Athenian generals favored an immediate attack upon the Persians, while the other five opposed it. By persuading Callimachus to support him, Miltiades committed the Athenians to a policy of aggressive action. Experience had taught him that however dangerous the Persian archers and cavalry might be at a distance and to undisciplined troops, at close quarters the armored Greek spearmen were their superiors. As the Persian land force began its overland march toward Athens, Callimachus gave the order to prepare for battle.

Tactics of the Battle of Marathon

The battle of Marathon was one of the earliest in recorded history which was won by tactical skill against superior numbers. The Persian army was at least two or three times as numerous as that of the combined Athenians and Plataeans. Thus, the allies ran the risk of being outflanked on both wings by the longer line of the invaders. To prevent this, the Athenians made their center long and thin and massed their strength on the wings. As they came within range of the Persian arrows, they charged the enemy on the run, and before the Persian archers could do much damage, the attackers were at close quarters. Long spears and heavy body armor gave the Athenians a decisive advantage. Their center gave way by prearrangement before the stronger Persian center, but the Persian wings were put to flight. Holding back their victorious wings, the Athenian commanders hurled them against the Persian center and crushed it. The invaders fled to their ships. The Persian losses were 6400 men, while that of the Athenians and Plataeans combined was 192. But the danger was not yet over. Picking up the fugitives, Datis sailed around Cape Sunium in an effort to surprise the city before its defenders could return to its relief. The generals, anticipating such a move, hurriedly marched their men across country and drew them up on the hills within sight of the harbor of Phalerum. When Datis learned that his surprise had failed, he turned about and sailed for

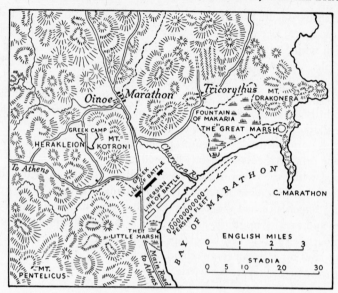

MAP OF BATTLE OF MARATHON

Asia. The victors burned their dead on the battlefield (Callimachus was among them), and raised a sepulchral mound over the fallen heroes. The Lacedaemonian reinforcement of two thousand men arrived too late to do more than compliment the victors, and then return home.

The battle of Marathon was one of the decisive battles of the world, but only in a qualified sense. It did not end the Persian menace, which returned in a worse form ten years later. Its real importance lies in its psychological effect upon the Athenian people. They had overthrown in fair fight and with inferior numbers a power which had frightened all Greece. "They were the first," said Herodotus, "to endure the sight of Median clothing and of those who wore it. Until then the Greeks were afraid of the very name of Mede." [1] In this heroic exploit the Athenian democracy was consecrated, for it was the courage and devotion of the middle and lower classes that had made it possible.

The End of Miltiades

Miltiades, in spite of the reputation which he had won at Marathon, came to a bad end. Presuming upon his services, he asked the assembly to

[1] Herodotus, History, VI, 112.

put him in command of a fleet and army. He did not disclose his intention, but promised that he would win rich rewards for the state. He led his force to Paros, where he tried in vain to extract blackmail from the people for supposed aid given to Datis. The enterprise failed, and Miltiades returned home discredited and mortally wounded. He was accused of having deceived the Athenian people, and although pity for his plight and gratitude for his services saved him from the death penalty, he was fined the large sum of fifty talents. He died soon afterward and his son Cimon paid the fine.

A Ten-Year Respite and Its Fruits (490–480 b.c.)

There can be no doubt that if Darius had had his way, another Persian attack would have followed soon after Marathon and under the command of Darius himself. This time there was to be no bungling by subordinates. Three years of intensive and gigantic preparations followed, but they were doomed never to gain their intended object. In 486 b.c., the Egyptians revolted and before they could be subdued, Darius died. His son Xerxes, who succeeded him, was of mediocre ability and required several years for the suppression of the Egyptian rebellion. For these reasons, a full decade elapsed before Persian warriors again entered continental Greece.

At Athens these years witnessed the triumph of democracy and the beginnings of the Athenian naval supremacy in the Aegean Sea. In 487, an ostracism disposed of Hipparchus, the leader of the tyrannist faction, and thereafter we hear of them no more. The Alcmeonidae also fell under the popular displeasure, and in 486 their chief, Megacles, was ostracized. In the same year it was provided that the archons should once more be chosen by lot, substantially as under the laws of Solon. As the men selected for the archonship under this system probably would be mediocrities at best, the command of the army was transferred from the polemarch to the generals. The Council of the Areopagus, which was recruited from ex-archons, was likewise certain to suffer progressive degeneration as its old members died and their places were taken by men chosen by lot. This change, however, came slowly and for some years the Areopagus displayed unusual ability.

Xanthippus, Aristides, and Themistocles

Three leaders now came to the front in Athenian political life: Xanthippus, Aristides, and Themistocles. All three favored a republic.

Xanthippus, a conservative, was ostracized in 484 B.C. The other two were democratic republicans, yet they differed widely in their policies. Athens was still engaged in a bitter struggle with Aegina, and by 483 it became apparent that another and more gigantic Persian attack was in preparation. The question among the Athenians was how this peril could best be met. Aristides (nicknamed "the Just" because of his well-known integrity) relied upon the support of the landowning farmers and believed in strengthening the heavy-armed infantry and leaving the navy about as it was. Themistocles, whose backers were merchants and manufacturers, naturally sponsored a policy of naval supremacy as the safest means of protecting the country against all her foreign foes and at the same time assuring her of foreign markets and a supply of imported food. Aristides was a man of respectable talents, but the event proved that Themistocles was a far-sighted statesman. Ever since 493, when he had held the archonship, he had been insisting that the true future of Athens lay upon the sea. Without control of the Aegean, the Persians could never hope to maintain an army of invasion large enough to conquer continental Greece. With such controls Athens could not only defend herself, but become the wealthiest and most powerful state in the Greek world.

Athens Builds a Fleet

Themistocles was not only a brilliant thinker, but a practical politician, and circumstances favored him. In 483, rich silver deposits were discovered at Maronea in the mining district of Laurium. The income from the mines was state property and the ordinary expenses of government were too small to require its use. Up to this time the universal Greek custom in such cases had been to distribute the surplus among the citizens. Themistocles broke with all precedents by proposing that the state keep the money and use it to build a fleet of warships. Apparently Aristides opposed the naval policy, for the next year he was ostracized. The story is told that while the voting was in progress an illiterate fellow asked Aristides to mark his ballot for him, and when he wished to know whose name to write down was told "Aristides." "What wrong has he done you?" Aristides inquired. "None at all," replied the voter. "I do not even know him, but I am tired of hearing him called 'the Just.'" The banished leader retired to Aegina, and the way was cleared for Themistocles to carry out his plans. Within two years Athens had almost two hundred warships of the class called *triremes* — the largest then in use. The step was taken none too soon, as in 480 B.C. the Persians returned.

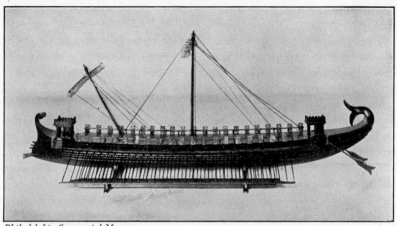

GREEK SHIP USED AT THE TIME OF BATTLE OF SALAMIS
Scale Model

The naval tactics of the Greeks and their neighbors were wholly different from any now in use. Warships could be propelled by either sails or oars, but because the former were so uncertain, before a battle the masts were taken down and entire dependence was placed in the oars. As we shall presently see, it was desirable that the vessel should be propelled as powerfully as possible; and the more rowers there were, the greater the power and speed of the vessel. If a ship were built too long, she would break in two in a heavy sea, hence, the oars had to be placed on two or more levels, and the hull was built higher to compensate for the enforced limitations upon its length. A vessel with two banks of oars was a *bireme* and one with three banks a *trireme*. There was no defensive armament except the planks of the deck and hull, and for offensive purposes nothing that corresponded in the slightest degree to modern naval artillery. Projecting from the prow of each ship was a bronze ram, which formed its chief offensive weapon. Usually a trireme carried thirty armored marines; and although earlier they had fought at close quarters with opponents on enemy vessels, in the fifth century they had little to do. A favorite maneuver was to charge the side of an enemy ship, drive the ram through it, and then back off, leaving it to sink. Various other tactics were employed, all involving the use of the ram. Only when an enemy ship was disabled did the marines have to board and capture it. Skill, discipline, and teamwork were indispensable.

The Great Crisis (480–479 b.c.)

The expedition which Xerxes led against the independent Greeks in 480 b.c. was no mere punitive campaign against a few cities, as its predecessors had been. It was the result of years of gigantic preparation and its aim was nothing short of the conquest of the peninsula. Several reasons influenced the movement. Athens was still unpunished for the burning of Sardis nearly twenty years before. The sons of Hippias and other Greek exiles were frequent visitors at the Persian court, and urged Xerxes to the enterprise. No doubt it was felt by the Great King's advisers that only by extinguishing the independence of the continental Greeks could the possession of Asiatic Greece be made secure. Back of it all must have been the urge to further conquests which seems to have been an inner law of Oriental states in all ages: that every strong ruler is also a conqueror and that states which cannot make new conquests are by the very fact labeled as decadent. Thus far Xerxes had, aside from the suppression of the Egyptian revolt, done nothing to prove his quality or win the loyalty of his people. He chose the Greek peninsula as a scene for what he hoped would be his first great triumph.

Persian Preparation for the Invasion of Greece

The Greeks knew in advance that the blow would fall and from what direction it was to be expected. In 483 b.c. Xerxes had caused a canal to be cut through the isthmus which joined the mainland to the promontory of Mount Athos, where the ships of Mardonius had been wrecked. Rumors began to arrive of bridges built by Persian engineers across Thracian rivers, of magazines of supplies collected to feed myriads of men, and of fleets and armies being organized in the coastal regions of Phoenicia and Asia Minor. In the autumn of 481 b.c., Xerxes himself arrived at Sardis, where he spent the winter getting all in readiness for what he fondly hoped would be a decisive victory the next summer.

The patriotic states of Greece did what they could to meet the peril, but they could do little. When, in the winter of 481–480, Persian heralds came to the peninsula, they received "earth and water" from about a third of the states, including Thessaly and all of Boeotia except Plataea and Thespiae. Many of those which did not openly espouse the Persian cause either did so secretly or remained neutral. Sparta, Athens and the other states of the Peloponnesian League were almost the only defenders of Hellenic liberty. Even among them, mutual jealousies made co-operation difficult. As they viewed the overwhelming forces at the disposal of their enemy, they fell victims to the blackest pessimism. The priests at Delphi decided that a Persian victory was inevitable, and began to predict ruin and desolation for the Athenians and others. It is a wonder that the defenders of Greek liberty displayed as much energy and courage as they did.

The Congress of Corinth

In the autumn of 481, the Athenians persuaded the Lacedaemonians to summon a congress of delegates from the loyal states to meet at Corinth. Every possible step was taken by this body to organize and strengthen resistance. All Greek states who willingly submitted to the invader were declared traitors and were threatened with destruction by their outraged countrymen. Interstate enmities were temporarily reconciled. Although Athens had a large army and the most powerful navy of all the Greek states, she voluntarily submitted to Spartan leadership on land and sea. Envoys from the congress invited the states which were not represented to join the movement, while spies were sent to observe the numbers and equipment of the enemy. Almost all the envoys returned unsuccessful, and the states which had originally formed the congress had to bear the burden alone. The spies fell into the hands of the Persians, who felt so confident of their strength that they took their captives through their camp, showed them the vast hordes at the disposal of Xerxes, and sent them back to carry the disquieting news to their fellow countrymen. Yet the congress was not entirely fruitless. When, in the spring of 480 B.C., the host of Xerxes began its march against the peninsular Greeks, they had achieved a measure of preparation.

The Strength of Xerxes' Forces

Subsequent generations made the expedition of Xerxes the theme of so many fantastic legends that it is difficult to separate facts from fiction. Herodotus, our chief Greek authority, would have us believe that it included 1,700,000 soldiers, several millions of slaves and camp-followers, 1207 warships, and 3000 transports. The numbers are impossibly large, but in all probability the army was several hundred thousand strong, and the fleet included from 500 to 600 ships. Every race and nationality under Persian domination, from Greek to Ethiopian, was represented, each with the characteristic arms and equipment of its people. The most effective portions of the land force were the native Persians, and of the navy, the Phoenicians.

A pontoon bridge afforded passage across the Hellespont for men and horses. As the invaders swept on through Thrace and Macedonia, the Greek allies made no effort to stop them. An army was sent to northern Thessaly to bar them from the peninsula, but the pass of Tempe, where it was posted, proved to be untenable, and the defenders returned to the Isthmus. The Thessalians, left without help, had no choice but to join the Persians. Themistocles, in the meantime, had evolved another plan of defense, which was adopted. The only practicable road from Thessaly into central Greece ran through the pass of Thermopylae, at the head of the Malian Gulf. At this point the road was only a narrow strip of beach at the foot of impassable cliffs. Superior numbers were of little use in such a position, and here the allied land forces were posted. The Greek fleet of nearly five hundred triremes was stationed in the narrow channel north of Euboea, the only route through which the Persian fleet could have direct access to the shore immediately behind the land forces of the defenders. At the same time, an Athenian fleet of fifty-three triremes was stationed at the southern entrance of the straits between Euboea and the mainland to prevent the main fleet from being taken in the rear. The plan was well made, but the Peloponnesians were only mildly interested in it, and sent but seven thousand men. Of these three hundred were Spartans, under their king, Leonidas. Ten times as many soldiers were available, as the events of the next year were to prove, and we must conclude that the Peloponnesian states were bent upon defending the Isthmus and abandoning central Greece to the enemy. No doubt it was only the fact that Athens furnished half the fleet that induced them to make even this feeble effort in her defense.

Thermopylae and Artemisium

It was July before the Persian army and fleet came to blows with the allies at Thermopylae and the promontory of Artemisium. A detachment of Persian ships was sent around Euboea to take the allied fleet in the rear, but a gale completely destroyed it, and at the same time wrecked hundreds of ships in the main fleet. In the sea fight which ensued the Greeks held their own. On land Xerxes hurled his choicest troops against the small Greek force for two days without avail. On the third day a traitor named Epialtes guided a Persian detachment over a by-path to the rear of the defenders. The bulk of the Greek army escaped, but seven hundred men from

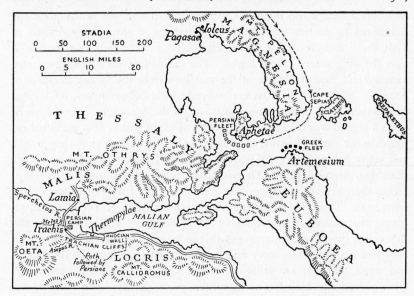

MAP OF BATTLE OF THERMOPYLAE AND ARTEMISIUM

the Boeotian city of Thespiae and the three hundred Spartans of Leonidas disdained to flee and were cut down to the last man.   When news of the disaster reached the fleet at Artemisium, it retired to the Saronic Gulf and took up its quarters in the Bay of Salamis.   Phocis was overrun, the Boeotians joined Xerxes (except the Thespians and Plataeans), and in a short time the Persian advance guard was in Attica.

The battle of Thermopylae was to become the theme of many a legend, for the heroism of the Spartans in the face of tremendous odds was never better illustrated.   Later, Simonides of Ceos composed in their honor the epitaph quoted in an earlier chapter.[1]   But the defeat and the destruction which it brought upon central Greece were unnecessary.   Could the Peloponnesian states have put into the field but half the men who fought the next year at Plataea, the army of Xerxes might easily have been stopped at Thermopylae.

The Destruction of Athens

After the defeat of the force at Thermopylae, the Peloponnesians seem to have returned to their original intention of defending the Isthmus and

[1] See Chapter 17, p. 306.

abandoned Attica and Boeotia to their fate. There was nothing for the Athenians to do but seek safety as best they might. They refused to "Medize," and the city was not defensible. For the bulk of the population the only safety lay in flight. The Council of the Areopagus came forward and paid the crews of the warships from the sacred treasures of Athena. Noncombatants were conveyed to the Peloponnesus, to Aegina, or to Salamis. A small garrison was left on the Acropolis. In subsequent years a legend was told that the oracle at Delphi had at first predicted entire ruin for the Athenians, then later had assured them that they would find safety behind "wooden walls." But the Oracle was capable of more than one interpretation. Themistocles argued that it referred to ships rather than to a stockade, and the great majority of the Athenians agreed with him. Thus this quibbling prediction proved a potent factor in securing the success of his policy of naval defense. The garrison on the Acropolis, it was said, interpreted this to mean a wooden barricade which they had erected. The story may have been true so far as the oracle was concerned, for there are other indications that the Delphic priests at this crisis played anything but an honorable part. Xerxes' men stormed the Acropolis, massacred the defenders, and burned the empty buildings of the city.

Meanwhile, the councils of the allies were torn with dissension. The Peloponnesians insisted that the defense be limited to the Isthmus, while the Athenians, Megarians, and Aeginetans objected to a policy which would make use of their resources and at the same time abandon them to the enemy. Disgraceful bickerings marked their council of war. At last, so the story goes, Themistocles had to threaten to take the Athenian refugees aboard the fleet and sail for Italy to prevent the Peloponnesian plan from being put into effect. To clinch the matter, he secretly sent a faithful slave to Xerxes to tell him of the projected retirement of the Greek fleet to the Isthmus and advising him to block the western exit from the Bay of Salamis. Xerxes sent his Egyptian squadron to guard the western exit, and there was nothing left for the Greeks to do but fight.

The Battle of Salamis

The battle of Salamis was fought about September 20, 480 B.C. As the Persian fleet pressed forward into the narrow strait between Attica and Salamis, the Greeks attacked its crowded ranks and sank or captured a large portion of the ships. Aristides and Xanthippus, both of whom had been recalled from exile just before the invasion, participated in the battle.

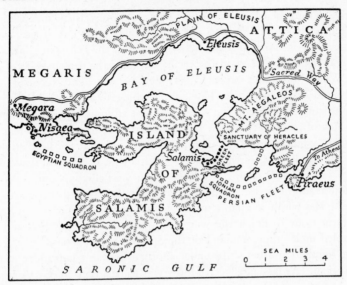

MAP OF BATTLE OF SALAMIS

The former landed a force of marines on the island of Psyttaleia and massacred a Persian garrison placed there to intercept shipwrecked Greek sailors. From a high throne on Mount Aegaleos, Xerxes witnessed the wreck of his seapower, and after the battle he caused the Phoenician sea captains to be beheaded. The allies now had control of the sea, for the Persian fleet, although not destroyed, retired to the Asiatic coast. Xerxes even feared for his communications with Asia. Themistocles, always more audacious than his colleagues, advised the allied captains to sail to the Hellespont and destroy the pontoon bridges upon which the Persians had crossed, but they refused. The Persian army withdrew into Thessaly, where Xerxes divided it. With one part he returned through Macedonia and Thrace to Asia, while he left the other under Mardonius to renew the war the following spring.

Athens Refuses a Persian Alliance

When the campaigning season of 479 opened, Mardonius undertook to finish the conquest of the Greek peninsula. He was aware that his only hope of success lay in breaking the solid front of the opposing alliance, and no doubt he had secret intelligence of the mutual jealousies of its members. Accordingly, he attempted to win the Athenians to his side. Alexander, the vassal king of Macedonia, was sent to promise them independence, enlarged territory, and Persian aid in rebuilding their city if they would become allies of Mardonius and help him against the Peloponnesians. The offer was rejected, and again the enemy occupied the deserted site of Athens. When Mardonius repeated his offer, he was again rebuffed. The Peloponnesians, meanwhile, had done nothing to help in expelling the Persians from Greece, and the Athenians sent an indignant protest against their lack of co-operation. At last the Spartan ephors began to fear that the strain would prove too much for Athens and that her fleet might be placed at the disposal of the invader. If this were to happen, it would be easy to land Persian troops at any point on the Peloponnesian coast that Mardonius might desire. This realization at last spurred the Spartans to action. The whole available military force of the Peloponnesian League was turned out to finish the war, and over one hundred thousand men assembled under the command of the Spartan regent Pausanias. A fleet of one hundred and ten ships under another Spartan commander guarded the Aegean. At last an effective blow was to be struck for Greek liberty.

The Battle of Plataea and the Revolt of Ionia

After destroying Athens a second time, Mardonius withdrew into Boeotia, and near Plataea the opposing forces came into contact with one another. Complicated maneuvers followed, in which, for a time, Mardonius had the advantage. The allied army began to suffer for want of water, and in order to remedy the situation, began to shift position. The Persians, thinking that their enemies were in flight, sent cavalry and archers to attack them and a general engagement began. For a long time the Lacedaemonian hoplites stood still under a hail of arrows while their diviners slew animals in a vain attempt to get favorable omens from the entrails. At last, after many of the soldiers had been killed or wounded, the omens changed. The Greeks charged the shield barricade of the enemy on the run. Mardonius was killed, the Persian camp was stormed, and only a remnant of the defeated army escaped through Thessaly, Macedonia, and Thrace to Asia. Peninsular Greece was free.

Meanwhile, the allied fleet had taken the offensive. Envoys from the Ionians induced its commander to cross the Aegean, and the Persian admirals, not trusting their Asiatic Greek crews, landed at Mycale near Miletus, beached their ships, and built a barricade around them. The allies followed, carried the barrier by assault, and destroyed the ships. The battle of Mycale, fought, according to tradition, on the same day as that of Plataea, proved the signal for a general revolt of the Asiatic Greeks. Before the end of the year the rebels, with the aid of the allied fleet, had cleared the coastal communities of Persian armed forces and officials. At the same time the capture of Sestos on the European side of the Hellespont had begun the task of reopening the commercial route to the Black Sea.

The impossible had been accomplished. A few communities of poverty-stricken Europeans, united only by flimsy bonds and rent with dissensions, had repelled the united strength of the Persian Empire. Afterward, legends were to cluster thickly about this heroic exploit, but the truth was miraculous enough. The sagacity of Themistocles, the steadfastness of the Athenians, and the valor and leadership of the Spartans had defeated the greatest and wealthiest state in the world. The feat had released a splendid force of pent-up energy in the Greek people, and had given them a pride and self-respect which were soon to create the richest and greatest culture that the world had ever seen.

The Crisis of Western Greece (540–474 b.c.)

While the Greeks of the Aegean coasts were fighting for their independence against Persia, their kinsmen in the West were sustaining an equally fierce struggle against their two civilized neighbors, the Carthaginians and Etruscans. Both had been settled in the western Mediterranean before the first arrival of the Greeks. The former were Phoenicians who, in the ninth century b.c., had occupied the choicest harbor site on the northern coast of Africa. By conquests and alliances they had mastered the whole African seaboard from Cyrenaica to the Atlantic, and had annexed the Phoenician cities on the southern shore of Spain. They had also founded a chain of colonies around the western tip of Sicily and had occupied the coastline of Sardinia. Their navy dominated the western Mediterranean and they enjoyed a practical monopoly of its commerce. The Etruscans had, about the time that Carthage had been founded, gone from some point in Asia Minor or the Aegean islands to Italy, where they had conquered the whole western coast from the Arno River to the Bay of Naples. While they were also seafarers, they confined their activities principally to piracy and trade in the sea bounded by Sicily, Italy, Sardinia, and Corsica. Hence, their interests did not clash with those of the Carthaginians, and in the sixth century the two peoples formed an alliance against the intruding Greeks.

Conflicts between the Greeks and their enemies began early. Soon after 600 B.C. we find the Carthaginians expelling Dorian colonists from western Sicily, and about the same time hostilities broke out between the people of Cyme and the Etruscans settled at near-by Capua. When the Phoceans, fleeing from the Persian invaders of Asia Minor, founded Alalia in Corsica, they were driven out by a combined force of Carthaginians and Etruscans (535 B.C.). The people of Massalia proved able to defend themselves against the allies; but they were thenceforth unable to continue their earlier program of expansion. Western Greece was thrown upon the defensive.

The Tyrannies of Acragas and Syracuse

At the opening of the fifth century, the principal cities of Greek Sicily were ruled by tyrants, of whom the chief were Theron of Acragas and Hippocrates of Gela. After the death of Hippocrates (491 B.C.), his place was taken by Gelon, one of his cavalry officers. Soon afterward a civil war broke out between the aristocrats of Syracuse and their serfs. Gelon, after intervening on the side of the aristocrats, became tyrant of Syracuse also, and before long controlled all southeastern Sicily. He deserted Gela and settled in Syracuse. The inhabitants of some of the conquered towns were deported to swell the population of the new capital, and ten thousand of the tyrant's mercenaries were also enrolled as citizens. The enlarged city was surrounded with the strongest walls to be found on the northern shore of the Mediterranean. A close alliance between Gelon and Theron, cemented by a series of intermarriages, united the two chief powers of Greek Sicily in a single foreign policy. This was fortunate, for in 480 Carthage made a determined effort to conquer the island.

The causes of the war of 480 B.C. between the two great Sicilian tyrants and the Carthaginians are not fully known. Greek historians inclined to the view that Carthage was urged on by the Persians. Again, a war between Theron and Terillus, tyrant of Himera, in which the latter was expelled from the country, afforded the foreigner an opportunity for intervention as the champion of Terillus. In any event, the invasion was but an incident in the century-long struggle between Greeks and Phoenicians for the mastery of Sicily.

The Battle of Himera

A Carthaginian mercenary army, said to consist of three hundred thousand men and commanded by Hamilcar, one of the two chief magistrates of Carthage, was convoyed to Sicily by a fleet which the Greeks asserted numbered three thousand warships. Probably the numbers are no more trustworthy than Greek statistics usually were, but we have no way of verifying them. Hamilcar laid siege to Himera, and Gelon advanced to its relief with an army of fifty-five thousand men. A decisive battle was fought before the city, lasting the entire day. The Carthaginian army was destroyed. Hamilcar, the Carthaginian prisoners related, had caused a huge fire to be lighted by the seashore, and as the battle raged he sought the favor of his gods by burning the bodies of sacrificed victims. When he saw that all was lost, he leaped into the flames. Slaves, spoils, and a huge war indemnity enriched the victors. Greek Sicily was free from the Carthaginian peril for seventy years, during which Syracuse and Acragas reached the peak of their prosperity.

Wars Between Cyme and the Etruscans

Gelon did not long survive his victory, but his brother Hieron, who succeeded him (478–466 B.C.), continued his work by aiding Cyme against the Etruscans. Wars between the Cymeans and their northern neighbors seem to have raged intermittently throughout the sixth century. In 505 B.C., Aristodemus, tyrant of Cyme, helped the Latins to defeat the Etruscans at Aricia and so struck a heavy blow in central Italy. In 474 B.C., however, the Etruscans besieged Cyme by land and sea. Hiero sent the Syracusan fleet to their aid, and in a naval battle off the harbor of Cyme, his ships completely destroyed the Etruscan fleet. The Syracusan tyrant dedicated a part of the spoil to Apollo at Delphi. Part of this spoil, a bronze helmet with an appropriate inscription, has been found by modern excavators. After 474, the steady decline of the Etruscan power freed the Italian Greeks from further danger for a generation. When next their freedom was threatened, it was by the native Italians.

19

****

Greek Society and Culture During the

Persian Wars

THE CULTURAL INFLUENCE OF THE WARS

SHORT as the decisive struggles in the Greek peninsula and Sicily had been, they profoundly influenced the tone and quality of Greek civilization. Much of the resistance to Xerxes had, it is true, been puny and half-hearted, but the triumph of the patriotic cause sent a wave of exuberant energy through those states which had participated in the movement. As the magnitude of their achievements dawned upon the loyal Greeks, they swelled with pride and thanksgiving. The gods were rewarded for their aid by rich offerings and hymns of praise. Men almost forgot the dubious part which the Delphic priests had played, and included Apollo in their outburst of gratitude. A new faith in divine power and justice came into being, and with it the Greeks acquired a new faith in themselves. We cannot, of course, believe that the Persian and Carthaginian armies were as large as the contemporary reports asserted, but what is really important is what the Greeks themselves believed. They did not doubt that 10,000 Athenians and Plataeans had routed 120,000 Persians at Marathon, that 7,000 Greeks had held 1,700,000 Persians at bay for several days at Thermopylae, and that 55,000 Greeks had annihilated 300,000 Carthaginians at Himera. To men who had performed such prodigies nothing was impossible. With this exuberant self-confidence came new wealth won as spoils from the enemy. Syracuse and Acragas were enriched by loot from the field of battle, by enslaved captives, and by a war indemnity. Athens reaped much spoil at Salamis, Plataea, and Mycale, and to this must be added the ransoms and other booty won from the Persians during the next thirty years, along with the tribute collected from the allies. Thus, the spirit of a large section of the Greek people was energetic and optimistic, and they had abundant resources to apply to the works of both war and peace. We shall now survey the development of Hellenic civilization under the impact of these new influences.

THE FINE ARTS

The Persian and Carthaginian wars had come at a time when the artistic genius of the Hellenes was just attaining maturity in architecture and sculpture. Both arts were soon employed to provide the gods with worthy places of worship. Because of the ravages of war, Asiatic Greece produced little work of merit, but in continental and western Greece, several temples were erected on a scale never before attempted, and decorated with statues and reliefs of high artistic excellence.

In Western Greece

At Acragas, Theron used the spoils of Himera to begin the construction of a series of splendid temples, which were not completed until long after his death. Chief among these was the temple of Zeus. It was of enormous dimensions and massive construction, 345 feet long by 165 wide. For some reason the architect abandoned the conventional floor plan, and instead of a peristyle, surrounded the building with an outer wall in which the columns were set as ribs. No other Greek city saw fit to follow this odd plan, but western Greece had several temples nearly as large. Thus, the Doric temple of Zeus at Selinus measured 367 by 161 feet. At Poseidonia, on the western coast of Italy, a fine Doric temple was built in honor of Poseidon during the first half of the fifth century B.C. It measured 193 by 81 feet. Owing to the fact that Poseidonia was deserted at an early date, this is one of the best-preserved remains of Greek architecture. In all the above-named buildings the proportions are heavy and squat. They were built of local limestone, covered with stucco, and decorated in gaudy colors. As a rule, they did not attain much beauty of line or proportion. In general the best work was done, and the greatest progress achieved, in continental Greece.

The Temples of Aphaea at Aegina and of Zeus at Olympia

At Aegina a small Doric peripteral temple was built in honor of the local goddess Aphaea about the time of the battle of Salamis. The material, as in the Sicilian and Italian temples, was local limestone except for the roof-tiles and sculptures, which were of Pentelic marble. Colonnade and entablature were gracefully proportioned. The metopes were left blank, but to compensate, the pediments were filled with groups of fully rounded figures representing battle scenes from the Trojan War. The sculptor had not yet learned to make his groups look natural or unconstrained in the awkward, three-cornered space, although the individual figures were excellent. They no longer stood in the stiff postures inherited from the artistic conventions of Egypt. Instead, he carefully rendered the tense muscles and varied positions of the fighting hoplite, the kneeling archer, and the wounded warrior.

Some time between 472 and 460 B.C., Libon, an architect of Elis, planned and executed a splendid temple of Zeus at Olympia. Again we find the builder forced by difficulties of transportation to use the coarse native limestone with stucco covering. The stylobate measured 210 by 91 feet, and the cella 105 by 52½ feet. The peristyle consisted of thirty-four Doric

University Prints

ATLAS BRINGING APPLES TO HERCULES
Metope from Temple of Zeus at Olympia

columns about thirty-four feet high and seven feet in diameter at the base. The interior of the cella was divided into three parts by two double-story colonnades which supported the roof. The metopes represented the labors of Heracles. They were probably the work of local artists, and while they retained traces of archaic stiffness, displayed considerable naturalism and beauty. The crowning glories of the building were the work of foreign sculptors. Both pedimental groups, as well as the chryselephantine (gold and ivory) cult-statue of the god, were executed by the Athenian Phidias and his two pupils, Paeonius and Alcamenes. The former did the eastern pedimental group, which represented the preparations for the chariot race between Pelops and Oenomaus. The latter wrought for the western pediment a group showing the battle of the Centaurs and the Lapithae, a masterful rendering of a scene of furious action, with the towering figure of Apollo dominating the whole. The cult-statue was not executed by Phidias until some years after the others. It was forty feet in height, the fleshy parts being of ivory and the hair and draperies of gold. The Greeks considered it one of the crowning triumphs of the sculptor's art and their art critics are unanimous in their praise of the godlike sublimity of the facial expression. Reproductions on coins and elsewhere indicate that they did not overrate it. After standing for more than eight centuries, the temple was gutted by fire and the fate of the statue is unknown. The surviving ruins, covered by a thick layer of mud laid down by the Alpheus River, were excavated during the last century. The best of the sculptures are now in Paris and Berlin.

The Argive and the Athenian Schools

In the same period Argos also had a flourishing school of sculptors, of which the most important member was Ageladas. Little is known of his work, but he was the instructor of three of the greatest artists of the fifth century: Myron, Phidias, and Polycleitus. From this fact we may conclude that he was an artist of extraordinary talents.

At Athens the artistic tradition of Peisistratid days gradually ripened into one which was much more virile, serious, and naturalistic than it had been under the tyrants. It was no longer contented with the portrayal of elegant dandies and frivolous dames. Soon after the expulsion of the tyrant, Antenor, who was probably the most accomplished sculptor in the city, was commissioned to make statues of the tyrant-slayers Harmodius and Aristogeiton. When Xerxes carried the group away, the Athenians asked Critius and Nesiotes, two of their most skillful artists, to make a substitute, of which copies are still extant. The heroes were represented as striding forward, brandishing sword and dagger. Although the musculature of the bodies was excellently molded, the heavy, expressionless face of Harmodius shows that the sculptors could not reproduce the outward signs of deep emotion. Another Athenian sculptor of the period, Calamis, produced excellent figures of gods and animals in bronze, but no authentic copies of his works survive.

Myron and his Unknown Contemporaries

Greatest of all the sculptors of the forty years following the Persian wars was Myron, a native of the Athenian deme of Eleutherae. His best works were executed in bronze. Several of his productions were sufficiently es-

University Prints

DISCUS THROWER
By Myron

teemed by the Greek and Roman connoisseurs to have been widely copied in marble, and some of these copies have survived. His "Discobolus" ("discus-thrower") represents with unsurpassed realism an athlete in the last tense moment before the discus flies from his hand. Equally powerful was a group showing the satyr Marsyas surprised by Athena in the act of picking up the flutes which the goddess had just thrown away. The criticism most frequently passed upon Myron's work is that he utterly failed to see the expressions which the situations portrayed by him would naturally have evoked upon the faces of his figures. His discus-thrower, for example, has a perfectly calm countenance in spite of the tenseness of his body.

Nearly contemporary with the above were two fine bronze statues from unknown hands — the "Charioteer of Delphi"and a figure of a god taken from the sea near the promontory of Artemisium. The former no doubt represented one of the brothers of Gelon, tyrant of Syracuse, and in the beginning formed part of a group with a chariot and four horses. While it retains some archaic features, the face possesses a seriousness and reserve strength which marks the subject as a man of character and ability, and the draperies are carefully and faithfully rendered. The god from Artemisium was most likely a figure of Zeus from some monument commemorating the naval battle of 480. The artist has represented him in the act of hurling a thunderbolt. The general effect is admirably animated and impressive in spite of its present mutilated condition.

Fresco and Pottery Painting

Advances in the art of fresco painting seem to have been as notable as those in sculpture. In the study of this branch of art, the modern student has no material remains of importance to guide him, and has to depend almost entirely upon literary sources, with a few hints gleaned from contemporary pottery paintings. When, about 470, the Athenians began to restore the buildings which bordered their market-place (the King's Porch, the Painted Porch, the Council Chamber, the Prytaneum), and when they built the temples of the Dioscuri and of Theseus, they summoned the foremost painters to decorate the interior walls. Chief of these was Polygnotus of Thasos. For the Painted Porch he executed his "Capture of Troy," while his colleagues painted a "Battle of Marathon" and a "Battle of the Greeks and Amazons." Later, Polygnotus adorned the treasury of the Cnidians at Delphi with a "Descent of Odysseus into Hades."

HARMODIUS AND ARISTOGEITON

From Richter, The Sculpture and Sculptors of the Greeks

Like the sculptors of the same period, Polygnotus seems to have exhibited a blend of archaic technique with keen artistic insight. He used only four colors — white, red, yellow, and black. His works had probably but few traces of perspective and shading. But ancient authorities agree that his keen dramatic sense enabled him to seize the exact moment in a story when most meaning could be compressed into a single scene, and the power to make each figure tell its own story through attitude and facial expression. Thus, his "capture of Troy" represented the day after the taking of the city, and its interest lay in character studies based upon the attitudes and expressions of the various persons depicted. A Greek epigram of later date stated that his Polyxena "carried in her eyelids the whole story of the Trojan War."

Even with some improvements in technique, the pottery painters failed to keep pace with the work of Polygnotus and his contemporaries. Occasionally they strove to imitate the great frescoes. As a rule they failed to catch their spirit and, in the endeavor, sometimes produced absurdities. Their best work consists of simple scenes drawn from everyday life.

CHARIOTEER OF DELPHI

POETRY AND THE DRAMA

In literature as in art, the first half of the fifth century was an age of rapid progress, in which the old and the new were curiously intermingled. Lyric poetry continued to be popular and was graced with the work of Simonides of Ceos, Bacchylides, and the prince of lyricists, Pindar. The same period saw tragic drama emerge from the choral lyric and not merely become an independent branch of literature, but produce several masterpieces of incomparable beauty and dramatic power.

Lyric Poetry

As a group, the lyric poets of the period were closely identified with the stately, conservative, aristocratic society which in their time was giving ground before the democratic influences generated by the Persian wars. They were interested in its family pedigrees, its athletic victories, and its pleasures, and their verses reflect these interests. They all found patrons either in the upper classes of peninsular Greece or in the rich and magnificent tyrants of Syracuse and Acragas. It is not surprising that their work

Do not try to play Zeus. You have everything if a portion of these good things come to you. Mortal aims are becoming to mortal men.[1]

The activities most becoming a gentleman were war and athletic exercises, and one was as glorious as the other. The champion runner, wrestler, or charioteer was deemed worthy of comparison with men whose laurels had been won on the battlefield. Although he could relate zestfully the stories of mortal maidens seduced by gods, Pindar was in some other phases of his religious thought intimate with the new tendencies of his day. He indignantly rejects the story that the gods had enjoyed a cannibal feast at the table of Tantalus. He believed in a state of rewards and punishments in the hereafter, and praised the Eleusinian Mysteries as an aid to the soul in its journey to the Elysian Fields.

His style is in keeping with his subject matter. Almost every sentence sparkles with brilliant phrases: Olympia is "Mother of gold-crowned games — Queen of Truth," Acragas is termed "Lover of splendor, most beautiful of mortal cities, home of Persephone," while Athena is "the gray-eyed goddess of the golden hair." The metaphors strike fire: war is "a rude hailstorm." One of his odes is "my liquid nectar, the Muses' sweet gift." A young man who has not attempted to compete in the games is "a cock who fights only at home." Pindar's odes follow a fairly uniform pattern: (1) an introduction, with an invocation of one or more gods and the statement of the occasion for the poem; (2) a myth or legend connected with the hero's family or city; and (3) a conclusion, in which the poet occasionally moralizes or introduces personal opinions.

Pindar's fame as a poet has never grown dim. Over a century after his death, his house in Thebes was the only one spared by Alexander the Great when he destroyed the city. The Roman writers, Horace and Quintilian, admired and imitated his brilliant imagery, his bold flights of imagination, and his pithy maxims. His style has strongly influenced many modern poets. He was the last great Hellenic lyricist. Indeed, already in his time men were beginning to use other forms of expression, more in keeping with the tendencies of the age.

The Tragic Drama Before Aeschylus

The ground lost by the personal lyric was rapidly occupied by the tragic drama. We have already seen the first stages of the process by which it developed from the choral lyric. About 500 B.C. it was still in an embryonic form, consisting of choral lyrics occasionally enlivened by dialogues

[1] *Ibid.*, *Isthmian*, V, 14–16.

between the leader of the chorus and the single actor. In the early years of the century, the most prominent tragedian was Phrynichus, none of whose works have survived. The presentation of tragedies was an affair of state, and the Athenian government paid for the training of the choruses by assigning a wealthy citizen to bear the cost of presentation as a part of his public duty (*choregia*). The archon decided which competitors were to be admitted to the final contest for the tragic prize. It became customary for each contestant to present what later Greek literary critics called a *tetralogy* — three tragedies and a *satyr drama* on related subjects. The *trilogy* of tragedies in this group formed what may almost be termed a single play of three acts, since they represented successive steps in the development of the story. The satyr drama (of which there is extant only one specimen, by an Athenian tragedian) was apparently a light farce, fantastic and impossible, intended to soothe the feelings of the audience after the grim horrors which so often formed the subjects of the tragedies. Greek tragedies usually had as their subjects myths of the gods or legends taken from the epics, although at times current events of great interest and importance might be substituted. Examples of the latter were the *Fall of Miletus* by Phrynichus, and the *Persians* by Aeschylus. In any event, tragedy was a religious rite, intended to honor the gods and instruct the audience, and never for mere amusement. The rules governing the presentation of tragic drama long remained unchanged.

Aeschylus, Creator of Tragic Drama

The decisive step which changed tragedy from a modified choral ode to true drama was taken by Aeschylus (525–456 B.C.). He was born of noble parentage at Eleusis in Attica. A patriotic citizen and a brave soldier, he fought at Marathon (where his brother Cynegirus was killed), at Salamis, and probably also at Plataea. His first tragedy was produced about 500, and sixteen years later he won the first prize. In 468, however, he was defeated by his younger rival, Sophocles. In his last years he seems to have become increasingly unfriendly to the democratic tendencies prevalent at Athens and spent some years at the courts of the Sicilian tyrants. He died at Gela, and was honored with an epitaph which he may have composed himself:

> Here lies Aeschylus, the son of Euphorion, an Athenian, in fruitful Gela. Marathon is a witness of his valor, and the long-haired Medes know it but too well.[1]

[1] Edmonds, *Lyra Graeca, Elegy and Iambus*, I, Aeschylus, frag. 4. By permission of the Harvard University Press.

He wrote at least seventy tragedies of which only seven are extant. Aristotle in the *Poetics* credits Aeschylus with two epoch-making improvements in tragedy:

1. He introduced a second actor, thus making it possible to tell a story in action.
2. He decreased the importance of the chorus and gave the chief place to the dialogue.

Thus, his works may be called the first true tragic dramas, but his choruses were still important and served a variety of purposes. Sometimes, as in the *Eumenides*, the chorus assumes a major part in the action. Again, it adds "atmosphere" to a scene by impersonating the spectators of an act, like the Argive elders in the *Agamemnon*. It may be utilized to stress the conflict of ideas which usually forms the plot, or it may express the ideas of the author. Normally the chorus parts were handled by twelve persons, and the lines were sung to the accompaniment of the lyre or the flute.

In the works of Aeschylus, religious interest is always uppermost, and the tone is one of solemn and superhuman grandeur. His sentences abound in compound words with a wealth of modifying adjectives, and rush along like a mountain torrent, overwhelming the listener with their majestic splendor. An example of this lurid grandeur is the last speech of Prometheus in the *Prometheus Bound:*

> The earth rocks, the echoing thunder-peal from the depths rolls roaring past me; the fiery-wreathed lightning-flashes flare forth, and whirlwinds toss the swirling dust. The blasts of the winds leap forth and set in hostile array their embattled strife; the sky is confounded with the deep. Behold, the stormy turmoil advances against me, manifestly sped by Zeus to make me tremble. O holy mother of mine, O thou firmament that dost revolve the common light of all, thou seest the wrongs that I suffer! [1]

His divine characters have a superhuman sublimity, and his human characters are heroes and demigods. Two themes constantly appear in his works — the punishment by the gods of insolence and pride and the hereditary curse which dogs the descendants of some great sinner from generation to generation until they either make atonement by humble obedience to the divine will or suffer extinction. Notwithstanding the atmosphere of gloom and terror which surrounded it, a Greek tragedy did not necessarily have an unhappy ending. In fact, Aeschylus usually unraveled his plots, solved his problems, and sent his audience away with their trust in the justice and goodness of the gods stronger than ever.

[1] Lines 1080–1093, Author's translation.

The "Oresteia"

To judge the dramatic gifts of Aeschylus fairly, one should begin with a study of his one complete surviving trilogy, which includes the *Agamemnon*, the *Choephorae* (Libation-Bearers), and the *Eumenides* (Furies). These are often termed collectively the *Oresteia*. In it we are told how the curse which had rested for generations upon the family of Pelops was lifted. The curse had originally come from the crime of Tantalus, the great-grandfather of Agamemnon, and each generation following him had deepened the guilt of the family by fresh deeds of violence, insolence, and horror. Agamemnon himself had sacrificed his daughter Iphigenia in order to gain a fair wind to sail the Greek fleet to Troy. This awful background was known to the audience, and is only incidentally alluded to in the drama, but the hereditary curse darkens the atmosphere throughout.

The scene of the *Agamemnon* is laid at Argos. The king returns from Troy, bringing with him the captive Trojan princess and prophetess Cassandra, whose fate is to foretell the truth without being believed. Clytemnestra, the queen and the villainess of the play, has during her husband's absence taken Agamemnon's cousin Aegisthus as a lover. On her husband's return, she dissembles her true feelings, welcomes him into the palace, and while he is in the bath entangles him in a net and kills him. Cassandra, who foretells the tragedy to the incredulous Argive elders, is also murdered. Then Clytemnestra stands forth in her true character, a tigress in human form, and boasts of her crime:

> I have done much pretending before to serve my purpose, and I am not ashamed to unsay it now. — Thus have I done the deed — I'll not deny it! I threw around him an impassible net, as if I were catching fish, so that he could not escape or ward off his fate. Twice I struck him, and with groans his limbs became limp. — As for me, I glory in the deed! [1]

The time of the *Choephorae* is some years later. After the murder of Agamemnon, Clytemnestra and Aegisthus ruled in Argos, while Orestes, the young son of Agamemnon and Clytemnestra, lived in exile in faraway Phocis. Spurred by the command of Apollo to avenge his father's death by slaying the guilty pair, Orestes returns in disguise, and, with the help of his sister Electra, puts to death his mother and her lover. In so doing he is but an instrument in the hands of the gods.

> . . . And as to the advice which nerved me to this deed, I offer as my chief security Apollo, the prophet of Delphi. He declared that if

[1] Smyth, *Aeschylus*. Loeb Classical Library (G. Putnam's Sons, New York, 1926), *Agamemnon*, ll. 1372 ff. By permission of the Harvard University Press.

I did it, I should stand clear of blame; but if I did not — well, I shall not name the penalty! For no bowshot could reach such a height of woe.[1]

But in avenging the crime against his father, he has committed what, according to one interpretation, was worse — the murder of his mother. The Furies — snake-haired underworld goddesses who avenge hideous and unnatural crimes — come to punish him, and he flees to Delphi to his protector Apollo.

The third play, the *Eumenides*, takes its name from the chorus of Furies who, throughout the play, pursue Orestes for his supposed crimes. Refusing to consider the positive command of Apollo which he had obeyed, they try to carry the unfortunate youth to the underworld to eternal punishment. At Delphi, Apollo gives him the ceremonial purification which removes the contamination caused by the shedding of blood. When the pursuers enter the temple, the kindly god puts them to sleep until Orestes can escape, and sends him under the guidance of Hermes to Athens to seek the help of Athena. The Furies, roused from their slumber by the angry ghost of Clytemnestra, follow him to Athens, and there submit the quarrel to the wise goddess of the Athenians. She cannot condemn Orestes, but is afraid to acquit him for fear that the Furies will curse Athens. She then establishes the Council of the Areopagus — a court to which she gives perpetual jurisdiction in murder cases, and refers Orestes' case to it. Apollo pleads for Orestes, the vote is a tie, and he is at last freed by the casting vote of Athena. The curse upon the House of Pelops has been lifted by Orestes' obedience to the divine will, and he may now return to rule over his people. The angry Furies are pacified by the soft persuasion of Athena and agree to bless her city and people. When this impressive justification of the ways of the gods to man had been completed, the harrowed feelings of the audience were soothed by the *Proteus*, a farce recounting the adventures of Menelaus with the ever-changing forms of the "old man of the sea."

We cannot hope to see in such a production all that an Athenian would have seen in it. The speeches lose much of their ring in a foreign tongue, and we cannot appreciate the patriotic pride which must have thrilled the first auditors of the play as they saw their divine patroness gain for them the eternal friendship of Argos and the blessings of the dread goddesses of the underworld. Even in its present alien setting it has an eternal human value and a poetic grandeur which place it among the world's literary masterpieces.

---

[1] *Ibid.*, edition cited, *The Libation Bearers*, ll. 1029–1033.

The "Prometheus Bound"

Another phase of the problem of divine justice is treated in the *Prometheus Bound*. Apparently it formed the central unit of a trilogy of which the first part was the *Fire-Bringing Prometheus* and the last the *Prometheus Unbound*. Both are now lost. The first told how the friendly Titan, Prometheus, angered Zeus by stealing fire from heaven in a hollow reed and giving it to men to lighten their toil. For this offense he was sentenced to be chained forever to a desolate crag near the Black Sea. In the opening scene of the *Prometheus Bound*, the culprit is brought in by two allegorical characters, *Strength* and *Force*, and his chains are riveted on by the sympathetic and unwilling fire-god Hephaestus. Left alone, Prometheus breaks into a stinging indictment of the tyranny and injustice of Zeus. The chorus, composed of the daughters of Oceanus, commiserate with the captive, and Oceanus himself, who soon appears, attempts to persuade him to follow the prudent course of submission to Zeus in the hope of winning pardon. But Prometheus, who has all the unconquerable pride of Milton's *Satan*, scorns the thought of humiliating himself, and only reviles Zeus more bitterly. A new victim of the injustice of the gods appears in the person of Io, a mortal maiden who has suffered cruelly from the love of Zeus and the jealousy of Hera. Prometheus, who has a gift of prophecy which is denied to Zeus, foretells that after long-continued wanderings she will at last find peace, and comforts her with the grim assurance that the divine tyrant will one day be overthrown by one of his children. More than this he will not tell. Zeus has heard that Prometheus knows the secret of the threatened danger to his throne and sends Hermes to demand that he disclose it. The Titan scornfully rebuffs this "lackey, a servant of an upstart tyrant," and amid the awful tumult of thunder, lightning, wind, and dashing waves sinks into Hades to suffer still worse tortures for his obduracy. But the story, we must remember, did not end there. In the *Prometheus Unbound*, the divine rebel, by holding closely the secret which Zeus must know at all costs and possibly by some conciliatory gesture, won freedom from his chains. We must not expect what a modern reader would call "realism" in a work dealing wholly with divine beings. By its very nature, it must preserve a tone becoming its theme and the cosmic sweep of the story. For this purpose, Aeschylus developed a style whose sustained grandeur only Milton has equaled.

The Persians

On occasion, Aeschylus could recount the events of his own time with as sure a touch as that which he displayed in narrating the doings of the gods or heroes of old. Eight years after the battle of Salamis, he produced the *Persians*, a paean of victory in honor of the great delivery which his country had experienced. It was the middle play of another trilogy, of which again the first and the third parts have been lost. Xerxes' defeat is represented as a judgment of the gods for his arrogant presumption; and the ghost of his father, Darius, is made to advise the Persians never to make another attempt against Greek independence. The play is remarkable for its account of the battle of Salamis, in which Aeschylus participated — a spirited passage, told with the vividness which only an eye-witness could impart. The Athenian audience must have thrilled with pride when the aged queen-mother Atossa asked the messenger,

Who is the shepherd and the master of their army?

to hear this reply:

They are not slaves nor subjects of anyone! [1]

Aeschylus did not, as a rule, take the trouble to make his characters realistically human. Generally they are personified abstractions which exemplify certain qualities or points of view. But occasionally he drew a portrait which, though done in harsh colors and on a titanic scale, was convincingly human. Such a one is Clytemnestra. Fundamentally, she is hard as adamant — a villainess who never feels a qualm of regret. Yet we hear her become sentimental over the woes of captured Troy, fawn upon the husband whom she is about to kill, insult the captive Cassandra with condescending pity, wail over her slain lover, and beg for her life from a son whom one cannot but feel she would have murdered at the first opportunity if he had heeded her prayers. She is a fiercer and harder character than Lady Macbeth, but in her way just as convincingly real.

Aeschylus was honored by subsequent generations of Athenians as few literary men ever were. Fifty years after the death of this great dramatist, the comedian Aristophanes selected him as the type of all that was best and noblest in the old-time Athens. It was decreed that his works might be presented at any dramatic contest, even after his death, an honor that only Sophocles and Euripides shared with him. Although the tragic drama was to progress far beyond the point to which he had brought it in artistic finish, none of his successors equaled him in grandeur of conception or lyric beauty. He fulfilled the original purpose of the drama — ethical instruction in terms of religious myths — better than either of his successors. Yet even before his death, Athens was outgrowing him. Sophocles had introduced still further innovations into the drama, some of which

[1] Aeschylus, *The Persians*, ll. 241–242.

Aeschylus imitated in his last plays. The democratic leaders were remaking the government of Athens along lines of which he disapproved, and educated men were coming under the influence of rationalist philosophies which acted as solvents of religious faith. The world which he knew was passing away before the rising splendors of the age of Pericles

Comedy

While tragedy was achieving its first great triumphs, comedy was just beginning to gain a respected place in Athens. Apparently it began as a procession of masked merrymakers, which filed into the theater before the presentation of a tragedy, singing a song in honor of Dionysus. The leader then made a humorous speech to the audience on topics of current interest. Comedy's earliest connection with primitive fertility rituals may be seen in the wild fun and plentiful vulgarity of songs and speeches (even of later comedy), and there are hint that in the beginning these were even more pronounced than in the latter part of the century, when the earliest of the surviving comedies were written. At some time previous to 450, comedy was given a legitimate place in the state dramatic exhibitions, and a trainer was assigned for each comic chorus. At the same time, Epicharmus and Sophron were developing a different type of comedy at Syracuse. This was the *mime*, a realistic representation of everyday life, sometimes in poetry and sometimes in prose. Of its character in this early period no more is known than about its relative, the Attic comedy. Both were to evolve into finished literary productions during the second half of the fifth century.

20

Greek Political History (479-445 B.C.)

IN SPITE OF THE HEAVY LOSSES of men and property which Athens had sustained at the hands of Xerxes, she had gained more from the struggle than she had lost. So great was her ascendancy in the Aegean region after the passing of the peril that the history of the half-century following the battle of Plataea is largely Athenian history. In this period she first assumed the rôles of protector of Greek independence and champion of democracy among her neighbors. For both parts she was exceptionally well fitted. As the chief naval power in the Greek world, she had the physical resources to wage wars far from home, while her strong army enabled her to hold her own in land fighting in the peninsula. Unlike Sparta, she was never deterred from distant enterprises by dangerous domestic problems. She had no depressed classes corresponding to the helots or perioeci to endanger her political stability with the threat of social revolution. Her political system did not provoke talented commanders to disloyalty as did the narrow and rigorous discipline of the Spartans, with its galling restrictions upon individual initiative. Already, before the outbreak of the struggle with Persia, she had built a thriving commercial and manufacturing economy which ably supported her imperialistic ventures. The struggle itself infused a fervent patriotism and a tireless energy into her citizens. During the half-century following the repulse of Xerxes, these qualities led her into more magnificent enterprises than any people of similar wealth and numbers had ever undertaken. Among neighbors who did not possess these advantages, she could hardly fail to assume the leadership.

FROM DELIAN LEAGUE TO ATHENIAN EMPIRE

Two years after the battle of Plataea the Hellenic League, which had defeated Xerxes and Mardonius, was no longer a factor in the Graeco-

Persian situation. The Peloponnesian states had never been very zealous in the cause, and when the enemy no longer directly threatened their independence, they were ready to withdraw from the conflict. For such a step the Spartans had reasons of their own. After the battle of Mycale, the islanders and Asiatic Greeks had joined the league, and the united force under Pausanias, the victor of Plataea, had continued the war. In 478, he won some success in Cyprus; then, sailing north, he besieged Byzantium. There the latent dissensions of the allies broke into an open quarrel. Power had made the Spartan officers haughty and Pausanias was the most offensive of them all. Besotted by pride, and chafing under the restrictions placed upon him by his government, he began to dream of transferring his allegiance to Xerxes and of ruling all Greece as a Persian vassal. He wrote a treasonable letter to lay his plans before the Persian king, and began to assume the airs of Oriental royalty. His haughty manner and his cruelty soon drove the allies to revolt. The Spartan ephors recalled the culprit to stand trial for treason, and although he escaped for the moment, he came to grief a few years later. The next year the Lacedaemonians withdrew from the war, recommending that the islanders and the Asiatic Greeks seek protection from Athens.

Athenian Plans for Fortification

The Athenians were ready to assume a place of leadership. Since the retreat of Xerxes, they had been steadily increasing their military strength. After the battle of Plataea they had returned to a devastated country and a ruined city. They began to build fortifications, and the Spartans, alarmed at their growing importance, came forward with a proposal for a unified system of national defense to meet future invasions. No city outside of the Peloponnesus was to be allowed to have walls. Those of Athens were not to be rebuilt, and Athens was to join Sparta in destroying those of the other cities of northern and central Greece. The reason given for this rather transparent scheme was that if the Persians should ever return, they would find no fortified places which they could transform into bases of operations. In case of invasion, the inhabitants were to find refuge in the Peloponnesus. Had the plan succeeded, it would have meant the complete control of the peninsula by Sparta and would certainly have blighted the prosperity of every city north of the Isthmus of Corinth. But Athens, whose policies were just then controlled by Themistocles, was in no mood to resign herself to permanent inferiority. With her powerful navy and large population, she needed only a fortified land base to defy all rivals.

Themistocles undertook to see that such defense was supplied. He had himself sent on a pointless mission to Sparta to discuss the Lacedaemonian proposition and directed the people to push the work with all haste in his absence. While he prolonged his embassy with all forms of dilatory tactics, the Athenians — men, women, and children — worked incessantly on the wall. The work was done crudely but effectively. Over half a century later, Thucydides wrote:

> To this day the structure shows signs of the haste with which it was built. The foundations are made of stones of all kinds, and in some places are not cut or fitted, but placed just in the order that they were brought by the various hands. Many columns from tombs and sculptured stones were also put in with the others.[1]

The wall was over six feet thick, probably less than twenty feet high, and enclosed a space about four miles in circumference. As siege warfare then stood, it was impregnable. When news arrived at Sparta that the work was completed, Themistocles confronted his chagrined hosts with the accomplished fact and returned home.

The Fortification of the Piraeus

Not long after, Athens completed another work of equal, if not greater, importance. As the city stood about four miles from the sea, there was danger that in time of war it might be starved into surrender. Until the invasion of 480, its harbor had been the open bay of Phalerum, where landing facilities were scarce and protection from bad weather poor. Just north of it lay the rocky peninsula of the Piraeus, which was surrounded by three excellent natural harbors. Already in his archonship (493–492), Themistocles had begun to fortify the peninsula and improve its harbor. He now had the work completed in the best form of construction then available. Huge stones, carefully dressed, were clamped together by bands of iron and lead. The wall was from six to ten feet in thickness, and although it was never more than half as high as Themistocles had planned it to be, it was one of the most formidable fortresses in the Greek world. The harbor mouths were defended by moles and towers. Thus fortified, the Piraeus was safe from capture so long as the fleet held the sea. All that was needed now to make the upper city equally secure was a safe line of communication between the two, but this was not provided until some years later.

[1] *History*, I, 90.

The Delian League

In 477, Athens stepped into the position of leadership which Sparta had just vacated. The islanders and Asiatic Greeks felt that they could not defend themselves against the Persians without aid from one of the great mainland states, and the Lacedaemonians, tired of the struggle which they could not conduct with credit, recommended them to the care of Athens. Out of the fragments of the Hellenic League, Aristides and Cimon proceeded to organize another confederacy with much stronger bonds of unity. Perpetual alliances were concluded between Athens and the newly liberated states, and the permanency of these agreements was emphasized when both parties threw lumps of iron into the sea and vowed to maintain their union until the iron arose and floated. The Athenians, on their part, promised to protect the other states and to maintain their existing forms of government unimpaired. A congress of representatives from the member states was to meet periodically at the temple of Apollo at Delos to consider matters of common interest. The presidency of the league was held by Athens. Unlike the earlier Greek leagues, which depended principally upon levies of ships and men from the members, the Delian Confederacy had a federal treasury, which was supported by regular contributions from the allied states.

The financial system of the league was based upon convertible units of money or service. A fleet of 200 triremes cost about 460 talents for a single campaigning season. This would average about 2.3 talents per ship, which seems to have been reckoned as a unit of contribution. Each state was expected to furnish a fixed number of units or fractions of a unit, either in ships or money. The apportionment was made by Aristides the Just and gave general satisfaction by reason of its fairness. The funds were administered by a board of "Treasurers of the Greeks," of which at least ten members were Athenians.

As this new and effective union was consummated, the war began to be waged with new vigor. Each year a fleet and army were fitted out to carry on the contest, and beneath this persistent hammering, the Persian power in the Aegean Basin soon began to crumble. In 466, the last Persian garrison was expelled from Europe and the route to the Black Sea was completely free from interference. In 469, an expedition under Cimon, the son of Miltiades, had sailed to Caria, and the next year gained a decisive victory at the river Eurymedon. The Greeks of the coast and many of the Carian natives joined the league.

The League Becomes an Empire

The task of freeing the Aegean coastline from the Persian yoke had not been completed before the confederacy which carried on the war had begun to change its nature. Usually a Greek league could not survive the danger which brought it into existence, unless dominated by an irresistible force. As repeated victories made the return of the Persians ever more unlikely, the islanders and the Asiatic Greeks began to long for rest. Communities where the upper classes were strong also resented the importance of democratic Athens. One city after another obtained leave to send money contributions instead of military and naval contingents. In such cases the deficiency was made good by larger contingents from the remaining states, which reimbursed themselves from the common treasury. Actually, the increased burden of personal service was borne largely by Athens. As a result, her forces were always kept at the peak of efficiency, while those who contributed only money found themselves with depleted finances and totally unprepared to meet any emergency alone.

Occasionally a state would tire of its obligations and revolt. Then the united forces of the loyal states would reduce it to subjection, force it to rejoin the confederacy, and take steps to see that no future misconduct occurred. The offending city would be charged a permanent tribute and an Athenian garrison installed. In extreme cases, part or all of its land would be confiscated and given to Athenian settlers. Thus, in 470, Naxos seceded and was reduced. Five years later, a dispute over the ownership of some silver mines on the mainland opposite Thasos led the Thasians to revolt, but after two years it also was reduced. The Thasians had to destroy their walls, surrender their ships of war, pay the arrears of tribute, promise regular payments in the future, and surrender the mines over which the dispute had occurred. One city after another made the same attempt, each with similar results. Many others voluntarily entered the tribute-paying class to escape personal service. By 445, only Lesbos, Chios, and Samos were still free allies. The other eight hundred communities were Athenian subjects.

A New Administrative System

Meanwhile, Athens had gradually transformed the administrative machinery of the league into that of an empire. About 473 she conquered Scyros, which had long been a nest of pirates, and colonized it with her settlers. She already held Lemnos and Imbros. These islands served as bases of operations and way stations on the route to the Black Sea. In 454, upon the motion of the Samians, the congress of the confederacy voted to move the treasury from Delos to Athens, and soon after this congress ceased to meet. The treasure was assimilated with Athenian state funds, and could be spent as the Athenian assembly might direct. The treaties made with conquered rebels usually reserved the trial of certain classes of lawsuits arising in such states for the Athenian courts, especially where the Athenian state or its officials were involved. The subject states lost the right to make treaties with other powers, although they long claimed the right to war with each other. Apparently some of these treaties provided for the use of Athenian standards of weight, measure, and coinage by the non-Athenian subjects. However, the rule was by no means universal, especially in Asia Minor. After the rise of Pericles, the empire was divided into five districts for the collection of the tribute. Athenian officials reapportioned the assessments every four years, and an aggrieved community might appeal to the assembly for a reconsideration of its decisions.

Even with these restrictions upon their freedom, the subject cities of Athens at first retained a large measure of self-government. This naturally varied considerably from city to city. For example, the Asiatic city of Erythrae had an Athenian garrison, whose commander acted as governor. Associated with him was a board of Athenian overseers. A council of one hundred and twenty citizens of Erythrae over thirty years of age was chosen annually by lot. All Erythraean officials swore to be faithful to Athens. Local courts tried cases, great and small. However, when a city proved rebellious, it was treated with extreme harshness. The cities of Euboea, whose rebellion brought Athens into grave danger in 446, lost control of most of their judicial business, which was transacted in the Athenian courts. Democratic governments were established in all subject cities, and Athens made it a fixed policy to encourage and protect the populace to the detriment of the aristocrats. "As things stand at present," said a speaker in the Athenian assembly many years later, "in every city the populace is your friend." [1] Events proved that it was so.

Necessity compelled Athens to assume the leadership of the Greeks of the Aegean Basin against Persia, and if their efforts were to be successful, the Delian League had to be held intact. Hence the policy of coercion was, for a while, quite justifiable. But as time went on, the character of the Athenian supremacy degenerated. The Athenian people gradually came to despise their unwarlike dependents and to treat them arrogantly, if not unjustly. Athenian imperialism became a stern driving force which,

[1] Thucydides, *History*, II, 47.

before its final fall, came to be both feared and hated. "The Athenians," says Thucydides, "made themselves hateful by applying coercion to men who were neither used to, nor in favor of, continuous labor." [1] As the need for efforts against Persia became less, they began to look upon the tribute as ordinary revenue and to spend it for their own domestic purposes. But the development of this tendency for the most part came at a later time.

The Decline of Sparta

The efforts put forth by the Spartans in repelling the Persians had not been very great and their losses were negligible, but the thirty years following the invasion of Xerxes was for them a period of weakness and unrest. The causes of this decadence were of several kinds, but most of them were aspects of their social and political system. After centuries of occupation of both Laconia and Messenia, the Spartiate class was still a small alien minority, domineering in various degrees over helots, perioeci, and Peloponnesian allies. The helots constituted a social volcano, which continually smoldered and at intervals burst into eruption. The perioeci, usually loyal, at times became discontented and developed grievances. In the allied cities the upper classes were usually friendly to the Lacedaemonians, but the populace was their enemy. Argos, which had preserved its independence against them, was an inveterate and irreconcilable foe. Even the Spartiate class itself was not free from unrest, and those most likely to feel it were the talented commanders who had been sent to do service abroad and had learned to resent the cramping restrictions under which they had to live while at home. The classes of "inferiors" were also bound to be dissatisfied with their lot, and to be fertile soil for the seeds of revolution.

The Conspiracy of Pausanias

The history of Sparta in the fifth century is largely the story of a struggle against these dangers. Pausanias, after his first trial for treason, did not cease to plot the overthrow of the Spartan government and of Greek independence. In addition to his conspiracy with Xerxes, he attempted to raise a revolution among the helots, promising them freedom and civic rights. Betrayed by one of his messengers, he fled for refuge to the temple

[1] *Ibid.*, I, 99.

of Athena. The ephors walled up the door, tore off the roof, and let him starve to death (472). The explosion of wrath which followed the discovery of so dangerous a plot also ruined Themistocles. In 473, his conservative enemy, Cimon, caused him to be ostracized, and he went to live at Argos. Learning of the designs of Pausanias, he seems to have encouraged them. When the Spartans discovered his complicity with their traitor, they sent to Athens to demand that he be punished. After a long series of adventures, he escaped to Persia, where he died a Persian vassal prince. Since no steps were taken by the Lacedaemonians to heal the festering sores of their state, new disturbances were certain to occur.

In the states of the Peloponnesian League, Spartan control was shaken by an alliance between Argos and some discontented Arcadian cantons. A Spartan victory over the combined forces of the enemy at Tegea (473) reduced the rebels to subjection, but a few years later the Argives were able to destroy both Mycenae and Tiryns, which were members of the Peloponnesian League. There matters rested for some years. The Lacedaemonians were outwardly friendly to Athens, but the steady growth of her league aroused their jealousy. In 464, they went so far as to promise aid to the revolting Thasians.

Results of the Earthquake at Sparta

Before the promise could be kept, Sparta had suffered a disaster which, for a time, reduced her to comparative impotence. A terrible earthquake desolated the Eurotas Valley, killing twenty thousand people and leaving only five houses standing in the capital itself. The helots had probably been in revolt shortly before the calamity, and they immediately rose again. In Laconia the outbreak was quickly quelled, but the Messenians, aided by some perioecic towns, successfully resisted their former masters for nearly five years. A Spartan force of three hundred men was annihilated. The rebels, when fortune at length began to desert them, retreated to the stronghold of Mount Ithome and were besieged there. For a long time they held out against all assaults, and the Lacedaemonians were compelled to ask aid from their allies, including Athens (462). The incident had momentous effects upon the interstate relations of the continental Greeks, but the allies had little better success than the Lacedaemonians. Not until 459 did the Messenians capitulate, and then they were allowed to leave the country.

Although Sparta was again mistress of the southern Peloponnesus, her losses in wealth and manpower had been so great that for a decade after the collapse of the rebellion she could hardly keep the Peloponnesian League itself intact. In the meantime, Athens was free to spread her influence in central and northern Greece as she had already done in the Aegean area.

THE ATHENIAN EMPIRE IN PENINSULAR GREECE

At Athens the building of the Delian League went hand-in-hand with democratization of the government and championship of democracy in neighboring states. We have seen how this form of government was spread through the states of the Aegean region. Our next task is to trace the progress of democracy in the imperial city itself and the efforts to establish it along with political supremacy among the states of the Greek mainland.

A New Political Economy

When the Athenians returned to their country after the defeat of Mardonius, their republic was an accomplished fact, though it was still a conservative republic, in which aristocratic influence was dominant. The system of census classes and the lack of payment for official services confined the tenure of office to a wealthy minority. The Council of the Areopagus, the stronghold of aristocracy and tradition, still exercised important functions in the state. As a whole, the aristocratic politicians had served their city well, but the times were against them. The war had been won by the navy, and the navy was a democratic institution, manned by men of the thete class, and backed by merchants and others of the middle and lower classes. It was not that these men hated the upper classes or desired to destroy their influence; instead, they merely wished to modernize the machinery of the state so as to give themselves a better position than they could attain under the old order. Once this point had been won, they were as ready as their opponents to employ men of the upper classes to administer this machinery. In fact, the navy found in the aristocratic Cimon its most talented commander. In foreign policy, the popular party opposed the further submission of Athens to the leadership of Sparta and favored her assumption of an independent rôle in Greek affairs.

New Leaders: Cimon and Ephialtes

Meanwhile, the old political leaders were passing from the scene and new ones were taking their places. In 472, the conservatives under Cimon had succeeded in driving Themistocles from public life. Aristides died in obscurity about 468. Their places in the popular party were taken by Ephialtes and Pericles. For over a decade these two, with their conservative rival Cimon, dominated Athenian politics. Of the three, Cimon was personally the most popular. In spite of his lack of formal education and his slowness of speech, he had an easy affability and charm of manner which endeared him to the masses. His generosity was boundless. With the wealth gained from the Persian wars he paid the ruinous fine imposed years before upon his father Miltiades and lavishly entertained his fellow tribesmen. His fields were unfenced, and all who were needy could help themselves to fruit. His military and naval exploits were brilliant, and he captured the popular imagination by bringing from Scyros to Athens a skeleton supposed to be that of the hero Theseus. Whenever he was in the city the votes of the sailors who had served under him usually gave him control of the assembly.

Ephialtes was an honest and intelligent man who led the democratic party for eleven years after the ostracism of Themistocles (472-461). He had no brilliant exploits or spectacular feats to place beside those of Cimon, and subsequent Greek historians knew little about him, although his accomplishments were many.

Pericles

The real political heir of Themistocles was Pericles, the son of Xanthippus. He was still a young man in 469 when he came forward as the supporter of Ephialtes. His father had been a staunch patriot and a successful commander in the great crisis of 480, and on his mother's side he was descended from the Alcmeonidae and Cleisthenes of Sicyon. In character and ability he far surpassed all contemporary Athenians and is still considered one of the great statesmen of the world. Although a competent general, he was not primarily interested in military affairs. In him the statesman was uppermost. He was incorruptibly honest and rarely flattered the passions of the populace to gain its support. Indeed, on occasion he could stand out courageously against popular policies of which he disapproved. So great was the public confidence in him that in one instance the citizens passed without examination a large sum of public money which he admitted having spent, merely because he asked them to do so and declared on his word of honor that it had been spent "for necessary purposes." It had probably been used to bribe a Spartan king to withdraw his army from Attica. His oratory was simple and unaffected, depending

Bettmann

· PORTRAIT BUST OF PERICLES

more upon the worth of his thoughts than upon studied delivery. His whole mature life was devoted to making and keeping Athens the mistress of the Greek world, and to do this he strove to free her from Spartan influence in foreign affairs and to make the common people supreme in domestic affairs.

During the early 460's, we hear little of political strife at Athens and may assume that it was not acute. But in 463, when Cimon returned from his conquest of Thasos, the democratic leaders prosecuted him on the charge of accepting bribes. The attack failed, and the next year the factions came to blows over a crucial question of foreign policy. The Spartans had thus far found it impossible to subdue their revolted Messenian helots and appealed for aid to Athens, as to their other allies. Ephialtes and Pericles opposed the request on the ground that the greatest rival of Athens was now powerless and should be kept so. Cimon, on the other hand, carried the day with an eloquent plea "that Greece should not be

made lame, nor Athens deprived of her yoke-fellow." At the head of a
force of four thousand heavy-armed infantry he marched to the relief of the
sorely tried Lacedaemonians. His good intentions were rendered fruitless
by the tactless and suspicious conduct of those whom he had come to aid.
The besieged still defied all efforts to dislodge them, and the Spartans, distrusting the good faith of Athens, bluntly told Cimon that they did not
need him, while they retained the other allies. The inexcusable rudeness
of the act cost the Lacedaemonians dearly. The Athenian public turned
furiously upon Cimon for exposing them to this insult, and in 461 they
ostracized him.

Strengthening the Commons

Shortly before the fall of Cimon, Ephialtes and Pericles had secured the
enactment of a series of laws which greatly strengthened the control of the
commons over the government. The Council of the Areopagus had hitherto succeeded, in spite of the work of Cleisthenes and other reformers, in
retaining most of its powers. As guardian of the laws it had wide super-
visory powers over administrative officials, and as a court of justice its
jurisdiction was extensive and ill-defined. Since it was composed of ex-
archons, it represented only the two highest property classes, and so the
aristocracy was assured of a potent check upon the activities of the sovereign Athenian people. It was now deprived of all its functions except
that of trying cases of homicide and sacrilege, which by reason of religious
conservatism would not be taken from it. Some of the powers which it
lost were transferred to the Council of Five Hundred, others to the assembly, and still others to the popular courts. The administration of justice was reorganized about the same time, and the leading part in it assigned to the citizen juries, with an archon to act as presiding officer over
each jury and to conduct preliminary investigations. The new system required much more of the juror's time than when he merely sat on a court
of appeals, and to make it effective, the jurors, many of whom were poor
men, had to be paid. Pericles secured the passage of a law giving to each
juror a daily wage of two obols for time spent in actual service. At the
same time, or soon after, members of the Council of Five Hundred, soldiers
and sailors on duty, and many of the lesser magistrates began to receive
pay. The common citizen could now participate personally and continuously in the government of the state and the benefits arising therefrom. A
few years later, the archonship was opened to the *zeugitai* (457). These
changes were not accomplished without a struggle. Although the details

are unknown, the bitterness of the contest may be judged from the fact that while it was in progress Ephialtes was assassinated by political opponents. Such occurrences were rare in Athenian history.

A Revolution in Foreign Policy

The snub which Sparta had administered to Athens brought about a revolution in Athenian foreigy policy. The alliance between the two states was repudiated, and Athens formed a league with Argos and the Thessalian Confederacy. As yet there was no open warfare, but it was not far off. Spartan preoccupation with the rebellion in Messenia allowed the affairs of the Peloponnesian League to fall into disorder. Corinth, now next in importance after Sparta, had begun to domineer over her smaller neighbors, Megara and Cleonae, and Aegina was left defenseless against Athenian attacks. Affairs in central Greece were no better. The Phocians had begun to pick quarrels with the little state of Doris, the ancestral home of the Spartiates and the other southern Dorians. In Boeotia, Thebes, under an oligarchic government, was trying to organize her neighbors into a large league under her own presidency. In 459, the Megarians, unable to defend themselves against Corinth or to secure from Sparta the redress of their wrongs, turned to Athens and sought her alliance. Control of this small neighbor state would be a great advantage to the Athenians. It would give them access to the Gulf of Corinth through the Megarian port of Pegae, and would enable them to use Megara as an advance post for the defense of their country against Peloponnesian aggression. But it meant war with Corinth and Aegina at the same time that Athens was on the verge of a new and titanic effort against the Persians in Egypt. It is indicative of their fiery energy and boundless self-confidence that the Athenians at once accepted the challenge.

Although the Megarian venture had been undertaken against formidable odds, it prospered. The Aeginetans were defeated, their city besieged, and they became subjects of Athens. A Corinthian army which invaded Megaris was destroyed. To protect Megara from further depredations, two walls, each a mile and a quarter long, were built to secure the road leading from the city to its seaport of Nisaea (458).

War with Sparta

Such an accession of strength to Athens could not meet with the approval of Sparta. In 457 she sent an army across the Gulf of Corinth, ostensibly against the Phocians but really to check the aggrandizement of her rival. After a short campaign in Phocis, the Lacedaemonian army, strengthened by contingents of Boeotian allies, encamped at Tanagra near the Athenian frontier. An Athenian army, with a force of Thessalian cavalry, marched against it. In the battle which ensued, the Thessalians deserted to the enemy, and the Athenians were defeated. The Lacedaemonians returned home, and two months later the Athenians again invaded Boeotia, defeated the Boeotians at Oenophyta, and forced the vanquished to become their allies. There, as elsewhere, democracies replaced the existing oligarchies.

Athenian Power Increases

The year 456 brought still further additions to the power of Athens in the peninsula. She sent a fleet around the Peloponnesus, burned the Spartan naval arsenal at Gytheium, and captured Naupactus on the northern shore of the Gulf of Corinth. This city was then settled by the exiled Messenian helots who fought against Sparta so bravely at Mount Ithome. By so doing, Athens secured an unimpeded commercial route to the west and at the same time strangled the western trade of Corinth. In 455 she formed an alliance with Troezen, a partly Ionian city on the coast of Argolis. A common anti-Spartan feeling had already drawn Phocis into the coalition.

At home, the Athenians had completed the fortifications begun under the influence of Themistocles by building two walls over four miles long and 550 feet apart to protect the road from the city to her port. These were the famous "Long Walls," and they made the upper city and the Piraeus a single impregnable fortress. Only a naval defeat could now put Athens in any danger.

With her fortifications, her fleet, her huge cash income from tribute and other sources, and her allies in the peninsula, Athens was one of the most powerful states in the Mediterranean Basin. The Aegean was an Athenian lake, whose islands and coasts were dominated by her either through alliance or outright possession. The Black Sea route, all-important as a source of supply for grain and other raw materials, was open to her alone. On the Greek mainland she had a wider and more powerful network of alliances than the Spartans had ever possessed. Nor did it appear that she had even then reached the limit of her strength, for she had warred successfully against both the Persians and her Greek enemies, and her efforts continued on a grand scale.

There were, however, weak points in this imposing structure which made its indefinite continuance unlikely. Almost everywhere it rested upon external force, and upon the support of the democratic parties, who could never have maintained control of their cities by their own unaided strength. No hope was held out to the allies either of gaining Athenian citizenship or of enjoying a voice in the determination of the policies of the confederacy. The first hope had been destroyed by the Athenian law of 451 which restricted citizenship to persons born of two Athenian parents, but probably few of the allied communities would have accepted citizenship if it had been offered to them. Local patriotism was too deeply rooted. On the other hand, Greek political thought had not evolved any effective means by which a confederation could be kept in unity and at the same time not be subservient to a single head. To preserve this position of leadership without incurring the hatred of the allies required more tact and regard for justice than the Athenians possessed. At the same time, constant warfare was exhausting their manpower, and any great disaster would be certain to deplete it dangerously.

The Persian War: The Peace of Callias

In 460, the Persian War had taken a new turn, which promised great things. A neighboring Libyan prince, Inaros, had induced the Egyptians to revolt against the Persian king and had appealed to Athens for aid. Her answer was to send two hundred ships, which had been assembled for an attack upon the Persian province of Cyprus, to aid the rebel. It was a fatal blunder; for after a campaign of nearly five years' duration, the whole fleet and an additional force of fifty ships which had been sent to relieve it were lost. Only a few stragglers escaped. Yet even this disaster did not bring Athens to her knees. In 457, Cimon had been recalled from exile upon the motion of Pericles, under circumstances which point to an agreement between the two rivals. Thereafter Cimon withdrew from domestic politics and devoted himself to military and naval affairs. For four years after the failure of the Egyptian expedition we know little of Athenian affairs, but there can be no doubt that the struggle between Athens and her Greek and Persian enemies continued intermittently. In 450, however, Cimon negotiated a five-year truce between his native city and the Spartans and Athens was left free to give her entire attention to the foreign war. The next year Cimon led a large fleet to Cyprus, and although he died before the decisive engagement was fought, his forces gained a signal victory by land and sea. The blow made Artaxerxes I ready to treat for peace. The so-called "Peace of Callias" (448) recognized the freedom of the Asiatic Greeks from Persian rule, although in deference to the vanity of the Great King this was said only indirectly. Athens ceased to attack his dominions and commercial relations were restored.

For Athens this was "peace with victory," and it came just in time. Her resources were nearly exhausted by over thirty years of incessant warfare and no commander could be found to take the place of Cimon. Affairs in Greece were again assuming a threatening aspect. The Lacedaemonians had had time to recover from their misfortunes and the sympathies of a large section of the continental Greeks were with them rather than with Athens.

In 447, the impending storm broke. A body of oligarchic exiles overthrew the pro-Athenian democracies in most of the cities of Boeotia, and Sparta espoused their cause. A premature attempt on the part of Athens to recover the lost ground resulted in a disastrous defeat for her army at Coronea (447). Many Athenian prisoners were taken, and Athens could recover them only by surrendering her claims in Boeotia. When this territory was lost, Phocis and Locris followed as a matter of course. Euboea and Megara revolted, and through Megara a Spartan army under King Pleistoanax advanced into Attica. The danger to Athens was serious, but Pericles met it with vigor and wisdom. The Spartan king retreated under circumstances which made it fairly certain that he was bribed, and the Athenians were free to crush the Euboean revolt, which was done thoroughly. At Histaea, the whole citizen body was expelled, and its possessions distributed among Athenian colonists. Other cities were punished with varying degrees of severity.

The Thirty Years' Truce

Athens had survived the crisis better than might have been expected, but she was nearly exhausted and needed rest. On the other hand, Sparta could hardly hope to capture the Athenian possessions beyond the sea. These facts made it easy for the rivals to conclude peace on the basis of the status quo. Athens surrendered all her claims to dominate the cities on the mainland of Greece except Plataea and Naupactus, and recognized once more the rights of the Peloponnesian League. Sparta recognized the sovereignty of Athens over the cities of the former Delian Confederacy. Neither was to receive deserters from the other, but unattached cities might join either group at will. Commerce between the cities of the opposing confederacies was to be free, and disputes between the two principals and their adherents were to be settled by arbitration. These terms were fair and secured for both a temporary and much-needed respite from war. The Aegean world was now completely dominated by rival coalitions of nearly equal power, while in the Spartan group Thebes and Corinth nourished especially bitter grudges against Athens. Under the circumstances, the arrangement was not likely to endure.

WESTERN GREECE (474–450 B.C.)

The Fall of the Tyrannies

In spite of the popularity which the victories of Himera and Cyme had secured for the tyrants of Syracuse and Acragas and the dazzling brilliance of their courts, neither was fated to found a lasting royal dynasty. Gelon had indeed gained the title of king from his grateful subjects, and Hieron, his brother, succeeded to it after Gelon's death. But while Hieron was a man of great ability, who patronized poets and artists, he was also jealous, suspicious, and quarrelsome. Theron of Acragas, whose government was mild and popular, died in 472, and thereafter discord between the two chief Greek cities of the island continued for some years. When Hieron died (466), the last support of one-man power in Sicily disappeared, and the tyrannies were everywhere overthrown. It was by no means easy to re-establish a settled society in cities which had recently suffered changes as revolutionary as those which the states of Sicily had undergone between 500 and 466 B.C. Large numbers of exiles were clamoring for the restoration of their confiscated property, which had in most cases been given to mercenaries and favorites of the tyrants. Any lasting settlement of this vexing question was bound to include some provision for the compensation of the losing party, and this was not easy to accomplish. For five years after the overthrow of the tyrannies, disorder reigned.

The Congress of Syracuse and Succeeding Unrest

In 461, a general congress of representatives from the Greek cities of Sicily met at Syracuse to consider the question. Its decisions were unusually fair and just and went far toward restoring peace. The exiles recovered their lost estates, but the "new citizens" (those enrolled as citizens and given estates by the tyrants) were provided with allotments of land in localities not yet occupied by Greek colonists. Moderate democracies were established in most of the cities and comparative peace returned.

The succeeding decade, however, brought new troubles — particularly the attempts on the part of the Sicel prince Ducetius to found a strong native state in the interior of the island. Twice he seemed likely to succeed, but his first effort was thwarted by the combined force of Syracuse and Acragas, and the second by his death. Thereafter, the natives of Sicily lapsed into a position of intermittent dependence upon the Greek masters of the seacoast.

In the Greek cities of Italy, the first half of the fifth century, while not free from troubles with the Italian natives and the Etruscans, was principally noteworthy for a succession of changes in government. The tyranny of Aristodemus at Cyme was ended by his death. That of Anaxilaus at Rhegium descended to his sons, whose guardian Micytheus ably governed the city until about the time of the overthrow of the tyranny at Syracuse, when a wave of democratic fervor swept over the Italian Greek cities, demolishing aristocracies and tyrannies alike. By the middle of the century most of them, like their sister cities in Sicily, were governed by moderate democracies, and the only vestiges of the old order were the few cities in which the Pythagorean brotherhoods still held control.

21

The Periclean Age: Government

THE THIRTY YEARS' TRUCE between Athens and Sparta had been in effect only fourteen years (445 to 431) when the Peloponnesian War began, but these years were of outstanding importance in the history of Greek culture. In this brief space the Greek people — especially the Athenians — achieved some of their most splendid triumphs in art, intellectual pursuits, and material well-being. Their civilization, during this short respite from strife, developed to an extent previously unknown. This period, lengthened by a few years at either extremity so that it coincides roughly with the third quarter of the fifth century B.C., is customarily known as the "Age of Pericles."

Like all other phrases coined to summarize the life of a people in a given period, this one must be used with caution. We must remember that the influence of Pericles was dominant only in Athens and her dependencies, and that in considerable sections of the Greek world it was scarcely felt. Neither in government nor in culture did the Greeks as a whole conform to Athenian standards. Then, as always, Hellas included every form of government from monarchy to democracy, and every stage of civilization from the most primitive agricultural and pastoral economy to wealthy urban communities with highly developed commerce, manufacturing, art, literature, and philosophy. Yet, when proper allowances have been made, the term still retains a high degree of validity, for Athens was indisputably the leading Greek state, and Pericles was the most influential and representative Athenian.

In government, it was a period of relative stability and peace, with few wars or revolutions to disturb its tranquillity. In the Greek peninsula and the Aegean region, the states were divided into two great classes: the oligarchic states, which were for the most part allied with Sparta, and the democratic, which with the exception of Argos were dependents of

Athens. In western Greece moderate democracies were the rule, although far-off Massalia was administered by an efficient oligarchy.

The calm which prevailed was more apparent than real, for old grudges had not been forgotten. The separation of so large a part of the Greek world into two mutually antagonistic alliances created a condition not unlike that of Europe in the early years of the present century, with a cataclysmic struggle as its inevitable outcome. But before the storm broke, Athens, the most progressive community in Hellas, had the opportunity to bring to perfection a civilization of which every phase was unique and splendid.

ATHENIAN POLITICAL HISTORY (445–431 B.C.)

Unless future discoveries increase our knowledge of fifth-century Greece, the political history of most of it can be written only in the barest outline, if written at all. Furthermore, if the facts were known, they would probably add little of importance to the record of human development. This statement, however, does not apply to Athens. Not only do we have a better record of her governmental affairs than of those of her neighbors, but in that record we read of her attempt to create a system of relationships which would care as efficiently as possible for the interests of all classes. For this reason our attention must be centered upon her, for her history, although not known in every detail, is moderately complete.

Party Strife: Ostracism of Thucydides

The triumph of democracy, while assured by the reforms of Ephialtes and Pericles, had not entirely silenced its opponents. There was still in existence at Athens an oligarchic party, small in numbers but embittered and aggressive. Its leader was Thucydides, the son of Melesias (not the historian, whose father's name was Olorus), and its program included the abandonment of the "empire," the strengthening of the army rather than the navy, friendship with Sparta, and the nullification, as far as possible, of the democratic innovations of the past half-century. Echoes of its criticisms of Pericles' policies have been preserved. It deplored the appropriation by Athens of the funds gathered as tribute from the subject states.

> The Greeks must resent it as an unbearable insult, they said, and consider themselves the victims of tyranny, when they see the treasure, which they have contributed for the purposes of war, spent by us upon our city, to gild her all over, and to adorn and deck her like a vain woman.[1]

[1] Plutarch, *Pericles*, chap. 12. John Dryden's translation; revised by E. Clough.

The oligarchs attacked Pericles himself, his family and friends, and seized every opportunity to circulate discreditable reports about them, calculated to appeal to popular prejudices. Thucydides organized his adherents into a compact group, who sought to make up for their scanty numbers by sitting together in a solid block in the assembly. The year after the Thirty Years' Truce was made, they tried to get rid of their arch-opponent by ostracism.

The attempt was ill-timed and its failure was inevitable. If Pericles' foreign policy had not been entirely successful, his domestic policies had gained overwhelming popular support. Paid juries, public works, free theater tickets, and colonies in conquered lands — each appealed to a wide circle of voters. He had plausible answers to all the objections of his opponents. Athens, he said, had assumed the burden of defending her allies. The tribute had been instituted to meet the expenses of this defense. If she performed her duty well, what she did with the surplus funds was no one's business but her own. As for Sparta, the populace did not need to be told that they had nothing in common with her, or that her triumph would mean the subjection of the masses. The struggle ended with the ostracism of Thucydides himself, and for some years his party was reduced to obscurity. Pericles was supreme, in that no opposing voice was raised against him in the assembly, but occasional prosecutions against his friends and scandalous stories about his own family life showed that the opposition still survived.

Founding of Thurii and Amphipolis

Although the imperialistic designs of Athens in the Greek peninsula had failed in 447–445, Pericles was by no means willing that she should abandon her interests in the outlying parts of the Hellenic world. Even before the conclusion of the truce with Sparta, he had promoted a plan to strengthen her influence in Italy. In 446, the descendants of exiles from Sybaris (destroyed by the men of Croton in 511) applied to Athens for aid in refounding their city. The Athenians invited a large number of prospective emigrants from the Peloponnesus and elsewhere to join with Athenian colonists in the enterprise. Among them were two men of note — the historian Herodotus and the engineer and philosopher Hippodamus of Miletus. In the fertile valley of the Siris River, Hippodamus laid out the model town of Thurii. Unlike the older Greek towns, whose streets were narrow and crooked, those of the new city were broad and straight and laid out on the checkerboard pattern as in the American Middle West.

Her government was equally progressive. From the laws of Athens and various other cities, the sophist Protagoras compiled a code which included universal, compulsory education and many other institutions of an enlightened character. But misfortune afflicted the colonists from the beginning. The Sybarites were soon expelled from the city, and dissensions broke out between the Athenians and their non-Athenian companions. The latter finally secured control and as far as the founders were concerned, the enterprise was a failure. Meanwhile, Athens had formed alliances with several other Italian and Sicilian Greek cities, and about 437 her conquest of the Amphilochian Argos, on the Ionian Sea, gave her a way station on the road to the West.

Pericles at Samos and in the Black Sea Region

Pericles was equally energetic in advancing Athenian interests in the Aegean and Black seas. In 440, Athens was in danger of losing all her Aegean subjects through the revolt of Samos. The cause of the trouble was a war between Samos and Miletus, in which the Milesians, being defeated, secured the help of Athens. That two Athenian dependencies could wage war with one another is in itself a proof of the laxity of Athenian suzerainty, and the Samian oligarchs had ample time to prepare for defense before steps could be taken to subdue them. The revolt spread to Byzantium, and the Persians offered the rebels aid. Pericles himself assumed command of the Athenian expedition sent to recover Samos, and after a preliminary defeat and nine months of arduous fighting reduced Samos to subjection. She lost her rank as a free ally and became a tribute-paying dependency. Byzantium likewise submitted. Athens emerged from the crisis stronger than ever, and Pericles was rewarded with distinguished honors.

Having made sure of the Aegean, Pericles next attempted to spread the power of his city into that great reservoir of wealth, the Black Sea region. Some years earlier, the Athenians had sent out a colony to Brea in Thrace, whose members were to retain Athenian citizenship and live under Athenian law. In the sixth century, the Thracian Chersonesus (Gallipoli peninsula) had received Athenian colonists also. A year or two after the surrender of Samos, Pericles led a powerful fleet to the aid of Sinope, which was endeavoring to expel her tyrant. This purpose accomplished, he took possession of both Sinope and Amisus, and in the former established six hundred Athenian colonists on lands confiscated from the tyrant's partisans. Friendly relations were established with the Greek cities and barbarian princes along the Black Sea littoral, and for many years only the ships of Athens or her allies could share in their commerce. Thus did Athens strengthen her hold upon the area from which came so much of her sustenance and to which she exported so many of her products.

On the southern coast of Thrace she undertook to protect her gold mines by founding the city of Amphipolis (436). The site was not far from the mouth of the Strymon River, and was easily defensible. Settlers from the cities of the Chalcidice, along with Athenians, were included in it. At the time it seemed to solidify the hold of Athens upon this valuable district and opened up opportunities for trade with the Thracian tribes of the interior.

GOVERNMENT IN PERICLEAN ATHENS

Under the influence of Pericles, Athens had become a democracy in the fullest Greek sense of the word. Not only was every adult male citizen qualified to vote and to hold office, but he was encouraged to do so by the prevalent policy of selecting officials by lot. Furthermore, the enormous resources of the state were employed to insure him protection, comfort, and amusement. Athenian democracy in the days of Pericles was a distinctive institution, differing not only from that established by Cleisthenes, but also from a modern democracy. For this reason it would be well to survey the system as it issued from the hands of Pericles and his collaborators.

Citizenship

The citizen body, after the law of 451 consisted of every person who could prove that he was the child of two Athenian parents. All others were excluded unless specifically naturalized by a decree of the assembly, and any foreigner asserting a false claim to the title might, upon conviction, be sold as a slave. This law was effective, for in 444 nearly five thousand names were stricken from the rolls. A citizen might lose his rights, either wholly or in part, in punishment for crime. Legal proof of Athenian citizenship was furnished by the father, who, as soon as possible after his son's eighteenth birthday, had him enrolled in the ancestral deme. Two years of compulsory military training followed, and at twenty he was a full-fledged citizen, with the right to vote in the assembly. Age qualifications kept him from holding important offices until much older, and for some positions there was at least a nominal income qualification, but in other respects he thenceforth enjoyed the privileges and performed the duties of a citizen.

The Assembly: Powers and Functions

The mainspring of government in Athens was the popular assembly. It was composed, as we have seen, of all adult male citizens who cared to attend, and its meeting place was on top of the Pnyx Hill on the western side of the city. Actually, only a small portion of those eligible to attend the assembly did so, since distance from Athens, military and naval service, and private business caused the absence of many citizens. Four regular meetings were held each prytany, and others could be called at the option of the Council of Five Hundred. Each of the regular meetings had a traditional program of business. No matter could be voted upon until it had been acted upon by the council, but any citizen could compel the council to act by securing a resolution to that effect from the assembly. Any member might speak, although preference was given to those over fifty years of age. Relatively few persons availed themselves of the right. To hold the attention of the audience one had to be a good speaker, or be in danger of being hissed from the platform. Then, too, he who spoke was advising the sovereign Athenian people, and was held strictly accountable for the outcome of his advice. A plausible orator might persuade them to do almost anything, but woe to him if his proposal brought misfortune upon the state. He was likely to be prosecuted for his error, and the punishment was death, exile, or a ruinous fine. Hence, it was well to know whereof one spoke, and few had the necessary eloquence, experience, and reputation for the task. Ostracism meetings were summoned annually in the market-place, and the leader of a troublesome minority faction was likely to be sent into honorable exile. It is one of Pericles' chief titles to glory that he was able to thread the treacherous waters of Athenian politics for better than a generation, through good fortune and bad, without losing the confidence of the people whom he served.

As the assembly was theoretically the sovereign Athenian people gathered in one body, the few limitations on its power were easily set aside. It elected many officials, specified the policies which they were to follow, and supervised their conduct. Once in each prytany the conduct of each official was reviewed by the assembly, and if the record was not approved, he was deposed from office and remanded to the courts for trial. It declared war, ratified treaties, levied taxes, and appropriated money. In one field, however, it was timidly conservative. Ready as it was to pass decrees on current administrative matters, it was reluctant to change or abolish existing laws. The enactments of Solon and later legislators had a quasi-sacred character not unlike that which Americans attach to their national constitution; and only by special procedure could the laws be changed. In the time of Pericles the assembly might, whenever it pleased, appoint a board of "law-drafters" (*nomothetai*) to frame a substitute for an existing law or to draft new legislation. Their work was laid before the council and assembly and acted upon like any other decree.

Decrees could be attacked by a procedure called *graphe paranomon*, or writ of illegality. Any citizen might, by swearing that he believed a proposed decree to be in conflict with an existing law, delay its passage until the case for and against it could be argued before a law court. An adverse decision meant that the decree at once became invalid and the proposer was liable for any punishment which the court might choose to inflict. On the other hand, if the prosecutor failed to receive one-fifth of the votes of the jury, he was liable to a fine of a thousand drachmas and was disqualified from bringing further charges of this character. Naturally, the question at stake was often the expediency of the proposal rather than its legality, and like ostracism, the graphe paranomon came to be used as a weapon of political warfare and a means of punishing political opponents.

The Council of Five Hundred (Boulé)

To understand the powers and duties of the council of Five Hundred (*Boulé*), it is necessary to remember that it acted as the executive committee of the assembly. The method by which its members secured their places has been described.[1] The council was too large to transact ordinary business as a single body and full meetings were exceptional. At the beginning of every official year each tribal delegation of fifty members had one prytany (a tenth of a year, thirty-five or thirty-six days) assigned to it by lot, during which it held daily meetings to receive ambassadors, reports from officials, dispatches from foreign governments, and serious accusations. It summoned meetings of the full council and assembly and prepared the business that was to come before them. One-third of these *prytaneis* had to be on duty day and night during this period. The council as a whole considered proposed laws and decrees before they were submitted to the assembly, supervised the magistrates, and passed decrees of its own which were valid for the current year. It had charge of public property, directed the construction of warships, and performed various

[1] Chapter 15.

other public duties. In short, it was the agency which co-ordinated the multifarious legislative and administrative activities of the state.

The Generals and Lesser Officials

Originally, the powers of the king had passed to the nine archons, but in the fifth century they in turn had seen most of these functions assumed by the ten generals (*strategoi*). Thenceforth, a few minor judicial and religious duties had to content the archons, while the generals fought wars, negotiated treaties, and shaped most of the policies of the state. At first they had been elected by their respective tribes to command the tribal military forces, but after 486 they were probably chosen at large by the whole people. Legally they were all equal in power, and the assembly assigned to each his individual tasks or his share in collective enterprises. But various factors combined to destroy this equality. Re-election for an indefinite number of times was permitted, and one who, like Pericles, served fifteen consecutive terms, was certain by reason of superior knowledge and popular support to dominate the board. Furthermore, the assembly could, and often did, invest one of them with extraordinary powers in time of crisis. Aside from the immediate conduct of war and foreign relations, the generals levied soldiers, collected property taxes, and assigned to wealthy citizens the expensive honor of the *trierarchy*. In a state where war and preparations for war held so prominent a place, these men were more important than any other group.

There were many lower administrative and military officials. As a rule, those whose duties required special ability were elected by the assembly, while those with only routine functions were appointed by lot. The Eleven had charge of the state prison and supervised executions and other punishments. The ten "receivers" (*apodektai*) were the heads of the state treasury and took charge of the money paid by several types of tax and fee collectors. Markets, harbors, and temples had their special overseers. In the army there were the ten *taxiarchs* to command the tribal regiments of infantry, *lochagoi* to act as subordinate infantry officers, and two *hipparchoi* to command the cavalry.

Courts and Juries; the Dikasteria

Perhaps the most characteristic feature of Athenian democracy was its judicial system. There again we find a double set of institutions — the archons and Council of the Areopagus as vestiges of the former aristocratic government, and the popular courts, representing the democracy. The Areopagus was by this time only a court for the trial of cases involving homicide and sacrilege: crimes which were thought to make their perpetrators unclean in the eyes of the gods. Its procedure was old-fashioned if not primitive, and is supposed to be accurately reproduced in the trial scene from the *Eumenides* of Aeschylus. In all lawsuits, whether civil or criminal, the archons received the complaints and conducted the preliminary investigations. They reduced the testimony to writing, certified it, and turned it over to the popular courts. In these they acted as presiding officers, but they lacked the power to declare and interpret the law which an English or American judge possesses.

The popular juries (*dikasteria*) were a distinctively Athenian institution. Each year 6000 men over thirty years of age were drawn by lot in equal numbers from each of the ten tribes. For purposes of service they were divided into juries of 201, 301, 401, and so on, the number varying with the importance of the case, and the odd number preventing a tie. Their procedure was the essence of democracy. The preliminary work having been done and the affidavits of the witnesses taken, each party in turn pleaded his case before the jury. No professional lawyers were permitted to participate, although women, foreigners, and minors were represented by Athenian citizen friends. Also, if a suitor were a very poor speaker, he might secure the aid of one more skilled in the art of oratory than himself. Speeches were admittedly casual affairs, and did not adhere closely to the point at issue. In fact, irrelevant personal abuse of an opponent was much appreciated by the jury if judiciously used, for each party's whole character and record was, in a sense, on trial. Ancestors and relatives of one's opponent also came in for their share of castigation. An oft-quoted example of such personal abuse is to be seen in Demosthenes' denunciation of his opponent Aeschines:

> Compare then, Aeschines, your life and mine, calmly and without rancor. Ask these jurors which fortune each of them would prefer. You taught reading; I went to school. You performed initiations; I was initiated. You danced; I paid for the chorus. You were a public scribe; I an orator. You were a third-rate actor; I a spectator. You failed in your part; and I hissed you.[1]

When, however, a speaker had actual evidence to support his claims, he would frequently interrupt his plea to ask the clerk to read the testimony of his witnesses. There was no cross-examination, but either party might challenge the other to answer certain questions or to submit his slaves to

[1] *On the Crown*, chap. 265.

torture to see if they would incriminate their master. Relatives of an accused person might appear before the jury in mourning to arouse its pity.

Verdicts and Sentences

When the pleading had been finished, the jury voted. In a criminal case this determined the guilt or innocence of the accused, and in a civil case whether plaintiff or defendant was in the right. If penalty or damages were fixed by law, that ended the matter, but where such was not the case, a curious device was used to reach a decision. The accuser proposed a penalty or sum due as damages and the defendant another (and lighter) one. The jury then voted a second time to determine which proposition it would accept, and the winning proposition stood as the decision.

It is easy to see the possible evils of such a system. The larger the jury, the greater the danger that mob hysteria would prejudice its decision and that grave injustice would result. As the jury was the judge of both law and fact, it follows that the law could be disregarded, and legal precedents would have slight influence. On the other hand, bribery and intimidation were difficult with so large a group, and under the existing conditions both might have influenced a smaller jury. An Athenian juror seems to have loved his work to the point of obsession. He was proud and self-important, for men of the highest rank had to humble themselves before him:

> For when I rise in the morning and am off to court, great strapping fellows are there to salute their judge humbly. A delicate hand that has been thrust deeply into the public treasury is placed in mine. He bows before me as he makes his prayer, and whines pitifully as he cries, "Pardon me, sir, if you ever stole anything yourself while managing the mess in a distant campaign, or if you yourself ever held an office." [1]

When his prejudices were not aroused, he had a fine sense of justice and fairness, and his disregard of legal technicalities was not always an unmixed evil.

Petty jurisdiction at Athens was in the hands of thirty itinerant justices, who visited all parts of the country and decided lawsuits on the spot. They were chosen, like other officials, for a year at a time. If both parties to a trifling dispute agreed, the case might be referred to arbiters; but if either party disagreed with their decision, an appeal might be entered and the matter brought before a regular jury.

[1] Aristophanes, *Wasps*, ll. 550–558.

Finance: The Liturgies

Athenian government finance was, in the fifth century, far more efficient than that of any other known Greek state. Athens had an income which, in the years following the Thirty Years' Truce, must have been around a thousand talents a year: an enormous sum for the time and place. About half of this was tribute from the allies, and one-sixtieth was the property of Athena. Her money formed an extraordinary reserve, to be used only in severe crises and then repaid. Royalties from the silver mines, duties on imports and exports, market and harbor dues, the tax on foreigners, court fees and fines, and confiscated property were some of the sources of income. No general property tax was levied except in cases of dire emergency, but those citizens whose assets totaled more than three talents were subject to a burdensome system of forced expenditures for public purposes (*leitourgia*). Chief among these were the *trierarchy, choregia, gymnasiarchia,* and *hestiasis.* A trierarch assumed command of a trireme for a year and had to bear a large share of the cost of maintaining the vessel. The expenditure involved was often as much as a talent a year. The *choregus* had to pay expenses of training and equipping the chorus for a tragedy, comedy, or dithyramb presented at one of the great religious festivals. Occasionally, as much as three thousand drachmas were spent for this purpose by a single individual. A *gymnasiarch* bore the cost of various athletic events, and an *hestiator* provided a feast for his fellow tribesmen. In a society which considered ten talents a great fortune, any one of these burdens was heavy, but they were undertaken willingly, and the minimum expenditures were often exceeded. In general, Pericles was a careful financier, and in spite of the heavy expenditures entailed by public works and official salaries, the beginning of the Peloponnesian War found the state possessed of a reserve of six thousand talents.

Local Government: The Deme

In addition to his duties to the central government, the Athenian citizen had a part in the working of his petty local unit, the deme. It often owned and administered property and it took care of a variety of local matters too small to interest the central government. It also served as a unit of local administration for such purposes as drafting soldiers and compiling lists of persons eligible for office. It is regrettable that we do not know more about the workings of these minute subdivisions, but aside from a few inscriptions and meager references by Athenian authors, their activities have disappeared from the human record. It was in the general

assembly that important questions of policy and administration were settled, but the demal assemblies, like New England town meetings, must
have played a large part in the training of the Athenian people for active
citizenship.

Unlike the voters in a modern democracy, who only take part in government at rare intervals, the Athenian citizen was constantly compelled to
participate personally in the task of self-government. In this field he felt
thoroughly at home, for he had either held office or served on juries, and
he knew public men and issues intimately. The state was so small that he
felt as if he personally counted for something, and his actions revealed the
feeling. Whether good or bad, they had a positive quality which grew
from the consciousness of worth and confidence that he knew what he was
doing.

Athenian Judgment of Periclean Democracy

Was Periclean democracy, as a form of government, good or bad? The
question may best be answered by reviewing two contemporary Athenian
judgments, one of which favors and the other opposes it. In its favor we
have the words of Pericles himself, spoken just after the opening of the
Peloponnesian War — the famous *Funeral Oration*. We learn its failings
from an anonymous lecture, evidently composed by one of the Athenian
oligarchs about 425 B.C., and long supposed to be the work of Xenophon.
The "Old Oligarch," as ts author has aptly been called, was evidently
well informed, and he is objective in his discuss on. From these two we
may at least secure the materials from which to form our own judgments.

The "Old Oligarch" begins by clearly announcing his purpose:

> Now as to the Athenian form of government, and the kind of con-
> stitution which they have chosen, I do not praise it . . . But given
> the fact that they have agreed upon this form, I propose to show that
> they have set about its preservation in the right way, and that
> those features which the other Greeks regard as blunders are the
> reverse.[1]

Athens, he says, does wisely in opening all offices to the commons, for to
them she owes her naval strength. The commoners do not attempt to
hold high military offices, for they know that it is to their advantage to
leave such responsibility in competent hands. Athens makes the masses
of the people prosperous, because the wealthy upper classes are everywhere
opposed to democracy. The Old Oligarch concedes that the people at

[1] Pseudo-Xenophon, *The Constitution of the Athenians*, chap. 1.

large are ignorant, brutal, turbulent, and dishonest. Such people cannot make good laws, but legislate for their own benefit, and one cannot blame them for doing so. They cannot trust the "better people" to exercise power.

> They will curb and chastise the commons. They will deliberate for the good of the city, and not let mad fellows sit in council or speak and vote in the assembly. That is true, but under the weight of such "blessings" the commons will soon be in slavery.[1]

In her diabolically clever efforts to perpetuate the power of the lower classes, Athens protects both slaves and foreigners. It is a misdemeanor to beat another man's slaves, even if they are so impudent that they will not step aside for you on the street. But there is a good reason for this. Slaves are as well dressed as poor freemen, and if beating of strange slaves were permitted, freemen might often be assaulted by mistake. Foreigners are protected because of the wealth which their labor brings to the city.

In like manner the Old Oligarch surveys other characteristic institutions of Athenian democracy. Athletic exercises have been degraded to a professional level, so that the rich have to bear the expense, while the poor participate. Festivals and sacrifices are paid for by the state, so that the poor may have a share in them. With her naval power, Athens can secure the good things of the whole world to supply her wants and build up her own power. The popular courts use their jurisdiction over the allies to humiliate men of wealth and standing and "to preserve the partisans of democracy and ruin her opponents." A steady stream of court fees and fines replenishes the fund for the payment of jurors. The democratic faction in each allied state is fostered because Athens cannot depend upon the loyalty of the "better people." The Old Oligarch does not blame the rabble for this. Every man should look out for his own interests, but no man of the better class should favor a government hostile to his welfare. Indeed, the speaker hints that it may some day be possible, with foreign aid, to overthrow this "rule of the worst."

Prejudiced and cynical as the diatribe is, it is also highly instructive. It proves that Athens, like other Greek states, had an oligarchic faction which, although driven from the political arena for a time, was rancorous, bitter, and ready to go to any extreme to overturn the hated system of which Pericles had so long been the leading exponent. We shall hear more of it when, at the close of the Peloponnesian War, it subjects the city to a reign of blood, spoliation, and terror.

[1] *Ibid.*, Chap. 9.

Pericles' Funeral Oration

The reverse of this dark picture is found in the words of Pericles, as reported by the historian Thucydides. It was the autumn of the year 431, and already the war which was to destroy the greatness of imperial Athens had begun. The oration is delivered at the public funeral given in honor of those who had fallen in battle during the year. Pericles begins by pronouncing a panegyric upon the greatness of Athens. Her government not only accords equal justice to all, but recognizes especial merit and allows every man, rich or poor, to exert his talents for the welfare of his country. The people combine individual freedom with respect for law and the rights of others. Their lives, unlike those of the Lacedaemonians, are distinguished by balance and reason. Work is relieved by play, and without making existence burdensome by endless military training they are able to defend themselves against all enemies. They use their wealth intelligently, and care for both material and spiritual interests without neglecting either. Public questions are settled by rational discussion, and danger is met, not with the courage of ignorance, but as the result of calm deliberation. Athens is the benefactress of all her friends and she makes friends by conferring benefits. She is the school of Greece, and the individual Athenian can adapt himself to the needs of any situation with ease and grace. To die bravely in defending such a state is the highest glory that mortals can achieve.

> I would have you daily fix your eyes upon the greatness of Athens, until love of her fills your hearts, and when you are impressed with the spectacle of her glory, think then that this empire has been gained by men who knew their duty and were brave enough to do it; who in the hour of conflict always feared dishonor; and who if ever they failed in an undertaking, would not allow their virtues to be lost to their country, but freely gave their lives as the fairest offering which they could present at her feet.[1]

To parents still in the prime of life, Pericles offers the comforting word that they may yet have other children to solace them and to fill the gaps in the ranks of their country's citizens. Those who have not this hope should reflect upon the happiness that was once theirs, glory in the fair name of the departed, and remember that they have not much longer to live. Sons and brothers of the dead heroes must strive to equal them in glory. Lastly, the greatest distinction to be achieved by a woman is not to show more weakness than is natural to her sex and "not to be talked about by men, whether for good or evil."

[1] Thucydides, *History*, II, 43.

An Evaluation

Which picture is nearer to the truth? Was selfish class interest or a disinterested patriotism the dominant note in Athenian life? For all their contradictions, the two descriptions have points of agreement, and where they differ, the facts of history show that Pericles was nearer to the truth than the "Old Oligarch." Certainly, the fifty years after the invasion of Xerxes was for Athens a period of achievement in many lines, which would not have been possible if her policies had been completely dominated by a selfish rabble seeking only to advance its own interests. Even Pericles would have accomplished little if he had not been supported by a citizen body composed for the most part of highly capable men, dominated by a spirit of self-sacrificing patriotism. In that age, at least, Athenian democracy was a success.

22

The Periclean Age: Economics and Society

SOCIAL CLASSES AND CLASS RELATIONSHIPS

IN SOCIAL HISTORY as in other things, there is little to be recorded for most of the Greek world during the third quarter of the fifth century B.C. This is owing, in part, to our ignorance of conditions, but it is also true that in many cities no important changes had occurred during that century. The same parties and classes were always in the ascendancy in these cities, generation after generation, and what was written of the sixth century might easily be substantially true of the fifth or fourth. In Athens and the cities of her empire, however, as well as in Sparta, interesting and significant changes were in progress.

Small Landholders, and Large

As a result of the Persian wars and the favoritism shown by Athens to the lower classes in her empire, many of the commoners had become the owners of small farms and building lots. Records of sales from Chios and Halicarnassus show that there were holdings worth as little as fifty drachmas, and the average price in the latter city was less than a thousand drachmas. Although the amount of land involved in each sale is unknown, it must often have been very small. The numerous cleruchies established by Athens on confiscated land contributed to swell the ranks of this group, for in almost every case the large landowners were the fomenters of rebellion and bore the brunt of the punishment. On the other hand, the allotments granted by the Athenian state were small. This policy, however, instead of solving the eternal problem of class relationships, greatly aggravated it. The pent-up wrath of the aristocrats waited only for a weakening of Athenian control to break out into rebellion, and it was later to prove an important factor in the overthrow of the empire by Sparta.

383

Meanwhile, Attica remained a land of small farms and small shops. In 431 b.c., out of a total of some 42,000 adult male citizens, 21,000 were cavalrymen or heavy-armed infantrymen and 20,000 were thetes. That leaves not over a thousand persons with incomes in the highest bracket, and even the wealthiest seldom had what we could call large estates. When the land was devoted to grape and olive culture, 25 acres would furnish the necessary 500 *metretes* of wine or oil, and 125 acres would yield the same number of *medimnoi* of grain. From 15 to 75 acres would provide an income for a cavalryman, and from 10 to 50 acres were enough for an infantryman. Even the thetes often held patches of land large enough to contribute materially to their support, and the largest estates were often widely scattered tracts.

There were, however, still parts of the Greek world in which large plantations were the rule. A noble at Acragas had storage space for 260,000 gallons of wine (presumably produced on his land), and we hear of other Sicilian Greeks each with as many as five hundred slaves. In Thessaly, an aristocrat had twelve talents of ready money and two hundred male serfs able to serve as soldiers. The Spartiates, in spite of the laws designed to prevent the concentration of land, were rapidly becoming separated into holders of huge tracts on the one hand and poverty-stricken "inferiors" on the other. In the Greek colonies on the north shore of the Black Sea, large grain farms seem always to have been the rule.

Wealthy Merchants

In a state like Athens, where manufacturing and commerce flourished, there was sure to be a large and important group whose wealth was entirely in money and merchandise. Athens had, even before the time of Pericles, given this class political equality with the landholders by placing a money value upon farm produce. This enabled the state to equate cash incomes with those derived from the land and to classify their recipients accordingly. Thus, a *medimnus* of grain and a *metretes* of wine or oil were valued arbitrarily at one drachma each, and the potter who received five hundred drachmas or more annually from his shop was rated as a *pentacosiomedimnus*. Similar measures assured political rights to wealthy merchants and craftsmen in Corinth, Aegina, and some other states. But in many cities the inherent aristocratic prejudice against manual labor and commerce intervened to deprive the moneyed classes of political influence. At Thebes no one could vote or hold office until he had been out of business for at least ten years. Even at Athens, laborers, craftsmen, and retail tradesmen were felt to be inferior beings, and the philosophers later reduced this prejudice to an inflexible dogma.

The Laboring Classes

We know little of the laboring classes in the Greek world, and what is known concerns for the most part the workers of Athens. The relative numbers of free workmen and slaves is, and will probably remain, unknown, for the statistics are scanty, fragmentary, and often unreliable.[1] A careful modern estimate places the number of slaves in Periclean Athens at about one hundred thousand, or approximately two-thirds of the number of citizens. Undoubtedly both the numbers of slaves and their status varied from city to city. There were some slaves in every community, and there were no doubt more in manufacturing and commercial than in agricultural areas. They had not yet, at least in Athens, become so numerous as to depress the social status or living standards of the free workmen. The theory formerly held by modern scholars, that Greek civilization rested entirely upon a basis of slave labor, is now known to be false. Slaves formed only a part of the Athenian working class and possibly not the most important part.

Treatment and Status of Slaves

Although Greeks were at times enslaved by reason of capture in war, crime, or abandonment in infancy, most of the slaves in fifth-century Greece were of barbarian birth. They came from many lands, and differed widely in age, physique, and previous training. The Greek slave-dealer graded his wares, so that each type might find the place which it was best fitted to fill. At Athens, men who were too old, too sullen, or too stupid for anything but rough labor were sold cheaply to contractors who put them to work in the stone quarries or the silver mines. Of the younger ones, the state would buy some for menial tasks connected with government or religion. Thus, the Athenian police force was composed of three hundred Scythian slaves, who were armed with bows and daggers, and served as night patrolmen. But the large majority of them went to private individuals to be trained for domestic service or for trades. Most of the younger men were bought by various industrial establishments, where they became valuable implements of production. As the shops were

[1] The statement of Athenaeus that Aegina had once had 470,000 slaves, Corinth 460,000, and Athens 400,000 is obviously a wild exaggeration.

small, they usually worked with their masters and with free workmen, and shared the same conditions and hours of labor as the latter. This, however, was not always the case. Some shops were operated by foremen, slaves, or resident foreigners, who were noted for harsh treatment of their charges. In other instances, masters bought slaves and rented them to others at a rate which allowed some profit. Again, an able and trusted slave might be allowed to choose his work or enter business for himself, paying his master part of the proceeds of his labor. Such slaves were called *choris oikountes* ("dwellers-apart"). They sometimes became sufficiently wealthy to have slaves of their own.

To understand the bright and dark sides of a slave's life, however, we must study his condition in detail. He was a piece of property, and as such could be sold, mortgaged, confiscated, or treated in other respects as an inanimate possession except where the state intervened to protect him. If he were injured by a third party, only his master might sue the culprit, and if he broke the laws he received corporal punishment instead of a fine. Masters everywhere had the right to beat their slaves, and in some places a freeman could beat the slave of another if he failed to make way for him on the street. Athens, however, extended the benefits of the laws to slaves. Their lives were protected and they could not be mistreated by strangers. If a master treated his slave cruelly, the latter could flee to a shrine and demand to be sold to a more humane master. But the Athenian courts would take a slave's testimony only under torture, though this seems at times to have been reduced to a solemn farce. Since the slave was property himself, he could not legally own property, but it was customary to allow him to keep his savings, and if he were energetic and resourceful he could eventually buy his freedom. Slaves could not marry, and if unions were consummated they had no standing in law. When all has been said, the slave's best protection was the self-interest of his master. It did not pay to starve him or to beat him too severely. To get the best service from him, one had to give him a stronger stimulus than mere fear could supply. Hence, the more intelligent owners often treated their slaves with consideration and held out the prospect of freedom as an incentive for good work. The slaves frequently conducted themselves with saucy freedom, but in times of crisis often showed devotion to their masters. Athens was never troubled with slave revolts. When freed, the former slave entered the class of resident foreigners, and occasionally his services to the state were so great that he was granted the supreme gift of Athenian citizenship. Hence the lot of the Athenian slave, though hard, was not as a rule unendurable.

The Metics: Free Laborers

The majority of free laborers in Athens belonged to the class of resident foreigners (*metoikoi*). Most of them were Greeks from other states, but like the slaves, they included many Thracians, Syrians, Phoenicians, Egyptians, Lydians, and representatives of other barbarian groups. The total number in the days of Pericles was much smaller than the number of citizens, but cannot be stated exactly. To attain metic status, one had to be a resident of the country, to have a citizen conduct his relations with the government for him (*prostates*), to pay a special poll tax of twelve drachmas a year, and to meet the liturgies, property taxes, and service in army and navy demanded from citizens. After the passage of the laws on citizenship in 451, the metics had small hope of ever becoming full-fledged Athenians, and they could not own land unless given the right by a special grant, but in most respects their position was satisfactory. Both Pericles (in the *Funeral Oration*) and the "Old Oligarch" agree that Athens welcomed them cordially. They associated with Athenians on equal terms in everyday life, and in industry and commerce, owing to the preoccupation of the citizens with the task of government, they had a marked advantage. Probably the largest workshop in the Piraeus was the arms factory of the metic Cephalos, which employed one hundred and twenty slaves. On public works the citizens seem to have done just enough to eke out their incomes from other sources, and the metics had the field largely to themselves. Stonecutting, metal-working, petty contracting, and common labor — each depended largely upon them for its personnel, and to them went the bulk of the financial returns. They had no prejudices against laborious or dirty work. Often a man practiced several trades, so that he could always find employment at one or another of them. In the shipping industry they surpassed Athenian citizens and the war navy of Athens owed much to them. It was only in businesses such as mining and timber-working, which depended upon the ownership of the land, that they were at a disadvantage, and there were some even in these industries.

Citizens as Workers and Businessmen

Having surveyed the conditions of the two classes which were competitors of the Athenian citizen-workman or businessman, we must now consider the economic activities of the citizens themselves. Under Pericles' guidance the state undertook to see that each able-bodied citizen had a chance to earn a living, and in this it was successful. With opportunities in the army, the navy, the temples and other public works, the juries, the paid service in various offices, and in private employment, no one needed to endure involuntary idleness. The widows and orphans of men killed in war, as well as disabled persons, were pensioned. Hence, the Athenian citizen enjoyed a large measure of what we currently call "social security." But he never was, or wished to be, steadily employed at manual labor. In the first place, he was often the owner of a piece of land which, while not enough to support him, provided a good share of his living. Then, too, wages were high enough that a man of simple tastes could live by working only a fraction of the time. The average wage for a workman was a drachma a day, regardless of the type of work done. A single man could live well on one hundred and twenty drachmas a year and a married man with two children on two hundred and eighty drachmas. Whether single or married, he could have plenty of free time to devote to public duties, festivals, and amusements. Under these conditions, it is not strange that few citizens cared to apply themselves to business more than enough to obtain a modest subsistence.

Theoretically, the Athenians had no prejudice against any kind of honest work. "With us," said Pericles in the *Funeral Oration*, "it is no disgrace to admit poverty. The true disgrace lies in doing nothing to avoid it." But like most of the human race, they did not take the trouble to be consistent. The upper classes still felt contempt for the tradesman and the laborer, although it was unwise to show it too openly. The small farmer had a similar feeling for men who were tied to exacting or unpleasant trades or who hawked their wares in the market-place. There was a law which forbade one citizen to reproach another for practicing an honest trade, but it was practically a dead letter. In fact, the comedians never tired of ridiculing Cleon's tanyard or of reminding their audiences that Euripides' mother sold herbs.

The Small Farmers

If the slaves, foreigners, and poor citizens performed the rough labor of Athenian society, the *zeugitai* carried on most of the farming. Distinctions between the rural and urban populations in Attica were clear-cut and profound, and the small farmers were the best representatives of the rural point of view. Although they were capitalists, who produced goods for both the foreign and domestic markets, their attitude toward life was not far different from that of Hesiod. They seldom went to town, and spent their lives in contact with Nature and with each other. The result was a conservatism so strongly rooted that nothing could change it. Their religion, which was as much a product of their environment as they were themselves, concerned itself intimately with their everyday worldly desires, and it fortified them in their dislike for innovations. Ancestor-worship in particular linked them to the past, and hardened them against new ideas unknown to their ancestors. In the assembly they neutralized the radicalism of the urban workingmen and merchants, and opposed imperialistic ventures which threatened to lead the state into serious hostilities. Yet they were a sturdy, self-respecting class, and in times of crisis the state never called upon them in vain.

Differences in Living Standards

In Athens the difference between wealth and poverty was not accentuated by sharp contrasts in standards of living. The man who had too many luxuries was unpopular with his poorer fellow citizens, and in a democratic society this was fraught with danger for him. A century later, Demosthenes remarked that the houses of Miltiades and Aristides were no finer than those of their neighbors. Probably the same was largely true of their food and clothing. Nor did the rich and the poor each concentrate in a separate section of the city, as they tend to do in modern cities. Indeed, the chief use of the surplus funds of the rich was to perform liturgies for the state. From these they derived only personal glory and the good-will of their poorer neighbors, but in this way they rendered themselves secure in the possession of their wealth. The aristocrats of Thessaly, Boeotia, and western Greece lived neither so moderately nor so safely as their Athenian counterparts. Their dwellings were luxuriously furnished and they gave sumptuous banquets. They kept blooded horses and competed in the great national games, although they paid for these advantages by living in continual fear of social revolution.

ECONOMIC ORGANIZATION

To understand the business life of the ancient world one must learn to think in simple terms and to divest oneself entirely of the ideas and terminology appropriate to the twentieth century. Even at its best, the Greek world was primarily agricultural, and depended upon commerce and manufacturing only to supply those necessities which could not be obtained by each household from its own resources. It was a society without power-driven machinery, mass production, or complex business organization, and its better-regulated households came as near as possible to complete self-sufficiency. Both the merchant and the craftsman had to meet the competition of foodstuffs, textiles, and other consumption goods produced, processed, and consumed within the same family. The former could only gain a monopoly of articles of luxury or imported wares, and the latter had no advantage over the homeworker except manual skill. Thus, neither could drive his domestic competitors from business. The organization of credit was equally primitive. Corinth must have had banks of a sort as early as 472 (when Themistocles deposited seventy talents in the bank of one Philostephanus); but it is doubtful if Athens had any during the period under discussion. Checks, drafts, and banknotes were unheard-of, and all payments had to be made in coin.

Food-Supply and Agricultural Methods

Except in fertile areas like Thessaly, Greek Sicily, and the communities along the Black Sea, securing an adequate food-supply was one of the major problems of every Greek city-state. Athens at all times forbade the exportation of homegrown grain, and took drastic steps to attract wheat and barley to her port. She produced only about one-fourth of the quantity of these commodities needed to feed her people; the remainder had to be imported. By far the greater part of this was barley, which in money and in food-value was worth only half as much as wheat. Wine and olive-oil, on the other hand, were produced for export, for they could be grown on rocky hillsides unfit for grain culture. In a normal year about a million and a half bushels of grain were imported from the Black Sea region, the Aegean islands, Sicily, and Egypt, and to protect the routes by which it came was perhaps the most pressing task of the Athenian state.

Agricultural methods had greatly improved in the century previous to the rise of Pericles. The spread of grape and olive culture had greatly increased the productive capacity of the land of Attica. The Persians had introduced alfalfa into continental Greece to the great benefit of the live-stock-growers. Crop rotation was beginning to take the place of the earlier practice of leaving half the land fallow each year, and fertilizers were coming into use. As a result of specialized agriculture, many of the Attic farmers bought their grain in the market with money realized from other products. Bee-culture, which furnished the only sweetening material known, was an important feature of Athenian agriculture and Attica had thousands of hives. Stock-raising flourished, but only in specialized lines. Cattle had never been plentiful in continental Greece, and the Athenians had to hire draft-oxen from Boeotia for their public works.

Horses were few and of little economic importance. Donkeys were used as burden-carriers, and almost every farmer had one. Sheep and goats fed in great numbers on the scrublands and on sterile mountainsides. They were almost the only source of milk-supply, and their wool was the commonest material used in the manufacture of clothing. The pig was the chief source of meat, as it could find its own subsistence and needed little care. Grass of any kind was scarce in Greece, and the sheep and goats, being compelled to browse upon the foliage and young shoots of the forests, contributed greatly toward aggravating the deforestation brought about by lumbering and charcoal-burning. Already, in the time of Pericles, Attica was beginning to suffer from a shortage of timber.

Athenian Commerce

Thanks to her navy and the enterprise of her people, Athens was the commercial center of the Greek world. "The greatness of our city," said Pericles, "draws the produce of the world into our harbor, so that to the Athenian the fruits of other countries are luxuries as familiar as those of his own." We have seen how she secured so much of her grain from other lands. In addition, she received from the coasts of the Black Sea salt fish, smoked and salted meat, hides, iron and steel, slaves, and various raw materials drawn from far in the interior of northern Europe and Asia. From near-by Greek states came fresh garden vegetables, fresh fish, eels, cheese, and live pigs. Even distant Etruria contributed bronzes and fine shoes, and Carthage, luxurious cushions. From Egypt, the Athenians received, in addition to grain, papyrus, linen, sailcloth, ropes, ivory, glassware, and other manufactured articles.

Markets and Traders

Once safely landed, this merchandise either might be sold directly to the consumer or delivered to one of several types of processer or retailer. The latter was known to the Greeks by the name *kapelos*, in contrast to the *emporos*, or large-scale merchant-importer and the *naukleros*, or merchant-ship owner. Some of them hawked their wares about the streets, but most had stalls in the market-place or near a temple like the Theseum. Their tongues were rude and fluent, their honesty was more than suspect, and the state subjected them to vigorous regulation. It rented stalls to them and undertook to protect the public from fraud. A board of market wardens (*agoranomoi*) regulated buying and selling, maintained a certain degree of order in the market, and strove to prevent the sale of poor-quality goods. A board of inspectors of weights and measures (*metronomoi*) undertook to see that purchasers got as much of each article as they paid for. Each commodity was sold in a separate part of the market and at an hour determined by the wardens. Interspersed with the shoppers were loafers whose object was entertainment, gossip, and discussion. The Piraeus had a similar market, noisier and more colorful than that of the upper city, and frequented by a motley crowd of foreigners. The Athenian markets were similar, with minor variations, to those of hundreds of other Greek cities.

The Greek peddler and trader found other opportunities for business at the great religious festivals, in the wake of armies, and among barbarian peoples. Those from the Black Sea cities and from distant colonies like Cyrene, Cyme, or Massalia must have rivaled the French-Canadian *coureurs-de-bois* in the extent of their travels into barbarian lands. They traversed most of Gaul, the Danubian lands, Russia up to the Ural Mountains, and northern Africa. From them the historians and geographers gathered much knowledge, and they disseminated among their rude customers the products of Greek workshops, as well as some of the finer Hellenic intellectual wares.

Manufactures and Industrial Organization

Athens enjoyed as great pre-eminence in manufacturing as in commerce, although in both cases she shared the field with her lesser rivals. Her pottery continued to monopolize large areas among both Greeks and barbarians, and its makers must have been continually pressed with orders. Household furniture, textiles, arms and armor, cutlery, leather goods, musical instruments, and sculptures in both bronze and marble were produced for export as well as for the domestic market. With the mastery of both raw materials and markets assured her by her command of the sea, Athens was able to provide work for thousands of men in her workshops, and the high quality of her products made the world willing to buy them.

Athenian industry was organized in small units and was conducted along informal lines. The arms factory of the metic Cephalos, which has been mentioned already, must have been at least three times larger than any other shop of its time. Many a craftsman carried on his trade alone or with the aid of members of his family, and seldom would there be as many as a dozen workmen employed. A few of these might be citizens, a slightly larger proportion metics, but the majority were slaves. Except for the potter's wheel and a few equally simple devices, there was no machinery.

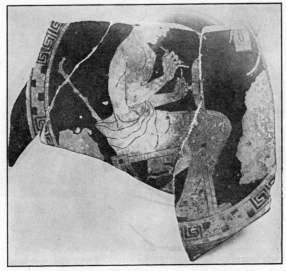

Museum of Fine Arts, Boston

A VASE PAINTER AT WORK

Every product was essentially hand-made, and every piece was necessarily different from every other.

Although the hours in such shops were long, conditions were not hard. The working pace was slow and leisurely. As the master worked with his men, he was not in a position to drive them harder than he did himself. A crowd of loafers watched the progress of the work and their chatter relieved its monotony. Holidays were frequent and slaves shared with their masters the sacrificial feasts. They were proud of their work, and some of the finest products of the Athenian potter's art may be their creations. As sculptors' assistants, they no doubt helped to produce the statues and reliefs which have given to the Age of Pericles so prominent a place in the history of art.

Athenian Public Works

At all times a large part of the work done in a Greek city was public work, directed and paid for by the government. In a few places even the manual trades were in this class and were performed by government-owned slaves. At Athens, the shipyards, arsenals, and public buildings employed large numbers of men, and the lavish building program of Pericles greatly

Berlin Museum

BRONZE FOUNDRY IN OPERATION

increased the number. All three classes of the population furnished their quotas, and democratic notions of equality prevailed among them. All workers, whether skilled or unskilled, slave or free, were paid at the same rate. The absence of machinery called for a good deal more concerted and monotonous effort by masses of men than does similar work in the modern world. To synchronize such effort, work songs were sung in unison, the motions of the men being regulated by the cadence of the air. In the ship-yards, whistle, pipe, and flute were used to give orders, as bugles are in a modern army.

The Silver Mines

From the viewpoint of labor, the dark spot in Athenian industry was the silver mines of Laurium. The operations were conducted by concession-aires to whom the state granted exclusive rights over certain tracts of mineral-bearing lands. In return they paid the state a portion of the out-put. The miners were slaves, the culls of the market. They were bought cheaply, and little care was taken to keep them in good health. With no tools but picks, chisels, hammers, and shovels they excavated shafts from two hundred to three hundred feet in depth, and followed the seams of ore in transverse passages not over three feet high and two feet wide. Light was provided by open lamps and there was no attempt to provide artificial ventilation. The work was done in continuous ten-hour shifts. The ore was sent to the surface in sacks, and was washed, ground, and smelted.

Museum of Fine Arts, Boston

SHOEMAKER AT WORK

Repeated refining brought it to a purity of 98.5 per cent before it was coined. A useful by-product was lead, which masons used in place of mortar to clamp stones together.

Lucky concessionaires, and owners who rented slaves to them, often made great fortunes from silver mining. In the time of Pericles, mine slaves cost no more than one hundred and fifty drachmas, and they were rented at the mines for about fifty drachmas a year and food. Thus, the gross income on such an investment was about thirty-three per cent. But such slaves wore out rapidly and no doubt runaways were frequent. Some years later, when the Spartans fortified a stronghold in Attica, twenty thousand of these unfortunates sought refuge with them. The greatest fortunes in Athenian history were made in silver mining. Callias the Rich had a capital of two hundred talents gained from it, and Nicias one hundred talents. Compared with these fortunes all others seemed insignificant. For the state, the industry provided an income of over one hundred talents a year, and a supply of silver which made possible the most reliable currency in the Greek world.   Athenian drachmas passed current all over the civilized world and their popularity did much to spread the use of Athenian goods.

LIVING CONDITIONS

We have had frequent occasion to discuss the urban life of the Greeks, but as yet little has been said about the appearance of a Greek city or the living standards of its inhabitants.   Analogies to modern life are few and misleading.   In most cases, the cities of continental Greece had grown haphazardly, as the need of defense and opportunity for economic betterment dictated.   The space allotted to houses and streets was limited to what could be surrounded by a wall, and the people were crowded closely together.   The streets were unbelievably narrow and crooked.   A rather important thoroughfare of old Athens, excavated a few years ago, was only fifteen feet wide, or one-fourth the width of a modest residential street in a Mid-Western American city.   Such a street might be paved with stone, although many were mere expanses of mud in winter and dust in summer, frequented by dogs and other animals.   Sewage and garbage were tossed into the thoroughfare, to the danger of passers-by, and the rains, the animal scavengers, and decomposition were the only means of cleaning it.   As a recompense, however, wheel traffic was rare, and the pedestrian was safer than in a modern city.   For the most part, his view was restricted to blank walls of sun-dried brick, sometimes coated with stucco.   The Greek was a strong believer in domestic privacy, and the only break in the outer walls of his dwelling was usually the street door, with possibly a window or two on the second floor, if there was one.   Some of the doorways and street intersections in Athens were provided with rude statuettes of Hermes, the protector of travelers.   Now and then a shrine, temple, or "sacred precinct" relieved the monotony of bare walls, for, although the more important temples were usually concentrated on the Acropolis, each neighborhood had its own minor places of worship.

Water-Supply

Although Athens had few sewers, she at least had a rudimentary municipal water-supply.   Early Athens, like her neighbors, had to depend upon wells, streams, springs, and cisterns for drinking water.   Peisistratus, however, built aqueducts to bring in a larger and better supply from the near-by mountains.   Once inside the city, the water was collected in reservoirs, from which channels distributed it to fountains in various parts of the city. To these fountains in the early morning came processions of women bearing water jugs, which they filled and carried away on their heads. Naturally, these places became centers for the distribution of neighborhood news as well as water. Other cities, such as Megara, Syracuse, and Samos, were proud of their aqueducts, but the Piraeus still had to rely upon cisterns fed by the winter rains, and many a city in the more barbarous sections of the Greek world depended upon the primitive and unsanitary devices of earlier ages.

Dwelling-Houses and Furniture

Greek dwelling-houses usually followed the floor plan of Minoan dwellings, with the rooms arranged about a central court. As nearly as can be determined, the great majority of the houses in both city and country were only one story high. Windows in the ground-floor rooms were rare, the light and air being admitted through the open doors. Some floors were paved with stone and still others with stucco or a kind of cement, but in the poorer dwellings one walked upon the bare earth. Many of the roofs were covered with closely packed clay, though tile roofs were not uncommon. The sun-dried brick walls afforded excellent protection against the stifling heat of a Greek summer, but very little against burglars. These marauders were expressively termed "walldiggers" (*teichorouchoi*), and their usual tools were picks and shovels. In the upper-class houses separate quarters were provided for men and women, but the cramped and squalid abodes of the poor made such segregation of the sexes impossible. The short and mild winters of the Aegean region did not encourage the Greeks to perfect artificial heating arrangements. Chimneys were unknown, and except for the kitchen fires, they had only jars of smoldering charcoal to soften the chill of a winter morning. In general they depended upon heavy woolen clothing, wine, solar heat, and patience to carry them over the uncomfortable interlude between two summers. At all times of the year, meetings of the assembly and law courts, dramatic performances, and other public gatherings were held in the open.

Household furniture was crude and scanty for both rich and poor, and housekeeping arrangements were primitively simple. There were bedsteads which were laced with leather thongs in place of springs, but they were innocent of sheets. There were chests, boxes, chairs, and tables, but no closets or cupboards. Hence, clothing and household utensils were usually kept in plain sight, and at best must have lent an untidy appearance to a room. Grain, wine, and oil were stored in huge jars, as in Minoan Crete.

Food, Oil, and Wine

Food habits had changed radically since the time of Homer. In the fifth century, fresh meat, which had appeared in such generous quantities on the tables of a Menelaus or an Odysseus, was rarely eaten by either rich or poor except at religious festivals. On the other hand, fish, eels, and oysters, which the Homeric heroes had disdained, were considered delicacies. Both fresh and salted fish were extensively consumed at Athens, the former caught in the near-by seas and the latter imported from the more distant coasts of the Aegean and Black seas. Wheat and barley formed the bulk of the diet of all classes. The former cost twice as much as the latter, however, and was thought to have twice its food-value. Wheat was usually made into bread and barley into porridge. Together they were classified as *sitos*, and their combined cost was reckoned as half of the food bill of the normal family. All other foods were combined under the term *opsonion*, or appetizers. These included meat, fish, vegetables, fruit, and cheese. The commonest vegetables were peas, beans, garlic, onions, and a variety of wild herbs eaten as salads. The available fruits were apples, quinces, figs, and pomegranates.

No discussion of Greek diet would be complete without emphatic mention of olive oil and wine. Only the choicest oil was used for food, the inferior grades substituting for soap, lamp fuel, and other purposes. For the Greek cook, olive oil served the purposes for which butter, lard, and numerous vegetable fats are now used, and without it he would have been helpless. It is not surprising that the Athenians considered the olive tree as the special gift of the goddess Athena, or that they protected it with drastic laws. As in modern Greece, Italy, Spain, and France, everyone drank wine. It took the place held in modern America by tea, coffee, milk, carbonated drinks, and intoxicants, and at every meal it was served in liberal quantities. But the Greek was by no means a drunkard. To drink undiluted wine was a mark of barbarism, and as a rule its strength was reduced to about forty per cent with water. In this form it stimulated the wits, loosened the tongue, and produced a sense of warmth in cold weather, without causing intoxication. It was only during carousals that the quantity and quality of the refreshments were such as to make the participants lose control of themselves. Yet every dinner party was likely to be followed by its *symposium*, or drinking party, which was enlivened by acrobats, flute-girls, courtesans, games, and the conversation of the guests. The symposium, with its wine, entertainment, and philosophic talk, serves as the artistic background for several of the finest dialogues of Plato.

On the whole, the Greeks were an abstemious people, both in food and in drink. In general, they ate three meals a day, as we do. Formerly their "dinner" had been eaten at midday, and in the fifth century the country people probably continued the practice. City dwellers, however, had made a change very much like that which has taken place in modern urban communities, and had their heaviest meal in the evening. Breakfast consisted of nothing more substantial than a slice of bread dipped in undiluted wine. The noon luncheon, while more substantial, was still light, and was often eaten by the man of the house away from home. In the evening, if no guests were present, the whole family ate together, the men reclining on couches and the women and children sitting on chairs. When guests came to dinner the women did not appear. Knives, forks, and spoons formed no part of Greek table equipment. Solid foods were cut into small pieces before being served and were conveyed to the mouth with the fingers. Liquids were either drunk or sopped up with bread. Athenian meals were so meager that foreign guests complained of arising from the table hungry. Spartan fare at the public messes was monotonous and badly prepared, but the Sicilian Greeks had a reputation in gastronomic matters as famous as that of the French in modern times, and Sicilian chefs were much in demand in continental Greece.

Clothing

In costume, the fifth-century Greeks still followed the general style introduced by the Dorian invaders seven centuries earlier.[1] Next to the body, both men and women wore the *chiton*, the feminine variety being fuller and more ornate than the masculine. Up to the fifth century, the prevailing style at Athens had been the long, trailing Ionic chiton, which was made of linen. Shortly before the time of Pericles, however, the plain woolen Dorian style had become dominant. Over it both sexes wore a type of garment called *epiblemata*, or "wraps." Of these, the most widely used was still the *himation*, described in an earlier chapter. Men doing active work wore the *chlamys*, a cloak fastened with a clasp over the

[1] See Chapter 11.

Metropolitan Museum

WOMAN WEARING IONIC CHITON
AND HIMATION

shoulder so as to leave both arms free. These garments were dyed in any one of several colors, the most precious being the famous "purple," actually a shade of red, made from the blood of the *murex*, and already mentioned as a discovery of the Minoans or Phoenicians. The hot climate and the absence of laundry soap made it impossible to keep garments as clean as modern taste demands. The commonest form of footwear was the sandal, a mere leather sole bound to the foot with leather thongs, but shoes and even boots were worn by soldiers, hunters, and workmen. Socks and stockings were unknown. Because of the filthiness of the streets, it was customary to leave foot-coverings at the door when entering a house, and the poorer people probably went barefoot at all times. There were no pockets in a Greek's clothing, and he sometimes carried coins in his mouth. Large sums were transported in leather bags. Except when traveling, neither sex wore any head-covering, although a woman might draw the corner of her *himation* over her head in bad weather. When on journeys, both sexes wore broad-brimmed felt hats (*petasos*), and a workman protected his head with a conical cap of felt or leather (*pilos*).

Hair and Beard Styles

Up to the Persian wars, Athenian men had let both hair and beard grow long. In the Age of Pericles, however, it had become customary for men to have their hair cut short and their beards trimmed. Barber shops were numerous and well patronized, and like every other place of public resort in Athens were frequented by swarms of genteel loafers eager to gossip and to learn the latest scandal of the metropolis. Women wore elaborate coiffures and confined their hair in nets. In addition, they painted their faces, worked over their eyebrows, and practiced the other arts of beautification known to their sisters in all ages and countries.

The ancient Greek had learned, as a modern scholar has well expressed it, "how to be civilized without being comfortable." When we list the articles which are considered indispensable to daily living, we are astonished by the number of them of which he was totally ignorant. Soap, sugar, tea, coffee, window glass, socks, underwear, clocks, watches, tin cans, artificial heating arrangements, springs in beds and chairs, refrigerators, sanitary plumbing — the list is interminable. His books were laboriously copied by hand, and he had neither newspaper nor periodicals. He traveled on foot, by horse or donkey back, or in a jolting chariot no better than a cart. Nor were the necessities which he possessed either cheap or easy to acquire. His food and clothing cost him far more effort than corresponding articles would exact of us. In illness or injury he had as a rule to depend upon home remedies to dull pain or to assist recovery. It is only when we keep his limited equipment and grinding poverty constantly in mind that we can appreciate the magnitude of his achievements.

Woman and the Family

With few exceptions the Greek world of the fifth century was a man's world, and the Greek city, "a man's club." In Athens the legal and social status of woman was much lower in the time of Pericles than it had been a century before. If she was a member of the citizen class, she remained throughout her life a ward of some male relative — father, brother, husband, or son. She was excluded from the general social life of the city and made no noticeable contribution to its culture. To understand her position, we must investigate the organization and government of the family, for her life was passed entirely within this narrow circle.

The Rights of a Husband and Father

The ruler of an Athenian family was, under normal conditions, the husband and father. If he died prematurely, his rights passed to guardians whom he named in his will. Except for his wife's dowry, he had complete control of the family property. At the birth of a child, he could accept or disown it without consulting anyone. If he chose the latter course, the baby was left at a street corner or near a temple, to die or to be rescued by some passer-by. Since girl babies were unwelcome, they were more often exposed than boys. The father publicly acknowledged his offspring before his relatives and his phratry, and gained citizenship for his sons by having their names registered with his deme. He chose husbands for his daughters and in his will selected a husband for his widow. Within the home his authority was as complete as law and custom could make it.

The Wife and Mother

The wife and mother was confined to the domestic circle. Propriety forbade her to be seen on the streets except in company with other women, usually female slaves, and then only on urgent business or at solemn festivals. In the theater she could attend the performance of tragedies, but was barred from the licentious comedies. Her associations with men were limited to close relatives, for, as we have seen, she did not meet her husband's guests socially. Athens subscribed heartily to Pericles' statement in the *Funeral Oration*, "That woman is best whose name is least spoken by men, whether for good or evil." But within her narrow sphere she was a person of importance. Work, war, or politics took her husband away from home much of the time, and the actual management of the household was left to her. Under her guidance her daughters and the household servants transformed raw materials into food and clothing. She trained barbarian slaves to perform useful tasks, tended them in sickness, checked and issued supplies, and mounted guard over furniture and household utensils. The education of her sons was largely in male hands, but she had undisputed sway over that of her daughters. If she performed those duties well, she was honored and respected.

Marriage

For the Athenian girl of citizen class, marriage was the only career, and her education was a preparation for it. Yet to her, as to the southern

European girl of today, it seldom if ever brought romance. The match was arranged by her father and the groom or his relatives, frequently with the aid of a professional matchmaker. The groom was often past thirty years of age and the bride from fourteen to sixteen. As he was already a man of the world and she an ignorant child, intellectual companionship was nearly impossible. No longer did her father receive a "bride-price" for her, as in Homeric times. Instead, he gave her a dowry, and if there were several daughters this might prove a severe strain on his finances. After marriage, the husband had the right to use his wife's dowry, but if he died or divorced her it was returned to her. Marriage was a purely domestic ceremony, of which the state took no account. The bride, after a ceremonial bath, partook of a banquet at her father's house. She was then veiled and rode in a chariot to her new home between the groom and best man. A noisy crowd of merrymakers followed. On arrival at her husband's home, she was showered with grain, fruit, and delicacies. She then retired to the bridal chamber with her husband; the pair ate a quince to-

Metropolitan Museum

A WEDDING PROCESSION

gether, after which the bride removed her veil. The bridesmaids lingered outside to sing an *epithalamion*, or marriage song.

Prostitution: The Hetairai

But if, as we have seen, romantic love was entirely divorced from courtship and marriage, what outlets did the Athenians afford to this sentiment? In the first place, marital faithfulness, in our sense of the term, was not expected of Greek husbands. Commercialized vice flourished everywhere. At Corinth more than one thousand women slaves owned by the temple of Aphrodite plied this trade; and in other cities it was conducted as a private enterprise. Of a somewhat higher type were the classes of women known at Athens as "companions" (*hetairai*). They were usually Greeks of alien birth, who ostensibly served as entertainers at dinner parties. They combined a large measure of what we would term immorality with personal beauty, lively wit, and pleasing manners. Apparently, they ranged all the way from women of the streets to mistresses of wealthy men. A famous example of the *hetairai* was the Milesian Aspasia, whose charming conversation and brilliant mind drew to her house some of the foremost intellectuals of Athens, including Socrates. A few of them even brought their wives. For many years she lived as the recognized mistress of Pericles (by law he was forbidden to marry her), and bore him a son.

Love Affairs Between Men

Another source of intimacies and companionship was love affairs between men. As the Greek youth passed his time almost exclusively in the company of his own sex, he frequently fell in love with male companions, composed verses in their honor, grew jealous of possible rivals, and, in short, exhibited all the symptoms normally reserved for the opposite sex. This practice existed all over the Greek world, and accounts for such famous friendships as those of Harmodius and Aristogeiton or Damon and Pythias. At its best this strange practice was pure and ennobling; but often it degenerated into revolting and unnatural vice.

In any description of a people's manners and morals one must beware of too facile generalizations. Most of the foregoing description necessarily applies to the upper and middle classes, whose activities furnished the materials for literature. The poor could not keep their women segregated, and for that reason, if for no other, probably lived less constrained lives than their wealthier fellow citizens. Furthermore, the tombstone inscriptions teach us that even among the latter conjugal affection was sometimes sincere and strong. And we must remember that the subjection of women at Athens was never as complete in fact as in law. Shrewd, purposeful, strong-willed women must have dominated weaker husbands, then as now. In short, unchanging and irrepressible human nature no doubt asserted itself at times to modify man-made institutions intended to suppress it.

SCHOOLS AND EDUCATION

Knowing the purpose of an Athenian girl's education, we may readily infer the methods applied to her training. Naturally, her teachers were her mother and the older women servants. The subject matter, while limited to the things which would make her a good housewife, varied widely with the personalities and interests of her teachers. The bride of a character in one of Xenophon's dialogues had been trained to spin, weave, and sew, had been lectured on the necessity of serious-mindedness, and had other-

Metropolitan Museum

SPINNING WOMEN AT WORK

wise been taught "to see and to hear as little as possible." Seclusion
tended to make Athenian women superstitious, and a girl was sure to pick
up the lore of ghosts, goblins, charms, and amulets from her childhood
associates. As a rule, she must have been tragically ignorant of the duties
which marriage thrust upon her, and these could be mastered only by long
and bitter experience. She had little opportunity to become literate and
must often have been unable to read or write. At Sparta, on the other
hand, a girl of citizen rank was expected to appear in public, to receive
athletic training, and after marriage to occupy a position of independence.
The education of girls in other Greek cities varied between these two extremes.

For the Athenian boy a better and more diversified education was available. The state, it is true, did not provide schools for him, although it
did supervise those founded by private enterprise, so far as the morals of
the teacher and the banning of injurious matter from the curriculum were
concerned. But there were many elementary schools, with tuition charges
to fit either ample or meager purses, and almost any free male could secure
the rudiments of a formal education. Boys entered school at about seven
years of age, and those whose parents could afford it were placed under the
care of monitors (*paidagogoi*). A *paidagogos* was an elderly and trustworthy slave of the family. His duties consisted of conducting his charge
to and from school, teaching him good morals and manners, and punishing
him for misbehavior. If he were conscientious, there was small chance for
his charge to get into trouble or contract bad habits.

The Elementary Curriculum

The curriculum taught in the elementary schools went under the general
name of *music*. It included writing, reading, some knowledge of simple
mathematical calculation, grammar, singing and playing on the lyre, and
considerable poetry. The pupils learned writing on boxwood tablets
coated with wax, by scratching letters on them with sharp points. These
had the advantage of easy erasure and could be used for a long time. Later,
the students wrote with pen and ink on the more expensive Egyptian
papyrus. The most important subdivision of "music" was poetry, which
the Greeks treated very differently from modern readers. While they did
not neglect beauty of form and expression, their chief interest was in the
subject matter, which they took literally. Homer had the first place
easily. His poems were used to teach lessons in military science, ethics,
and religion. Hesiod taught lessons in agriculture and other rustic arts.

Museum of Fine Arts, Boston   *Metropolitan Museum*

GREEK PLAYING LYRE   A GREEK SCHOOL BOY

Archilochus, Sappho, and the other great national poets each had his or her honored place in the curriculum. Their works were memorized, discussed, and used to form the character of the student. Foreign languages had no place in the Greek schools, but from the poets the student learned to make the best use of his mother tongue.

Little is known about the Greek teaching and practice of what we term music, except that it had a prominent place in the curriculum and careful attention was given to proper instruction in the art. Airs were composed in any one of several "modes," which corresponded roughly to our keys. The emotions of the Greeks responded powerfully to both vocal and instrumental music and each mode was characterized as having a different influence upon an audience. The Lydian mode, soft and plaintive, was sometimes called effeminate; the Phrygian mode was supposed to excite the hearer to an orgiastic frenzy, while the Dorian mode made the listener manly and warlike. In addition to its ethical influence, music was a source of entertainment at public gatherings and banquets.

Gymnastics

As young manhood approached, gymnastic training assumed an ever greater importance in a boy's life. Group games, while played for amusement, were not a part of formal training, but the boy seriously practiced running, jumping, wrestling, boxing, javelin-throwing, and archery. For these sports, the youth went to a *palaistra*, or public gymnasium, where he had a special trainer. His aim was to produce a strong, supple body, fit to serve the state in peace and in war. At eighteen he became an *ephebus*, or army cadet. From that point on we need not follow him, but it is important to note that throughout his youth character formation rather than skill or knowledge was the paramount aim of Athenian education and to this aim it was well adapted.

****

23

The Periclean Age: Literature, Philosophy, and Science

SOPHOCLES AND THE TRAGIC DRAMA

NOT ONLY IN ATHENS, but in all the more advanced portions of the Greek world, the political stability and economic prosperity of the Periclean Age were concurrent with a splendid outburst of creative genius in art, literature, and intellectual discovery. Prose literature invaded the fields of history, philosophy, and science. Lyric poetry declined, but the tragic drama continued to evolve from the stark grandeur of Aeschylus into the more graceful and human, but equally beautiful and stirring, productions of Sophocles.

Sophocles (496–406)

Sophocles, the second great master of Attic tragedy, was born in the deme of Colonus (which he was later to immortalize in the closing scene of the *Oedipus* series) six years before the battle of Marathon. He lived an unusually happy and carefree life until the age of ninety, with abundant wealth, high social prestige, honor, political preferment, and stimulating intellectual contacts with the great thinkers who thronged his native city. He received the first prize in tragedy twenty times (five more than Aeschylus) and was elected to some of the highest offices of the state. He composed over a hundred tragedies, of which only seven are extant.

The subject matter of Sophocles' tragedies and the ideals which he taught were, in general, the same as those of Aeschylus, but in dramatic technique and human interest the younger poet made great advances over the older. Previously it had been the rule that only two actors should

Keystone

STATUE OF SOPHOCLES

appear on the stage at a time. Sophocles added a third. He shortened his choruses, thus increasing the importance of the dialogue, and heightened the attractiveness of his productions by using painted scenery. Aeschylus had made each trilogy a play of three acts, but the resulting plots had such a cosmic grandeur that even an Athenian audience may have found it hard to appreciate them. Although the rules of the contest for the tragic prize compelled Sophocles to present three units of tragedy at a time, he made each unit a separate play, often writing on more than one subject. Within the smaller field thus delimited, he was able to make the plot more easily comprehensible to the spectator. He abandoned the torrential mouth-filling phrases of the older poet and developed a simple and lucid style of his own, with a grandeur which depended upon sublimity of ideas rather than upon forms of expression.

The difference between the two tragedians is something deeper than form and style. Sophocles brings his characters to life. They are heroic, though not superhuman, and they are ruled by human motives and sentiments. Love, hate, greed, cunning, jealousy, stupidity, and anger play their parts in the development of his stories, and direct divine intervention is rare. More than once he makes the tragedy of a situation appear in the ignorant confidence of a hero about to be engulfed by catastrophe. His characters are drawn from the same Late-Mycenaean tradition as those of Aeschylus, and the same deeds of insolence and crime bring down the same curses upon the guilty and their descendants. Yet Sophocles divided his interest between recognition of divine justice and sympathy for its victims, who may be personally innocent of wrong-doing. As in real life, we find human law clashing with divine law, and the victim of this dilemma must face terrible punishment, whichever he chooses to obey. In short, while Sophocles interprets religion in an orthodox fashion, he emphasizes the human strivings and sufferings to which the will of the gods may give rise; and one sometimes feels that the action of a Sophoclean drama can be accounted for by the workings of human nature and the conditions of life, without divine intervention.

The Oedipus Drama

Let us first see how he treats the theme so popular with Aeschylus — the hereditary curse. It forms the subject of two of the surviving plays — the *Oedipus Rex* and the *Oedipus at Colonus* — and appears in the background of a third — the *Antigone*. Laius, king of Thebes, sinned by carrying off Chrysippus, the son of Pelops, for which he incurred the wrath of the gods. In punishment for his deed, it was decreed that he should become the father of a son who would kill his father and marry his mother. When Oedipus was born, Laius tried to thwart the divine will by mutilating the child's feet and leaving him to die on a mountainside. But in vain! The shepherd who was to have carried the babe to his death gave him to another shepherd who carried him to Polybus, the childless king of Corinth. Having been reared as the child of Polybus, in ignorance of his real parentage, Oedipus himself was informed by the Delphic oracle of the crimes which he was destined to commit. Horrified, he fled from Corinth, vowing never to return while Polybus and his queen were alive. On a lonely road in Phocis he met an old man who with a few attendants was hastening toward Delphi. It was King Laius, his real father, but Oedipus did not know him. The stranger haughtily ordered the young man off the road; a quarrel arose, and Oedipus unwittingly fulfilled the first part of the curse by slaying his father. Still seeking to thwart the divine will, Oedipus went on to Thebes. The land was being depopulated by the Sphinx — a monster with a woman's head and the body of a lioness. To everyone whom she met she propounded a riddle, and anyone who failed to solve it correctly was eaten alive. So far no one had solved it, but in Oedipus she met her match. When she asked him, 'What animal walks on four feet in the morning, two at noon, and three at eventide?" he answered, "Man. He crawls on all fours in infancy, walks on two feet in manhood, and on two feet and a staff in old age." The Sphinx, chagrined at the discovery of her secret, committed suicide. The grateful Thebans made Oedipus their king and gave him their widowed queen, Jocasta, in marriage. The second part of the curse was fulfilled, yet the criminal was still in ignorance of his plight.

The "Oedipus Rex"

As Sophocles' audience already knew the story, he could begin, according to convention, in the middle. The *Oedipus Rex* opens at the point when a plague has broken out in Thebes and the people come to their king to ask for help. He has already sent Creon, the brother of Jocasta, to Delphi to ask Apollo how the calamity may be averted. The god replies that the murderer of Laius has polluted the city by his presence, and that if he is expelled from the land the plague will cease. In a transport of generous indignation, Oedipus curses the criminal, and summons the blind prophet Teiresias to tell who the guilty one is. To his horror and astonishment he learns that it is no other than himself. In a towering rage he accuses Creon and Teiresias of plotting his overthrow, but a comparison of stories convinces him that the charge is true. Jocasta meanwhile urges her husband to disregard all prophecies. To prove her point she cites the prophecy delivered to Laius. It had been proved false, for the child is dead, and Laius has been slain by robbers. A messenger from Corinth arrives. Polybus is dead and Oedipus has been chosen king in his stead. Another proof of the falsity of oracles! When Oedipus still hesitates to return to Corinth for fear that he may marry his mother, the messenger assures him that he is not really the son of Polybus, but a foundling whom he himself had received from one of Laius' herdsmen. The herdsman, when questioned, confirms the story. As the awful truth becomes apparent, the distracted Jocasta rushes out and hangs herself and Oedipus gouges out his eyes. The oracle is vindicated, and the curse incurred by Laius finds two innocent victims in addition to the real criminal.

Sophocles' character sketches are delicate and convincing. Oedipus himself is of the very stuff of which the heroes of tragedy are made: generous, frank, and kindly, but hot-tempered, headstrong, and rash. Jocasta is a devoted wife, extremely skeptical of prophets and oracles, and her quick intuition senses the truth before her husband can see it. The plot is admirably constructed, and the whole play is filled with tragic irony arising from the spectacle of good and well-intentioned people drawn without their knowledge or consent into a web of crime and misery. It ranks among the greatest plays in all literature, but in many respects it is as terrible an indictment of divine justice as the book of Job.

The "Oedipus at Colonus"

Many years after his first *Oedipus* drama, Sophocles wrote the *Oedipus at Colonus*, in which he carried the dark story to the end. In it we see Oedipus as a blind beggar, with only his daughter Antigone to tend him. They come to the shrine of the Furies in Sophocles' native deme of Colonus to seek the hospitality and protection of the Athenians. Hard as their lot has been, it has brought to the forlorn old man a measure of peace. He sees the awful past in a new light, and realizes that although under other circumstances his acts would have been crimes, they have brought no guilt upon him because they were committed in ignorance. Furthermore, the gods have decreed that after he has departed this life he shall be a semidivine hero, with power to protect the land in which his last days are spent. He is anxious to confer this boon upon the Athenians, but his Theban relatives, who know the benefits to be gained from his presence, are at last anxious to secure his return home. His undutiful sons, Eteocles and Polynices, have quarreled, and the latter is an exile plotting to regain the Theban kingship with the aid of King Adrastus of Argos. It is now Oedipus' turn to rebuff his former persecutors. Creon, the brother of Jocasta, attempts to persuade the exiled Oedipus to return to Thebes, but in vain. Then Polynices tries to win the support of the father whom he had helped to drive from home, and only gains a renewal of his curse upon filial ingratitude. At last the innocent sufferer is taken alive into the lower world, leaving to his protectors the benefit of his aid for all time to come. The play contains finely drawn characters and a beautiful description of the scenery of Sophocles' native place.

The "Antigone"

In the *Antigone* Sophocles shows the irrepressible conflict which may exist between human law and the divine will. The curse upon the house of Laius was not allayed when Oedipus and Jocasta were forced to their doom. As we have seen, their sons Eteocles and Polynices quarreled over the kingship, and the latter was driven into exile. Gathering an army under the leadership of seven Peloponnesian kings, Polynices attempted to oust his brother from the Theban throne. In the ensuing battle the brothers slew each other and their uncle, Creon, became king. He decreed that Eteocles should be properly buried, but that the corpse of Polynices should remain unburied. To a Greek, this meant that the spirit of Polynices would never rest and must wander about as a malignant ghost. Upon his kinsfolk devolved the duty of performing the funeral rites, and his sister Antigone defied Creon's will to do what divine law commanded. In the play, her timid sister Ismene pleads with her not to risk her life in such a hopeless enterprise, for women, as the weaker sex, are not expected to override the will of the male:

> We must remember that we are women, unable to cope with men; and since we are ruled by those stronger than ourselves, we must endure this and worse.[1]

Antigone chooses the harder path of duty, knowing the consequences:

> Henceforth I shall not ask for your help. . . . Let whatever you will seem right to you, I shall bury him. Death so incurred is an honor. For that death-deserving crime of piety I shall lie at his side, loving and loved. It is far better to satisfy the powers of the under-world than those on earth, for in the underworld I shall abide forever. So, if you will, scorn the will of heaven.[2]

She suffers a horrible death as the reward for having acted according to her conscience, but her murderer is punished by the suicides of his wife and son (to whom Antigone was betrothed) and is left alone in the world. As the desolate old man leaves the stage, the chorus chants:

> Wisdom first of all works for man's good. Heaven makes no allow-ance for man's irreverence. By dealing heavy blows in return for the great speeches of the boaster it teaches men wisdom in their old age.[3]

Thus, our poet puts before us the hates, the fears, the loves, the vain struggles of mankind, and the stern, inscrutable ways of the gods. If he lacks the sublimity and the splendid faith of Aeschylus, he far surpasses him in artistic perfection, human interest, and kindly sympathy. In him the stormy heroism of the Persian wars has softened into the more polished and peaceful culture of the Age of Pericles.

[1] *Antigone*, ll. 61–64.   [2] *Ibid.*, ll. 69–77.   [3] *Ibid.*, ll. 1348–1351.

HERODOTUS AND THE BIRTH OF HISTORY

Although verse continued to be widely used throughout the fifth century B.C. as a vehicle for the expression of non-poetic ideas, prose made slow but steady encroachments upon its domain. It was adopted by several philosophers, by some, if not all, writers on scientific subjects, and by those whose interest was in recording the past. History thus became definitely divorced from epic poetry and mythography, and took the first steps toward the creation of a scientific method.

The First Historians

The impulse toward the writing of history which Hecataeus had given in the late sixth century was communicated to several writers in different parts of the Greek world. Sometime before 450, Charon of Lampsacus, a Greek from the northern shore of Asia Minor, produced a history of Persia down to the death of Darius I, or perhaps later. A similar work was written by Dionysius of Miletus, and a third by Scylax of Caryanda. All these have been lost, and there is little reason to think that they possessed any great merit either of style or accuracy. The first real historian, the "Father of History," was Herodotus.

The "Father of History" was born about 484 B.C. in the Asiatic-Greek city of Halicarnassus, which had originally been Dorian in language and customs, but had been Ionicized. Interest in the past had already led one of his relatives to compose an epic poem on the colonization of Ionia. At the age of thirty-two, Herodotus was exiled for political reasons. After spending some years in traveling through the Greek world — Egypt, Asia Minor, Babylonia, and Persia — he went as a colonist to Thurii in Italy. Little of his later life is known, and he probably died about 425 B.C.

The Scope of Herodotus' Work

The task which Herodotus set for himself was that of recording the story of the wars between the Greeks and the Persians. In his own words:

> What Herodotus of Halicarnassus has learned by investigation is told here, in order that the past may not become obliterated from man's mind by time, and that the great and wonderful deeds of both Greeks and foreigners may not lack fame, especially the causes for which they made war on each other.[1]

[1] *History* I, 1.

Metropolitan Museum

PORTRAIT BUST OF HERODOTUS

To accomplish this purpose he traced the contacts of the Greeks with the Asiatics from legendary times down to the capture of Sestos in 478 B.C., with emphasis on the critical years and events after the outbreak of the Ionic revolt. The scope of the work indicates that he did not consider the Graeco-Persian wars an isolated phenomenon, but rather a phase of an age-old struggle between the two rival civilizations, and it is in this spirit that the story is told. After briefly recounting a series of legendary wrongs committed by the Greeks on the one hand and the Phoenicians and Trojans on the other, he describes the rise of Lydia, the Lydian conquest of Asiatic Greece, the rise and expansion of the Persian Empire, the Ionic revolt, and the subsequent attempts of Darius and Xerxes to subjugate continental Greece. The original organization of the work is a matter of question, but long after the author's death it was divided into nine "books," as we find it today.

With a theme of such epic grandeur, Herodotus had the wisdom to borrow many points from Homer in his plan of organization. The plot of the story dominates everything, but he knew that it was unwise to adhere rigidly to the subject to the exclusion of subsidiary facts. Such a plan, concentrated and unrelieved, would overtax his readers' power of attention. Likewise, in a world where books were few and the reader's historical and geographical background was usually non-existent, this lack had to be supplied before his main theme could be understood. Hence, he breaks in upon the thread of narrative with digressions upon geography, and upon the manners, customs, and historical past of each people whom he treats. To the general reader, Herodotus' *History* may seem to be a jumble of casually related or unrelated facts which do not come to the point until the latter half of the work. But in reality it is closely knit, with all its parts integral to the general result. Moreover, the digressions themselves furnish us with a mass of data on the cultural life of the ancient world, which has been of immense value to modern sociologists and anthropologists.

His Philosophy of History

Not only does Herodotus organize his material: he has a philosophy of history. It is nowhere stated, but he drives it home with an endless wealth of illustrative anecdotes. He believes, like Aeschylus and Sophocles, that excessive power and prosperity lead men to pride and insolence for which the gods punish them. Between the Greeks and the Asiatics, he hints, there are fundamental psychological differences which account for two totally different civilizations. Whatever the personal worth of individual Asiatics — and some of them are as brave and as wise as any Greek — they collectively lack the balance and moderation characteristic of the Greek people, and they have no sense of the dignity of man or of free government. At best, their kings, with one or two exceptions, were arrogant boasters; at worst, they were capricious and cruel tyrants. To illustrate this, he draws for us a series of portraits and character sketches, varying from the amiable but conceited Croesus to the arrogant, cruel, and lustful Xerxes. Herodotus does this by narrating their acts or letting us hear them speak, and seldom by outright description. At the very end, in a seemingly irrelevant anecdote, he puts into the mouth of the great Cyrus words which, in his opinion, go far to explain the victory of the Greeks:

> Soft lands breed soft men. Marvelous fruits of the earth and good and warlike men do not grow on the same ground.[1]

[1] *History*, IX, 122.

Historical Accuracy

But if Herodotus is so heavily indebted to Homer and the tragedians, can we trust him to discover and tell the truth with the care which we demand of a historian? The first point to be made in answer to this question is that he obviously intended to tell a true story, and that he applied every canon of criticism known to him to the conflicting mass of data at his disposal. His written sources were probably limited to Hecataeus, Charon, and other historians of the preceding generation, Egyptian chronicles consulted at second hand through interpreters, and occasional inscriptions. Most of his data, especially in the last four books, came from oral tradition. In utilizing these questionable sources he displays a mixture of naïveté and shrewdness. He goes out of his way to prove the reliability of oracles, but is otherwise inclined to be skeptical of divine intervention in mundane affairs. Like other educated Greeks of his time, he is vastly impressed by the claims to wisdom of the Egyptians and Babylonians. Beyond a doubt he used Hecataeus' book as a guide to the understanding of both countries and verified it by questioning priests, temple servants, and guides. The two former groups were often ignorant and credulous, and the last were no more truthful than their modern counterparts. Add to this the fact that many of his conversations were carried on through interpreters, and we can see why in his account of Egypt he inextricably jumbles sober history with fable. Some of the apocryphal anecdotes of Egyptian kings are as spicy and entertaining as Boccaccio or the *Arabian Nights*. In Babylon, the guides must have told him preposterous yarns about the customs of the land. He relates:

> They carry their sick to the market-place, for they make no use of physicians. If anyone has suffered from the same disease or has seen someone else suffering from it, he goes up and discusses it with the sick, offering comfort and telling by what means he himself was cured or saw the other person cured. No one may pass by a sick man without asking what his disease is.[1]

Yet even in Egypt, his critical sense did not always desert him, and he brands as lies some of the stories which he heard there. In the Greek world he was more at home and better able to evaluate his sources. His accounts of Greek history and customs are in general much more reliable than his essays on Oriental history. He shows decided partiality toward Athens, but this does not prevent him from doing justice to the Aeginetans, the Lacedaemonians, or the other members of the coalition which overthrew Xerxes' forces. Some confusion is likely to arise in the reader's

[1] *History*, I, 197.

mind from his practice of stating all the variant stories which he has heard about an event. When a choice is possible, he indicates which of these he believes, but if he cannot determine the truth, he leaves the decision to the reader.

No mere analysis will do justice to Herodotus' style. His stories are told with a charming simplicity and clarity which captivate the average reader, while a more discerning mind may perceive a grandeur of conception, a wealth of human interest, and a concealed art which make him the equal of the greatest masters of the art of story-telling. The critical method was greatly improved by his successors, but never again were the Greeks to produce a historian with his combination of broad outlook, charm of style, and high ideals.

Other Historians

Although Herodotus' *History* is the only work of its kind which has survived from the Age of Pericles, he was not the only historian of that epoch. In Lydia, Xanthus recorded in Greek prose the story of his country's past. Antiochus of Syracuse wrote a history of western Greece which was extensively used by later writers, and from which much of our knowledge of that region is indirectly drawn. Most ambitious of all, Hellanicus of Lesbos composed a work covering the same ground as Herodotus, with a system of chronology which had the appearance of exactness. Had his dates been reliable, this feature of Hellanicus' book would have marked a distinct advance over the chronological inexactness of Herodotus, but such was not the case. In general the judgment of the Greek reading public seems to have been that Hellanicus lacked the qualities which made Herodotus so great a recorder of the past.

PHILOSOPHY AND SCIENCE

We have seen the Greek thinkers of the sixth century creating philosophy as they strove to comprehend the natures of the gods, the physical universe, and mankind. The movement continued in the fifth century, and man long pursued the same quest with the same methods as Thales, Pythagoras, and Xenophanes. While Ionia still produced prominent philosophers, the center of activity in this field had shifted to western Greece, where it was to be found until near the end of the century. None of the prominent thinkers of the period were from Athens.

The Eleatics

In the Italian-Greek city of Elea there flourished a succession, or "school," of philosophers among whom Parmenides (born about 515) and Zeno (born soon after 500) were pre-eminent. The former, repudiating the theory of Heracleitus that the universe is in a state of perpetual flux, propounded the proposition, "*Being* exists, and *not-being* does not exist." That which exists is the only element subject to study. Matter is eternal and indestructible and has neither beginning nor end. Zeno developed this theory still further, propounding a series of ingenious paradoxes to demonstrate the impossibility of Heracleitus' view.

Empedocles

Midway between the two opposing groups stood the striking and bizarre figure of Empedocles of Acragas (494–434), who combined the charlatan, the politician, and the philosopher. He appeared in public crowned with flowers, gaudily dressed, asserting that he could control the weather, endow men with eternal youth, and bring the dead to life. It was alleged that men worshiped him as a god. As a political leader he helped to establish a democracy at Acragas after the overthrow of the tyranny. In the strife between the advocates of a static universe and a dynamic, changing one, he partly agreed with both and not wholly with either. Being, he asserted, is indeed eternal and indestructible, but matter is not all of one kind. It exists in four forms — earth, air, fire, and water. Matter cannot pass from one of these forms to another, nor can any of these be broken down into any simpler form. The visible world, he taught, is a series of combinations of these elements in varying proportions. These combinations are formed and dissolved by two forces, which he called love (attraction) and hate (repulsion). By their action the universe has gone through a succession of cycles of growth and disintegration. It is, therefore, in a state of constant flux; but the extent and kind of the changes which may occur are limited by the possible number of combinations of the four elements which may take place. In religion, Empedocles was a mystic, whose beliefs were remarkably similar to those of Pythagoras.

Anaxagoras

The opinions of Empedocles on the four elements were controverted by Anaxagoras of Clazomenae (500–428). This Ionian philosopher taught for many years at Athens, where he had Pericles for a pupil. Accused of impiety by the enemies of Pericles, he fled to Lampsacus, where he taught until his death. Anaxagoras propounded yet another answer to the problem which Empedocles and the Eleatics had attacked. All matter, he asserted, is composed of "seeds," which contain all the possible qualities which matter may assume. Thus, any particle of matter carries within itself the power to change into any substance whatever. At one time these seeds were so thoroughly mixed that matter had no form, but was in absolute chaos. Outside of this chaotic mass, however, was a cosmic mind (*nous*) — a universal intelligence. It began to act upon the mass, which thereupon separated into sections, in each of which like seeds predominated. In this way arose the ordered universe which we know, with its infinite variety of substance and its harmonious arrangement. Anaxagoras, having used his "cosmic mind" to set the universe going, relied entirely upon natural law to explain its current workings. Whereas the populace regarded the sun as a god, he taught that it is a mass of glowing rock. The moon, he said, is composed of earth. In a similar way he explained all natural phenomena. Some of his views profoundly influenced Socrates.

The Atomic Theory: Leucippus and Democritus

The quest for rational explanations of the universe did not end with these thinkers. At Abdera in Thrace, Leucippus of Miletus taught, probably for the first time, the theory that all matter is made up of infinitesimal and indivisible units called atoms. The atomic theory, however, owed its complete formulation and development to a pupil of Leucippus — Democritus, born about 450. Although Democritus' writings have all perished, we recognize him as one of the greatest philosophers of the ancient world. The universe, he taught, is made up of two parts — atoms and empty space. The atoms are of different sizes and of different character, and they fall endlessly through space. As atoms of a similar kind come together, the material universe is formed, but the resulting combinations are also perpetually disintegrating and entering into new forms. Hence, the universe is indeed in a state of continual flux. The ordering force in this process is not a god or a universal mind, but "necessity" (natural law). Man's body and soul are both made up of atoms and at death they disintegrate like all material things. Democritus went farther and undertook to explain the nature of perception and of knowledge. To a considerable extent he anticipated Berkeley, Hume, and Kant in teaching that sense perception results when certain atoms strike our sense organs. All that we know about the outside world is the result of these impacts, and we can never be sure that the knowledge thus gained is accurate. It is "dark knowledge"; and all that we can really know ("white knowledge") is the atomic composition of the universe.

These philosophical systems represent perhaps the most ambitious attempt ever made by man to storm the gates of knowledge with no weapon other than his unaided intellect. The fifth-century philosophers had no foundation upon which to build except the casually ascertained facts and alleged facts about the material universe which passed current among their contemporaries. Yet upon this shaky substructure they reared, by sheer force of intellect, elaborate and imposing explanations of all natural phenomena. They blithely solved all the problems which the universe presents to human reason with a sophomoric certainty which present-day thinkers, possessed of an enormously greater body of knowledge and with physical equipment undreamed of in the ancient world, cannot feel. Their influence upon their own age was not extensive. Practical rationalists sneered at the dogmatism with which these philosophers defended their nebulous creations, and feared that they would undermine public morality by destroying religion. Conservatives condemned them as blasphemers. The problems which they had undertaken to solve were too vast and baffling for their age, and our own age has not fared materially better in working out solutions for some of them. It is not surprising that, in the next generation, Greek philosophers turned their attention to the narrower but more practical sphere of man and his relations to his fellows.

Science in Fifth-Century Greece

If Greek science was less prominent than philosophy during the fifth century, it was by no means stagnant. Although hampered by popular superstition and complete lack of laboratory equipment, both medicine and astronomy made considerable progress, and in geometry discoveries were numerous and constant.

Medicine; Hippocrates of Cos

The medical profession in fifth-century Greece existed, as in other lands and ages, on two levels — the scientific and the superstitious. As early as the sixth century, physicians like Democedes of Croton, while not perhaps free from superstition, had accumulated much useful and practical knowledge about human ills. On the other hand, the common people were usually left to the tender mercies of quacks whose methods were entirely superstitious and irrational. Partaking of both schools were the priests of Asclepius, the god of medicine. Each of his temples served as a hospital and sanitarium, and the attendant priests had the advantage of appearing to cater to popular superstition while, in some cases, at least, pursuing rational methods. Thus, at Cos, Cnidus, and other centers of the cult, manuals, founded apparently upon sound principles, were compiled for the use of these practitioners.

Out of this environment came the "Father of Scientific Medicine," Hippocrates of Cos (460–377). His ancestors had been priests of Asclepius, and he was brought up in the profession. He traveled widely, practicing in Thasos, Abdera, Thessaly, Athens, and other cities. He wrote a number of manuals for the instruction of physicians, including the *Aphorisms, Prognostics, Sacred Disease, Wounds in the Head, Regimen in Acute Diseases*, and *Airs, Waters, and Places*. Hippocrates entirely rejected superstition in both theory and practice. "Every illness," he says, "has a natural cause, and without natural causes none occur." He scornfully repudiates the theory that epilepsy is a visitation from the gods (the "Sacred Disease"), and recognizes its hereditary character. He kept careful clinical records, of which the following is an example:

> A woman who lodged in the house of Aristion was affected with quinsy. Her complaint began in the tongue; speech inarticulate; tongue red and parched. On the first day, felt chilly, and afterwards hot. On the third day, rigor and acute fever; a reddish and hard swelling on both sides of the neck and chest, extremities cold and livid; respiration elevated; drink returned through her nose; she could not swallow; saliva and urinary discharges suppressed. On the fourth day all of these symptoms were more acute. On the sixth day she died of the quinsy.
>
> Explanation of the characters: It is probable that the cause of death was the suppression of the discharges.[1]

In setting broken bones and in wound-surgery generally, Hippocrates' knowledge and skill were as great as those of any physician down to the sixteenth century A.D. While unacquainted with modern antisepsis, he used cauterization to remove infections and malignant ulcers. In disease he relied upon laxatives, diet, and similar mild remedies rather than upon harsh and potent drugs.

[1] *Epidemics*, III, sect. II, case 7, translated by Francis Adams.

Anatomy, Physiology, and Professional Ethics

While Hippocrates' knowledge of anatomy was, for his time, quite respectable, his physiology was overclouded with philosophic theories. He believed that the human body is composed of four substances, or "humors" — blood, phlegm, yellow bile, and black bile. When in good health the body has struck a balance between these humors, but if any one of them becomes too plentiful, the balance is upset and illness ensues. They also determine the temperament of each individual, which is either "sanguine," "phlegmatic," "bilious," or "melancholy," according to whether blood, phlegm, yellow bile, or black bile is in the ascendant. This doctrine persisted in the medical profession until about A.D. 1800, and even now, when it has been rejected, survives in a number of words indicating the states of mind with which it was formerly associated. Hippocrates realized that the superior knowledge of the physician may be used for evil as well as for good, and the school of medicine which he founded insisted strongly upon a high standard of professional ethics as a safeguard against the dangerous possibilities which this situation created. In the famous "Hippocratic Oath" (which reflects his views even if he did not actually write it), he makes the young doctor of medicine promise to use his knowledge only for good, to abstain from abusing his patients, to respect the confidences which they entrust to him, and to abstain from prescribing or administering poisons or medicines designed to produce abortions. The presence of this oath on the wall of many a modern physician's office proves that his ideals have stood the test of time. Progress in medicine and its allied fields continued long after Hippocrates' death, but no one of his successors did as much as he to advance it.

Mathematics and Astronomy

While the primitive system of notation in use among the Greeks made progress in arithmetic almost impossible, interest in geometry was intense. In fact, it offered an ideal field for the exercise of abstract reasoning, which fared so badly when used to unravel the secrets of the physical universe. Perhaps this was why Anaxagoras, Democritus, and others whose chief titles to fame are their philosophical hypotheses achieved striking results in geometry. In addition to them, Hippocrates of Chios, Hippias of Elis, and the Athenian astronomer Meton made additions to the extensive knowledge already accumulated by the Greeks. Three problems were particularly interesting to the fifth-century geometers: to construct a square of the same area as a given circle, to trisect an angle, and to double

GREEK VASE SHOWING CLASS ROOM SCENE

the volume of a given cube. It would appear that Meton solved the first of these. Several books of *Elements* were compiled, that of Hippocrates of Chios being the best-known. None of these have survived, but they were undoubtedly used by Euclid when, a century later, he wrote the textbook upon which so much of present-day geometry is founded.

Astronomy concerned itself principally with the practical problem of evolving a dependable calendar. The traditional Athenian calendar was lunar, the year beginning at the first new moon after the summer solstice (early in July). Twelve lunar months, however, equaled only 354 days, and as the chief purpose of a calendar is to enable men to predict the seasonal climatic changes with certainty, it was necessary to add an extra (intercalary) month at intervals to bring the lunar year into line with the solar year. This was done rather haphazardly until Meton attempted to reduce the practice to a system. He devised a cycle of nineteen years, in the course of which seven intercalary months would be added to various lunar years. At the end of each cycle the lunar and solar years would end at the same time. This reckoning made the solar year consist of 365 and 5/19 days, or a half-hour more than the true length. Yet Meton was too advanced for his time, and his calendar was not adopted by the Athenian state until after his death.

THE SOPHISTS AND HIGHER EDUCATION

The disfavor with which the Greek public regarded the philosophers, together with the apparent uselessness of their hypotheses in everyday life, prevented them from becoming leaders in higher education. Yet the increasing complexity of civilization made such education indispensable. In democratic states it was necessary for those who sought political honors and suitors before the lawcourts to be fluent speakers, and most people could become so only after long training. Business and political relations called for a broader knowledge than could be attained casually or in the elementary schools. Hence, a new class of teachers arose whose object was to supply the needs of the new age. These were the *sophists* ("teachers of wisdom"). They distinguished themselves from the philosophers by making teaching a profession, by accepting payment from their students, and by the practical character of their instruction.

The Sophists in Sicilian and Continental Greece

The first sophists appeared in Greek Sicily shortly after the restoration of the democracies there. In 466, Corax of Syracuse published a book called *The Art of Speech*, in which he described the structure of a convincing oration and brought out potential arguments which both parties to a lawsuit might use to their respective advantage. He was soon followed by Gorgias of Leontini, who, after a successful career in his native land, taught in Athens and Thessaly. Gorgias specialized in diction rather than in logic or analysis and was noted for his florid, poetical style.

So useful were the sophists that they were soon teaching in continental and eastern Greece as well as in the West. Protagoras of Abdera (485–410) taught in his native city and in Athens. His courses were not confined to oratory, but included grammar, ethics, and whatever was of advantage to his students in any line. Both his fees and his professional standards were high. He charged as much as ten thousand drachmas for a single student, and the teacher promised to make his students "better at the end of the first day of instruction than before, and better at the end of the second day than they had been the first." He seems to have used a question-and-answer method of argument somewhat like that later immortalized by Socrates, who may have learned it from him. His enemies accused him of teaching his pupils to prove that black was white. He was the most famous of a large group of professional teachers who either made Athens their home or occasionally visited it. We shall have occasion to evaluate their influence upon the Greek mind in a subsequent discussion.

SUMMARY

It will be seen from the preceding pages that the Periclean Age was a time of intense and varied intellectual activity. It was not limited to any one part of the Greek world. Ionia, the Aegean islands, and western Greece participated in it as well as Athens, and in many respects they surpassed her. In some respects it was an age of transition. The old faiths and loyalties of which Sophocles and Herodotus were the spokesmen existed side by side with the critical thought of the scientists and sophists. Temporarily, there was room for both; but later the Greeks were to discover to their cost that the two were mutually exclusive.

24

The Periclean Age: Art and a Summary

IMPERIAL ATHENS ADORNS HERSELF

The Acropolis

WHEN, IN 479 B.C., the wave of Persian invasion retreated from the soil of Attica, it left the city a tumbled mass of ruins. The old temple of Athena, the new temple in her honor begun about 500 B.C., the marble-faced gateway constructed by Peisistratus, and all other works which had adorned the Acropolis, had been gutted by fire, defaced, and leveled with the ground. The center of Athenian civic and religious life must have remained in this condition for more than a generation after the battle of Plataea. Meanwhile, the Athenians had rebuilt and fortified their city, driven the Persians from the Aegean coasts and islands, and founded their "naval empire." These labors, together with the exigencies of everyday business, absorbed their energies so fully that the gods had to wait until quieter times for the rebuilding of their shrines. Even so, the Acropolis was too important to be neglected entirely. In 465, Cimon utilized the spoils taken from the enemy at the battle of the Eurymedon to build a retaining wall along the south side, where its natural strength was least. It was in some places as much as twenty-one feet thick at the base and forty-five in height. Themistocles had already either rebuilt or repaired the north wall and Cimon had restored the fortified gateway. Thus, the Acropolis not only became once more a defensible site, but Pericles was later able to increase the area of level ground at its top by cutting down the elevations and filling in the space back of the walls.

Probably the first step toward restoring the religious importance of the Acropolis was taken by the sculptor Phidias. At some time before 450 B.C., he wrought from spoils of the Persian wars a colossal bronze statue of the warrior-goddess Athena, which stood near the gateway at the northwest corner of the Acropolis. Including the pedestal, it was about thirty feet

RESTORATION OF THE ACROPOLIS AT ATHENS

high.   The goddess was represented as standing erect with spear, helmet and shield, her breast decorated with the aegis and Gorgon's head.   The reflection of the sun on her spear point could be seen far out at sea.   Modern scholars call this statue the *Athena Promachos* ("Athena the Champion"). Seven centuries later it was carried to Constantinople, where it stood until its destruction in A.D. 1203.

With this exception, the rehabilitation of the Acropolis as the religious center of Athens was the work of Pericles, assisted by the architects Ictinus, Callicrates, and Mnesicles, and by the sculptor Phidias.   Under his direction a vast plan was worked out for the embellishment of the Acropolis and for honoring the patron deities of the state by the erection of splendid temples and a large ornamental gateway.   The plan was too ambitious to be executed completely, but the portion which was realized converted the Athenian citadel into a vision of beauty seldom, if ever, equaled. The structures completed before Pericles' death which time has partially spared are the Parthenon, the "Temple of the Wingless Victory," and the Propylaea, or gateway.

The Parthenon

It was only natural that the crowning glory of the Acropolis should be the temple of Athena, the patron goddess of the state.   Almost midway between the eastern and western ends, and not far from the southern edge, were the foundations and ruined materials of the temple which the Persians had destroyed before it was completed.   Upon this site Ictinus and Callicrates reared a magnificent structure which we call the *Parthenon*, or "Temple of the Virgin Goddess."   It was built between the years 447 and 438 B.C.

By this time the white, translucent marble of Paros had lost much of its earlier popularity, and Pericles' assistants chose instead the native Pentelic marble.   This latter is coarse-grained, and pure white when first quarried. It contains, however, a slight quantity of iron, which causes it to change to a rich, cream color when exposed to the weather.   As always in ancient Greece, transportation from quarry to building site presented a formidable problem.   The Pentelic quarries are not more than a dozen air miles from Athens, but the ancient road was much longer because of the inequalities of the terrain.   Like most Greek roads, it was miserably poor, and the only

Brown Brothers

RESTORATION OF THE NORTHWESTERN ENTABLA-
TURE OF THE PARTHENON

means of conveyance were ox-drawn vehicles. On these the blocks which were to form the walls were hauled to the city by teams of from twenty to thirty oxen. The drums from which the columns were to be made were hewn at the quarries into cylinders weighing about three tons each. On the site the blocks were dressed so carefully that no mortar was needed to close the joints, which originally were almost invisible to the naked eye. Once in position, the blocks were held in place by iron clamps soldered with lead, which were fitted into slots cut in their sides. The drums of a column had the upper and lower surfaces carefully dressed, and in the center of each surface a hole was bored. As each successive drum was placed in position, an olive-wood plug was fitted into the center hole of its lower surface and the upper surface of the one beneath it. It seems then to have been revolved about this central point until the joint was a perfect, airtight fit. So accurate was this work that some of the plugs have been protected from decay for nearly twenty-four hundred years, and are now in the Acropolis Museum at Athens. After the column was completely built, the flutings were cut. The beams of the roof and ceiling were of wood and the roof was composed of marble tiles.

The Parthenon was an amphiprostyle temple surrounded by a colonnade, built in Doric style, with a few Ionic features. Compared with the sanctuaries of Egypt, Babylon, or even of western Greece, it was of modest proportions, being only 228 feet long and 101 feet wide at the top of the stylobate, with a height of 65 feet from the floor to the comb of the roof. The peristyle consisted of 46 columns (17 on each side and 8 on each end, the corners being counted twice), 34¼ feet in height and 6¼ in bottom diameter. As in other Greek temples dedicated to the Olympian gods, the main entrance was at the east end, although there was also a west door. In front of each entrance, within the colonnade, was a prostyle of six Doric columns somewhat smaller than those of the peristyle. The cella consisted of two rooms, one considerably larger than the other — the *Hecatompedon* ("Hundred-foot Chamber") on the east, and the *Parthenon* ("Virgin's Chamber") on the west. The Hecatompedon was the sanctuary of the goddess, measuring approximately 100 by 63 feet. It was divided lengthwise into three aisles by two two-story Doric colonnades which supported the roof. In the center aisle stood the great gold and ivory statue of the deity, the work of Phidias. The west room was a storage chamber for the property of Athena, the other state gods, and the state itself. Its roof was supported by four columns.

University Prints

PARTHENON STYLOBATE SHOWING CURVATURE

The Parthenon Sculptures

The sculptures of the Parthenon consisted of an outer Doric frieze, and Ionic frieze on the outside of the wall of the cella, and two fine pedimental groups. Phidias was the director of this part of the work, and he, no doubt, drew the plans for the whole series and may have executed personally some of the more important sculptures. The others were done by various stonecutters of Athens, and show a wide difference in skill on the part of their makers. The general level of quality is high, displaying a maturity which bespeaks a long artistic tradition. Although superbly naturalistic, the figures are entirely free from violent action, contorted muscles, or other expressions of nervousness or unrest on the part of their makers. They breathe a spirit of calm self-restraint as marked as that of the *Funeral Oration*. They are not, however, merely designed to relieve the monotony of bare walls. Beginning with the Doric frieze and passing thence through the east and west pediments to the Ionic frieze, they

BATTLE OF CENTAUR AND LAPITH
Metope from the Parthenon

formed a pagan *Bible* in stone — an unfolding story of the divine government of the world and of Athens. The first book is to be found in the
scenes carved in high relief on the metopes of the Doric frieze. It is the
story of a struggle between the opposing forces of chaos and of universal
order. In some scenes, the Olympian gods battle with the uncouth, earth-
born giants. In others, the Greeks struggle with those primeval feminists,
the Amazons. The subject of most of the surviving scenes was the famous
fight between the human and civilized Lapithae and the bestial centaurs
at the wedding feast of King Pirithous.

The sculptures of the pediments were fully rounded figures, held in position by metal clasps. The story told by the metopes was continued on the
east pediment, which portrayed the birth of Athena from the split forehead of Zeus. The central portion was destroyed at an early date, so that
we can only guess at the details, but the main features of the scene portrayed on the west pediment are well known. It represented the contest
between Athena and Poseidon for the mastery of Athens. The contend-

ing deities stood near the center of the scene, each flanked by a chariot with four spirited horses, and a crowd of reclining divinities and heroes. Athena had just struck the ground with her spear, causing the first olive tree to spring up. Poseidon, with trident poised, was about to make his bid for the coveted honor by creating the horse, but his evident dismay showed that he already foresaw defeat.

The ionic frieze ran completely around the cella walls just below the ceiling. Its total length was 594 feet, and its height about 3¼ feet. It was executed in very low relief, none of the figures standing out more than two inches from the background. Yet within this limited space the sculptors succeeded in creating the illusion of figures moving in several planes, side by side. The subject of the frieze was the great Panathenaic procession, which every year carried up to the temple of the goddess a sacred robe woven for her by the maidens of Athens. Over the east door groups of gods were seated, watching the assembled Athenians as they honored their divine protectress. Toward them the procession advanced from both sides. Following the north and south walls, one saw practically the same scenes: magistrates and marshals, girls bearing baskets of offerings, sacrificial animals, chariots with armed warriors and drivers, and in the rear, cavalcades of knights mounted on wildly careering horses which they managed with consummate skill. On the west side were still more knights in the act of forming ranks before beginning their march up the Acropolis road. Processions are often wearisome, even in real life, but here the supreme genius of the designer and the skill of the sculptors overcame the usual fault. Of the hundreds of human and animal figures, no two are alike. The finish was exquisitely careful, even the veins under the skins of the horses and the bony structure of their faces being worked out with photographic exactness. Today we can see this wonderful panorama only in a mutilated and fragmentary state, and the bright paint and the numerous bronze and gold parts which once adorned it, such as the reins of the horses, have long since vanished. What must have been its beauty when the Panathenaic procession of 438 B.C. wound its way up the Acropolis road to dedicate the Parthenon!

Within the cella, as previously mentioned, stood the statue of the goddess — the only part of the work which can be definitely assigned to Phidias. It towered to a height of thirty feet from the top of its eight-foot pedestal and completely dominated the room. The fleshy parts were made of ivory and the draperies were of pure gold over a wooden frame. Athena was here, as in the "promachos" statue, represented as a warrior deity, with helmeted head, a shield under her left hand, and a six foot image of

University Prints

POSEIDON, APOLLO, AND ARTEMIS WITNESS THE PANATHENAIC PROCESSION
Part of Ionic Frieze of the Parthenon

the goddess of victory held in her right. The pose was, in accordance with the ancient religious convention, somewhat stiff and archaic.

The Parthenon's Structure and Subsequent History

The Parthenon owes its beauty to a number of factors, not all of which are immediately apparent to the casual observer. Despite its small height, the advantageous position which it occupies makes it visible for a long distance. The mellow hue of the marble, together with the bright paint which originally covered parts of its surface, must have fitted well into the sun-drenched surroundings. Now, when the colors have vanished and the building is in ruins, the beauty still lingers. The whole structure is exquisitely proportioned. At first glance it seems to have nothing but straight lines until further examination discloses that there is not a single long straight line in it. Each column has an *entasis*, or swelling, near the middle of the shaft, equal to one-fifty-fifth of its lower diameter. Each shaft leans inward about one two-hundred-fiftieth of its height. The same is true of the cella walls. Immediately in front of the doors, the edge of the stylobate is three inches higher than at the corners, and at the middle of each of the long sides it is four inches higher. The same principle is

employed throughout the building. These deviations were intentional.
They can be sensed rather than seen, for it requires close investigation to
discover even the largest of them. Their effect is to relieve the appearance
of rigidity which might result from perfectly straight lines, and they add
subtly to the beauty of the structure. Unlike the cathedrals of western
Europe, the Parthenon does not direct the thoughts of the spectator upward toward an unseen world. The deity whom it sheltered was the personification of a greater and finer Athens, and in keeping with this concept,
her shrine was made to cling closely to the earth of which she was the mistress. Situated as it was, it formed a fitting crown for the greatest city in
the Mediterranean world.

The subsequent history of the Parthenon has been extremely varied.
For eight centuries it served as a temple of Athena. At some time in the
fifth century A.D., it was rededicated as "the Church of the Holy Wisdom"
— a name which sounds suspiciously like that of its former mistress, the
goddess of wisdom. A vaulted roof replaced the original one, the middle
wall was pierced with doors, and the peristyle was left roofless. At the
east end an apse was added. In the thirteenth century the Roman Catholic
Dukes of Athens converted it into the "Great Church of Saint Mary." In
the fifteenth century the invading Turks made it over into a mosque and
erected a minaret near the southwest corner. Thus it remained until
1687, when the Venetians under Morosini besieged Athens. Informed by

University Prints

PARTHENON FROM THE NORTHWEST, ATHENS

a deserter that the Turks had stored their powder in the Parthenon, Morosini's gunners dropped a bomb into it, and the resulting explosion wrecked the central portions of the cella and peristyle. In 1801, Lord Elgin, the British ambassador to Constantinople, secured permission to remove some sculptured figures from the ruins. He took portions of the friezes and the pedimental groups to London and today they are to be seen in the British Museum under the name of the "Elgin Marbles."

The Propylaea

Having provided Athena with a fitting abode, Pericles and his collaborators set out to construct at the west end of the Acropolis an impressive entrance to the sacred enclosure above. Mnesicles undertook to lay out a splendid gateway flanked by massive wings, which would occupy the whole space from the wall of Themistocles to that of Cimon. The plan was so ambitious that it was never entirely carried out. Political opposition to Pericles, religious prejudice evoked by the fear that old shrines might be destroyed to make way for the new structure, and the outbreak of a new war with Sparta, all contributed to prevent the execution of the work. Hence the *Propylaea*, or gateway to the Acropolis, remained unfinished, but between 437 and 432, Mnesicles reared a structure so beautiful that even today, after being battered by the storms of more than twenty-three hundred years, it evokes the admiration of modern art-lovers.

The Propylaea was built of Pentelic marble, with occasional courses of black Eleusinian limestone to furnish a color contrast. It consisted of three parts — a central gateway, a large northern wing, and a small southern wing which was never finished. The central portion was built upon a rapidly rising grade which complicated the problem of the architect. As one approached from the west, one saw two marble staircases, separated in the center by a roadway of native rock nearly fourteen feet wide, which traversed the whole length of the building. At the top of each flight of steps was a marble porch. A single roof, supported by six Doric columns, covered both porches and the roadway. Passing through this western porch, one entered a covered hall, divided into three parts by a double row of Ionic columns. At the east end of the central hall was a transverse wall pierced by five doors. Through one of them the visitor passed out to the east porch, similar to the west, but not so deep. The north wing was entered through a Doric porch laid out at right angles to the main porch. Back of it was a room, the *Pinacotheca*, which served as a depository for votive pictures. Of the south wing, only the porch was built. The Doric

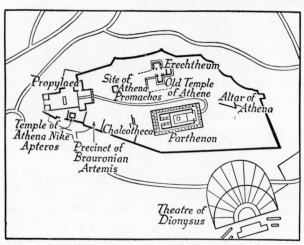

MAP OF THE ACROPOLIS

frieze and the pediments were without sculptures, but were richly ornamented with red, blue, and gold paint.

In the Middle Ages, when the Acropolis again became a fortified center,
this splendid product of Mnesicles' genius suffered repeated desecrations.
The Fourth Crusaders built a wall between the columns of the west porch,
converted the north wing into a record office, and reared a tower over the
south wing. Later, a Turkish governor took up his quarters in the tower,
and in 1645 an explosion of gunpowder destroyed the central structure.
The Greek government has wisely confined its efforts to clearing away the
débris and safeguarding the ruins as they stand.

The "Temple of the Wingless Victory"

On a bastion which flanked the approach of the Propylaea on the south,
Callicrates, at an unknown date, erected a tiny Ionic temple in honor of
Athena as goddess of victory. Since the Athenians had no desire to be
deserted by this much-needed deity, they portrayed her without wings.
The "Temple of the Wingless Victory" was only 27 feet long, 18 feet
wide, and 13¼ feet high from stylobate to architrave. It was amphiprostyle in plan, each prostyle consisting of four columns. The frieze
probably represented the battles of the Persian wars, with Athena on the
east front advocating her people's cause in the council of the gods. It
must have been an architectural gem, and it remained intact until just be-

University Prints

TEMPLE OF WINGLESS VICTORY, ATHENS

fore the Venetian attack of 1687. In that year the Turks tore it down and used the blocks to strengthen the fortifications of the Acropolis. In 1835–36, however, the materials were reclaimed, and the temple rebuilt in the condition in which it exists today.

Such was the Acropolis as Pericles left it — a beauty spot without an equal in the world. The mellow tint of the marble, cut and fitted with meticulous precision, contrasted pleasantly with the bright, barbaric colors of the painted surfaces. The graceful, lifelike figures of gods, men, and beasts told in eternal stone the story of Athenian devotion to Pallas Athena, and of the divine favor with which that devotion was repaid. Five centuries later, Plutarch said of the artistic creations of the Periclean Age:

> There is a kind of bloom of newness upon these works, which preserves them from the ravages of time, as if some immortal spirit and undying vitality mingled with their substance.[1]

Other Athenian Buildings

But the Acropolis was not the only spot in Athens to be beautified during the ascendancy of Pericles. To the south of it he constructed a music

[1] Plutarch, *Pericles*, 13. Dryden's translation.

hall (the *Odeum*) of wood, with a rounded roof shaped, according to tradition, like the top of Xerxes' tent. It contained seats for the audience of
the musical contests which Pericles held each year at the Panathenaea. A
structure which departed so widely from Greek architectural conventions
did not escape the notice of the comedians. Soon after the ostracism of
Thucydides, Cratinus wrote:

> The potsherds have ceased to fly, and Pericles, our long-headed
> Zeus, appears, wearing the Odeum on his head . . .[1]

— an allusion to the peculiar shape of the statesman's head and to his
habit of wearing a helmet to conceal it.

On a low knoll some distance northwest of the Acropolis, an unknown
artist laid out, at about the same time that the Parthenon was under construction, the temple popularly known as the *Theseum*, or temple of
Theseus. While it is practically certain that it was not dedicated to the
Athenian hero, and its real significance is unknown, the traditional name
has persisted for want of a better one. The Theseum was built of Pentelic
marble, with the exception of the lower step of the stylobate (Piraeic limestone) and the Ionic frieze (Parian marble). It was not large. The stylobate measured 103½ by 45 feet, while the columns of the peristyle were
3⅓ feet in diameter and 19 feet high. The peristyle consisted of six Doric
columns at each end and thirteen on each side, the corners being counted
twice. Inside was a double temple in antis, the cella consisting of a single
room. No traces have been preserved of the sculptures which once adorned
its pediments. Of the metopes, only those of the east front and the adjoining portions of the north and south sides were sculptured. They represented the labors of Theseus and Heracles. The partly finished Ionic frieze
which surrounded the walls of the cella portrayed a series of battle scenes.
The importance of this temple lies chiefly in the fact that it is the most
perfectly preserved of all known Greek shrines, but artistically it falls far
below the splendid structures on the Acropolis.

Pericles' activities as a builder were not limited to the city of Athens.
At Eleusis he had Ictinus rebuild the temple of Demeter. Under his spon-
sorship a fine sanctuary was erected in honor of Poseidon on the headlands
of Sunium, and one of *Nemesis* (Retribution) in the northeastern deme of
Rhamnus. How many other temples were similarly built or repaired in
rural Attica can never be known. When Pericles' enemies accused him of
"adorning Athens like a vain woman," they were only expressing, in an
unfriendly spirit, a well-known fact.

[1] Quoted by Plutarch.

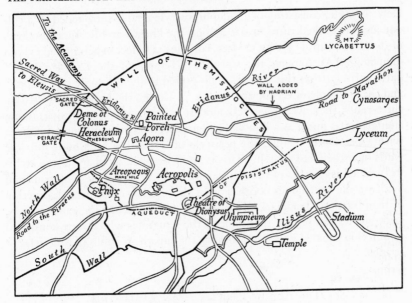

MAP OF CITY OF ATHENS

Art in Other Greek Cities

While Athens under Pericles' leadership was the greatest and most refined center of artistic endeavor in the Greek world, she was by no means
the only one. In fact, the great master Phidias himself left products of
his chisel in several other cities which he visited in the years just following
the completion of the Parthenon. It may have been at this time that he
executed the gold and ivory statue of Zeus at Olympia, and no doubt about
the same time he completed works for the Thebans, Eleians, and Ephesians.
His pupils, Alcamenes and Paeonius, continued the tradition which he had
established. The latter made, in the early years of the Peloponnesian War,
a fine image of the goddess of victory, which was set up at Olympia and the
remains of which still survive.

Western Greece produced little first-rate sculpture at any time, even during the Age of Pericles. In Greek Sicily the cities continued the construction of the temples, large and small, begun by Gelon, Theron, and their
fellow tyrants. In general, the Sicilian Greeks seem to have built slowly.
Thus, the temple of Apollo at Selinus, begun before 500, was still unfinished when, in 409 B.C., the city was destroyed. A considerable amount of
work was done on it during the third quarter of the fifth century. It was

Doric in style, consisting of an amphiprostyle temple surrounded by a colonnade. It ranked third in size among the known architectural products of the Greek world (371 by 177 feet, columns 53½ feet in height and 11¼ in diameter). At Acragas the so-called "Temple of the Lacinian Hera" dates entirely from this period, as do probably the "Temple of Concord" and the "Temple of Castor and Pollux." Unlike the buildings erected by the tyrants, these were relatively modest in size, not one of them attaining a length of as much as a hundred and fifty feet. Syracuse honored Athena with a fine Doric temple, the peristyle of which has been built into the walls of a Christian church. This is an incomplete summary of the architectural achievements of the Sicilian Greeks, for in cities like Messina and Syracuse the continuous occupation of the site has caused the destruction of many artistic landmarks. Of Asiatic Greece about the same may be said, but we can be sure that none of the structures which were consigned to oblivion equaled in finish or beauty the superb creations of Mnesicles or Ictinus.

The Age of Pericles — An Evaluation

In the foregoing chapters we have studied one of the most glorious periods in the artistic and intellectual history of mankind. Brief as was its duration, and precarious as was the political and social equilibrium upon which it rested, it produced temples and statues whose very ruins have an ineffable beauty, and dramatic, historical, and philosophical works whose influence still lives. The discerning student, whether he surveys the prancing horsemen of the Parthenon frieze or reads the *History* of Herodotus, finds a picture of self-control, order, and faith in the destiny of man and his universe. If here and there we catch glimpses of doubt and strife, they do not in any sense dominate the period. Even the geniuses of the age were free from the neurotic restlessness characteristic of their kind in our own time. Although it came between two ages of bitter class strife, the Age of Pericles suffered little from this scourge of Greek society. Its place in Greek history was very much like that of the nineteenth century in the modern world. Both were all too brief. It is useless to judge the Athenian, Spartan, or Syracusan of the fifth century by our own standards: economic, social, ethical, or intellectual. They kept slaves, and had an entirely different standard of sex morality. They practiced exposure of unwanted babies, and, in Athens at least, secluded their women. But we cannot condemn them for these practices, any more than some future age can condemn us for not conforming to standards which do not yet exist.

However, we may quite properly undertake to point out the strong and weak features in their institutions and conduct, from the vantage-ground given us by our knowledge of subsequent history.

The Weak Points in Periclean Greece

As we have seen, the class hatred between the few and the many was not ended, but only dormant. It needed but little encouragement to start once more upon its career of destruction. In matters of government finance, all Greek states were weak, and most of them were more dishonest, or certainly much cruder and franker, than our modern national states. Athens had to depend largely upon two sources — tribute, and income from the Laurium mines — of which strokes of hostile fortune might easily deprive her. Upon these uncertain foundations she had reared a topheavy structure of governmental services which could not be contracted to fit a shrunken income. In the background of the states of New Greece there were, because of their wide distribution and their partiality for seacoast locations, a number of dangerous foreign enemies — Italian and Sicilian tribes, Gauls, Carthaginians, Persians, Thracians, and others. Disunion within their gates subjected the Greeks to even greater dangers than attack from without. It was a group of exiles from Epidamnus who, about 435, joined the savage Illyrians in an attack upon their native city. The quarrel thus generated brought the most glorious period in Greek history to an end.

25

The Great Peloponnesian War

(431-404 B.C.)

Its Background

In our preoccupation with the splendor of the Age of Pericles, we must not forget that its central point was only a short interval of peace between two periods of intense intercity warfare. The Thirty Years' Truce, during which Athens and other Greek cities achieved so much along cultural lines, did not last half the stipulated time. Fourteen years after it was concluded, Athens and the Peloponnesian allies were once more at war. This time the struggle ended only when the Athenian Empire had been destroyed, much of the Greek world devastated, and the remainder fatally weakened. The great Peloponnesian War (for, as we have seen, there had been others, and were to be still more) marked a turning-point in Hellenic history, and its tragic importance warrants extensive treatment.

Causes: Opposing Interests and Grudges

Under the conditions which existed in 431, a decisive struggle between Athens and the Lacedaemonians was natural if not inevitable. Each was the head of an extensive confederacy, and together they included nearly all the important Greek communities east of the Ionian Sea. These groups stood for opposing ideals of government and social organization. Furthermore, Athens had several quarrels of old or recent date with various members of the Peloponnesian League — particularly Corinth, Megara, and Thebes. These cities looked with jealous fear upon the growing power and aggressive spirit of their democratic neighbor. The peacemakers of 445 had foreseen the possibility of such friction and had provided for the settlement of disputes by arbitration, but a time was sure to come when the rising passions of men could not be controlled so easily.

The Corinthian and Megarian Enmities

Perhaps the bitterest enemy of Athens in continental Greece was Corinth. Her people had been driven from one market after another by Athenian competition, and in the 430's this pressure continued unabated. Two incidents illustrate the relations of these rival powers. The Corinthian colony of Corcyra was an important way station on the road to western Greece. Corinth and Corcyra had taken opposite sides in a civil war which had broken out in a colony founded jointly by the two in near-by Epirus. War broke out between them and the Corcyreans obtained an alliance with Athens. An Athenian fleet helped to beat off a Corinthian attack on Corcyra. As Corcyra was not an ally of Sparta, Athens had not technically violated the Thirty Years' Truce, but the threat to Corinthian interests in the West was so real that technicalities availed little in preventing further strife. Again, one of the subject allies of Athens in the Chalcidice was the Corinthian colony of Potidaea. In spite of her dependence upon Athens, Potidaea was still governed by magistrates sent out annually from Corinth. In 432, Athens found it necessary to demand that Potidaea dismiss her Corinthian magistrates, and that she give other guarantees of obedience. Potidaea refused, and an Athenian army besieged her.

The quarrel with Megara was equally serious. There are indications that there had been border raids on both sides, and finally Pericles decided upon sharp and decisive action. Probably in 432, he induced the Athenian assembly to pass a decree excluding the Megarians from all the markets of Athens and her allies. This meant practical starvation for them, and it was keenly resented as evidence of Athenian arrogance and tyranny.

The Theban Angle and Spartan Intervention

Thebes had a long-standing grudge against Athens because the latter had championed the independence of Plataea, which Thebes wished to control. As hatred of Athens grew among the allies of Sparta, an incident occurred which made war inevitable. The oligarchic faction at Plataea arranged to admit a detachment of Theban soldiers into the city by stealth in the night, overthrow the democracy, and make Plataea an ally of Thebes. At first the attempt prospered, but the Plataeans rallied, overcame the intruders, and forced them to surrender. Then, in defiance of solemn promises, they massacred all their prisoners. Athens sent aid to the Plataeans, which still further offended Thebes.

Meanwhile, Sparta's disgruntled allies were imploring her intervention in their quarrels. In October, 432, a congress of the Peloponnesian League was convened at Sparta, in which the allies aired their grievances and demanded the aid of their suzerain in redressing them. An influential minority of the Spartans were opposed to war, but in the end the war party carried the day. A succession of embassies was sent to Athens, each with more exacting demands than its predecessor. At last the Athenians received an ultimatum to the effect that they must rescind the Megarian decree, end the siege of Potidaea, and restore the independence of their subjects, or go to war. Athens chose war.

It is probable that in some respects the rising storm was welcome to Pericles. At home his position was challenged by both the extreme conservatives and the radicals. The former resented his unorthodox religious views and democratic ideas; the latter felt that he was too conservative, especially in foreign affairs. His friends Phidias and Anaxagoras had been prosecuted on trumped-up charges, the former dying in prison and the latter being compelled to flee from the city. Even Aspasia had been called to court for impiety, and had narrowly escaped conviction. No doubt some of the more aggressive features of his policy were in a measure forced upon him by the necessity of retaining the support of groups who would otherwise have deserted him. War offered a way of escape from intolerable domestic problems. At any rate, the spring of 431 saw Athens and her empire embarked upon a decisive struggle with Sparta and her allies.

The First Phase (431-421)

From a formal viewpoint, Athens fought two wars with the Peloponnesian allies between 431 and 404, with an eight-year truce intervening, but in reality the struggle was continuous. Such was the judgment of the contemporary historian Thucydides, and, on the whole, modern scholars agree with him. He tells us that it was the most severe and calamitous war in recorded Greek history.

> Never had so many cities been taken and desolated, sometimes by barbarians and sometimes by the contestants. Never had there been so many banishments and so much bloodshed, now in battle and again in revolutions. There were earthquakes of unheard-of extent and violence, more numerous eclipses of the sun than ever before, severe drouths in several places, and as a consequence, famines. Most disastrous and fatal of all was the plague. All these things occurred in the late war.[1]

[1] Thucydides, *History*, I, 23.

Pericles' Plan of Warfare

The nature of the war was largely determined by the fact that Athens was strong in naval power and money and relatively weak in soldiers, while her enemies were weak in maritime and financial resources and strong in military force. When the war began, Athens had a huge reserve of coined money, and her annual revenues were probably nearly as large as the combined incomes of her opponents. Her fleet of three hundred triremes, reinforced at need by contingents from Chios, Corcyra, and Lesbos, gave her undisputed control of the sea. But her field army of 15,800 men and her garrison force of 16,000 old men, boys, and metics was not over half the size of the forces which her enemies could put in the field. On the mainland of Greece her only allies were Plataea, Naupactus, and some Thessalian communities. Opposed to her were all the Peloponnesian states except Argos and Achaea, all the Boeotians except Plataea, Phocis, Locris, Ambracia, Megara, and some smaller communities. Thus, Sparta controlled the peninsula and could raid Attica itself, but she could never take Athens or the Piraeus so long as the Athenian fleet remained intact. Athens, with her control of the sea, could live on imported food without suffering vital injury from the ravaging of her farms. By way of retaliation, she could destroy the overseas commerce of her enemies, and raid their coasts almost at will. Hence, the logical policy for her was to fight a war of exhaustion, guarding her empire against attack, dealing blows when practicable, and avoiding risky enterprises which might weaken her. So, at least, thought Pericles, and such was the policy of the Athenian state while he directed its affairs.

The Evacuation of Rural Attica

No sooner had the war begun than a Peloponnesian army under the Spartan king Archidamos, said to number sixty thousand men, invaded Attica. As it approached, the Athenians acted upon the advice of Pericles and carried all movable property out of harm's way. Their livestock was sent to Euboea and other islands, while other belongings — even the woodwork of their houses — were transported into the city. It was a sore blow to the country folk, who were torn from their accustomed surroundings and compelled to start life anew in the city. Their new dwellings were quarters in the homes of friends, towers on the wall, temples, and wretched mud hovels. In these they subsisted precariously by practicing petty trades, by the wages of military and naval service, and by jurors' pay.

Their buildings, crops, and other costly land improvements were abandoned to the enemy.

As the ravages of the invaders spread through northern Attica, Pericles refused to seek a pitched battle with them. He caused the cavalry to patrol the lands nearest the walls, and at the same time struck hard blows in return. The siege of Potidaea was rigorously pressed, Megara was raided, and the Athenian fleet ravaged the coasts of the Peloponnesus. The same tactics were followed by both sides in 430, 428, 427, and 425. The Attic countryside was ruthlessly devastated and portions of the Peloponnesus fared no better. Early in 429, Potidaea surrendered. The inhabitants were exiled and an Athenian colony took their places. Aegina shared the same fate. In 429, the Peloponnesians besieged Plataea. Thus far only the smaller states had suffered the extreme horrors of war. Between the chief antagonists the struggle was still indecisive.

The Plague

But a force more formidable than the Peloponnesians now threatened Athens. In 430, some ships returning from Egypt brought to her port the germs of a virulent epidemic disease (probably bubonic plague), which spread from the Piraeus to the city. Its victims developed a violent fever, broke out with boils, suffered from internal disorders, and nearly always died within eight days from the time they were stricken. Those who recovered often lost their fingers and toes and were temporarily insane. Medical attention did them no good. In the wretched hovels of the poor and the quarters of the refugees it raged unchecked, and even the wealthier citizens were not immune. Society temporarily disintegrated as fear brought the worst qualities of human nature to the surface. The sick were left to die unaided and the dead lay unburied in streets and temples. Dying wretches crawled about the streets and drowned in cisterns while trying to quench their raging thirst. At the same time many who expected momentarily to be stricken plunged into shameless revelry and debauchery in order to get what pleasure they could from the short space of life left them. In 429 and 428, the plague renewed its ravages, and perhaps a fourth of the population of Athens perished. Apparently it scarcely touched other localities.

The End of the Periclean Era

Such a crushing misfortune temporarily wrecked Athenian morale. In a fit of hysteria, the assembly deposed Pericles and fined him for alleged misconduct in office. Then, seeing their folly, the people re-elected him to the same office with extraordinary powers. But public and private misfortunes had broken the spirit of the statesman. Both his legitimate sons had died. At last he secured the legitimization of Pericles, the son born to him by Aspasia. In 429, he himself succumbed to the epidemic which had claimed so many other victims.

His death marked the end of an era in Athenian history. The years that followed produced many able politicians and some good men; but none of them possessed his farsighted statesmanship, and few of them his incorruptible honesty. Throughout the Athenian citizen body the trials of war and plague had produced a new mentality, in which the self-control of former days was lacking. Hysteria, violence, cruelty, cynicism, unreasoning confidence alternating with abject cowardice — all became increasingly apparent as the years passed. Yet with all these bad qualities not a little of the splendid patriotism of the preceding generation survived to nerve the Athenians for the tasks before them.

For some years after the death of Pericles, the war degenerated into a series of raids and skirmishes, in which the forces engaged were small and the goals were often petty. Thus, the Athenian army in the Chalcidice after the fall of Potidaea numbered only twenty-two hundred men of all arms; and the fleets rarely exceeded fifty galleys. Between 430 and 425, a small Athenian fleet and army, operating from the bases of Naupactus and Corcyra, blockaded the mouth of the Corinthian Gulf and gained several victories over Sparta and her partisans in northwestern Greece. Other armies of the same description fought against the friends of the Lacedaemonians in Sicily or raided the Peloponnesian coasts.

Lesbos' Attempted Rebellion

Meanwhile, the Athenians put down a formidable rebellion within their empire. Lesbos was one of the two last communities of the former Delian League to retain the status of an independent ally, and its wealth and naval power made it extremely important. The oligarchic faction at Mytilene, the chief city of the island, took advantage of the preoccupation of Athens with war and pestilence to withdraw from the Athenian alliance, and they drew all but one of the other Lesbian communities with them (428). Athens besieged Mytilene, and at last the democratic faction in the city compelled the oligarchs to surrender. The fate of the city was to be settled by the Athenian assembly. The leading political figure in Athens at the moment was Cleon the tanner, a wealthy businessman, with

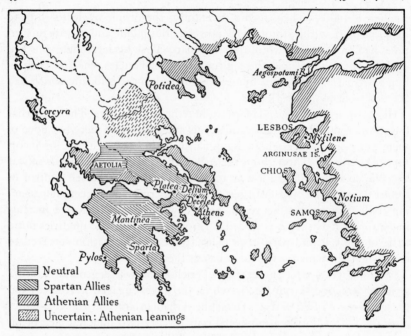

MAP OF THE GREEK PENINSULA AND THE AEGEAN REGION AT THE OUTBREAK
OF THE PELOPONNESIAN WAR IN 431 B.C.

coarse manners, a gift for rabble-rousing oratory, and considerable talents
in war and government. His policies were exactly the opposite of those of
Pericles, for he favored aggressive war to be ended only by decisive victory.
He believed that the allies could be held true to their duty only by a policy
of terrorism, and under his influence the assembly passed a decree con-
demning all the Mytilenean men to death, while the women and children
were to be sold as slaves. A trireme was sent with the fatal message, but
the next day a revulsion of feeling occurred. Another meeting was summoned, the previous decree rescinded, and a milder substitute passed. The
ship which carried the second mandate arrived just in time to prevent the
wholesale massacre which Cleon had planned, although the final judgment
was by no means mild. A thousand of the more guilty rebels were executed, the walls of the city were torn down, and the land confiscated for
the benefit of Athenian colonists.

On the Peloponnesian side even less mercy was shown to conquered enemies. In 427, Plataea surrendered. All the men (the women and children

had previously been sent safely to Athens) were put to death, the buildings demolished, and the land was let out to Theban colonists. Athens also occasionally used this drastic punishment for cities which had rebelled under particularly irritating circumstances.

Civil War

The cruelties practiced by foreign enemies were mild compared with those caused by civil strife. The war greatly aggravated this traditional evil of the Greek people, for since each of the chief contestants favored a type of government opposed to that sponsored by the other, potential revolutionists could always hope for outside aid. One of the most horrible examples of this scourge occurred at Corcyra (427–425). The Corcyrean oligarchs, instigated by Corinth, attempted to overthrow the democracy of their native city. They began by murdering a prominent Athenian sympathizer and sixty members of the council suspected of similar leanings. Then they attacked the popular party and at first got the upper hand. However, the leaders of the commons won the support of the rural slaves, and with their aid the oligarchs were defeated. Spartan intervention was blocked by the arrival of an Athenian fleet, and the people proceeded methodically to massacre their aristocratic opponents. Thucydides writes:

> During the seven days that Eurymedon [the Athenian admiral] stayed with his ships, the Corcyreans continued to massacre those of their fellow citizens whom they regarded as enemies. Although they were accused of attempting to overthrow the democracy, some were slain because of private grudges, and others by their debtors because of the debts owing to them. Thus death raged in every form, and, as usual in such cases, violence knew no limits. Sons were killed by their fathers, and suppliants were dragged from the altar or butchered upon it. Some were even walled up in the temple of Dionysus, and died there.[1]

The Athenians finally patched up a truce with the Corcyrean democracy for a few of the oligarchs, but two years later these latter were treacherously murdered by the popular faction.

The year 425 at last brought to the Athenians an advantage which seemed to place peace within their reach. Led by Demosthenes, a brilliant general who had won several victories as commander of the Athenian forces in the northwest, a detachment was landed at Pylos on the coast of Messenia. There they built a fort and beat off a Spartan attack. In the

---

[1] *History*, III, 81.

course of the fighting, the Lacedaemonians landed a force of 420 Spartans and attendant helots on the near-by island of Sphacteria. The Athenians now blockaded Sphacteria and besieged its garrison. The Lacedaemonians were dismayed at the prospect of losing so large a portion of their effective manpower. They concluded an armistice and sent to Athens to sue for peace. The militarists, led by Cleon, blocked the negotiations, and the siege went on. Finally, Cleon began to criticize Demosthenes and his colleagues at Pylos. He himself could, he boasted, capture Sphacteria in twenty days if given the chance. The Athenians took him at his word, and to the consternation of his enemies he succeeded. Of the Lacedaemonians, 292 became prisoners, 120 being Spartiates. The sensation produced in the Greek world by the surrender of Spartans on the battlefield was profound. Pylos became a base for raiding parties of Messenians from Naupactus, who induced many of their fellow countrymen to desert, and carried their depredations even into Laconia. During the same year the Athenians fortified Methana on the eastern coast of the Peloponnesus, and in 424 they conquered Cythera, an island just off the coast of Laconia. Their garrisons at Naupactus and Corcyra blocked the entrance to the Corinthian Gulf. Athenian naval supremacy was beginning to bear fruit.

In pitched battles on land, however, the Peloponnesians and Boeotians continued to hold their own. In 424, an Athenian army invaded Boeotia to aid democratic plotters there. A fort was constructed at Delium, but at the approach of a Boeotian army, the invaders were compelled to fight and were disastrously defeated.

Sparta Invades Athenian Territory

The same year Athens suffered a much heavier blow in the Chalcidice and Thrace. Sparta's ablest officer was Brasidas, who combined daring and military skill with diplomacy and ingratiating manners. The ephors, seeing that the only vulnerable points in the Athenian Empire were those that could be reached by land, collected a motley force of helots and mercenaries, and put them under Brasidas' command with orders to incite revolts among the northern subjects of Athens.

Such a step was timely on the part of Sparta, for Athens had recently adopted a policy which was sure to cause discontent among her dependents. Because of huge expenditures caused by the war, she was badly in need of funds, and her reserves were well below the danger line. Just as Brasidas was on the point of setting out on his expedition, a revision of the tribute lists was carried out, which seems to have doubled or trebled the sums exacted from individual states, and which may have increased the total to nearly fifteen hundred talents. In view of the decreased purchasing power of money and the increased prosperity of many of the allies, this measure was not particularly oppressive, but it was certain to cause discontent and to pave the way for such an enterprise as that which Brasidas was now undertaking.

Passing through Boeotia, Phocis, and Thessaly without difficulty, the Spartan commander appeared in Chalcidice, where most of the cities opened their gates to him. Continuing eastward, he scored a signal triumph by winning over the important city of Amphipolis. The historian Thucydides, who commanded a small fleet in the northern Aegean, failed to reach Amphipolis before the Lacedaemonians, and for this reason the Athenians banished him.

A Year's Truce and Eventual Peace

Both sides were now weary of war, and in 423 a truce was made for the ensuing year; but Sparta and Athens had each a war party, which insisted upon a decisive victory as the prelude to peace. The leaders of these militarist groups were Brasidas and Cleon, and so long as each remained influential in the affairs of his native city there was little hope for peacemakers. Brasidas refused to observe the truce at all, and Cleon waited only for it to expire before renewing the struggle vigorously.

It was fated that these two should destroy each other. In 422, Cleon led an expedition of Athenians and allies to recover the revolted communities. He had won some notable victories, but in a battle before Amphipolis, his force suffered complete defeat. Both he and Brasidas were among the slain. While each of them was in a way an able and patriotic leader, their deaths came opportunely for the cause of peace.

The Peace of Nicias (421) was the work of the conservative party at Athens and of King Pleistoanax and a similar group at Sparta. It was in the form of a fifty years' truce, based upon the principle of mutual restitutions. Athens was to surrender all recent conquests except the port of Megara and a few naval bases in northwestern Greece. The Lacedaemonians were to return Amphipolis and to raise no objection if the other cities of Thrace and the Chalcidice joined Athens as free allies. There were also provisions for changes and additions in the treaty by the consent of both parties. Shortly afterward the recent enemies formed a defensive alliance.

There can be no doubt that peace was welcome everywhere. The comedian Aristophanes greeted it with a paean of joy which must have found echoes in the hearts of the Greek people. He dwells particularly upon the delight of the country folk, cooped up for ten years inside the city walls.

> Yes, yes! All the farmers may return to their homes, with their implements and gear. Leave your javelins behind. Sword and spear are useless. Everything overflows with the good gift of peace. Sing paeans, as you march away to work in the field today.[1]

Our comedian relates with zest the grief of the arms manufacturers (the "munitions makers" of their time), since the market for their wares is gone. Thebans and Megarians, long deprived of an outlet for their goods, again flock to Athenian marts, bringing their fish, eels, salt, vegetables, and fruit. Life can resume its accustomed course once more.

For all this unfeigned joy, the peace was a hollow one. Not one of the basic issues which disturbed the Greek people had been settled and the hatreds to which the war had given rise still persisted. It was, in the strictest sense, only a breathing space, to be followed by a still more ruinous war.

PEACE, IMPERIALISM, AND WAR (421–415)

For seven years after the conclusion of the Peace of Nicias, Sparta and Athens were nominally at peace. This was attributable not so much to improved feeling between the former contestants as to the fact that each was busy with problems which the war had created. Athens had not subdued her revolted subjects in the Chalcidice and Thrace, and in the case of Amphipolis she was unable to do so. Claiming that Sparta was bound by the treaty to guarantee its restoration, she retained Pylos and her other Peloponnesian conquests.

Opposition to Sparta by the League

Sparta was threatened with even more serious trouble. The war had caused dangerous discontent within the Peloponnesian League, and the sacrifices necessitated by the Peace of Nicias had been made by Sparta's allies rather than by herself. Corinth, Megara, and Elis were seriously disaffected, and Argos, after a century of sullen obscurity, was once more ready to cross swords with her old enemy. A coalition of these malcontents was soon formed, and Athens, although still formally at peace with Sparta, gave the project as much encouragement as possible.

Yet, strong as was the opposition to Sparta in southern and central Greece, by 418 it had collapsed, and thereafter she was stronger than she

[1] Aristophanes, *Peace*, ll. 551 ff.

had been for half a century. Like most Greek alliances, this one was unstable. Corinth and Sicyon had never joined it, and resumed their allegiance as soon as the Spartans showed fight. A single battle (Mantinaea, 418) restored the Spartan hegemony. Oligarchies were set up in Argos and Sicyon, the Peloponnesian League was strengthened, and Athens had once more to face powerful opposition in southern Greece.

Athenian Foreign Policy and Party Politics

Athenian foreign policy after the Peace of Nicias became more and more the plaything of party politics. The conservatives, led by Nicias, favored peace and good relations with Sparta. The radical democrats, on the contrary, sponsored an aggressive imperialistic and anti-Spartan policy, which might at any moment lead Athens into another war. At first the radicals were led by Hyperbolus the Lampmaker, who by all accounts was a dishonest politician without much ability or any principles. Before long, however, he was ousted from his position by Alcibiades. For some years the history of Athens revolved largely around the personalities of Nicias and Alcibiades.

Nicias' character was well suited for the part which he had to play. He was one of the wealthiest men in Athens. His honesty was beyond question and he was scrupulous and cautious to the point of timidity. There was a vein of superstition in his temperament which was later to cause his ruin. In politics he was too slow-witted to cope with unscrupulous opponents.

Alcibiades was the direct opposite of his opponent in almost every respect. He was a relative of Pericles, in whose home he had been reared. It might well be said that he lacked only character to make him great. His personal beauty, quick wits, and disregard for convention made him the idol of the masses and of the younger social set as well. He drank heavily and seems to have got into an endless succession of scrapes, but the Athenian public forgave him everything. His talents in war and politics were exceptional, and had he possessed the honesty and devotion to duty of Pericles, he might have rivaled the latter's achievements. As it was, his levity and selfishness contributed to the ruin both of himself and of his country.

The Argive Alliance and Its Results

Alcibiades had been a friend of the Spartans until a personal slight made him their enemy. In 420, he had succeeded in negotiating a treaty with Argos, nominally one of defensive alliance only, but actually a silent partnership with the anti-Spartan coalition in the Peloponnesus. Such a step might at any time lead Athens into war, and it probably would have done so if the Spartans had not been unusually forbearing. Even so, the defeat of the allies and the establishment of the oligarchy at Argos left Athens isolated and faced with the ill-will of the Lacedaemonians.

So disastrous a failure abroad weakened the prestige of the Athenian war party. Alcibiades failed to be re-elected to the generalship, and in 417 the adherents of peace began to clamor for an ostracism meeting. Alcibiades was their prospective victim, but he was too cunning for them. By a brilliant stroke he induced Nicias to join forces with him against Hyperbolus. The latter was ostracized and thus the imperialists were left in the clutches of a much abler and more dangerous leader than the one whom they had lost. Possibly it was disgust with this farce which led the Athenians thenceforth to abandon ostracism as a means of settling disputes. Meanwhile, strife between Nicias and Alcibiades continued.

In 416 there occurred an incident which illustrates the cynical brutality of the group which Alcibiades now led. The island of Melos was inhabited by a Dorian population who, while allies of Sparta, had been scrupulously neutral throughout the recent war. An Athenian fleet and army entered its harbor, and the leaders delivered an ultimatum to the effect that Melos must acknowledge the leadership of Athens and pay tribute. The Melians refused and their city was besieged. It was soon betrayed into the hands of the besiegers, the men massacred, and the women and children sold into slavery. Athens then sent a colony to occupy the island.

THE ATHENIAN EXPEDITION AGAINST SYRACUSE (415-413 B.C.)

The sack of Melos was hardly completed when Athens became involved in an enterprise which was doomed to end in irreparable disaster. In the winter of 416-415, an embassy came from the Sicilian city of Segesta to seek Athenian aid against the Dorian Greek colony of Selinus. As Selinus was a satellite of Syracuse, to grant this request was equivalent to undertaking a war with Syracuse and all other Sicilian Dorian cities. This would be the most stupendous task upon which Athens had ever entered. Athenian representatives were sent to Sicily to investigate. They came back thoroughly converted to the idea of carrying the war into Sicily. Early in 415, the proposal came before the assembly for final action.

The Expedition Voted

Immediately it became a bone of contention between Alcibiades who favored it, and Nicias who opposed it. In this contest the odds were all in favor of Alcibiades. The populace went wild with enthusiasm at the prospect of a rich and easy conquest. Nothing else was talked about in the public loafing places of the city, and men lost all sense of caution or prudence concerning it. In vain Nicias opposed it. When he tried to frighten the assembly by pointing out how many men and ships would be required, it blithely voted for the largest number that he named. Then it elected him, Alcibiades, and a veteran general named Lamachos, to head the expedition.

Just before the Athenian armada sailed, a terrible scandal rocked the city. In a single night almost all the small images of Hermes which stood in the doorways and public squares were mutilated by unknown persons. The religious sensibilities of the people were shocked, and it was feared that this outrage was but the prelude to an oligarchic revolution. In the disordered state of the public mind, such an occurrence provoked an attack of mass hysteria. Investigation did not immediately discover the criminals, but suspicion fell upon Alcibiades as one of them. His enemies bided their time, knowing his popularity with the soldiers and sailors. Later the matter was revived.

In late June of 415, the expedition set sail. It consisted of 134 triremes, 130 supply-ships, and 6400 troops — the largest force ever equipped by a Greek state for foreign service. Its reception by the Greek cities of Italy was, at best, cool. Not one of them admitted the Athenians within its walls, but at least none of them attacked the strangers. In Sicily a few small Ionian cities joined forces with them. Segesta sent no aid of any kind and it was found that her promises had been false. Divided in opinion, the Athenian leaders were slow to begin operations.

The Arrest and Escape of Alcibiades

Meanwhile, the enemies of Alcibiades had been busy undermining him. An informer accused him not only of mutilating the Hermae, but also of parodying the Eleusinian Mysteries at a drinking party. A state trireme was sent to recall him to Athens for trial. On the return voyage he escaped and eventually made his way to Sparta. The Athenians, in a panic, sentenced him to death with confiscation of property. This was a colossal blunder, for, whatever his faults, he was their ablest military leader and politician. For several disastrous years afterward, he was their implacable enemy.

Acting upon the advice of their renegade guest, the Lacedaemonians took two fateful steps. The first was to send to Syracuse an able general named Gylippos, who took charge of the defense. At the same time, Corinth and some other states of the Peloponnesian group sent armed forces to Syracuse. Furthermore, the Lacedaemonians seized and fortified Decelea, a fortress in northern Attica, and maintained a permanent garrison in it. Thus, the Athenian countryside became unsafe for habitation, the working of the silver mines at Laurium was interrupted, and twenty thousand slaves deserted the Athenians. For the remainder of the war, Athens was a besieged city.

Failure of the Expedition

After the recall of Alcibiades, affairs in Sicily continued to go badly. In the beginning Syracuse was unprepared, and might have been taken by an immediate attack, but the opportunity passed and did not return. Under the energetic guidance of Gylippos, the approaches to the city were fortified, and some of the works of the besiegers were stormed. Lamachos was killed in battle, while Nicias conducted his operations timidly and inefficiently. At last, late in 414, he petitioned his government to recall him and either to evacuate Sicily or to send large reinforcements. The Athenians were not ready to abandon the enterprise and instead of recalling Nicias, they sent the able and energetic Demosthenes to be his colleague, with seventy-three triremes and eight thousand additional soldiers.

When Demosthenes arrived, the Athenian cause in Sicily was as good as lost. Gylippos had practically destroyed the siege lines around Syracuse and had defeated the Athenian fleet in the harbor. The fame of his successes had drawn nearly all the Greek cities of Sicily into a coalition with Syracuse, from which she was deriving considerable aid. Demosthenes made valiant, though fruitless, efforts to stem the tide. An assault on the Syracusan fortifications failed utterly, and at last retreat became imperative. But retreat was possible only if carried out quickly, for the enemy forces were growing daily larger. At a critical moment, an eclipse of the moon occurred (August, 413), and the superstitious Nicias, deluded by the soothsayers, refused to sanction a retreat until four weeks had elapsed after the portent. This time was spent by Gylippos in blocking all possible ways of escape for his enemies. Two battles in the harbor of Syracuse destroyed the Athenian fleet, and as the survivors of the ill-fated expedition retreated by land, they were, with few exceptions, surrounded and compelled to surrender.

The vengeance of the victors was merciless. Nicias and Demosthenes were tortured and put to death. Thousands of the prisoners were kept as slaves by their captors and many were confined in the stone quarries outside Syracuse. Their condition was indescribable, crowded together in filthy surroundings, exposed to every change of temperature, underfed and with little water, the living beside the dead. After some months of this living death, the survivors were sold as slaves. In all, Athens had lost two hundred triremes and fifty thousand men in this stupendous catastrophe, and thenceforth the Greek world no longer feared her.

THE LAST PHASE (413–404 B.C.)

For Athens, the Sicilian *débâcle* marked the beginning of the end, and only the exhaustion of her enemies delayed it for nine more years. In the eyes of the Greek world, Athens had now become a tyrant city, the oppressor of her subjects, and the enemy of city-state liberty. The news of her crushing misfortune accordingly raised a wave of rebellions throughout her dependencies, and many states hitherto neutral took courage and declared war on her. The struggle became a crusade "to make the world safe for the city-state," with Sparta as its leader. To climax the rising tide of Athenian misfortunes, Persia began to furnish the Lacedaemonians with money and even with armed forces. Only a miracle could now save Athens from defeat.

Athens Reorganizes Her Defenses

In the face of these misfortunes, the Athenians displayed a resolute courage which goes far to redeem their character as a people. The influence of the radical democrats, whose folly had brought on the disaster, declined, and the oligarchic party began to raise its head. Before the end of 413, the powers of the Council of Five Hundred were shorn by the election of ten *probouloi*, who, under the assembly, had charge of war, diplomacy, and finance. Some men of oligarchic sympathies were chosen to the board of generals. Meanwhile, the state turned with herculean energy to the task of defending herself and holding her dependencies. As the garrison of Decelea dominated much of Attica, a fort was built at Sunium to protect homeward-bound grain ships from attack. The last reserve funds of the state were spent in building a new fleet to retain control of the sea. The expenses of government were pared closely.

The Allies' Revolt

Athens had need of all possible energy and courage, for the year 412 witnessed a long series of disasters. A Lacedaemonian fleet, with Alcibiades as one of its commanders, sailed to Ionia, and its appearance caused an extensive revolt among the Asiatic and insular Greeks. At Miletus, its commanders signed the first of three treaties with the Persian satrap Tissaphernes. Persia was to furnish the enemies of Athens with pecuniary and other aid, and neither party was to make a separate peace with the Athenians. A later treaty provided that the Persian king was to have possession of all Asiatic Greece in return for his assistance. Yet Athens made some headway against the adverse tide. A revolution at Samos expelled the pro-Spartan oligarchic party and restored the island to its former allegiance. The Athenians, in gratitude, restored Samos to the status of a free ally. Henceforth, it became the headquarters of Athenian forces operating on the eastern side of the Aegean. Lesbos was also recovered.

It was obvious that Athens could not long maintain the struggle if Persian gold continued to fill the treasuries of her enemies. Alcibiades prepared to use this fact for his own purposes. He had worn out his welcome at Sparta and had reason to fear that his former hosts might murder him. Hence, he desired to make peace with his countrymen and return home. The chief Persian agent for Greek affairs was Tissaphernes, the satrap of Lydia. With him Alcibiades formed an acquaintance and soon sought his protection. From the court of the satrap he got into communication with the oligarchic party at Athens. Unfettered by facts, he promised to bring the Persians over to the Athenian side if the latter would change their government from democracy to oligarchy. As the winter of 412–411 wore on, one Athenian ally after another revolted, and in desperation men began to listen to the promises of the renegade. The oligarchic leaders — Antiphon, Peisander, Phrynichos, and Theramenes — planned a revolution in order to win the promised Persian aid. Before it could be consummated, the negotiations with Persia collapsed, but by that time the plotters had gone too far to retreat.

The Revolution and Fall of the Four Hundred

Among the officers stationed at Samos there existed an oligarchic club, of which Peisander was a member. In May of 411, he and some associates set out for Athens to accomplish their purpose. Before their arrival, the oligarchic clubs in the city had prepared the way for them by assassinating the chief democratic leaders. Then by trickery and terrorism the oligarchs induced the assembly to approve their scheme. A provisional council of four hundred members assumed the direction of the state, preparatory to drawing up a list of citizens qualified to participate in the new government. It was to consist of all who were able to serve as cavalry or heavy-armed infantry at their own expense. It was understood that not less than five thousand names would be on the roll. In reality this was merely a subterfuge. Of the four leaders principally responsible for the revolution, only Theramenes seems to have intended seriously to call the five thousand at all. The others expected to control the state indefinitely through the four hundred.

From the first, the Athenian oligarchy committed gross blunders and suffered disgraceful misfortunes. The army at Samos immediately repudiated it, and under leaders of its own constituted itself the assembly of the Athenian democracy. In this capacity it recalled Alcibiades and elected him general. Peace negotiations with Sparta instituted by the oligarchs broke down disastrously. Euboea revolted and established its independence. Finally, sensing the growing hostility to them, the extreme oligarchs plotted to betray the city to Sparta. The army at Samos, under the influence of Alcibiades, demanded that the five thousand be summoned as an assembly of the Athenian people. Theramenes deserted his colleagues and a reaction followed. Several of the leaders of the oligarchs were assassinated or executed, the remainder escaped to go into exile, and the assembly of the five thousand took over the government. Working through a complicated system of revolving committees, its efficiency won the praise of both Thucydides and Aristotle. In April of 410, encouraged by a naval victory, the Athenians restored the full democracy. Meanwhile, Alcibiades' election to the office of general had been confirmed, the sentence against him was revoked, and his property was restored.

Athens' Black Sea Route Attacked

It was well for the Athenians that they composed their differences so quickly, for a new and dire peril threatened them. Up to the late autumn of 411, the Spartan alliance had merely sought to rob Athens of her tribute-paying allies, without attempting any decisive blow. But a new Lacedaemonian admiral, Mindaros, instituted a radical change of policy. He centered his attack upon the most vital spot in the Athenian Empire — the "wheat route" to the Black Sea. To close it was to starve Athens into submission. He began by winning over Cyzicus on the Sea of Marmora, but the Athenians twice defeated him and recovered the city. In the spring of 410, Alcibiades overtook the Peloponnesian fleet in the same waters and practically annihilated it. Mindaros died fighting and the survivors of his fleet had to depend upon the bounty of a neighboring Persian satrap.

When the extent of the disaster became known at Sparta, her government proposed peace. Each party was to keep what it then possessed, except that the Athenians should surrender Pylos and the Spartans Decelea. Hard as these terms were for Athens, they were the best that she could hope for. The restored democracy was no wiser than the old one had been. Under the influence of Cleophon the lyre-maker — a low demagogue of the type of Hyperbolus — the offer was rejected and the war went on. Henceforth, the erratic and hysterical tendencies of the Assembly were to constitute the gravest obstacle to Athenian success.

But the fortunes of Athens continued to rise throughout 409 and 408. The island of Thasos, which had revolted, was recaptured. Along the Dardanelles and the Sea of Marmora, Alcibiades won an astonishing series of successes. One after another, the revolted cities were recaptured, until at last his achievements were crowned by the taking of Chalcedon and Byzantium, at the entrance to the Bosporus. The Black Sea route was once more safe in Athenian hands.

Lysander and Cyrus

With the beginning of the year 407, however, Spartan prestige began to revive, for which two men were chiefly responsible. Lysander, the son of a Spartiate father and a helot mother, atoned for his irregular birth by transcendent genius in war and diplomacy. Possibly because of his illegitimate origin, he had a bold disregard for the traditions of his native city, and when necessary he could be both unscrupulous and cruel. Cyrus, the younger son of King Darius, was a kindred spirit. Through his mother he had secured an appointment as viceroy of all Asia Minor, with authority over all the satraps of the peninsula. A charming manner, Oriental subtlety, insatiable ambition, and a broad mind contributed toward making him a great leader and a formidable antagonist. His orders were to supply Sparta liberally with money, and he saw to it that a steady stream of gold and silver flowed into her coffers. With such backing, Lysander could construct a powerful fleet and was able to pay his rowers more than the Athenians could pay theirs.

Against these able and dangerous enemies the Athenians had no commander of equal ability except Alcibiades, and they lost him through their own folly. Late in 407 or early in 406, he was in command of a fleet on the coast of Asia Minor. When compelled to be absent for some days from his command, he forbade the subordinate who was to represent him to engage in battle on any pretext whatever. The latter, in his chief's absence, attacked the Spartans at Notium, and was defeated with the loss of fifteen ships. The blame for this trifling reverse fell upon Alcibiades and the reaction against him at Athens was violent. Not daring to face the hysterical populace, he went into voluntary exile in Thrace. A few years later he fell a victim to the vengeance of the Spartans and Persians.

Athens' Last Victory

Even with her best commander gone, Athens was to win one more great victory. In 406, with an empty treasury and depleted manpower, she was still able to fit out about one hundred and fifty triremes, filling out their crews with metics and slaves. With these her commanders met the Spartan fleet of about one hundred and twenty ships at the Arginusae Islands, between Lesbos and the Asiatic mainland, and gained an important victory. Over half the enemy ships were sunk with their crews, while the Athenians lost only twenty-five ships. Just as the battle ended, a northerly gale swept down upon the scene, and the crews of twelve of the disabled vessels, who might otherwise have been saved, were drowned. The Athenian commanders were also prevented from giving funeral rites to the bodies afloat on the water. When the news of this mishap reached Athens, popular anger rose to a frenzy. In defiance of legal precedent, the eight generals in command were deposed and committed for trial. Two escaped into exile; the other six, including Pericles, the son of Pericles and Aspasia, were executed. Again Sparta offered peace and again Cleophon's influence led Athens to refuse the offer.

The Collapse and Surrender of Athens

The victory at Arginusae had been gained while Lysander was not in command of the Spartan fleet, but the year 405 saw him once more in action as admiral of the fleet operating in the Dardanelles. Capturing Lampsacus, he made it his headquarters, while the Athenian commanders took up their position at Aegospotami, on the European side. There they endeavored to force Lysander to fight, which he refused to do. Each day they cruised in front of Lampsacus, and each afternoon they beached most of their ships and went ashore. Alcibiades, who lived in the neighborhood, warned them of the danger that they incurred by this carelessness. He was rewarded with a snub and his advice went unheeded. On the fifth day of

University Prints

THE MOURNING ATHENA

these maneuvers, the watchful Lysander waited until his enemies were off their guard, sailed over, and captured one hundred and sixty ships almost without resistance. All the Athenian citizen prisoners — some three thousand in number — were ruthlessly butchered and funeral rites denied to their corpses. Twenty ships, under the command of a general named Conon, escaped. Conon fled to Cyprus, whence he was later to emerge to do Athens good service.

The disaster of Aegospotami sealed the doom of Athens. Her fleet was gone, her treasury empty, and her food-supply cut off. Xenophon writes:

> When the Paralos [one of the state dispatch boats] arrived at Athens in the night, the story of the disaster was told. The lamentation spread from the Piraeus up the Long Walls to the city, one man passing the news to the next. No one slept in Athens that night.[1]

After this, the end was only a question of time. Lysander blocked the Piraeus and an allied army besieged the city by land. After a siege of eight months, starvation forced the Athenians to unconditional surrender (404). Thebes and Corinth, the most bitter and inveterate enemies of Athens, clamored for the complete destruction of the fallen city, but Sparta, whether from mercy or policy, was more lenient. Pleading that Athens had done the Greek cause good service in the Persian wars, the government of Lacedaemon agreed to spare the city and its people. Even so, Sparta's conditions were harsh enough. The fortifications of the Piraeus, together with the Long Walls, were to be dismantled. Athens gave up all but twelve of her ships, and agreed to surrender control of her foreign relations in war and peace to Sparta. All exiles were to be restored. As a satellite of Sparta, Athens would naturally have to adopt some form of oligarchic government.

Thus ended the crusade to make "the world safe for the independent city-state." As the stones of the Long Walls fell crashing to earth, the victors gave way to the wildest rejoicing, for it was felt that the Greeks had at last regained their liberty. The story of the disillusionment which awaited them is yet to be told.

[1] *Hellenica*, II, 2, 3.

26

A New Phase of Greek Civilization

THE BIRTH OF INDIVIDUALISM

THE GENERATION of GREEKS which grew to maturity during the Peloponnesian War saw the passing of the refined and conservative culture of the Periclean Age. Greek civilization now entered upon a new phase, the product of turmoil, suffering, and doubt. In the new intellectual and ethical system, the dominant factors were skepticism and individualism. As so often happens in apparently abrupt cultural changes, the outstanding features of the new age had been present, though suppressed, in the preceding period. Party strife reappeared with a virulence unknown since the Persian wars. Imperialism dropped the mask of beneficence which it had worn in the Athens of Pericles, and became again the shameless exploitation of the weak by the strong. Panic fears, mass hysteria, and ferocious cruelty toward conquered enemies marked the conduct of the war. The educated classes lost their unreasoning faith in the gods and the traditional moral standards and subjected their dearest beliefs to searching criticism. Naturally, the result of all this intellectual ferment was a wide variety of conclusions. In religion, they ranged from the reaffirmation of old faiths to complete atheism; and in morals, from the lawless ambitions of Alcibiades and Critias, or the impudent rascality of some of Aristophanes' characters, to the patriotic heroism of Thrasybulus and the reforming zeal of Socrates.

An Age of Intellectual Doubt and Alertness

The tendency to question all accepted beliefs made the age one of intense intellectual activity, the results of which in a large measure compensated for the lost calm and confidence of the Age of Pericles. The ills from which governments and society suffered drew man's attention to the study of political science and ethics. Art took on new forms. In place of the stately majesty which had characterized the Parthenon sculptures, it gained a convincing realism and human appeal which the work of the preceding age had lacked.

Political life as it was expressed in the city-state was indubitably decadent, and the Hellenic national character had lost the balance and self-control which produced statesmen such as Solon, Pittacus, and Pericles. Intellectually and artistically, however, it was to continue for a long time in undiminished splendor and to flower in a series of triumphs which are among the finest features of our Hellenic heritage.

The Decline of the City-State

Causes

The Peloponnesian War revealed the first indications of a process which was to change the whole tone of later Greek culture: the decline of the independent city-state. Several factors combined to initiate this development. The war caused the destruction or depopulation of a large number of cities. It was not a duel between single states, but a contest between two great alliances, in each of which the component units were largely submerged. Naturally, the claims of small states to independent sovereignty were treated with slight respect, and before the struggle ended, many of them had sunk to the rank of dependencies.

Furthermore, the broader intellectual horizon of the period directed the attention of the educated classes to events far beyond their own borders, making it impossible for them to center their thinking solely upon local institutions. Beyond a doubt, the Athenian intelligentsia were rapidly becoming hostile to the democratic form of government. A mania for Spartan customs prevailed, varying from the practice of boxing for fashionable young aristocrats to the idealization of the Lacedaemonian constitution by the philosophers. While this fad was less pervasive than similar ones are in these days of universal education, it nevertheless put democracy distinctly on the defensive.

Even more important was the disintegrating influence of individualism which penetrated the middle and lower classes deeper than did the hobbies of the intellectuals. At Athens, during the Age of Pericles, the claims of the state had been uppermost in the minds of all classes, and although the liturgical system (trierarchies, choregia, and so on) must have borne heavily upon the wealthier citizens even then, there was little or no complaint against it. Now, however, the wealthy began to resent the financial burdens which hindered them from keeping pace with a rising standard of living, while the poor, who had been reduced to distress by war, urged the further extension of the system and the increase of state expenditures from which they were in a position to profit. Xenophon represents an impoverished aristocrat as reconciled to the loss of his property because, among other things, his poverty freed him from the constant demands of the government for the performance of liturgies and the threat of lawsuits:

> Now when I was rich . . . I was forced to pay those pettifogging lawyers who swarm in this town like locusts. . . . I was obliged to bear liturgies at my own expense, nor could I go abroad to travel to avoid that expense. The government is now no longer jealous of me, nor I of it.[1]

The withdrawal of the better elements of the population from political life was another result of individualism. Young men of talent refused to enter political careers, and the leadership of the assembly fell into the hands of demagogues like Cleon and Hyperbolus, most of whom were middle-class businessmen. Personal abuse of opponents, a loud voice, and frantic gesticulation marked the new school of oratory, of which the populace voiced its approval with applause and its disapprobation with derision. Under such leadership its decisions became more and more hasty and ill-considered, and were at times shockingly cruel and unjust.

Political Misuse: The Oligarchic Clubs

Another unhealthy symptom in Athenian public life was the formation of oligarchic clubs, which undertook to manipulate the courts and elections in favor of their members. Occasionally, these organizations even resorted to assassination, as in the revolution of 411–410. Under such conditions, it is not surprising that the democracy was twice overthrown in the later years of the war, nor that its operations became increasingly rash and unwise.

If the discussion has thus far been centered about Athens, it is not because the situation in other parts of the Greek world was essentially better. Our data do not permit as full a description of the conditions elsewhere, but the outbreaks of revolutions at Corcyra, Syracuse, and other places indicate that, as a whole, they were even worse. These tendencies increased during the following century, with at times tyrannies, massacres, and other evidence of class hatred.

[1] Xenophon, *Symposium*, chapter 4; condensed.

The Sophists and the New Intellectualism

We have seen how the sophists began their activities as teachers of oratory and debating. By the end of the fifth century, they had broadened their scope to include all knowledge useful to a man in business or public life, and the entrance of the wealthy middle class into political careers greatly increased the number of their clientèle. A few of these, like Protagoras, may have done some original thinking, but the majority merely systematized and disseminated the teachings of the philosophers. In an age of skepticism and disillusionment they were noted for the pitiless thoroughness with which they dissected the traditional beliefs of their pupils on politics, ethics, cosmology, and religion. Such a process, beneficial as it might be in some cases, was full of danger. As a rule, the criticism was wholly destructive. The conservatives accused the sophists of teaching their pupils to "make the worse cause appear the better," and of making them both atheists and villains.

Popular Prejudices Against the New Education

The popular view of sophistic instruction, which must be accepted with extreme caution by the modern student, is well expressed in the *Clouds* of Aristophanes. They destroyed their pupils' religious beliefs. The comedian represents Socrates as keeping a school where opinions similar to those of the sophists are taugh . He derides the belief that the gods punish perjurers, and illustrates his point by proving that some of the leading Athenian politicians are perjurers. The only deities which he recognizes are the Clouds, who teach men arguments with which to defraud their creditors. How far this picture was intended to apply to Socrates personally, and how far it was a generalized description of subversive educational tendencies, cannot be ascertained, but the important fact is that such tendencies were prevalent.

Undoubtedly there was a certain amount of avowed atheism in Athens. Critias, a disciple of Socrates and afterward the leading figure among the Thirty during the revolution of 404–403, explained the gods as figments of the imagination invented by some cunning ruler to frighten rebels and evil-doers:

> There was once a time when the life of men was without order, and like that of the animals — enslaved to brute force, and without regard for the good, or chastisement for the bad. Then I think men established laws as means of punishment, that Justice might rule and Insolence be her slave, and retribution was inflicted upon wrong-doers.

When the laws restrained them from open deeds of violence, they did them secretly. Then I think some cunning wise man thought out the plan of devising gods for mankind, that the bad might feel awe, even if in secret they should do or say or think evil.[1]

The gods, then, were mere bogies to be used to frighten the credulous.

The Skepticism of the Sophists

Less radical than the atheists, but not much less hated by the conservatives, were the skeptics. We have mentioned Protagoras and Gorgias. The former, according to Plato, taught that "Man is the measure of all things." By this he meant that if A believes an object to be white, and B thinks it black, both may be right. This makes truth merely a personal matter. Gorgias asserted that nothing exists; that if it did, we could not know it; and that if we did know it, we could not communicate our knowledge to others. The ethical consequences of these doctrines must have been, in strict logic, the destruction of distinctions between right and wrong, for it is easy to deduce that man can never know the real difference between them, and that whatever choice he wishes to make is right to him. We may infer from the pages of Plato that there were prominent persons in Athens at this time who held the view that "might is the only right." One of the speakers in his *Republic* anticipates Nietzsche by twenty-three hundred years when he says, "Justice is nothing but what is advantageous to the most powerful."[2]

Such statements had more than a purely academic importance. Acts like the unprovoked destruction of Melos in 416 prove that the philosophy of violence was being adopted as a maxim of state policy. Thucydides, in his immortal account of the conference between the Athenian and Melian representatives, makes the former say: "Right, as this world goes, is only a question between those who are equal in power. The strong do what they can, and the weak endure what they must."[3] Among the educated classes in Athens and the rest of Greece moral chaos was as complete as the political chaos which accompanied the war.

SOCRATES AND THE PHILOSOPHY OF MAN

Opposed to this wave of destructive criticism was the powerful influence of Socrates (469–399). Paradoxically, although his personality is one of

[1] Critias, *Sisyphus* Frag. Cited in Botsford and Sihler, *Hellenic Civilization*, no. xi, 3.

[2] Plato, *Republic*, I, 338 ff.   [3] Thucydides, *History*, V, 105.

the best known from the ancient world, it is practically impossible to give anything approaching an exact account of his teachings. No doubt there is a good reason for this. His character was dynamic, attractive, and diversified, and he had the power to stimulate thought in the most varied types among his hearers. Yet he never seemed to have formulated his

Bettmann

PORTRAIT BUST OF SOCRATES

teachings into a system, and has left no writings by which he can be judged. We have to rely for our knowledge of his ideas upon the works of his disciples, and each writer seems to have colored his accounts with his own views. Only in the brief notices of Aristotle and the caricature presented by Aristophanes in the *Clouds* have we any data from outside this circle; and although both furnish us with valuable hints, the former wrote at least fifty years after Socrates' death, while the latter must have distorted the character of his victim for the comic effect.

Socrates the Person

With protruding eyes, pug nose, and thick lips, this pioneer in the philosophy of man was reputed to be the homeliest person in Athens. He had once learned the trade of stonecutter, but had soon given it up for the more congenial vocation of frequenting public places and asking questions. This was not a lucrative occupation, since Socrates refused to accept pay for his services. We may sympathize with his wife Xanthippe, whose nagging of her thriftless spouse has given her an unenviable notoriety in subsequent ages. Meanwhile, Socrates, benignly tolerant of her castigations, spent most of his time away from home, tormenting all and sundry with his disturbing inquiries. Old and shabbily dressed, he had a charm of manner, a genial and kindly wit, and a nobility of character which drew to him a group of young men from the highest social circles of the city. Plato, Alcibiades, the sons of Pericles, Critias, Xenophon, and many others were proud to be called his friends. At times he would stand motionless for hours, either lost in thought or overcome by a nervous disorder akin to catalepsy. But he was a brave soldier, he could drink elegantly and moderately at dinner parties, and he was the equal of any in a contest of wits. On one occasion we hear of his proving to a conceited young dandy that his own homely features were, by reason of their functional usefulness, more beautiful than the other's classic profile. He was scrupulously pious toward the gods worshiped by his neighbors, but his religious views were by no means in entire agreement with theirs. Among other things, he believed that he had a guardian spirit which warned him of danger and directed the course of his life.

Socrates' Attitude and Method

Any account of the teachings of Socrates which will avoid the most doubtful points must be relatively brief. One fact seems to stand out in all our accounts: during his later years, at least, man and his problems were always at the center of his consciousness, in contrast to his predecessors' concern with the physical universe. Man's chief problem is how to achieve right conduct. The Delphic oracle had once told an inquirer that there was no one wiser than Socrates, but when Socrates took stock of his wisdom, he found that he had none. Inquiry revealed that others were as ignorant as he, but he was aware of his ignorance, while they foolishly thought themselves wise. Thereupon he set out to provoke them by constant questions into a critical examination of their own lives and thoughts. Accosting some passer-by or chance acquaintance, he would insist that the person define justice or some other virtue. To give a definition was no defense against this pest. Every point in the answer became the subject of other questions, until the exasperated victim found that he had been led to contradict his first statement. Apparently, Socrates then made an attempt to lead the bewildered ones by the same method to new and sounder positive conclusions, but one may question how far the second half of the process was successful. Destructive criticism is usually more impressive and efficient than constructive reasoning.

Why the mania for definitions? The answer is, that to Socrates, virtue was synonymous with knowledge, and evil with ignorance. He constantly used the analogy of the manual trades. It was no more possible, he asserted, for a man to be virtuous without understanding the nature of virtue than for a potter to ply his craft without understanding the nature of pots and jars. The same analogy led him to criticize the practice — dear to the Athenian democracy — of choosing officials by lot. How much further his criticism went in this direction is uncertain, but he seems to have been hostile to democracy in general.

Popular Hostility: His Trial and Death

The Athenian masses did not care to be accused of ignorance nor to have their dearest opinions stigmatized as fallacies, especially when these charges were proved by the relentless Socratic logic. To them, Socrates was merely another enemy of the traditional order of things, like the sophists and the radical tragedian Euripides. We find Aristophanes holding him up to ridicule and hatred in the *Clouds* as an atheist and destroyer of morality. Alcibiades and Critias, both of whom were his disciples, had turned out to be villains. After the latter had taken the lead in the massacre which disgraced the reign of the "Thirty," [1] Socrates was a marked man. In 399, he was accused of atheism and of "corrupting the youth." He was convicted, and his ill-timed contempt of the court led it to impose the death penalty demanded by his accusers. Socrates was seventy years old and ready to die. Disdaining opportunities to escape, he calmly drank the cup of hemlock.

Unless we remember that what Socrates was as a man is more important than what he taught, the secret of his career escapes us. His disciples acquired from him the thirst for truth, but they satisfied it with a wide variety of doctrines. The impulse to creative thought which flowed from him led Plato to formulate the theory of ideas and develop the philosophy of values, made the prosaic Xenophon a moralist, and long after his death impelled the cynics, stoics, and epicureans to give diverse answers to the

[1] See *infra*, Chapter 28.

question which he had so persistently raised: "What is life's highest good?" Through Plato, he exerted an indirect influence upon Aristotle. Philosophy was permanently enriched because this queer, homely old man had lived.

The Athenian Viewpoint

When all has been said, had the Athenian court which convicted Socrates any justification for its verdict? In all probability the charge was a veiled reference to his well-known hatred of democracy, which, however, by the amnesty of 403 could not be made a ground of accusation. In 399, democracy at Athens was still on an insecure footing, and it was inadvisable to tolerate any longer the teaching which had produced the two great betrayers of popular government. It is probable that the accusers never intended to put Socrates to death. By Athenian law, a convicted person had the right to propose one penalty and the accuser another. All that the jury could do was to choose between them. When Socrates' accuser proposed the death penalty for him, he was probably trying to compel Socrates to put forth as an alternative a heavy fine or exile. Socrates countered by suggesting a very small fine, coupled with a reward for his services to the state. To have done otherwise than vote for the death penalty would have been to stultify the verdict already reached. What could the jury do but accept the more severe penalty? The Athenians had suffered deeply in the years preceding the trial, and two of their worst betrayers had been Socrates' pupils.

EURIPIDES, THE DOUBTER AND PESSIMIST

The age of doubt and criticism which appeared at the beginning of the Peloponnesian War could not produce drama which would ring with the cosmic faith and optimism that characterized the works of Aeschylus and Sophocles. Its fears, its questionings, and the broader humanitarianism of its better minds found expression in the tragedies of Euripides (480–406). Chronologically, most of his life belongs to the Age of Pericles, as he was nearly fifty when the war began; but there is reason to feel that from the beginning of his literary career he was out of touch with the spirit of the times, a prey to pessimism and doubt. Euripides was well educated, having studied under Anaxagoras and other prominent teachers. From them he imbibed a rationalist viewpoint and a fluent command of language. His

PORTRAIT BUST OF EURIPIDES

own sad and thoughtful temperament — reflected in the facial expression of his portrait busts — was the remaining element in a remarkable personality. His whole life had in it the touch of tragedy. It was rumored that both his wives were unfaithful. He did not participate in Athenian politics, like his contemporary Sophocles. The intellectual circle to which he belonged was unpopular, and he was exposed to criticism and ridicule. Probably he lacked the cheerful self-possession which made Socrates rise above similar hostility. When more than seventy years of age, he went to the court of King Archelaus of Macedonia, where he died. Of his ninety-one tragedies, only five received first prizes. Nineteen tragedies and a satyr drama have come down to us.

While compelled by tradition to use plots drawn from mythology and legend, Euripides was an innovator, both in style and dramatic technique. He did not group his works into trilogies, but made each an independent dramatic unit. He retained the chorus (probably from necessity) and occasionally used it to good effect, but his dialogues are proportionately more important than those of Sophocles. Possibly because his audience was no longer conversant with the stories which supplied the subjects to the tragedians, he began his plays with long explanatory prologues which furnish the background of the action. A comparison of his treatment of these themes with those of Aeschylus and Sophocles will show that he added to his plots a distinct melodramatic touch. Aristophanes ridicules him for his frequent use of disguises, his introduction of blind beggars upon the stage, his use of the sudden appearance of a god to straighten out tangled situations and bring about unhoped-for happy endings, and *impasses*, such as the scene in the *Orestes* in which the hero threatens to kill Hermione unless her father secures his release.

The " Electra" and the " Orestes"

A review of the *Electra* and the *Orestes* (which treat the same subjects as the extant trilogy of Aeschylus) will make clear the innovations in style and plot which Euripides could effect with a theme which had been frequently treated by his predecessors. In the former, Electra had been given in marriage by Clytemnestra and Aegisthus to Auturgus, a humble and noble-hearted peasant who, in respect for her aristocratic birth, allows her to keep her virginity. When Orestes and Pylades arrive on their errand of vengeance, they are entertained in the humble dwelling of Auturgus. They slay Aegisthus while he is sacrificing. Clytemnestra is lured to her daughter's house by the false report that Electra has become a mother. Instead of the splendid villainess portrayed by Aeschylus, she is a kindly, solicitous parent, who looks with horror upon the hardships of her daughter's life. Her children slay her, and immediately her divine brothers, Castor and Pollux, appear to the murderers and make known to them the will of the gods. Electra is to be married to her brother's friend. The faithful Auturgus is to be made rich, and Orestes himself, cleansed of the blood-guilt and acquitted by the Council of the Areopagus, is to have a kingdom in Arcadia.

In the *Orestes* the melodramatic element is even stronger. The citizens of Argos condemned Orestes and his sister to death for the murder of their mother. Their aunt and uncle, Helen and Menelaus, and their grandfather, Tyndarus, arrive; and they all discuss the merits of the deed in the best sophistic style. Orestes and Pylades seize Helen as a hostage to insure their safety, but the gods carry her away. They then seize her daughter Hermione. At this critical moment the god Apollo appears, gives Hermione in marriage to Orestes and Electra to Pylades, and tells Menelaus that his wayward spouse has been taken to heaven.

Characteristics of Euripidean Drama

Every important character in Euripidean drama is an orator and logician, and perhaps Euripides' greatest weakness is the tendency to overload his lines with displays of eloquence. Thus, in the *Andromache*, Menelaus and Hermione are prepared to murder the heroine and her son, but before they strike the fatal blow their weakness for fine speaking leads them into a debate with their intended victim which continues until help arrives and they fail to accomplish their purpose.

The faults of Euripides should not, however, blind us to his many excellences. The first of these is his genuine sympathy for the unfortunate and the oppressed. Especially does he feel for the hapless victims whom the fortunes of war have condemned to slavery and shame. His anger against the perpetrators of these outrages became intense. In the *Hecuba* and the *Trojan Women* we are shown the horrors which followed the capture of Troy: the boy Astyanax murdered in cold blood, the aged Hecuba and the widowed Andromache awaiting a life of servitude, and Polyxena — more fortunate than they — slaughtered as a sacrifice to the shade of Achilles. The *Trojan Women* was presented after the sack of Melos, and it may have been inspired by pity for the unfortunate Melians.

Euripides did not confine himself to a realization of the despair of these unfortunates. He could understand the unreasoning lust for vengeance which made them lash out at their tormentors, caring little how much they themselves suffered if they might repay their wrongs in kind. Such a one is Medea. Wedded to Jason, who owes all to her, she finds herself repudiated in favor of another. She rebels against the inequality which makes woman a perpetual dependent of man:

> Of all things that have life and sense, we women are the most unfortunate. First we must buy a husband at too high a price, and set over us a tyrant, which is worse than the first. This is a most important issue, whether our choice is good or bad. For divorce is discreditable to a woman, nor can we disown our husbands.[1]

> And yet they say that we live safely at home, while they are at war. Sorry reasoning: I would rather go thrice into battle than suffer childbirth once.[2]

When her home is broken up by her husband's infidelity, she longs only for revenge:

> Hence I only ask this one favor of you — your silence, if perchance I can plan some way or other to take vengeance upon my husband for

_____

[1] *Medea*, ll. 231–237.   [2] *Ibid.*, ll. 248–251.

this cruel treatment. For though a woman be fearful enough in other things, and a coward at the sight of a sword, yet when she finds her honor wronged, no heart is filled with deadlier hate than hers.[1]

Having slain her sons, her rival, and the latter's father, she exults:

> *Medea:* Call me a lioness if you will, or by the name of Scylla, whose home is in Etruscan caverns. For in my turn I wounded your heart as justice prompted.
> *Jason:* You grieve, and share my woes.
> *Medea:* To be sure I do; but my grief is soothed because you no longer boast.[2]

Although Euripides at times delineates demoniac women athirst for vengeance, and makes much of sex-problem plays, as in the *Hippolytus*, he seems, on the whole, to prefer the finer types of feminine character. His *Alcestis* introduces us to a noble and self-sacrificing wife who gives her life to save that of her husband. Andromache, Electra, and Hecuba — each in her own way displays true grandeur of character. Indeed, there are few finer figures in ancient literature than the widowed queen of Troy, who, reduced to slavery and about to be led from the smoking ruins of her native city, encourages her fellow victims to make the best of their lot.

Euripides Writes of the Gods and the Moral Law

Euripides' sense of right and wrong extends even to the acts of the gods. In the *Hippolytus* he makes the goddess Artemis denounce the insidious plot by which her sister Aphrodite has brought about the downfall of the chaste Hippolytus and his stepmother. But the tone of condemnation is even stronger in the *Ion*, which treats one of the innumerable legends that made the gods the ancestors of aristocratic families. Ion was the eponymous ancestor of the Ionians and therefore of the Athenian people. He was the son of Apollo and of Creusa, the daughter of the king of Athens. Abandoned by his mother, he was carried to Delphi and was reared in the temple of his father, in complete ignorance of his parentage. When Creusa and her husband Xuthus come to Delphi to inquire about the cause of their childlessness, Apollo takes advantage of the fact to palm off his illegitimate son upon Xuthus as the latter's own offspring. Although the Greeks were much more tolerant toward such matters than succeeding generations, this solution of the delicate problem probably did not satisfy Athenian theatergoers. In one of the speeches, Ion thus characterizes the lawless loves of the gods:

[1] *Ibid.*, ll. 258–266.   [2] *Ibid.*, ll. 1358–1362.

. . . Whosoever of the human race does wrong, the gods punish his crimes severely; but how can it be just for you to break the laws which you have written for mankind to obey? It can never be; but suppose that you, Poseidon, and Zeus who rules the heavens should make atonement to mankind for those whom you have wronged by force. Your temples would be emptied to pay the fines imposed upon you for your base deeds. For when you pursue pleasure regardless of what is seemly, you do wrong. No longer is it right to call men wicked if they imitate the conduct of the gods.[1]

In his old age Euripides wrote the *Bacchae*, which marks a return to more orthodox religious views. In the meantime, he had established a reputation as an "atheist," which is often the subject of comment by his arch-opponent Aristophanes.

The admirers of Euripides at Athens were chiefly the "intellectuals," but the Syracusans had such high regard for him that in 413 they freed Athenian prisoners who could teach them parts of his dramas from memory. In Hellenistic and Roman times his popularity continued to grow, and even today there are many who rank him first among Athenian dramatists.

ARISTOPHANES, THE CONSERVATIVE SCOFFER

The conservative cause, although attacked at so many points, was not without its champions, and of these the best-known and most effective was the comedian Aristophanes (about 447–380). Of the man himself we know relatively little. He seems to have come from a respectable country family and he must have had a good education, as his works indicate a broad knowledge of the best literature. Plato makes him one of the guests at the banquet described in the *Symposium*. From his association with the highly intellectual circle of Socrates and his friends, we are forced to conclude that his aversion to the new intellectual trends of his time was not owing to ignorance or stupidity, but to deliberate, reasoned choice. His first comedy (now lost) was produced in 427, and his last, the *Plutus*, in 388. He composed over forty plays, of which eleven are extant.

We have seen some of the outstanding characteristics of the early Athenian comedy: lack of plot, obscenity, improbability, boisterous fun, and political and personal allusions. Some of these characteristics were too firmly entrenched in popular favor to be dispensed with, but Aristophanes, to judge from our scanty knowledge of his predecessors, made important changes both in treatment and subject matter. Without any revolutionary changes in form, he introduced an intellectual element

[1] *Ion*, ll. 436–451; condensed.

which raised comedy to the level of real drama. All but two of his works were classified by Graeco-Roman critics as part of the "Old Comedy."

The Pattern of the Comic Drama

Few of Aristophanes' comedies have well-developed plots, although they usually follow a clearly marked, conventional pattern. There is a prologue in which the setting of the play is given, followed by the entry of the chorus. Then comes a contest between the two chief characters, followed by a pause. During this interlude occurs the *parabasis*, in which the chorus makes a long address to the audience, expressing the author's views on current topics or asking the judges to give him the prize. The parabasis is followed by a loosely connected series of incidents, usually the logical results of the contest in the first part. The normal ending is a revel, a feast, a wedding, or some rude horse-play. At times, however, the poet alters the arrangements of these parts.

Aristophanic humor is of various kinds. First we find some stock pleasantries, apparently the common property of all the comic writers, which are usually obscene. Our comedian intimates in several places that he considered these antiquated and offensive witticisms to be cheap and stale, but that his audience expected them and could not do without them. He has not, however, told us the true reason for the obscenity of the early Greek comedy. It was, as we have seen, a ritual in honor of the deities of fertility, and as such had to be lascivious in order to accomplish its purpose. The Athenians were at all times less fastidious than polite modern society, but the respectable people did not ordinarily indulge in the vulgarity which appears in their comedies. The comedian also parodies the works of his fellow dramatists — especially Euripides — with ease and effectiveness. He likewise ridicules politicians, odd or depraved fellow citizens, and at times even the gods. Here again is a practice foreign to modern ideas of propriety. We cannot understand how a pious worshiper can ridicule a divinity as Aristophanes does Dionysus in the *Frogs*. But the incongruity is more apparent than real. Where religious emotion is strong and plays a part in the daily lives of the people, a stress develops which has to be relieved. Accordingly, in countries where this condition prevails, the people often relax the strain, as our medieval Catholic ancestors did, by an annual festival in which religious rites were made the subject of coarse buffooneries and parodies. When it is over, they return to their habitual attitude of respect. Aristophanes also creates scenes which defy every canon of possibility, like the flight of Trygaeus to heaven on the back of a beetle. Some of his pleasantries grate harshly upon the modern ear, and others have a local tang which only a contemporary Athenian could appreciate; but even through the mists of twenty-three centuries, we catch exquisite bits of humor which will never lose their appeal as long as men know how to laugh.

Understanding Aristophanes' Humor

The moral attitude of Aristophanes is hard to understand unless we are able to distinguish between coarse language and immoral sentiments. The difference is a very real one, and Aristophanes has much of the former, with little or none of the latter. He condemns Euripides for his use of sex-problem plots. His indignation against the quibbling logicians who sought to distort the truth in order to win arguments is real and strong. He castigates the new education largely because of what he considers its intellectual dishonesty. His moral outlook is essentially the traditional Athenian one, which aimed at the production of good citizens and brave soldiers, and at times he urges its claim with an earnestness which shines through the mask of buffoonery.

Comedies and Satires

No mere review of Aristophanes' comedies can give an adequate impression of them. Four — the *Acharnians*, the *Knights*, the *Peace*, and the *Lysistrata* — have as their general subject the Peloponnesian War and the urban demagogues who fomented it. The first three were written before the Peace of Nicias, and contain bitter denunciations of the leaders of the war party — notably Cleon and Hyperbolus. The *Lysistrata*, produced in 411, is less personal. It represents the Athenian women engaging in a strike against their belligerent husbands and forcing them to make peace. The *Wasps* is a fierce attack upon the jury system which placed the lives and fortunes of litigants at the mercy of groups of arrogant, ignorant, gossip-loving old men.

The new education is the subject of the *Clouds*, with Socrates as the butt of the comedian's wit. The dramatic tendencies exemplified in the tragedies of Euripides come in for their share of satire. Euripides himself is the subject of the *Thesmophoriazousae* — a light farce — and of the *Frogs*, which is a critical evaluation of his career, written a few months after his death. Parodies upon Euripides' lines and dramatic devices occur so frequently in other Aristophanic comedies that a rival comedian,

Cratinus, coined the expression "Euripidaristophanism" to describe Aristophanes' style.

After the end of the Peloponnesian War, our comedian turned his attention to another field. Already in 414, the *Birds* had transported the audience in imagination to Cloud-Cuckoo-Town in the midst of the air, but this fantastic vein was not followed. His last two plays are satires upon current intellectual fads and social conditions. The *Women of the Assembly* (392) is a caricature upon the kind of utopian communism later immortalized in Plato's *Republic*, and the *Plutus* (388) shows the blind god of wealth recovering his sight and attempting to undo the mistakes which he made in the distribution of this world's goods. In these we have passed into another age. They belong to the Middle Comedy.

An Evaluation

Among later Greeks and Romans, as well as in the modern world, one of the chief obstacles to a sympathetic understanding of Aristophanes' works has been the local references found in all but the last two of them. He wrote for an Athenian audience, which was steeped in the traditions of the Old Comedy. To these traditions we must attribute his lascivious language, his rude clowning, and the many allusions to queer and ludicrous fellow citizens which we, naturally, cannot appreciate. He lived in an age of changing intellectual and political standards and of violent partisanship, and he fought the losing battle for conservatism with bitter rancor. While these qualities, no doubt, added to the poet's popularity in fifth-century Athens, they naturally do not appeal to readers in other ages and countries. Quite aside from them, however, he had excellences which must always place him high among the world's great literary artists. Scattered through his plays are bits of humor whose appeal is as strong now as ever, and the absolute improbability of some of his scenes place him with Rabelais and Dean Swift, in a select class of masters of imaginative writing. Here and there we find in his comedies passages of incomparable lyric beauty which are rarely equaled in any age or tongue. Of all the fifth-century comedians, his works alone have survived, and we may well acquiesce in this silent verdict of subsequent ages.

THUCYDIDES, A CRITICAL HISTORIAN

The rationalistic spirit, which was part of the new education, revolutionized the attitude of educated Greeks toward history. For the present and recent past there was an increasing abundance of written records and government documents, from which the facts could be ascertained. For the more remote past there was available a logical method for the critical evaluation of legends and epics. In addition to these advantages, the study of rhetoric had made possible the use of a more mature, compact style than that of Herodotus. Mental discipline had likewise taught educated men to view facts with greater objectivity than ever before. These tendencies found expression in the *History of the Peloponnesian War*, written by the Athenian, Thucydides (about 471–400).

Thucydides had all the advantages which could aid in fitting him for his work. He was an aristocrat by birth, a relative of Cimon and Miltiades, and the owner of extensive estates in Thrace. He was trained in oratory and philosophy by the ablest teachers of his time. During the early years of the Peloponnesian War he held the office of general in the Athenian service. In 424, his failure to protect Amphipolis from Brasidas led to his banishment. He did not return to Athens until after the war, and he lived only a few years after his recall. During the period of his exile, he probably made his home on his Thracian estate, although his history shows that he traveled widely in search of material. The time and manner of his end are uncertain.

His Scope and Method

The task which Thucydides set for himself was quite limited. His work is divided into eight books, but only part of the first deals with events before the days of Pericles, and they are told only in outline. The war forms the central theme, primarily in its military and political aspects. There is a good reason for this choice of subject matter, even aside from the natural interest of a contemporary and participant. It permitted him to apply a rigidly critical method to his work which would have been impossible if he had treated the extensive field which Herodotus covered.

At the very outbreak of the war, Thucydides tells us, he became convinced of its importance and began to collect data from which to write a history of it. His material was gathered as soon as possible after the events which he planned to describe. Every account was carefully checked:

> With reference to the story of events, far from permitting myself to derive it from the first source that came to hand, I did not even trust to my own impressions. It rests partly on what I saw myself, partly on what others saw for me. The accuracy of the report was always tested by the most severe and detailed tests possible. My conclusions cost me some labor, because of the want of coincidence between the

reports of the same event by different eye-witnesses. This arose sometimes from imperfect memory, sometimes from undue partiality toward one side or the other.[1]

It was a serious undertaking, and not intended merely for amusement:

> The absence of romance in my history will, I fear, lessen its interest somewhat; but if it is judged useful by those inquirers who desire an exact knowledge of the past as an aid to the interpretation of the future, I shall be content. For in the course of human affairs the one must resemble, if it does not exactly reflect the other. In fine, I have written my work, not as a prize essay, but as an eternal possession.[2]

In common with subsequent Greek and Roman historians, Thucydides frequently reports speeches purporting to have been delivered by important characters in the events which he narrates. He explains the practice thus:

> As regards the speeches of this history, some were delivered before the war began, others while it was in progress. Some were heard by myself, while I gathered others from various sources. It was always hard to remember them. My own habit has been to make the speaker say what was proper to the occasion, of course adhering as closely as possible to what he actually said.[3]

We must not, therefore, consider the speeches which he reports as actual transcripts. What value can be placed upon them? Thucydides uses them as an artistic means of setting forth ideas, policies, and the characters of the speakers themselves. The famous *Funeral Oration* of Pericles, to which allusion has already been made,[4] is an exposition of the ideals of Athenian democracy as Pericles conceived them to be, with some additions by Thucydides himself. Again, the attitude of the allies of Sparta toward Athens is stated in the speech of the Corinthian envoys at the conference at Sparta, and the Athenian case, in the answer of the Athenian envoys.[5] In the speeches on the treatment of the Mytileneans (427), Cleon expounds with frank and brutal cynicism the theory of predatory imperialism maintained by terror, and his opponent, Diodotus, answers with a speech which is not less cynical because it argues for more humane conduct on the basis of expediency.[6] It would be difficult to accomplish the purpose of the author more effectively.

Criticism of Thucydides' Viewpoint

Modern historians, with their strong interest in the social and economic phases of history, are inclined to blame Thucydides for his neglect of such

---

[1] *History*, I, 22.   [2] *Ibid.*   [3] *Ibid.*
[4] Chapter 21.   [5] *History*, I, 68–70.   [6] *Ibid.*, III, 37–49.

factors. Thus, he cites, as the fundamental cause of the Peloponnesian War, Sparta's fear of the growing power of Athens, and as immediate causes three "diplomatic incidents" of political character. At first glance these strictures seem justified, but we must beware of too hasty judgment. The economic organization of the Greek world was very simple, and its influence upon policies and diplomacy must be stated in entirely different terms from those in current use. No doubt the modern historian errs as far in one direction when considering the ancient Greeks as Thucydides does in the other.

Scarcely ever does Thucydides give a moral judgment as his own opinion, and speeches which he reports are almost equally lacking in this respect. He has not a word of pity for the Plataeans massacred by the Spartans, nor for the Melians put to the sword by the Athenians. He deplores the resurgence of party strife during the war and traces its effects with a master hand, but one feels that throughout he is concerned with its historical importance and not the crimes which are committed during its course. He views the Athenian Empire as a predatory state living at the expense of its subjects, but even the enemies of Athens do not, in his pages, charge her with immoral conduct toward her dependencies. He seems to be interested only in the wisdom or folly of actions, not in their ethical implications. Religion is treated in a similar manner. Oracles are coldly analyzed in the attempt to determine their influence upon the course of events: the writer occasionally displays a withering skepticism on the whole subject. He was a product of the new education, which was nothing if not skeptical and rationalistic.

But if Thucydides is lacking in moral and religious fervor, he can describe events with a vivid realism seldom equaled. His account of the plague at Athens, or of the defeat of the Athenian expedition against Syracuse, achieves pathos by its graphic simplicity and without apparent effort. In him, Greek historiography attained a degree of excellence in style and method unequaled until modern times.

THE NEW AGE IN ART

The intellectual ferment which characterized the age of the Peloponnesian War, with its emphasis upon the individual and its pitiless analysis of all things human and divine, was reflected in the evolution of new forms in all branches of the fine arts. The regularity, self-restraint, and calm dignity which distinguished the works of Ictinus and Phidias were gradually lost by a generation which lacked the balanced character that appreciated such works. As a compensation, the art of the new period gained a naturalness, a freedom from convention, and a technical perfection previously unknown.

The Erechtheum

At Athens, the calamities which accompanied the war severely curtailed the building program of which the Parthenon, the Propylaea, and the Temple of the Wingless Victory were the outcome. The only important temple built after 431 was the so-called *Erechtheum*, located on the Acropolis, just north of the Parthenon. The date of its beginning is unknown, but it was completed between 409 and 407, perhaps as a project to furnish work for the starving commons. It was dedicated to Athena in her capacity of guardian of the city (Polias), and to the Athenian hero Erechtheus, who was here identified with the god Poseidon.

In plan and construction, the Erechtheum was a radical departure from all architectural conventions. It was built on sloping ground, the east end being about ten feet higher than the west end. The material used was Pentelic marble, except for the background of the frieze which was of dark gray Eleusinian limestone. The cella measured seventy-four by thirty-seven feet and was divided into three rooms. It had no peristyle, and instead of one or two entrances located at the ends, it had four. The east and north doors were shaded by Ionic porticoes, while the door on the west had none. The present west wall is plainly not the original, and we can only imagine what its appearance may have been.

The Caryatid Porch

The south entrance was shaded by the famous Caryatid Porch, one of the most unusual creations of the Greek artistic genius. It was surrounded by a marble balustrade, which was entered through an opening on the east side. On this balustrade stood the figures of six young women who supported the roof with their heads. So common is the sight of women bearing burdens on their heads in the Mediterranean world that the device seems simple and natural. The pose of the figures was dignified and graceful. There was no appearance of strain, and the arrangement of the draperies, with the thick mass of hair at the necks, gave the impression of stability. Perhaps for psychological effect, the roof which they held up was lightened by the omission of the frieze.

After undergoing various vicissitudes as a church and a Turkish harem,

Brown Brothers

THE CARYATID PORCH

the Erechtheum was reduced to ruins during the War of Greek Independence. A few years earlier, however, in 1812, Lord Elgin had moved one of the maiden figures from the Caryatid Porch to the British Museum, and it has since been replaced by a terra-cotta replica. Even in the present condition the remains of this wonderful building are a monument to the fruitful genius of the age that produced it.

The Temple of Apollo at Bassae

Athens was not alone in the possession of worthy habitations for the gods. Some time after the beginning of the Peloponnesian War, Ictinus, the architect of the Parthenon, laid out a remarkable temple of Apollo at Bassae in Arcadia. Here again we see a notable freedom from hampering conventions. Because of the configuration of the site, it faced north instead of east. The peristyle was Doric, but inside the building there were, instead of the internal colonnades found in the Parthenon, a series of projecting pilasters, terminating in "engaged" Ionic columns; in the center between two of these projections was a single Corinthian column — probably the oldest in existence.

Sculpture and Painting

Sculpture was not less responsive to the tendencies of the age than was architecture. Various new methods developed, in which we can see the faint beginnings of the "schools" which appeared in the next century. At Athens the bastion on which stood the Temple of the Wingless Victory was surrounded by a balustrade, on which were carved reliefs representing

University Prints

DORYPHOROS
After Polycleitus

the goddess of victory in various attitudes. The best-known of these reliefs is "Nike Fastening Her Sandal." It lacks the superhuman majesty
of the gods of Phidias, but instead we see a purely human grace and beauty
that has as strong an appeal to modern esthetic taste.

In the work of Polycleitus of Argos (last half of the fifth century) the
influence of the prevailing intellectualism is to be seen. He attempted to
work out a mathematical ratio between the various parts of the human
body, using the width of the middle finger as the unit in multiples of which
all measurements were expressed. This system he embodied in a treatise
called the *Canon*, and as an example of his method he produced a nude figure
of a young man holding a spear, the "Doryphoros." As we have only
Roman copies of this work, it would be rash to dogmatize upon its appearance, which is somewhat heavy and sluggish. Other works of his which
survive in Roman copies are the "Diadumenos" — a victorious athlete
binding a fillet about his head — and the "Wounded Amazon." Both
display well-marked peculiarities of pose and execution, the latter especially being characterized by an air of artificiality. In spite of this, Polycleitus was among the most popular sculptors of the ancient world.

Our knowledge of Greek painting for any period previous to the Macedonian occupation of Egypt is gained entirely from descriptions by Roman
and Greek writers. They tell us that revolutionary progress was made in
this field during the last third of the fifth century. Up to that time, figures
were usually drawn in outline and colored in flat tones. Before the end of
the Peloponnesian War, the Athenian Apollodorus began to practice a new
technique. He painted easel pictures, and his figures were shaded to produce the impression of depth. This device was adopted by Zeuxis of Heraclea, who apparently carried it much farther than did its inventor. Equally
important was Parrhasius of Ephesus, although we cannot be sure that he
used the discovery of Apollodorus. Our evidence justifies the conclusion
that painting was making forward strides comparable to those made by
sculpture fifty years earlier.

27

Sparta, Thebes, and Persia (404-362 B.C.)

THE FRUITS OF A GREAT CRUSADE

THE FORTY-TWO YEARS which followed the fall of the Athenian Empire is a dreary period which acquires meaning only when we consider it as evidence of the bankruptcy of the traditional Greek system of independent city-states and political parties. The rejoicing with which the Greek world at large greeted the success of the Lacedaemonian crusade to restore the liberty of the city-state was short-lived. Hardly had the object been achieved when it was discovered that the victor had simply stepped into the position formerly occupied by the vanquished, adding new evils to those which the subjects of Athens had had to endure, and largely increasing the area of exploitation. Most of the money which had financed the building of the Spartan fleet had come from Persia, and in return the Spartans had pledged themselves to surrender the Asiatic Greeks to the Persian king. This pledge was kept, but the fate of those who were sold into subjection was mild compared with that of the other former subjects of Athens and of Athens herself.

An Oligarchic Reign of Terror

Class and party supremacy were now reversed. Sparta was the champion of oligarchic government as Athens had been of democracy, and the establishment of her supremacy meant, at the very least, a complete overthrow of the popular governments established by Athens in her dependencies three-quarters of a century earlier. The bitterness of class hatred made it inevitable that the aristocrats, long depressed and nursing their grievances, would wreak their vengeance upon their opponents with no light hands. In this they would have the backing of their Spartan suzerain. In Sparta, the leading spirit and the principal authority on foreign policy was Lysander, who chiefly determined the course of events in the Greek peninsula and on the Aegean islands in 404–403. In each of the former subject cities of Athens except those given to Persia, he established a board of ten citizens of the oligarchic party for the ostensible purpose of revising the constitution and of ruling in the Spartan interest until the work was completed. These "decarchies" were backed by Spartan garrisons under commanders called *harmosts*, who in some cases were helots. The decarchs were mere tools of Lysander, animated by the blind hatred of the Greek aristocrats for their fellow citizens of the opposite party. An orgy of executions and confiscations took place, with prominent democratic leaders as the victims. Nor were the "liberated" cities free from tribute, for we are informed that Sparta, in spite of the poverty that resulted from the Peloponnesian War, collected from them a thousand talents a year to pay the costs of occupation.[1]

Athens Under the Thirty

At Athens, a board of thirty was chosen for the same purpose as the decarchies in the other cities of the Spartan Empire. Its members seem for the most part to have represented the intelligentsia (the pupils of the sophists and philosophers) rather than the old aristocracy. Critias, the most notorious of the group, was a former disciple of Socrates. Of his master's teachings he retained only a strong dislike of democratic institutions, coupled with a cynicism and cruelty all his own. Theramenes, a more moderate member of the Thirty, had already figured as a stormy petrel of Athenian politics, having been instrumental both in establishing and overthrowing the Four Hundred and in the prosecution of the generals after the battle of Arginusae. How far he was a rogue and how far a man of principle it is hard to determine, but he was at least opposed to unnecessary bloodshed. It was to be expected that the Thirty would exterminate a few political opponents, and to these they added a number of informers and other disreputable characters. Then, by degrees, they showed their real intent. The machinery of government was put entirely into the hands of their supporters. A citizen roll of three thousand, all personal adherents of Critias, was compiled, and any person whose name was not on the roll could be put to death without trial. Only the listed three thousand could possess arms. Political hatred was now reinforced by greed, and wealthy citizens and metics, without regard to their opinions, were killed and their property confiscated. When Theramenes protested,

---

[1] Diodorus, XIV, 10, 2.

Critias overawed the council by a display of armed force, struck his opponent's name from the roster of citizens, and compelled him to drink the hemlock. Fifteen hundred men were slain in eight months, but Critias and his henchmen, fortified by a Spartan garrison on the Acropolis, seemed to have no idea of ending the massacre.

Restoration of Athenian Democracy

The wild excesses of the Thirty made a reaction inevitable. Thebes and Megara were crowded with Athenian exiles, and discontent with Sparta caused these cities to welcome them. Thrasybulus, already prominent in the overthrow of the Four Hundred, gathered a band of seventy fellow exiles and with unsurpassed heroism declared war on the tyrants. Seizing a border fortress, he beat off an attack of the Spartan garrison and the oligarchs; then, with his forces increased to a thousand he entered the Piraeus, defeated the troops sent against him, and took possession of the stronghold of Munychia. Critias was slain and the Thirty retreated to Eleusis. The Spartans had tired of the policies of Lysander and forced him into exile. King Pausanias was sent to regulate the affairs of Athens, and effected a reconciliation which led to a restoration of the democracy and a general amnesty. In 401, the Athenians retook Eleusis and slew the survivors of the Thirty. Athens was once more at peace and had her old form of government, although she was still a dependency of Sparta. About the same time the decarchies were replaced by regular oligarchies in the other Aegean cities, but there, also, Spartan control continued. The worst was over, but the Greek world had had a bitter awakening from its rosy dreams of restored freedom.

THE EXPEDITION OF CYRUS AND THE TEN THOUSAND GREEKS
(401–399 B.C.)

The ascendancy which Persia had acquired in Greece during the later stages of the Peloponnesian War continued for nearly forty years. This position was not owing to a revival of her strength, for every king since Darius I had left the Persian Empire weaker than he had found it; and so it continued, with one exception, to the end. The best and most vivid evidence of the decline is the story of the rebellion of the younger Cyrus and the return of his Greek mercenaries, as told in the *Anabasis* of Xenophon. The rebellion itself was of a kind common in Oriental monarchies, and its immediate historical consequences were not important. Yet the sidelights which it furnishes upon the condition of the Persian Empire around 400 and upon the conduct of Greek mercenaries in general make the *Anabasis* a significant document.

The Expedition of the Younger Cyrus

At the death of Darius II in 404, his clever and aggressive younger son Cyrus, at the instigation of the queen mother Parysatis, had attempted to supplant his weak elder brother, Artaxerxes, as heir to the throne. The plot failed, but Parysatis saved Cyrus from death and he returned to his satrapy of Lydia. There he waged a private war with the neighboring satrap Tissaphernes, and used this as a pretext to collect about thirteen thousand Greek mercenaries and a much larger force of Orientals. Pretending that he meant to fight the independent Pisidians of central Asia Minor, he marched his forces farther and farther inland. The prince of Cilicia, an hereditary vassal of Persia, took good care to stand well with both Cyrus and Artaxerxes. He made a show of resistance to the rebel, but gave him secret aid. At Tarsus the Greeks began to suspect the real object of the expedition, and mutinied, but the trickery of one of their commanders and the promise of a raise in pay brought order again. Crossing Syria, Cyrus invaded Babylonia, and at Cunaxa, about eighty miles north of Babylon, met the army of his brother. In the battle which followed, the Greeks carried all before them, but Cyrus, rashly leading a charge against his brother's bodyguard, was killed. His army broke up, and Tissaphernes, enticing the Greek commanders into a conference, took them prisoners by treachery. Artaxerxes had them put to death. Left leaderless in the midst of a hostile country, the mercenaries elected new commanders, of whom Xenophon was one, forced their way up the Tigris River and across the Armenian Mountains, and arrived at the coast of the Black Sea some eighty-five hundred strong. Thence they traveled by slow stages back to the Aegean.

On their march they found that the mountaineers of the country which we call Kurdistan were independent of the Persian king, having recently destroyed one of his armies. Paphlagonia and Bithynia, on the shores of the Black Sea, were also free. All these countries had at one time been included in the Persian Empire. A royal family rent by dissensions and harem intrigues, satraps who fought civil wars with each other without hindrance from their master, subject peoples breaking away to form independent states, and a few thousand leaderless mercenaries who successfully cut their way through hundreds of miles of Persian territory in defiance of the king: such is Xenophon's picture of the state which pretended to rule western Asia. If it continued to dominate the Greeks of Asia and Europe, they had no one but themselves to blame.

THE WAR BETWEEN SPARTA AND PERSIA (400–387 B.C.)

The rebellion of the younger Cyrus placed the Spartans and the Asiatic Greeks in an uncomfortable position; for both of them, supposing that the king's brother represented the king's interests, had befriended him, and now they were astonished to find themselves respectively enemies and rebels. The Asiatic Greeks, fearing the vengeance of Artaxerxes, appealed to Sparta for aid. In 400, she sent an army to their assistance and war began.

Sparta, a Decadent State

Sparta was in no condition to sustain a struggle abroad. Her full citizenship did not exceed two thousand men. Contacts with the outside world had seriously deranged the economic system of the state, causing the concentration of the land in the hands of the few, with the consequent impoverishment of the remainder. Men of the Spartiate class found it increasingly difficult to keep up their contributions to the public messes, and failure in this meant disfranchisement. Such men were called "inferiors," but in spite of their degradation they still had to perform their civil duties. They felt their humiliation keenly and were a constant source of danger to the state. The perioeci and helots were in no better mood. In 397, an "inferior" named Cinadon formed a dangerous conspiracy against the government, involving the massacre of the Spartan group and the overthrow of the class system. It was betrayed by one of the participants, but the evils which gave rise to it still continued to exist. In addition to this social volcano at home, the Spartans faced the universal hatred of the outside Greek world. Athens still smarted from her recent defeat. Just before the outbreak of the war with Persia, the Lacedaemonians had attacked Elis, and after a two years' struggle had subjected her. Thebes and Corinth, formerly staunch Spartan allies, refused to contribute their quotas of troops for service in Asia. Argos nursed an age-old resentment. All were waiting for a favorable opportunity to take vengeance, and all were willing to accept Persian aid in securing it.

In spite of these adverse conditions, the war went well for the Spartans and their allies for several years. The original expeditionary force was increased by the survivors of the "Ten Thousand" and by contingents from the Asiatic Greek cities. Persian counsels were divided and their energies paralyzed. In 396, the Spartan king, Agesilaus took command in Asia, and for two years achieved almost continuous success. Xenophon has pictured Agesilaus as the hero of the Pan-Hellenic effort against Persia, but we need not accept the portrait as authentic. He was a narrow-minded, somewhat crude Spartan, who was not a genius even in military affairs. However, he was a capable officer, fighting a divided foe. At the end of his second campaign he had liberated nearly all the Asiatic Greeks from Persia, and dreamed of extensive conquests in the interior. But his successful offensive was interrupted by the inevitable recurrence of strife in Greece itself, and soon he had to return to defend his country against her neighbors.

The "Corinthian" War

The Persians by this time thoroughly understood the weaknesses of Greek character. The year after Agesilaus began his campaign in Asia, they dispatched a Rhodian Greek envoy with fifty talents to Greece to foment war in the rear of the enemy. The response was hearty and immediate. Athens, Thebes, Corinth, Argos, and some smaller states formed a coalition against their oppressor, and war once more devastated the ruined country. The year 395 saw several Spartan victories in Boeotia and one defeat (Haliartus), in which Lysander lost his life. The net result was that Sparta lost her hold upon Boeotia. Another shrewd move of the Persians was to build a fleet with which to dispute Spartan control of the sea. Two hundred triremes were prepared in the harbors of Phoenicia and placed under the joint command of the satrap Pharnabazus and the Athenian Conon, a survivor of the battle of Aegospotami. In 394, Conon met the Spartan fleet off Cnidus on the coast of Asia Minor, killed the commander, and sank or captured sixty ships. Agesilaus had been recalled to Greece, but his victory over the allies at Coronea did not restore the balance which had been upset by this overwhelming naval defeat. Conon and Pharnabazus sailed about the Aegean, overthrowing the harmosts and garrisons and proclaiming liberty to the islanders. In 393 they ravaged the coasts of the Peloponnesus, after which Conon sailed to Athens and with Persian money and the labor of his sailors helped the Athenians to rebuild their Long Walls and the fortifications of the Piraeus. Athens was again a first-class power, and she at once began preparations to recover her possessions and alliances in the Aegean. Lemnos, Imbros, and Scyros, long ago colonized by the Athenians, were recovered. In 389, an Athenian fleet sailed through the northern Aegean and the Propontus, renewing the former alliances with Byzantium, Chalcedon, the Thracian Chersonesus (Gallipoli peninsula), Thasos, and Samothrace. Thus, the all-important "wheat route" to the Black Sea was once more in her possession.

On the mainland of Greece, the Spartans suffered a sharp reverse in the year 390. A new system of tactics that had been developed during the latter years of the fifth century was utilized by the commanders of the mercenaries. Heavy-armed infantry was supplemented by various light-armed troops, particularly of the type called *peltasts*. These men wore little or no armor and carried light shields and long spears. They gained much more in mobility than they lost in protection, and under the command of *condottieri* like the Athenian Iphicrates, they repeatedly proved their value. By this time the Spartans were concentrating their attack upon Corinth and Argos, now closely united, whose fortifications blocked the road into central Greece. Near Corinth the peltasts of Iphicrates attacked and destroyed a Spartan battalion, killing two hundred and fifty Spartan citizens. Aside from the blow to her military prestige, Sparta lost one-eighth of her adult male citizens in this disaster. The tactical revolution which was to culminate in the Macedonian system of Philip and Alexander was under way.

The "King's Peace"

The dreary struggle dragged on. Fortune favored first one side and then the other. All the Greek participants were nearing exhaustion. The revival of Athenian strength caused the Persians finally to veer toward their late enemy, for they wished to maintain a balance of power in Greece which they could manipulate to their own interest. In 387, Sparta sent Antalcidas to Susa as her envoy, and he prevailed upon Artaxerxes to sanction a treaty of mutual advantage. The same year the satrap Tiribazus read to the envoys of the Greek states assembled at Sardis the royal decree in which these terms were embodied:

> King Artaxerxes thinks it just that the cities of Asia, together with the islands of Clazomenae and Cyprus should belong to him; and that the rest of the Greek cities, great and small, be independent, except Lemnos, Imbros, and Scyros. These shall belong to Athens, as of old. Against anyone who shall reject this treaty, I myself, with others of like mind, shall fight, by land and by sea, with ships and with money.[1]

[1] Xenophon, *Hellenica*, V, 1, 31.

There was nothing to do but accept these terms. Persian gold and diplomacy, together with the perennial dissensions of the Greeks, had succeeded where a century earlier Persian steel had failed. The word of the Persian king was now law in European Greece, less obviously but almost as surely as in Asia. The Asiatic Greeks settled down under a government which enslaved them, but gave them order and commercial opportunities, while their European brethren experienced for another generation the miseries of disorder and violence.

SPARTA AS THE EXECUTRIX OF THE "KING'S PEACE" (387–371 B.C.)

Had the "King's Peace" been interpreted only in its most obvious sense — that of upholding the independence of the states not surrendered to Persia — it would undoubtedly have proved a boon to the war-torn Greek peninsula, but such was not to be the case. It must have been supplemented by "secret articles" whose provisions become apparent only when the subsequent history of the treaty is studied. Beginning with the later years of the Peloponnesian War, and continuing until 387, the Persian policy in Greece had been one of fomenting coalitions of lesser states against any one state that was powerful enough or disposed to give her trouble in Asia. Then a change occurred. Thereafter she chose the most powerful state as her representative, upheld its influence over the others and held it responsible for preventing aggressions against the king's dominions. The beneficiary of the policy from 387 to 371 was Sparta, to whom was committed the task of "guaranteeing" the independence of the other states.

Sparta as an Agent of Persia

With a subtlety and inconsistency strangely comparable to modern diplomacy, the Lacedaemonians construed the treaty as a mandate to break up all leagues and alliances in Greece except the Peloponnesian League of which they were the heads, and to regulate the internal governments of these states which had been left independent under its terms. Opportunities of both kinds were plentiful. Thebes had succeeded, during the later years of the Peloponnesian War, in organizing a strong Boeotian League under her leadership. She was immediately compelled to disband it. Corinth had voluntarily united with Argos, but was forced to dismiss her Argive garrison, take back her exiles (equivalent to the restoration of an oligarchy), and rejoin the Peloponnesian League. On vague charges of past disloyalty, war was declared against Mantinaea in Arcadia, and the city was broken up into villages dependent upon Sparta. At Phlius in the northern Peloponnesus, the democratic leaders were put to death and an oligarchy established.

These high-handed acts were crowned by two outstanding outrages — the destruction of the Olynthian League and the seizure of the Acropolis of Thebes. After the fall of the Athenian Empire, the Greek cities on the northern coast of the Aegean found themselves exposed to the risks of piracy on the sea and depredations by their Thracian and Macedonian neighbors on land. Olynthus, the most prosperous city of the Chalcidice, gradually built up a close federation of neighboring towns based upon a common citizenship and equality of civil rights for the citizens of all member communities. So equitable was this arrangement that even the enemies of the federation admitted the universal loyalty of its members to it. Force or persuasion was constantly adding new communities to the organization, and so strong had it become that it could treat as an equal with the Macedonian kings, whose capital, Pella, it had seized. Thus far it had proved to be one of the most promising political experiments ever conducted on Hellenic soil, but it was sure to arouse antagonism among neighbors jealous of their independence. Deputies from Acanthus and Apollonia, seconded by King Amyntas of Macedonia, complained to Sparta of the threat to their sovereignty. The Lacedaemonians declared war, and after a four years' struggle (383–379) succeeded in breaking up the league and enrolling its separate communities as their allies. Shortly after the outbreak of the Olynthian War, a party of Spartan soldiers on their way to the Chalcidice were induced by a Theban oligarch to seize the Cadmeia of Thebes by treachery. The leader of the Theban democrats was sent to Sparta to be executed, and Thebes entered the Spartan alliance. Lacedaemonian harmosts and garrisons also occupied other Boeotian towns.

The Spartan "Empire"

By 379, under pretext of safeguarding city-state independence, Sparta had built an "empire" which included all of the Peloponnesus, Megara, Boeotia, Locris, Phocis, part of Thessaly, and the former members of the Olynthian League. She had the backing of the Persians on the east and of Dionysius I, tyrant of Syracuse, on the west. Thus, her position now appeared to be impregnable. In reality it was built upon a foundation of sand, for nowhere were the Spartans capable of giving or supporting good government among their dependents. Even Xenophon, who is partial to the Lacedaemonians, furnishes us with ample evidence that their régime was one of violence and terror. The Athenian publicist Isocrates, writing about 380, thus describes the wretched condition of the Greek world:

> Pirates hold the seas, mercenaries occupy the cities, and instead of warring against foreigners in behalf of their country, the citizens fight with each other inside the walls. More cities have been taken in war than before the treaty was concluded, and because of the frequency of revolutions the inhabitants of the states live in greater despondency than the exiles.[1]

Plainly the Lacedaemonians had learned nothing and forgotten nothing since the days of Lysander and the decarchies. The very year which saw Spartan power at its height witnessed the beginning of its decline. The first break came to Thebes, where returning exiles slew the oligarchic leaders, expelled the Lacedaemonian garrison, and restored the democracy. Thereafter the most prominent figures in Theban politics were for a number of years Epaminondas and Pelopidas, who created a powerful army, invented a new and effective system of military tactics, and organized anew the Boeotian League. The Spartan harmost of Thespiae about the same time made a treacherous attempt to seize the Piraeus, thus driving Athens into an alliance with Thebes.

The Second Athenian Confederacy

Athens had been recovering her sea power gradually ever since Conon's victory at Cnidus. At the same time she was reestablishing her alliances in the Aegean. The earliest steps in this process have been traced. The "King's Peace" proved but a momentary obstacle to it. By 377 the movement was again in full swing, and that year a resolution was passed by the Athenian assembly providing a plan for a new confederacy. No state which owed allegiance to Persia could join it. Elaborate safeguards were provided to prevent the revival of oppression of the allies such as they had charged against Athens in the preceding century. No tribute was to be collected and no Athenian might own land in an allied state. Although Athens held the presidency, she agreed to grant the allies collectively the same weight as herself in determining the policies of the league. Precisely because of these precautions, the new confederacy was weaker than the old one had been, but for a time it was popular. In four years, over seventy states of the Aegean coast and islands joined.

[1] Isocrates, *Panegyricus*, 115 ff.

Gradual Decline of Spartan Power

Thebes, supported by Athens and her new confederacy, fought the common enemy for six years (377–371). The fortunes of war varied, but neither state gained decisive advantage. In 374, a settlement was nearly reached, but broke down. Then the time arrived for the realignment of powers which always occurred periodically in the internal wars of Greece. Thebes was growing too powerful, and Athens feared her arrogant ambition. No longer Sparta, but the Boeotians, constituted the chief menace, and in 371 the Athenians made peace. By the terms of the treaty the "King's Peace" was reaffirmed, though voluntary leagues and alliances were legalized. Thebes, however, insisted upon signing for the whole of the Boeotian League, and when prevented from doing so continued the war.

The decline of Spartan fortunes had been hastened by the rise of a new power in the north. Jason became tyrant of the Thessalian city of Pherae, and constituted himself the head of a united Thessalian League, with a mercenary force of six thousand men and a conscript army of twenty thousand infantry and six thousand cavalry. In 379, the Spartans admitted their inability to check him, and thereafter, until his death in 370, Jason of Pherae controlled Thessaly, acted as an overlord of Epirus, and allied himself with Macedonia, Thebes, and Athens at different times on equal terms. His power was purely personal, and after his assassination it dissolved.

The failure of the negotiations between Thebes and Sparta left the former, with the half-hearted assistance of Jason of Pherae, to stand against the united might of the Peloponnesian League. The match was not an uneven one. Epaminondas was the foremost general of his age, and the Boeotian army was of excellent quality. In the summer of 371, the Spartan king Cleombrotus invaded Boeotia with ten thousand men, of whom seven hundred were Spartan citizens. At Leuctra, Epaminondas confronted him with six thousand Boeotians, including the famous "Sacred Band" of three hundred Thebans, who were men of desperate valor. The tactics of Epaminondas marked a further departure from traditional standards. His cavalry was superior to that of the Spartans. It had been usual to draw up heavy-armed infantry in a battle line with an even depth of eight or twelve ranks, but he massed the Sacred Band on his left (opposite the Spartan king and citizen force) in a phalanx fifty ranks deep, at the same time holding back the other Thebans and the Boeotian allies. The Boeotian cavalry drove that of the Lacedaemonians from the field, and the Sacred Band struck the Spartan right wing with an impact that completely demolished it, killing a thousand of the enemy, including Cleombrotus and four hundred Spartan citizens. The advancing Boeotians then drove the enemy into their camp, until they acknowledged their defeat by evacuating Boeotia. Jason of Pherae arrived too late to participate in the battle.

The End of Spartan Supremacy

While Sparta was able to maintain her independence after the battle of Leuctra by reason of her isolation and her iron discipline, her military supremacy was ended. In a stirring passage, Xenophon relates that when the news of the defeat at Leuctra arrived at Sparta, the ephors forbade all signs of mourning, and that the relatives of the slain appeared in the streets with cheerful faces while those of the survivors showed humiliation. Even this heroic morale was powerless to rise superior to so overwhelming a disaster. Hardly a thousand male citizens now remained, and their energies would henceforth be fully occupied in the suppression of domestic discontent and in defense of the homeland. Spartan domination had been an unmitigated evil in Greece, and the tragic aspect of the situation was that the victors were as incompetent as the vanquished to found a Greek state system upon reason and justice. The years following Leuctra were to be as dreary as those that had preceded it.

THE THEBAN SUPREMACY (371-362 B.C.)

Thebes was now supreme in central Greece. Before the end of 370, she had organized a confederacy which extended from the borders of Aetolia on the west to include the island of Euboea on the east. Athens, of course, remained outside the new organization. Immediately after the battle of Leuctra, she called a peace congress of neutral states which ended in a pledge of mutual assistance against aggressors, but it was barren of good results. The weakening of Spartan prestige resulted in a wave of democratic revolutions which swept over the Peloponnesus. At Argos the oligarchic party was massacred. The Mantinaeans began to rebuild their city, and the Arcadians organized a league with a new city, Megalopolis, as its capital. When the Tegeans resisted incorporation into the new federation, they were compelled to join and Spartan efforts to save them failed. Democratic exiles returned to many cities, and soon only Corinth, Sicyon, and Phlius retained their oligarchies and Spartan sympathies. When an appeal to Athens by the anti-Spartan states in the Peloponnesus failed to bring aid, they had recourse to Thebes, who was eager to carry her operations into the immediate neighborhood of Sparta. In November, 370, a Theban army, which was increased by allied contingents to forty thousand men, passed the Isthmus, and remained in the Peloponnesus for several months. Epaminondas was in command.

The Reorganization of the Peloponnesus

The work of Epaminondas in the south shows a deliberate policy to weaken Sparta permanently. Laconia was ravaged from end to end, although Sparta herself resisted capture. The confederate army then assisted in the fortification of Mantinaea and Megalopolis and in placing the Arcadian League on a firm basis. Its next task was the liberation of Messenia, which had been for three centuries an integral part of Lacedaemon. A new city, Messene, was built on the slopes of Mount Ithome and strongly fortified. The Messenians, after centuries of humiliating subjection, resumed their place among the free peoples of Greece with an ease which has surprised modern scholars, and in 368 a Messenian was crowned victor in the footrace at the Olympic Games — a contest to which only free Greeks were admitted.

Sparta was henceforth impotent and her already acute social problem was vastly intensified by the loss of Messenia, which constituted the most fertile portion of her territory. Evil as her influence in Greek affairs had been in the half-century preceding her fall, she had been the only power capable of keeping order in the Peloponnesus and of defending Greece from foreign invasions. The time when an alien invader could conquer the peninsula was brought definitely nearer by her collapse.

The balance of power now having been upset completely by the rise of Thebes, Athens reversed her policy and joined with Sparta and Dionysius I of Syracuse to restrain the upstart. The usual diplomatic maneuvering ensued during the year 368, including a fruitless peace conference called at Delphi by the Greek agent of a Persian satrap. The year ended with another conference, called this time in the palace of Artaxerxes at Susa, and attended by delegates of all the contending powers. Pelopidas represented Thebes, and he so far surpassed his opponents as to secure from Artaxerxes a royal decree recognizing the Boeotian League and the freedom of Messenia, with no mention of the Arcadian League. This meant that Thebes virtually replaced Sparta as the Persian agent in Greece. When the other states refused to abide by the settlement, it became ineffective and the struggle continued.

In the north the circumstances were exceptionally favorable to the extension of Theban influence. The confusion which followed the death of Jason of Pherae and the weakness of Macedonia resulted in the intervention of a Boeotian army under Pelopidas which brought Thessaly and Macedonia into the Theban sphere of influence. Philip, later the king of Macedonia and founder of her greatness, was taken to Thebes as a hostage when fifteen years of age and remained there for three years. Probably it was there that he learned the lessons in war and diplomacy which later enabled him not only to organize a strong state and conquering army, but to play the crafty game of Greek politics with a masterly hand. In 364, Pelopidas was killed while on an expedition into Thessaly, but the next year the Thebans thoroughly subdued it.

Thebes Challenges the Athenian League

Thebes could not hope to extend her supremacy to the Aegean islands as long as the Athenian fleet controlled the sea. Accordingly, in 364, she completed a fleet of a hundred triremes with which Epaminondas sailed to dispute the Athenian title. Athens was no longer popular with her allies, whom she had once more begun to domineer, and the first year the Theban fleet seduced several of them from their allegiance, including Byzantium, the all-important key to the Black Sea wheat country. But this expedition gained no victories, and Thebes soon needed all her resources to fight the enemies that her own harsh conduct had roused against her in continental Greece. The next year Athens regained all the malcontents except Byzantium.

The year 364 probably marked the height of Theban fortunes. Macedonia, Thessaly, the central Greek states, Arcadia, Argos, and Messenia, were dependencies or allies of the mistress of Boeotia. Her power, however, was no more firmly rooted than that of Sparta had been, and the cause of her unpopularity was the same. Like her predecessors, she favored one party in her dependencies and allowed it to domineer over, if not grievously oppress, the other. In Achaea, as early as 367, a Theban attempt to transform the oligarchies into democracies had driven the oligarchs to ally themselves with Sparta. The Arcadian League soon became discontented with a protectress who did not secure Persian recognition for the league, and who interfered with its local independence. In Boeotia itself in 364, the city of Orchomenus was accused of disloyalty, its men slain, and the women and children sold as slaves. Such an act shocked the conscience of the Greek people. Harmosts and garrisons upheld Theban influence as they had formerly upheld that of Sparta. As city-state independence was no longer suited to the conditions of the time, it fared no better than before, but Hellenic public opinion was still overwhelmingly in favor of it. As a consequence, the independent cities were a unit in opposing the threat to their sovereignty. It was only a question of time until a break would occur.

In 363, affairs in the Peloponnesus began to assume a threatening aspect. The Arcadian League was disintegrating into two sections, the northern, or pro-Spartan, and the southern, or anti-Spartan. Athens, Sparta, Elis, and the Arcadian malcontents formed a coalition to end Boeotian interference in the Peloponnesus. The spring of 362 found Epaminondas in the south with a strong army to aid Argos, Messenia, and the few faithful Arcadian states. His campaign was only moderately successful, as he failed to take Sparta or Mantinaea, and his provisions ran short. His enemies were gathering, and only a victorious pitched battle would save his army from disaster. With consummate strategy he lured the enemy into an attack upon him at Mantinaea. The armies were about equal in numbers, each having nearly twenty-five thousand men. The tactics of Leuctra were repeated and the enemy fled, but Epaminondas was among the slain. With his last words he had advised his countrymen to make peace, which they did.

Fall of the Theban Supremacy

The genius of Epaminondas made possible the Theban supremacy, which died with him. He was the winner of its victories and the author of its most farsighted policies. It is unfair to blame him for the worst of the Theban mistakes, as some of them were made in direct disregard of his advice, and others while he was absent or in temporary disgrace. Despite his personal greatness, he left continental Greece worse off than he found it. Up to the battle of Leuctra, the Peloponnesus was the most orderly part of the Hellenic world, but at the death of Epaminondas, and largely because of his efforts, it was as chaotic as the rest. The free state of Messenia was his only lasting memorial. The remainder of Greece was weakened by the struggle which he initiated and it did little good to Thebes. As an imperialist state, she ranked below Athens and Sparta in ability and her supremacy was correspondingly short-lived.

SUMMARY

The period between the close of the Peloponnesian War and the death of Epaminondas demonstrated conclusively the inability of the great states of continental Greece to found a state system based upon reason and justice. Each attempt had been marked by greater disorder and more misery than the preceding one, and proved less enduring. It was not because the Hellenic mind was incapable of conceiving larger political units than the city-state, for a few thinkers like Isocrates had envisioned a Pan-Hellenic union. Negotiations and arbitration had been tried, as we have seen in the several peace conferences mentioned in preceding pages. Indeed, it is questionable whether city-state particularism alone will account for the political decadence which came upon the Greeks in the fourth century, for at an earlier period these small sovereignties had existed in amity with each other. It required the precise combination of city-state particularism, selfish individualism, and the party system which prevailed in the peninsula to explain the dreadful succession of wars, revolutions, executions, confiscations, and other calamities which prepared Greece for the Macedonian conquest.

Was the party system a cause or a result? Must we not trace the whole matter back to certain fundamental traits of Greek character which, acting under the conditions of fourth-century life, caused an economic and social maladjustment that rendered strife or slavery the only alternatives? Even so, some future historian may puzzle over the disordered world of the nineteen-thirties and the nineteen-forties in an effort to discover the causes of its lapse from cosmic sanity, and then, as now, the ultimate reason will probably be an insoluble mystery. The greatest wonder is that in the midst of so much disorder and misery the Greeks could attain such triumphs in art, literature, and philosophy as those we shall study presently.

28

Western Greece in the Fourth Century B.C.

SICILY TO THE RISE OF DIONYSIUS I

IN THE PRECEDING CHAPTER we have seen how the city-state system in the Greek Peninsula crumbled under the impact of wars between cities and parties, Persian interference, and growing individualism. In the West the same cultural trends observable in old Greece affected the Hellenic population, and Carthage was for them an even more formidable enemy than Persia was for the eastern Greeks. But the western Greeks had an added disadvantage from which their brethren in the Greek peninsula were free. Their settlements formed a mere fringe about the coasts of southern Italy and Sicily, exposed to attacks from the interior of the dispossessed Italic and Sicilian natives. Under these conditions, the savage party strife and city-state imperialism characteristic of the age became doubly ruinous, and the fortunes of western Hellas suffered an almost continuous decline. In this, as in preceding periods, the Sicilian city of Syracuse occupied the center of the stage.

Syracuse, a Radical Democracy

From the death of Hiero I in 466 until the failure of the Athenian expedition in 413, Syracuse had been governed by a moderate democracy of a type peculiar to the western Dorian cities, but the common people profited by the part which they had taken in the defense of the city to establish a radical democracy in its place. The new government aided the Spartans against Athens, continued to intervene in the quarrels of the Greek and native communities of the island, and experienced the usual political strife at home. It was the wrong period for such actions, and the Sicilian Greeks soon regretted their short-sighted pugnacity.

There are many phases of the history of the western Greeks which cannot be thoroughly understood because so little is known about their Italian,

Gallic, Etruscan, and Carthaginian neighbors. For centuries Carthage was one of the great powers of the civilized world, yet for long periods her internal history is almost a blank, and such information as we possess is furnished quite incidentally by historians of other nationalities. Thus, we can only guess at the reason for her inactivity in Sicily for the seventy years following the disaster which her army experienced at Himera in 480.[1] It may have been attributable to internal disorders, for Carthaginian government in Africa was unpopular, and both her native and Phoenician subjects often rebelled when defeats experienced by their oppressors abroad seemed to promise success to their efforts. Or it may have been fear of the dominant Athenian navy that restrained her. At any rate, in 409 she was again ready to make a bid for the mastery of Sicily. Hannibal, the grandson of the Carthaginian general who fell at Himera, landed near Lilybaeum with a mixed force of citizens and mercenaries which contemporary rumor estimated at two hundred thousand to five hundred thousand men. With this army he besieged the Greek city of Selinus. Disdaining the timid maxims of Greek siege-craft, he hurled his barbarian troops at the doomed city for nine days in cont nuous assaults, and finally stormed it before any relief could be obtained from Syracuse. The luckless population experienced nameless horrors at the hands of Hannibal's brutal Gallic and Spanish mercenaries, and the walls and public buildings were destroyed. A similar fate awaited Himera, on the northern coast. Despite half-hearted attempts of the Syracusans and other Sicilian Greeks to relieve it, the city was taken by assault and those of the people who did not escape on allied ships fell into the hands of the enemy. With cold cruelty, common to the Semites but rarely found among the Greeks, Hannibal sacrificed three thousand of the male cap ives to the spirit of his grandfather. Then he returned to Africa. The sorry part played by Syracuse in this war was caused primarily by the bitter strife between the radicals and conservatives within her own walls, which two years lat r burst forth as civil war.

In 406 the Carthagin ans returned. Thi time they laid siege to the great city of Acragas. A confederate Greek army of thirty-five thousand

---

[1] Political conditions at Carthage may help to account for her quiescence. From a later period we learn that there were two political parties. The mercantile aristocracy favored an active program of expansion which woulɑ open up new markets. The landlords, on the other hand, opposed foreign wars. After the battle of Himera, the family of the defeated commander was forced into exile, and Hannibal himself had spent his youth as a fugitive in a Sicilian Greek city. Probably his family belonged to the mercantilist party, and after the fiasco of 480 this party would be driven from power by its less aggressive rival. But the mercantilists must have regained the ascendancy shortly before 409.

men advanced from Syracuse to relieve it, but a series of unparalleled
blunders nullified its efforts. All that was accomplished was to rescue the
Acragantines, leaving the city to be sacked by the enemy. The only alternatives for the Sicilian Greeks seemed to be slavery or extermination.

THE TYRANNY OF DIONYSIUS I (405–367 B.C.)

The succession of shameful and appalling disasters which the Sicilian
Greeks suffered between 409 and 406 shook the confidence of the Syracusans
in their government, and at such a time a Greek city-state was ready for
revolution or tyranny. In this crisis there appeared a eader in the person
of Dionysius, the son of Hermocrates. Our own age, with its collectivist
dictators, is unusually well fitted to understand th s type of character.
Although of the lower classes, he had enjoyed a good education and his
understanding of mob psychology must have been profound. With brilliant eloquence and utter disregard of truth, he could sway assemblies in
any direction he wished. Even after his worst acts, he could, by a few
clever gestures, regain his popularity. Apparently, he was moved by
neither love of his native city nor Hellenic patriotism, for much of his behavior was in callous disregard of both. He was equally devoid of common humanity. Only greed and love of power appear to have influenced
him, although there are modern attempts to interpret his acts as profound
statesmanship. It is as reasonable to ascribe similar motives to the conduct of Critias or Alcibiades, who, like him, were products of the Age of
Individualism. Unlike so many other tyrants in all ages of the world, he
was entirely free from gross personal vices, and even displayed a taste for
literature. In his spare moments he wrote a number of tragedies, one of
which received a prize at Athens.

Dionysius Becomes Tyrant of Syracuse

Taking advantage of the shame and indignation of his fellow citizens
over the Acragantine disaster, Dionysius accused the Syracusan generals
of treason and secured their deposition. A new board was elected, of
which he was a member. His persuasive oratory secured the recall of all
political exiles, who naturally became his partisans. He won the support
of the army by promises of increased pay. Then, accusing his colleagues
of collusion with the enemy, he secured their dismissal and his own election as sole general with extraordinary powers. Shortly afterward, skillful mendacity induced the people to vote him a guard of six hundred
mercenaries, which he raised to one thousand. Before the end of 405, the

panicstricken and deluded citizenry found that they had a master, and in bartering away their freedom they had not even obtained a competent military leader. The first campaign of Dionysius ended as disastrously as those of his predecessors, and in a disgraceful treaty he granted to the Carthaginians possession of the rest of Sicily in return for recognition of his control over Syracuse and the freedom of a few other Greek cities.

The next eight years (405–397) were spent by Dionysius in consolidating his power at home. Two rebellions were crushed and the property of the aristocratic rebels was confiscated. The island of Ortygia, which commanded the city and harbor of Syracuse and had previously been the home of Syracusan aristocrats, was transformed into an impregnable fortress, in which only the tyrant and his mercenaries and henchmen might live. The citizen body was reconstituted. Many non-Hellenic mercenaries, along with emancipated slaves and persons transported from outlying cities, were granted civic rights. To these new citizens were given farms carved from confiscated estates, to which their titles were, of course, only good so long as Dionysius remained in power. By such measures, and by the ruthless execution of some ten thousand malcontents, he put down opposition and secured a body of devoted partisans. Syracuse was surrounded by stronger walls than those of any other European city, while her arsenals were stocked with arms and armor for eighty thousand infantry and three thousand cavalry, and the latest and most efficient siege machinery. A navy which ultimately included four hundred triremes and some larger vessels enabled him to repel his enemies on the seas.

To finance this titanic program, Dionysius resorted to the most cruel and oppressive expedients. The populations of several Greek cities were sold into slavery. A twenty per cent annual capital levy was imposed upon property-holders. Temples were despoiled of their treasures, and the coinage was debased. Extortion and confiscation made up what was lacking.

Dionysius' War With Carthage

In 397, having completed his preparations, Dionysius resumed the war with Carthage. Posing as a champion of Hellenism against the barbarian, he began hostilities by encouraging a series of outrages against enemy citizens in his dominions and by courting popularity in other ways. The war lasted five years (397–392). At one time Dionysius penetrated to the western extremity of Sicily, while at another he was besieged in Syracuse. He won a sweeping victory over the Carthaginian Himilco, but allowed his enemy to escape — in return, it is said, for a bribe of three hundred talents. In fact, he could not afford to be too victorious, for if the danger of a Carthaginian attack were removed, the excuse for further existence of his tyranny would be gone. Peace found him in possession of all but a small part of Sicily. Two more wars with Carthage resulted in small losses for the Syracusan power, and at the end of Dionysius' reign he held about two-thirds of the island.

Toward the Greeks of Sicily and Italy he was a hard master, who actually seemed to prefer to associate with the barbarians rather than with his own people. He sold the population of Naxos, Catana, and Rhegium into slavery, and depopulated Hipponium, Caulonia, and Leontini to swell the population of Syracuse. With Locri, on the Ionian shore of the "toe" of Italy, he was on terms of alliance, for it had furnished him a wife; but toward Rhegium, which controlled the Italian side of the Strait of Messina, he displayed implacable enmity. An unsuccessful siege of Rhegium in 391 marked the beginning of hostilities. The Greeks of the threatened area had formed a league under the leadership of Croton to withstand the Lucanian invader from the back country, and it now took the field to repel the Greek invaders from across the strait. Dionysius' answer was to ally himself with the Lucanians. A war lasting four years made him master of the Italian coast of the Ionian Sea as far north as Croton, and of the western coast to Terina. Tarentum and her immediate neighbors were too far distant and too strong to be reached, and with them he remained on terms of friendship if not of alliance.

Alliances, Conquests, and Colonization in Italy

But the interest of the Syracusan tyrant in Italian affairs did not stop there. The Etruscan Confederacy in northwestern Italy was harassed by both the native Italians and Gauls. With the latter, Dionysius formed an alliance which enabled him to ravage the coasts of Etruria (where he took booty worth fifteen hundred talents from a single temple), to found a naval station in Corsica, and to take possession of the island of Elba. On the Adriatic Sea he built Issa and Pharos along the Illyrian coast, and Ancona and Hadria on the Italian side. His hold upon the Adriatic region was strengthened by alliances with several Italian tribes, and with the Epirote prince Alcetas. The Syracusan navy was the largest in the western Mediterranean and diverted much trade to the harbor of Syracuse. In the Aegean he aided the Spartans to enforce the "King's Peace," and was a member of the anti-Theban alliance formed during the 360's. When

Dionysius died in 367, he was one of the most powerful sovereigns in the civilized world.

The character of the tyrant of Syracuse has been described. Aside from personal aggrandizement, his achievements in no respect justified the huge efforts which he exerted. The nature of his position compelled him to pay too much attention to the maintenance of his personal power, and he gave scant heed to the welfare of his subjects. He was not a Hellenist, for his dealings with the enemies of the western Greeks were notorious. His enormous confiscations, destruction of Greek cities and the sale of their people into slavery, oppressive taxation, pillaging of temples, and failure to protect his dominions from periodic Carthaginian ravages must have left the Italian and Sicilian Greeks in a worse condition than they were at the beginning of his reign. In Syracuse, he indulged in the usual despotic pastime of erecting showy buildings, but intellectually his subjects did little to match the splendid achievements of their eastern brethren. The philosopher Plato, with singular optimism, strove to convert him to the notion of founding an ideal Platonic state, but the experiment ended in disaster for the philosopher, who was said to have been deported and sold into slavery. If Dionysius had lived for a few more years or had had successors equal to himself, Syracuse might have become the capital of an empire embracing most of the Hellenic peoples, with much barbarian territory in addition. But the great opportunity for an enterprising monarch to bring the continental Greeks into subjection did not arise until the battle of Mantinaea ended the Theban supremacy, and by that time he had been dead five years. His successor was unequal to the task. To judge from the visible consequences of Syracusan imperialism, we may pronounce it fortunate that this work of conquest and unification was reserved for others.[1]

DIONYSIUS II, DION, AND TIMOLEON (367–336 B.C.)

As so often happened in Greek tyrannies, the heir of Dionysius I was lacking, both by temperament and education, in the ability to hold what

---

[1] Many take a more favorable view of Dionysius I than this. For example, J. B. Bury (*Cambridge Ancient History*, VI, 134–136) calls him "the most important Greek statesman between Pericles and Philip II." He admits that Dionysius in all probability betrayed the Syracusans at least once during his wars with Carthage, and that he "was not interested in the development of Hellenic civilization." In common with some other students of the period, Professor Bury considers Dionysius a champion of Europe in general rather than of the Greeks. The opinion expressed in the text is based upon the data which precede it.

his father had won. Dionysius II was weak, self-indulgent, and at times vicious. During his father's lifetime he had been deprived of all education in the art of government because of paternal jealousy. At first Dion and Philistus, formerly ministers of his father, attempted to guide him, but they soon quarreled, and Dion was forced into exile. In 357, he returned as a rebel and thereafter confusion reigned. For ten years intermittent civil war raged, and the Greek cities of Italy and Sicily fell under the sway of independent tyrants. In 347, Dionysius II regained a shadow of power in Syracuse, but that was all. Carthage again threatened war, and the western Greeks were in a state of misery and terror.

Sicily Liberated

It was under these conditions that Corinth, the "mother-city" of Syracuse, came to the rescue. In 344, she dispatched to Sicily a force of seven hundred mercenaries under Timoleon, one of the finest characters in Greek history. No previous experience or transcendent genius fitted him for the task of bringing peace and freedom to tortured Sicily, but with common sense, high principles, and unusual good fortune he was able to accomplish it. Dionysius ended his days as a schoolmaster in Corinth, the tyrants were expelled from the other cities, and moderate democracies were established. In 341, Timoleon administered a crushing defeat to the Carthaginians, and two years later they made peace. A federation was established to protect the Sicilian cities from further Carthaginian aggression. Immigration from other parts of Hellas offset the losses caused by war and disorder. Most remarkable of all, in 337, Timoleon laid down his powers and retired to private life. It is sad to relate that in less than twenty years almost all the political effects of his work had vanished, but in the meantime Greek Sicily enjoyed a prosperity unknown for a long time before his coming.

THE FURTHER DECLINE OF THE ITALIAN GREEKS

The break-up of the "empire" of Dionysius I brought little relief to the hard-pressed Hellenic colonies along the Italian coast of the Ionian Sea. Gradually Dionysius II lost control of his overseas possessions, but the attacks of the Italic mountaineers still continued, and resistance to them had been weakened by the repressive policies of the tyrant. About 356, a group of these invaders organized the Bruttian League, with its capital at Consentia, and conquered many Greek cities along the "toe" of the peninsula.

Rhegium, Croton, Locri, and Thurii still maintained their independence, however, and farther east, Tarentum, Heraclea, and Metapontum seem to have defended themselves successfully against the Lucanians and Messapians.

Mercenaries from Greece

The Tarentines, enervated by prosperity and feeling unequal to the task of defending themselves, relied upon *condottieri* from the Greek homeland rather than upon their own citizen troops. In 346, they called upon their "mother-city" for aid, and King Archidamus came to the rescue with a mercenary army. His endeavor eventually ended in disaster, for the king and most of his army were killed in battle in 340. The next appeal was to Alexander of Molossis, an Epirote prince and relative of Alexander the Great. A few outstanding successes were gained against the enemy, but Alexander was not actuated by altruistic motives, and it soon became apparent that he intended to found an empire of which Tarentum and her allies were to form a part. Civil war broke out between the Tarentines and their protector, and Alexander, defeated in battle by the Italians, was assassinated. Twice more the story was repeated in all essentials, with the Spartan Cleonymus and the Epirote Pyrrhus as the chief actors. The outcome was always about the same. The Italian Greeks could not defend themselves without outside aid, and they could not trust such auxiliaries when they came. Relief from the menace of attack by the inland tribes was to come only when Rome, the stabilizing force among the Italian peoples, succeeded in uniting the Greeks and their enemies under her all-embracing power.

29

****

The Rise of Macedonia

Eastern Greece and Her Neighbors

The death of Dionysius I and the dissolution of the Theban Confederacy which followed the battle of Mantinaea signalized definitely the failure of city-state imperialism as a means of effecting the political consolidation of the Greek people. There was now no important state which had not attempted to perform the task, and all had failed. Yet to the modern scholar it seems clear that the day of independent, isolated, and mutually hostile city-states was nearing its end. Conditions in the world of the fourth century were definitely hostile to the system, and the question after 362 B.C. was whether equal and voluntary confederation or foreign conquest would accomplish the task at which Athens, Thebes, Sparta, and Syracuse had failed.

Political Thought and Experience Concerning Federations

We must not, of course, assume that the fourth-century Greeks saw this as clearly as we do now. The publicist Isocrates was, indeed, aware of it, and addressed eloquent appeals, first to the Athenians and then to Philip of Macedonia, to provide leadership for the movement toward a Pan-Hellenic Federation. Demosthenes, as we shall see, had a similar aim. But Plato and Aristotle, who rank among the world's greatest minds and who were formulating their philosophies during the period under discussion, continued to write and think about city-state government as if its perfection were still the central problem of the statesmen. Indeed, the previous experience of the Greek people with political groupings larger than the individual city-state had been disappointing. Each attempt had, in its turn, degenerated into an instrument of oppression by the state which had sponsored it. The Hellenic temperament and political tradition made this nearly

514

inevitable. Free federation was, therefore, a remote possibility, but foreign conquest was, under the prevailing conditions, more than probable.

Foreign Aggressors: Caria and Macedonia

The weakness of Persia, although momentarily relieved by the fierce energy of Artaxerxes Ochus (359–338), rendered the possibility of her active intervention in Greek affairs very remote, but two other neighbors, Mausolus of Caria and Philip of Macedonia, were sufficiently near and aggressive to be real sources of danger. Mausolus was a Hellenized vassal of the Persian king, who controlled extensive territories in southwestern Asia Minor. Although outwardly loyal to his master, he acted almost like an independent sovereign, maintaining his own fleet and army and conquering several of the Aegean islands for himself. He probably instigated the revolt of the Athenian allies which broke out in 357 and which cost Athens most of her overseas possessions. His death in 353 removed the potential threat to Greek independence, leaving the word "mausoleum" as the chief reminder of his career in later times. The Macedonian peril was more persistent.

Macedonia, like Caria, lay in the twilight zone of lands which were neither definitely Greek nor entirely foreign. Whether or not the Macedonians should be classed as Greeks has been a matter of dispute in both ancient and modern times. Their Hellenic partisans accepted them as kinsmen and their enemies stigmatized them as barbarians. Their country lay at the northwest corner of the Aegean Sea and included the valleys of the Axius and Haliacmon rivers, with an indefinite sphere of influence reaching into the upper valleys of these streams and the hill country between them. On the south, Macedonia was bounded by Thessaly and the Gulf of Thessalonica, and on the east, it bordered upon Thrace. It was a wild, undeveloped land, whose people were centuries behind their Greek neighbors in cultural development. In the more fertile areas agriculture was practiced, but the majority lived by hunting and stock-raising. Commerce and manufactures were practically non-existent. There were few cities in the land except Greek colonies along the coast which were independent of the Macedonian king and prevented his access to the sea. In the lowlands there were large estates tilled by free peasants and owned by aristocratic landlords. King and court were largely Hellenized, but it was a crude and primitive form of Greek civilization that prevailed. Polygamy was still practiced by the kings, and drunkenness, violence, and assassinations were common. The uplands were inhabited by half-barbarous clans and tribes

ruled by hereditary princes, who yielded reluctant obedience to strong low-
land kings and flouted weak ones. Beyond these unruly vassal states were
the even more barbarous Illyrians, Paeonians, and Thracians, who ravaged
the border lands or allied themselves with rebel vassals as occasion offered.
Thus, the Macedonian crown was an insecure one, and many of the kings
before Philip II had perished in battle or by assassination.

Macedonian rulers had participated in Greek politics since the Persian
wars. The Athenian Empire had for some time rendered them helpless
until Archelaus I (413–400) took advantage of the Peloponnesian War to
build a strong and progressive state. His death was followed by disorders
and dynastic disputes, and Amyntas II (393–369) had to struggle throughout his reign against Illyrians, the Olynthian League, rebellious high-
landers, and pretenders to the throne. Before his death, conditions had
improved, but of his two older sons, one was killed by his mother and the
other fell in battle with the Illyrians. In 359, the youngest son Philip
pushed aside an infant nephew and seized the crown. Macedonia was now
ready to play a worthy part in world affairs.

The Consolidation of Macedonia (359–356 b.c.)

The reign of Philip II (359–336) marked his country's "coming-of-age."
At his accession he was twenty-four years old and already had had a varied
experience. He had been a hostage among the Illyrians and spent three
years of exile at Thebes in the days of Epaminondas. Later he assisted his
brother and predecessor in the government of the country. In character
he was an odd mixture of the civilized man and the barbarian. He appreciated Greek culture, kept Greeks at his court, and could, when convenient,
show charming courtesy. He had acquired an astonishing knowledge of
the weaknesses of Greek character, and could outwit their most acute
practitioners in the dubious arts of politics and diplomacy. For Athens
he had an unfailing respect, which led him to deal tenderly with her in
spite of her persistent opposition to his policies. On the other hand, his
bibulous habits, colorful marital escapades, and occasional acts of callous
cruelty betrayed the savagery that lay close beneath the veneer of civilization. But whether Greek or barbarian, he was an organizing genius whose
restless ambition drove him through every danger and hardship to the
achievement of objectives far beyond the view of other men. At the same
time he could wait patiently for opportunity to accomplish his purposes.
He could be cruel and perfidious, or kindly and forgiving, as circumstances demanded, and he seldom failed to read the minds of others cor-

rectly. The sources from which our knowledge of his career is drawn must be used with caution, for it is inevitable that they should be strongly prejudiced either for or against him. The adverse bias is particularly plain in the orations of his bitter enemy, Demosthenes.

Philip's Liberation of Macedonia

Philip came to the Macedonian throne at a time of desperate crisis. His predecessor had just been defeated and slain by the Illyrians, who were ravaging the country. The vassal states were disloyal, and five pretenders disputed his right to the crown. Within two years he had cleared the land of invaders, disposed of the pretenders, and begun the organization of the finest army which the world had thus far known. He was now ready to undertake a program of aggrandizement.

The Macedonian army, as gradually reorganized by Philip, embodied the effective combination of the most up-to-date varieties of armament and tactical formations then known. Under former kings it had consisted chiefly of cavalry drawn from the aristocratic landlord class, who held the proud title of "companions" of the king. Philip added the famous *Macedonian phalanx*. It was composed of heavy-armed infantry, and its arms and formation included features adopted from both Iphicrates' peltasts and the Theban phalanx of Epaminondas. The armor of the phalangite was lighter than that of an ordinary Greek hoplite, but, instead of the short stabbing spear of the hoplite, which was not over seven feet long and was wielded with one hand only, the phalangite carried a lance some twelve or sixteen feet in length, using both hands. The phalanx was drawn up in more open order than an ordinary Greek battle line and was about sixteen ranks deep. So long as it held its formation, it could bear down opposition by sheer weight and pushing power. Philip's army also included ordinary heavy-armed infantry, lightarmed archers and slingers, and the most efficient siege machinery then known. In battle, the phalanx usually held the enemy's front in check, while the "companion" cavalry struck the decisive blow, but this arrangement could be varied to meet any situation. Constant training and campaigns kept this force in top condition, and it was inspired by the personal presence of the king, who shared its hardships and rewarded its efforts. By drawing into his army men from the turbulent vassal states and inspiring them with patriotic fervor, Philip developed a national sentiment in these outlying regions which went far toward creating a united Macedonian people.

Early Conquests

With order restored at home, the new king was able to undertake the rounding-out of his frontiers. In 357, he seized the district on his eastern frontier which included Amphipolis and the gold mines of Mount Pangaeus, near which he founded the city of Philippi. Before long the mines were yielding him an income of a thousand talents a year ($1,700,000), to which must be added the ordinary revenues of the crown, proceeds from the sale of the spoils of war, and, later, customs duties from the seaports which he captured. Thus, he had far greater resources than any of the Greek city-states, and could not only support his fleet and army, but could bribe Greek politicians to represent his interests or traitors to deliver up besieged cities.

THE MACEDONIAN CONQUEST OF GREECE (356–338 B.C.)

The rise of a strong power in the north was a threat to the independence of the Greeks, but preoccupation with other matters prevented them from seeing this fact in time to check the menace. The year 357 saw the outbreak of two wars which were to have calamitous effects: the revolt of the Athenian allies and the Sacred War against Phocis. The former was probably fomented by Mausolus of Caria, who took advantage of the discontent occasioned by tactless acts of the Athenians and by their recent conquest of Euboea and the Thracian Chersonesus (Gallipoli peninsula). By forming an alliance with the oligarchic factions in the Athenian dependencies, the Carian prince was able to foment a rebellion of some of the principal states, including the all-important city of Byzantium. Athens mismanaged her military operations, her government was short of funds, and her people were reluctant to exert the effort necessary to win the war. After a disastrous struggle lasting three years, she was compelled to recognize the independence of the rebels, and most of her other maritime allies immediately deserted her. The war cost the Athenians a thousand talents in money, along with other losses, and it prevented them from taking early steps to protect their possessions on the Thracian coast from Philip.

The Sacred War Against Phocis; Philip Against Athens

The Sacred War was to convulse central Greece for a decade. Phocis had for ages been at war with her neighbors, Locris, Thebes, and Thessaly. These states controlled the Delphic Amphictyony, and, apparently under

Theban leadership, began to use this organization to settle old political scores. A number of wealthy Phocians were heavily fined for sacrilege alleged to have been committed against Apollo, and the Spartans were assessed five hundred talents for their seizure of the Theban Cadmeia twenty-seven years before. The Phocian victims refused to pay, and one of them, Philomelus, raised a mercenary army and seized Delphi. Sparta and Athens gave him support. By appropriating the temple treasures, the Phocians secured funds to pay their mercenaries, and so long as these funds lasted they were more than a match for their neighbors. Thus, all the powers from Thessaly southward were rendered impotent to check Macedonian encroachments, and Philip was later given an opening which enabled him to gain a foothold in the peninsula.

While meeting the perils of the first two years of his reign, Philip had courted Athens, but the understanding did not last long. Soon he began seizing Greek cities on his borders which Athens claimed as allies or subjects. She retaliated in 357 by declaring war. Hostilities between Philip and the Athenians lasted eleven years. For the latter, it was a lost contest from the start, for the Macedonian king was a master of underhand diplomacy, and he could pursue his objectives with a consistency which an unstable democratic assembly, torn between conflicting parties and policies, could never hope to attain. At the outset he tricked the Athenians into helping him to secure Amphipolis and Pydna, and soon afterward he formed an alliance with the Olynthian League, which had revived after the decline of Sparta. Gradually he advanced his boundaries eastward along the Thracian coast. On the southwest he intervened in the stormy politics of Thessaly, where another tyrant of Pherae, aided by the Phocians, was struggling for the mastery of the country. After a preliminary defeat, Philip drove the Pheraean tyrant from the country and in 351 became general of the Thessalian League. During this period Athens did little or nothing.

Several causes combined to produce the sorry showing made by Athens in this war, and of these one in particular demands consideration. From 355 to 350 the leading spirit in her politics was Eubulus, a cautious and conservative financier and an advocate of peace. In some fields he accomplished much, for in addition to bringing the fleet once more up to three hundred triremes, he built roads, secured a water-supply for the city, and encouraged her commercial interests in various ways. One of his measures, however, largely nullified the good accomplished by the others. Since the days of Pericles the state had supported religious festivals, including the drama, and the money reserved for this purpose was known as the *Theoric*

Fund. Eubulus, feeling it necessary to buy popular support for an otherwise sound program, carried a law providing that the whole excess revenue of each year should be paid into this fund and making it a capital offense to move the repeal of the arrangement. Thereafter, for many years the state was rendered impotent in any crisis by a shortage of funds; for the people refused to vote for other purposes money which normally would be expended on their pleasures.

Demosthenes

The chief opponent of Eubulus, and the most bitter enemy of Macedonia, was Demosthenes (384–322). The son of a prosperous manufacturer, orphaned in childhood, he had been defrauded by his guardians of most of his inheritance. Eager for vengeance, he had studied oratory in order to prosecute the embezzlers, and had overcome great physical handicaps by sheer will power. The story of how he cured himself of stammering by speaking with his mouth full of pebbles has been an example of indomitable perseverance to all subsequent ages. He became the greatest orator in Athens, with a compelling eloquence that carried all before it. Unlike the opportunist Eubulus, Demosthenes looked beyond the field of local politics to the larger one of Hellenic affairs. There he saw the threat to Greek independence embodied in the rise of two aggressive monarchies in the near-by regions. He realized that the only escape from the danger of foreign conquest depended upon the formation of a league of states strong enough to repel the invaders. It was the duty of Athens to take the lead in the enterprise, and for this her citizens would require the self-sacrificing heroism of their ancestors of the preceding century. In some respects this ideal was impracticable under the existing conditions. The Athenian people had become individualistic and self-centered and were unwilling to make the sacrifices necessary to its realization. Aside from this, the object was intensely practical. Certainly, if the Greeks were to remain free, this was the only way that their freedom could be preserved. Demosthenes, seeing in Philip the most threatening enemy of Athens and of Greece, prepared to goad his fellow countrymen into action.

In 351, the Athenian orator opened his campaign with the address known as the *First Philippic.* Philip had mastered Thessaly, his cruisers were raiding the Aegean possessions of Athens, and a piratical foray had recently been made upon the coast of Attica itself. The speaker bids his fellow countrymen take courage. Philip has won successes against them because they have not yet begun to fight. He draws a lively picture of the passive curiosity with which they listen to rumors that their enemy is sick or dead. What would it profit them if it were true? "Should this man meet with mishap, you will soon create another Philip if you act thus; for he has been exalted not so much by his own strength as by your negligence."[1] He then takes up the specific measures necessary to check the enemy. Transports and ships of war must be kept in readiness; and a force of two thousand infantry and two hundred cavalry, of which one-fourth ought to be Athenian citizens, should be prepared at all times to relieve points threatened by attack. Generals must be chosen for their ability to command armies rather than for their fine appearance in religious processions. With biting irony directed at the Theoric Fund, he reminds his hearers that, although they cannot defend their possessions, they have the finest festivals in the world. Activity, courage, and self-sacrifice will save them, and nothing else will. His advice was well received, but as the danger was too remote to be immediately threatening, nothing was done.

The "Olynthiac Orations"

Two years later, Demosthenes was again upon the speaker's platform. The Olynthians were discontented and made peace with Athens in 352; but not until 349 was Philip ready to punish them for their defection. As Olynthus and her allies controlled the Chalcidic peninsula, which shut off a large part of his kingdom from the sea, he was determined to secure it. Olynthus, in terror, appealed to Athens for aid. Demosthenes, ever ready to check the rising Macedonian power, delivered his three *Olynthiac* orations urging the Athenians to send immediate relief. Athens herself, he reiterates, has by her apathy built the power of Philip. He is forever on the move, intriguing, negotiating, fighting, while his enemies sit tamely at home and do nothing. The orator reminds them that some time before in an emergency they had decreed the sending of forty ships, with a large force of citizens and a campaign chest of sixty talents, to the point which was in danger. "That was in the fifth month. The remainder of the year passed, and three months of the next year. Then, after the Mysteries, you reluctantly sent Charidemus with ten empty ships and five talents in money."[2] Not decrees, but action, will be their salvation.

Aid was sent to the Olynthians, but too late. Most of the Chalcidic cities were saved by immediate surrender to the Macedonian king. Olynthus and a few other places held out and were besieged. The oligarchic

---

[1] *First Philippic*, 42, 11.   [2] *Third Olynthiac*, 4 and 5.

party in each was in communication with Philip. Traitors opened the gates, and the unfortunate Olynthians were visited with sack and ruin (August, 348). An Arcadian partisan of Macedonia received thirty captive women and children as a present from his friend the king, and heart-rending stories were told of the fate of other prisoners.

Philip Triumphant: The Peace of Philocrates

Philip was now supreme, either as lord or ally, over a territory reaching from the southern boundary of Thessaly to the Hellespont and far into the back country. In central and southern Greece his partisans were in control of many cities, for he was the patron of oligarchies, and all men of property were likely to view him with favor. His war against the Phocians drew the Thebans to his side, and where none of these means prevailed there was always bribery. Athenian efforts against him had been fruitless. When, after the fall of Olynthus, Eubulus attempted to form a Pan-Hellenic League along the lines advocated by Demosthenes, it was unsuccessful. The Phocians, after a succession of alternate victories and defeats, had begun to quarrel among themselves, so that none of their allies could continue to co-operate with them. Hence, Athens was ready for any sort of honorable peace, and she found Philip willing to negotiate. He was engaged in a war with Thrace and needed leisure to deal with the Phocians. In spite of the long war, he still cherished the hope of securing Athens for an ally in the prosecution of his larger schemes for the formation of a Pan-Hellenic League.

The Peace of Philocrates (346), which took its name from its chief Athenian advocate, left to each contestant the territories which he should hold at the time of its ratification. Athens kept the Thracian Chersonesus and with it control of the all-important Black Sea route, but Philip gained title to the conquests which he had made during the war. A defensive alliance was arranged between the late enemies. The allies of each were to be permitted to become parties to the agreement. This clause raised the question of the Phocians, who were allies of Athens, but against whom Philip was particularly bitter. By suave mendacity, either he or his Athenian partisans (their respective degrees of responsibility are still in dispute) deluded the assembly into believing that Philip did not intend to punish the Phocians, but rather their enemies, the Thebans. Thus, they were excluded from the peace, with momentous consequences. As the Thebans had been friendly to Philip throughout, it required considerable naïveté to accept this explanation, but the Athenians did so.

Philip would have been glad to make the peace a lasting one, provided that the Athenians would co-operate in, or at least remain neutral toward, his subsequent enterprises. The pro-Macedonian party among them would have been willing to accede to his views. Isocrates, the aged publicist, who a generation earlier had written his *Panegyric* to prove that all of the Greeks should unite under Athenian leadership, forget their quarrels, and wage war upon the Persians, now repeated the plea in his *Address to Philip*. The second plea, however, has this difference from the earlier one: in 346 the Macedonian king, and not Athens, was to take the lead in the unification. Aeschines, who up to this time had been a virulent opponent of Philip and had served with Demosthenes on the embassies which negotiated the treaty, was so charmed with the personality, and, so Demosthenes alleged, the bribes of the Macedonian ruler, that he become his ardent partisan and a leader of the "Philippizing" party. Indeed, the second embassy, sent to secure ratification of the pact, was composed almost entirely of his friends, Demosthenes being the sole exception, and they seem to have acceded completely to his wishes. By delaying their journey for nearly two months, they enabled Philip to reduce to subjection the Thracian prince Cersobleptes, who ranked as an Athenian ally, without violation of the treaty terms. They likewise failed to report to their government the plans which Philip was maturing for the crushing of Phocis. When finally news of the Phocian expedition came, it was from Philip himself, who invited the Athenians to help him in settling the Sacred War, but under Demosthenes' influence Athens refused.

The Punishment of Phocis

Phocis was helpless. Her general, Phalaecus, made a separate treaty with Philip which allowed the former and his mercenaries to leave the country. The remainder of the Phocians capitulated after little or no resistance. The Amphictyonic Council sentenced them to have their cities broken up into villages, to repay in annual installments of sixty talents each the money taken from the temple of Delphi, and to lose their votes in the council. The latter were given to Philip, who signalized his reception as a legitimate Greek by presiding at the Pythian Games. The fate of Phocis was bad enough, but it would have been worse if Philip had not moderated the zeal of the Thessalians and Thebans. By his settling of the Sacred War he had gained much. He was now the protector of the Delphic oracle and held a foothold south of the Pass of Thermophylae. It was only in recognition of an accomplished fact when shortly afterward he had his title of "general" in Thessaly changed to that of "archon" and installed governors to administer the district in his name.

The six years which followed the Peace of Philocrates were marked at Athens by a bitter struggle between the friends and enemies of Macedonia, with the latter gradually gaining the ascendancy. Demosthenes prosecuted Aeschines for receiving bribes from Philip in connection with the embassy to Macedonia, and all the efforts of Eubulus and his friends secured the acquittal of the accused by only thirty votes out of a jury of 1501. Hypereides, a supporter of Demosthenes, drove Philocrates into exile by means of another prosecution. Little by little, relations with Macedonia became marked by an irritable, belligerent attitude on the part of Athens, which must have tried Philip's patience severely. Athenian agents, Demosthenes among them, traversed the Peloponnesus, attempting to rouse the people against Macedonia. Their success was small. Philip posed as the protector of Argos, Messenia, and the Arcadians against Sparta, and to the Peloponnesians, the Spartan danger still outweighed all others. Philip and his Peloponnesian partisans protested to Athens against these activities, and it was in reply to this message that Demosthenes delivered his *Second Philippic* (344). In it he accused the Macedonian king of attempting to encircle Athens with unfriendly states and of plotting her destruction. Events were to show that his view was groundless, but Demosthenes was probably sincere. Clashes between Philip's enemies and partisans occurred in many cities, and hatred and suspicion increased. It was merely the semblance of peace, as none of the important issues at stake had been settled.

Further Macedonian Conquests; The Ascendancy of Demosthenes

In the north, the march of Macedonian conquest was steady and impressive. Epirus was reduced to vassalage. Thrace, which since 346 had been in vassalage to Philip, was reduced to a province, and a beginning was made toward the conquest of the region between the Balkans and the lower Danube. The occupation of Thrace brought Philip close to the Thracian Chersonesus, and Athens felt that her route to the Black Sea was threatened. "Incidents" began to occur, increasing the already great tension between the two powers. Finally, in 340, Philip planned an attack upon the Thracian Chersonesus, and when Perinthus and Byzantium, Greek cities allied with him, refused to aid in the enterprise, he besieged them in succession. Athens sent them aid and Philip declared war.

The anti-Macedonian party at Athens saw that a decisive struggle was imminent and prepared for it. Demosthenes' *Third* and *Fourth Philippics*, his oration *On the Chersonesus*, and his reply to Philip's declaration of war were delivered in the years 341 and 340. Another effort was made to organize a Pan-Hellenic coalition and a congress of allies was held at Athens in 340. As Thebes and most of the Peloponnesian states still held aloof, little was accomplished. Meanwhile, the Persian king became alarmed and sent aid to Perinthus and Byzantium. The sieges dragged on into 339 and finally Philip was forced to abandon them. At Athens, Demosthenes carried a resolution repealing the law of Eubulus on the Theoric Fund, another reorganizing the system of naval liturgies, and others putting the navy on a war footing.

The war between Philip and the Athenians, which had smoldered for a year, broke out in 339. The Delphic Amphictyony declared another "Sacred War," this time against the Locrians of Amphissa. When neither Thebes nor Athens would participate, the Amphictyons called upon Philip to execute their decree. As Thebes was friendly to the Locrians, this move abated her pro-Macedonian zeal. Her hostility increased when he seized Elatea, a stronghold in Phocis which commanded the road to both Thebes and Athens. Demosthenes was not slow to see the opportunity for securing Theban co-operation in the war. When Philip sent an embassy to Thebes asking for either active aid against Athens or a free passage for his army through Boeotia, Demosthenes and an Athenian embassy succeeded in winning the Thebans to their side by an offer of immediate military support against the common enemy. The decisive moment in the struggle was near, and Athens had scored an important preliminary success.

The sequel is soon told. In the summer of 338, Philip outmaneuvered the allied generals, forced his way into Boeotia, and met the enemy at Chaeronea. Each force numbered over thirty thousand men; but the Macedonian army was composed of veterans and was better organized than that of the allies, and Philip was far superior to their generals. The Theban Sacred Band was annihilated, and the Athenians lost a thousand men killed and two thousand prisoners.

The battle of Chaeronea ended the opposition to Philip in Greece, with the exception of a weak attempt on the part of Sparta. He made surprisingly mild use of his victory. Such vengeance as he took was at the expense of Thebes, a former friend who had proved false. Her prisoners of war were sold into slavery. The anti-Macedonian democracy had to give way to an oligarchy, the Boeotian League was dissolved, and a Macedonian garrison was installed in the Cadmeia. Athens suffered little. Her prisoners of war were sent back without ransom and the bodies of her dead

were given up. She kept Lemnos, Imbros, Scyros, Delos, and Samos.
Sparta lost some of her remaining territory and the rest was ravaged, but
her government and institutions were not disturbed. Chalcis, Corinth,
and Ambracia received garrisons.

The Pan-Hellenic League

Having insured himself against further Greek opposition, Philip was
now ready to undertake a drastic reorganization of the Greek political
system. Late in the year 338 he summoned a congress of representatives
from the whole peninsula and the Aegean islands to meet at Corinth. Its
purpose was to ratify a plan for the long-discussed Pan-Hellenic League.
This time it was to be organized under his own presidency. All but Sparta
responded, although the Athenians did so reluctantly. The plan was
Philip's work, with perhaps suggestions from Isocrates and other Greek
partisans, and it displayed a farsighted statesmanship rare in Hellenic
history. Each member of the League was to enjoy complete autonomy and
was to be guaranteed against any change in its existing form of government. All attempts at revolution and interference with property rights
were outlawed. The league was to function through a representative
council in which membership was probably apportioned according to
military strength. There was to be a common army and navy, each state
contributing a definite quota, and a heavy fine was decreed against states
that failed to meet their obligations. No tribute was to be collected. The
league was to be in permanent alliance with Macedonia, but her king was
not a member of the council. War and peace were in its hands, although
obviously Philip's suggestions on these matters would be followed. In
fact, the declared purpose of the league was war on the Persians. The
avowed reason for this was revenge for former Persian invasions of Greece,
but the real reason was that given by Isocrates in his *Address to Philip*: the
necessity of providing lands on which the numerous exiles that filled the
Greek world could find homes. Thus, just as Great Britain has made many
of her conquests by utilizing the bellicose Scots and Irish who would otherwise cause her trouble, so Philip intended to disperse the excess fighting
men of Greece who had for two generations been conducting the ruinous
intercity wars.

The Death of Philip

Although the organizer of the Pan-Hellenic League, Philip was never to
lead it in an expedition against Persia. The advance forces had already

been sent across the Hellespont and the king was nearly ready to follow, when, at the festivities attending the marriage of his daughter, he was assassinated by one of his guards. The reason for this act has never been revealed. No one ever realized more fully the Nietzschean precept "to live dangerously" than Philip in his matrimonial relations. His official queen, the volcanic Olympias, had long tolerated the presence of his other wives, but his recent marriage to a certain Cleopatra had deeply offended her. Although a reconciliation had been effected, some contemporaries charged her with having planned her erring husband's removal. Others thought that the Persians had a hand in the deed. At any rate, the subjection of the Near East was to be reserved for an even greater conqueror than Philip.

The End of Greek Independence; The City-State Endures

The formation of the Pan-Hellenic League by the Macedonian king merely marked a stage in the decline of the city-state, but neither the first nor the last. The system to which it belonged had been successively subverted by Athens, Sparta, and Thebes before Philip of Macedonia overthrew it; but so well did it correspond to the needs of the Hellenic temperament that it survived this attack as well as the earlier ones. In the third and second centuries the city-state was the basic unit of which the Achaean and Aetolian leagues were formed, and later it played a similar part in the Roman Empire. The days of Greek independence were past. Gifted as they were, the Greeks were too individualistic to form a larger political unit than the city-state, and it was not strong enough to maintain its position under fourth-century conditions. The system which Philip established was one of the most promising attempts at Pan-Hellenic co-operation ever made. Had its founder lived a few years longer, it might have acquired some hold upon the affections of the people, but it could not do so when attached to the world-monarchy of Alexander the Great. Its memory is a lasting tribute to the genius of the great statesman who founded it.

Subsequent historians, ancient and modern, have frequently tried to judge the dispute between Philip and Demosthenes as if one were entirely right and the other wrong. Such judgments are futile. The latter stood for an independent Greek people, united by voluntary bonds; the former for an involuntary union effected by conquest. Although they agreed upon the necessity of a united Greece, their ideals differed so widely as to be irreconcilable. Each fought courageously, skillfully, and persistently for what seemed right to him. We need not condemn either in order to appreciate the greatness of the other.

30

Economic, Social, and Political Conditions

in Greece (404-338 B.C.)

THE CHARACTER OF THE PERIOD

THE POLITICAL HISTORY of the Greek people in the century preceding the Macedonian conquest has been sketched in the foregoing chapters. We must now examine the more important phases of the civilization of this troubled age. Previously we have seen it as a dreary succession of wars, revolutions, plots, tyrannies, assassinations, confiscations, foreign interventions, and gradual decline to servitude. These unpleasant facts, however, do not comprise the whole story. While social institutions suffered severely under the impact of such calamities, economic life was far from decadent, and in the realms of art and intellect the achievements of the Greek people were as great as in former ages.

Loss of Community Spirit

The fourth century, like the last quarter of the fifth, was an age of individualism, and hence an age of stark contrasts and infinite variety. Large fortunes were made in commerce, industry, real estate, and banking. With this wealth men procured comforts and luxuries unheard of a century before, but they did not as a rule give willingly to the state on the scale known to their grandfathers. The poor, possessed in their way of the same desires, came more and more to regard the state as a sponge whose sole purpose was to absorb the wealth of their more fortunate fellow citizens for purposes of redistribution. Party strife and class warfare lost none of their former virulence amid such surroundings, and not infrequently gave rise to the usual revolutions and bloodshed.

wool and put the ladies to work. Soon he had restored his household to prosperity. Lysias, the son of Cephalos the wealthy armorer, was stripped by the Thirty of his paternal estate. He took to writing legal orations for a living. Women of good family, we are told, worked as day laborers at vintage time or hired out as nursemaids.

At the same time, men of means began to buy run-down farms, put them into good condition, and then either operate them with slave and hired labor or sell them at a stiff advance in price. Such a one was Ischomachos, of whose affairs Xenophon gives so fine a picture. Commerce began to revive, aided by the wise policies of government and the industry of the people. The Laurium silver mines were reopened and made profitable. After 395, when the Long Walls were rebuilt, reviving political power aided the process. Athens never again became the mistress of the Aegean region, but she became once more a busy hive of industry, commerce, and wealth.

The Grain-Supply

As always, the food-supply was the matter of first importance. In a normal year, Athens consumed nearly three million bushels of wheat and barley. Attica produced about one-fifth of this amount, and her island possessions in the Aegean supplied her with an additional tenth. The remainder came from the Black Sea region, Sicily, Cyprus, and Egypt. It taxed the ingenuity of lawmakers and financiers to attract sufficient imports of food to the Piraeus. Loans to shipowners and merchants were manipulated to the uttermost to achieve this end. One of the chief sources of supply was the "Kingdom of the Cimmerian Bosporus," which included the land on both sides of the entrance to the Sea of Azov. Its princes were Greek in language and customs, and Athens cultivated their friendship assiduously. In return for gifts and honors, they granted to Athenian grain ships freedom from customs duties, priority of loading, and other valuable concessions. Occasionally, they even made outright presents of grain to the Athenian people. Once brought to the Piraeus, two-thirds of each cargo had to be left there, and the remainder could be moved on only if the Athenian market was glutted.

The Athenian retail grain-dealers were also subject to draconic laws. They were disliked and berated by the public, who suspected them of profiteering and other sharp practices. The "Comptrollers of the Grain-Supply" (*sitophylakes*) subjected them to minute inspection. They could not accumulate large stocks, and their gross profit could not exceed one obol for each medimnus handled. Even so, the uncertainties of the supply caused violent fluctuations in price, with occasional acute shortages. At such times public-spirited citizens — occasionally the grain-dealers themselves — would import quantities of foodstuffs and sell them far below the market price. On one occasion, when wheat had risen from the normal price of five drachmas per medimnus to sixteen drachmas, a number of persons, united in the common cause, bought ten thousand medimnoi and sold them at five drachmas each. Other cities usually fared no better than Athens in regard to food-supply. On the contrary, many of them fared worse, owing to bad management, unstable currency, and shortsighted dishonesty in dealing with foreign merchants and importers.

After the loss of her empire, Athens was compelled to balance her accounts with the outside world by means of silver from her mines, goods from her workshops, and the profits of her merchants and shipowners in foreign markets. Her silver was still the basis for the most stable currency in the Greek world. Her potteries retained a large part of the export market, although local competition in a number of places had cut down the demand for her ceramic wares. Household furniture, arms and armor, woolen cloth, clothing, leather goods, and many articles of bronze or silver helped to pay for the goods which she imported.

Industrial Organization

The industries which produced these articles were still operated much as in the Age of Pericles, with numerous small shops in each field. The father of the orator Demosthenes owned an arms factory, which employed thirty-two or thirty-three slaves. His total investment was one hundred and ninety minas, with an annual profit of thirty minas. He also owned a couch factory, which employed twenty slaves. It represented a capital of forty minas, and produced a net income of twelve minas a year. The shoe-shop of Timarchos employed nine or ten workmen and a foreman, with a profit of two obols per day from each worker and three from the foreman. From Laurium we hear of a certain Pantaenetos, who with thirty slaves operated a mining concession worth one hundred and five minas.

But if these enterprises were all small-scale affairs, the returns were very high. As we may easily see, the father of Demosthenes received from his two shops a profit of over eighteen per cent a year. Thirty per cent was by no means uncommon. However, one must deduct from this gross profit the cost of dead, sick, aged, or runaway slaves, which was a considerable item.

Money-Lending and Banking; Loans

Those who did not care to invest in industrial enterprises could always lend their available funds at interest. Fourth-century Greece had considerable liquid capital, and a serviceable system of credit had been invented for its utilization. Banks, which had been few in the Age of Pericles, were now plentiful everywhere. Beginning as money-changers, a trade made necessary by the bewildering variety of city-state currencies, the bankers had come to accept deposits, make loans, transmit funds, and perform most of the functions of a modern banker. Strict honesty, prudence in making investments, and administrative ability were the necessary qualities of a banker; for him who possessed them, the Greeks completely forgot class prejudice. At Atarneus in Asia Minor, one Hermias, the slave of a banker, won his freedom, took over the business, and came to rule his city as a vassal of Persia. He was highly educated and was the friend of Aristotle. Two of the best-known bankers of fourth-century Athens were Pasion and his successor, Phormion. Pasion was the slave of the banker Archestratos. He gained his freedom, set up a bank of his own, became wealthy, and was granted Athenian citizenship for his services to the state. His slave, Phormion, followed in his footsteps. After Pasion's death, Phormion married his widow, acted as guardian to his children, and operated the business. He, too, became an Athenian citizen, honored and respected. Soon every important town had its bankers.

As a class, Athenian bankers were conservative businessmen whose favorite investment was real estate mortgages. On such loans the rate of interest was twelve per cent. Industry and commerce had to depend upon the funds furnished by another class of investors, who took great risks in order to win larger returns. Particularly the metics, who could not own land and therefore could not foreclose delinquent real estate mortgages, found themselves forced into this more hazardous form of finance.

A favorite investment with these adventurous capitalists was loans on ships and cargoes. Many shipowners and merchants seem to have operated almost entirely on borrowed capital, refinancing their operations for each voyage. It was usually agreed that if the vessel and its contents were lost, the loan was to be considered cleared, and thus the same transaction was at once a loan and a form of marine insurance. Storms, pirates, privateers, and rascals who defrauded their creditors made the path of the lender a thorny one, and suits to enforce payment were numerous in the Athenian courts. Hence, the rate of interest was high — twenty-two to thirty per cent for voyages into the Black Sea.

Wages and Prices

In this age of more plentiful currency, wages and prices were much higher than in the Age of Pericles. In the earlier period workmen of all kinds, except assistants, received a drachma a day, but in 329 the laborers at Eleusis were paid one and one-half drachmas a day, while skilled workmen got two to two and one-half drachmas. Architects, sculptors, and other technicians now received much higher pay than the others. The architect in charge at Eleusis had an annual salary of seven hundred and twenty drachmas a year, or two a day without the lay-offs which the other workmen had to take. Piecework, which calls for increased skill and energy, had begun to replace the older day rate. But real wages remained practically stationary. Wheat advanced from three drachmas a medimnus to five, and other prices rose proportionately. Tradesmen and craftsmen could support their families in comfort, and even save a little money, if they were thrifty, but the rising standard of living increased the temptation to spend everything on current needs.

Public Finance; Taxation

The weakest element in Greek economic life, then as always, was public finance. In Athens the prosperous days of the empire had left the state with a costly tradition of payments to officials, social services, and entertainment which was, now that the tribute had ceased to come, a heavy burden. Naturally, there was no thought of retrenchment. Instead, the state added to its load by paying the poor for attendance at assembly. After 329, the rate was three obols apiece for each session or an aggregate of about thirty talents a year. Warfare had been made more expensive by the practice of hiring mercenaries, who had to be paid high wages to prevent mutiny or desertion. The practice of impounding all surplus funds of the state at the end of each year for the Theoric Fund added to the stringency, as we have already seen.[1] It was becoming more and more difficult to induce the wealthy to accept the expensive liturgies. All these factors increased the financial difficulties of the state and sharpened the hatred of the rich, who bore the burden of supporting the state, against the poor whose votes laid this burden upon them and who benefited most from the money raised. With inadequate financial support, fleets and armies were seriously hampered and often failed. We hear of Timotheus, who commanded the fleet which operated against Sparta about 375, finan-

[1] Chapter 29.

cing it with money borrowed on his personal security. Even the integrity of the law courts suffered.

> You have often heard these men say [stated an orator to an Athenian jury], whenever they wished you to condemn someone unjustly, that unless they are condemned you will get no pay.[1]

One result of this financial disorder was the extension and more frequent collection of the extraordinary property tax — *eisphora* — a capital levy graduated according to the wealth of the payer. It was not levied every year, but only in times of financial crisis, yet these crises came with alarming frequency. Demosthenes' guardians paid on his behalf three talents on a total capital of fifteen talents — a rate which would equal twenty per cent of the whole. While poorer people paid smaller sums, all who had incomes of one hundred and fifty drachmas a year or more were liable to some extent. Taxpayers were divided into groups (*symmoriai*) of approximately equal aggregate wealth, each of which paid an equal share of the tax and apportioned it among its members. Later, it became the rule for the three hundred richest citizens to pay the whole amount of the tax in advance, and then to collect it from the others. This rule resulted in endless lawsuits, evasions, and recriminations. In addition to this direct tax, the customs duties and other indirect taxes were doubled or trebled.

Other states were, so far as may be judged from the evidence, worse off than Athens in financial matters. The reign of Dionysius I at Syracuse was notorious for the oppressiveness of his taxation and the cynicism with which he avoided paying his debts. He confiscated property, sold the inhabitants of conquered cities into slavery, and debased his coinage — all to supply funds for the support of his government. Byzantium distinguished herself by her readiness to resort to dishonest practices in filling her treasury. Many other states were nearly as bad. While such policies had always characterized Greek governmental finance to some extent, their increasing use in the fourth century is eloquent testimony to the disorder and decadence into which these local governments had fallen.

FOURTH-CENTURY SOCIETY

While the basic social institutions of the Greeks continued to present the same general appearance as formerly, they were in reality profoundly influenced by the disorder of the times and the growing individualism of the people. Family organization remained almost everywhere the same

[1] Lysias, *Against Epicrates*, 1.

in theory and social classes changed but little. But within the old framework profound changes had taken place. More and more, men consulted their own comfort and convenience, and cared little for the welfare of the state, clan, or family. The rising standard of living tempted them either to avoid the sacrifices necessary to rearing a family altogether or to limit the number of their children. Concubinage and prostitution had always been common, but they now enjoyed a popularity greater than ever before. Hetairai moved unchallenged in good society. As the children of irregular unions were rarely allowed to live, it is not surprising that Greek cities were already beginning to suffer from a decline in population which nothing could check.

The Decline of the Middle Class

A significant sign of the times was the decline of the middle class and the separation of the population into extremes of wealth and poverty. The wars had everywhere borne heavily on the small, free landholder whose lands suffered devastation and whose time was taken with military service. New economic conditions called for adjustments which many of these unfortunates were unable to make, and they sank into the class of landless tenants or sold their lands and went to live in the cities. In their new homes a few succeeded in acquiring wealth from commerce or industry, but the majority swelled the ranks of the proletariat which lived from the doles paid by governments or clamored for revolution. The more complex business organization of the times tended to concentrate even the small city workshops in the hands of relatively few wealthy people. Hence, the people of moderate property became fewer and fewer as the years passed. In Athens the proportion of thetes in the population rose from forty-five per cent in 431 to fifty per cent about 355, and fifty-seven per cent in 322. Elsewhere the decline was even sharper and more rapid. Previously, the middle class had acted everywhere as a balance wheel to government and an umpire between rich and poor. Its decline intensified the hatred between the extremes and embittered the strife of social classes.

Mobility of the Population

The Great Peloponnesian War and the calamities which followed it produced unusual mobility of population. Every capture of a city and every successful revolution sent scores, hundreds, or thousands of homeless wretches forth into exile. Some of these were cared for by political friends in other cities, and many of them were, no doubt, enabled by later changes of fortune to return to their homes. Even in such cases, the wastage of life and property was enormous and the majority did not fare so well. They were reduced to robbery, beggary, slavery, or mercenary service. All parts of the Greek world seem to have been plagued with the presence of bands of homeless vagrants, persons demoralized and rendered desperate by want, who were a menace to social order. It was partly for the purpose of furnishing these unfortunates with homes that Isocrates urged Philip of Macedonia to conquer lands from the Persian Empire.

From such homeless folk, and from men who had been unfitted for peaceful callings by years of continuous warfare, the mercenary armies of the period were recruited. We have seen the younger Cyrus easily gather thirteen thousand Greek mercenaries for his expedition against his brother. Dionysius I of Syracuse, Jason of Pherae, and the Phocian generals in the Sacred War, all depended heavily upon such materials for their armed forces. As the fourth century progressed, Athens came more and more to depend upon them in place of the unwilling citizen levies.

Social Evolution

Besides these patent evidences of social change — the fruits of destruction and violence — there was much which can only be defined as the consequences of social evolution — the operation of forces which had been at work in Greek life for centuries. In no community was this more apparent than in Sparta. Some of the difficulties encountered in keeping intact her outworn social and political system have been mentioned. This could be done only by repressive measures which did little or nothing to remove the causes of the evil from which she suffered. The constant shrinkage of the citizen body and the concentration of lands in the possession of a few persons continued unchecked throughout the fourth century. Thus, in the Persian War the Lacedaemonians could, without difficulty, put five thousand Spartiates into the field, but by the year 390 the number had shrunk to two thousand, and fifty years later to less than one thousand. While this was in part attributable to losses in war, a more potent cause was the rise of large estates, with a corresponding increase in the number of "inferiors." The sale and bequeathal of land were now legal and forty per cent of it was owned by women. The loss of Messenia had intensified the evil. How dangerous the discontent of the "inferiors" could be may be inferred from the conspiracy of Cinadon, and there can be little doubt that many attempts against the government were suppressed without the knowledge of them ever becoming public. In the Macedonian period, Sparta was able for a time to maintain her independence, but that was all.

In Athens the concentration of property was not so great, nor were its results so calamitous, as at Sparta. This was largely because of the greater freedom of the Athenian, who could supplement his income from the soil by other means. But the class of Athenian small farmers was not prosperous and it tended to disappear. When the Athenians began to rehabilitate their farms after the war, the poorer landholders had not sufficient capital to plant the necessary vines and olives, without which little of the arable land of Attica could be farmed profitably. They could acquire such capital only by going into debt, and for a poor man, debt meant ruin. Hence, many of them sold their land and the remainder eked out a living under adverse conditions. The law of inheritance added to the evil by providing for the continued division of farms among heirs, so that they soon became too small to support their owners. Then the capitalists stepped in, bought up the fragments, and constituted what were, for Attica, large estates. As tenant-farming was never a success in that region, the estates were worked by hired laborers and slaves. The new owners, with sufficient capital at their disposal, could restore the vines and olive trees which made Attic agriculture profitable. Thus, the tendency was for the land to return to a few owners, as in the early sixth century.

In Thessaly the manorial system of earlier ages was still in force, but it was no longer unchallenged. Jason of Pherae and his successors made it part of their program to free the serfs. This plan succeeded in the region under their immediate influence, although it failed in Thessaly as a whole. The lords were no longer mere gluttons and drunkards, but displayed an interest in literature, oratory, art, and philosophy.

The Asiatic Greeks

The Asiatic Greeks gradually accommodated themselves to the capricious despotism of Persia. Her satraps lacked the high sense of duty of the first Persian rulers, and the central government was unable to control them as strictly as in the days of Darius I. They fought among themselves and rebelled against their master, and at the same time their subjects were the victims of cruel and arbitrary conduct. One of the most enlightened and affable of them, Cyrus the Younger, had in his harem two Greek girls whom he had kidnapped from their parents. Many young persons of both sexes were reduced to slavery by other Persian officials. To some extent the economic prosperity which Asiatic Greece enjoyed consoled her for her wrongs. Her inclusion in the Persian Empire gave to her people commercial opportunities from which they profited greatly, especially after the "King's Peace." Between that event and the Macedonian invasion, wealth and population increased in all the more important cities, and in several of them splendid buildings testified to their material prosperity.

GOVERNMENT

In general, the traditional forms of government in the Greek world suffered but little institutional change in the fourth century, although revolutions often resulted in the substitution of one form for another. Likewise they displayed the same tendencies and the same weaknesses as in the last quarter of the fifth century, but in a more advanced stage. The chief of these were: (1) growing individualism on the part of the citizens; (2) sharper and more destructive class strife; and (3) a tendency to combine individual states into extensive leagues and federations.

Individualism had attacked the integrity of the city-state from two directions. It produced powerful personalities, such as Alcibiades, Lysander, Dionysius I, and Jason of Pherae, who had little or no respect for tradition and rudely brushed aside restraints upon their personal ambitions. On the outskirts of Hellas, Philip II of Macedonia and Mausolus of Caria, animated by a similar spirit, were casting covetous eyes upon the cultured but politically inept Greeks. Tyranny enjoyed renewed popularity in many states. On the other hand, the poor and moderately wealthy classes had become too selfish to make the constant sacrifices which the independent city-state required of them. Instead, they wished the state to furnish them an easy and attractive living. The upper classes looked upon one-man rule as a way of escape from the fear of unjust spoliation by their covetous fellow citizens. These groups, no longer united by pursuit of a common ideal as in the Athens of Pericles, began once more to hate each other with bestial ferocity.

Class Hostility and Strife

In the fourth century, Athens and Sparta had not ceased to champion respectively the democratic and oligarchic factions in neighboring states. When Thebes began to assert imperialistic pretensions (after 378), she generally favored the popular faction in cities under her influence. As a consequence, the wars of these states fanned into flame the smoldering class warfare of the Greek peninsula. This strife had been sharpened by the decline of the middle class. Its bitterness was in many cases aggravated by the extreme claims of the lower classes, who wanted nothing short of the cancellation of all debts and the redistribution of the land. Even the more moderate leaders advocated services and doles for the poor which could be realized only by confiscatory taxation upon the rich. The latter, in desperation, began to retaliate. In some cases they formed secret societies to protect their interests and in others they called in foreign aid. These oligarchic clubs existed in many places. Their members aided each other in lawsuits, endeavored to control elections, and plotted revolutions. The bitterness of their hatred for their persecutors is shown vividly by the oath which some of them administered to their members:

> I will be an enemy of the people; and in the Council I will do it all the harm I can.[1]

On the other hand, the orator Isocrates says:

> The very poorest persons would be less pleased by securing the wealth of the rich for their own use than by depriving them of it.[2]

With such attitudes governing both sides, the stark ferocity of fourth-century class strife might be expected to equal or surpass the sorry record of previous ages in this respect. Our study of the decarchies in the cities of the Aegean region and of the Thirty at Athens has shown us what the upper classes were capable of when they were in power. Their opponents were no more merciful. At Corinth the popular party instituted a massacre of aristocrats and tried to join their city in an organic union with Argos. The survivors of the massacre betrayed the city to the Lacedaemonians, with another massacre as the consequence (390). Rhodes, Mytilene, and the Asiatic Greek cities were all scenes of repeated revolutions as fortune swayed between Sparta, Athens, and Persia in the 390's. The overthrow of Sparta at Leuctra was the signal for a popular revolution at Argos, in which twelve hundred of the upper classes were slaughtered and their property confiscated. These are by no means the only examples of this terrible scourge. It is not surprising that men of property everywhere embraced the idea that subjection to Philip of Macedonia was preferable to the constant terror in which they lived.

Leagues and Federations

If civil war and class strife were unmitigated evils, the formation of leagues and federations of states for mutual defense promised much good.

---

[1] Aristotle, *Politics*, V, 9, 11.   [2] *Archidamus*, 67.

We have mentioned the formation of the Boeotian, Arcadian, Olynthian, and Second Delian leagues. About 390, the Achaeans of the northern Peloponnesus organized the Achaean League, a close federation based upon community of dialect and institutions. Occasionally, allied cities went so far as to grant not only civil rights to each other's citizens, but also *isopoliteia*, or reciprocal rights of citizenship. This was a pledge that the alliance would be a lasting one.

Such groupings were a step toward the political unification of the aimlessly bellicose Hellenes, and in time they might have secured peace for the distracted land. But the circumstances of the time and the Greek national temperament were against them, and most of such movements were short-lived. Too often they were the work of single cities, and the so-called "allies" were really only subjects of the leading state. Then, too, Sparta was the persistent enemy of all such groups except the Peloponnesian League, which she controlled. The "King's Peace" was a severe setback to them, and in the ensuing wars most of them were dissolved. As this phenomenon was continually repeated, it became apparent that only superior force on the part of some strong state could make such a league permanent. To Macedonia fell the doubtful honor of putting this policy into execution.

Athenian Government

Attributable in part to the one-sided emphasis of our evidence and in part to its intrinsic interest, any study of Greek constitutional history becomes largely a study of the Athenian constitution. Of Thebes, Taras, and many other important Greek cities, little is known. Spartan government remained nearly static at the expense of development in all other lines. Even Syracusan government, in spite of the catastrophic changes which it suffered, has little of interest. But whether in praise, denunciation, or objective narration, the Greeks have left us a comprehensive and interesting account of the Athenian polity, and the surviving inscriptions have added largely to the fund of knowledge. Evidently this one-sided emphasis is justified by the relative intrinsic interest of the subject.

Compared with most of the other Greek states in the troubled fourth century, Athens presents a picture of calm and order. Her return to democracy after the rule of the Thirty was accomplished with astonishingly little bloodshed and disorder. Only a few of the most culpable oligarchs — those who were guilty of bloodshed and spoliation — were put to death. To the remainder, an amnesty was granted and scrupulously observed. Even the money borrowed by the beaten faction from Sparta was repaid. But the awful experience had cured the great majority of the Athenians of any anti-democratic tendencies which they had entertained. Thereafter, the rule of the people was accepted by all except a few philosophers, who continued to denounce it and to idealize Lacedaemonian institutions in the seclusion of their lecture halls. The list of officials, with minor exceptions, remained the same as before the rise of the Thirty, and the laws of Solon, with additions, were the basis of the legal structure of the state. The changes in Athenian government, which will be noted farther on, were adaptations of the existing institutions to the circumstances of the time.

The restored Athenian democracy established strong safeguards about the rights of property. Every year the archons and the jurymen took an oath to protect every person in the enjoyment of his rightful possessions, and in a literal sense this pledge was scrupulously kept. Athens was never, during the period between the restoration of the democracy and the Macedonian conquest, convulsed by the fierce class hatred which was the bane of her neighbors.

The apparent friendship between rich and poor was, however, somewhat deceptive. The Athenian commons were soothed by the thought that the state (in which they were, so to speak, majority stockholders) could lay hands upon the property of the rich at any moment through taxes, liturgies, fines, or gifts. In the law courts it was a good policy for a speaker to call attention to the wealth and luxury of his opponent, and for a rich man to plead poverty or to tell how much money he had spent for the state and for his fellow citizens. This can only mean that the possession of wealth was regarded with a jealous eye by the populace who made up the jury. However, the rule of the Thirty had taught the wealthy classes that there were worse evils than democracy, and so they made no concerted movement against it.

Legislation: *The Nomothetai*

A curious change took place in the process of legislation. At some time during the first half of the century, the assembly practically surrendered to a reorganized board of *nomothetai* its right to change old laws and make new ones. At the first session of each year the magistrates recommended any changes in the laws which they deemed desirable. If a majority of the assembly voted the change should be made, a committee of 501 or 1001 nomothetai was chosen at the fourth meeting of the first prytany. The assembly laid down the procedure which the committee was to follow and appointed representatives to defend the law as it then stood. Any citizen might then propose a new law, or changes in the old law, on the point indicated in the original resolution of the assembly. A regular trial ensued, the champion of the new law endeavoring to demonstrate its superiority to the old one, and the defenders upholding the *status quo*. If a majority of the nomothetai favored the proposed change, it became effective at once, without further action by the assembly. But at any point in the proceeding, opponents of the proposed change could still resort to the "writ against illegality," as in the fifth century.

Professionalism in Government

The increasing professionalism of the age influenced the government of Athens both in war and peace. With the increase of mercenary armies there arose a school of generals who made war a scientific pursuit, which required natural aptitude and long training. The day of the amateur politician-general was nearly done, and the fact profoundly altered the functions and relative importance of the officials of the state. The generals now tended to confine their attention to military affairs. Diplomacy, finance, and other branches of administration were handled by civilians without military knowledge or ambitions. To this class belonged Eubulus and Lycurgus, experts in finance, and Demosthenes, who today would rank as a diplomat. None of them held the office of general while performing his public functions, and the first apparently served only on committees of the council or assembly chosen to look after special funds. This system should have insured greater efficiency in government, but its good effects were largely nullified by demoralization of the people through their shortsighted solicitude for personal gain in the form of doles and wages. However wise the officials might be, they had, in most cases, neither the popular support nor the financial backing necessary to great success.

Professionalism also invaded the law courts. The law still provided that each suitor must plead his own case in person, but it had lost all meaning. For those who could afford such services, there were professional speech-writers (*logographoi*) who prepared the pleas, playing a part roughly analogous to that of a modern attorney. It was these "ghost-writers" who really waged the legal battles of the period. Sometimes, if a client was a notoriously poor speaker, they even appeared in person to assist him. They were forbidden to receive compensation for their services, but this law also had become a dead letter. Lysias, Demosthenes, Isocrates, and others grew wealthy from the fees which they collected.

In short, the Athenian people had changed their viewpoint and ideas so radically that they were no longer fit for the role of leaders in continental Greece and defenders of her independence. Athens was still a great and wealthy state, the most refined and cultured in the Greek world. But her people would never again be capable of the heroic self-sacrifice and intelligent planning which had been the foundation of her position in the Age of Pericles. Henceforth, she was to be distinguished for art, oratory, and philosophy rather than for her ability to conquer and to rule. Unfortunately for the Greek world, no other state arose to take the place which she had vacated. The day of the city-state as a sovereign entity passed with the battle of Chaeronea. The future now lay with larger and more powerful units of organization.

****

Fourth-Century Greece: Art and Literature

ARCHITECTURE

IN THE CENTURY following the fall of the Athenian Empire, the Greeks continued to display their taste and skill as builders by the masterly use of old forms and the invention of new ones. Athens, it is true, was unable to continue her ambitious building program after the loss of her imperial tribute, and many other states were equally impoverished by the ravages of the war. Moreover, secular interests were turning men's thoughts from temples to theaters and other public buildings. A new style, the Corinthian, was added to the existing Doric and Ionic forms, and the buildings of the period, while not so beautiful or so splendid as the best creations of the Periclean Age, have claims to consideration in their own right.

The Corinthian Style

In spite of Greek legends and modern speculations, the origin of the Corinthian style of architecture is not definitely known. It may have been an evolution from the Ionic, which it strongly resembled in the character of the flutings and in some other respects. The distinguishing feature of a Corinthian capital was its covering of acanthus leaves executed in high relief. The style, as a whole, was characterized by profuse ornamentation. Up to about 330, it was employed only on interior colonnades, but afterward for exterior work as well. The earliest structures in which the Corinthian style was used exclusively were the exquisite little "Choragic Monument of Lysicrates," in Athens, and the *Philippeum* of Olympia. Its greatest popularity was attained in the Hellenistic and Roman periods.

The Tholos

At Delphi and in the Peloponnesian city of Epidaurus, the architects utilized a floor plan which the Greeks had long known but never used extensively — the *tholos*, or round temple. In both cities these structures were surrounded by Doric colonnades surmounted by the usual architraves and Doric friezes. The metopes of the Delphian tholos appear to have contained figure sculptures, while those at Epidaurus were decorated with rosettes. Inside the cella walls of each was a circular Corinthian colonnade. These round temples adopted a floor plan with structural features hitherto associated with a rectangular building. It is impossible to say to what deities the temples were dedicated.

The Theater of Dionysus

The same period witnessed the construction of the first stone theaters. At Athens, the Theater of Dionysus, located on the southern slope of the Acropolis, was rebuilt in stone about 330. Later Greek and Roman alterations have left some points of the original plan uncertain, but the fundamental features are fairly clear. It consisted of three parts — the stage, the orchestra, and the auditorium. The stage was in this period located at ground-level and was an oblong space, back of which was a building (the *skené*) which contained the dressing-rooms and wings. The front wall of this structure formed the background of the stage. In front of the stage was the semicircular orchestra, which was occupied by the chorus. The auditorium also formed a semicircle, concentric with the circumference of the orchestra. The seats were partly cut out of the solid rock of the hillside and were arranged in tiers, each higher than the one in front of it. Twelve radial stairways divided them into thirteen wedge-shaped sections, each of which was divided into three parts by transverse passages. The seats had no backs and were without upholstery. Stage, orchestra, and auditorium were open to the sky. Later, the stage was raised above the level of the ground and other refinements were introduced. The radius of the auditorium was 165 feet, and its capacity was at least fourteen thousand persons. Epidaurus also had its stone theater, built about 400 by Polycleitus, the son of the sculptor. It is one of the best preserved in the Greek world and has never undergone extensive alterations, as has its Athenian counterpart.

The Thersilion

The foundation of the Arcadian League and of the city of Megalopolis (370) led to the erection of another interesting building — the Thersilion, or assembly hall of the league. It was one of the few places of public assembly in ancient Greece which offered protection from the weather — a huge rectangular building, some 215 feet long and 170 feet wide. The roof of so extensive a structure had to be upheld by some sixty columns, which offered serious handicaps to visibility between a speaker and his audience. This fault was partly overcome by an ingenious arrangement of the columns in lines converging toward a focal point near the entrance. The floor level converged from three sides toward the same point, as in the auditorium of a theater. In front of the building was a portico which acted as the rear wall of the stage of a large open-air theater.

Doric and Asiatic Greek Temples

In spite of these innovations, old forms of construction were still used to advantage. The temple of Apollo at Delphi was rebuilt in the traditional Doric style, but very little of it now survives. At Tegea, the sculptor Scopas laid out a fine temple in honor of Athena Alea, which has now been thoroughly excavated. The stylobate measured 154 by 72 feet, and the colonnade consisted of 34 Doric columns, each 26 feet high. But while the columns preserved the traditional Doric characteristics of fluting and capital, they were more slender than those of earlier structures of the same style, and the *echini*, which in older Doric structures were high and had a curved edge, were low with straight beveled edges. Most of the metopes were left blank, but there were two fine pedimental groups. The eastern group represented the hunting of the Calydonian boar, while the western one portrayed the battle between the Tegean hero Telephos and Achilles. Inside the cella, Scopas employed a device similar to that found in the cella of the temple of Apollo at Bassae. In each corner was a pilaster, with a richly wrought Corinthian capital, engaged in the wall. The decorations were quite elaborate and the workmanship of the building as a whole showed as fine a sense of line and harmony as that of the temples of the Athenian Acropolis.

Asiatic Greece adhered closely to the Ionic style in temple architecture. But her greater wealth and Asiatic love of ostentation often led her architects to strive for grandeur and striking effects rather than for artistic beauty. Two outstanding examples of this tendency were the temple of Artemis at Ephesus ("Diana of the Ephesians") and that of Apollo at Branchidae near Miletus. Both were of great size (342 by 164 feet and 359 by 159 feet, respectively, at the top of the stylobate), and both had double exterior colonnades. Some of the columns of the temple of Artemis had their lower double drums covered with relief sculptures — a practice

Brown Brothers

RESTORATION OF THE MAUSOLEUM AT HALICARNASSUS

rarely, if ever, followed elsewhere. A unique feature of the temple of Branchidae was a small but complete prostyle temple 48 feet long and 28 wide, placed inside the cella.

Quite different from these colossal structures was the Ionic temple of Athena Polias ("Guardian of the City") at Priene. It was small (122 feet by 64 feet on the stylobate), but it was exquisitely proportioned and delicately finished. Like most of the other Asiatic temples, it had very little exterior decoration.

The Mausoleum

It is fitting that an account of fourth-century Greek architecture should close with a description of the famous Mausoleum, or tomb of the Hellenized Carian prince Mausolus, at Halicarnassus. Architecturally, its importance lies in the fact that it represents the adaptation of Greek structural principles and methods to the spirit and purposes of the Near-Eastern peoples. It was built of marble. On a rectangular base one hundred feet long and eighty wide rose a cella surrounded by an Ionic colonnade. The marble roof, which was shaped like a stepped pyramid, was seventy feet high. On its summit stood a sculptured group representing Mausolus and his queen Artemisia standing in a four-horse chariot. The sculptures, which must be reserved for separate treatment, were the work of the foremost sculptors of the day.

SCULPTURE AND PAINTING

If architecture may be said to have declined in importance among the fine arts of fourth-century Greece, sculpture had certainly become more important than ever. It was thoroughly progressive and representative of the spirit of the age. Fifth-century sculptures were frequently decorations for buildings or closely associated with them; the extant remains are more often reliefs than fully rounded figures. In the fourth century, sculpture in the round became increasingly popular, and many of the most famous works were now entirely dissociated from any particular building. Striking advances were made in technical methods. Increasing use of the drill enabled the artist to make deep incisions in marble, which were impracticable when he depended entirely upon the hammer and chisel. The effect of this innovation was to be seen in the deeper folds of draperies and in the heavy masses of hair which adorned the heads of figures shaped by

Museum of Fine Arts, Boston

HEAD OF ZEUS
Found at Mylasa

Praxiteles and his contemporaries. Tense emotion and violent action were studied and reproduced by the foremost sculptors in a way which seems to reflect the unsettled conditions of the age. Portrait busts and statues of prominent men reflect the growing interest in the individual, and the decline of religious awe and fervor is to be seen in the charming humanity and benignity of the statues of the gods.

Athenian Sculptors

Even amid the poverty and suffering which followed the fall of her empire, Athens did not cease to produce sculptors of outstanding merit. Such a one was Cephisodotus. About 375, to celebrate the recent treaty with Sparta, he carved from marble a group representing the goddess of peace holding the infant god of wealth in her arms. Only Roman copies of this masterpiece survive. The costume of the goddess — a Doric chiton — was reminiscent of the preceding century, but the other characteristics

University Prints

PEACE HOLDING THE INFANT WEALTH IN
HER ARMS

clearly revealed its true date. The deeply cut folds of the cloth, arranged with studied accuracy, the kindly expression of the deity's face, the playful air of the child, and the suggestive symbolism of the "horn of plenty" which he holds, all reveal a depth and sophistication of thought which could not have belonged to an earlier period. It was a new type of sculpture, and although others were to bring it to maturity, all its essential features were present in the work of Cephisodotus.

A further development in this style is to be seen in the work of the Athenian Praxiteles. Like Cephisodotus, he worked chiefly in marble, and his statues were in demand all over the Greek world. In his works the spirit of fourth-century Athens found its fullest and most beautiful expression. Unlike Phidias and his contemporaries, Praxiteles largely disregarded the major deities and specialized in the minor Olympian gods and the spirits of the woods and fields. He cared nothing for dramatic scenes, stormy emotion, or violent action. Instead, his gods were placid and thoughtful, and their usual attitude was one of rest. In most cases they leaned upon a support, with back and knees bent. Destiny has been kinder to Praxiteles than to his contemporary sculptors, for whereas we can judge their works only by inferior Roman copies, the original of his "Hermes and the Infant Dionysus" is still extant. In it we are not introduced to distant, awe-inspiring deities. Hermes, a physically perfect and exquisitely beautiful youth, stands in an attitude of complete relaxation, gazing absent-mindedly at the infant sitting on his left arm, and dangling an object from his right hand, possibly a bunch of grapes, just out of the baby's reach. The modeling and finish of this work show how infinitely superior the original works of the Greek masters were to the Roman copies upon which we are usually compelled to rely.

Excellent as we may consider the "Hermes," it was but a minor work of Praxiteles. Probably his masterpiece was the "Aphrodite of Cnidus." The goddess was portrayed in the nude, about to enter the bath. Ancient art critics are unanimous in their praise of its beauty of modeling, finish, attitude, and facial expression. In fact, it was so popular that later sculptors widely imitated it, and the nude goddess became a standard, even hackneyed theme. Other outstanding works of Praxiteles were his "Apollo the Lizard-Slayer," two statues of Eros, the god of love, and one of a satyr, which he set up in Athens. His Eros, a somewhat effeminate boy with wings, also fixed a type which his successors frequently imitated. Indeed, a considerable number of sculptors of the generations that followed were so strongly influenced by Praxiteles that it is proper to speak of their works as belonging to "Praxiteles' School."

HERMES HOLDING THE INFANT DIONYSUS
By Praxiteles

Far different were the genius and methods of Praxiteles' great contemporary and rival, Scopas of Paros. He is known to have worked extensively on the friezes of the Mausoleum, and probably planned the reliefs of the temple of Athena Alea at Tegea. Copies of two works known to be his are now in existence. He was the portrayer of passion and strenuous action. Faces of statues attributed to him have, as a rule, furrows about the noses and mouths, wrinkled brows, and an impassioned upward gaze. His "Maenad" (woman in a Dionysiac frenzy) has her head thrown back and hair and garments streaming behind her in the wind. Associated with him on the Mausoleum sculptures were Timotheus, Bryaxis, and Leochares. Since it is impossible to say for what parts of the surviving remains each was responsible, the work should be treated as a whole.

The Mausoleum Sculptures

The architectural features of the Mausoleum have been described. Of its three friezes, one showed a chariot race, another the battle between the

Centaurs and the Lapithae, and the third the struggle of the Greeks with the Amazons. Of the first two, so little has survived that they cannot be intelligently evaluated. But of the third, some seventeen slabs, about eighty feet in all, have been preserved and are now in the British Museum. These show such differences of style and execution that they are probably the work of different artists, but they have so much in common that they can be treated as a unit. There is in them none of the calm and happy serenity of Praxiteles. The individual figures are lean and muscular, and they are engaged in a desperate struggle. Here an Amazon is seated backward on her horse and strikes at her foes as she gallops along. In another place a Greek warrior, beaten to his knees, strives to ward off with his shield the blows of his assailants. An Amazon, unable to defend herself, extends her hands to her assailant in a plea for mercy, but as he lowers his weapon another Amazon advances to strike him in the back. Taut muscles, flying cloaks, lifted swords, and careering horses create a scene of animated action with few parallels in Greek artistic history.

Lysippus and the Portrait Statues

To the list of great names in fourth-century sculpture the Peloponnesus contributed that of Lysippus of Sicyon. Working entirely in bronze, he was one of the most prolific artists the Greek world ever produced, with an estimated output of fifteen hundred statues. His work was characterized by delicacy of modeling, meticulous attention to detail, and by the slender proportions of his figures. He was one of the first successful por-

University Prints

BATTLE OF THE GREEKS AND AMAZONS

trait sculptors, and so highly valued was his work in this field that Alexander the Great would not allow anyone else to make a plastic representation of him. Lysippus' portraits of Alexander would seem, therefore, to be the prototypes of all or nearly all the copied busts and statues of the Macedonian conqueror which have come down to us. His images of gods, unlike those of Praxiteles and Scopas, were majestic and awe-inspiring. In this field he is best known for his colossal statue of Zeus at Taras and for statues of Heracles ranging from colossi down to a tiny figure intended for a table ornament. His *Apoxyomenos* (athlete scraping oil and dust from his body) survives in inferior Roman copies, but we probably have a good Greek copy of his statue of the athlete Agias. His influence upon subsequent sculptors was immense, and to it no doubt we owe much of the realistic sculpture of the Hellenistic and Roman periods.

University Prints

ATHLETE SCRAPING HIMSELF
After Lysippus

Lysippus was not the only master of portrait sculpture in the latter part of the fourth century. The sculptures of the Mausoleum included a spirited and convincing likeness of Mausolus — not a Greek in either physique or costume, but a splendid, forceful personality, every inch a ruler of men. From some unknown hand we have a series of likenesses of Socrates which reproduce with ludicrous faithfulness his homely features and plain apparel. Sculptors also carved idealized portraits of the great men of former times — Sophocles, Euripides, Herodotus, and Pericles. Some of these show that their makers were deep and understanding students of character, and that they knew how to impress it upon the human features.

Attic Tombstones

Even the commoner forms of sculpture displayed a large measure of artistic power and beauty. Between the beginning of the century and the year 317, there were placed in the Ceramicus Cemetery at Athens a series of tombstone reliefs, which combine a high degree of technical perfection with the quality of restrained pathos carried to heights seldom attained in any other age or country. Death is alluded to only indirectly. Usually we see only the last touching farewell of the deceased to his loved ones, but in the "Stela of the Knight Dexileos" we find him portrayed in his last gallant fight against the Spartans, charging on horseback and spearing a fallen enemy.

Painting: Character and Schools

Greek painting in the fourth century progressed to a degree of maturity comparable to that of sculpture. Pottery painting declined and after 300 almost disappeared. Easel pictures replaced the earlier wall paintings, and the encaustic process (the mixing of colors with hot wax) became a serious rival of the older fresco and tempera processes. Its chief advantage was that it kept the colors fresh and bright for long periods of time. The *chiaroscuro* technique of Apollodorus was perfected still further. Painters began to study perspective, thus making possible the production of large and complicated scenes.

Three schools of painting developed: the Athenian, Sicyonian, and Ionian. Of these, the first was apparently characterized by its devotion to symbolical and mythological subjects and by emphasis upon composition and facial expression. Too little is known about it to burden the memory of the casual student with the disjointed fragments. The school of Sicyon

GRAVE RELIEF OF DEXILEOS

was noted for its evenly divided interest between artistic theory and practice. Its greatest master, Pausias, employed the encaustic process to represent scenes from everyday life in a series of charming miniatures.

The Ionian school owes its glory chiefly to Apelles, the court painter of
Alexander the Great, and probably the greatest painter of the ancient
world. His subjects were largely those to be expected from an artist in his
position — portraits of Alexander and his generals and allegorical and
mythological scenes. Perhaps his masterpiece was a scene representing the
naked Aphrodite wringing the water from her hair just after rising from
the sea. He combined technical perfection with grace and beauty of conception and execution.

Of all this wealth of paintings only a few third-hand and fourth-rate
copies survive in the wall paintings and mosaics of Pompeii and other Ro-

man sites. Even these show that the Greek painters of this great age were masters comparable to the greatest figures of Renaissance Italy. Pre-eminent among these remains is a damaged mosaic copy of a work by an unknown fourth-century artist, representing Alexander the Great and his opponent Darius at the battle of Issus. Even in its present state, it proclaims the supreme genius of its creator. The resistless charge of the Macedonian horseguards, the Persian cavalier pierced by Alexander's lance as he strives to protect his king, the other Persian noble who has dismounted from his horse so that Darius may escape on its back and who faces certain death for his loyalty, the threatening spears of the advancing phalanx, and Darius, the despicable object of so much devotion, gazing helplessly at the foe — all combine to make this one of the world's greatest battle-pieces. If, as we may suppose, the original author was a relatively unimportant figure among the painters of his time, what must have been the beauty and dramatic interest of the works of Apelles?

ORATORY

We have seen that the study of the art of correct and effective speaking was introduced into Athens by Gorgias and others.[1] Once begun, the advantages of this art assured its teachers of a numerous clientèle and a large income. For those who lacked the time or the ability to prepare their own speeches for the assembly or the law courts, professional writers were ready to prepare speeches and perhaps coach the speakers in their delivery. Numerous textbooks taught the principles of the art. It is no wonder that the fourth century was the golden age of judicial and political oratory.

Structure, Method, and Styles

In the hands of these professional practitioners, the public oration became a complex and formal creation. Korax of Syracuse had first divided it into five parts: introduction, narration, argument, subsidiary remarks, and conclusion. This division became a fundamental rule of composition. The scarcity of reliable documentary evidence and the reckless mendacity of the witnesses led suitors in the courts to rely heavily upon the "doctrine of probability" as a check upon opposing testimony. Thus, if A is a dwarf and is accused of assaulting B, a professional pugilist, A can show the court how unlikely he would be to attempt such an act. But if the case is reversed, B is not without a defense on the same grounds. He will

[1] Chapter 23.

ALEXANDER AND DARIUS AT THE BATTLE OF ISSUS

reply that it is improbable because his superiority of strength would immediately cause him to be suspected. Teachers stated imaginary cases, and their students composed speeches for both plaintiff and defendant. Antitheses, balanced sentences, flowery expressions, and many other devices were used to make the spoken word an effective means of persuasion.

At various times three styles were in favor with Attic orators: the "rugged," used by those of the period prior to about 380, the "middle" of Demosthenes, and the "smooth" of Isocrates. The first was slow and dignified, with relatively little care expended on formal structure. The "middle" and "smooth" styles paid progressively more attention to easy and pleasing diction. However, the style of an oration had frequently to be varied to suit the personality of the person who was to deliver it. This consideration was very important in the preparation of judicial speeches for clients.

The Ten Attic Orators

Later Greek literary critics selected ten Athenian orators, teachers of oratory, and logographers as constituting the élite of the profession. These were Antiphon (died 411), Andocides (born about 440), Lysias (440?–380?), Isocrates (436–338), Isaeus (420–?), Demosthenes (384–322), Aeschines (born 390), Lycurgus (born about 390), Hypereides (389–322), and Deinarchus (born 369). Only a few of these need be discussed in detail.

Lysias was the son of the wealthy metic Cephalus, and lived for some years at Thurii, where he studied under Sicilian teachers. During the Peloponnesian War he returned to Athens. The Thirty confiscated the family estate, killed his brother, and drove Lysias himself into exile. Thereafter he took up speech-writing as a means of livelihood. Twenty-eight of his genuine works survive, but of these only one was delivered by him in person. It was an arraignment of Eratosthenes, the man responsible for his brother's death. It is a powerful indictment, both of the man and of the system under which he pursued his career, and its power is achieved by simple narration of the facts, without much denunciation. Elsewhere Lysias took so much pains to suit his speeches to the personalities of those who were to deliver them that his own personality is largely submerged. He was noted for the purity of his diction, vivid description, subtle characterization, tact, and good humor.

Isaeus was, like Lysias, a metic. He was not interested in politics, but pursued the career of a lawyer, and his specialty was cases dealing with inheritances. His speeches were characterized by a consciously sophisticated style and by logical arguments with copious citations of evidence and quotations of the laws. Eleven of his genuine speeches survive. For us his importance lies largely in the fact that he was one of the teachers of Demosthenes.

It was the work of Isocrates to impart to Greek oratory the highest degree of formal polish. After a decade of experience as a logographer, he opened a school of oratory at Athens, and devoted the remainder of his long life to instruction in public speaking, with a few excursions into the field of political pamphleteering. Isocrates trained his students to speak upon political rather than upon legal questions, and his courses must have included much material which we would term political science and ethics, in addition to the art of speaking. He was an advocate of Pan-Hellenic unity for the purpose of attacking Persia. To disseminate his views he composed, in the form of orations, a number of political pamphlets, of which the most prominent were the *Peace*, *Panegyricus*, *Philip*, and *Areopagiticus*. Each was a carefully elaborated work of art with smoothly flowing, polished, and rhythmical sentences. Isocrates was one of the earliest of the *epideictic* ("display") orators, who composed speeches merely to show off their powers of composition and delivery, without regard to the importance of the subject. Unfortunately this type of oratory was widely imitated in Hellenistic and Roman times.

By far the most important of the Athenian orators, both as a speaker and a statesman, was Demosthenes. We have already studied his public career, and the orations which were a part of it. In addition to them he composed, in the capacity of a logographer, a great many speeches to be delivered in the courts by his clients. His style was midway between the unpolished efforts of the earlier orators and the elegant, artificial periods of Isocrates. He never sacrificed clearness of meaning for elegance, and he seldom divided his material into stereotyped categories prescribed by the textbooks. With the single aim of convincing his hearers, he mingled narrative, argument, emotional appeals, and other types of material with entire disregard of precedents, and fused the whole into a coherent unity, animated by the white-hot fervor of his emotion. He did not flatter his audiences. No more scathing criticisms of Athenian morale in the face of the Macedonian peril can be found anywhere than are contained in the *Philippics*, the *Olynthiacs*, and the other orations of Demosthenes delivered during the struggle with Philip II. That he was able to persuade his fellow citizens without flattery or distortion speaks volumes for his convincing eloquence and sincere patriotism.

Demosthenes' "Oration on the Crown"

The supreme oratorical effort of Demosthenes, and possibly the greatest speech ever delivered by a Greek, was his reply to Aeschines, commonly called the *Oration on the Crown*. In 336, a man named Ctesiphon proposed that the Athenian state reward Demosthenes for his services to it by the gift of a golden crown. Aeschines prosecuted Ctesiphon for proposing an illegal decree, but the suit lay dormant for six years. When it was finally brought to trial, Demosthenes, whose public career was the real issue at stake, spoke for Ctesiphon. Step by step he reviewed his acts and policies, pausing midway in his exposition to draw a word-picture of his opponent full of coarse and vitriolic denunciation. He closed with a prayer that the gods convert his enemies to sounder views, and that if they refused to see the light, they should be utterly destroyed. Aeschines received so few votes that he became liable to the punishment provided in such cases, and retired into exile at Rhodes.

Demosthenes' subsequent career will be dealt with in its proper place, but the art of which he had been so great an ornament never again produced his equal among the Greeks. Oratory has for its legitimate aim the persuasion of the orator's audience, and persuasion is only possible where men are free to choose their course of action. After the Macedonian conquest the Greeks were no longer able to do this. Only the florid and empty epideictic style survived and throve, and it degenerated into verbal juggling. When next a great orator appeared in the Mediterranean world, it was in the Roman Republic. The true successor and spiritual heir of Demosthenes was Cicero.

HISTORY AND THE DIDACTIC ESSAY

While the influence of Thucydides continued to be felt in the century which followed his death, other forces were at work to modify or submerge both his style and method. Of these the most important were philosophy and rhetoric. The first centered man's attention upon ideals rather than facts, and the second profoundly influenced methods of presentation. It is not surprising that an age of suffering and unrest should be interested in political science, as sick people usually are in medicine; but this interest tended to destroy the power of objective observation and to make the historian also a propagandist. The rhetorical influence was apparent in a certain straining after interesting methods of presentation, including the administration of praise and blame to historical characters, trite moralizing, and the too frequent use of imaginary orations. Characteristic of an age of great personalities was a growing interest in biography, which accounts for the *Evagoras* of Isocrates (a rhetorical life sketch of a Cypriote Greek prince), the *Agesilaus* of Xenophon, and the *Philippica* of Theopompus.

The Followers of Thucydides

The Thucydidean tradition was continued by Philistus of Syracuse, who lived under the rule of Dionysius I and Dionysius II. He wrote a history of Sicily from the earliest times to the destruction of Acragas by the Carthaginians, and followed it with another, nearly as long, on the reigns of the Syracusan tyrants. In the early part of his work he relied too readily upon doubtful traditions, and throughout he was addicted to recording portents and prodigies. But in spite of these faults he had many of the qualifications of a great historian. He understood politics from the inside, and Cicero praises him for pithiness, brevity, and shrewdness. His works have perished, but large excerpts seem to have survived in the compilation of a later writer, Diodorus Siculus.

In continental Greece the influence of Thucydides may be seen in an anonymous work, of which a fragment has been found in Egypt. It covers parts of the years 396–395. The style is simple and lucid, the attitude objective, and the selection of material discriminating. Whoever the author may have been, we may well regret that so little of his work survives.

Xenophon

Xenophon (431–355), the Athenian continuer of Thucydides' history, was only slightly influenced by his historical ideals and practice, and the influence became progressively less in his later works. He was a pupil of Socrates, although he appears to have understood little of the latter's philosophy. We have seen that he took a prominent part in the retreat of the Ten Thousand Greeks. His pro-Spartan views caused him to be exiled from Athens in 393, and he lived for many years in Elis on an estate granted to him by the Lacedaemonians. After the battle of Leuctra, he was driven from this refuge and spent his last years in Corinth.

Xenophon's most important work, the *Hellenica*, continued the history of the Greeks from the point where Thucydides had left it (411) to the battle of Mantinaea (362). In spite of a superficial resemblance to his great predecessor, he had little or none of his critical acumen, objectivity of outlook, and understanding of causes. While reasonably adequate in its treatment of the closing years of the great Peloponnesian War, the *Hellenica* degenerates rapidly in its narration of the events which were, for the author, contemporary history. Xenophon was a friend and follower of the Spartan king Agesilaus and an uncritical admirer of Lacedaemonian institutions. His whole outlook was so strongly influenced by the Spartans that in places his work becomes little more than a partisan pamphlet. Thus, in his account of Theban affairs he slights both Epaminondas and Pelopidas inexcusably, and he pictures Agesilaus as a far greater soldier and statesman than events show the Spartan ruler to have been. Since the *Hellenica* is the only contemporary history of the early fourth century which has survived, the student has to depend upon it, but always it must be used with caution.

In the fields of personal memoirs and didactic essay writing Xenophon rates much higher. His *Anabasis* is an interesting and lively document, full of vivid, eye-witness descriptions of strange countries and peoples and of sketches of men and events. His *Memoirs of Socrates* was written to clear the memory of his friend and teacher of the charges made by his accusers. In it the philosopher is portrayed as an edifying and conventional moralist, without any new or original ideas at which the Athenian people needed to take alarm. It has none of the sparkle of Plato's dialogues, but it probably embodies some aspects of Socrates' personality which Plato neglected. Three other sketches — the *Economicus*, the *Symposium*, and the *Apology* — introduce Socrates as a speaker, but their historical value is at best slight. In the field of the didactic essay, Xenophon composed a number of pieces, including the *Lacedaemonian Constitution*, *Revenues of Athens*, and some technical treatises. He was also the author of a historical romance — the *Cyropaedia* or *Education of Cyrus* — in which he set forth his philosophy of education. He was one of the most versatile and prolific writers in the ancient world, although in no field did he attain first rank.

The Pupils of Isocrates

Isocrates, whose nearest approach to historical writing was his panegyric on Evagoras, nevertheless trained two prominent fourth-century historians, Ephorus and Theopompus. The former, whose life covered approximately the half-century between 380 and 330, was a native of the Asiatic Greek city of Cyme. In keeping with the Pan-Hellenic interests of his teacher, he composed a "universal history" of the Greeks from the

Dorian invasion to the siege of Perinthus (340). As a historian he had some virtues, including freedom from prejudice and industry in amassing facts. Particularly valuable were his researches in geography. On the other hand, his work was dull and uninspired, and the little that we know about him shows that his theories of the causes of events were often trivial and absurd. Although his work has perished, much of the material which it contained is found in quotations by later Greek and Roman authors.

Theopompus (about 380–315) was a native of Chios. Whether for political reasons or because of his unpleasant disposition, he spent much of his life in exile. His first work was a continuation of Thucydides, extending to 395. The rise of Macedonia, however, directed his attention to contemporary history. Feeling, like Isocrates, that a new age was beginning, and that it would be dominated by the personality of Philip II, he began a colossal *Philippica* ("History of the Age of Philip"). It was padded with letters and speeches, and no doubt was filled with the rhetorical flourishes which the author had learned from Isocrates. As a Macedonian partisan, Theopompus berated democracies everywhere. Long digressions on every conceivable subject interrupted the course of the action. His works, like those of Ephorus, are lost, but again we have large excerpts and numerous quotations in the works of later authors.

DRAMA

After Euripides there were no more tragedians of note. Tragedies of sorts continued to be presented in the Athenian Dionysia up to about 300, but the state recognized their inferiority by permitting and encouraging revivals of the works of the old masters. Tragedy had run its course.

Comedy, on the contrary, continued to grow, and evolved new forms to meet the changed times. The last years of the fifth century had seen a sharp reaction against the personal abuse and scurrility which had formerly characterized that branch of the drama. As personalities lost interest, general ideas (embodied in the form of stock characters) took their place. The Parabasis, or address of the chorus to the audience, was discontinued. The Old Comedy was dead, and the Middle Comedy (about 400 to 336) had taken its place. Of the numerous plays that fell within this class, only one unequivocal specimen remains — the *Plutus* of Aristophanes (388).

The "Plutus"

The problem which the comedian attacks in this, the last of his extant plays, is nothing less than: What sort of world would it be if wealth went only to the deserving? Plutus, the blind god of wealth, meets an Athenian named Chremylus, who is angrily pondering the fact that only rascals grow rich. All this is owing to the blindness of Plutus, who cannot see to whom he is giving his bounty. Chremylus undertakes to restore the god's sight by treatments at the healing shrine of Asklepios at Epidaurus. Poverty appears in the shape of a gaunt and ragged woman. She urges Chremylus to leave the god as he is. Are not all the good things that mankind enjoys a result of the poverty that spurs them to effort? Cure the god, and no one will any longer work. In vain. Chremylus has Plutus treated and he recovers his sight. A typically Aristophanic series of incidents follows, showing the changed conduct of Plutus now that he can see. Cured of his blindness, he is the most powerful of all the gods. Zeus is deserted by his priests and even by his fellow deities, for wealth rules the universe. Chremylus and his neighbors prosper, and informers, misers, and their kind get what they deserve. "Money makes the mare go." Athenian comedy had begun the process of evolution which was to result in its later degeneration to sentimental romance.

32

Fourth-Century Greece: Philosophy

GREAT as were the accomplishments of the Greek people in many activities during the last seventy-five years of their independence, the splendor of their achievements in the field of abstract thought far surpassed all others. In this period we find the first philosophers whose ideas still have a direct and profound influence upon modern man, especially those towering intellectual giants, Plato and Aristotle.

Our previous studies have shown upon what foundations the philosophic thought of this period was built. We have seen how earlier thinkers learned to explain natural phenomena without the aid of mythology. The sophists had taught their pupils close and exact reasoning. Socrates had improved the reasoning process still further, and had turned the attention of his circle from external nature to man and his problems. When he died, the new current of thought had not yet had time to congeal into a coherent system, and his successors were left free to continue what he had begun with the tools of thought which he and his predecessors had invented.

THE LESSER FOLLOWERS OF SOCRATES

The generation following the death of Socrates produced a bewildering variety of new theories which professed to be interpretations of his thought. Several of his more aspiring disciples seized upon various phases of his personality or ideas as embodying the core of his teachings, and proceeded to expand them into comprehensive systems of thought. Aside from Plato, whose school must be reserved for separate treatment, the chief socratic sects were the Megarians, the Cynics, and the Cyrenaics.

The Megarian School and the Cynics

Euclid, the founder of the Megarian school, was among the older followers of Socrates, and taught in his native city both before and after his master's death. But Euclid had also studied the works of Parmenides before meeting Socrates, and he attempted to combine both systems in an intricate synthesis which identified *goodness* with *existence*. In the hands of his successors this doctrine degenerated into fruitless quibbling and sophistical hairsplitting. Stilpo, a later Megarian, was the teacher of Zeno who founded the Stoic school.

In the Piraeus there lived a metic named Antisthenes, the son of an Athenian father and a Thracian slave woman. In spite of a rough and boorish temperament, he fell under the spell of Socrates' personality, and attempted to interpret the teachings of the master to future generations. After Socrates' death he opened a school in a suburban gymnasium known as the *Cynosarges*, from which probably came the name *cynics*, by which his followers were known. To Antisthenes the essence of socratic thought was man's independence from worldly goods, comforts, and pleasures. The wise man gains this independence, he taught, by voluntarily renouncing as many as possible of the artificial aids to well-being and by returning to the ways of nature. He will see the hollowness of all conventions and of the prejudices which are associated with them. Family ties and patriotism mean nothing to him, for he is a citizen of the whole world. He is as happy in rags as in silk, and he contents himself with the plainest food and poorest lodging. Over such a man, Fortune has no power, for of what can she deprive him that he has not already given up? Antisthenes professed contempt for all theoretical knowledge and especially for the views of Plato.

Far better known than Antisthenes was his successor, the eccentric and theatrical Diogenes. The modern world is well acquainted with the records of his odd doings — living in a tub, searching with a lamp in the daytime for an honest man, and ordering Alexander the Great to stand out of his sunlight. The Cynics were missionaries of the simple life, who wandered from town to town: ragged beggars who delivered pithy and colorful sermons to crowds on the street-corners and in the market-places. In general their moral influence was good, despite the presence of quacks and charlatans in their ranks. Cynicism continued to flourish down to the coming of Christianity, but a century after its origin, its salient doctrines were taken over by the Stoics.

The Cyrenaics

Diametrically opposed to this ascetic gospel was the ideal of Aristippus of Cyrene, who also professed to get his inspiration from Socrates. The chief good, he taught, is the pleasure of the present moment. Past and future are but shadows and have no real existence, but the present is ours and we should enjoy it to the full. All pleasures are equally good and honorable, but the wise man will not become the slave of any of them and will avoid passion and desire because of the pain which they give. Apparently the *Cyrenaics*, as the group came to be called, were indifferent to religion. Later the same ideas were to reappear in a modified form in Epicureanism.

Plato (429–347)

By far the greatest of the disciples of Socrates was Aristocles, generally known by his surname of *Plato*, or the "Broad-Browed." He belonged to one of the most aristocratic families of Athens, related on his mother's side to the ill-famed Critias. After applying himself briefly to poetry,

PORTRAIT BUST OF ARISTOTLE   PORTRAIT BUST OF PLATO

music, and athletics, he came under the influence of Socrates and devoted himself thenceforth to philosophy. After Socrates' execution, Plato left Athens in disgust, and traveled in Egypt, Cyrene, and western Greece. While abroad, he seems to have studied mathematics at Cyrene and Pythagorean philosophy with some of the brotherhoods of that sect in Italy.

He may also have absorbed some of the priestly lore of Egypt. Later, he made two voyages to Syracuse, where he hoped to induce the tyrants of the city to make it over into an ideal state. Both efforts ended in failure. About 387, Plato opened a school in the Academy, a park north of Athens, and he continued to act as its head until his death in 347.

The "Dialogues" of Plato

With the exception of a collection of letters which are probably forgeries, the only surviving works attributed to Plato are thirty-five dialogues. Several of these, too, may be the works of others. In all except the *Laws*, Socrates is the principal speaker. As previously indicated, it is impossible to determine exactly the relative proportions of socratic and platonic thought in this collection, and this fact must be kept in mind in studying either of them.

At his best, Plato has high claims to the title of a literary artist. He disdains dry, philosophical exposition and uncouth technical terms. Instead, he introduces us to realistic and protracted debates between flesh-and-blood people on the problems of life and man's relation to the universe. The *Dialogues* are filled with fine character sketches and delightful scenes. In the *Republic* we meet Cephalus, the wealthy and philosophic old armorer of the Piraeus, and Thrasymachus, a sophist, pictured as a coarse, rude ranter. Aristophanes, Protagoras, Alcibiades, and others pass before us in review, but above all we have the picture of Socrates himself. To Plato he was always the ideal philosopher, meeting each problem with exquisite courtesy, kindly wit, and profound wisdom. There are few more moving scenes in all literature than the description in the *Phaedo* of the old philosopher's last hours, as he calmly discussed with his friends the problem of the life after death, and then fearlessly drank the hemlock. Again, in the *Symposium*, we are given a view of the dinner party of Agathon, where the guests learnedly discuss the nature of love, and the drunken Alcibiades delivers a rousing eulogy of Socrates.

The dialogue as a means of philosophic exposition is open to grave objections. The reader is wearied by the endless logic-chopping, and by page after page of socratic monologues, broken only by occasional tokens of assent from the victims of Socrates' questioning. His reasoning is not always above reproach, and we wonder that some of it was allowed to go unchallenged. But in spite of these weaknesses, the *Dialogues* rank high among the literary masterpieces of the world.

Plato's Cosmology: The Theory of Ideas

Plato's approach to the world of men and things is from the realm of the ideal. Of the sciences, only mathematics was of use to him; his preference for it apparently sprang from the fact that it is relatively remote from the realm of the five senses. Beginning with the socratic doctrine, "Knowledge is virtue," he attempted to discover what were the true objects of knowledge — in other words, what was the nature of the universe. Out of this search grows the theory of creation which he expounds in the *Timaeus*. In the beginning the one true god (Plato was essentially a monotheist) had to deal with a chaotic and disorderly mass of matter and with an eternal and immutable set of forms or *ideas*. In these ideas were contained the spiritual models for all the qualities which were to give form and meaning to the visible world, but as yet they had not become actualized. God first mixed the ideas with baser elements to form a *world-soul*, which was to be the animating principle of the material world. He formed lesser gods and entrusted to them the task of creating vegetation, the lower animals, and man. Into all created objects were injected portions of the world-soul, which animated them and determined their characters. Here Plato came to the primary conclusion that the outer world is not mere matter. It is a well-ordered system, governed by law, and on that basis comprehensible by human intelligence.

From this theory Plato drew his views on the nature and destiny of man. The human soul has within it fragments of the pure and perfect ideas, which are the animating and shaping forces of the universe. These ideas impel the soul toward wisdom, which is the same as goodness. Since all truth is bound up in the ideas, and the human soul both partakes of their nature and has been in contact with them in a pure state before it was born, it instinctively recognizes them in its new environment. Hence, we tend intuitively to group individual objects into classes, each of which embodies some common quality which is the earthly reflection of a cosmic idea. Thus, we combine all human beings under the general heading "man," and the desirable qualities of a multitude of objects under that of "goodness." The ideas "man" and "goodness" are everlasting parts of divine truth, and the earthly beings or qualities to which they are applied are only mundane reflections of these ideas. Learning, he believed, is the awakening of our memories of truths known in a pre-existent state, and he whose memories of the great truths of the universe are strongly awakened cannot be other than good.

The Problem of Evil: Transmigration

But the soul is composed of baser as well as of finer stuff, and the proportion varies with the individual. Each of us has lived many times before, and in each previous existence we have either added to the proportion of fine "soul-stuff" by right living or to that of baser material by living viciously. Between each death and the succeeding rebirth, a thousand years elapse, and this period is spent in reaping the rewards or suffering the punishments merited by our past lives. Then each soul is allowed to choose the kind of life which it will live in its next incarnation, and the moral state which it has attained in the previous incarnation largely determines its choice. Once a choice is made, it is irrevocable. A soul addicted to the pursuit of truth and high ideals may escape from the round of birth and death. If for three successive incarnations it has followed the best life, then it is born no more, but enjoys eternal happiness contemplating the great universal truths — the ideas.

Plato's Political Theory: the "Republic"

Such a theory divides mankind sharply into classes on the basis of character, and a political philosophy based upon it is bound to be profoundly aristocratic. Such an aristocracy of character is described by Plato in the most famous of his dialogues, the *Republic*. It is significant of his idealistic approach to everyday problems that he does not avowedly base his description of the ideal state upon existing political institutions. The best state, he says, is the one which best serves the ends of *justice*, and by plotting the course which abstract justice will take in human society, he traces the outlines of a perfect polity.

Plato's ideal state is a Greek city-state, in which every person is placed in the position for which he is designed by nature. Its population is divided into two general classes — those who work and those who fight, govern, and philosophize. The division, however, is made upon the basis of personal fitness as determined by rigid, state-conducted tests, and not according to birth or personal favoritism. All children are to receive the same type of preliminary education, whether boys or girls, and regardless of parentage. In late adolescence, a preliminary examination will eliminate the majority, who will at once pass into agricultural employment or the manual trades. After some years of additional training, those who pass the first test will be subjected to a second. Those who fail in it will henceforth serve the state as soldiers. The few who have passed both tests will receive further and more elaborate training, then pass some years as soldiers and administrators, and finally, at the age of fifty, will become magistrates. Absolute equality of the sexes is to prevail and all types of employment are to be open to women.

To the lower class, Plato would allow both private property and monogamous private families, but the two upper classes are dealt with more rigorously. They have neither private property nor homes of their own; their mating is closely supervised by the state, and they are not even to know which are their own children. By such means our philosopher hopes to free his ruling classes from the personal greed and narrow family loyalty which have so often been the ruin of other aristocracies.

In order to accomplish his political and social ends, Plato would recast the educational system along lines curiously like those followed in modern totalitarian countries. All literature must be expurgated, so that only edifying matter will be left. History and legend must be treated similarly, no regard being had for objective truth, but only for their value as character-building agents. Deception should at times be used to keep the system running smoothly. In other ways the hypothetical curriculum was much like that current in the Athenian schools, except that gymnastic exercises and, for the higher classes, philosophy would be stressed more than was probably done in real life.

Plato's ideal society, which in spite of its philosophic character bore an obvious resemblance to Spartan institutions, may not have been intended to serve as the basis for actual political and social experimentation, and at any rate, his views gradually became more conservative. In the *Laws*, published in his old age, he modifies the picture considerably, abandoning the communistic and other radical features of the *Republic*, and substituting a national army for his earlier warrior caste.

Plato's Influence

It is hard to convey an adequate idea of the enormous extent and duration of Plato's influence. He has been, throughout the twenty-three hundred years since his death, one of the most potent molders of human thought in the Occidental world — the philosopher *par excellence* of ideas and ideals. The Academy continued to present his teachings, with modifications, until the sixth century A.D. Among his Roman admirers were Cicero and Virgil. In the third century A.D., the Neoplatonists diluted his philosophy with Oriental mysticism, and in this form it became the most popular and vital force in the declining Graeco-Roman paganism. Later, it profoundly influenced Christianity. In the Middle Ages it was largely eclipsed by the doctrines of Aristotle, but the Renaissance restored the fame of Plato, and he has continued in high favor among thinkers ever since. Seldom has any philosopher so profoundly influenced the mind of Western civilization.

ARISTOTLE (384–322 B.C.)

It is one of the ironies of history that Plato's most searching critic was a former student of the Academy. Aristotle was born in Stagira, a small Greek city of the Chalcidice. His father, Nicomachus, was at one time the personal physician of King Archelaus of Macedonia. At eighteen years of age, Aristotle entered the Academy, where he remained for nineteen years. After Plato's death he spent some years at the court of Hermias, the tyrant of the little Asiatic city of Atarneus and a former schoolmate at the Academy. Still later he was summoned to Pella to become the preceptor of Alexander, the crown prince of Macedonia. The boy seems to have developed a warm affection for his instructor, and possibly Alexander's later spectacular career as a conqueror and statesman owed something to Aristotle's teaching. In 335, Aristotle returned to Athens. Near the city stood a gymnasium called the Lyceum, and in it he opened a school somewhat like the Academy. As much of his teaching was done while walking about with his students, his system of thought came to be known as the *Peripatetic* system, from the Greek work *peripatein*, meaning "to stroll about." After Alexander's death, Aristotle's pro-Macedonian views made him the target of the patriotic party, which drove him from the city with threats of prosecution. He died at Chalcis the next year (322).

A Prolific Writer

Aristotle is credited by later Greek writers with the authorship of a thousand "books," or inscribed rolls of papyrus. Many of these were sometimes included in a single book, as we use the term. About 162 "books" bearing his name have survived, but some of them are obviously not from his pen. No doubt much which was originally credited to him was the work of his pupils and assistants, for Aristotle was an organizing genius, who could direct the efforts of many anonymous assistants toward the attainment of his own ends, and he probably got credit for much that was their work. Again, it seems likely that many of the works which actually represented his ideas were left unfinished, either as outlines or as lecture notes, and that his successors at the Lyceum cast them into their

present form. He wrote dialogues but they have perished. All the surviving works are strictly expository, and are closely reasoned, logical, and
dull. In them we find cold intellect and ruthless investigation instead of
the graphic description, sparkling wit, and lofty enthusiasm of the platonic *Dialogues*.

Never in the history of the world has there been such a synthesis of existing knowledge as that which Aristotle carried out. There is hardly a
field of Greek knowledge which he failed to explore. His findings are
carefully classified, interpreted, and co-ordinated with a regard for essentials and underlying principles which only a titanic intellect and tireless
industry could achieve.

His Criticisms of Platonism

While Aristotle agrees with Plato in recognizing a single supreme deity,
with a number of lesser gods, he entirely rejects Plato's view of the creation
of the world. God is a very remote and self-contained spirit, he says, and
the world has always existed. He treats the universe as if it were entirely
mechanical and governed by natural laws, hence, his god is not a personalized deity. The theory of ideas fares but little better. He denies that
the ideas have any independent existence, and considers them only as attributes of objects. There is no such thing as abstract *whiteness*, but there
are white houses, white snow, white linen, and so on, with whiteness
merely a common factor in diverse objects. Similarly, such terms as *goodness*, *truth*, and *justice* are names which we use to characterize the actions
and beliefs of men, and not earthly reflections of extra-mundane things.
Briefly, the problems of life should be attacked from the viewpoint of
life itself, rather than as appendages to a cosmic scheme of things. Such
an attitude is close to the scientific method.

To see how Aristotle's views affected his practice, we must examine his
works on ethics, political science, and natural science. Plato had begun
with a set of ideas whose validity he admitted, and from them had deduced
his views of life and of the universe. Aristotle attempted to confine himself to the inductive method of reasoning, ascertaining individual facts
through observation or experiment and from these forming his generalizations. In the *Nicomachean Ethics* he discusses individual conduct. He assumes that the aim of good conduct is happiness, which he defines as "the
working of the soul in the way of excellence." This consists of "living
well and doing well." One must have a fair share of this world's goods
and freedom from outright suffering, but beyond these essentials the recipe

for a good life is to be found largely in the word *moderation*. In the response to normal human appetites and impulses, either an excess or a deficiency constitutes a vice. Thus, concerning readiness to meet danger, an excess is foolhardiness, and a deficiency is cowardice. Both are vices. The mean between these extremes is the virtue courage. With regard to giving, excess is prodigality, and deficiency is stinginess. The mean is liberality, a virtue. Our philosopher repudiates the socratic and platonic theory that "knowledge is virtue." It is not enough to know what is good, for there is in human nature an irrational element which leads us to do what we know is wrong. Hence, he who would live virtuously must have and practice self-control. Yet this "wisdom of life" is, after all, not enough to insure the truest happiness. One must also free his mind from the shackles of his human environment, and contemplate eternal and universal truth, in order to win the greatest possible felicity. Therefore, the life of contemplation offers man the richest rewards of all. Since the human race is gregarious, one must associate with others of one's kind. Friendship — particularly that of good men for the sake of goodness — is the realization of man's highest and best impulses. "Friends are like one soul in two bodies." Thus, true and enlightened self-interest includes the love of one's friends.

The "Politics"

"Man," says Aristotle, "is a political animal." Hence, no study of his conduct is complete without a survey of the means by which he is governed. This is the subject of the *Politics*. True to his factual bent, Aristotle prepared for his task by having his students and assistants make detailed reports on 158 city-state constitutions. One of these studies, the *Athenian Constitution*, is extant. It consists of a historical survey, together with a description of Athenian government as it was in Aristotle's day. From these studies Aristotle derived the data upon which he based his principles of government and a lavish wealth of examples with which to illustrate them.

The *Politics* opens with a discussion of social and economic institutions. Not all persons are of equal ability, and in an orderly society each should be given the place which he can best fill. First is the freeman, who should be the ruler of his wife, children, and slaves. Women are inferior to men in wisdom and character, but have a certain amount of both. Children are temporarily lacking in both qualities by reason of their immaturity, and slaves have so little of either that their only usefulness lies in the services which they can render to others.

> Hence it is evident that although moral virtue is common to all those whom we have named, yet the temperance of a man and of a woman are not the same, though Socrates thought otherwise. For the courage of a man lies in commanding, and that of a woman in obeying, and the same is true in other respects. . . . As a child is incomplete, it is clear that his virtue is not to be referred to himself in his present state, but to what he will be when complete, and to his teacher. In like manner, the virtue of a slave is to be referred to his master.[1]

Free artisans are also inferior, he believes, to farmers and men of leisure. Worst of all are the bankers and others who live off the interest of invested funds. His justification for this opinion is curious. Interest is the *offspring* of money, and that lifeless coin should have offspring is supremely unnatural. A well-regulated state should not allow artisans or businessmen to participate in its government.

Private property and the monogamous family are necessary to an efficient social order. Plato was wrong when he said that communism of wives and property would produce universal benevolence. One result would be universal negligence, for "what is everybody's business is nobody's business." Another probable result would be the weakening of all bonds of affection among men.

> For as a very little sweetening, being added to a great deal of water, is imperceptible after the mixture, so must all the family bonds and the names by which they are called be weakened in such a community.[2]

In addition, all manner of crimes would be committed through ignorance or jealousy. Such an institution would defeat its own purpose.

Aristotle's Types of Government

Like Plato, Aristotle seems to consider the Greek city-state the highest type of political organization.

> A city is a society of persons joining together with their families and children for the sake of living as happily and independently as possible.[3]

It can be governed well in any one of three ways — by a monarchy, an aristocracy, or a popular government of a conservative type (*politeia*). But each of these forms can be perverted. When a monarchy becomes arbitrary and despotic, it is a tyranny. A government in which wealth rather than personal fitness has become the passport to political power is an oli-

[1] *Politics* I, 13.1260 A.   [2] *Ibid.*, II, 4.1262 G.   [3] *Ibid.*, III, 9.1280 B.

garchy, and one which is run by and in the interest of the rabble is a democracy.[1] Any of the legitimate forms can be good, and there are degrees of badness even among the perversions. It is the task of the lawgiver to fashion institutions so as to achieve the greatest good possible under the circumstances.

Economic and social conditions profoundly influence government. Where a few have great wealth and the majority are poor, oligarchy is certain to appear. Substantial equality of wealth, on the other hand, favors democracy. The lawmaker who wishes to found a stable government should take these forces into account and either construct a government fitted to existing economic and social conditions or vice versa. Where the rich or well-born have a preponderance of authority, it is necessary that they should avoid offensive conduct toward their inferiors, and particular care should be taken to prevent feuds between noble families, which often result in revolutions. The growth of a moneyed class in an aristocratic state is sure to undermine the position of the governing group, and the natural tendency of the upper classes to decrease in numbers is always a peril to their continued ascendancy. Thus, a knowledge of economic and social forces is a necessary preliminary to the study of political science.

The chief problem which confronted the city governments of the Greeks was, after all, the danger of revolution, and to it Aristotle devotes a whole book of the *Politics*. No government is stable unless the majority of the governed wish it to continue in its present form. Each variety of government is subject to its own special dangers, and each variety can be strengthened by guarding against those to which it is subject. Class warfare is best prevented by the growth of a strong middle class, which will act as a mediator between the extremes of wealth and poverty. The last three books of this masterly treatise are devoted to such topics as public meals, fortifications, religion, eugenics, and public education.

Much of the material in the *Politics* is so thoroughly Greek that it lost all practical value when the Greeks ceased to be independent, but the book as a whole will continue to be of value to students of political science so long as human nature remains unchanged. In it Aristotle gave to mankind the first scientific study of government. His practice of considering each case on its merits, and his maxim that each form of government is designed for a particular set of circumstances, are lasting contributions to political

---

[1] A similar discussion of the various classes of governments is found in Plato's *Republic*, Book VIII, from which Aristotle may have drawn some of the material summarized here.

thought. It is significant that two of the most successful governments in history — the Roman Catholic Church and the British Empire — have been administered by persons whose thinking has been shaped by the study of Aristotelean philosophy.

Aristotle on Natural Science

In the field of natural science, Aristotle was less competent than in ethics and political science. Here, indeed, his general point of approach was correct, and his researches were conducted on a colossal scale. Alexander the Great seems to have furnished him with ample funds for the purpose and to have aided him in other ways. These advantages were partly nullified by the conditions of the times. Aside from astronomy, mathematics, and medicine, the Greeks had almost no scientific tradition and had evolved no method of scientific inquiry. They had neither laboratory equipment nor instruments of precision for measuring reactions. Worst of all, perhaps, was the Hellenic addiction to unsupported hypotheses in fields where direct observation and experiment alone could determine the truth. Aristotle, who to some extent realized the dangers of this seductive pastime, strove to overcome it in his own work, but the habit frequently got the best of him. Furthermore, he had to contend with a mass of pseudo-information in the shape of travelers' tales and other stories which he could not check and which often sounded enough like the truth to deceive all but the actual observer. In the face of such difficulties it is remarkable that he achieved so much and made so few mistakes in several fields of natural science.

Astronomy, Biology, and Logic

Aristotle's astronomy illustrates his handicaps as a scientist. He had, of course, no telescope, spectroscope, or other precision instruments, and so he resorted to a series of guesses, almost all of which were wrong. He considers the earth to be the center of the planetary and stellar systems, and explains the movements of the heavenly bodies by supposing that they are attached to concentric, transparent spheres, which revolve about the earth. This theory was challenged by some later Greek astronomers, but in the medieval universities it was hailed with delight as confirming the similar statement in the Old Testament. It thus contributed to retard progress in astronomy until the seventeenth century A.D.

In biology his opportunities were better, and his success correspondingly greater. Not content with piecemeal descriptions of individual specimens, he undertook a general classification of all living things. In all, he describes some 520 species of land and marine animals, often with an accuracy which could only have been gained by dissection of specimens. His *History of Animals* is a work of bold generalizations and illuminating observations. He assumes the essential unity of all animal life and places man in his proper position among viviparous mammals. Where his opportunities permitted, he describes animal anatomy with fair accuracy. His physiological knowledge, on the other hand, is poor. He believes the heart to be the seat of the intelligence, and regards the brain as an organ for regulating the temperature of the blood, similar to the function of an automobile radiator. Food is "cooked" in the intestines. Women have fewer teeth than men. He believes in the spontaneous generation of eels from putrid mud. A rudimentary theory of organic evolution runs through his work, but it is too much involved in philosophic subtleties to be of value as a stimulus to further discoveries.

In the fields of logic and argumentation his chief contribution is the *syllogism*. It consists of three propositions: a major premise, a minor premise, and a conclusion. The major premise is a general statement, attributing a certain quality to a whole class of objects. The minor premise places one or more individuals within the class previously mentioned, and the conclusion (which deduces that the individual possesses the quality previously attributed to the whole class) follows logically from the relation of the other two. An example would be as follows:

> Major premise: All men are bipeds.
> Minor premise: John is a man.
> Conclusion: John is a biped.

The syllogism, of course, is not primarily a device for reasoning but rather a touchstone by which the validity of our thinking is tested. It is too slow and clumsy for everyday use, and in practice we suppress one or even both premises.

Space will not permit more than a few surveys of the vast amount of work done by this extraordinary man, and we must pass without special mention his work in metaphysics, psychology, literary criticism, rhetoric, and several other fields.

Aristotle's influence upon subsequent generations of thinkers would be hard to overestimate. The Lyceum continued to present his views until the sixth century A.D. His scientific studies inspired the biologists, physicians, and astronomers of Egyptian Alexandria for three centuries after his

death. The schoolmen of medieval Europe learned the art of reasoning
from his logical treatises and accepted uncritically such of his scientific
works as came their way. Not until the seventeenth century, when scientists advanced beyond his method and discovered new experimental instruments, did his reputation as a scientist suffer eclipse. But even today
his observations still arouse the admiration of scientists when they understand the conditions under which he had to work. In a deeper sense his
influence still lingers. He is the champion of the factual and inductive
approach to the problem of knowledge, just as Plato is the protagonist of
the idealistic and deductive method. Every man, in so far as he attempts
to gain wisdom, favors the method of one or the other, but in more ways
than we realize, all of us are indebted to the combined wisdom of both.

33

****

Alexander the Great: The Macedonian

Conquest of the Near East

THE DEATH of Philip of Macedonia left the stage set for one of the most
profound political and cultural revolutions in human annals — the conquest of western Asia and Egypt by the Macedonians and their allies, the
continental Greeks. This momentous event has exerted a lasting influence
upon the subsequent history of the conquered peoples, the conquerors, and
the human race in general. It subjected the peoples of the Near East to
Greek cultural influences for a period which varied in different localities
from two hundred to a thousand years, and caused a potent reciprocal
interaction of the Hellenic and Oriental civilizations. The center of economic gravity now shifted from the poorly endowed Greek peninsula to
the Mediterranean islands and the near-by coasts of Asia and Africa; the
Greek tradition of independent city-state republics was forced to give way
before a trend toward larger political units and absolute monarchy.

So profound a change in human affairs did not take place without pre-
monitory signs. The Greeks and Persians had been in contact with each
other for over two centuries before Alexander the Great invaded Asia.
Greeks had traversed the Persian Empire, had served as mercenaries in its
armies, and had lived at the court of its rulers. As we have seen in the case
of Xenophon and the Ten Thousand, the Greeks had had ample opportunity to know the weakness of the Persians. At the same time they had
themselves begun to outgrow the narrow bonds imposed by the system of
city-states, and their culture had entered a broader and mellower stage
than that of the fifth century. For fifty years the Greeks had submitted
to an informal Persian suzerainty. More recently, the League of Corinth
had placed them under the domination of a people closely related to them,

with the fresh energy, vitality, and qualities of leadership which fourth-century Greece had lost. Previous wars and revolutions had displaced large numbers of Greeks and made them willing to migrate to any place where they might find good homes. All that the Graeco-Macedonian side needed was good military leadership, and that was supplied by one of the world's outstanding generals, Alexander the Great.

ALEXANDER THE MAN

Alexander was the son of Philip II by the Epirote princess Olympias, and his personal qualities partook of the characters of both parents. Olympias was a woman of violent and passionate temperament, capable of savage cruelty when her anger was aroused, but possessed withal of a strain of mysticism and romanticism which her son inherited. Through her, Alexander traced his ancestry to the Homeric hero Achilles. Through his father he claimed descent from the demigod Heracles. Much of his behavior can be explained by the fact that he took pride in these family

University Prints

PORTRAIT BUST OF ALEXANDER THE GREAT

traditions and tried to emulate his reputed forebears. When swayed by anger, he was a veritable wild beast, but ordinarily he kept his temper carefully under control. In his better moments he was capable of a chivalrous courtesy toward opponents and a loyalty to friends, which has been all too rare among the great leaders of any age or people. Once his mind was made up, he pursued his course with indomitable resolution and rarely abandoned a project until he had brought it to completion. He had even greater gifts than his father as a soldier and administrator, and, in addition, an open-mindedness which enabled him to deal sympathetically with the customs and traditions of strange peoples. His resourcefulness, both in war and peace, was boundless. In his military career he met all types of enemies under every conceivable circumstance, but he was never at a loss to devise successful tactics. Thanks to Aristotle and other Greek tutors, he had been imbued thoroughly with Greek literature and philosophy and regarded himself as the champion of Greek interests until late in his career. He was a barbarian by inheritance, a Greek by training, and a genius in his own right.

His Youthful Experience

Alexander was twenty years old when he mounted the Macedonian throne, but he was already rich in experience. At sixteen he had acted as regent of the kingdom in his father's absence, and at eighteen he had led the attack on the Athenians and Thebans at Chaeronea. He had gone into exile with his mother when Philip's marriage to Cleopatra threatened his position, but was later persuaded to return. And so, having tasted of both power and adversity, Alexander was called upon in 336 to fill his father's place as king of Macedonia, general of the League of Corinth, and leader of the projected war of revenge upon the Persian Empire.

ALEXANDER CONSOLIDATES HIS POSITION

In spite of an apparently clear title to the crown, Alexander's inheritance was by no means either safe or certain. As usual in Macedonia, several pretenders disputed his claim. The Balkan tribes, and above all the Greeks, had not yet become accustomed to subjection and were seething with revolt. When the Athenians heard the news of Philip's death, they held a thanksgiving festival, and Demosthenes began to organize a new league of Macedonia's enemies, including Persia. Even the Thessalians showed signs of indecision. All along the northern frontier, enemies were preparing to take advantage of the unsettled conditions. Unless the new king could avert these dangers, his crown, and also his life, would be in peril.

First Expeditions

Alexander acted with whirlwind speed. His father's murderers were punished and the pretenders disposed of. His next task was to prevent an open break with the Greeks. Leaving his northern enemies for the moment, he hastened to Thessaly and secured his election to his predecessor's position of archon. In quick succession the Delphic Amphictyony, the Boeotians, the Athenians, and the Peloponnesians were brought into line, and before the end of the year 336 the congress of the League of Corinth had elected him to the post which Philip had held. As yet no one was punished for subversive activities.

With Greece once more under control, Alexander turned to the northern frontier. A lightning thrust subdued the tribes along the lower Danube, and then the Illyrians and Taulantians to the northwest of Macedonia were defeated. The Celtic tribes near the head of the Adriatic Sea heard of the young Macedonian king's brilliant feats and concluded an alliance with him. The northern frontier was safe, but it was not a moment too soon, for new trouble had broken out in Greece.

The Theban War

While Alexander had been absent in the north, the Persians had not been idle. In 336, a palace revolution had placed upon the throne Darius III, a collateral relative of the royal family. As the Macedonian general Parmenion was already in Asia at the head of an invading army, Darius determined to meet the danger in the traditional manner by stirring up a war in Greece against the aggressor. Envoys were sent to continental Greece with large sums of money, but they had no success until a report arrived that Alexander had been killed by the Thracians. Then the Thebans revolted, killed some Macedonian officers, and besieged their Macedonian garrison. While Athens had not yet officially declared for the rebels, Demosthenes personally had taken part in promoting the Theban outbreak, and the trouble was likely to spread if not quickly taken in hand.

In an incredibly short time Alexander covered the distance between northern Macedonia and Thebes. On the way he was joined by the

Boeotians and Phocians — long-standing enemies of the rebellious city. When the Thebans refused to submit, Alexander attacked and took their city. Its fate was referred to the congress of the league, apparently represented only by the states which had sent contingents to Alexander's army. The decision was that Thebes should be destroyed. Thousands of her citizens had been killed in the assault. Alexander saved the temples and the house of the poet Pindar, and freed all members of the pro-Macedonian faction, but the remainder of the city was destroyed, and thousands of women and children were sold as slaves. After this fearful lesson to Greek malcontents, Alexander could afford to deal leniently with those who were less deeply compromised. Even Demosthenes escaped punishment for his part in the affair. Awful as the fate of Thebes had been, it served its purpose. In the years that followed, although the sympathies of the Greeks were undoubtedly with Persia, they thought it wise to remain quiet. The expedition against the Great King could now be begun in earnest.

The Conquest of the Persian Empire

Early in the year 334, Alexander crossed the Hellespont to assume personal direction of the Asiatic campaign. Thus far Parmenion had had but little success. When the king took charge, his forces controlled only a landing-place on the Asiatic side of the Sea of Marmora. Hence, Alexander had to start the whole campaign almost from the beginning. To protect the northern frontier and to overawe the Greeks, he left Antipater, a faithful and competent officer of Philip's school, as regent, with an army of twelve thousand infantry and fifteen hundred cavalry.

Persian Resources

At first glance, the odds in the coming struggle seemed to favor the Persians decisively. The army of invasion numbered no more than thirty thousand infantry of all kinds and five thousand cavalry. Alexander had little money and was heavily in debt. Although the Greeks submitted sullenly to his domination, they offered little co-operation and were ready at any favorable moment to create a diversion in favor of Persia. The Persian fleet of four hundred ships controlled the sea, and Alexander's own fleet, which numbered about one hundred and sixty ships, was of little use to him. To attain success, he would have to penetrate long distances into the interior of Asia and to establish lines of communication with the homeland. Against him were the wealth and the manpower of the Persian

Empire, both of which were many times larger than those of Macedonia and which had the added advantage of fighting on territory with which her commanders were thoroughly acquainted.

But the advantages were not all with the Great King. The very extensiveness of his dominions made them unwieldy. His nobles were numerous and warlike, but his armies had made scarcely any progress in the art of war for two centuries. The ranks consisted for the most part of unwilling and poorly organized levies from the subject peoples. There was no native Asiatic force with the disciplined effectiveness of a Greek phalanx, and the only expedient which the Persians had ever devised for encountering Greek armies was to hire other Greeks as mercenaries. Anything like the integrated perfection of the Macedonian army was unheard of and unthinkable. In addition, the control of Darius III over many of the peoples of western Asia was slight or non-existent. It was rare for the more warlike mountaineers to acknowledge Persian supremacy. Egypt had only recently been reconquered after a long period of independence and its people were still smarting from the humiliations to which they had been subjected by Artaxerxes Ochus. Above all, Darius III was a weakling, who repeatedly fled from battlefields while his soldiers were still fighting bravely for him. Having none of the other qualities of a general, he was forced to oppose Alexander, one of the outstanding military geniuses of all time, and in this difference between the two commanders lay the decisive factor of the war.

The Conquest of Asia Minor

True to his conception of his mission as the champion of Hellenism against the Asiatic barbarians, Alexander personally landed near the site of Troy and sacrificed to the shades of Achilles and other Homeric heroes. Rejoining his army, he encountered a force of some forty thousand men, half of whom were Greek mercenaries, which the Persian satraps of Asia Minor had gathered and posted behind the little river Granicus. In a short, fierce fight he defeated them, and massacred or enslaved the Greeks who were traitors to the national cause. His victory destroyed the only field army of the enemy in Asia Minor. But the other Asiatic Greek cities were garrisoned and controlled by pro-Persian oligarchies. As Alexander advanced, most of them surrendered to him without a blow, but at Miletus and Halicarnassus the Persians gave up only after hard fighting. Everywhere the oligarchies were replaced by democracies, the freedom of the cities was restored, and they were admitted to the League of Corinth.

Having traversed the western coast of the peninsula, Alexander turned to the northeast and followed a semicircular route through its mountainous central region. At Gordium, in Phrygia, he spent the winter of 334–333. In one year he had completed the conquest of that portion of Asia Minor which the Persians had controlled.

Meanwhile, the Rhodian Greek Memnon, the ablest of Darius' generals, had been placed in command of the Persian fleet. With it he attempted to impede the progress of the invaders by aiding the besieged cities and carrying the war into Greece. As Alexander had sent his fleet home, Memnon was able to capture several of the Aegean islands and to cause the Macedonians considerable alarm. But he soon died, and Alexander's conquest of the coast cities eventually deprived the fleet of bases and compelled it to disband.

The Campaign of 333: Cilicia Occupied

Hardly had the spring of 333 arrived when the young conqueror was on the move. By a swift advance he was able to seize the passes which led into Cilicia, and soon occupied the province. At Tarsus, after a bath in the icy waters of the river Cydnus, he contracted a fever which nearly cost him his life. Weeks were lost while he hovered at the point of death, and when he recovered, Darius III was in northern Syria with an army reputed to consist of six hundred thousand men. At last the Persians were ready to strike an effective blow for the defense of their empire.

It was early autumn when Alexander occupied the passes leading into Syria and set out to locate the enemy. The Persians had in the meantime crossed the mountains into Cilicia. Before Alexander was aware of the fact, they had cut the Macedonians' line of communications and had slain their sick and wounded. Alexander faced about, and near the city of Issus both armies prepared for battle. The strength of the Persian army was, of course, far below six hundred thousand, but it was considerably greater than the forces under Alexander's banner. As at the Granicus, the Persian front was protected by a stream, the Pinarus, and like his satraps, Darius stiffened his line with a force of Greek mercenaries. As usual, the decisive move of the battle was the resistless charge of the "companion" cavalry under Alexander himself against the Persian left wing, which gave way under the shock, allowing the "companions" to attack the Greek mercenaries in the center. Darius fled, the whole Persian line gave way, and the victors captured the Persian camp. As Darius had followed the Oriental custom of taking his family with him on campaigns, his mother,

University Prints

ALEXANDER SARCOPHAGUS SHOWING BATTLE OF MACEDONIANS AND PERSIANS

wife, and three children were among the prisoners. The conqueror treated them with chivalrous courtesy.

The battle of Issus was decisive in several respects. It secured Alexander's hold on Asia Minor and opened the road to Syria and Egypt. The severity of the blow to the Persian Empire may be judged from the fact that soon after the battle, Darius sent twice to his opponent to beg for peace. In his second offer he promised to pay a ransom of ten thousand talents for his family, to give Alexander his daughter in marriage, and to cede to him all Persian lands west of the Euphrates River. Parmenion advised Alexander to accept, but Alexander had larger aims. "There cannot be two suns in the sky, and there cannot be two kings in Asia," he is reported to have said. Henceforth, his ambition for world-conquest began to outweigh his philhellenic enthusiasm. At the same time the news of his victory quieted the Greeks temporarily (except Sparta), and tribute and the spoils of war solved his financial problems.

Succeeding Campaigns

With no Persian field army near them, Syria, Phoenicia, and Palestine submitted readily to their new lord. But Tyre and Gaza were exceptions. The Tyrians wanted to preserve neutrality between the contestants, but

Alexander would accept nothing short of submission. After a desperate struggle of seven months' duration, the city was captured, the inhabitants killed or sold into slavery, and the site converted into a Macedonian stronghold. Gaza, led by a eunuch named Batis, resisted heroicaliy, but likewise suffered destruction.

In Egypt, Alexander had no opposition to fear. The cruelties practiced by Artaxerxes Ochus eleven years before had completed the alienation of the people from their Persian allegiance, and they hailed Alexander as a deliverer. He carefully flattered them by assuming the titles of a native Pharaoh and by sacrificing to their gods. Near the northwest corner of the Nile Delta, on the coast opposite the island of Pharos, he laid out a new city, which he named Alexandria after himself. From every point of view the site was admirably chosen. The new city had two excellent harbors and was the natural point of junction for the commerce of the Mediterranean coasts, the Nile Valley, and the Indian Ocean. From that day to this it has been one of the world's greatest commercial centers.

At this point Alexander undertook a pilgrimage characteristic of the romantic strain in his temperament. More than three hundred miles west of the Nile, in the midst of the North African Desert, lay the oasis of Ammonium, the seat of a famous oracle of the Egyptian god Amen-Re. Alexander went there, with a small following, to consult the oracle, as his reputed ancestors Perseus and Heracles were said to have done. As king of Egypt he was a god *ex officio*, and the priests caused him to be saluted as one. Thenceforth he took his patent of divinity very seriously. The ram's horns which were part of the insignia of Amen were frequently portrayed on his head on coins and elsewhere. Later the idea of divine kingship was habitually asserted by his Hellenistic successors.

Darius Gathers Another Army

With the Mediterranean coast securely in his possession, Alexander was now ready to complete his conquest of the Persian Empire. In the spring of 331, he collected his forces at Tyre and thence marched northward through Syria to the Euphrates. Skirting the northern edge of the Syrian Desert, he crossed both the Euphrates and Tigris and then turned southward through Assyria. There Darius awaited him with another army, collected during the two years which had elapsed since the battle of Issus. The army was drawn largely from the eastern and central portions of the empire and included two features which the invaders had not yet encountered. Darius was equipped with a herd of fifteen Indian elephants, to be used in much the same way as are modern tanks. He had also revived the old device of using chariots with long scythes projecting from the ends of the axles. These were expected to throw the Macedonian phalanx into disorder and to prepare for a decisive charge of cavalry. The numerical strength of the Persian army is unknown, but rumor placed it at a million infantry and two hundred thousand cavalry.

Near the village of Gaugamela, about three hundred miles north of Babylon, Alexander's army came into contact with the enemy. As he was certain to be outflanked by the much larger Persian army, he posted a reserve force behind his battle line, with orders to face about and form a square if the enemy should attack his rear. The fighting was much hotter and longer than at Issus. The elephants and chariots proved tactical failures. Again the headlong charge of the "companion" cavalry made the decisive break in the Persian line. But Alexander's line was also broken by the Persian cavalry, and even his camp was for a moment in the possession of the enemy. The usual cowardice of Darius, however, made him the first to flee from the field. When night fell, the survivors of his army were in flight, leaving their camp and baggage in the hands of the victors.

The battle of Gaugamela (sometimes called Arbela after the near-by Assyrian city) broke the power of Darius completely. Never again was he able to gather an effective army, and although five more years were to elapse before the conquest of his dominions was completed, the resistance to Alexander was henceforth local and sporadic rather than national. Alexander could now with justification call himself "King of Asia."

Alexander Occupies Babylonia and Persia

The Macedonian king lost no time in harvesting the fruits of victory. A month after the battle he was in Babylon, where he conciliated the priests and people as effectively as in Egypt. Early in the year 330, he took possession of Susa, Persepolis, Pasargadae, and Ecbatana — the royal capitals and sacred cities of the Medes and Persians. There he gained the hoarded treasures of the Persian kings, which amounted to several hundred million dollars, with a purchasing power many times greater than the same sum would have at present. Most important of all, large numbers of the Persian nobles lost confidence in their government and submitted to the new lord. He treated them with marked consideration and even appointed some of them to important posts in the civil administration. At all times the military and financial posts were reserved for Macedonians and Greeks. Finally, as a symbol of the end of the Persian Empire, he burned the palace at Persepolis and massacred or enslaved the inhabitants of the city.

Having secured the Persian and Median cities, Alexander's next task was to run the fugitive Darius to earth. The latter, accompanied by a small military force and a group of his nobles, fled northward to the shore of the Caspian Sea and then turned eastward toward his provinces of Parthia and Bactria. Alexander followed in rapid pursuit, but he was never to see his enemy alive. The Persian nobles, disgusted with their timid and vacillating king, first imprisoned and then stabbed him, leaving the corpse to be found by the pursuers. One of the assassins, Bessus, assumed the royal title and continued the resistance to Alexander in Bactria and Sogdiana, the provinces in the extreme northeastern part of the empire. Alexander, characteristically, gave the fallen monarch a royal burial and punished Bessus with barbaric severity. Later he added Darius' daughters to his harem.

The War in the Northeastern Provinces

The Macedonians now entered upon the conquest of the northeastern part of the Persian Empire. At this point the character of the struggle changed radically. Hitherto the invaders had fought with the armies of the Persian state, but now they faced a national struggle for independence, led in large part by local chiefs and supported by the body of the population. These eastern Iranians were closely related to the Persians in blood and culture and had the same Zoroastrian religion. They had been contented under their former government and would have none of Alexander. He was compelled to spend over three years in breaking their resistance. Marches and countermarches, sieges, rebellions of peoples who had previously submitted, and conflicts with the nomads of the steppes made up the military history of the period. Alexander had to make his army capable of increasingly swift movement to cope with this guerrilla warfare. For this purpose he enlisted Asiatic light cavalry and other forces armed in the Persian fashion. To hold conquered districts to their allegiance, he founded many colonies, often named Alexandria with the name of the neighboring native people added, which he peopled with discharged Greek and Macedonian veterans and other Greek immigrants. So intensive was this colonization that in the next century Bactria and the surrounding districts became the seat of a Greek kingdom which lasted for over a century. When the conquest was completed, Alexander celebrated his reconciliation with his new subjects by marrying a Bactrian princess, the beautiful Roxana.

Hostility in Alexander's Ranks

While engaged in the struggle with the eastern Iranians, he first became aware of serious discontent among his immediate followers. Following his habit of ruling each people according to its native traditions, he had begun to adopt the pomp and state of a Persian king and had shown great favor to individual Persians. Among the practices which he was striving to introduce at his court was that of *proskynesis*, whereby each person who approached him was to fall prostrate on the ground before him. To the Macedonians this was a mark of degradation and they deeply resented it. His old companions were likewise offended by the airs of divinity which he assumed on public occasions, and his limitless ambition for further conquests frightened and antagonized them. It was plain that in the empire which he was founding, they would have to share the first place with their former enemies. In 330, a conspiracy against his life was discovered, and it happened that Philotas, the son of his veteran general Parmenion and an officer of high rank, had known of the plot but had not reported it. Philotas was condemned to death by the army. Thereupon, Alexander himself ordered the execution of Parmenion. Sometime later another conspiracy was discovered among the royal pages. Callisthenes, the nephew of Aristotle and the official historian of the expedition, had been the tutor of several of the culprits and was known to be opposed to proskynesis. He, too, was finally put to death.

The conclusive proof of the growing hostility between the Macedonian king and his former friends was his murder of Cleitus, who had saved Alexander's life at the battle of the Granicus. At a drinking party, when both were far gone in their cups, Cleitus began to reproach him for his new behavior and to compare him unfavorably with his father Philip. At last Alexander, maddened by such stinging rebukes, seized a spear and killed his friend. When he realized what he had done, his grief passed all bounds. For three days he would see no one and neither ate nor drank. But it was only his intimate companions who resented his new ways. The rank and file of the soldiers still idolized him.

Invasion of India

With the conquest of eastern Iran completed, the young conqueror's ambition was still unsatisfied. His previous campaigns had carried him into what is today Afghanistan, and from there he meant to conquer India, though he had little or no conception of its size. The Indus Valley was at

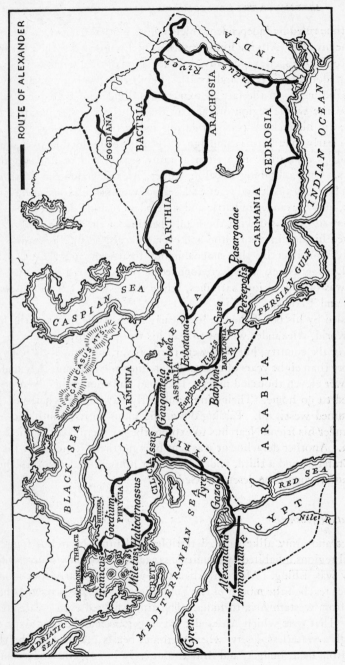

ROUTE OF ALEXANDER

MAP OF ALEXANDER'S EMPIRE

that time ruled by independent chiefs whose mutual feuds opened the way for the invader. Allying himself with a chief whose name the Greeks pronounced Taxiles, Alexander invaded the region of the Punjab with an army of Macedonians, Greeks, and Asiatics, numbering one hundred and twenty thousand men. In the face of tremendous difficulties he reduced to subjection the whole region drained by the Indus and its tributaries. Nowhere did his reckless personal daring and fertility of resource stand out more clearly than in this campaign, in the course of which he overcame the difficulties of warfare in a tropical rainy season and of Indian military tactics. Once, climbing a scaling-ladder, Alexander jumped down alone into a besieged castle and received a serious wound. Taxiles' enemy, King Porus, met Alexander in battle and suffered a crushing defeat, but the victor was so impressed with the manly bearing of the Indian king that he restored his dominions to him and even enlarged them. Porus was completely won over by this magnanimous treatment and became a loyal vassal. New Greek cities were founded in the conquered territory. Some of it was organized into satrapies, while the rest was left to vassals like Porus and Taxiles.

Misled by his belief that he had nearly reached the limits of the habitable world, Alexander wished to lead his troops on to complete the conquest of the country, but they were tired of war and refused to go farther. In more than eight years of constant marching and fighting, they had covered over eleven thousand miles. They had had enough of adventure and wanted to go home. Their king reluctantly gave up his cherished plan, and turned westward. Passing down the Indus to its mouth, he sent a fleet under his friend Nearchus to explore the northern coast of the Indian Ocean. Another detachment was sent by a northern route under his general Craterus; and a third, under Alexander himself, undertook the march overland through the deserts of Gedrosia.

The Return Journey

Fleet and army alike suffered terrible hardship. Nearchus found the coastal regions inhabited by primitive savages, whose only source of food-supply was fishing. After an exhausting voyage of nearly four months, the fleet reached the mouth of the Euphrates, having rediscovered the sea route from western Asia to India. The army suffered even greater privations. That part which Alexander led in person marched for sixty days through a waterless desert, where men and beasts perished by the thousands from heat, hunger, and thirst. But early in 324, Alexander and the survivors of his fleet and army were back in Persia, where the task of creating a stable government for his dominions awaited him.

ALEXANDER THE STATESMAN

It was time, indeed, that the ruler of the empire returned. During the conquest, his government of conquered lands had been a series of makeshifts. As in any absolute monarchy, only the presence of the ruler could prevent oppressive conduct by his subordinates. The mixed staff of Macedonians, Greeks, and Persians which he left to administer his territories probably never expected his return alive from Bactria and India. Corruption, extortion, oppression, and insubordination were everywhere prevalent. His treasurer, Harpalus, fled rather than face an inquiry into his conduct. Satraps had enlisted mercenary armies, plundered tombs and temples, and put his subjects to death without trial. Alexander acted with vigor and severity. Some of the culprits were executed, others were deposed, and soon a semblance of order and justice was restored.

The Extent of the Empire

From Babylon, which was marked out as the future royal residence, Alexander now ruled an empire which included approximately the former territories of Macedonia, Greece, and the Persian Empire, together with a part of India. On the other hand, northeastern Asia Minor from the Bosporus eastward, which had been a part of the Persian Empire, was never conquered by the Macedonians. It was soon broken up into independent states under native rulers or Persian nobles who had settled there before the time of Alexander. Even so, his empire constituted the most extensive group of territories ever ruled by a single man.

Alexander was now no longer the doctrinaire and exclusive Hellenist that he had been in 334, and in the short span of life left to him after his return he attempted to establish his rule upon a broader basis than one of mere Macedonian and Greek support. Experience had shown him the good qualities of the Iranian peoples, and he now saw that their co-operation was necessary if his extensive dominions were to hold together. Henceforth, he endeavored to place them upon a plane of equality with his European subjects in the army and in the civil administration, and to fuse them, with the Greeks and Macedonians, into a single imperial people. For this purpose they were enlisted as soldiers, armed and disciplined in the Macedonian fashion, and efforts were made to break down national and local prejudices which interfered with his plans.

The Marriages of Susa, and Mutiny

To celebrate the reconciliation of Europe with Asia, Alexander staged a striking pageant — the mass marriages of Susa. In a single evening he and eighty of his principal officers married Persian women. He himself married two brides — one from each branch of the Persian royal house, and his dearest friend, Hephaestion, married a sister of one of them. Ten thousand of the common soldiers had already set the example for their leaders by taking Persian brides, and to each of them the king gave a dowry. He had already founded Greek colonies in Asia, and he was said to be contemplating Persian colonies in Europe.

Some of these innovations were as unpopular with the masses of the soldiers as the Persian court etiquette had been with the nobles. When it became known that their king contemplated discharging ten thousand veterans who were unfit for duty and sending them home, discontent grew into mutiny. The whole army cried out that it would go home and leave Alexander to the protection of his "father" Amen, a scornful allusion to his claim to divinity.

First, after taking the precaution of having his guards arrest and kill the ringleaders of the movement, Alexander made his men a speech. He reminded them that his father, Philip, had found them wretched shepherds, tending their flocks on mountainsides in constant fear of their neighbors, and had made them the masters of Greece. He himself, he said, had shared their hardships and dangers and had made them the masters of a vast empire. If they wished to leave, they were all discharged. They might go home when they wished and tell the people that they had left their king to be guarded by conquered barbarians. Retiring to his quarters, he proceeded to enroll Persians to fill the vacant places in the army, both high and low. This was too much. The mutineers came in a body to beg for pardon, and a grand reconciliation took place, but Alexander discharged the veterans and proceeded with his plans as if nothing had happened.

Relations With the Greeks

If relations between the king and his soldiers were not always pleasant, the tension between him and the Greeks mounted steadily. While the war with Darius was at its height, King Agis of Sparta made a determined effort to break up the League of Corinth, but he was defeated and slain by the regent Antipater, and Sparta was compelled to join the league. Greek mercenaries had fought in all the Persian armies and other evidences of anti-Macedonian feeling were plentiful. When Harpalus fled from the just wrath of his master, he brought to Athens seven hundred talents which he had stolen.   The Athenian state acted very properly in its dealings with the refugee, but Demosthenes and others were accused of taking bribes from him amounting to half the total.   For this the orator was fined and imprisoned, but he finally escaped and went into exile.   In 324, Alexander took the Greek situation in hand.   His first demand was that each state worship him as one of its patron gods.   To this they made no objection.   Then, on his own authority, he ordered all of them to allow their exiles to return home.   This was a gross violation of the constitution of the League of Corinth, and it was widely and bitterly resented.   The matter was still under discussion when Alexander died.   There can be no doubt that, had he lived, he would have reduced Greece to strict subjection, possibly at the cost of war.

Alexander's Death

Death found the great conqueror contemplating still greater conquests. Plans appear to have been maturing for an expedition into the western Mediterranean and vast projects of exploration were under way.   Then, in the autumn of 324, Hephaestion died.   The blow was a heavy one for Alexander.   He gave his friend an extravagantly splendid funeral, and thereafter resumed his plans, but death was at hand for him too.   An attack of fever, contracted in the Babylonian marshes, sent him to his bed. For days he insisted on continuing his regular business, but grew no better. When it became known that he was dying, the whole force of Macedonians stationed in Babylon forced the palace gates and filed silently past his bedside.   On June 13, 323, he died, not yet thirty-three years of age.

In evaluating Alexander's influence upon history, it may be best to begin with the negative side of the account.   The great object of his later career — the foundation of a lasting empire based upon the support of Macedonians, Greeks, and Persians — was not attained.   His empire hardly outlasted its founder, and the leaders to whom its fragments fell were usually not in sympathy with his policies toward the Asiatics.   He failed to conciliate the Greeks, although he sincerely made the attempt, and Greece was later to be the "Achilles' heel" of Macedonia.   Both Greece and Macedonia were the weaker as a result of his conquests, which drew their strongest and most enterprising people away to Egypt and Asia for a century or more after his death.

When all of these deductions have been made, his constructive achievements were stupendous. By seizing and distributing the hoarded wealth of the Persisn kings and by opening new trade routes to central Asia and India, he wrought a far-reaching revolution in the economic life of the Mediterranean world. His marches through the little known parts of central and southern Asia and the exploring expeditions which he fitted out added greatly to the geographical knowledge of the Greeks and their neighbors. Above all, in the regions which he conquered, he made possible the growth of Hellenistic civilization. He founded, it is said, seventy Greek cities in Asia, and his successors probably more than doubled the number. In these colonies the Greeks were brought into contact with the surrounding Orientals, and some of the Orientals likewise adopted Greek culture. Greek art, literature, and philosophy took root all over southwestern Asia and in Egypt, and the Greek tongue in a simplified state became the international language from India to the Atlantic Ocean. The educated classes of this wide region now had a common medium for the exchange of ideas and the fact affected both East and West. Greek art, literature, and music influenced the Asiatics as far east as India and possibly even China; and Asiatic religions — particularly Christianity — took advantage of the new medium of communication to spread into Europe. Thus, in some degree Alexander realized his desire to amalgamate European and Asiatic cultures.

The "Successors" and the Dissolution of the Empire

The death of Alexander, so soon after the winning of his empire, doomed it to speedy dissolution. With its many diverse peoples, extensive area, and poor means of communication, it had no cohesive force except the transcendent genius of its creator. The Macedonians seem to have idolized him personally, but condemned his policies. Most of the military commanders were a hard, ambitious, and unscrupulous group, who had bowed to the indomitable will of the great ruler but now felt free to make their own fortunes. Of the whole group, only the Macedonians Antipater and Perdiccas and the Greek Eumenes were interested in preserving the empire intact under the old dynasty.

The Regency and the Rise of the Successors

When Alexander died, he had no sons, but a few weeks later Roxana bore him an heir. As a compromise between the old Macedonians of the army and Alexander's immediate staff, both the young Alexander and his epi-

PTOLEMY
The son of Lagus

leptic uncle Philip Arrhidaeus were declared joint sovereigns, with Perdiccas as regent.   The arrangement failed, largely because of the jealous
ambition of the Macedonian war lords.   Ptolemy, the son of Lagus, who
had been made satrap of Egypt; Seleucus, the satrap of Babylonia; Antigonus the One-Eyed, satrap of Phrygia; and Lysimachus, the satrap of
Thrace — each assumed the prerogatives of an independent sovereign.
Greece burst into revolt (the Lamian War), with the indomitable Demosthenes once more in the forefront, but the rising was put down by Antipater.   Athens had to accept an oligarchic constitution and Demosthenes
killed himself to escape capture.   In an attack upon Ptolemy, Perdiccas
was killed.   Antipater did not long outlive him.   Old Olympias, the
mother of Alexander, slew Philip Arrhidaeus, and after the death of Antip-

ater, his son Cassander killed both Olympias and the young Alexander. The legitimate claimants to the throne were exterminated.

Antigonus the One-Eyed

The years 318 to 301 inclusive were marked by the attempt of Antigonus the One-Eyed to unite the whole Empire under his own rule. He was an able soldier and administrator, but his age was against him, and he had no claim to rule except his ability to enforce obedience. Ptolemy made himself impregnable in Egypt. Seleucus mastered Babylonia and the eastern provinces. Lysimachus controlled the eastern part of the Balkan peninsula, and Cassander set himself up in Macedonia with weak suzerainty over Greece. Both Antigonus and his opponents began to call themselves kings. Antigonus claimed the whole empire, while they were content with their respective dominions. In 301, the coalition got the upper hand. At Ipsus, in Phrygia, they closed in on Antigonus, who fell fighting. The empire was irretrievably divided.

When the victors of Ipsus divided the spoils, they created a new political map of the Near East which was to endure for a long time — in some places until the Roman conquest. To Egypt, Ptolemy had now added Cyrene, Cyprus, Palestine, and isolated cities on the coast of Asia Minor. Seleucus controlled Syria, Babylonia, southern Asia Minor, and the Iranian Plateau eastward to the Hindu Kush Mountains and the central Asiatic steppes. Lysimachus added western Asia Minor to his original holdings, and Cassander had to content himself with Macedonia and the suzerainty over Greece. Within his own territories, each was an absolute sovereign. A new state system had come into existence with the beginning of a new Hellenistic world.

Selected Bibliography

THE FOLLOWING LIST OF BOOKS is designed to furnish a guide to supplementary reading on the topics covered in the present volume, on the advanced undergraduate level. It is not intended to be exhaustive. Periodical articles, all foreign language material, books which have been entirely superseded, and a number of others which the author has not found particularly well adapted to the purpose, have been intentionally omitted. Instructors will doubtless feel that some additions should be made to it, and there is no reason why in such cases they should hesitate to do so.

GEOGRAPHY

A. *Descriptive*

Burton, Harry E., *The Discovery of the Ancient World*. Cambridge, Mass., 1932.

Kiepert, Heinrich, *A Manual of Ancient Geography*. London, 1881.

Leake, William M., *Disputed Questions about Ancient Geography*. London, 1857.

Newbigin, M. I., *The Mediterranean Lands*. New York, 1924.

Semple, Ellen Churchill, *The Geography of the Mediterranean Region: Its Relation to Ancient History*. New York, 1931.

Schmitz, Leonard, *A Manual of Ancient Geography*. Philadelphia, 1857.

Tozer, H. F., *Classical Geography*. New York, 1877.

Tozer, H. F., *History of Ancient Geography*. New York, 1897.

B. *Atlases*

Atlas of Ancient and Classical Geography. New York, 1908. (Everyman's Library.)

Kiepert, Heinrich, *Atlas Antiquus*. 12th rev. ed., Berlin, 1902.

Shepherd, W. R., *Historical Atlas*. 7th rev. ed., New York and London, 1929.

C. *Bibliography*

Bury, J. B., and others, *The Cambridge Ancient History*, volumes I–VI, inclusive. Exhaustive bibliography with each volume.

Dutcher, G. M., and others (editors), *A Guide to Historical Literature*. New York, 1931.

See also the book reviews of *The American Historical Review, Classical Philology, The American Journal of Philology, The American Journal of Archeology*, and similar publications.

General Works on Ancient History

The Cambridge Ancient History, edited by J. B. Bury, S. A. Cook, and F. E. Adcock. 12 vols. and 4 vols. of plates. Vols. I–VI and I–II of plates on the Orient and Greece. Cambridge, England, and New York, 1924–1929.

Rostovtzeff, M., *History of the Ancient World*. Vol. I, the Orient and Greece. Vol. II, Rome. 2d ed., Oxford, 1929.

Sources and Methods for the Study of Ancient History

Barnes, H. E., *History of Historical Writing*, chaps. 1–2. Norman, Okla., 1938.

Beer, Henri, and Febvre, Lucian, Article, "History," in *Encyclopedia of the Social Sciences*, Vol. VII.

Carpenter, Rhys, *The Humanistic Value of Archeology*. Cambridge, Mass., 1933.

Glover, T. R., Article, "Historiography — Antiquity," in *Encyclopedia of the Social Sciences*, Vol. VII.

Lamprecht, Karl (translated by E. A. Andrews), *What Is History?* New York and London, 1905.

Langlois, Ch., and Seignobos, Ch. V. (translated by G. G. Berry), *Introduction to the Study of History*. New York, 1912.

Leavenworth, C. S., *Lessons of History*. New Haven, 1924.

Robinson, J. H., *The New History*. New York, 1912, chap. 1.

Shotwell, J. T., Article, "History," *Encyclopaedia Britannica*, 14th ed.

Stawell, F. M., and Marvin, F. S., *The Making of the Western Mind*. New York, 1923.

Thorndike, Lynn, *History of Medieval Europe*. Revised ed., pp. 1–16. Boston, 1928.

Towner, R. H., *The Philosophy of Civilization*. 2 vols. New York and London, 1925.

Toynbee, A. J., *A Study of History*. London, 1939.

Prehistory

Burkitt, M. C., *The Old Stone Age*. Cambridge, Mass., 1933.

Childe, V. Gordon, *The Dawn of European Civilization*. London and New York, 1925.

de Morgan, Jacques, *Prehistoric Man*. New York, 1925.

Elliott, G. F. Scott, *Prehistoric Man and His Story*. London, 1920.

Goldenweiser, A. A., *Early Civilization: An Introduction to Anthropology*. New York, 1922.

MacCurdy, George Grant, *Early Man*. London, 1937.

MacCurdy, George Grant, *Human Origins*. 2 vols. New York and London, 1924.

Osborn, Henry F., *The Men of the Old Stone Age*. New York, 1916.
Peake, Harold, and Fleure, Herbert John, *Merchant Ventures in Bronze*. New Haven and London, 1931.
Quennell, Marjorie and C. H. B., *Everyday Life in the New Stone Age, Bronze, and Early Iron Ages*. London, 1936.
Quennell, Marjorie and C. H. B., *Everyday Life in the Old Stone Age*. 2d ed., rev., London, 1926.
Sollas, W. J., *Ancient Hunters*. 3d ed., New York, 1924.
Tyler, John M., *The New Stone Age in Northern Europe*. New York, 1922.

THE ORIENT

I. General Histories
Hall, H. R., *Ancient History of the Near East from the Earliest Times to the Battle of Salamis*. London and New York, 1913.
Hogarth, David, *The Ancient East*. London and New York, 1915.
Maspero, Sir G. C. C., *The Dawn of Civilization in Egypt and Chaldea*. 5th ed., London, 1910.
Maspero, Sir G. C. C., *The Struggle of the Nations*. 2 vols. 2d ed., London, 1910.
Maspero, Sir G. C. C., *The Passing of the Empires* (edited by A. H. Sayce and translated by M. L. McClure). London, 1910.
Myres, John L., *The Dawn of History*. London and New York, 1911.

II. Egypt
Breasted, James H., *Ancient Records of Egypt*. 5 vols. Chicago, 1906–07.
Breasted, James H., *History of Egypt*. 2d ed., reprint, New York, 1924.
Breasted, James H., *Development of Religion and Thought in Ancient Egypt*. New York, 1912.
Carter, Howard, and Mace, A. C., *The Tomb of Tut-ankh-Amen*. 3 vols. London, 1922–33.
Conder, Major C. R., *The Tell-el-Amarna Tablets*. London and New York, 1893.
Erman, Adolf (translated by H. M. Tirard), *Life in Ancient Egypt*. New York, 1894.
Moret, Alexandre, *In the Time of the Pharaohs*. New York and London, 1911.
Moret, Alexandre, *The Nile and Egyptian Civilization*. New York, 1928.
Petrie, Wm. M. F., *History of Egypt*. 7 vols. Vols. I–III. London, 1898–1905.
Shorter, Alan W., *Everyday Life in Ancient Egypt*. London, 1932.
Winckler, Hugo, *The Tell-el-Amarna Letters*. New York and Berlin, 1896.

III. Assyria and Babylonia
Babelon, Ernest, *Manual of Oriental Antiquities*. London, 1889.
Delaporte, L. J., *Mesopotamia: The Babylonian and Assyrian Civilizations*. (Translated from the French of 1923 by V. G. Childe.) New York, 1925.

Gadd, C. J., *History and Monuments of Ur.* New York, 1929.

Hilprecht, H. V., *Explorations in Bible Lands.* Philadelphia, 1903.

Jastrow, Morris, Jr., *The Civilization of Babylonia and Assyria* (Westbrook Lectures). Philadelphia and London, 1915.

Johns, Claude H. W., *Ancient Assyria.* Cambridge, England, 1912.

King, L. W., *History of Sumer and Akkad* (*History of Babylonia and Assyria,* Vol. I). London, 1923.

King, L. W., *History of Babylonia from the Foundation of the Monarchy to the Persian Conquest* (*History of Babylonia and Assyria,* Vol. II). London, 1915.

Luckenbill, D. D., *Ancient Records of Assyria and Babylonia.* 2 vols. Chicago, 1927.

Olmstead, A. T., *History of Assyria.* New York and London, 1923.

Peters, J. P., *Nippur.* 2 vols. New York and London, 1897.

Rogers, R. W., *A History of Babylonia and Assyria.* New York and Cincinnati, 1901.

Winckler, Hugo, *A History of Babylonia and Assyria* (translated by J. A. Craig). New York, 1907.

Woolley, C. Leonard, *The Sumerians.* 4th printing. Oxford, 1930.

IV. *Syria and Palestine*

Barton, George A., *A History of the Hebrew People.* New York and London, 1930.

Clay, Albert T., *The Empire of the Amorites.* New Haven, 1919. (Yale Oriental Series.)

Day, Edward, *The Social Life of the Hebrews.* New York, 1907.

Hogarth, D. G., *The Kings of the Hittites.* London, 1926.

Hosmer, James K., *The History of the Jews.* London, 1901.

Kent, Charles F., *History of the Hebrew People.* New York, 1906.

Kittel, R., *A History of the Hebrews.* 2 vols. London, 1896.

Olmstead, A. T., *History of Palestine and Syria.* New York and London, 1931.

Rawlinson, George, *History of Phoenicia.* London and New York, 1889.

V. *Media and Persia*

Cameron, George C., *History of Early Iran.* Chicago, 1936.

Ragozin, Zenaide A., *The Story of Media, Babylonia, and Persia.* New York and London, 1936.

Huart, Clement, *Ancient Persia and the Iranian Civilization* (translated from the French of 1925 by M. R. Dobie). New York, 1927.

Rogers, Robert, *History of Ancient Persia.* New York and London, 1929.

Vaux, W. S. W., *Persia from the Earliest Period to the Conquest of the Arabs.* London, 1893.

GREECE

I. *Source-Books and Readings*

Botsford, G. W., and Sihler, E. E. (eds.). *Hellenic Civilization: Sources and Studies.* Edited by J. T. Shotwell. New York, 1915.

Howe, Geo., and Harrer, G. A. (eds.). *Greek Literature in Translation*. New York, 1927.
Thallon, Ida C. (Mrs. Hill) (ed.). *Readings in Greek History*. Boston, 1914.

II. *Complete Works*

Note: All of the books listed below have been translated into English — most of them several times. While there is a wide range of difference in the merits of the various translations, all of them are good enough to be of material aid to an undergraduate student who wishes to become acquainted with Greek literature at first hand. Most of the books listed below can be secured at reasonable prices in the Bohn and Everyman editions. The specialist will, for research purposes, find the Loeb Classical Library and the Oxford Library of Translations better adapted to his purpose. The former, with its Greek or Latin text and translation in parallel columns, is especially useful to one who is sufficiently well acquainted with the language of the original to check the translation as he reads.

A. *Histories*
1. Arrian, *The Anabasis of Alexander*, and the *Indica*. The first treats the campaigns of Alexander the Great, and the second describes the voyage of Nearchus from India to Babylonia.
2. Herodotus, *The History*. The central theme is the wars of the Greeks with the Persians up to the year 479 B.C., but the previous history, geography, manners, and customs of the nations involved receive lengthy treatment.
3. Plutarch, *Parallel Lives of Famous Greeks and Romans*. A series of biographies of celebrated Greeks and Romans, arranged in pairs — a Greek and a Roman — whose careers seemed to the author to be similar. Written in the first century A.D., but based upon older works now lost.
4. Thucydides, *History of the Peloponnesian War*. Tells the story of the war from its beginning down to the year 411 B.C.
5. Xenophon, *The Hellenica*. A history of the Greeks from the point where Thucydides breaks off down to the year 362 B.C.
   By the same author, the *Anabasis*. A memoir of the rebellion of the Younger Cyrus, and of the march of the Ten Thousand Greeks.

B. *Poetry and the Drama*
1. Aeschylus, *Tragedies*. Seven complete plays survive, along with fragments of others.
2. Aristophanes, *Comedies*. Eleven of the original forty-three are extant.
3. Euripides, *Tragedies*. Nineteen of the original ninety-one are extant.
4. Hesiod, *Works and Days*, *Theogony*, and minor works.

5. Homer, The *Iliad* and the *Odyssey*.
6. The Lyric Poets. The collection *Lyra Graeca* (Loeb Classical Library, 1922–28, 3 volumes) contains the extant works of all the Greek lyric poets except Pindar.
7. *The Palatine Anthology* contains extracts and complete poems from the works of the important Greek poets and dramatists.
8. Pindar, *The Epinician Odes*.
9. Sophocles, *Tragedies*. Seven of his plays survive.
10. Theognis, *Elegies*.

C. *Science and Philosophy*
1. Aristotle, *Complete Works*. Includes *Logical Treatises, Ethical Treatises, Politics, Physics, Economics, Poetic Inspiration, History of Animals,* etc.
2. Hippocrates, *Medical Treatises*.
3. Plato, *The Dialogues*.

D. *Oratory*
1. Aeschines, *Orations*. Of particular interest is his speech against Ctesiphon.
2. Demosthenes, *Orations*. In addition to his well-known *Public Orations*, he wrote a great many for parties to private lawsuits. These usually pass under the name of *Private Orations*.
3. Isocrates, *Orations*. The best-known are the *Panegyric*, the *Peace*, the *Areopagiticus*, the *Panathenaicus*, and the *Philip*. Some of these are not truly orations, but essays.
4. Lysias, *Orations*. The most important for the student of history is that against Eratosthenes.

D. *Travel and Art-History*
1. Pausanias, *Description of Greece*.

                                    General

A. *Classical Encyclopedias and General Reference Works*
Smith, Sir William, *Dictionary of Greek and Roman Biography and Mythology*, 3d ed., revised by G. E. Marendin, 3 vols. London, 1909.
Walters, Henry B., *Classical Dictionary of Greek and Roman Antiquities*. Cambridge, Eng., and New York, 1916.
Whibley, Leonard (ed.), *Companion to Greek Studies*, 3d rev. ed. Cambridge, Eng., 1916.

B. *General Histories*
Abbott, Evelyn, *History of Greece*, 3 vols. London and New York, 1895–1901.
Bury, J. B., *History of Greece to the Death of Alexander, the Great*, 2d rev. ed. London, 1913.

Curtius, Ernst, *History of Greece*, 5 vols. rev. ed. New York, 1892 and 1907. (Translated by Sir A. W. Ward.)

Grote, George, *History of Greece*, 12 vols. new ed. London and New York. 1906.

Holm, Adolf, *History of Greece*, 4 vols. New York, 1894–1898. (Translated by F. Clark.)

Zimmern, A. E., *The Greek Commonwealth*, 5th ed. Oxford, 1931.

Prehistoric

Baikie, James, *The Sea-kings of Crete*. London, 1913.

Burn, A. R., *Minoans, Philistines, and Greeks*. New York, 1930.

Evans, Sir Arthur, *The Palace of Minos*, vols. I–IV. London and New York, 1921–28.

Glotz, Gustave, *Aegean Civilization*. New York, 1925.

Hall, H. R., *Aegean Archeology*. London, 1915.

Hawes, Charles Henry, and Hawes, Harriet Boyd, *Crete the Forerunner of Greece*. London and New York, 1910.

Lang, Andrew, *The World of Homer*. London and New York, 1910.

Mosso, Angelo, *The Palaces of Crete and Their Builders*. London, 1907.

Murray, Gilbert, *Rise of the Greek Epic*, 3d rev. ed. London, 1924.

Ridgeway, Sir William, *The Early Age of Greece*, vols. I–II. New York and London, 1930–31.

Seymour, Thomas D., *Life in the Homeric Age*. New York, 1907.

Tsountas, Chrestos, and Manatt, J. S., *The Mycenean Age*. Boston, 1897.

Archaic

Freeman, Kathleen, *The Work and Life of Solon*. Cardiff, 1926.

Jardé, A. F. V., *The Formation of the Greek People* (translated from the French by M. R. Dobie). New York, 1926.

Linforth, Ivan M., *Solon the Athenian*. Berkeley, Calif., 1919.

Ormerod, H. A., *Piracy in the Ancient World*. London, 1924.

Ramsay, Sir William M., *Asiatic Elements in Greek Civilization*. Edinburgh, 1927.

Seltman, Charles T., *Athens, Its History and Coinage Before the Persian Wars*. Cambridge, Eng., 1924.

Ure, Percy N., *The Greek Renaissance*. London, 1921.

Fifth and Fourth Centuries

Abbott, Evelyn, *Pericles and the Golden Age of Athens*. New ed. New York, 1925.

Bromby, Charles H., *Alkibiades*. London, 1905.

Ferguson, W. F., *Greek Imperialism*, chaps. 1–3. Boston, 1913.

Glover, T. R., *From Pericles to Philip*. New York and London, 1917.

Grant, A. J., *Greece in the Age of Pericles*. New York, 1897.

Grundy, J. B., *The Great Persian War*. London, 1901.

Grundy, J. B., *Thucydides and the History of his Age*. London, 1911.

Henderson, G. W., *The Great War Between Athens and Sparta*. London, 1926.

Hogarth, D. G., *Philip and Alexander of Macedon*. New York, 1897.

Laistner, M. L. W., *History of the Greek World, 479–323 B.C.* London, 1936.

Marshall, Frederick H., *The Second Athenian Confederacy*. Cambridge, Eng., 1905.

Pickard-Cambridge, Arthur W., *Demosthenes and the Last Days of Greek Freedom*. London and New York, 1914. (Heroes of the Nations Series.)

Woodhouse, Wm. J., *King Agis of Sparta and His Campaign in Arcadia in 418 B.C.* Oxford, 1933.

The Macedonian Supremacy

Cary, Max, *The Legacy of Alexander: A History of the Greek World from 323 to 146 B.C.*, chaps. 1–3. New York, 1932.

Jouguet, P., *Macedonian Imperialism and the Hellenization of the East* (translated by M. R. Dobie), Parts I and II. New York, 1928.

Wheeler, B. I., *Alexander the Great*. New York, 1900.

Wilcken, U., *Alexander the Great* (translated by G. C. Richards). New York, 1932.

The Outlying Lands

Freeman, E. A., *History of Sicily: Phoenician, Greek, and Roman*. New York, 1882–1917. (Story of the Nations Series.)

Minns, Ellis I., *Scythians and Greeks*. Oxford, 1913.

Rostovtzeff, M. I., *Iranians and Greeks in Southern Russia*. Oxford and New York, 1922.

Government

Agard, W. R., *What Democracy Meant to the Greeks*. Chapel Hill, N.C., 1942.

Barker, Ernest, *The Political Thought of Plato and Aristotle*. London and New York, 1906.

Bonner, Robert J., *Lawyers and Litigants in Ancient Athens*. Chicago, 1929.

Bonner, Robert J., and Smith, Gertrude, *The Administration of Justice from Homer to Aristotle*. Chicago, 1920.

Bonner, Robert J., *Aspects of Athenian Democracy*. Berkeley, Calif., 1933.

Botsford, G. W., *The Development of the Athenian Constitution*. Boston, 1893.

Calhoun, Geo. C., *The Growth of Criminal Law in Greece*. Berkeley, Calif., 1927.

Fustel de Coulanges, N. D., *The Ancient City* (translated by W. Small). 10th ed. Boston, 1901.

Fowler, W. Warde, *The City State of the Greeks and Romans*. Reprint. London, 1907.

Glotz, Gustave, *The Greek City and Its Institutions* (translated by N. Mallinson). New York, 1930.
Greenidge, A. H. J., *A Handbook of Greek Constitutional History*. London and New York, 1896.
Minar, E. L. Jr., *Early Pythagorean Politics in Practice and Theory*. Baltimore, 1942.
Myres, John L., *The Political Ideas of the Greeks*. Cincinnati, 1927.
Tod, Marcus N., *International Arbitration Among the Greeks*. Oxford, 1913.
Ure, P. N., *The Origin of Tyranny*. Cambridge, Eng., 1922.
Vinogradoff, Sir Paul, *The Jurisprudence of the Greek City*. Oxford, 1922.
Whibley, Leonard, *Political Parties at Athens During the Peloponnesian War*. Cambridge, Eng., 1889.
Whibley, Leonard, *Greek Oligarchies, Their Character and Organization*. New York and London, 1896.

Economics

Boeckh, August, *Public Economy of the Athenians* (translated by Antony Laub). New York and Cambridge, Eng., 1857.
Calhoun, Geo. C., *The Business Life of Ancient Athens*. Chicago, 1926.
Gardiner, Percy, *History of Ancient Coinage, 700–300 B.C.* Oxford, 1918.
Glotz, Gustave, *Ancient Greece at Work* (translated by M. R. Dobie). New York, 1926.
Hasebroek, Johannes, *Trade and Politics in Ancient Greece* (translated from German). Chicago, 1934.
Michell, Humphrey, *The Economics of Ancient Greece*. New York and Cambridge, Eng., 1940.
Toutain, J. F., *The Economic Life of the Ancient World* (translated by M. R. Dobie). New York, 1930.

Private Life and Customs

Blümmer, Hugo, *The Home Life of the Ancient Greeks* (translated by Alice Zimmern). New York, 1893.
Guhl, Ernst, and Koner, Wilhelm, *The Life of the Greeks and Romans*. New York, 1902.
Gulick, Charles Burton, *The Life of the Ancient Greeks*. New York, 1902.
McClees, Helen, *The Daily Life of the Greeks and Romans*. New York, 1925.
Mahaffy, John P., *Social Life in Greece from Homer to Menander*. London, 1907.
Robinson, Cyril E., *Everyday Life in Ancient Greece*. Oxford, 1933.
St. John, James A., *History of the Manners and Customs of Ancient Greece*. London, 1842.
Tucker, T. G., *Life in Ancient Athens*. New York and London, 1906.

Literature

Bates, W. N., *Sophocles, Poet and Dramatist*. Philadelphia, 1940.
Bowra, C. M., *The Early Greek Elegists*. (Martin Classical Lectures, v. 7), Cambridge, Mass., 1938.

Bury, J. B., *The Ancient Greek Historians*. New York, 1909.
Capps, Edward, *Homer to Theocritus*. New York, 1901.
Finley, John H., *Thucydides*. Cambridge, Mass., 1942.
Flickinger, Roy C., *The Greek Theatre and Its Drama*. 2d ed. Chicago, 1922.
Goodell, Thomas D., *Athenian Tragedy: A Study in Popular Art*. New Haven, 1920. (Yale Classical Series.)
Harrison, Ernest, *Studies in Theognis*. Cambridge, Eng., 1902.
Jebb, R. C., *The Growth and Influence of Classical Greek Poetry*. Cambridge, Eng., 1893.
Little, A. M., *Myth and Society in Attic Drama*. New York, 1942.
Mahaffy, Sir John P., *A History of Classical Greek Literature*. 2 vols., 2d ed. London, 1883.
Murray, Gilbert, *Aristophanes: A Study*. Oxford, 1933.
Murray, Gilbert, *Euripides and His Age*. New York, 1933.
Murray, Gilbert, *A History of Ancient Greek Literature*. New York, 1897.
Pearson, Lionel, *The Early Ionian Historians*. Oxford, 1939.
Perry, T. S., *A History of Greek Literature*. New York, 1890.
Pickard-Cambridge, A. W., *Dithyramb, Tragedy, and Comedy*. Oxford, 1927.
Powell, J. U., and Barber, E. A., *New Chapters in Greek Literature*. Oxford, 1921.
Prentice, W. K. *Those Ancient Dramas Called Tragedies*. Princeton, 1942.
Symonds, J. A., *Studies of the Greek Poets*. 2 vols. London, 1902.
Wright, W. C., *A Short History of Greek Literature from Homer to Julian*. New York, 1907.

Education, Philosophy, and Science

Bakewell, C. M., *A Source-Book in Ancient Philosophy*. New York, 1907.
Burnet, John, *Greek Philosophy*, Part I, *Thales to Plato*. London, 1914.
Cornford, F. M., *From Religion to Philosophy*. London, 1912.
Freeman, F. M., *The Schools of Hellas*. London, 1907.
Gomperz, Theodor, *Greek Thinkers: A History of Ancient Philosophy*. 4 vols. (Translated by L. Magnus and G. G. Barry.) London, 1901–12.
Green, W. C., *Moira*. Cambridge, Mass., 1944.
Heath, Sir Thomas L., *A History of Greek Mathematics*. 2 vols. Oxford, 1921.
Jaeger, W. W., *Paideia: The Ideals of Greek Culture* (translated from the German by Gilbert Highet). Vol. I, New York, 1939. Vol II, Oxford and New York, 1943. Vol. III, 1944.
Moon, Robert C., *Hippocrates and His Successors*. London and New York, 1923.
Rogers, A. K., *The Socratic Problem*. New Haven, 1928.
Shorey, Paul, *What Plato Said*. Chicago, 1933.
Singer, C. J., *Greek Biology and Medicine*. Oxford, 1922.
Taylor, Alfred E., *Aristotle*. New York, 1912.
Zeller, Eduard, *A History of Greek Philosophy from the Earliest Times to the Time of Socrates* (translated by S. F. Alleyne). 2 vols. London, 1881.

Zeller, Eduard, *Socrates and the Socratic Schools* (translated by C. J. Reichel). 3d rev. ed. London, 1885.

Zeller, Eduard, *Plato and the Older Academy* (translated by S. F. Alleyne and A. Goodwin). 3d rev. ed. London and New York, 1888.

Zeller, Eduard, *Aristotle and the Earlier Peripatetics* (translated by B. F. C. Costello and J. H. Muirhead). 2 vols. London, 1897.

Art

Anderson, W. J., and Spiers, R. P., *The Architecture of Greece and Rome* (rev. by W. B. Dinsmoor). New York, 1927. Part I.

Beazley, J. D., and Ashmole, Bernard, *Greek Sculpture and Painting*. New York, 1932.

Buschor, Ernst, *Greek Vase-Painting*. New York, 1922.

D'Ooge, Martin, *The Acropolis of Athens*. New York, 1908.

Gardiner, E. N., *Olympia, Its History and Remains*. Oxford, 1925.

Gardner, E. A., *A Handbook of Greek Sculpture*. 2d ed. New York, 1915.

Gardner, Percy, *The Principles of Greek Art*. Rev. ed. London and New York, 1926.

Harrison, Jane E., *Introductory Studies in Greek Art*. London, 1892.

Hill, G. F., *Historical Greek Coins*. New York, 1906.

Milne, J. G., *Greek Coinage*. Oxford, 1931.

Powers, H. H., *The Message of Greek Art*. New York, 1925.

Richter, G. M. A., *The Craft of Athenian Pottery*. New Haven, 1923.

Richter, G. M. A., *The Sculpture and Sculptors of the Greeks*. New Haven, 1930.

Tarbell, F. B., *A History of Greek Art*. New York, 1925.

Walters, H. B., *A History of Ancient Pottery* (Greek, Roman, and Etruscan). 2 vols. New York, 1905.

Religion

Cornford, F. M. (compiler), *Greek Religious Thought from Homer to the Age of Alexander*. New York, 1923.

Fairbanks, Arthur, *A Handbook of Greek Religion*. New York, 1910.

Farnell, L. R., *The Cults of the Greek States*. 5 vols. Oxford, 1896–1909.

Farnell, L. R., *The Higher Aspects of Greek Religion*. New York, 1912.

Harrison, Jane E., *Prolegomena to the Study of Greek Religion*. Cambridge, Eng., 1903.

Murray, Gilbert, *Five Stages of Greek Religion*. 2d rev. ed. New York and London, 1925.

Moore, C. H., *The Religious Thought of the Greeks from Homer to the Triumph of Christianity*. 2d rev. ed. Cambridge, Mass., 1925.

Nilsson, M. P., *Greek Religion*. Oxford, 1925.

Persson, A. W., *The Religion of Greece in Prehistoric Times* (Sather Classical Lectures, Vol. XVII). Berkeley and Los Angeles, 1942.

Rohde, Erwin, *Psyche: The Cult of Souls and Belief in Immortality Among the Greeks*. New York, 1925.

Zielinski, F. F., *The Religion of Ancient Greece* (translated by O. R. Noyes). Oxford, 1926.

Index